BEST PRACTICES SERIES

The Privacy Papers

Managing Technology, Consumer, Employee, and Legislative Actions

THE AUERBACH
BEST PRACTICES SERIES

Broadband Networking
James Trulove, Editor
ISBN: 0-8493-9821-5

Business Continuity Planning
Ken Doughty, Editor
ISBN: 0-8493-0907-7

**The Complete Book
of Remote Access:
Connectivity and Security**
Victor Kasacavage, Editor
ISBN: 0-8493-1253-1

**Designing a Total
Data Solution:
Technology, Implementation,
and Deployment**
Roxanne E. Burkey and
Charles V. Breakfield, Editors
ISBN: 0-8493-0893-3

**High Performance Web
Databases: Design,
Development, and
Deployment**
Sanjiv Purba, Editor
ISBN: 0-8493-0882-8

**Making Supply Chain
Management Work**
James Ayers, Editor
ISBN: 0-8493-1273-6

**Financial Services
Information Systems**
Jessica Keyes, Editor
ISBN: 0-8493-9834-7

**Healthcare Information
Systems**
Phillip L. Davidson, Editor
ISBN: 0-8493-9963-7

**Multi-Operating System
Networking: Living with UNIX,
NetWare, and NT**
Raj Rajagopal, Editor
ISBN: 0-8493-9831-2

Network Design
Gilbert Held, Editor
ISBN: 0-8493-0859-3

Network Manager's Handbook
John Lusa, Editor
ISBN: 0-8493-9841-X

**New Directions in Internet
Management**
Sanjiv Purba, Editor
ISBN: 0-8493-1160-8

**New Directions in Project
Management**
Paul Tinnirello, Editor
ISBN: 0-8493-1190-X

**The Privacy Papers: Managing
Technology, Consumer,
Employee, and Legislative
Actions**
Rebecca Herold, Editor
ISBN: 0-8493-1248-5

Web-to-Host Connectivity
Lisa Lindgren and Anura Gurugé,
Editors
ISBN: 0-8493-0835-6

**Winning the Outsourcing
Game: Making the Best Deals
and Making Them Work**
Janet Butler, Editor
ISBN: 0-8493-0875-5

AUERBACH PUBLICATIONS

www.auerbach-publications.com
TO ORDER: Call: 1-800-272-7737 • Fax: 1-800-374-3401
E-mail: orders@crcpress.com

BEST PRACTICES SERIES

The Privacy Papers

Managing Technology, Consumer, Employee, and Legislative Actions

Editor

REBECCA HEROLD

AUERBACH PUBLICATIONS

A CRC Press Company

Boca Raton   London   New York   Washington, D.C.

Chapter 27 "A New Paradigm Hidden in Steganography," appeared in the *Proceedings of the New Security Paradigms Workshop,* Ballycotton, County Cork, Ireland, on September 12–22, 2000, pp. 41–50. ACM Press. Used by permission.

Chapter 47, "Data Privacy Directive 95/46 EC: Protecting Personal Data and Ensuring Free Movement of Data," copyright ©2002 by Lawrence D. Dietz. Used by permission.

Library of Congress Cataloging-in-Publication Data

The privacy papers : managing technology, consumer, employee, and
   legislative actions / editor, Rebecca Herold.
       p. cm. — (Best practices series)
   Includes bibliographical references and index.
   ISBN 0-8493-1248-5 (alk. paper)
    1. Privacy, Right of—United States. 2. Data protection—Law and
legislation—United States. 3. Disclosure of information—Law and
legislation—United States. 4. Confidential communications—United
States. I. Herold, Rebecca. II. Best practices series (Boca Ration, Fla.)
KF1262 .P754 2002
342.73′0858—dc21
                                                    2001056060
                                                        CIP

This book contains information obtained from authentic and highly regarded sources. Reprinted material is quoted with permission, and sources are indicated. A wide variety of references are listed. Reasonable efforts have been made to publish reliable data and information, but the author and the publisher cannot assume responsibility for the validity of all materials or for the consequences of their use.

Neither this book nor any part may be reproduced or transmitted in any form or by any means, electronic or mechanical, including photocopying, microfilming, and recording, or by any information storage or retrieval system, without prior permission in writing from the publisher.

All rights reserved. Authorization to photocopy items for internal or personal use, or the personal or internal use of specific clients, may be granted by CRC Press LLC, provided that $1.50 per page photocopied is paid directly to Copyright clearance Center, 222 Rosewood Drive, Danvers, MA 01923 USA. The fee code for users of the Transactional Reporting Service is ISBN 0-8493-1248-5/02/ $0.00+$1.50. The fee is subject to change without notice. For organizations that have been granted a photocopy license by the CCC, a separate system of payment has been arranged.

The consent of CRC Press LLC does not extend to copying for general distribution, for promotion, for creating new works, or for resale. Specific permission must be obtained in writing from CRC Press LLC for such copying.

Direct all inquiries to CRC Press LLC, 2000 N.W. Corporate Blvd., Boca Raton, Florida 33431.

Trademark Notice: Product or corporate names may be trademarks or registered trademarks, and are used only for identification and explanation, without intent to infringe.

Visit the Auerbach Web site at www.auerbach-publications.com

© 2002 by CRC Press LLC
Auerbach is an imprint of CRC Press LLC

No claim to original U.S. Government works
International Standard Book Number 0-8493-1248-5
Library of Congress Card Number 2001056060
Printed in the United States of America 1 2 3 4 5 6 7 8 9 0
Printed on acid-free paper

Dedication

To Tom and my beautiful boys … Noah Theodore and Heath Xavier

Contributors

MICHAEL H. AGRANOFF, *Attorney, Stafford Springs, Connecticut*

MOHAMMAD AL-ABDULLAH, *IT Security Analyst, American Management Systems, Fairfax Virginia*

LESLIE G. ARONOVITZ, *Director, Health Care—Program Administration and Integrity Issues, Department of Health and Human Services, Washington, D.C.*

LAWRENCE F.M. CAPUDER, SR., CPA, CISA, CIA, CMA, CPIM, *President, Sterling Arbor Consulting, Strongsville, Ohio*

LI WU CHANG, *Center for High Assurance Computer Systems, Naval Research Laboratory, Washington, D.C.*

MICHAEL J. CORBY, CISSP, *Consulting Director, M Corby & Associates, Inc., Worcester, Massachusetts*

MITCH DEMBIN, *Program Director, Cyber Attack Tiger Team, Exodus Communications, San Diego California*

JAMES X. DEMPSEY, *Senior Staff Counsel, Center for Democracy and Technology*

LAWRENCE D. DIETZ, *Marketing Intelligence Director, Symantac Corporation, Campbell, California*

VICTOR S. DORODNY, M.D., PH.D, *Patient Advocate, Southfield, Michigan*

KARL J. FLUSCHE, CFE, *Computer Forensic Analysis Consultant, Plano, Texas*

EDWARD H. FREEMAN, JD, *Attorney, West Hartford, Connecticut*

FREDERICK GALLEGOS, CISA, CDE, CGFM, *Adjunct Professor, Computer Information Systems Department, California State Polytechnic University, Pomona, California*

ROBERT L. GRAY, PH.D., *Chair, Qualitative Methods and Computer Information Systems Department, Western New England College, Springfield, Massachusetts*

SUSAN HANSCHE, CISSP, *Senior Manager, Troy Systems, Inc., Fairfax, Virginia*

WILLIAM T. HARDING, PH.D., *Associate Professor of Management Information Systems, Texas A&M University, Corpus Christi, Texas*

REBECCA HEROLD, CISSP, *Information Security Consultant, Van Meter, Iowa*

ERIN KENNEALLY, JD, *Forensic Analyst, Pacific Institute for Computer Security, San Diego, California*

MICKI KRAUSE, CISSP, *Manager, Information Securities Systems, PacifiCare Health Systems, Cypress, California*

Contributors

AMIN LEIMAN, CISA, *Senior Manager, Information Risk Management, KPMG, Los Angeles, California*

GARTH E. LONGDON, *Center for High Assurance Computer Systems, Naval Research Laboratory, Washington, D.C.*

BELDEN MENKUS, CISA, *Editor, EDP Audit, Control, and Security, Manchester, Tennessee*

MARTIN MILLER, *Manager, Computer Assurance, Deloitte & Touche, Seattle, Washington*

IRA S. MOSKOWITZ, *Center for High Assurance Computer Systems, Naval Research Laboratory, Washington, D.C.*

THOMAS R. PELTIER, CISSP, *Information Security Consultant, Detroit, Michigan*

RALPH SPENCER POORE, CISSP, CISA, CFE, *Chief Technology Officer, Privacy Infrastructure, Inc., Arlington, Texas*

ANITA J. REED, CPA, *Tampa, Florida*

DUANE E. SHARP, *President, SharpTech Associates, Mississauga, Ontario, Canada*

PETER STEPHENSON, *Information Security Consultant, Auburn Hills, Michigan*

FARLEY STEWART, *President, CEO, Internet Products, Inc., San Diego, California*

JOHN R. VACCA, *Information Technology Consultant, Pomeroy, Ohio*

JOHN B. VAN BORSSUM, CISA, CFE, *Vice President, iSecurePrivacy, Pasadena, California*

MIGUAL O. VILLEGAS, CISSP, CISA, *President, iSecurePrivacy, Pasadena, California*

BENJAMIN WRIGHT, *Author, Dallas, Texas*

MARIE A. WRIGHT, PH.D., *Associate Professor, Western Connecticut State University, Southbury, Connecticut*

Contents

Contents

Contents

Contents

Foreword

If you ask a hundred people today what their privacy concerns are, you will get a hundred widely varying answers. The spectrum of privacy concerns is tremendously large, ranging from public video surveillance, to e-mail monitoring, to addressing a multitude of privacy laws that are now in place worldwide, to protecting children on the Internet, to identity theft, ...and the list goes on and on. A significant subset of these concerns must be addressed by businesses and organizations. When executive management makes the assignment to address "privacy" within the organization, the assigned person is faced with the grueling task of deciding, first, what privacy means to his or her organization, and then identifying all the related privacy issues to tackle, and assigning priorities. Then, in most cases, they must determine how to get the biggest ROI to help support their privacy and security initiatives.

I put this book together by collecting articles that would help **me** if faced with this type of challenge. I must admit that I am an information-phile; it was difficult to exclude any of the literally hundreds of articles and government documents I found about privacy. However, after combing through mountains of articles, I have selected what I hope will be the most helpful for you in your privacy endeavors. I was able to actively use much of the information to help my colleagues, co-workers, and clients during the three months it took to put this book together. I think you will find all the information to be gems, and I hope you consider many of the articles to be diamonds.

The first two sections, I and II, deal with the history of privacy concepts. These are followed by Section III, which is dedicated to addressing the numerous privacy aspects within business organizations. This section provides many articles covering privacy-related policies, training issues, international issues, legal issues, and the handling and management of private information. This will be a good place for you to look first if you were just dubbed the privacy icon within your company.

Section IV addresses privacy tools and related technology. Encryption and cookies immediately come to mind. However, there is also a treasure of a steganography chapter, plus some great discussion of data mining and third-party security certifications. This will serve you well when your technology departments make plans to implement or upgrade such systems, or when they come to you looking for guidance on how to implement them to ensure that privacy regulations are followed.

Section V addresses the huge mass of laws and regulations related to privacy within the United States. With the Health Insurance Portability and Accountability Act (HIPAA) and Gramm-Leach-Bliley (GLB) requirements at the forefront of many organizations' to-do lists, it is a good time to consider all the other privacy-related laws and regulations that must also be addressed. This section not only discusses HIPAA and GLB in detail, but also provides a listing of existing U.S. privacy-related laws, as well as a listing of proposed laws. Plus, there is an interesting evaluation of Carnivore and its privacy implications.

Section VI covers the even larger collection of international privacy-related laws. This section focuses first on the European Union Directive and Safe Harbor initiatives. Following this, a very long list of resources for privacy laws throughout the world is provided.

The final section, VII, is a listing of Web sites, agencies, and Internet mail lists that you can use in fulfilling your privacy objectives.

The writers of the chapters in this book are phenomenal. Their experience and expertise are readily apparent in the valuable information they provide the reader regarding how to address privacy issues. They know that privacy, and the related security, must be a business enabler. However, to be successful with this effort, decision makers must understand the impact and priority that security and privacy must have within their companies. Organizations must place a priority on assigning security and privacy responsibilities to their personnel and create positions for them (such as Chief Information Security Officer and Chief Privacy Officer) high enough within the company to truly have impact, to achieve organizational compliance, and to ensure that related issues are considered when making business decisions. I hope this book can help you to provide the impetus and justification for security and privacy initiatives and get the resulting funding approved to help you demonstrate ROI.

I have included several Internet Web sites (URLs) as further references. These URLs were active at the time this book was compiled. However, keep in mind that URLs occasionally change or "disappear." It is my hope that the ones chosen within this book will still be active for many years. If you find a site is no longer available, however, I appreciate your understanding that the nature of the Internet may result in such changes.

As you consider your privacy challenges, keep in mind that the biggest challenge to achieving success is making the people within your organization know how to do business in a secure way to maintain privacy.

Technology alone cannot be the panacea for all your privacy problems. If you think you have addressed all your privacy issues just because you have implemented encryption, or have posted a privacy policy on your Web site, then I hope this book serves as an eye-opener for you.

I want you to be successful. I want you to use this book to achieve success. I hope you find this to be a valuable asset in achieving your work goals.

REBECCA HEROLD
December 2001

Preface

Today, more than ever, organizations are coping with the increased concerns of privacy issues. And it is not just consumer fears about how information collected by Web sites will be used or misused. There are broader concerns about data collected for direct response marketing, privacy of financial and health records, and identify theft and fraud. Employees are also raising questions about acceptable use of phones, e-mail, the Web, and if and when employers can monitor use. Employers find that without policies governing the use of these assets, they have no legal basis for action against employees. Any company conducting business across borders needs to know how foreign laws will affect transactions with customers and prospects. There is ever-increasing legislation dictating what organizations can and cannot do. Corporate espionage is a growth industry, putting at risk such sensitive information as intellectual property, product development and marketing plans, and customer files. Finally, government has the ability to collect more information about more individuals and organizations than ever before.

The Privacy Papers is a book for C-level executives, IT managers, HR managers, security officers, privacy officers, and legal professionals. It covers all aspects of the technology and the legislation that both enable privacy and place it at risk. As a guide to how to do it right, *The Privacy Papers* presents sample policies for employee training, awareness, and acceptable use; covers why companies must protect data and how to do it; describes the technology that makes information more private; and lists and summarizes major federal and international privacy legislation.

Introduction

Edward H. Freeman

In a 1981 episode of the classic situation comedy *Taxi*, Louie DiPalma, the comically repulsive dispatcher, was apprehended spying on the female cab drivers through a peephole into the Ladies Room. Louie was quickly fired from his job. In a story that could only occur in a sitcom, he was rehired before the final commercial.

Throughout *Taxi*'s run, Louie was a thoroughly detestable character (within the confines of television comedy, of course). As the petty despot of the decrepit garage, he stole from his employers, extorted money from the cabbies, and performed countless acts of trivial churlishness. This episode was the only time that he lost his job. He was only able to get it back by begging and ultimately telling of a time when his own privacy was violated.

Our society has developed a strong sense of privacy and the limits of acceptable behavior in our relationships with others. Louie's actions caused the female cabbies no physical injuries or financial loss. Their reputations were not compromised in any way. If he had not been "caught in the act," they would not even have been aware of the violation. Yet, his actions as a Peeping Tom were considered so vulgar that his employment was terminated.

This book deals with issues of personal and corporate privacy in the workplace, on the Internet, in other countries, in this Age of Databases. These issues are very complex and controversial, with the legitimate needs and desires of various groups and individuals often in direct opposition. To resolve these conflicts, an understanding of the human needs and history of privacy is essential. An incorrect or inappropriate decision can have serious repercussions for an organization's reputation and financial stability.

THE NEED FOR PRIVACY

Privacy is one of many abstract, conceptual terms that defy simple definition. The classic definition, as outlined in an 1890 law review article, states that individuals have "the right to be let alone."[1] Privacy is the expectation that individuals have in maintaining a personal space, free from outside interference. Information told in confidence should not be disclosed to others. Disclosure may cause embarrassment and emotional distress to a person of reasonable sensitivities. "Privacy, as a whole or in part, represents the control of transactions between person(s) and other(s), the ultimate aim of which is to enhance autonomy and/or to minimize vulnerability."[2] Privacy has always been present in human development. All early societies had some level of privacy, with different levels of emphasis.

Why do people feel that there is a need and a right for privacy? In a 1980 law review article, Ruth Gavison defined privacy as an integral aspect of the human need for control of one's life:

> Control suggests that the important aspect of privacy is the ability to choose it and see that the choice is respected. All possible choices are consistent with enjoyment of control, however, so that defining privacy in terms of control relates it to the power to make certain choices rather than to the way in which we choose to exercise this power.[3]

Privacy needs are constantly changing. Faced with a personal problem, an individual may choose to keep to himself. He may choose to share his feelings with a close friend, psychiatrist, or spiritual leader. He may even turn to a complete stranger (e.g., a bartender in a strange city).

It is precisely the right to control who knows what that makes privacy a fundamental part of our liberties. If we lose the basic ability to choose when to remain private and when to talk to others, we cannot exercise many other basic freedoms. Without this level of control, we have lost our fundamental constitutional rights to decide personal situations for ourselves.

PRIVILEGE AS A PRIVACY RIGHT

The courts recognize the right to discuss certain concerns with experts in confidence. The rules of attorney–client privilege allow specific types of information to be kept confidential from the other side in litigation. Some individuals cannot be forced to testify and certain information cannot be entered into court as evidence. When one requires a lawyer, priest, physician, or psychologist, he must be able to speak freely and confidentially, knowing that his words will never be repeated. If the client fears that what he tells his attorney can be used to his detriment, he might withhold crucial information. The attorney, then, might give incorrect or inappropriate advice.

In its most general form, the attorney–client privilege forbids the court from forcing an attorney to disclose information that the client has revealed to the attorney in confidence. If the attorney makes a statement that violates the attorney–client privilege, it cannot be used to the client's detriment. The privilege belongs solely to the client. If the client waives the privilege, the attorney would be required to testify.

The attorney–client privilege is the oldest privilege, going back at least to the days of Elizabeth I. Its supporters maintain that a client generally consults an attorney to receive accurate, informed professional advice. As one court phrased it:

In a society as complicated as ours and governed by laws as complex and detailed as those imposed upon us, expert legal advice is essential. To the furnishing of such advice, the fullest freedom and honesty of communications of pertinent facts is a prerequisite. To induce clients to make such communications, the privilege to prevent their later disclosure is said by courts and commentators to be a necessity. The social good derived from the proper performance of the functions of lawyers acting for their clients is believed to outweigh the harm that may come from the suppression of the evidence in specific cases.[4]

If all conditions are met, private communications between the attorney and the client are permanently protected unless the client waives the privilege. "Once the privilege has been held applicable, protected information may not be the subject of compelled disclosure regardless of the need or good cause shown for such disclosure."[5]

In recent years, the courts have often interpreted attorney–client privilege strictly and have limited its scope. Courts feel that the privilege impedes the full disclosure of the truth. The Supreme Court is aware that attorney–client privilege must have a predictable set of rules if its purpose is to be maintained.[6] The Court has not, however, established a set of clearly defined rules, preferring instead to decide on a case-by-case basis.

SOURCES FOR PRIVACY LAW

The development of privacy rights has been a slow and deliberate process reaching back thousands of years. Numerous writings have formulated these rights.

Biblical Law

The foundations for the legal recognition of privacy and the boundaries between the public and private realms of social lives date back to Ancient Greece. Such rights are also recognized in the *Mishnah,* the code of Jewish law compiled in the second century of the Common Era. The *Mishnah* (Baba Batra 3:7) states:

> In a shared courtyard, a man should not build a door facing another person's door nor a window facing another person's window. If it is small, he should not enlarge it.

We can see the importance of the privacy of an individual's behavior in a private space. Not only is the intrusion upon privacy forbidden, but the creation of circumstances wherein privacy intrusion can take place is also forbidden.

Invasion of privacy is tantamount to trespass or theft, and similarly punishable. There are ample precedents through centuries of Jewish legal writings to indicate that the individual is entitled to prevent the public from intruding upon or sometimes even knowing about his private doings, correspondence, and other aspects of his private domain.[7]

Other passages deal with repeating gossip. Leviticus 19:16 states: "Thou shalt not go up and down as a tale bearer among thy people." One may not pass on any information concerning a person to a third party, no matter how that information has been obtained. Even if the statement is true, gossip is considered a violation of privacy.

Under extreme circumstances, information can be passed on:[8]

- If not passing on the information will definitely cause financial damage or personal tragedy
- The information must be believed to be accurate
- The intent of the person passing the information must be to prevent financial damage or personal tragedy, not for some personal motive
- If the damage will be averted only if the information is passed on

The U.S. Constitution

The word *privacy* does not appear anywhere in the U.S. Constitution. When the founding fathers drafted the Bill of Rights, they realized that no document could possibly include all the rights that were granted to the American people.

The first eight Amendments list specific rights granted to the people. For example:

- The First Amendment protects the rights of freedom of speech, press, and association.
- The Third Amendment prohibits the quartering of soldiers in one's home.
- The Fourth Amendment bans unreasonable searches and seizure of property.
- The Fifth Amendment gives citizens the right to remain silent and to avoid self-incrimination.

The Ninth Amendment declares, "The enumeration in this Constitution, of certain rights, shall not be construed to deny or disparage others retained by the people." These retained rights are not specifically defined in the Constitution. Courts have consistently pointed out that many rights are not specifically mentioned in the Constitution, but are derived from specific provisions. The Supreme Court held that several amendments already extended privacy rights. The Ninth Amendment then could be interpreted to encompass a right to privacy. It says, in essence, "If it is not stated in the Constitution, then it is a right reserved by the people."[9]

The Fourteenth Amendment was adopted in 1868. It is generally recognized as the source of most modern privacy interests. It was intended to provide substantive and due process rights for millions of black Americans who had been slaves. It provides that no state "shall deprive any person of life, liberty, or property, without due process of law; nor deny to any person within its jurisdiction the equal protection of the laws." These words have formed the basis for extending privacy rights that "bar certain government actions regardless of the procedures used to implement them."[10]

De May v. Roberts

In 1880, Dr. John De May attended the birth of Alvira Roberts' fourth child in rural Michigan. Dr. De May brought Alfred Scattergood, an unmarried jeweler and watch repairman, along to the birth. Mrs. Roberts thought that Scattergood was a medical student or medical assistant. In truth, he was an unmarried jeweler and watch repairman. When Mrs. Roberts learned the truth, she sued De May and Scattergood. Despite their claims that they should not be found liable for acts "involving solely the question of taste or propriety," a jury awarded Mrs. Roberts $5000.

De May and Scattergood appealed the decision to the Michigan Supreme Court. The court affirmed the jury's decision. Mrs. Roberts "had a legal right to the privacy of her apartment at such a time, and the law secures to her this right by requiring others to observe it and to abstain from its violation."[11]

De May is generally considered the first U.S. case in which the right to privacy was mentioned explicitly. It was also the first case to award damages for violating that right. *De May* was decided when privacy was becoming an established right and a legal concept.

The Right to Privacy

In Boston during the 1890s, Mrs. Samuel D. Warren, a leading local socialite, was considered an outstanding party hostess. Before long, the local newspapers began printing her guest lists and descriptions of her décor and food. On different occasions, the *Saturday Evening Gazette* reported that Mrs. Warren had given a dinner party for 12 friends and that she and her husband had transformed their home into a "veritable floral bower" for a wedding breakfast for his cousin.

The Warrens, both of whom came from politically prominent families, were outraged at the intrusiveness of the Boston press. Samuel Warren, a respected attorney, asked his friend and former law partner, Louis D. Brandeis (later a Supreme Court judge), to write an article on privacy with him. The article appeared in the *Harvard Law Review* in 1890. It is generally credited with creating the "right to privacy" and, consequently, the right to sue for "invasion of privacy."[12]

In their article, Brandeis and Warren stipulated that individuals have the "right to be let alone." For the first time, legal scholars advanced an articulate legal theory to meet the threats of new technology. Their theory of privacy rights evolved from the common law, developed over centuries. Common law protected a person not only from the physical attack on life and property, but also from intangible attack as well.

Warren and Brandeis recognized that an increasingly technical and intrusive society would require new protections for privacy. They also realized that invasion of privacy would usually cause emotional harm rather than physical injury, but argued that the damage was just as serious and should be compensated through legal action. In an extremely relevant section, they said:

> The press is overstepping in every direction the obvious bounds of propriety and decency. Gossip is no longer the resource of the idle and of the vicious, but has become a trade, which is pursued with industry as well as effrontery. To satisfy a prurient taste the details of sexual relations are spread broadcast in the columns of the daily papers. To occupy the indolent, column upon column is filled with idle gossip, which can only be procured by intrusion upon the domestic circle.

Courts soon began to accept Warren and Brandeis's arguments and the legal right to privacy was born. In 1905, a Georgia court held that the unauthorized use of a person's photograph for commercial purposes was a violation of a person's privacy interest.[13] By 1947, only nine jurisdictions recognized a common law right of privacy. Progress was sometimes slow until the 1960s, but the article first established the concept of privacy as a legal principle.

Griswold v. Connecticut

In this landmark case, the Supreme Court finally recognized a constitutional right to privacy.[14] A Connecticut statute made it a crime to use or counsel anyone in the use of contraceptives. A New Haven doctor and the executive director of the local Planned Parenthood had been arrested and each fined $100 for counseling married couples regarding birth control.

Most of the justices in *Griswold* concluded that the Constitution provides a fundamental right to privacy, which in turn includes the right to decide whether to use contraceptives. The only way to enforce such a statute was to "allow the police to search the sacred precincts of marital bedrooms for telltale signs." Justice William O. Douglas found that the spirit, structure, and specific provisions of the Bill of Rights created "zones of privacy" that are broad enough to protect aspects of personal and family life.

PRIVACY AND TECHNOLOGY

In 1844, Samuel F.B. Morse invented a new way of transmitting telegraphic messages by way of electronic pulses that could be translated into text.

Within a generation, the country was traversed with telegraph lines, allowing for speedy communications to most areas.

The telegraph was arguably the first technological advance to affect our conception of privacy. If an ordinary letter were received with the envelope intact, both the sender and the recipient could assume that no one along the way had read the letter. The sender of a telegram had to trust that the telegraph operator would keep the message contents confidential, although he could easily read messages without the risk of an opened envelope. Unlike the postal service, a copy of every message could be retained, as well as a billing record. During the Civil War, both sides regularly tapped each other's telegraph lines. It was inevitable that telegraph company's copies of received messages would be requested as evidence in trials. Special codes were later developed to ensure privacy.

CONCLUSION

History has shown that new technology brings on new concerns for maintaining and protecting our privacy rights. In modern society, where individuals are not afraid to speak up and bring litigation, companies are accountable when their employees and policies do not measure up to the current standards. Embarrassing and expensive lawsuits are real concerns. Many organizations have created high-level executive positions to deal exclusively with privacy issues.

This book presents a detailed analysis of privacy issues in the modern workplace. It is hoped that these chapters and references will lead to a more thorough knowledge of the legal, historical, ethical, moral, and business needs for comprehensive privacy policies and procedures within your organization, and serve as a tool and reference to assist you with what you will soon discover are widely varying privacy-related issues.

Notes

1. Samuel D. Warren and Louis Brandeis, The Right to Privacy, *Harvard Law Review,* 4, 193, 1890.
2. Stephen T. Margolis, Conceptions of Privacy, *Journal of Social Issues,* 33(3), 10, 1977.
3. Ruth Gavison, Privacy and the Limits of Law, *Yale Law Journal,* 89, 421, 1980.
4. *United States v. United Shoe Mach. Corp.,* 89 F. Supp 347, 358 (D. Mass.1950).
5. *In re* Grand Jury Investigation (Sun Co.), 599 F.2d 1224, 1233 (3d Cir. 1979).
6. *Upjohn Co. v. United States,* 449 U.S. 383, 393 (1981).
7. Alfred S. Cohen, Privacy: A Jewish Perspective, *Journal of Halacha and Contemporary Society,* 1(1), 53–102, Spring 1981.
8. J. David Bleich, Privacy of Personal Correspondence, *The Jewish Law Annual,* 128–131, 1980.
9. Robert Ellis Smith, *Ben Franklin's Web Site,* Providence: Privacy Journal, 2000, 258.
10. *Daniels v. Williams,* 474 U.S. 327, 331 (1986).
11. *De May v. Roberts,* 46 Mich. 160, 165-166 (1881).
12. Ellen Alderman and Caroline Kennedy, *The Right to Privacy,* New York: Alfred A. Knopf, 1995.
13. *Pasevich v. New England Life Ins. Co.,* 122 Ga. 190 (1905).
14. *Griswold v. Connecticut,* 381 U.S. 479 (1965).

Section I
Business Organization Issues

Chapter 1
E-Mail: Balancing Corporate Assets and Employee Privacy
Michael H. Agranoff

Employers, employees, and their outside contractors have widely differing expectations with regard to the access, use, and disclosure of electronic mail (e-mail). The matter of balancing the company's interests and the rights of employees is a corporate responsibility, one with which IS management can help by instituting policy. This chapter examines e-mail privacy within the context of existing laws and recommends some appropriate policies that are fair — both to the organization and to its individual employees and contractors.

OVERVIEW

Modern computer technology has created a revolution in office productivity. Like all revolutions, it has side effects; in particular, computers make it easier to invade an individual's privacy. Former U.S. Supreme Court Justice William Brennan wrote, more than a decade ago, "The central storage and easy accessibility of computerized data vastly increases the potential for abuse of that information."

For the most part, the worst fears about technology and invasion of privacy have not been realized; nonetheless, there remains a natural conflict between the need to protect company assets and the need to protect individual privacy in the workplace. Most companies deal adequately with this situation through informal means, by following accepted customs and exercising business prudence. More frequently, however, companies are advised to establish internal privacy codes and policies that address the misuse of computerized information. Under such policies, companies can collect data on individuals only for legitimate business purposes. Furthermore, the data collected should be the minimum needed to do a job, and

0-8493-1248-5/02/$0.00+$1.50
© 2002 by CRC Press LLC

persons should consent to (or at least be aware of) the data collection. Individuals must also be allowed to correct erroneous data and give their own view on any disputed data.

By and large, the office workplace has avoided labor disputes. Most modern companies accept the idea of employee privacy, even if they have not enacted formal privacy policies. Labor relations matters for offices do not generally make newspaper headlines.

All this changed with the 1990 Alana Shoars case. The lawsuit alleged that Shoars was illegally fired by her employer, Torrance, California-based Epson America, Inc., after she discovered that an Epson manager had placed a tap on all internal e-mail and had printed confidential employee e-mail. Shoars alleged that she was dismissed when she protested this practice to senior management. In addition to Shoars's wrongful discharge and defamation action against her employer and some of its managers, a separate class action was filed by Epson employees for invasion of privacy.

The law in this area is not well established. However, companies need not wait for a decision from the California courts before taking action on the issue of privacy and e-mail. This chapter attempts to define the minimum policies that corporate and IS management should institute with regard to e-mail privacy. The emphasis is on policies that must be set responsibly, not merely as a reaction to one unfortunate case. Most people would agree that a company must take steps to protect its assets. No matter how solid an organization's financial position, laxity in this area can spell downsizing — if not disaster — for a company.

Corporate management may need to retrieve employee e-mail for any of the following legitimate reasons:

- To find lost messages
- To assist employees, at their request or with their consent, in the performance of their job duties when they are out of the office
- To study the effectiveness of the e-mail system as a whole and institute revisions if needed
- To comply with an investigation into suspected criminal acts
- To recover from system failures or other emergencies
- To ensure that company computing resources are being used for company business only

These reasons for accessing corporate records, including e-mail, are legitimate and may be necessary for the efficient and proper operation of the workplace. After all, a well-run workplace preserves employment. It is not surprising that the courts are reluctant to interfere in any private or public organization's operations that have either been accepted over the years or are not manifestly illegal. In a 1987 workplace privacy case, the

U.S. Supreme Court upheld the lower courts' decision, which stated that any work-related search by an employer satisfies the Fourth Amendment's reasonableness requirement. The courts have generally recognized the plethora of contexts in which employers can intrude, to some extent, on an employee's expectation of privacy.

PRIVACY AND THE LAW

Many people assume that privacy is a constitutional right. However, it is not. There are many definitions of privacy: it is variously referred to as the right to be left alone, the right to be free from unreasonable personal intrusion, or the individual's right to determine what personal information can be communicated and to whom.

The U.S. Constitution does not mention privacy, however; and there is no evidence that its founders considered the topic. Only in this century did the U.S. Supreme Court state that the Constitution implies a right to privacy in certain situations. The protection of a person's general right to privacy (i.e., the right to be left alone) is relegated largely to the law of the individual states.

The traditional privacy protection offered by the states is part of the general system in common law. In most states, a person may be liable for damages for invasion of privacy if that person intentionally intrudes on someone else's solitude or private affairs and the intrusion could be characterized as highly offensive to a reasonable person. Courts are usually reluctant to find liability unless the victim had a reasonable expectation of privacy in his or her activities.

New forms of electronic communication have greatly increased the potential for invasion of privacy, however. Many states, as well as the federal government, have recognized that traditional constitutional law and state common law are inadequate to protect individuals against new types of privacy violations that can occur with cellular telephone service and e-mail networks, for example. As a result, federal laws have been passed, such as the Electronic Communications Privacy Act of 1986, as well as various state statutes.

SPECIFIC LEGAL CONSIDERATIONS FOR E-MAIL

It is natural to wonder whether existing privacy laws prohibit corporate management from collecting, printing, or reading the e-mail sent by employees. The general answer is that they do not and that no one can be held liable, in a court of today, for doing so. (It is important to emphasize, however, that law varies, depending on the factual situation, the jurisdiction involved, and new judicial opinions rendered that interpret the Constitution, statutes, or common law.) The following sections, which examine how laws protect against similar invasions of privacy, help to explain the various legal considerations involved in e-mail privacy.

Constitutional Law's Balancing Test

If an employer reads e-mail sent by employees, could that action be considered an unreasonable personal search? A 1987 U.S. Supreme Court case, *O'Connor v. Ortega,* suggests that such a finding would be most unlikely.

In the O'Connor case, a psychiatrist employed by a state hospital was suspected of managerial improprieties. While this employee was on administrative leave, hospital officials searched his office, on the grounds that they were conducting an inventory of state-owned property. Items were taken from his office during the search that were later used against him in administrative hearings that resulted in his discharge.

The U.S. Supreme Court held that government employees have a reasonable expectation of privacy, at least in their desks and file cabinets; however, the employer did not always need a search warrant, as law enforcement officials would, to examine these spaces. The Court wrote that "requiring an employer to obtain a warrant whenever the employer wished to enter an employee's office desk, or file cabinets for work-related purpose could seriously disrupt the routine conduct of business and would be unduly burdensome.... [A search is usually acceptable] when there are reasonable grounds for suspecting that the search will turn up evidence that the employee is guilty of work-related misconduct, or that the search is necessary for a noninvestigatory work-related purpose, such as to retrieve a needed file."

The Supreme Court adopted a balancing test, finding that strict Fourth Amendment warrant and probable-cause requirements were not appropriate for the workplace. In the future, a case may reach the Supreme Court in which a government employer is accused of reading employee e-mail. Although it is impossible to predict Supreme Court decisions, it seems unlikely that the Court would reverse its stated reluctance to disrupt the routine conduct of business and require that management obtain a search warrant. There are various reasons not to expect a reversal of this decision, including the following:

- The U.S. economic climate has worsened since 1987. If anything, this situation reduces anti-business sentiment that might otherwise have pressured for a reversal.
- Three justices, two of whom dissented in this case, have since retired. They have been replaced by three, apparently conservative justices (i.e., Kennedy, Souter, and Thomas).

- In many organizations, the use of e-mail has become an accepted office routine. There is no reason to believe that the Supreme Court would treat e-mail any differently than it treats desks and file cabinets.

No Protection for Private Employees

Whatever federal constitutional protection exists for workplace privacy can be invoked only against a government employer, not against a private employer. The Supreme Court has not stated this in so many words; it is simply understood. A lower federal court case (*Simmons v. Southwestern Bell Telephone Co.*) found that for the workplace, protection extends only to government intrusions into a person's privacy. This view has not yet been seriously challenged.

Private employers may not always be exempt, however. It is possible that a private employer could perform so much government-related work that its activities would be considered state action and the employer held liable for federal constitutional misdeeds. There are also several cases in which private employers with no possible state-action connection have been held to federal constitutional standards; these, however, have been primarily in the civil rights area.

In short, it is safe to say that federal constitutional protection is unavailing for workplace privacy, especially in the case of private employers. It is always possible that any one state's constitution could offer protection within that state, but this is a perpetual gray area in U.S. law.

STATE COMMON LAW

If a private employer intentionally reads e-mail sent by an employee, it might appear that the employer would be liable for invasion of privacy, because such an intrusion into private affairs could be deemed highly offensive to a reasonable person. However, most state courts hold that to recover for invasion of privacy, individuals must demonstrate that they had a reasonable expectation of privacy in the activity that allegedly was intruded on.

Employees of both private or public companies may have difficulty showing a reasonable expectation of privacy in their own e-mail for several reasons. Among the reasons are that:

- E-mail is considered part of the organization's computer system and therefore a corporate asset, and not a personal resource.
- Passwords do not make computer input secure from certain managers (who might have authority to override communications) or systems programmers (who may be able to circumvent controls to gain access).

7

- Because e-mail is often used to send a memo to several people, it is not practical to expect any real degree of privacy. Employers would have to institute different policies according to the number of addressees.
- It is a reasonable and generally known policy that management must be able to collect and store e-mail in the event it must be retrieved for emergency purposes or for legitimate investigations.

For these reasons and because of the depressed business climate, liability for invasion of privacy through the reading of workplace e-mail seems unlikely under state common law under circumstances reasonably foreseeable, but it cannot be ruled out entirely for all states. If, for example, corporate management were to publicize e-mail to deliberately and publicly embarrass an employee, common law actions against the employer might be possible.

FEDERAL STATUTORY LAW

Existing federal statutes (i.e., laws passed by Congress) do not satisfactorily address the question of e-mail privacy. For example, although many people are aware of the federal statute called the Privacy Act, few are aware that all it protects against is the disclosure of personal information that has been collected by federal agencies. The Privacy Act was originally intended to establish far-reaching federal privacy standards and guidelines; however, enthusiasm waned during the era of deregulation, given the lack of an identifiable crisis. Because of its many built-in expectations and sporadic enforcement, the Privacy Act is little more than a historical curiosity.

U.S. Mail

It is natural to ask if e-mail can be afforded the same protection as U.S. first-class mail. The answer is an unequivocal no. An item takes on legal status according to what it is or does (or purports to be or do), depending on legal definitions. For example, a document is or is not a will, depending on form and circumstances; what the writer of the document says it is does not bind the courts.

First-class mail is defined by federal statute. Business e-mail does not even arguably meet that definition. The appellation "mail" means little; this type of messaging system could just as easily be labeled Business Electronic Telephone and Memo System (or BETAMS). The point is that an acronym, name, or buzzword does not bind the courts.

Furthermore, although first-class mail receives strong protection, even it can be inspected under proper Fourth Amendment procedures (e.g., probable cause and search warrants). The idea that first-class mail has absolute immunity is a modern myth. E-mail does not qualify for absolute protection under any theory.

The Federal Wiretapping Act

The Wiretapping Act (Title III of the Omnibus Crime Control and Safe Streets Act) must be considered to place the Shoars e-mail case in perspective. The Wiretapping Act, in general, prohibits the interception of wire or oral communications. It also prohibits the disclosure of the contents of any illegally obtained information. There are exceptions, however. A recent case illustrates the difficulty of using the Wiretapping Act against employers.

In this case, a hospital emergency medical technician stationed in an emergency medical service (EMS) trailer called another technician who was stationed in the EMS main office, located inside the hospital. The communication was made over a special EMS telephone extension, and the conversation included disparaging remarks about EMS supervisory personnel. The conversation was recorded in the EMS dispatch center through a generally known recording mechanism. Persons undisputedly heard, disclosed, and used the contents of the recording.

The technicians sued for monetary damages, which is allowed as a civil remedy under the Wiretapping Act. The U.S. District Court found for the hospital, and the technicians appealed. Although the 11th Circuit Court of Appeals held that there was indeed a wire communication that was intercepted, disclosed, and used, the court upheld judgment for the hospital under the so-called telephone extension exception. According to the court, the conversation between two technicians was not a personal call. It occurred during office hours, between co-workers, over a specialized extension, and it concerned scurrilous remarks about other employees in their capacity as supervisors. The court recognized the potential contamination of the work environment as a matter in which the employer has a legal interest. Therefore, there was no liability under the Wiretapping Act.

This example suggests that an employee has a heavy burden of proof in actions brought against employers on grounds of wiretapping. Because e-mail is often viewed as an extension of the telephone, and because of the other reasons mentioned, it seems unlikely that the Supreme Court would hold for employees in a similar case.

The Electronic Communications Privacy Act

Congress passed the Electronic Communications Privacy Act (ECPA) in 1986. Title I of the ECPA updates the Wiretapping Act by including protection for new forms of electronic communications in addition to wire or oral communications.

The ECPA might appear to protect against the interception of e-mail; however, it has no provisions that increase employer liability beyond the general scope of the Wiretapping Act. Although it has been suggested that the Shoars case could be used to test the extent of the ECPA, as of this writing no court decisions indicate that the ECPA would in fact apply to employers. All previous arguments against employer liability for e-mail privacy violations seem to be unchanged by the ECPA.

The Privacy for Consumers and Workers Act

People often ask if general laws to protect workers' rights could be used to protect workers against violations of e-mail privacy. As luck would have it, a bill has been in the works for several years with the stated purpose of preventing potential abuses of electronic monitoring in the workplace. The bill is known as the Privacy for Consumers and Workers Act (PCW).

The PCW was last introduced into the U.S. House of Representatives in September 1991 by Representative Douglas K. Bereuter (R–NE) and sent to the House Committee on Education and Labor for consideration. The PCW was introduced in earlier House and Senate sessions and failed to pass. Similar bills have been introduced in various state legislatures. A 1991 *Harvard Law Review* note described the PCW as follows:

> Specific provisions of [the PCW] prohibit secret monitoring and require employers to inform workers of how monitoring statistics are collected and assessed and of when they are actually being monitored. Employers must also notify customers whose telephone conversations are monitored that they are being overheard. [The PCW] bars employers from basing individual performance evaluations or disciplinary action solely on monitoring statistics, unless the employee can review them. Also, monitoring statistics may not be used as the sole basis for production quotas.[1]

The passage of an e-mail privacy law would require careful legislative deliberation, supported by input from business and industry leaders. Several versions of the PCW have drawn opposition from business groups, partially because the act does not remove the confusion that surrounds electronic monitoring and electronic mail interception. For example, the term "electronic monitoring" is defined so broadly in the PCW that it could include routine computer security records, generated by logging and audit programs, that track activity by ID numbers. Corporate management could be forced to supply written advance notice of security system details and be subject to restrictions. As a result, standard computer security measures could become subject to costly administrative or court action.

Under the PCW, employers would be required to describe, in advance, the interpretation of statistical printouts and their relation to work performance. In a lawsuit, companies could potentially be bombarded with endless pretrial discovery requests by lawyers searching for anything that might, as the PCW is written, even remotely lead to relevant evidence. Employers would also be required to disclose to prospective employees, during a personal job interview, information regarding monitoring that might affect their work. This could open the door for prospective, sophisticated computer hackers.

Finally, employees would have to be permitted access to personal data obtained by electronic monitoring. There is no exemption for data generated by audit and security programs. Those who would argue that the intent of the PCW is merely to stop unwarranted snooping neglect to fully consider the fact that, regardless of the intent of the law, lawyers can use their powers to bring about results that legislators might not have originally intended.

ETHICAL CONSIDERATIONS

Because the legal system does not yet provide an answer to the question of e-mail privacy rights, an organization may decide to write its own express policy. Exactly what degree of privacy people desire is not always clear. A workable consensus might develop if policies are seen as fair to both companies (including owners, creditors, and customers) and individual employees.

Americans have a fundamental belief in the idea of fair play and justice. The concept of due process revolves around letting individuals know precisely what they are charged with and giving them a fair opportunity to defend themselves against the charge. Therefore, when management sets a corporate policy on e-mail privacy, a requirement is that employees be informed under what conditions their e-mail is being or can be monitored.

Informing Employees

The Computer Security Act of 1987 established a 12-member National Computer System Security and Privacy Advisory Board that, in theory, advises the Department of Commerce on computer security and privacy issues. The board's chairperson wrote in a letter to an agency of Commerce, recommending that:

> [U]sers of federal electronic mail systems be informed of the level of privacy to be accorded their messages[hellip]. The Board believes that every agency ... should establish a policy prohibiting casual reading of electronic mail by [system administrators and system programmers]. Access ... should be permitted only as required by emergency or system failure circumstances.[2]

The letter also stated that management personnel can have access to the mail of others. Because much e-mail traffic is in the nature of interoffice mail and is related to the business of the organization, individuals sending or receiving electronic messages should have no expectations of privacy unless the organization has taken specific steps to ensure it.

A debate on whether e-mail is an extension of the telephone, the U.S. mail, interoffice mail, fax machines, or some combination thereof cannot be resolved in this chapter; the status of employee e-mail has not been declared by an appropriate governmental body. In the meantime, companies should not hesitate to assert their legitimate right to protect their assets, but only in a manner consistent with established business practices and the principles of due process.

RECOMMENDED COURSE OF ACTION

More companies can be expected to take action and develop policies regarding the privacy of company e-mail. The recommendations that follow are intended to help IS managers, EDP auditors, and information security managers, whose companies may be reviewing e-mail policies, but they should not be mistaken for legal advice. Competent in-house or outside counsel should be consulted before instituting a policy in this area. The following are general recommendations:

- Companies must implement their e-mail privacy policies with appropriate procedures and guidelines.
- The policies and procedures should be developed and monitored by the IS department and its security function, in conjunction with the legal department and possibly the personnel department.
- It may be appropriate for the policies to be approved by, and formally promulgated under the authority of, senior management. This determination must be based on a company's degree of employee orientation and overall decision-making philosophy.
- Detailed procedures and guidelines should be reviewed at least once a year. The legal department must participate directly. Nonlegal staff members must be aware that the law varies in different jurisdictions. Even a definitive U.S. Supreme Court decision might have unexpected ramifications in a different factual pattern. Meaningful, regular review can prevent policies from becoming outdated.

Minimum Policy Recommendations

Each organization must determine its own policies; overall, simpler is better. Companies are advised to develop the minimal number of policies to meet their objectives and to implement the least restrictive procedures necessary to carry out these policies.

Not for Personal Use. A policy must specify clearly and explicitly, and as strongly as possible, that company resources are for business use, not for personal use. A patient effort to enforce this policy may be required, especially if the business culture has operated to the contrary for years.

The Risk of Disciplinary Action. The policy must clearly state that misuse of company resources, including e-mail, can result in disciplinary action. Management has the duty to monitor e-mail for possible misuse of resources, and such action should not be construed as invasion of privacy. A policy should explain corporate management's responsibility to its owners, customers, creditors, and the employees themselves in this regard; employees ultimately benefit from a company that conserves its assets.

Employee Common Sense. A policy must advise employees, in positive and definite terms, of the degree of security and privacy that is afforded their e-mail. For example, a policy might state that when employees use a company resource for the purpose of business communication, they can expect no privacy in their e-mail.

To counter possible employee resistance, the e-mail policy must emphasize management's legitimate access needs and dissuade employees from using e-mail for incidental personal messages or endeavors. If a communication must be private, employees can be asked to use common sense and to put their communication in interoffice mail marked "Personal and Confidential" rather than use the company computer.

Privilege Coupled with Responsibility. An e-mail policy must emphasize that security administrators and systems programmers have special responsibilities that go along with their special privileges. They have no right to abuse their authority by accessing e-mail, except at the direction of management. They cannot casually browse through files for their own amusement.

Employee Appeals. Employee complaints must be heard because that is one way that overzealous or abusive management actions can be rooted out. Most non-union companies have no mechanism to handle employee complaints that a supervisor has dismissed. In such a case, an employee appeal committee can be established to hear any employee complaint dismissed by the first and second levels of supervision. This practice need not destroy company discipline but can be used to warn the company of problems before they become catastrophes.

Notes

1. Note appearing in "Addressing the New Hazards of the High Technology Workplace," *Harvard Law Review,* 104, 1898 and 1908, 1991.
2. Letter from Willis Ware, chairperson of the National Computer System Security and Privacy Advisory Board, to John W. Lyons, director of NIST, June 1991.

Chapter 2

Control Issues in an E-Mail Personal Privacy Invasion Prevention Policy

Belden Menkus

Problems associated with the invasion of personal privacy can arise in an organization if the users of its electronic mail (e-mail) system are confused about the basis of their use of the system. To prevent such confusion, organizations need to establish, implement, and enforce a written policy that states positively the basis of the use of its e-mail system by employees, customers, and suppliers.

The IT auditor's role is to counsel the organization's senior executives on the need for such a policy, the appropriate content of the written statement, and the means for ensuring compliance with the policy. And, of course, the IT auditor should anticipate routinely reviewing and reporting the nature and scope of that compliance. IT auditors should not be responsible for the direct implementation or enforcement of the policy.

This chapter recounts some developments regarding pornography being sent through organizational e-mail systems and relates these developments to the issue of protecting personal privacy from invasion. This chapter discusses the development and implementation of an *E-Mail User Personal Privacy Invasion Prevention Policy* for the organization. It concludes with a strategy for resolving policy violations.

THE PORNOGRAPHY ISSUE

The protection of personal privacy in an individual's on-the-job use of e-mail has been described by both politicians and civil libertarians as an issue of safeguarding individual rights in this environment. It is a concern

0-8493-1248-5/02/$0.00+$1.50
© 2002 by CRC Press LLC

that is significant for its own sake. However, there is an underlying issue in e-mail personal privacy protection that should not be ignored. It is not widely discussed. It is a desire by many of the consumers of pornography to conceal their on-the-job involvement with this material as it is made available over the Internet.

The development of the Internet has been accompanied by an almost explosive worldwide growth in the creation and distribution of pornography. For the most part, the dissemination of this material is unregulated and untaxed. Contemporary pornography is of two categories. One type portrays largely what the Law describes as relations between consenting adults. (Those relations that do not involve consent are considered to be a form of rape. A consideration of them is beyond the scope of this chapter.) The second type of commercial pornography depicts what a BBC (British Broadcasting Corporation) news service account has described as scenes of children being raped and sexually assaulted. The production and distribution of pornography have drawn the attention of law enforcement activities worldwide. (The people who play a role in this activity have been reported to be major users of sophisticated encryption products.) Access to its sources through the Internet has introduced this material into some workplaces. (A side issue of this introduction is the organization's potential vulnerability to charges of permitting or promoting a hostile work environment.)

Typical of the range of what might be involved in the distribution of pornography over the Internet are the reported activities of Pentaguard, an organization of computer hackers. Pentaguard has defaced, according to a report by the Associated Press news service, numerous World Wide Web sites because these locations did not contain either pornographic materials or MP3 (MPEG Audio Layer 3) compressed music storage files. (MP3 is a form of digital audio signal encoding that was developed in 1991 by Germany's Fraunhofer Institute. Its use has been spread worldwide by the Internet.) Involved in the claimed Pentaguard attacks were at least 26 Web sites operated by various government organizations in China, Kuwait, Romania, Vietnam, and the country of Georgia. (The more than 48 U.S. government agency maintained sites that Pentaguard claimed to have defaced included those operated by the National Cemetery Administration and the Alaska office of the Interior Department. Also, Pentaguard claimed to have successfully invaded the computer systems of the California State Assembly Republican Caucus.)

Among the non-government enterprises that have been reported to have experienced problems with employee involvement with sexually explicit e-mail messages are software producer Computer Associates International, components of the Cable and Wireless telecommunications organization, and Liverpool-based insurer Royal and Sun Alliance. (Roger Lyons, the general secretary of The Manufacturing, Science, and Finance

Union, which represented some of the Alliance employees, described the discharge of 10 of these individuals and the disciplining of an additional 77 employees as extremely heavy-handed. Paul Atkinson, an Alliance executive, denied this charge and indicated that the individuals had violated clearly defined written policies on what was termed the misuse of the Internet at work.) The United Kingdom incidents reflected e-mail message monitoring that was done by these organizations under that country's Regulation of Investigatory Powers Act.

Representative of the apparent scope of the traffic in pornography were the international operations that have been reported by the BBC news service of the Wonderland Club pornography distribution network. This network was active in 12 countries for at least two years before its operations were the focus of a coordinated law enforcement intelligence action, according to Detective Chief Inspector Bob McLachlan, who heads the London Metropolitan Police Pedophile Unit. In Scotland and England alone, the BBC account indicated, 13 people were arrested in this incident. (Two of these were individuals who had control of the computers at the Phoenix Activity Centre, a children's care facility in Middleton, a suburb of Greater Manchester.)

An Illustration

There are indications that the on-the-job viewing by individual employees of Internet pornography can become obsessive. The *Montreal Gazette* has reported that Dominic Petruzzi, a technical inspector at CAE Electronics, a Montreal engineering organization that manufactures flight simulators, had been dismissed by CAE for spending excessive time on the job visiting Internet pornography sites. (The dismissal had been appealed unsuccessfully on Petruzzi's behalf by Canada's Communications, Energy, and Paperworkers Union.) As often happens, the on-the-job pornography viewing was done during regular work hours, and the viewer's actual job was then performed during those hours in which overtime premium income could be accumulated.

At issue in the Petruzzi incident, according to the *Montreal Gazette* account, was the record that during a six-month period in 1999, Petruzzi had spent 329 hours (the equivalent of eight weeks of eight-hour days, five days a week) viewing pornographic material on these sites. In one month during this period, Petruzzi was recorded as having spent 120 hours, the equivalent of three weeks of regular work time, in this activity. It was reported by the *Montreal Gazette* that Petruzzi had claimed 123.7 additional hours of overtime during that same month. (According to CAE executives, Petruzzi's job responsibilities did not require any computer use. Rather, for 14 years, he had been employed to examine the actual assembly and wiring of the electrical-mechanical systems of the individual flight simulators.)

ESTABLISHING A WRITTEN POLICY

Dealing conclusively with personal privacy problems related to e-mail use will require concrete action on the part of senior executives. Attempts by organizations to avoid these problems by indirect suggestions or by vague or weasel-worded statements have not been shown to be effective thus far.

Senior executives should formulate, implement, and enforce a formal written organizational policy regarding e-mail user privacy. This written policy should assert positively the organization's essentially unrestricted ownership of its e-mail resources, including all of the actual e-mail messages. In particular, the employee's use of e-mail should be defined as a privilege that is associated with the individual's continued employment and that there is no absolute right of an employee to use this resource. Generally, those employees, customers, and suppliers who use the organization's e-mail resources should have the same sort of privacy expectations that they would have in using the organization's regular mail, telephone, and courier services. The policy should make it clear to these individuals in an unambiguous fashion that their right to privacy is not absolute in all cases. The policy should be so plain that the organization's e-mail users will understand that all of the communication processes that pass through the organization can be subject to either traffic analysis or content analysis, and that the basis for doing this will be determined by, and at the discretion of, the organization's senior executives or their designated representatives.

POLICY STATEMENT CONTENT

The organization's appropriate acts such as monitoring, traffic analysis, and content analysis that are referred to in the policy statement are not acts of spying on the users of the e-mail system. (At least one source has proposed that if an IT auditor does not understand the difference, he or she may need to consider transferring to another type of occupation.) So, in connection with that, the policy statement should make these two commitments:

1. Every effort will be made to avoid violating the employee's reasonable expectation of personal privacy. (The operative word here is *reasonable*. In particular, the organization should obligate itself to comply with all of the legal requirements for preserving the employee's rights within the bounds of reason.)
2. The least intrusive methods for monitoring the operation of the system will be utilized.

The policy statement should define the conditions under which communications that move through any part of the e-mail process will be accessed. It should identify who the information that is disclosed from the system can be shared with, and the conditions under which this sharing will occur. In implementing this policy, a general declaration of the organization's intent might be inserted as a banner that is displayed when a user enters this system. An example of such a declaration is as follows:

> The organization makes this electronic mail system available to its employees and its customers for conducting its official business. Using this system is a privilege, not a right. The records created through the use of this system are the property of this organization. This system and its records do not belong personally to any of its employees, its customers, or its suppliers. The organization reserves the right to monitor in a reasonable manner the operation of this system, to access all of the records within it, and to retain or dispose of those records when and how it desires to do so. The individuals who utilize this system may make occasional and incidental use of it to send and receive personal messages. In doing so they acknowledge the organization's ultimate ownership of this system and its rights regarding its use.

A number of related procedures and practices can be specified. For example, those e-mail messages that are sent and received in connection with one's employment should not be considered as absolutely personal and private. Moreover, the indiscriminate accessing of another employee's e-mail messages without the permission of that individual should be no more acceptable a form of conduct than would be eavesdropping on telephone conversations or other forms of personal contact between individuals.

Responsibility for E-Mail Message Content

The individuals who are using the e-mail message handling mechanism should be aided in understanding that even what may be thought of as personal communications between employees may be subject to so-called discovery proceedings in routine legal actions. An organization's legal counsel will be prepared, most likely, to emphasize to its senior executive that the organization may be liable for the consequences of even the incidental actions and statements of its employees. This may be true even when these individuals are not acting as the organization's agent, say, even in a matter of possible slander or claimed misrepresentation in dealings with its customers, competitors, or suppliers.

Encryption

The policy statement terms should clarify such things as the conditions under which messages that are sent through the e-mail mechanism may be encrypted. An organization is free either to define the conditions under which messages may be encrypted or to entirely prohibit the use of cryptography in this mechanism. The choice that has been made should be presented in the policy statement in an unambigous fashion.

POLICY IMPLEMENTATION

The terms of the policy statement can be set in motion through a variety of communication techniques. These can include the distribution of its text in a training manual; the posting of its contents on a public bulletin board, the organization's intranet mechanism (if one exists), or in the employee cafeteria or lounge; and in an agreement that is signed at the time of employment and that may be renewed annually.

The successful implementation of an e-mail user personal privacy invasion protection policy depends on the larger issue of the organization's management of its electronic records.

Data Ownership

It has become common for e-mail message handling servers to become congested with material that is highly personal and trivial in nature. In turn, preventing the recurrence of such congestion requires that a mechanism be established for consistently distinguishing between employee personal information and the organization's own data. (Individuals should not be permitted to control such data beyond the limits of their assigned job responsibilities.)

Successfully implementing this policy statement will require the periodic routine auditing of employee personal e-mail accounts to ensure that data that properly belongs to the organization is not being marked inappropriately as being personal in nature. (The possible contradiction that must be resolved is that the individual who administers the e-mail system must be prevented, by task definition or by a system design feature, from monitoring routinely and indiscriminately the content of individual employee electronic messages. At the same time, the person who administers the system must be required to take reasonable precautions to protect the privacy of those who use the system. Here, too, the operative word is *reasonable*.) However, as a matter of organizational policy, the e-mail system administrator or other responsible representatives may have access to message content. This may occur, for example, when:

- An employee has been away from his or her assigned workplace for an extended period of time.
- It is necessary to ascertain and resolve technical problems that affect the system's operation.
- A suspicion of the possible misuse of the system exists.

- It is conducted in conjunction with an approved internal or outside investigation of relevant system activities.

Those employees or customers who feel that such practices (along with the routine auditing mentioned earlier in this chapter) constitute an invasion of their personal privacy should be instructed to maintain their private e-mail message contacts at their place of residence or through the facilities of a commercial ISP enterprise where the cost of the service is paid for by this employee or customer.

Message Content Protection

In turn, the organization that is operating this e-mail system is obligated to support its users in maintaining such content security measures as protecting their passwords or the content of their messages from disclosure to unapproved third parties. (This will require, in most instances, the maintenance of effective controls over message content access, including the prompt changing of a password when such an action is requested.)

Message Content Retention Control

To relieve both the e-mail system operation congestion and the liability exposure in connection with the discovery proceedings mentioned earlier in this chapter, system users should be required to remove all of their messages from the system in a prompt manner. The policy statement should require that individual messages not be retained in the system for extended periods of time. To place such a requirement in operation, the statement could authorize the individual who administers the e-mail system to remove any information that remains in it for, say, more than 90 days. Where a user of the system desires to maintain the content of a specific message for a longer period of time, the policy statement should require that the material be moved promptly to some other electronic message storage medium. It remains true, as it has been for decades, that the message that is not maintained for an unreasonable period of time will not either embarrass someone or be required to make a trip to the courtroom.

To minimize the occurrence of such problems, violations of the e-mail policy statement should be resolved as promptly as possible when they arise.

HANDLING POLICY VIOLATIONS

The IT auditor will find it wise to avoid becoming responsible for either the implementation or the actual enforcement of the organization's e-mail policy statement. However, the IT auditor can anticipate being asked both to report violations of the policy when they are disclosed in a regular review and to advise the organization's senior executives on how to respond aggressively to such incidents.

Policy violations reflect, typically, both a failure of the relevant control and the existence of a probable IT security defect. A five-element strategy can provide an effective response to such a situation. (A comparable approach can be used to respond to the identification of a possible fraud.) The components of this strategy include:

1. *Act promptly but with care.* A timely reaction can guarantee that the impact of the incident does not broaden and that there is not an unreasonable delay in remedying the situation. However, one should also ensure that hasty action is avoided. For example, the incident may not be what it appears to be and the presumed policy violator may be innocent of any wrongdoing. The individual's intent may be a concern. Someone else may be the actual offender. And, hasty action against the wrong individual may lead, as has happened in some of the incidents mentioned earlier in this chapter, to unfortunate conflicts with employee representative groups. This reaction may be accompanied, as well, by a claim by the affected individual of emotional stress that stems from alleged defamation or discrimination.

2. *Seek guidance from the organization's legal counsel.* Do not act precipitously. Do not assume the existence of legal rights that do not exist in fact. Ensure that the relevant policy has been applied consistently, both in this incident and in the past. It may be wise to secure legal advice about when and how to react and respond if the organization's past practices have been lax or inconsistent. For example, determine what evidence should be gathered about the incident.

3. *Confirm the facts.* Do not rely on first impressions or on employee gossip. Gather evidence about the violation as unobtrusively as is feasible. Be sure of the facts. As noted earlier in this chapter, the presumed policy violator may be innocent of any wrongdoing.

4. *Limit the knowledge that others gain to what is at issue.* Do not gossip. Apply the long-held military organization of handling sensitive information on a need-to-know basis. Avoid sharing even the broadest details of the incident with others, even those outside the organization itself.

5. *Confront the individual.* Ideally, the contact should take place away from the workplace, with at least two witnesses present when this contact takes place, and it should be done in a manner that avoids any possible claim of embarrassment or harassment. Provide the individual with an opportunity to explain and defend the action. This confrontation should be framed as an exercise in due process.

Chapter 3
Developing an Organizational Internet Policy

Lawrence F.M. Capuder, Sr.

Businesses worldwide are going online to expand their public relations, marketing, and customer support activities. The most ambitious have already taken the plunge into Internet commerce, and are engaging in sales transactions over the Internet and the World Wide Web. To minimize exposure to the inevitable security risks inherent in fledgling Internet communications, organizations should develop and adopt a comprehensive Internet policy to direct employees' use of this powerful tool. Information systems (IS) auditors, as representatives of an organization's security and control function, are typically invited to join an organization's policy development team. This chapter focuses on issues that auditors should consider when developing an Internet policy, and provides a sample Internet policy as a benchmark for the policy development process.

INTRODUCTION

The explosive growth of the Internet has employees in all types of organizations focused on using this tool to facilitate their work. Moreover, the Internet is having a profound effect on the way companies do business. In the most advanced companies, it has inspired reengineering efforts and the creation of commerce technology divisions to facilitate the exploitation of the Internet's seemingly limitless access to new markets. By nature, the new frontiers of Internet trade are widely accessible and have relatively loose controls. Thus, Internet-related activities expose organizations to a variety of security risks that may be generated from both inside and outside the company. Security and control measures to help organizations protect themselves are still evolving, and related laws have yet to catch up with security risk discoveries. As most Internet-related tasks performed in the course of business are accomplished by individual employees, they

0-8493-1248-5/02/$0.00+$1.50
© 2002 by CRC Press LLC

can be extremely difficult to oversee or control internally. Therefore, issuing an organizationwide Internet policy is an essential starting point for controlling in-house Internet use and minimizing a company's exposure to security risks.

Because of the technical nature of this area, management will often invite IS auditors to play a significant role in developing Internet policies or evaluating them once they are issued. This chapter outlines important issues for IS auditors to consider when developing an organizational Internet policy. It also provides a sample Internet policy that can serve as a benchmark for the policy development process.

UNDERSTANDING ORGANIZATIONAL CULTURE AND TECHNOLOGICAL INFRASTRUCTURE

Corporate management might be tempted to ask: Does our organization really need an Internet policy? The answer is a resounding "yes." Even companies that do not rely on extensive Internet use in their business activities must control the activities that do occur, as well as the growth of new activities, to protect themselves from Internet-specific security risks. Whether the Internet policy should be an autonomous policy is based on an organization's needs and goals. It may viably be included as a subset of the organization's data security and integrity policy or other related regulations, such as those governing electronic mail or information network interconnectivity. The important matter is that the organization addresses Internet issues in some formal and comprehensive way, and that it makes its policies clear to all personnel.

Before an organization can begin to develop its Internet policy, that organization must first understand its own culture, current Internet use, and technological infrastructure. Cultural considerations dictate how much risk the organization is willing to assume, how many controls its employees are accustomed to having imposed on them, and how important the use of technology is to its competitive advantage. The extent and type of Internet use dictate what types of controls are necessary or possible. The technological infrastructure indicates what types of security tools and exposures exist. Ideally, the organization should form an interdisciplinary team to explore these issues and to help develop the Internet policy. This team should include representatives of management, operations personnel, administrative staff, and information systems (IS) experts, including those specializing in security and control.

One cultural consideration, for example, is if a high-technology organization is reluctant to place too many constraints on Internet use. This type of organization's employees are inclined to use the latest technology to its utmost capacities. The organization may want to encourage these tendencies because its employees may transform their familiarity with high technology into a competitive advantage. On the other hand, a conservative, low-technology organization with few Internet users may be more willing to create policies that limit Internet use. It may want to ease onto the Internet slowly, controlling access until strategies for exploiting Internet opportunities are developed. This latter organization may choose to sit on technology's "bleeding edge," that is, to allow other companies to be Internet pioneers until the Internet becomes more commercially viable with fewer risk exposures. The furthest extreme of the latter organization is one that issues a policy stating that its employees will not use the Internet at all.

The policy development team should also study the organization's current Internet use and technological infrastructure. It might consider interviewing key personnel or conducting a survey to determine the answers to the following questions:

- How many employees are using the Internet?
- What types of transactions are employees conducting?
- How do employees currently access the Internet?
  - How many gateway networks to the Internet does the organization operate? (There may be gateways of which management is not aware.)
  - What means do employees use to access the Internet when in the office? What means do they use from other sites for business-related activities?
  - What other alternatives do employees have for electronic mail? To what extent do outside organizations provide these services?
- What security and control measures are currently in place?
  - How strong is the security on the organization's gateway networks?
  - What Internet-related application programs does the organization have? How strong are the application programs' controls?
  - How does the organization audit the Internet gateway network and the organization's gateway network?
  - What Internet-related security incidents has the organization already faced?
  - How does the organization monitor Internet use and security incidents? What tools does the organization use to do so?
- How much money is currently being spent on Internet use?
  - What is the total annual cost for Internet, e-mail, and other online information services? These costs include commercial gateway and Internet use and in-house hours spent on related projects.
  - Is the organization wasting funds by using duplicate or expensive services?
  - Is the organization's accounting system set up to track such costs?

- What are the commercial advantages that the Internet creates for the organization?
- Who has the organizational responsibility for major Internet-related decisions?
- What does the organization's business plan or IS strategy say about the organization's future use of the Internet?
- Are there plans in place or any applications currently under development?

A SAMPLE ORGANIZATIONAL INTERNET POLICY

Exhibit 1 presents a sample organizational Internet policy. The generic ABC Company Internet Policy covers a broad spectrum of issues and is designed as a basic guide for those involved in Internet policy development. Of course, each organization should tailor this policy to fit its individual needs. Management may want to take drastically different stances on some issues — to choose different levels of managers for authorized approvals, for example, or to delete issues that are not applicable to their organization's operations. Some organizations find it beneficial to include a glossary of terms in the policy. For example, in the generic ABC policy, terms that may require definitions for employees unversed in Internet terminology include company-approved gateway and application programs. Again, the most important factor is that a coherent policy is established.

THE BENEFITS OF PROVIDING A SUPPLEMENTAL INTERNET PROCEDURES AND GUIDELINES HANDBOOK

Many organizations find that issuing an Internet policy alone does not provide adequate guidance to personnel. These organizations also provide an Internet procedures and guidelines handbook that contains detailed instructions on how to handle a variety of specific Internet-related activities. These procedures and guidelines can be as detailed as needed based on an organization's exposure to the Internet. Issues to be addressed in a procedures and guidelines document of this nature include, but are not limited to, the following:

- Procedures for creating and maintaining firewalls to prevent external parties from obtaining access to unauthorized portions of the organization's Internet gateway computer and other networks
- Procedures for logical and physical access control at both the network and system levels, including appropriate password controls and security administration
- Archiving and backup procedures for e-mail and Internet application databases

Exhibit 1. ABC Company Internet Policy

ABC Company recognizes the commercial benefits of its employees using some aspects of the Internet. However, casual or reckless use of the Internet may expose the company to substantial security risks and escalating usage costs. Therefore, the company has issued the ABC Company Internet Policy to direct employee Internet activities. All employees should carefully review the policy and act according to the regulations presented; any requests for variations from the policy must be approved in advance by the Chief Information Officer. ABC Company employees who violate this policy will be subject to disciplinary action, up to dismissal. The most current version of the policy will reamin posted at the policy bulletin board.

- ABC Company comployees will access the Internet only in performing legal, business-related tasks. All personal use of the Internet is prohibited.
- ABC Company employees needing to perform business-related tasks on the Internet will access them only through company-approved gateways.
- All gateways to the Internet, application programs, and databases accessible through the Internet must have adequate security and controls.
- All new Internet-related application programs must be approved by the Chief Information Officer prior to development or acquisition.
- ABC Company employees must have written approval from their manager before having an Internet electronic mail address through a company-approved gateway. The company information services function will be responsible for activating these accounts.
- ABC Company employees will avoid sending electronic mail, bulletin board messages, or discussion group messages that could cause legal or competitive exposures to the company based on their content.
- ABC Company employees who download data, text, video, graphics, voice clips, programs, or any other resource from the Internet should use prudent procedures to prevent computer virus crises and to follow laws and copyright agreements.

- File protection to prevent unauthorized modification or deletion of critical Internet-related application programs, data, and password files
- A company-approved encryption method if the organization chooses to use cryptology to protect sensitive data and programs when stored or transmitted
- Security violations monitoring procedures
- A list of company-approved Internet gateways
- A review of controls on Internet gateway providers, including right-to-audit clauses in provider contracts

SAMPLE POLICY BREAKDOWN AND DISCUSSION

The following discussion breaks down the ABC Company Internet Policy regulation by regulation, and cites reasons why organizations should consider including these basic regulations in their own Internet policy.

Organizational Philosophy

> ABC Company recognizes the commercial benefits of its employees using some aspects of the Internet. However, casual or reckless use of the Internet may expose the company to substantial security risks and escalating usage costs. Therefore, the company has issued the ABC Company Internet Policy to direct employees' Internet activities. All employees should review the policy carefully and act according to the regulations presented; any requests for variations from the policy must be approved in advance by the Chief Information Officer. ABC Company employees who violate this policy will be subject to disciplinary action, up to dismissal. The most current version of the policy will remain posted at the policy bulletin board.

It is beneficial to begin any Internet policy with an organizational philosophy statement. This statement should, ideally, relate to personnel the organization's general position on Internet use; the ABC Company, for example, states that some usage is deemed beneficial and necessary. However, by including the reasons why strict usage guidelines are necessary, and detailing how the policies will be enforced, the company effectively conveys the gravity of policy adherence. Other organizations' philosophy statements might read much differently. For example, some companies may wish to state that the company encourages all employees to aggressively use the Internet for appropriate business purposes. Others may wish to stipulate that, because the Internet has limited practical applications for their organization, usage will be strictly curtailed. Non-commercial organizations, such as governments, should carefully tailor their organizational philosophy statements to adhere to the appropriate protocols.

Business-Only Use

> ABC Company employees will access the Internet only in performing legal, business-related tasks. All personal use of the Internet is prohibited.

Organizations should always establish, immediately, that Internet usage is acceptable only for business-related activities. Companies pay, often dearly, for Internet access, storage, and online services, and have the right to limit Internet use to business-related tasks. However, this policy may be difficult to enforce without a systematic review of employees' e-mail accounts, a notion that raises the volatile issue of employees' rights to privacy. An organization may choose to stipulate in its procedures and guidelines handbook that management reserves the right to read an individual's electronic mail files in the course of a justified, business-related investigation or upon termination. Regardless of how a company decides to enforce the business-use-only policy, that company cannot fairly attempt to regulate it without including it in the company Internet policy.

Limiting Access to Company-Approved Gateways

ABC Company employees needing to perform business-related tasks on the Internet will access them only through company-approved gateways.

Organizations should strongly discourage employees from conducting business-related Internet activities on their home computers or personal Internet gateway accounts. It is vital that the organization be able to monitor all gateways that it uses to ensure that proper securities and controls are in place. The organization should consider including a list of all company-approved gateways in its procedures and guidelines handbook.

Gateway and Application Security and Controls

All gateways to the Internet, application programs, and databases accessible through the Internet must have adequate security and controls.

Organizations should introduce the concept of security and control in their Internet policy. Although many employees may be uneducated in Internet security practices, it should be made clear in the policy that safety strategies exist and must be learned by all Internet users. Detailed guidance on adequate security and control measures and how Internet users can be sure controls exist should be included in the more comprehensive prodedures and guidelines document, but the issue should be raised in the Internet policy.

Application Growth

All new Internet-related application programs must be approved by the Chief Information Officer prior to acquisition or development.

Controlling Internet application growth internally can greatly reduce an organization's Internet-related expenses; thus, a statement outlining the proper approval procedure for new applications should be included in the Internet policy. Controlling application growth also ensures that the organization's security and control specialists, its IS auditors, can be involved in the implementation of all new applications. The IS team's involvement in the acquisition of new applications is the only way to ensure that the organization designs appropriate internal controls in new systems. By the same token, the organization may find that it should adapt its systems development methodology for Internet-related applications.

Approval for Electronic Mail Addresses

ABC Company employees must have written approval from their manager before having an Internet electronic mail address through a company-approved gateway. The company information services function will be responsible for activating these accounts.

By issuing tight controls over which employees are issued e-mail addresses, organizations can monitor the internal growth of Internet use. Knowing which employees have access to company-approved gateways will also prove helpful in tracking users who have exposed the company to security risks.

Content of Messages Sent Over the Internet

> ABC Company employees will avoid sending electronic mail, bulletin board messages, or discussion group messages that could cause legal or competitive exposures to the company based on their content.

The content of messages that employees send and receive through the Internet can cause several exposures to the organization, and the issue should therefore be addressed in the Internet policy. A potentially hazardous message might:

- Contain confidential information that could lead to a competitive disadvantage if viewed by unauthorized persons
- Suggest that employees are speaking on behalf of the organization if they are not authorized to do so
- Have content that could embarrass or criminally implicate the organization

Ideally, the organization's procedures and guidelines handbook should provide clear directions for message content. Many companies require that employees not identify the company's name in Internet transmissions. Others require the following disclaimer at the bottom of any employee's Internet message that contains an opinion: "The opinions expressed are those of the writer and not those of my employer." Of course, those authorized to speak for the organization would not have to provide such disclaimers. Providing guidelines on legal and sensitive content is difficult because of its broad scope and subjective nature, respectively. The employer may want to cite various examples of illegal or offensive content, and obtain the assistance of legal counsel to help write these particular guidelines.

Downloading Precautions

> ABC Company employees who download data, text, video, graphics, voice clips, programs, or any other resource from the Internet should use the appropriate procedures to prevent computer virus crises and to follow laws and copyright agreements.

Computer virus nightmares tend to be widely publicized, and most organizations already have at least some security measures in place to prevent them. The Internet policy should extend the mandate for safe practices to download information from the Internet, and should also direct employees to follow all copyright laws specific to downloading information. The procedures and guidelines supplement can include specific recommendations for safe downloading practices, such as:

- Using anti-viral software to check downloaded files
- Downloading only to stand-alone microcomputers, as opposed to network disk drives
- Downloading only from well-known and reputable sources
- Following all licensing agreements, paying the necessary fees, obeying import or export restrictions, and avoiding unlicensed software

OTHER CONSIDERATIONS WHEN DEVELOPING AN INTERNET POLICY

Although each organization must consider its own unique culture, preexisting infrastructure, and any other applicable factors when developing an Internet policy, the following considerations generally apply to all organizations: e-mail alternatives and causes of runaway Internet expenses.

E-Mail Alternatives

The choice of which electronic mail system to use — Internet, in-house, or vendor supplied — must be made with both an organization's budget and security needs in mind. The organization must answer the question: What is the most cost-effective means to send e-mail messages with a security level appropriate for the message type? The organization's chosen e-mail system may directly influence Internet policy development. For example, consider an organization in which all employees need to have general access to in-house e-mail. This organization's Internet policy may stipulate that all interoffice e-mail travel through the in-house system. The rationale is that this e-mail is likely to be the most confidential and that the organization can better control security on its computer systems. A related policy statement might be that employees should limit Internet e-mail messages to communications with persons outside the organization, with the added restriction that they be nonconfidential in nature or encrypted.

Common Causes of Runaway Internet Expenses

While developing an Internet policy, development teams should keep in mind the following common sources of Internet-related cost overruns:

- Personnel using an external gateway when the organization provides its own
- Different organizational facilities using different external gateway providers when the organization could easily consolidate under one provider

- Excessive use of online services, including those used for personal benefit and enjoyment at company expense
- Duplicate applications throughout the company

CONCLUSION

Ultimately, the formation of an organizational Internet policy is an essential first step for any business embarking on Internet commerce. IS auditors, whose expertise in IS security and control will be tapped by management for input on policy development, should embrace the opportunity to contribute to Internet security at its earliest stages. Auditor involvement from the inception of the development process will ensure that the organization is fully protected from security risks, and will undoubtedly facilitate the auditor's future Internet-related IS auditing.

Chapter 4

Computer Forensics and Privacy: At What Price Do We Police the Internet?

Ralph Spencer Poore

Like the *djinn* of legend, once the genie is out of the bottle, its power is unleashed for both good and evil. Our interconnectivity through the Internet enables cost-effective data transmission to almost any point on the planet. When the data facilitates lawful commerce or promotes human rights, the enchanting magic validates the technology. When the data facilitates murder and mayhem or governmental oppression, then the baneful curse condemns the technology. A completely free society — if it is to survive — requires citizens who exercise self-restraint and who are willing to accept the consequences of failures of that self-restraint. At some threshold of failures, however, citizens demand of their government protection from each other. At some point, such protection curtails the freedom of its citizens, and the citizens find themselves in a police state. Thus, the pendulum swings between anarchy and totalitarianism, between unbridled freedom and censorship, between anonymity (i.e., no accountability) and Big Brother (i.e., no privacy). To achieve a balance of costs and benefits, we must first understand the problems we hope to solve.

First, the philosophical: Is a piece of stone good or evil? Humans are creators and users of tools. Even with simple tools (e.g., a stone axe), the wielder of the tool can do weal or woe. Some technologies may have greater potential for harm than others (e.g., nuclear weapons), but how they are used determines whether they are a bane or a boon. Are we not better served having nuclear weapons to destroy a potentially planet-killing asteroid than

0-8493-1248-5/02/$0.00+$1.50
© 2002 by CRC Press LLC

we would be if we had no technology to prevent our extinction? Perhaps that question can find its answer only in a history we have yet to write — that is, if we avoid destroying ourselves with the technology.

The Internet is a tool — a potent tool worthy of safeguards. The safeguards, however, must not destroy the tool's potential for benevolence in an effort to prevent malevolence.

HOW MESSAGES WORK

Many common software products embed codes in the files they create. These codes range from simple headers that make the type of file more easily identifiable to complex, cryptographic codes or hashes associated with the license or serial number of the specific copy of the product used to create the file. The embedded headers may point to parameters or values set in the product and may even include the name of author of the file to the extent that such a value has been set. The use of digital signatures to protect the integrity of the message may also provide information about the sender of the message. Even a person attempting anonymity may inadvertently create an evidence trail leading directly back to that person.

Exhibit 1 contains an example of a simple e-mail message sent using Microsoft Outlook. The route taken by the message, the originator of the message, and the recipient of the message (as well as additional recipients in this case) are clearly shown in the header. However, the header information goes far beyond "from" and "to" information. It includes software version and release-level information for each product in the traced route. It includes time and date stamps and message identifiers (sufficient information to obtain a copy of the message from an intervening node if the store-and-forward node keeps the copy long enough). It includes the subject line and a unique message identifier that incorporates the sender's e-mail address. Finally, it includes a user identifier (UIDL) that provides a locally unique identifier for the message that may aid in tracing the message within the system of origin. Of course, a knowledgeable perpetrator can easily forge or alter these headers, and successful delivery of the message does not require most of the fields. However, many criminals use technologies they do not understand, leaving evidence they did not know they were leaving. The information security professional who is aware of these sources potentially gains an advantage.

Let's examine Exhibit 1. The fields within this header generally have a fieldname ending with a colon (:). RFC 2076 (revised June 2000 by Jacob Palme), as of the time of my writing, provides a good compilation of common Internet message header fields. You may find it a good reference, especially in support of a wider variety of fields than are in my example. The series of "Received:" fields gives a trace route that includes domain

Exhibit 1. MIME Message Header from MS Outlook

Received: from crius.flash.net (crius.flash.net [209.30.2.40])
   by bunyip.flash.net (8.9.3/Pro-8.9.3) with ESMTP id QAA04424
   for <rsp00re@flash.net>; Fri, 18 Aug 2000 16:54:50 -0500 (CDT)
Received: from vision.connect.net (vision.connect.net [199.1.91.168])
   by crius.flash.net (8.9.3/8.9.3) with ESMTP id QAA24372
   for <ralph@ralph-s-poore.com>; Fri, 18 Aug 2000 16:54:50 -0500 (CDT)
Received: from oemcomputer ([209.95.3.21]) by vision.connect.net
   (Post.Office MTA v3.5.3 release 223 ID# 569-52317U5000L500S0V35)
   with SMTP id net; Fri, 18 Aug 2000 16:53:29 -0500
From: "Douglas Peacock" <Dougie@YourCommand.com>
To: "Millie Kanahan" <mkanahan@greyhawkdiscoveries.com>
Cc: "Ralph Poore" <ralph@ralph-s-poore.com>, "Adam Sinclair" <as66466@aol.com>
Subject: Privacy Information
Date: Fri, 18 Aug 2000 16:51:38 -0500
Message-ID: <LPBBJJFLJFMGGDDIAOLGGELFCDAA.Dougie@YourCommand.com>
MIME-Version: 1.0
Content-Type: text/plain;
   charset="iso-8859-1"
Content-Transfer-Encoding: 7bit
X-Priority: 3 (Normal)
X-MSMail-Priority: Normal
X-Mailer: Microsoft Outlook IMO, Build 9.0.2416 (9.0.2910.0)
Importance: Normal
X-MimeOLE: Produced By Microsoft MimeOLE V5.00.2314.1300
X-UIDL: 3db67a180a01072a9cb6299228fc22a0

names and IP addresses as well as mail software product and release information. The "ESMTP id" is a Simple Mail Transfer Protocol extension for uniquely identifying the message to the local sending system. The "Date:" field provides a time frame down to the second. The "Message-ID:" field provides a globally unique identifier for the message that also includes the identity of the sender. The fields that begin with "X-" are so-called nonstandard extensions, but are Microsoft *de facto* standards. Because the collection of these fields can narrow the search for a specific machine by identifying the software used in creating the message, these fields provide additional clues that may assist the information security professional's investigation.

DOCUMENTS AND ATTACHMENTS

Many widely used software applications today use OLE encapsulation. When originally created in 1991, OLE was an acronym for "Object Linking and Embedding." However, since release 2, the product has expanded so far beyond its original purpose that the original name no longer encompasses its full functionality. Just as "Radio Corporation of America" became so much more that "RCA" became the name in its own right (no longer just an acronym), so has OLE become the name for Microsoft's component integration technology and no longer just an acronym. With OLE, Microsoft products embed volumes of information in the files they create. Microsoft Word and Excel, for example, embed information about the operating environment, software release level, time and date of document creation, time and date of last modification, time and date last printed, date last accessed, and even a globally unique document identifier. If the parameters were set, the document may include the author's name, the organization's name, change history, file name, title of document, subject of document, and names of file templates.

Exhibit 2 describes the Table of Associated Strings (STTBFASSOC) found in Microsoft Word 6 (and later versions) documents. Although the exact coding may change from version to version, the table reflects the content available in such documents. In addition, the File Information Block (FIB) in versions 8 and above contains useful data and indices, including a pointer to STTBFASSOC. Some of this content is available through the "Properties" selection under "File" when the document is open. Other values are accessible only through tools such as the Visual Basic Editor (VBE) or third-party tools such as Caolan McNamara's (caolan.mcnamara@ul.ie) *MSWordView*. Another source describing Word and other Microsoft file structures in detail is the program developer's reference site www.wotsit.org.

Embedded data is not limited to Microsoft products. IBM/Lotus products also contain valuable information for computer forensics. Any product that uses a "wrapper" technology — even if the purpose of the wrapper is to protect the secrecy of the document's contents — embeds data that may help you prove the identity of the originator, the system on which the data was created, or the application used to create the data (usually including the specific version and release level and often including the serial number or globally unique identifier that can point to a specific copy or license holder). The use of digital signatures, digital fingerprints (i.e., cryptographic hashes), and message digests (e.g., MD5 or SHA) may also provide a link back to the originator even if the identity the originator used was false. When such values remain static from document to document or from message to message, they allow the investigator a means of correlating each instance. These values tend to be programmatically accessible, making real-time tracing of messages or transmitted files possible. The FBI may be able to accomplish this with Carnivore in the context of Internet message traffic. An organization could do this for its own network and extend this to searching through files on servers (or, potentially, on client machines

Exhibit 2.   MS Word 6 STTBFASSOC (Table of Associated Strings)

The following are indices into a table of associated strings:

Index Field Name	Index	Description
ibstAssocFileNext	0	Unused
ibstAssocDot	1	Filename of associated template
ibstAssocTitle	2	Title of document
ibstAssocSubject	3	Subject of document
ibstAssocKeyWords	4	Keywords of document
ibstAssocComments	5	Comments of document
ibstAssocAuthor	6	Author of document
ibstAssocLastRevBy	7	Name of person who last revised the document
ibstAssocDataDoc	8	Filename of data document
ibstAssocHeaderDoc	9	Filename of header document
ibstAssocCriteria1	10	Packed string used by print merge record selection
ibstAssocCriteria2	11	Packed string used by print merge record selection
ibstAssocCriteria3	12	Packed string used by print merge record selection
ibstAssocCriteria4	13	Packed string used by print merge record selection
ibstAssocCriteria5	14	Packed string used by print merge record selection
ibstAssocCriteria6	15	Packed string used by print merge record selection
ibstAssocCriteria7	16	Packed string used by print merge record selection
ibstAssocMax	17	Maximum number of strings in string table

as well). If any file with a known author is found to match the "anonymous" file or message by matching a field known to contain a static, high-integrity value, the investigator potentially gains a valuable clue.

POLICY CONSIDERATIONS

When I investigate "anonymous" messages or documents sent to alleged victims (e.g., when someone threatens to harm a client's employee or attempts to extort money or perpetrate some other fraud), I first advise my clients to keep all the messages or documents and to make a copy of them through a file copy tool (as opposed to saving a copy through the mail or document software product itself). I am amazed, however, at the many times when the recipient will delete the message (especially the initial threat, perhaps believing that if by ignoring it the problem will go away on its own). Although we may be able to recover the deleted file, the delay in reporting the initial message or document can prove disastrous to the investigation. Many store-and-forward nodes overlay files, giving the investigator only a small window during which a copy can be made. Some open relay servers strip information when they accomplish the relay. Only by getting back to that server quickly can all the evidence be protected.

I recommend that organizations maintain a copy of all incoming messages for at least 24 hours. They should also have a policy requiring employees to notify management immediately upon the receipt of a threatening, abusive, harassing, or libelous message or an unlawful solicitation. With quick notification and a rapid reaction team (potentially including law enforcement contacts, as search warrants or similar court orders may be necessary), you have the best chance to backtrack a perpetrator. In addition, you can begin collecting messages from the same sender, giving you the opportunity to correlate message content.

ENCRYPTED MESSAGES OR DOCUMENTS

Some perpetrators may attempt to encrypt the documents or messages they send to limit receipt to a specific party. In such cases, decryption at intermediate nodes may not be commercially feasible. In these cases, making a copy of the encrypted file remains necessary but is insufficient. A cleartext copy must be saved from the receiving application. Best practice would include an independent witness to this process who could testify to the correlation between the encrypted copy and the cleartext copy. The use of encryption, however, may give investigators an additional element of proof. Whether they use a product such as PGP or they rely on S/MIME, header information and embedded keying material as well as the cryptogram (i.e., enciphered message) itself may help to prove the identity of the perpetrator or at least the system on which the document or message was encrypted.

PRIVACY

The techniques used in investigating message traffic can also be used to abuse individuals' privacy. The information security professional should develop clear guidelines for investigations that include notice to any employees whose messages or documents were used in the investigation. The timing of these notices must take into consideration the nature of the investigation and whether the employee is a suspect or not. However, when the investigation is completed (unless a court order or administrative ruling requires otherwise), every employee whose document or message was captured for the investigation should receive a formal notice. The organization's overall privacy policy should clearly indicate that all incoming and outgoing messages are subject to monitoring and become or remain the intellectual property of the organization. In this complex and changing area of law, you need to work closely with your firm's legal counsel who, in turn, may wish to seek legal advice from an attorney specializing in privacy-related law. A good source of information on privacy and links to other privacy-related sites is available at www.epic.org.

SUMMARY

In the title to this chapter, I introduced the question, at what price do we police the Internet? Clearly, a price exists if we allow criminals unrestricted and unaccountable use of the Internet. The internetworking of our organizations, with each organization's network boundaries becoming grayer and grayer, amalgamates our organizations with the Internet. If we each do our part to protect our own organizations' networks, we will reduce the risk to the world at large. To the extent that "bad actors" remain within the Internet community, we need to balance the law enforcement needs with our citizens' privacy expectations. The goal of anarchists, terrorists, and the mischievous is usually the reaction caused by their actions, not the direct effect of their actions. If we allow processes such as Carnivore to become routine and acceptable compromises of privacy to make law enforcement easier, we incrementally give away our privacy. Because we have the ability to hold most message senders accountable using existing tools and investigative techniques, do we need to further enable message traffic analysis or do we need to build better policy and technology safeguards against the misuse of what we already have?

Chapter 5
Policies for Secure Personal Data

Michael H. Agranoff

Many believe that computer use in large organizations poses a threat to individual privacy. Most U.S. businesses favor self-regulation instead of computer security legislation to ensure a reasonable level of security for personal data. This chapter explores the need for policies that will be complied with and illustrates some of the technical and administrative issues to be considered along the way. Meaningful policies for secure personal data require organizational commitment to both privacy principles and technical security measures.

OVERVIEW

George Orwell's classic novel *1984* raised the specter of a supergovernment peering into the private lives of all individuals. As it happened, shortly after the publication of that work, the computer revolution began to take shape. Many people thought that private industry would replace Big Brother as the threat to individual privacy.

Yet many would agree today that the worst fears about technology and invasion of privacy have not been realized. For example, there has been no implementation of a national database. In fact, international computer security authority Donn B. Parker has offered the opinion that computer use has sensitized people to the privacy issue and generated new practices and public debates, to the point that "increasing computer usage is improving personal privacy, not destroying it."

That viewpoint assumes that new regulations and codes of conduct will protect, control access to, and preserve the integrity of personal information in computers to a far greater degree than such information can be protected when stored on paper in file cabinets. The idea that increasing computer use improves personal privacy only holds true, however, if proper regulations and codes of conduct are in place. The ability of computers to match information about people, combined with computer networking

0-8493-1248-5/02/$0.00+$1.50
© 2002 by CRC Press LLC

capabilities, creates in effect a mininational data bank, which does not augur well for personal privacy in the absence of specific and enforceable regulations. Therefore, the goal should be for businesses to develop corporate policies for secure personal data, presenting straightforward regulations and codes of conduct to protect personal information in a cost-effective, responsible manner.

THE PRIVACY DEBATE

Many people have an intuitive idea of what *privacy* means, yet different people interpret the term in different ways. The right of privacy is often variously expressed as:

- The right to be left alone
- The right to be free from unreasonable personal intrusion
- An individual's right to determine what personal information can be communicated, and to whom

People are often surprised to learn that privacy is not a constitutional right. It is not mentioned in the U.S. Constitution, and there is no evidence that the Founding Fathers considered the topic. Rather, privacy rights largely developed in the twentieth century, as a mixture of state common law, federal and state statutes, and constitutional law.

An organization wishing to develop policies for secure personal data could quickly become bogged down in trying to decide exactly what kind of information should be protected. Budget constraints may make it appear pointless to spend money to protect an interest that is not judged to be that important. The organization must clarify for itself exactly what interests it wishes to protect. It is important to understand that when computers are involved, two major issues must be addressed: unreasonable intrusion and due process.

Protection Against Unreasonable Intrusion

Permitting others to intrude on their private affairs is one price Americans pay for being members of a highly mobile, commercial society. For example, if individuals wish to have health insurance, they must allow insurers to review their medical and hospital records. To obtain commercial or mortgage credit, consumers must allow others to have access to records that indicate their spending habits.

Most people would agree that these are reasonable intrusions. When, then, do they become unreasonable? It seems, at the very least, that individuals should know what kind of data is being gathered about them and give their consent (which may be implied from the individual's applying for employment or credit). Individuals should also be able to trust that the organization gathering such data will not release it to unauthorized persons but will take active steps to ensure that all employees are properly trained and supervised in this regard. Privacy codes should address the issues of data collection and confidentiality, emphasizing the personal responsibility of those who deal with computerized data to safeguard personal information. This responsibility should not be avoided on the grounds that "the computer did it."

Protection Against Lack of Due Process

Americans have a fundamental belief in the idea of fair play and justice. The American constitutional notion of due process revolves around letting individuals know precisely what is charged against them and giving them a fair opportunity to defend themselves against the charge.

When a computer is involved, people have the right to demand that accurate information is maintained on them. Otherwise, adverse decisions may be made against them without the opportunity to state their side of the story. Indeed, individuals might not even know that there has been a charge made against them. It is, of course, possible that an innocent mistake was made; if so, it should be corrected. It is also possible that a legitimate dispute exists between the data gatherer and the subject, in which case the subject should at least have his or her say. To store erroneous data on individuals without their knowledge, and without offering them the opportunity to correct the data, offends traditional ideas of fundamental fair play and justice.

Privacy codes should therefore emphasize the personal responsibility of managers dealing with computerized data. Management might consider itself responsible for fairness in the gathering, storage, and dissemination of personal data. This responsibility should not be avoided on the grounds that it is someone else's problem. It is possible that the organization could be held liable if personal data were disclosed to an unauthorized person; however, without formal standards, the law is unclear in this regard.

E-Mail Privacy

As a general rule, the courts do not like to get involved in workplace privacy issues. Traditionally, employers, whether public or private, have been allowed great leeway in protecting their business and financial interests by almost any means not clearly illegal. Various cases, both state and federal, have upheld the right of employers to search desks, lockers, file cabinets, and interoffice mail without a search warrant. There are limits if conduct is truly outrageous; but clearly, the courts do not have time to get involved in the management decision process.

Questions may arise as to whether employers should be able to read the electronic mail sent by employees. Because e-mail uses company facilities to transmit business matters, it cannot have the same degree of protection as first-class U.S. mail. Furthermore, companies have legitimate reasons to read e-mail, such as finding lost messages, studying system effectiveness, protecting against fraud and misuse, and recovery. Nonetheless, people do not give up all privacy expectations simply by coming to work.

Privacy codes regarding e-mail should therefore emphasize that business resources are not intended for personal use and should stress employee self-interest in cutting costs. Employees should be told that if communications must be private, they should be placed in interoffice mail marked "Personal and Confidential." One can hardly have an expectation of privacy in an e-mail letter that might have numerous recipients. Finally, managers and administrators must not abuse their authority; they have no right to rifle through employee items for their own amusement or on ill-conceived fishing expeditions.

TRANSBORDER DATA FLOWS

Privacy is also a concern with what is commonly known as transborder data flows. If privacy is not ensured here, it could result in a potential barrier to the free flow of information between nations. Some European countries require an export license for the transfer of personal data because these countries believe that if personal information is violated in another country, it is an infringement on the basic rights of the citizens and a violation of the nation's sovereignty. The 1981 Guidelines of the Organization for Economic Cooperation and Development (OECD) stated that its European member countries should take all reasonable steps to ensure uninterrupted and secure transit for the transborder flow of personal data, but should not develop policies that would create severe obstacles to such flow. If its guidelines are followed and adequate remedies provided for violations, then the free flow of data in commerce should not be a problem. (The European OECD Guidelines are described in this chapter under the major heading, Successful Privacy Codes.)

SELF-REGULATION OF PRIVATE COMPANIES

Most corporations would prefer to develop their own internal privacy codes, rather than be subject to government regulation and audit. This is true whether or not the corporation is a multinational. It follows that international guidelines should be adhered to if they do not present an insurmountable problem.

It seems preferable for corporations to have one privacy code rather than different codes for dealing with different countries. For example, in most respects, corporations should not find it difficult to comply with the general European OECD guidelines. However, many corporations may find it difficult to carry out the assignment of a data controller, or similar authority, that is accountable for privacy compliance as is called for in the European OECD guidelines. Historically, U.S. firms have fragmented this authority, as privacy and data security have not been given top priority. It is definitely time for accountability for information privacy to be established.

It is fair to state that both Europeans and Americans believe in basic due process and in protection against unreasonable intrusion. The difference may be that Americans are less likely to legislate these beliefs, preferring voluntary compliance. Organizations should try to implement policies for secure personal data that will bring about compliance.

SUCCESSFUL PRIVACY CODES

The following organizations have set up their own security codes for protecting personal data.

The Canadian Independent Computing Services Association

The Canadian Independent Computing Services Association (CICS) developed a code, *Privacy Principles for Data Processors,* that has been passed by management and recommended to its members for implementation within its individual companies. This code can act as a guide to corporations that are considering implementing their own internal privacy codes. It reads as follows.

The following principles guide data processing firms in handling client information.

- Information received from a client:
  — Remains the property of the client
  — Will be used only for the purpose for which it was intended
  — Will not be disposed, transferred, sold, or made available to any other party or parties without the specific permission of the client
  — Will be retained only for the limited time necessary for the performance of its functions
- The management of the data processing firm will:
  — Have all employees sign written undertakings to use client information only in accordance with the principles outlined above
  — Secure all data in all reasonable ways against theft or abuse of any kind
  — Restrict use of client data to those employees who require it to fulfill their obligations to the client

The OECD Guidelines

The European OECD has promulgated guidelines for privacy protection and transborder flows of personal data. The OECD specified that these are minimum standards that should be supplemented by additional security measures. These guidelines include the following provisions:

- Personal data should be collected in limited amounts only, and (where appropriate) with the knowledge or consent of the person concerned.
- Data should be obtained by lawful and fair means.
- Data should be accurate, complete, and up-to-date, to ensure its relevance to the purpose for which it was collected.
- Data should be collected only for legitimate purposes, and then not used for other purposes.
- Data should not be disclosed to others, except by consent or in accordance with law enforcement.
- Reasonable security safeguards should exist to ensure protection of data against unauthorized modification, disclosure, or destruction.
- A data controller should be accountable for complying with the preceding principles.

Conferees at a privacy and data protection conference sponsored by the International Chamber of Commerce in 1984 upheld these basic principles and further specified that any data subject should be entitled to the following protections:

- To be informed if an organization is holding data on the individual
- To examine such data on request
- To be able to correct or delete the data if appropriate

The European Council of Ministers

The Council of Ministers of the Committee of Experts on Human Rights of the Council of Europe adopted the following principles for protection of individual privacy in the private sector. Although more than 20 years old, the following principles seem remarkably apt today:

- The information stored should be accurate and kept up-to-date. In general, information relating to the intimate private life of persons or information that might lead to unfair discrimination should not be recorded or, if recorded, should not be disseminated.
- The information should be appropriate and relevant with regard to the purpose for which it has been stored.
- The information should not be obtained by fraudulent or unfair means.
- Rules should be laid down to specify the periods beyond which certain categories of information should no longer be kept or used.

- Without proper authorization, information should not be used for purposes other than those for which it has been stored, nor communicated to third parties.
- As a general rule, the people concerned should have the right to know the information stored about them, the purpose for which it has been recorded, and particulars of each release of this information.
- Every precaution should be taken to correct inaccurate information and to erase obsolete information.
- Precautions should be taken against any abuse or misuse of information, and data banks should be protected from unauthorized access.
- Access to the information stored should be confined to persons who have a valid reason to know it.
- Statistical data should be released only in aggregate form and in such a way that it is impossible to link the information to a particular person.

DATA SECURITY PROCEDURES

It is wholly unsatisfactory to publish policies for secure personal data if these policies will not be taken seriously. Grand statements supporting data privacy and accuracy mean very little unless there are the necessary automated and manual procedures to enforce the policies. These include password protection, authorization procedures, physical security controls, encryption, and other security mechanisms.

Password Protection

An adequate password system is integral to data security. Software is needed that limits computer access to properly authenticated individuals.

Passwords should be unique to each individual authorized to access the system and should be changed regularly. Passwords should not be rotated back and forth among users and should not be easy to guess. Software-based formulae might be used to weed out easily guessed combinations. Of course, passwords should be at least six characters long.

Passwords should be subject to management inspection to ensure that they have not been written down or otherwise compromised. Other measures to protect passwords include suppressing passwords on the terminal, encrypting them on the access control file, subjecting passwords to terminal idle time log-off after a minute or so, and logging passwords for errors, with the terminal shut down or the ID disabled as appropriate. There may be highly sensitive applications for which a password system would be inadequate and signature authentication or another identification technology would be preferred.

Plainly, it is not enough to establish privacy principles and then state that they will be enforced by adequate passwords. The organization must implement authentication methods that offer the best protection in ensuring data privacy. Audut trails should be used to identify problems or monitor suspected violations.

Authorization Procedures

It is necessary to limit authorized users to those files (and other resources) that are necessary for them to perform their jobs. In addition to authentication measures, authorization procedures must be in place. Most organizations have authorization software in one form or another, but it is a mistake to assume that software guarantees protection.

Not all authorization schemes are created equal. Some merely burden legitimate users and offer little or no real protection against hackers. Authorization software must be established and maintained, for each file or resource, by a knowledgeable person who is responsible for the security of that file or resource. Periodic checks against lists of authorized users, as verified by the personnel department, will help ensure that the list remains accurate. There should also be techniques to screen personnel who could be in a position to circumvent authorization procedures. Systems programmers could, without supervision or accountability, override or bypass the security system. Computer operators could read sensitive residue left in core, or the software could be read as part of terminal backup procedures. Although most computer crime reports focus on outside hackers, insiders represent great potential vulnerability. No class of persons should be exempt from accountability.

Authorization software may be rendered ineffective by add-on hardware and software if the security system is not hardware and software independent. Therefore, the security function must be involved in systems testing.

Clearly, authenticating users is not enough. Users must be restricted to necessary resources, but this is far more difficult to implement than password protection. An independent auditing team, even one using a tiger team approach in which attempts are made to breach file security, is essential to ensure data security.

Terminal Security Measures

Terminal security largely involves a mixture of physical security and proper management controls. For example, when possible, terminals should be in a secure area, an area not generally open to the public. When terminals must be placed in public locations, such as reception areas, the terminal should be turned off, or even locked if possible.

For sensitive functions, entry can be restricted to terminals located in secured areas. All terminals should be programmed to log off if certain conditions occur, such as several incorrect passwords in a row or excessive idle time. A properly qualified security official should be authorized to reinstate the terminal; this should not be a routine, low-level function.

Other Procedures

Even with adequate password protection, authorization software, and terminal security measures, a system that has no data encryption is at risk. For example, individual passwords should be encrypted. Messages should be considered for encryption during transmission, with encryption keys securely controlled by responsible persons. In addition, if the encryption algorithm has been developed by an outside agency, it may be wise to ensure the integrity of that agency and be certain that the encryption is not compromised by a trap door in the application. In addition, effective data security includes the following procedures:

1. A contingency plan that has been tested and kept up to date
2. Timely follow-up of violation reports
3. Computer security audits conducted by individuals who do not report to data processing but who are as well versed in the system, as are the systems programmers
4. Background checks on employees in sensitive positions
5. Regular security education and awareness programs featuring classroom instruction and general organizational publicity efforts
6. Personnel policies such as job rotation, separation of duties, and encouragement of reporting unusual behavior at work
7. Business interruption insurance
8. Virus protection programs
9. Establishment and maintenance of a corporatewide security policy and procedures manual

Perhaps most important, a senior manager must assume overall responsibility for computer security and privacy protection. This manager should not have concurrent computer performance responsibilities that might create a conflict of interest.

POLICIES FOR SECURE PERSONAL DATA

Policies for secure personal data require, at a minimum, two elements:

- *Commitment to internal privacy code principles.* An organization should not develop policies until it knows precisely what it is trying to protect and what principles it will adhere to. Otherwise, the policies will tend to be ignored when they come up against organizational realities. Privacy code principles, based on protection

49

against unreasonable intrusion and due process principles, may be a good starting point. It should be remembered, however, that each organization is different and must adopt its own principles.

• *Commitment to meaningful data security.* It is useless for an organization to develop policies, however sound, if the technology is unable to support those policies. Laws against bank robbery and theft would be meaningless if banks left money in the open with no guards, vaults, or alarms to protect it. A commitment to data privacy unsupported by the necessary technological and administrative methods is just as foolish and deceives the public, senior management, and the board of directors. Independent information security management is a must.

RECOMMENDED COURSE OF ACTION

Most organizations believe that they must take responsibility for the computer systems they create and that this responsibility includes taking reasonable measures to secure the personal data stored in such systems. The problem is in deciding what measures are reasonable. Organizations should consider this problem in steps. First, they must determine privacy code principles by defining major goals and the personal responsibilities of those involved. Second, they must determine what technical and administrative measures are required to meet these goals. Password, authorization, and administrative schemes that merely look good on paper are not the answer. It is inevitable that choices will be made on the basis of cost considerations, but organizations must implement internal privacy codes if they believe that voluntary compliance is better than government mandate. In all cases, the assignment of specific individual responsibility for information privacy and security is essential for success in a large organization.

Chapter 6
Making Security Awareness Happen

Susan Hansche

This chapter focuses on the initial step of providing computer and information system security — developing and implementing an effective security awareness program. Then it presents a complete IT security training program.

THE SECURITY AWARENESS PROGRAM

One might wonder why security awareness is not considered the same as training. The simple answer: because the desired outcome of each is different. The goal of a security awareness program is to heighten the importance of information systems security and the possible negative effects of a security breach or failure. During an awareness campaign, the end user simply receives information. It is designed to reach a broad audience using various promotional techniques. In a training environment, the student is expected to be an active participant in the process of acquiring new insights, knowledge, and skills. When designing and developing an information technology (IT) security training program, there is a wide range of options that are based on specific job requirements and the daily management, operation, and protection of information systems.

Information technology is apparent in every aspect of our daily life — so much so that in many instances, it seems completely natural. Can you imagine conducting business without e-mail or voice mail? How about hand-writing a report that is later typed using an electric typewriter? As one is well aware, computer technology and open-connected networks are the core components of all organizations, regardless of the industry or the specific business needs.

Information technology has enabled organizations in the government and private sectors to create, process, store, and transmit an unprecedented amount of information. The IT infrastructure created to handle this information flow has become an integral part of how business is conducted. In fact,

0-8493-1248-5/02/$0.00+$1.50
© 2002 by CRC Press LLC

most organizations consider themselves dependent on their information systems. This dependency on information systems has created the need to ensure that the physical assets (e.g., the hardware and software) and the information they process are protected from actions that could jeopardize the ability of the organization to effectively perform official duties.

Several IT security reports estimate that if a business does not have access to its data for more than ten days, it cannot financially recover from the economic loss.

While advances in IT have increased exponentially, very little has been done to inform users of the vulnerabilities and threats of the new technologies. In March 1999, Patrice Rapalus, Director of the Computer Security Institute, noted that "corporations and government agencies that want to survive in the 'Information Age' will have to dedicate more resources to staffing and training of information system security professionals." To take this a step further, not only must information systems security professionals receive training, but all employees who have access to information systems must be made aware of the vulnerabilities and threats to the IT system they use and what they can do to help protect their information.

Employees — especially end users of the IT system — are typically not aware of the security consequences caused by certain actions. For most employees, the IT system is a tool to perform their job responsibilities as quickly and efficiently as possible; security is viewed as a hindrance rather than a necessity. Thus, it is imperative for every organization to provide employees with IT-related security information that points out the threats and ramifications of not actively participating in the protection of their information. In fact, federal agencies are required by law (Computer Security Act of 1987) to provide security awareness information to all end users of information systems.

Employees are one of the most important factors in ensuring the security of IT systems and the information they process. In many instances, IT security incidents are the result of employee actions that originate from inattention and not being aware of IT security policies and procedures. Therefore, informed and trained employees can be a crucial factor in the effective functioning and protection of information systems. If employees are aware of IT security issues, they can be the first line of defense in the prevention and early detection of problems. In addition, when everyone is concerned and focused on IT security, the protection of assets and information can be much easier and more efficient.

To protect the confidentiality, integrity, and availability of information, organizations must ensure that all individuals involved understand their responsibilities. To achieve this, employees must be adequately informed of the policies and procedures necessary to protect the IT system. As such, all end users of information systems must understand the basics of IT security and be able to apply good security habits in the daily work environment. After receiving commitment from senior management, one of the initial steps is to clearly define the objective of the security awareness program. Once the goal has been established, the content must be decided, including the type of implementation (delivery) options available. During this process, key factors to consider include how to overcome obstacles and face resistance. The final step is evaluating success; and this article now focuses on the steps in developing an IT security awareness program.

SETTING THE GOAL

Before beginning to develop the content of a security awareness program, it is essential to establish the objective or goal. It may be as simple as "all employees must understand their basic security responsibilities" or "develop in all employees an awareness of the IT security threats the organization faces and motivate the employees to develop the necessary habits to counteract the threats and protect the IT system." Some may find it necessary to develop something more detailed, such as:

Awareness Program Objectives

Employees must be aware of:

- Threats to physical assets and stored information
- Threats to open network environments
- Federal laws they are required to follow, such as copyright violations or privacy act information
- Specific organization or department policies they are required to follow
- How to identify and protect sensitive (or classified) information
- How to store, label, and transport information
- Who they should report security incidents to, regardless of whether it is just a suspected or an actual incident
- E-mail and Internet policies and procedures

When establishing the goals for the security awareness program, keep in mind that these goals should reflect and support the overall mission and goals of the organization. At this point in the process, it may be the right (or necessary) time to provide a status report to the chief information officer (CIO) or other executive and senior management members.

DECIDING ON THE CONTENT

An IT security awareness program should create sensitivity to the threats and vulnerabilities of IT systems and also remind employees of the need to protect the information they create, process, transmit, and store. Basically, the focus of an IT security awareness program is to raise the security consciousness of all employees.

The level and type of content depend on the needs of the organization. Essentially, employees need to be told what they need to protect, how they should protect it, and how important IT systems security is to the organization.

IMPLEMENTATION (DELIVERY) OPTIONS

The methods and options available for delivering security awareness information are very similar to those used for delivering other employee awareness information (e.g., sexual harassment or business ethics). And although this is true, it may be time to break with tradition and step out of the box — in other words, it may be time to try something new.

Think of positive, fun, exciting, and motivating methods that will give employees the message and encourage them to practice good computer security habits. Keep in mind that the success of an awareness program is its ability to reach a large audience through several attractive and engaging materials and techniques. Examples of IT security awareness materials and techniques include:

- Posters
- Posting motivational and catchy slogans
- Videotapes
- Classroom instruction
- Computer-based delivery, such as CD-ROM or intranet access
- Brochures/flyers
- Pens/pencils/keychains (any type of trinket) with motivational slogans
- Post-it notes with a message on protecting the IT system
- Stickers for doors and bulletin boards
- Cartoons/articles published monthly or quarterly in in-house newsletter or specific department notices
- Special topical bulletins (security alerts in this instance)
- Monthly e-mail notices related to security issues or e-mail broadcasts of security advisories
- Security banners or pre-logon messages that appear on the computer monitor
- Distribution of food items as an incentive. (For example, distribute packages of the gummy-bear type candy that is shaped into little snakes. Attach a card to the package, with the heading "Gummy Virus Attack at XYZ." Add a clever message such as: "Destroy all viruses wiggling through the network — make sure your anti-virus software is turned on.")

The Web site http://awarenessmaterials.homestead.com/ lists the following options:

- First-aid kit with slogan: "It's healthy to protect our patient's information, it's healthy to protect our information."
- Mirror with slogan: "Look who is responsible for protecting our information."
- Toothbrush with slogan: "Your password is like this toothbrush: use it regularly, change it often, and do not share it with anyone else."
- Badge holder (retractable) with slogan: "Think Security"
- Key-shaped magnet with slogan: "You are the key to good security!"
- Flashlight with slogan: "Keep the spotlight on information protection."

Another key success factor in an awareness program is remembering that it never ends — the awareness campaign must repeat its message. If the message is very important, then it should be repeated more often, and in a different manner each time. Because IT security awareness must be an ongoing activity, it requires creativity and enthusiasm to maintain the interest of all audience members. The awareness materials should create an atmosphere that IT security is important not only to the organization, but also to each employee. It should ignite an interest in following the IT security policies and rules of behavior.

An awareness program must remain current. If IT security policies are changing, the employees must be notified. It may be necessary and helpful to set up technical means to deliver immediate information. For example, if the next "lovebug" virus has been circulating overnight, the system manager could post a pre-logon message to all workstations. In this manner, the first item the users see when turning on their workstations is information on how to protect the system, such as what to look for and what not to open.

Finally, the security awareness campaign should be simple. For most organizations, the awareness campaign does not need to be expensive, complicated, or overly technical in its delivery. Make it easy for employees to get the information and make it easy to understand.

Security awareness programs should (be):

- Supported and led by example from management
- Simple and straightforward
- Positive and motivating
- A continuous effort
- Repeat the most important messages
- Entertaining
- Humorous where appropriate — make slogans easy to remember
- Tell employees what the threats are and their responsibilities for protecting the system

In some organizations, it may be a necessary (or viable) option to outsource the design and development of the awareness program to a qualified vendor. To find the best vendor to meet an organization's needs, one can review products and services on the Internet, contact others and discuss their experiences, and seek proposals from vendors that list previous experiences and outline their solutions to your goals.

OVERCOMING OBSTACLES

As with any employee-wide program, the security awareness campaign *must* have support from senior management. This includes the financial means to develop the program. For example, each year management must allocate dollars that will support the awareness materials and efforts. Create a project plan that includes the objectives, cost estimates for labor and other materials, and time schedules and outline any specific deliverables (i.e., 15-minute video, pens, pencils, etc.). Have management approve the plan and set aside specific funds to create and develop the security awareness materials.

Keep in mind that some employees will display passive resistance. These are the employees who will not attend briefings, and who will create a negative atmosphere by ignoring procedures and violating security policies. There is also active resistance when an employee may purposefully object to security protections and fight with management over policies. For example, many organizations disable the floppy drive in workstations to reduce the potential of viruses entering the network. If an employee responds very negatively, management may stop disabling the floppy drives. For this reason, it is important to gain management support *before* beginning any type of security procedures associated with the awareness campaign.

Although there will be resistance, most employees (this author is convinced it is 98 percent) want to perform well in their jobs, do the right thing, and abide by the rules. Do not let the nay-sayers affect security efforts — computer security is too important to let a few negative people disrupt achieving good security practices for the organization.

Frustrated at this point? It is common for companies to agree to an awareness program but not allocate any human or financial resources. Again, do not be deterred. Plan big, but start small. Something as simple as sending e-mail messages or putting notices in the newsletter can be a cost-effective first step. When management begins to see the effect of the awareness material (of course they will notice — you will be pointing them out), then the needed resources may be allocated. The important thing is to keep trying and doing all that one can with the available resources (or lack of them).

Employees are the single, most important asset in protecting the IT system, and users who are aware of good security practices can ensure that information remains safe and available.

Check out the awareness tip from Mike Lambert, CISSP, on his Web page: http://www.frontiernet.net/~mlambert/awareness/. Step-by-step directions and information are provided on how to develop "pop-up announcements." A great idea!

EVALUATION

All management programs, including the security awareness program, must be periodically reviewed and evaluated. In most organizations there will be no need to conduct a formal quantitative or qualitative analysis. It should be sufficient to informally review and monitor whether behaviors or attitudes have changed. The following list provides a few simple options to consider.

1. Distribute a survey or questionnaire seeking input from employees. If an awareness briefing is conducted during the new-employee orientation, follow up with the employee (after a specified time period of three to six months) and ask how the briefing was perceived (i.e., what do they remember, on what would they have liked more information, etc.).
2. While pouring a cup of coffee in the morning, ask others in the room about the awareness campaign. How did they like the new poster? How about the cake and ice cream during the meeting? Remember: the objective is to heighten the employee's awareness and responsibilities of computer security. Thus, even if the response is, "That poster is silly," do not fret; it was noticed and that is what is important.
3. Track the number and type of security incidents that occur before and after the awareness campaign. Most likely, it is a positive sign if there is an increase in the number of reported incidents. This is an indication that users know what to do and who to contact if they suspect a computer security breach or incident.
4. Conduct "spot checks" of user behavior. This may include walking through the office, checking to see if workstations are logged in while unattended or if sensitive media are not adequately protected.
5. If delivering awareness material via a computer-based delivery (e.g., loading it on the organization's intranet), record user names and completion status. On a periodic basis, check to see who has reviewed the material. One could also send a targeted questionnaire to those who have completed the online material.
6. Have the system manager run a password-cracking program against the employees' passwords. If this is done, consider running the program on a stand-alone computer and not installing it on the

network. Usually, it is not necessary or desirable to install this type of software on a network server. Beware of some free password-cracking programs available from the Internet because they may contain malicious code that will export a password list to a waiting hacker.

Keep in mind that the evaluation process should reflect and answer whether or not the original objectives/goals of the security awareness program have been achieved. Sometimes, evaluations focus on the wrong item. For example, when evaluating an awareness program, it would not be appropriate to ask each employee how many incidents have occurred over the past year. However, it would be appropriate to ask each employee if he or she knows whom to contact if a security incident is suspected.

SUMMARY

Employees are the single, most important aspect of an information system security program, and management support is the key to ensuring a successful awareness program.

The security awareness program needs to be a line item in the information system security plan. In addition to the operational and technical countermeasures that are needed to protect the system, awareness (and training) must also be an essential item. Various computer crime statistics show that the threat from insiders ranges from 65 to 90 percent. This is not an indication that 60 percent of the employees in an organization are trying to hack into the system; it does mean that employees, whether intentionally or accidentally, may allow some form of harm to the system. This includes loading illegal copies of screen-saver software, downloading shareware from the Internet, creating weak passwords, or sharing their passwords with others. Thus, employees need to be made aware of the IT system "rules of behavior" and how to practice good computer security skills. Further, in federal organizations, it is a law (Computer Security Act of 1987) that every federal employee must receive security awareness training on an annual basis.

The security awareness program should be structured to meet the organization's specific needs. The first step is to decide on the goals of the program — what it should achieve — and then to develop a program plan. This plan should then be professionally presented to management. It is hoped that the program will receive the necessary resources for success, such as personnel, monetary, and moral support. In the beginning, even if there are not enough resources available, start with the simple and no-cost methods of distributing information. Keep in mind that it is important just to begin, and along the way seek more resources and ask for assistance from key IT team members.

The benefit of beginning with an awareness campaign is to set the stage for the next level of IT security information distribution, which is IT security training. Following the awareness program, all employees should receive site-specific training on the basics of IT security. Remember that awareness does not end when training begins; it is a continuous and important feature of the information system security awareness and training program. (For more information, see *Building an Information Security Awareness Program* by Mark B. Desman, Auerbach Publications, 2002.)

THE INFORMATION SECURITY TRAINING PROGRAM

Training is more formal and interactive than an awareness program. It is directed toward building knowledge, skills, and abilities that facilitate job capabilities and performance. The days of long and, dare one say, boring lectures have been replaced with interactive and meaningful training. The days when instructors were chosen for their specific knowledge, regardless of whether they knew how to communicate that knowledge, have disappeared. Instructional design (i.e., training) is now an industry that requires professionals to know instructional theories, procedures, and techniques. Its focus is on ensuring that students develop skills and practices that once they leave the training environment will be applicable to their job. In addition, training needs to be a motivator; thus, it should spark the student's curiosity to learn more.

During the past decade, the information systems security training field has strived to stay current with the rapid advances of information technologies. One example of this is the U.S. National Institute of Standards and Technology (NIST) document, SP800-16 "IT Security Training Requirements: A Role- and Performance-Based Model." This document, developed in 1998, provides a guideline to federal agencies developing IT security training programs. Even if an organization is in the private sector, NIST SP800-16 may be helpful in outlining a baseline of what type and level of information should be offered. For this reason, a brief overview of the NIST document is included in this article. Following this overview, the article follows the five phases of the traditional instructional systems design (ISD) model for training: needs analysis and goal formation, design, development, implementation, and evaluation. The ISD model provides a systematic approach to instructional design and highlights the important relationship and linkage between each phase. When following the ISD model, a key significant aspect is matching the training objectives with the subsequent design and development of the content material. The ISD model begins by focusing on what the student is to know or be able to do after the training. Without this beginning, the remaining phases can be inefficient and ineffective. Thus, the first step is establishing the training needs and outlining the program goals. In the design and development phase, the content, instructional strategies, and training delivery methods are decided. The implementation phase includes the actual delivery of the material. Although the evaluation of the instructional material is usually considered something that occurs after completing the implementation, it should be considered an ongoing element of the entire process. The final section of the article provides a suggested IT security course curriculum. It lists several courses that may be needed to meet the different job duties and roles required to protect the IT system. Keep in mind that course curriculum for an organization should match the identified training needs.

NIST SP800-16 "IT Security Training Requirements: A Role- and Performance-Based Model" (Available from the NIST Web site http://csrc.nist.gov/nistpubs/)

The NIST SP800-16 IT Security Learning Continuum provides a framework for establishing an information systems security training program. It states that after beginning an awareness program, the transitional stage to training is "Security Basics and Literacy." The instructional goal of "Security Basics and Literacy" is to provide a foundation of IT security knowledge by providing key security terms and concepts. This basic information is the basis for all additional training courses.

Although there is a tendency to recognize employees as specific job titles, the goal of the NIST SP800-16 IT Security Learning Continuum is to focus on IT-related job functions and not job titles. The NIST IT Security Learning Continuum is designed for the changing workforce — as an employee's role changes or as the organization changes, the needs for IT security training also change. Think of the responsibilities and daily duties required of a system manager ten years ago versus today. Over the course of time, employees will acquire different roles in relationship to the IT system. Thus, instead of saying the system manager needs a specific course, SP800-16 states that the person responsible for a specific IT system function will need a specific type of training.

Essentially, it is the job function and related responsibilities that will determine what IT system security course is needed. This approach recognizes that an employee may have several job requirements and thus may need several different IT security training classes to meet the variety of duties. It can be a challenge to recognize this new approach and try to fit the standard job categories into this framework. In some organizations, this may not be possible. However, irrespective of the job function or organization, there are several IT security topics that should be part of an IT system security curriculum. Always keep in mind that the training courses that are offered must be selected and prioritized based on the organization's immediate needs.

In an ideal world, each organization would have financial resources to immediately fund all aspects of an IT security training program. However, the reality is that resource constraints will force an evaluation of training needs against what is possible and feasible. In some cases, an immediate training need will dictate the beginning or first set of training courses.

If you are struggling with how to implement a training program to meet your needs, training professionals can help to determine immediate needs and provide guidance based on previous experiences and best practices.

Management Buy-In

Before the design and development of course content, one of the first challenges of a training program is receiving support from all levels of the organization, especially senior management. Within any organization are the "training believers" and the "on-the-job-learning believers." In other words, some managers believe that training is very important and will financially support training efforts, while others believe that money should not be spent on training and employees should learn the necessary skills while performing their job duties. Thus, it is an important first step to convince senior managers that company-provided training is valuable and essential.

Senior management needs to understand that training belongs on the top of everyone's list. When employees are expected to perform new skills, the value of training must be carefully considered and evaluated.

To help persuade senior management on the importance of sponsoring training, consider these points:

- Training helps provide employee retention. To those who instantly thought that "No, that is not right. We spend money to train our employees and then they leave and take those skills to another company," there is another side. Those employees will leave anyway; but, on average, employees who are challenged by their job duties (and satisfied with their pay) and believe that the company will provide professional growth and opportunities will stay with the company.
- Find an ally in senior management who can be an advocate. When senior managers are discussing business plans, it is important to have someone speak positively about training programs during those meetings.
- Make sure the training program reflects the organizational need. In many instances, one will need to persuade management on the benefits of the training program. This implies that one knows the weaknesses of the current program and that one can express how the training program will overcome the unmet requirements.

- Market the training program to all employees. Some employees believe they can easily learn skills and do not need to take time for training. Thus, it is important to emphasize how the training will meet the employee's business needs.
- Start small and create a success. Management is more likely to dedicate resources to training if an initial program has been successful.
- Discover management's objections. Find out the issues and problems that may be presented. Also, try to find out what management likes or does not like in training programs, then make sure the training program used will overcome these challenges. Include management's ideas in the program — although it will be impossible to please everyone, it is a worthy goal to meet most everyone's needs.
- Be an enthusiastic proponent! If you do not believe in the training program and its benefits, neither will anyone else.

ESTABLISHING THE INFORMATION SYSTEM SECURITY TRAINING NEED

After receiving management approval, the next step in the development of a training program is to establish and define the training need. Basically, a training need exists when an employee lacks the knowledge or skill to perform an assigned task. This implies that a set of performance standards for the task must also exist. The creation of performance standards is accomplished by defining the task and the knowledge, skills, abilities, and experiences (KSA&Es) needed to perform the task. Then compare what KSA&Es the employees currently possess with those that are needed to successfully perform the task. The differences between the two are the training needs.

In the information systems security arena, several U.S. government agencies have defined a set of standards for job functions or tasks. In addition to the NIST SP800-16, the National Security Telecommunications and Information Systems Security Committee (NSTISSC) has developed a set of INFOSEC training standards. For example, NSTISSC has developed national training standards for four specific IT security job functions: Information Systems Security Professionals (NSTISSC #4011); the Designated Approving Authority (NSTISSI #4012); System Administrator in Information System Security (NSTISSC #4013); and Information System Security Officer (NSTISSC #4014). The NIST and NSTISSC documents can be helpful in determining the standards necessary to accomplish the information system security tasks or responsibilities.

Once the needs analysis has been completed, the next step is to prioritize the training needs. When making this decision, several factors should be considered: legal requirements; cost-effectiveness; management pressure; the organization's vulnerabilities, threats, information sensitivity, and risks; and who is the student population. For some organizations (i.e., federal agencies, banking, health care), the legal requirements will dictate some of the decisions about what training to offer. To determine cost-effectiveness, think about the costs associated with an untrained staff. For example, the costs associated with a network failure are high. If an information system is shut down and the organization's IT operations cease to exist for an extended period of time, the loss of money and wasted time would be enormous. Thus, training system administrators would be a high priority. Executive pressures will come from within, usually the chief information officer (CIO) or IT security officer. If an organization has conducted a risk assessment, executive-level management may prioritize training based on what it perceives as the greatest risks. Finally, and what is usually the most typical determining factor, training is prioritized based on the student population that has the most problems or the most immediate need.

Due to the exponential technological advances, information system security is continually evolving. As technology changes, so do the vulnerabilities and threats to the system. Taking it one step further, new threats require new countermeasures. All of these factors necessitate the continual training of IT system professionals. As such, the IT Security Training Program must also evolve and expand with the technological innovations.

In conducting the needs analysis, defining the standards, prioritizing the training needs, and finalizing the goals and objectives, keep in mind that when beginning an information system security training program, it is necessary to convince management and employees of its importance. Also, as with all programs, the training program's success will be its ability to meet the organization's overall IT security goals, and these goals must be clearly defined in the beginning of the program.

Developing the Program Plan

Once the training needs are known, the plan for the training program can be developed. The program plan outlines the specific equipment, material, tasks, schedule, and personnel and financial resources needed to produce the training program. The program plan provides a sequence and definition of the activities to be performed, such as deliverables for specific projects. One of the most common mistakes that training managers make is thinking they do not need a plan. Remember this common saying: If you do not plan your work, you cannot work your plan.

Another mistake is not seeking approval from senior management for the program plan. An integral part of program planning is ensuring that the plan will work. Thus, before moving to the next step, review the plan with senior managers. In addition, seeking consensus and agreement at this stage allows others to be involved and feel a part of the process — an essential component to success.

INSTRUCTIONAL STRATEGY (TRAINING DESIGN AND DEVELOPMENT)

The design of the training program is based on the learning objectives. The learning objectives are based on the training needs. Thus, the instructional strategy (training delivery method) is based on the best method of achieving the learning objectives.

In choosing an instructional strategy, the focus should be on selecting the best method for the learning objectives, the number of students, and the organization's ability to efficiently deliver the instructional material. The key is to understand the learning objectives, the students, and the organization.

During the design and development phase, the content material is outlined and developed into instructional units or lessons. Remember that content should be based on what employees need to know and do to perform their job duties. During the needs analysis, the tasks and duties for specific job functions may have been established. If the content is not task-driven, the focus is on what type of behaviors or attitudes are expected. This involves defining what performance employees would exhibit when demonstrating the objective and what is needed to accomplish the goal. The idea is to describe what someone would do or display to be considered competent in the behavior or attitude. The course topics must be sequenced to build new or complex skills onto existing ones and to encourage and enhance the student's motivation for learning the material.

A well-rounded information system security training program will involve multiple learning methods. When making a decision about the instructional strategy, one of the underlying principles should be to choose a strategy that is as simple as possible while still achieving the objectives. Another factor is the instructional material itself — not all content fits neatly into one type of instructional strategy. That is, for training effectiveness, look at the learning objectives and content to determine what would be the best method for students to learn the material. One of the current philosophies for instructional material is that it should be "edutainment," which is the combination of education and entertainment. Because this is a hotly debated issue, this author's advice is not to get cornered into taking a side. Look at who the audience will be and what the content is, and then make a decision that best fits the learning objective.

When deciding on the method, here are a few tips:

- Who is the audience? It is important to consider the audience size and location. If the audience is large and geographically dispersed, a technology-based solution (i.e., computer-based [CD-ROM] or Web-based training [delivery over the Internet]) may be more efficient.

- What are the business needs? For example, if a limited amount of travel money is available for students, then a technology-based delivery may be applicable. Technology-based delivery can reduce travel costs. However, technology-based training usually incurs more initial costs to design and develop; thus, some of the travel costs will be spent in developing the technology-based solution.
- What is the course content? Some topics are better suited for instructor-led, video, Web, or CD-ROM delivery. Although there are many debates about what is the best delivery method (and everyone will have an opinion), seek out the advice of training professionals who can assess the material and make recommendations.
- What type of learner interaction is necessary? Is the course content best presented as self-paced individual instruction or as group instruction? Some instructional materials are better suited for face-to-face and group interaction, while other content is best suited for creative interactive individualized instruction. For example, if students are simply receiving information, a technology-based solution may be more appropriate. If students are required to perform problem-solving activities in a group, then a classroom setting would be better.
- What type of presentations or classroom activities need to be used? If the course content requires students to install or configure an operating system, a classroom lab might be best.
- How stable is the instructional material? The stability of content can be a cost issue. If content will change frequently, the expense of changing the material must be estimated in difficulty, time, and money. Some instructional strategies can be revised more easily and cost-efficiently than others.
- What type of technology is available for training delivery? This is a critical factor in deciding the instructional strategy. The latest trend is to deliver training via the Internet or an intranet. For this to be successful, students must have the technological capability to access the information. For example, in instances where bandwidth could limit the amount of multimedia (e.g., audio, video, and graphic animations) that can be delivered, a CD-ROM solution may be more effective.

Regardless of the instructional strategy, there are several consistent elements that will be used to present information. This includes voice, text, still or animated pictures/graphics, video, demonstrations, simulations, case studies, and some form of interactive exercises. In most courses, several presentation methods are combined. This allows for greater flexibility in reaching all students and also for choosing the best method to deliver the instructional content. If the reader is unfamiliar with the instructional strategies available, refer to "Making Security Awareness Happen: Appendices" (82-01-04) for a detailed definition of instructor-led and technology-based training delivery methods.

While deciding on what type of instructional strategy is best suited for the training needs, it is necessary to explore multiple avenues of information. Individuals should ask business colleagues and training professionals about previous training experiences and evaluate the responses. Keep in mind that the instructional strategy decision must be based on the instructional objectives, course content, delivery options, implementation options, technological capabilities, and available resources, such as time and money.

Possible Course Curriculum

Appendix B (82-01-04) contains a general list of IT security topics that can be offered as IT system security training courses. The list is intended to be flexible. Remember that as technologies change, so will the types of courses. This list merely represents the type of training courses that an organization might consider. Additionally, the course content should be combined and relabeled based on the organization's particular training needs.

"Making Security Awareness Happen: Appendices" (82-01-04) contains more detailed information for each course, including the title, brief description, intended audience, high-level list of topics, and other information as appropriate. The courses listed in Appendix B are based on some of the skills necessary to meet the requirements of an information system security plan. It is expected that each organization would prioritize its training needs and then define what type of courses to offer. Because several of these topics (and many more) are available from third-party training companies, it is not necessary to develop custom courses for one's organization. However, the content within these outside courses is general in nature. Thus, for an organization to receive the most effective results, the instructional material should be customized by adding the organization's own policies and procedures. The use of outside sources in this customization can be both beneficial and cost effective for the organization.

EVALUATING THE INFORMATION SYSTEM SECURITY TRAINING PLAN

Evaluating training effectiveness is an important element of an information system security training plan. It is an ongoing process that starts at the beginning of the training program. During all remaining phases of the training program, whether it is during the analysis, design, development, or implementation stage, evaluation must be built into the plan.

Referring back to NIST SP800-16, the document states that evaluating training effectiveness has four distinct but interrelated purposes to measure:

1. The extent that conditions were right for learning and the learner's subjective satisfaction
2. What a given student has learned from a specific course
3. A pattern of student outcomes following a specified course
4. The value of the class compared to other options in the context of an organization's overall IT security training program

Further, the evaluation process should produce four types of measurement, each related to one of the evaluation's four purposes; the evaluation process should:

1. Yield information to assist the employees themselves in assessing their subsequent on-the-job performance
2. Yield information to assist the employee's supervisors in assessing individual students' subsequent on-the-job performance
3. Produce trend data to assist trainers in improving both learning and teaching
4. Produce return-on-investment statistics to enable responsible officials to allocate limited resources in a thoughtful, strategic manner among the spectrum of IT security awareness, security literacy, training, and education options for optimal results among the workforce as a whole

To obtain optimal results, it is necessary to plan for the collection and organization of data, and then plan for the time an analyst will need to evaluate the information (data) and extrapolate its meaning to the organization's goals.

One of the most important elements of effective measurement and evaluation is selecting the proper item to measure. Thus, regardless of the type of evaluation or where it occurs, the organization must agree on what it should be evaluating, such as perceptions, knowledge, or a specific set of skills. Because resources, such as labor hours and monies, are at a premium for demand, the evaluation of the training program must become an integral part of the training plan.

Keep in mind that evaluation has costs. The costs involve thought, time, energy, and money. Therefore, evaluation must be thought of as an ongoing, integral aspect of the training program and both time and money must be budgeted appropriately.

SUMMARY

Information technology system security is a rapidly evolving, high-risk area that touches every aspect of an organization's operations. Both companies and federal agencies face the challenge of providing employees with the appropriate awareness, training, and education that will enable employees to fulfill their responsibilities effectively and to protect the IT system assets and information. Employees are a company's greatest assets and trained employees are crucial to the effective functioning and protection of the information system.

This chapter has outlined the various facets of developing an information system (IS) security training program. The first step is to create an awareness program. The awareness program helps to set the stage by alerting employees to the issues of IT security. It also prepares users of the IT system for the next step of the security training program, providing the basic concepts of IT security to all employees. From this initial training effort, various specialized and detailed training courses should be offered to employees. These specific training courses must be related to the various job functions that occur within an organization's IT system security arena.

Critical to the success of a training program is having senior management's support and approval. During each step of the program's life cycle, it is important to distribute status reports to keep all team members and executive-level managers apprised of progress. In some instances, it may be important (or necessary) to receive direct approval from senior management before proceeding to the next phase.

The five steps of the instructional process are relevant to all IS security training programs. The first step is to analyze the training needs and define the goals and objectives for the training program. Once the needs have been outlined, the next step is to start designing the course. It is important to document this process into some type of design document or blueprint for the program. Because the design document provides the direction for the course development, all parties involved should review and approve the design document before proceeding.

The development phase involves putting all the course elements together, such as the instructor material, student material, classroom activities, or, if technology-based, storyboarding and programming of media elements. Once course development has been completed, the first goal of the implementation phase is to begin with a pilot or testing of the materials. This allows the instructional design team to evaluate the material for learner effectiveness and rework any issues prior to full-scale implementation. Throughout the IS security training program, the inclusion of an evaluation program is critical to the program's success. Resources, such as time and money, must be dedicated to evaluate the instructional material in terms of effectiveness and meeting the learning and company's needs. Keep in mind that the key factor in an evaluation program is its inclusion throughout the design, development, and implementation of the IT security training program.

Several examples of training courses have been suggested for an IS security training program. Keep in mind that as technology changes, the course offerings required to meet the evolving IT security challenges must also change. These changes will necessitate modifications and enhancements to current courses. In addition, new courses will be needed to meet the ever-changing IT system advances and enhancements. Thus, the IS security training program and course offerings must be flexible to meet the new demands.

Each organization must also plan for the growth of the IT professional. IT security functions have become technologically and managerially complex. Companies are seeking educated IT security professionals who can solve IT security challenges and keep up with the changing technology issues. Currently, there is a lack of IT security professionals in the U.S. workforce; thus, organizations will need to identify and designate appropriate individuals as IT security specialists and train them to become IT security professionals capable of problem solving and creating vision.

As one faces the challenges of developing an information system security training program, it is important to remember that the process cannot be accomplished by one person working alone. It requires a broad, cross-organizational effort that includes the executive level bringing together various divisions to work on projects. By involving everyone in the process, the additional benefit of creating ownership and accountability is established. Also, the expertise of both training personnel (i.e., training managers, instructional designers, and trainers) and IT security specialists is needed to achieve the training goals.

Always remember the end result: "a successful IT security training program can help ensure the integrity, availability, and confidentiality of the IT system assets and its information — the first and foremost goal of IT security."

APPENDIX A: INSTRUCTIONAL STRATEGIES (TRAINING DELIVERY METHODS)

Instructor-Led

The traditional instructional strategy is instructor-led and considered a group instruction strategy. This involves bringing students together into a common place, usually a classroom environment, with an instructor or facilitator. It can provide considerable interaction between the instructor and the students. It is usually the least expensive as far as designing and development of instructional material. However, it can be the most expensive during implementation, especially if it requires students to travel to a central location.

Text-Based

Text-based training is an individual, self-paced form of training. The student reads a standard textbook (or any book) on the training content. Text-based training does not allow for interaction with an instructor. However, the book's information is usually written by an individual with expertise in the subject matter. In addition, students can access the material when it is needed and can review (or re-read) sections as needed.

Paper-Based or Workbook

Paper-based or workbook training is a type of individual, self-paced instruction. It is the oldest form of distance learning (i.e., correspondence courses). Workbooks include instructional text, graphical illustrations, and practice exercises. The workbooks are written specifically to help student's learn particular subjects or techniques. The practice exercises help students to remember what is covered in the books by giving them an opportunity to work with the content. In some cases, students may be required to complete a test or exam to show competency in the subject.

Video-Based

Video-based training is usually an individual, self-paced form of instruction. The information is provided on a standard VHS video cassette tape that can be played using a standard VHS video cassette recorder (VCR). If used as a self-paced form of instruction, it does not allow for interaction with the instructor. However, if used in the classroom, a video can be discussed and analyzed as an interactive exercise. Video does allow for animated graphics that can show processes or a demonstration of step-items. It is flexible as far as delivery time and location and, if necessary, can be repeated.

Technology-Based, Including CBT and WBT

Technology-based training is also an individual, self-paced instructional strategy. It is any training that uses a computer as the focal point for instructional delivery. With technology-based training, instructional content is provided through the use of a computer and software that guides a student through an instructional program.

This can be either computer-based training delivered via a floppy disk or CD-ROM or loaded on a server, or it can be Web-based training delivered via the Internet or an intranet.

Computer-based training (CBT) involves several presentation methods, including tutorials, practice exercises, simulations or emulations, demonstrations, problem-solving exercises, and games. CBT has many positive features that can be of importance to agencies that need to deliver a standard set of instructional material to a large group of students who are in geographically separate areas. The benefits of CBT include immediate feedback, student control of instructional material, and the integration of multimedia elements such as video, audio, sounds, and graphical animations.

After the initial CBT development costs, CBT can be used to teach any number of students at any time. Customized CBT programs can focus only on what students need to learn, thus training time and costs can be significantly reduced. In addition, CBT can enable one to reduce or eliminate travel for students; thus, total training costs can also be reduced. As a self-paced, individualized form of instruction, CBT provides flexibility for the student. For example, the student can control the training environment by selecting specific lessons or topics. In addition, for some students, the anonymous nature can be nonthreatening.

Although CBT has many benefits, it is important to remember that CBT is not the answer to all training needs. It some situations, it can be more appropriate, effective, and cost efficient. However, in other situations, it may produce a negative student attitude and destroy the goodwill and goals of the training program. For example, students who are offered CBT courses and instructed to fit it into their schedule may believe they are expected to complete the training outside of the workday. These same students know that taking an instructor-led course allows them to complete the training during a workday. Therefore, they may view CBT as an unfair time requirement.

Computer-based training includes computer-assisted learning (CAL), which uses a computer as a tool to aid in a traditional learning situation, such as classroom training. The computer is a device to assist the instructor during the training process, similar to an overhead projector or handouts. It also includes computer-assisted testing (CAT), which assesses an individual through the medium of a computer. Students take the test at the computer, and the computer records and scores the test. CAT is embedded in most computer-based training products.

Web-based training (WBT) is a new, creative method for delivering computer-based training to widespread, limitless audiences. WBT represents a shift from the current delivery of CBT. In the CBT format, the information is usually stored on the local machine, server, or a CD-ROM. In WBT, the information is distributed via the World Wide Web (WWW) and most likely is stored at a distant location or on an agency's central server. The information is displayed to the user using a software application called a browser, such as Internet Explorer. The content is presented in the form of text, graphics, audio, video, and graphical animations. WBT has many of the same benefits as CBT, including saving time and easy access. However, one of the key advantages of WBT over CBT is the ease of updating information. If changes need to be made to instructional material, the changes are made once to the server, and then everyone can access the new information. The challenges of WBT are providing the technical capability for the student's computer, the agency's server, and the available bandwidth.

APPENDIX B: SUGGESTED IT SYSTEM SECURITY TRAINING COURSES (EXHIBIT 1)

INFOSEC 101 IT Security Basics

Brief Description. This course should describe the core terms and concepts that every user of the IT system must know, the fundamentals of IT security and how to apply them, plus the IT system security rules of behavior. This will allow all individuals to understand what their role is in protecting the IT systems assets and information.

Intended Audience. This course is intended for all employees who use the IT system, regardless of their specific job responsibilities. Essentially, all employees should receive this training.

List of Topics. What Is IT Security and Why Is It Important; Federal Laws and Regulations; Vulnerabilities, Threats, and Sensitivity of the IT System; Protecting the Information, Including Sensitive but Unclassified and Classified Information; Protecting the Hardware; Password Protections; Media Handling (i.e., how to process, store, and dispose of information on floppy disks); Copyright Issues; Laptop Security; User Accountability; Who to Contact with Problems; and other specific agency policies related to all users of the IT system. Note that if the agency processes classified information, a separate briefing should be given.

Note: Because most agencies will require this course for all employees, it is a good example of content that should be delivered via a technology-based delivery. This includes video, computer-based training via CD-ROM, or Web-based training via the agency's intranet.

INFOSEC 102 IT Security Basics for a Network Processing Classified Information

Brief Description. This course describes the core terms and concepts that every user of the IT system must know, the fundamentals of IT security and how to apply them, and the rules of behavior. It is similar to INFOSEC 101 except that it also provides information pertinent to employees who have access to a network processing classified information.

Intended Audience. This course is intended for all employees with access to a network processing classified information.

List of Topics. What Is IT Security and Why Is It Important; Federal Laws and Regulations; Vulnerabilities, Threats, and Sensitivity of the IT System; Protecting Classified Information; Protecting the Hardware, Including TEMPEST Equipment; Password Protections; Media Handling (i.e., how to process, store, and dispose of classified information); Copyright Issues; Laptop Security; User Accountability; Who to Contact with Problems; and other specific agency policies related to users of a classified IT system.

INFOSEC 103 IT Security Basics — Annual Refresher

Brief Description. This is a follow-on course to the IT Security Basics (INFOSEC 101). As technology changes, the demands and challenges for IT security also change. In this course, the agency will look at the most critical challenges for the end user. The focus of the refresher course will be on how to meet those needs.

Intended Audience. This course is for all employees who use the IT system.

List of Topics. The topics would be specific to the agency and the pertinent IT security challenges it faces.

INFOSEC 104 Fundamentals of IT Security

Brief Description. This course is designed for employees directly involved with protecting the IT system. It provides a basic understanding of the federal laws and agency-specific policies and procedures, the vulnerabilities and threats to IT systems, the countermeasures that can help to mitigate the threats, and an introduction to the physical, personnel, administrative, and system/technical controls.

Intended Audience. The course is for employees who need more than just the basics of IT security. It is an introductory course that can be used as a prerequisite for higher-level material. This could include system administrators, system staff, information officers, information system security officers, security officers, and program managers.

Note: This course can be taken in place of the INFOSEC 101 course. It is designed as an introductory course for those employees who have job responsibilities directly related to securing the IT system.

INFOSEC 201 Developing the IT System Security Plan

Brief Description. By law, every IT federal system must have an IT system security plan for its general support systems and major applications. This course explains how to develop an IT System Security Plan following

Exhibit 1.   Suggested Information System Security Training Courses

Course Number and Content Level	Course Title	Intended Audience	Possible Prerequisite
INFOSEC 101 Basic	IT Security Basics	All employees	None
INFOSEC 102 Basic	IT Security Basics for Networks	All employees with access to a network processing classified information	None
INFOSEC 103 Basic	IT Security Basics — Annual Refresher	All employees	INFOSEC 101
INFOSEC 104 Basic	Fundamentals of IT Security	Individuals directly responsible for IT security	None
INFOSEC 201 Intermediate	Developing the IT System Security Plan	Individuals responsible for developing the IT system security plan	INFOSEC 101 or 103
INFOSEC 202 Intermediate	How to Develop an IT System Contingency Plan	Individuals responsible for developing the IT system contingency plan	INFOSEC 101 or 103
INFOSEC 203 Intermediate	System/Technical Responsibilities for Protecting the IT System	Individuals responsible for the planning and daily operations of the IT system	INFOSEC 101 or 103
INFOSEC 204 Intermediate	Life Cycle Planning for IT System Security	Managers responsible for the acquisition and design of the IT system	INFOSEC 101 or 103
INFOSEC 205 Intermediate	Basic Information System Security Officer (ISSO) Training	Individuals assigned as the ISSO or alternate ISSO	INFOSEC 101 or 103
INFOSEC 206 Intermediate	Certifying the IT System	Individuals responsible for the Designated Approving Authority (DAA) role	INFOSEC 101 or 103, INFOSEC 203

Course	Title	Audience	Prerequisites
INFOSEC 207 Intermediate	Information System Security for Executive Managers	Executive-level managers	None
INFOSEC 208 Intermediate	An Introduction to Network and Internet Security	Individuals responsible for network connections	INFOSEC 101 or 103, INFOSEC 203
INFOSEC 209	An Introduction to Cryptography	Individuals responsible for network connections information and security	INFOSEC 101 or 103, INFOSEC 203 or 205
INFOSEC 301 Advanced	Understanding Audit Logs	Individuals responsible for reviewing audit logs	INFOSEC 101 or 103, INFOSEC 203 or 205
INFOSEC 302 Advanced	Windows NT 4.0 Security	Individuals responsible for networks using Windows NT 4.0	INFOSEC 101 or 103, INFOSEC 203
INFOSEC 303 Advanced	Windows 2000 Security	Individuals responsible for networks using Windows 2000	INFOSEC 101 or 103, INFOSEC 203
INFOSEC 304 Advanced	UNIX Security	Individuals responsible for networks using UNIX	INFOSEC 101 or 103, INFOSEC 203
INFOSEC 305 Advanced	Advanced ISSO Training	Individuals assigned as the ISSO or alternate ISSO	INFOSEC 205
INFOSEC 306 Advanced	Incident Handling	Individuals responsible for handling IT security incidents	INFOSEC 101 or 103, INFOSEC 205
INFOSEC 307 Advanced	How to Conduct a Risk Analysis/Assessment	Individuals responsible for conducting risk analyses	INFOSEC 101 or 103, INFOSEC 205

the guidelines set forth in NIST SP 800-18 "Guide for Developing Security Plans for Information Technology Systems."

Intended Audience. The system owner (or team) responsible for ensuring that the IT system security plan is prepared and implemented. In many agencies, the IT system security plan will be developed by a team, such as the system administrator, information officer, security officer, and the information system security officer.

List of Topics. System Identification; Assignment of Security Responsibilities; System Description/Purpose; System Interconnection; Sensitivity and Sharing of Information; Risk Assessment and Management; Administrative, Physical, Personnel, and System/Technical Controls; Life Cycle Planning; and Security Awareness and Training.

Note: The design of this course should be customized with an agency-approved methodology and a predefined set of templates on how to develop an IT system security plan. The students should leave the class with agency-approved tools necessary to develop the plan.

INFOSEC 202 How to Develop an IT System Contingency Plan

Brief Description. The hazards facing IT systems demand that effective business continuity plans and disaster-recovery plans be in place. Business continuity plans define how to recover from disruptions and continue support for critical functions. Disaster recovery plans define how to recover from a disaster and restore critical functions to normal operations. The first step is to define one's agency's critical functions and processes and determine the recovery timeframes and trade-offs. This course discusses how to conduct an in-depth Business Impact Analysis (BIA) (identifying the critical business functions within an agency and determining the impact of not performing the functions beyond the maximum acceptable outage) that defines recovery priorities, processing interdependencies, and the basic technology infrastructure required for recovery.

Intended Audience. Those employees responsible for the planning and management of the IT system. This may include the system administrator, information officer, security officer, and information system security officer.

List of Topics. What Is an IT System Contingency Plan; Conducting a Business Impact Analysis (BIA); Setting Your Site (hot site, cold site, warm site); Recovery Objectives; Recovery Requirements; Recovery Implementation; Backup Options and Plans; Testing the Plan; and Evaluating the Results of Recovery Tests.

Note: The content of this course should be customized with an agency-approved methodology for creating an IT system contingency plan. If possible, preapproved templates or tools should be included.

INFOSEC 203 System/Technical Responsibilities for Protecting the IT System

Brief Description. This course begins by explaining the vulnerabilities of and threats to the IT system and what is necessary to protect the physical assets and information. It focuses on specific requirements such as protecting the physical environment, installing software, access controls, configuring operating systems and applications to meet security requirements, and understanding audit logs.

Intended Audience. Employees who are involved and responsible for the planning and day-to-day operations of the IT system. This would include system administrators, system staff, information officers, and information system security officers.

List of Topics. Overview of IT System Security; Identifying Vulnerabilities, Threats, and Sensitivity of the IT System; Identifying Effective Countermeasures; Administrative Responsibilities (e.g., management of logs and records); Physical Responsibilities (e.g., server room security); Interconnection Security; Access Controls (identification and authentication); Group and File Management (setting up working groups and shared files); Group and File Permissions (configuring the system for access permissions); Audit Events and Logs; and IT Security Maintenance.

INFOSEC 204 Life Cycle Planning for IT System Security

Brief Description. The system life cycle is a model for building and operating an IT system from its inception to its termination. This course covers the fundamentals of how to identify the vulnerabilities of and threats to IT systems before they are implemented and how to plan for IT security during the acquisition and design of an IT system. This includes identifying the risks that may occur during implementation of the IT system and how to minimize those risks, describing the standard operating procedures with a focus on security, how to test that an IT system is secure, and how to dispose of terminated assets.

Intended Audience. This course is designed for managers tasked with the acquisition and design of IT systems. This could include contracting officers, information officers, system administrators, program managers, and information system security officers.

List of Topics. Identify IT Security Needs During the Design Process; Develop IT Security in the Acquisition Process; Federal Laws and Regulations; Agency Policies and Procedures; Acquisition, Development, Installation, and Implementation Controls; Risk Management; Establishing Standard Operating Procedures; and Destruction and Disposal of Equipment and Media.

Note: The course focus should be on the implementation and use of organizational structures and processes for IT security and related decision-making activities. Agency-specific policies, guidelines, requirements, roles, responsibilities, and resource allocations should be previously established.

INFOSEC 205 Basic Information System Security Officer (ISSO) Training

Brief Description. This course provides an introduction to the ISSO role and responsibilities. The ISSO implements the IT system security plan and provides security oversight on the IT system. The focus of the course is on understanding the importance of IT security and how to provide a security management role in the daily operations.

Intended Audience. Employees assigned as the ISSO or equivalent. This could be system administrators, information officers, program managers, or security officers.

List of Topics. Overview of IT Security; Vulnerabilities, Threats, and Sensitivity; Effective Countermeasures; Administrative Controls; Physical Controls; Personnel Controls; System/Technical Controls; Incident Handling; and Security Awareness Training.

Note: Each agency should have someone designated as the Information System Security Officer (ISSO) who is responsible for providing security oversight on the IT system.

INFOSEC 206 Certifying and Accrediting the IT System

Brief Description. This course provides information on how to verify that an IT system complies with information security requirements. This includes granting final approval to operate an IT system in a specified security mode and ensure that classified or sensitive but unclassified (SBU) information is protected according to federal and agency requirements.

Intended Audience. Individuals assigned the Designated Approving Authority (DAA) role and responsibilities. This includes program managers, security officers, information officers, or information system security officers.

List of Topics. Federal Laws and Regulations; Agency Policies and Procedures; Understanding Vulnerabilities, Threats, and Sensitivities; Effective Countermeasures; Access Controls; Groups and File Permissions; Protection of Classified and SBU Information; Protection of TEMPEST and Other Equipment; The Accreditation Process; Incident Handling; Life Cycle Management; Standard Operating Procedures; and Risk Management.

INFOSEC 207 Information System Security for Executive Managers

Brief Description. This course provides an overview of the information system security concerns for executive-level managers. It emphasizes the need for both planning and managing security on the IT system, how to allocate employee and financial resources, and how to lead the IT security team by example.

Intended Audience. Executive-level managers.

List of Topics. Overview of IT System Security; Federal Laws and Regulations; Vulnerabilities and Threats to the IT System; Effective Countermeasures; Need for IT Security Management and Oversight; and Budgeting for IT Security.

Note: This course content should be customized for each agency to make sure it meets the specific needs of the executive-level management team. It is anticipated that this would be several short, interactive sessions based on specific topics. Some sessions could be delivered via a technology-based application to effectively plan for time limitations.

INFOSEC 208 An Introduction to Network and Internet Security

Brief Description. In this course, the focus is on how develop a network and Internet/intranet security policy to protect the agency's IT system assets and information. The focus is on how to analyze the vulnerabilities of the IT system and review the various external threats, how to manage the risks and protect the IT system from unauthorized access, and how to reduce one's risks by deploying technical countermeasures such as firewalls and data encryption devices.

Intended Audience. Employees involved with the implementation, day-to-day management, and oversight responsibilities of the network connections, including internal intranet and external Internet connections. This could include system administrators, system staff, information officers, information system security officers, security officers, and program managers.

List of Topics. Overview of IT Network Security and the Internet; Introduction to TCP/IP and Packets; Understanding Vulnerabilities and Threats to Network Connections (hackers, malicious codes, spoofing, sniffing, denial-of-service attacks, etc.); Effective Countermeasures for Network Connections (policies, access controls, physical protections, anti-virus software, firewalls, data encryption, etc.); Developing a Network and Internet/intranet Security Policy; and How to Recognize an Internet Attack.

INFOSEC 209 An Introduction to Cryptography

Brief Description. The focus of this course is to provide an overview of cryptography. This includes the basic concepts of cryptography, public and private key algorithms in terms of their applications and uses, key distribution and management, the use of digital signatures to provide authenticity of electronic transactions, and non-repudiation.

Intended Audience. Employees involved with the management and security responsibilities of the network connections. This could include system administrators, system staff, information officers, information system security officers, security officers, and program managers.

List of Topics. Cryptography Concepts; Authentication Methods Using Cryptographic Modules; Encryption; Overview of Certification Authority; Digital Signatures; Non-repudiation; Hash Functions and Message Digests; Private Key and Public Key Cryptography; and Key Management.

INFOSEC 301 Understanding Audit Logs

Brief Description. This is an interactive class focusing on how to understand and review audit logs. It explains what types of events are captured in an audit log, how to search for unusual events, how to use audit log tools, how to record and store audit logs, and how to handle an unusual audit event.

Intended Audience. Employees assigned to manage and provide oversight of the daily IT system operations. This includes system administrators, information officers, and information system security officers.

List of Topics. Understanding an IT System Event, Planning for Audit Log Reviews; How to Review Audit Logs; How to Find and Search Through Audit Logs; Using Third-Party Tools for Audit Log Reviewing; How to Handle an Unusual System Event in the Audit Log.

Note: As a prerequisite, students should have completed either INFOSEC 203 or INFOSEC 205 so that they have a basic understanding of IT security concepts.

INFOSEC 302 Windows NT 4.0 Server and Workstation Security

Brief Description. This course focuses on how to properly configure the Windows NT 4.0 security features for both the server and workstation operating systems. Students learn the security features of Windows NT and participate in installing and configuring the operating systems in a hands-on computer lab.

Intended Audience. This course is designed for employees who are responsible for installing, configuring, and managing networks using the Windows NT 4.0 server and workstation operating system. This may include information officers, system administrators, and system staff.

List of Topics. Overview of the Windows NT 4.0 Server and Workstation Operating Systems; Identification and Authentication Controls; Discretionary Access Controls; Group Organization and Permissions; Directory and File Organization and Permissions; Protecting System Files; Auditing Events; Using the Windows NT Tools to Configure and Maintain the System.

Note: As a prerequisite, students should complete INFOSEC 203 so they have a basic understanding of IT security concepts.

INFOSEC 303 Windows 2000 Security

Brief Description. This course is similar to INFOSEC 302 except that it focuses on how to properly configure the security features of the Windows 2000 operating system. Students learn the security features of Windows 2000 by installing and configuring the operating system in a hands-on computer lab.

Intended Audience. This course is designed for employees who are responsible for installing, configuring, and managing networks using the Windows 2000 operating system. This may include information officers, system administrators, and system staff.

List of Topics. Overview of the Windows 2000 Operating System; The Domain Name System (DNS); Migrating Windows NT 4.0 Domains; Identification and Authentication Controls; Discretionary Access Controls; File System Resources (NTFS); Group Organization and Permissions; Directory and File Organization and Permissions; Protecting System Files; Auditing Events; Using the Windows 2000 Tools to Configure and Maintain the System.

Note: As a prerequisite, students should complete INFOSEC 203 so they have a basic understanding of IT security concepts.

INFOSEC 304 Unix Security

Brief Description. In this hands-on course, students will gain the knowledge and skills needed to implement security on the UNIX operating system. This includes securing the system from internal and external threats, protecting the UNIX file system, controlling superuser access, and config-uring tools and utilities to minimize vulnerabilities and detect intruders.

Intended Audience. This course is designed for employees who are responsible for installing, configuring, and managing networks using the UNIX operating system. This may include information officers, system administrators, and system staff.

List of Topics. Introduction to UNIX Security; Establishing Secure Accounts; Storing Account Information; Controlling Root Access; Directory and File Permissions; Minimizing Risks from Unauthorized Programs; and Understanding TCP/IP and Security.

Note: As a prerequisite, students should complete INFOSEC 203 so that they have a basic understanding of IT security concepts.

INFOSEC 305 Advanced ISSO Training

Brief Description. This course provides an in-depth look at the ISSO responsibilities. The focus is on how to review security plans, contingency plans/disaster recover plans, and IT system accreditation; how to handle IT system incidents; and how specific IT security case studies are examined and evaluated.

Intended Audience. This is intended for ISSOs who have completed INFOSEC 205 and have at least one year of experience as the ISSO.

List of Topics. Oversight Responsibilities for Reviewing IT System Security Plans and Contingency Plans; How to Handle IT System Incidents; and Case Studies.

INFOSEC 306 Incident Handling

Brief Description. This course explains the procedures for handling an IT system security incident. It begins by defining how to categorize incidents according to risk, followed by how to initiate and conduct an investigation and who to contact for support. Key to handling incidents is ensuring that equipment and information is not compromised during an investigation. Thus, students learn the proper procedures for safekeeping assets and information.

Intended Audience. This course is designed for employees who are responsible for handling IT security incidents. This could include information officers, information system security officers, security officers, and individuals representing a computer incident response team.

List of Topics. Understanding an IT System Security Incident; Federal Laws and Civil/Criminal Penalties; Agency Policies and Penalties; The Agency-Specific Security Incident Reporting Process; Security Investigation Procedures; Identifying Investigative Authorities; Interfacing with Law Enforcement Agencies; Witness Interviewing; Protecting the Evidence; and How to Write an IT System Security Incident Report.

Note: As a prerequisite, students should complete INFOSEC 205 so that they have a basic understanding of IT security concepts.

INFOSEC 307 How to Conduct a Risk Analysis/Assessment

Brief Description. This course explains the process of conducting a risk analysis/assessment. It reviews why a risk analysis is important, the objectives of a risk analysis, when the best time is to conduct a risk analysis, and the different methodologies to conduct a risk assessment (including a review of electronic tools) and provides plenty of hands-on opportunities to complete a sample risk analysis. A critical element of a risk analysis/ assessment is considering the target analysis and target assessment. The unauthorized intruder may also be conducting an analysis of the information system risks and will know the vulnerabilities to attack.

Intended Audience. Individuals tasked with completing a risk analysis. This could include the information officer, system administrator, program manager, information system security officer, and security officer.

List of Topics. Overview of a Risk Analysis; Understanding Vulnerabilities, Threats, and Sensitivity and Effective Countermeasures of IT Systems; Objectives of a Risk Analysis; Risk Analysis Methodologies; Federal Guidance on Conducting a Risk Analysis; Process of Conducting a Risk Analysis; Electronic Risk Analysis Tools; Completing Sample Risk Analysis Worksheets (asset valuations, threat, and vulnerability evaluation; level of risk; and countermeasures); and Reviewing Target Analysis/Assessments.

Note: This course may be offered in conjunction with INFOSEC 201 and INFOSEC 206.

Chapter 7
The Case for Privacy

Michael J. Corby

NOTHING NEW

> Any revelation of a secret happens by the mistake of [someone] who shared it in confidence.
>
> — La Bruyere, 1645–1694

It is probably safe to say that since the beginning of communication, back in prehistoric times, there were things that were to be kept private. From the location of the best fishing to the secret passage into the cave next door, certain facts were reserved only for a few knowledgeable friends. Maybe even these facts were so private that there was only one person in the world who knew them. We have made "societal rules" around a variety of things that we want to keep private or share only among a few, but still the concept of privacy expectations comes with our unwritten social code. And wherever there has been the code of privacy, there has been the concern over its violation. Have computers brought this on? Certainly not! Maintaining privacy has been important and even more important have been the methods used to try to keep that data a secret. Today in our wired society, however, we still face the same primary threat to privacy that has existed for centuries: mistakes and carelessness of the individuals who have been entrusted to preserve privacy — maybe even the "owner" of the data.

In the past few years, and heightened within the past few months, we have become more in tune to the cry — no, the public *outcry* — regarding the "loss of privacy" that has been forced upon us because of the information age. Resolving this thorny problem requires that we re-look at the way we design and operate our networked systems, and most importantly, that we re-think the way we allocate control to the rightful owners of the information which we communicate and store. Finally, we need to be careful about how we view the data that we provide and for which we are custodians.

PRIVACY AND CONTROL

The fact that data is being sent, printed, recorded, and shared is not the real concern of privacy. The real concern is that some data has been

0-8493-1248-5/02/$0.00+$1.50
© 2002 by CRC Press LLC

implied, by social judgment, to be private, for sharing only by and with the approval of its owner. If a bank balance is U.S.$1240, that is an interesting fact. If it happens to be my account, that is private information. I have, by virtue of my agreement with the bank, given them the right to keep track of my balance and to provide it *to me* for the purpose of keeping me informed and maintaining a control point with which I can judge their accuracy. I did not dive them permission to share that balance with other people indiscriminately, nor did I give them permission to use that balance even subtly to communicate my standing in relation to others (i.e., publish a list of account holders sorted by balance).

The focal points of the issue of privacy are twofold:

- How is the data classified as private?
- What can be done to preserve the owner's (my) expectations of privacy?

Neither of these are significantly more challenging than, for example, sending digital pictures and sound over a telephone line. Why has this subject caused such a stir in the technology community? This chapter sheds some light on this issue and then comes up with an organized approach to resolve the procedural challenges of maintaining data privacy.

RUDIMENTS OF PRIVACY

One place to start examining this issue is with a key subset of the first point on classifying data as private: What, exactly, is the data we are talking about? Start with the obvious: private data includes those facts that I can recognize as belonging to me, and for which I have decided reveal more about myself or my behavior than I would care to reveal. This includes three types of data loosely included in the privacy concerns of information technology (IT). These three types of data shown in Exhibit 1 are: static, dynamic, and derived data.

Static Data

Static data is pretty easy to describe. It kind of sits there in front of us. It does ot move. It does not change (very often). Information that describes who we are, significant property identifiers, and other tangible elements are generally static. This information can of course take any form. It can be entered into a computer by a keyboard; it can be handwritten on a piece of paper or on a form; it can be photographed or created as a result of using a biological interface such as a fingerprint pad, retina scanner, voice or facial image recorder, or pretty much any way that information can be retained. It does not need to describe an animate object. It can also identify something we have. Account numbers, birth certificates, passport numbers, and employee numbers are all concepts that can be recorded and would generally be considered static data.

Exhibit 1.   Types of Private Data

1. Static data
    a. Who we are:
        i.   Bio-identity (fingerprints, race, gender, height, weight)
        ii. Financial identity (bank accounts, credit card numbers)
        iii. Legal identity (Social Security number, driver's license, birth certificate, passport)
        iv. Social identity (church, auto clubs, ethnicity)
    b. What we have:
        i.   Property (buildings, automobiles, boats, etc.)
        ii. Non-real property (insurance policies, employee agreements)
2. Dynamic data:
    a. Transactions (financial, travel, activities)
    b. How we live (restaurants, sporting events)
    c. Where we are (toll cards, cell phone records)
3. Derived data:
    a. Financial behavior (market analysis)
        i.   Trends and changes (month-to-month variance against baseline)
        ii. Perceived response to new offerings (match with experience)
    b. Social behavior (profiling)
        i.   Behavior statistics (drug use, violations or law, family traits)

In most instances, we get to control the initial creation of static data. Because we are the one identifying ourselves by name, account number, address, driver's license number or by speaking into a voice recorder or having our retina or face scanned or photographed, we usually will know when a new record is being made of our static data. As we will see later, we need to be concerned about the privacy of this data under three conditions: when we participate in its creation, when it is copied from its original form to a duplicate form, and when it is covertly created (created without our knowledge) such as in secretly recorded conversations or hidden cameras.

Dynamic Data

Dynamic data is also easy to identify and describe, but somewhat more difficult to control. Records of transactions we initiate constitute the bulk of dynamic data. It is usually being created much more frequently than static data. Every charge card transaction, telephone call, and bank transaction adds to the collection of dynamic data. Even when we drive on toll roads or watch television programs, information can be recorded without our doing anything special. These types of transactions are more difficult for us to control. We may know that a computerized recording of the event is being made, but we often do not know what that information contains, nor if it contains more information than we suspect. Take, for example, purchasing a pair of shoes. You walk into a shoe store, try on various styles and sizes, make your selection, pay for the shoes, and walk out with your purchase in hand. You may have the copy of your charge card transaction, and you know that somewhere in the store's data files, one pair of shoes has been removed from their inventory and the price you just paid has been added to their cash balance. But what else might have been recorded? Did the sales clerk, for example, record your approximate age or ethnic or racial profile, or make a judgment as to your income level. Did you have children with you? Were you wearing a wedding band? What other general observations were made about you when the shoes were purchased? These items are of great importance in helping the shoe store replenish its supply of shoes, determining if they have attracted the type of customer they intended to attract and analyzing whether they are, in general, serving a growing or shrinking segment of the population. Without even knowing it, some information that you may consider private may have been used *without your knowledge* simply by the act of buying a new pair of shoes.

Derived Data

Finally, derived data is created by analyzing groups of dynamic transactions over time to build a profile of your behavior. Your standard way of living out your day, week, and month may be known by others even better than you may know it yourself. For example, you may, without even planning it, have dinner at a restaurant 22 Thursdays during the year. The other six days of the week, you may only dine out eight times in total. If you and others in your area fall into a given pattern, the restaurant community may begin to offer "specials" on Tuesday, or raise their prices slightly on Thursdays to accommodate the increased demand. In this case, your behavior is being recorded and used by your transaction partners in ways you do not even know or approve of. If you use an electronic toll recorder, as has become popular in many U.S. states, do you know if they are also computing the time it took to enter and exit the highway, and consequently your average speed? Most often, this derived data is being collected without even a hint to us, and certainly without our expressed permission.

PRESERVING PRIVACY

One place to start examining this issue is with a key subset of the first point on classifying data as private: What, exactly, is the data we are talking about? Start with the obvious: private data includes those items that we believe belong to us exclusively and it is not necessary for us to receive the product or service we wish to receive. To examine privacy in the context of computer technology today, we need to examine the following four questions:

1. Who owns the private data?
2. Who is responsible for security and accuracy?
3. Who decides how it can be used?
4. Does the owner need to be told when it is used or compromised?

> You already have zero privacy. Get over it.
>
> — Scott McNealy, Chairman: Sun Microsystems, 1999

Start with the first question about ownership. Cyber-consumers love to get offers tailored to them. Over 63 percent of the buying public in the United States bought from direct mail in 1998. Companies invest heavily in personalizing their marketing approach because it works. So what makes it so successful? By allowing the seller to know some pretty personal data about your preferences, a trust relationship is implied. (Remember that word "trust"; it will surface later.) The "real deal" is this: Vendors do not know about your interests because they are your friend and want to make you happy. They want to take your trust and put together something private that will result in their product winding up in your home or office. Plain and simple: economics. And what does this cost them? If they have their way, practically nothing. You have given up your own private information that they have used to exploit your buying habits or personal preferences. Once you give up ownership, you have let the cat out of the bag. Now they have the opportunity to do whatever they want with it.

"Are there any controls?" That brings us to the second question. The most basic control is to ask you clearly whether you want to give up something you own. That design method of having you "opt in" to their data collection gives you the opportunity to look further into their privacy protection methods, a stated or implied process for sharing (or not sharing) your information with other organizations and how your private information is to be removed. By simply adding this verification of your agreement, 85 percent of surveyed consumers would approve of having their profile used for marketing. Not that they ask, but they will be responsible for protecting your privacy. You must do some work to verify that they can keep their promise, but at least you know they have accepted some responsibility (their privacy policy should tell you how much). Their very mission will ensure accuracy. No product vendor wants to build its sales campaign on inaccurate data — at least not a second time.

Who decides use? If done right, both you and the marketer can decide based on the policy. If you are not sure if they are going to misuse their data, you can test them. Use a nickname, or some identifying initial to track where your profile is being used. I once tested an online information service by using my full middle name instead of an initial. Lo and behold,

I discovered that my "new" name ended up on over 30 different mailing lists, and it took me several months to be removed from most of them. Some still are using my name, despite my repeated attempts to stop the vendors from doing so. Your method for deciding who to trust (there is that word again) depends on your preferences and the genre of services and products you are interested in buying. Vendors also tend to reflect the preferences of their customers. Those who sell cheap, ultra-low-cost commodities have a different approach than those who sell big-ticket luxuries to a well-educated executive clientele. Be aware and recognize the risks. Special privacy concerns have been raised in three areas: data on children, medical information, and financial information (including credit/debit cards). Be especially aware if these categories of data are collected and hold the collector to a more stringent set of protection standards. You, the public, are the judge.

If your data is compromised, it is doubtful that the collector will know. This situation is unfortunate. Even if it is known, it could cost them their business. Now the question of ethics comes into play. I actually know of a company that had its customer credit card files "stolen" by hackers. Rather than notify the affected customers and potentially cause a mass exodus to other vendors, the company decided to keep quiet. That company may be only buying some time. It is a far greater mistake to know that a customer is at risk and not inform them that they should check their records carefully than it is to have missed a technical component and, as a result, their system was compromised. The bottom line is that *you* are expected to report errors, inconsistencies, and suspected privacy violations to them. If you do, you have a right to expect immediate correction.

WHERE IS THE DATA TO BE PROTECTED?

Much ado has been made about the encryption of data while connected to the Internet. This is a concern; but to be really responsive to privacy directives, more than transmitting encrypted data is required. For a real privacy policy to be developed, the data must be protected when it is:

- Captured
- Transmitted
- Stored
- Processed
- Archived

That means more than using SSL or sending data over a VPN. It also goes beyond strong authentication using biometrics or public/private keys. It means developing a privacy architecture that protects data when it is sent, even internally; while stored in databases, with access isolated from those who can see other data in the same database; and while it is being stored in program work areas. All these issues can be solved with technology and should be discussed with the appropriate network, systems development, or data center managers. Despite all best efforts to make technology respond to the issues of privacy, the most effective use of resources and effort is in developing work habits that facilitate data privacy protection.

GOOD WORK HABITS

Privacy does not just happen. Everyone has certain responsibilities when it comes to protecting the privacy of one's own data or the data that belongs to others. In some cases, the technology exists to make that responsibility easier to carry out.

Vendor innovations continue to make this technology more responsive, for both data "handlers" and data "owners." For the owners, smart cards carry a record of personal activity that never leaves the wallet-sized token itself. For example, smart cards can be used to record selection of services (video, phone, etc.) without divulging preferences. They can maintain complex medical information (e.g., health, drug interactions) and can store technical information in the form of X-rays, nuclear exposure time (for those working in the nuclear industry), and tanning time (for those who do not).

For the handlers, smart cards can record electronic courier activities when data is moved from one place to another. They can enforce protection of secret data and provide proper authentication, either using a biometric such as a fingerprint or a traditional personal identification number (PIN). There are even cards that can scan a person's facial image and compare it to a digitized photo stored on the card. They are valuable in providing a digital signature that does not reside on one's office PC, subject to theft or compromise by office procedures that are less than effective.

In addition to technology, privacy can be afforded through diligent use of traditional data protection methods. Policies can develop into habits that force employees to understand the sensitivity of what they have access to on their desktops and personal storage areas. Common behavior such as protecting one's territory before leaving that area and when returning to one's area is as important as protecting privacy while while in one's area.

Stories about privacy, the compromise of personal data, and the legislation (both U.S. and international) being enacted or drafted are appearing daily. Some are redundant and some are downright scary. One's mission is to avoid becoming one of those stories.

RECOMMENDATIONS

For all 21st century organizations (and all people who work in those organizations), a privacy policy is a must and adherence to them is expected. Here are several closing tips:

1. If your organization has a privacy coordinator (or chief privacy officer), contact that person or a compliance person if you have questions. Keep their numbers handy.
2. Be aware of the world around you. Monitor national and international developments, as well as all local laws.
3. Be proactive; anticipate privacy issues before they become a crisis.
4. Much money can be made or lost by being ahead of the demands for privacy or being victimized by those who capitalize on your shortcomings.
5. Preserve your reputation and that of your organization. As with all bad news, violations of privacy will spread like wildfire. Everyone is best served by collective attention to maintaining an atmosphere of respect for the data being handled.
6. Communicate privacy throughout all areas of your organization.
7. Imbed privacy in existing processes — even older legacy applications.
8. Provide notification and allow your customers/clients/constituents to opt out or opt in.
9. Conduct audits and consumer inquiries.
10. Create a positive personalization image of what you are doing (how does this *really* benefit the data owner).
11. Use your excellent privacy policies and behavior as a competitive edge.

Chapter 8
Attorney–Client Privilege and Electronic Data Transmission

Edward H. Freeman

The American legal system supports the ancient legal doctrine of attorney–client privilege, which establishes that conversations and materials sent between the attorney and the client are confidential. The attorney–client privilege allows the client to discuss legal concerns candidly with his attorney and receive sound and accurate legal advice, knowing that the court cannot force the attorney to disclose any information or documents.

Attorney–client privilege is not absolute. Specific circumstances must exist before it can be invoked. It can be waived by the client or by certain actions that would indicate that the privileged information was not meant to be privileged at all.

The increased use of new technology (e-mail, data encryption, the Internet, faxes, and cellular telephones) has created a new set of circumstances regarding attorney–client privilege. Both lawyers and clients must be aware of the rules of the new technology to prevent forced disclosure of highly sensitive facts and documents.

This chapter is written for nonlawyers. It discusses the attorney–client privilege and how the courts deal with it. Newer technological advances are included. It will give specific advice to organizations that use the technology to transmit information to their attorneys. Actual court cases will be presented as examples throughout this chapter.

0-8493-1248-5/02/$0.00+$1.50
© 2002 by CRC Press LLC

ATTORNEY–CLIENT PRIVILEGE

The American court system is based on the adversarial system of justice. When a dispute arises, each party must prove its own case and simultaneously attack the other party's case. The litigants usually will hire attorneys who are specially trained to gather evidence, organize the issues, and represent the party in court.

Under the adversarial rules, the judge is unbiased and independent. He or she will render a decision based on the law, the facts, and the evidence presented by the parties. The judge will not gather evidence or attempt to do independent research to discover facts that were not brought out during the trial. The judge is not a mediator, although he or she will encourage the parties to reach an out-of-court settlement if possible.

The judge's responsibilities are

- To hear the facts presented by each side of the dispute
- To ensure that the procedure is conducted fairly
- To maintain order in the courtroom
  - To exclude certain types of evidence according to appropriate state and federal law
  - To determine which contentions and claims made by each party represent the truth
- In a jury trial, to instruct the jury on relevant matters of law
  - In a nonjury trial, to render a verdict based on the facts and questions of law submitted to the court

The outcome of any legal proceeding is determined by questions of fact and propositions of law. Evidence is the material from which inferences are drawn to prove the truth or falsity of a disputed act. It consists of testimony, writings, material, or objects that are presented to the senses to prove the existence or nonexistence of a fact.[1]

For evidence to be introduced at trial, it must be admissible. For example, if a defendant confesses to committing murder only after being beaten by the police, the confession is not admissible as evidence. The judge and jury would be ordered to disregard the confession. If other evidence existed to show the defendant's guilt, it could be admitted, but the coerced confession would not be allowed.

To reach a fair and informed decision, courts prefer that both sides have full access to the facts relevant to a case. Discovery is a method of gathering information in which the parties to a dispute can examine information held by the other side. The attorney for each side will present a list of documents that the other side must produce. Discovery rules are much more lenient than the rules of trial evidence. Quite often evidence gathered during discovery is inadmissible as evidence during trial.

Complete disclosure of the facts of a case encourages a result based on the merits of the case, not on surprise tactics or seemingly new evidence. (The television version of courtroom drama, where Raymond Burr stuns the court before the final commercial with shocking new evidence, is quite rare.) Discovery also encourages the parties to reach a voluntary, out-of-court settlement of the case, which the courts usually consider the best resolution.

The courts do recognize, however, a certain level of protection for revealing information. The rules of privilege allow specific types of information to be kept confidential from the other side. Some individuals cannot be forced to testify nor can certain information be entered into court as evidence or during discovery. Privileges include:

- Priest–penitent
- Physician–patient
- Psychologist–patient
- Accountant–client
- Spousal

Each state recognizes the attorney–client privilege in its statutes. In federal court proceedings, the courts will look to the Federal Rules of Evidence and case law to determine claims of privilege.

In its most general form, the attorney–client privilege forbids the court to force an attorney to disclose information that the client has revealed to the attorney in confidence. If the attorney makes a statement that violates the attorney–client privilege, it cannot be used to the client's detriment. The privilege belongs solely to the client. If the client waives the privilege, the attorney will be required to testify.

The attorney–client privilege is the oldest privilege, going back at least to the days of Elizabeth I. Its supporters maintain that a client generally consults an attorney to receive accurate, informed professional advice. As one court phrased it:

> In a society as complicated as ours and governed by laws as complex and detailed as those imposed upon us, expert legal advice is essential. To the furnishing of such advice, the fullest freedom and honesty of communications of pertinent facts is a prerequisite. To induce clients to make such communications, the privilege to prevent their later disclosure is said by courts and commentators to be a necessity. The social good derived from the proper performance of the functions of lawyers acting for their clients is believed to outweigh the harm that may come from the suppression of the evidence in specific cases.[2]

Exhibit 1.   Requirements to Establish Attorney–Client Privilege

1. The person who claims the privilege is a client or has sought to become a client.
2. The person to whom the communication was made
   a. is a member of the bar, or his subordinate, and
   b. is acting as a lawyer in connection with this communication.
3. The communication is a fact about which the attorney was informed
   a. by his client
   b. with no strangers present
   c. to receive
      i.   an opinion on law or
      ii. legal services or
      iii. assistance in some legal proceeding
   d. not for the purpose of committing a crime
4. The privilege had been
   a. claimed by the client
   b. not waived by the client

If the client fears that what he tells his attorney can be used to his detriment, he may withhold crucial information. The attorney then may give incorrect or inappropriate advice.

Four major conditions must be satisfied for the privilege to be fulfilled, as shown in Exhibit 1.

If all conditions are met, communications between the attorney and the client are protected permanently, unless the client waives the privilege. "Once the privilege has been held applicable, protected information may not be the subject of compelled disclosure regardless of the need or good cause shown for such disclosure."[3]

In recent years, the courts often have interpreted attorney–client privilege more strictly and have limited its scope. Courts feel that the privilege impedes the full disclosure of the truth. The Supreme Court is aware that attorney–client privilege must be a predictable set of rules if its purpose is to be maintained.[4] The Court has not established a set of clearly defined rules, instead preferring to decide on a case-by-case basis.

When a third party is assisting the lawyer in rendering legal services, (i.e., a paralegal, accountant, or detective) communications between the client and that third party also may be privileged. In *United States v. Kovel*,[5] the Second Circuit Court of Appeals extended the attorney–client privilege to communications between a client and a third party retained by the attorney to provide accounting-related services.

A law firm had hired Kovel, a former Internal Revenue Service agent, to help advise its clients. He met with a client who was under grand jury investigation and received a personal financial statement from the client, along with a letter indicating its purpose. The grand jury subpoenaed

Kovel, who refused to answer questions about his meetings with the client and the effect of certain transactions. He was held in contempt of court and sentenced to one year in prison.

The matter was appealed to the Second Circuit, where the contempt decision was reversed. Just as other parties have been recognized as necessary to providing legal services — secretaries, clerks, and messengers — so should accountants. Consequently, when an attorney retains an accountant to provide services that enhance the legal advice being provided, the attorney–client privilege extends to the accountant.

A case for applying attorney–client privilege to accountants and other professionals can be made when:

- An attorney–client relationship exists.
- An accountant is retained by the attorney.
- The accountant renders services that abet the provision of legal services.
- The parties do not waive the privilege.

There are other points that should be taken into account when the attorney–client privilege is utilized. It is important to realize that all cases of waiver are decided on the merits of that particular case.

- A waiver may occur although the client did not intend to waive the privilege. For example, if the client tells a friend what he told the lawyer, attorney–client privilege is lost and a waiver will occur.
- If a third party is present during a conversation between the attorney and the client, the court could decide that the communication was not intended to be truly confidential.

EAVESDROPPING AND ENCRYPTION

As discussed earlier, the attorney–client privilege can be forfeited if either party fails to take reasonable steps to protect the privileged information. The courts strictly have limited the attorney–client privilege and hold that "disclosures that are inconsistent with maintaining the confidential nature of the attorney–client relationship waive the privilege."[6]

E-mail, faxes, and cellular telephones have opened new methods for eavesdropping and inadvertent disclosure of privileged information. Inadvertent disclosure can take many forms, ranging from inadvertently faxing a privileged document to the opposition's attorney to sophisticated espionage methods found in a James Bond movie. What types of inadvertent disclosure will waive the attorney–client privilege?

The Electronic Communications Privacy Act (ECPA) of 1986 was adopted to address the legal privacy issues that were evolving with the growing use of computers and other innovations in electronic communications. The ECPA updated legislation passed in 1968 that had been designed to clarify what constitutes invasion of privacy when electronic surveillance is involved. The ECPA extended privacy protection outlined in the earlier legislation to apply to radio-paging devices, e-mail, cellular telephones, private communication carriers, and computer transmissions.

As a rule, criminal eavesdropping does not create a waiver of the attorney–client privilege. This is supported fully by the ECPA, which provides that "No otherwise privileged wire, oral, or electronic communication intercepted in accordance with, or in violation of, the provisions of this chapter shall lose its privileged character."[7]

Absolute security for attorney–client communications does not exist. No encryption method is 100 percent effective. Instead, the courts will focus on both the precautions taken to preserve the confidentiality and the party's reasonable expectation of privacy.

A lawyer probably would be negligent if he or she discussed a client's business affairs in a crowded restaurant or on an elevator and someone overheard the conversation. The lawyer probably would not be negligent if the same discussion occurred in his office with the door closed. There would be no negligence even if someone were listening through the door, the room were bugged, or an intruder could hear the conversation through an open air vent.

One court found that the attorney–client privilege had been waived by inadvertent disclosure, relying on these five factors to determine whether a document loses its privilege:

1. The reasonableness of the precautions taken to prevent inadvertent disclosure in the view of the extent of the document production
2. The number of inadvertent disclosures
3. The extent of the disclosure
4. Any delay and measures taken to rectify the disclosure
5. Whether the overriding interests of justice would or would not be served by relieving a party of its error[8]

Cellular Telephones

Although there is a great deal of disagreement, most authorities feel that cellular telephone conversations are not protected under attorney–client privilege. Several state bar associations discourage attorneys from transmitting privileged information over cellular telephones because the method of communication is not sufficiently secure. The Association of the Bar of the City of New York has warned its members to "exercise caution when engaging in conversations containing ... client confidences by cellular or cordless telephones of other communication devices readily capable of interception, and to consider taking steps sufficient to ensure the security of such conversations."[9] Devices such as a police scanner have been known to intercept cellular telephone conversations. This rule may be less applicable now that more sophisticated encryption methods are available.

Special care should be taken with highly confidential materials. A lawyer should inform a client that he is using a cellular telephone and offer to call later from a standard telephone if that would be more convenient.

Cordless Telephones

Cordless telephones are especially subject to eavesdropping because an FM receiver (baby monitor or police band) can hear them. Although they are covered by ECPA, they provide no reasonable expectation of privacy. Neither the client nor the attorney should ever use cordless telephones for privileged conversations. A higher level of encryption now exists, which should make cordless telephones more secure.

Faxes

Intercepted faxes would be protected under the ECPA in the same manner as calls made from a standard telephone. If an attorney or a client accidentally sends a confidential message to the opposing attorney or client, waiver of the attorney–client privilege is likely. The client would have an excellent cause of action for malpractice against the attorney.

E-Mail

The major issue then is whether e-mail is a sufficiently secure means of communication so that e-mail messages are considered to be made in confidence and protected by the attorney–client privilege. To date, there have been no direct court cases and the commentators are divided on the issue.

Encrypted e-mail is probably the most secure means of communication available today and should be treated with the same level of privilege as telephone conversations. Until the matter is resolved, e-mail communication between attorney and client should be used cautiously. Clients should insist that their attorney encrypt highly sensitive e-mail to foil those attempting to read intercepted messages. Such messages are at least as secure as standard telephone lines and should remain privileged. As the encryption technology becomes easier to use, encoded messaging should become the industry standard.

RECOMMENDATIONS

Attorney–client privilege is a crucial part of the judicial system and is much too valuable to be squandered because of carelessness. Even if the court rules that the attorney–client privilege has been maintained, disclosure could destroy an organization's credibility and reputation. Although the main responsibility for maintaining confidentiality belongs to the attorney, a prepared client will take appropriate steps to maintain the privilege.

Organizations would be wise to follow these guidelines when communicating with attorneys:

- Be extremely careful when transmitting documents by any method. The attorney–client privilege may be lost if a fax is sent to the wrong party. The preparation and transmittal of highly confidential documents should not be left to the third-shift mailroom clerk, but should be handled only by highly trusted and competent personnel.
- The attorney–client privilege allows one to be totally candid with his or her attorney. Use this privilege to its fullest. An attorney cannot give a client proper legal advice unless the client tells him or her everything.
- Use encryption technology such as PGP when sending e-mail to an attorney. If an organization is highly technical, advise the attorney on the best ways to maintain confidentiality. If not comfortable with the methods recommended by the attorney, suggest a more reliable technology.
- All documents that are transmitted to an attorney should be labeled "confidential" or "attorney–client privileged." They also should alert unintended recipients to disregard the information to which they mistakenly have been exposed.
- Telephone calls should be made in a private office with the door closed. There is no expectation of privacy from a standard office cubicle and there is no way of knowing who is eavesdropping.
- Ask the attorney if he or she is using a cellular or cordless telephone and, if necessary, request that he or she calls back. Also, insist that highly confidential documents not be transmitted by e-mail unless they are encrypted.
- Be sure that all confidential correspondences are sent directly to the attorney, even if they are required by another member of the attorney's team, for example, an accountant or detective. The attorney will forward the message if necessary. The traditional privilege between a client and an accountant is not nearly as strong as the attorney–client privilege, so it is best to rely on the highest level privilege.
- Never send any correspondence directly to opposing counsel or to the opposing party. Never speak to opposing counsel unless an attorney is present. If contacted directly by opposing counsel for any

reason, tell an attorney immediately. This is an especially severe violation of legal ethics.

• Be especially wary of former employees, building workers, and the Dumpster. Shred documents on a regular basis. Remind current employees periodically of their responsibility of confidentiality.

CONCLUSION

E-mail and other electronic methods of transmitting information are valuable resources for speeding attorney–client communications. Attorneys must be aware of the risks and must take proper steps within their offices to ensure that a breach of confidentiality does not occur.

Although the attorney–client privilege is primarily the responsibility of the attorney, clients also should be aware of their obligations. Great care should be taken to maintain this privilege, especially when electronic transmission of privileged information is involved. Clients must be aware of the risks associated with the use of e-mail and must take proper steps to ensure that a breach of confidentiality does not occur.

Notes

1. California Evidence Code, §140.
2. *United States v. United Shoe Mach. Corp.,* 89 F. Supp. 347, 358 (D. Mass. 1950).
3. *In re Grand Jury Investigation (Sun Co.),* 599 F.2d 1224, 1233 (3d Cir. 1979).
4. *Upjohn Co. v. United States,* 449 U.S. 383, 393 (1981).
5. 296 F.2d 918 [2d Cir. 1961].
6. *Jones,* 696 F.2d at 1072.
7. 18 U.S.C.A. §2517(4).
8. *United States v. Keystone Sanitation Co.,* 885 F. Supp. 672 (M.D.Pa 1994).
9. Gruber, H. M., E-Mail: The Attorney–Client Privilege Applied, 66 *Geo. Wash. L. Rev.* 624 (1998) [quoting N.Y. Bar Association, Formal Opinion No. 1994-11 (1994)].

Chapter 9

Computer Crime and Analysis of Computer Evidence: It Ain't Just Hackers and Phreakers Anymore!

Karl J. Flusche

On June 17, 1993, the state of Virginia executed Andrew J. Charbrol, a former Navy officer, who tracked down, stalked, and murdered Melissa Harrington as revenge for her filing a sexual harassment charge against him, which ended his marriage and his career in the Navy. The electronic journal he kept on his computer was a key piece of evidence used to show how the crime was premeditated. His stalking of her and his plans to murder her were detailed in this journal.[1]

In May 1993, the disappearance of 10-year-old George "Junior" Burdynski, Jr., of Brentwood, Maryland was linked to a suspected child molester by the discovery of the missing boy's name among dozens of boys' names the child molester kept on his home computer — names of children he had molested in the past several years.[2]

In just 20 days, a fake automated teller machine (ATM) machine set up by three men in a Connecticut shopping mall recorded the account numbers and personal identification numbers (PIN) of hundreds of unsuspecting customers — but gave out no money. Instead, the operators of the fake ATM machine used the recorded credit card numbers and their home computer, with an inexpensive card read/write device, to duplicate legitimate debit cards. They then used these "clone" cards to take more than $100,000 from valid ATM machines, verifying the transactions with the PINs as entered by the victims on the fake ATM.[3]

0-8493-1248-5/02/$0.00+$1.50
© 2002 by CRC Press LLC

Clearly, computer crime is no longer exclusively the realm of the adolescent computer "hacker" who bypasses passwords to enter corporate computers searching for data files and games, as depicted in such movies as *Wargames* and *Sneakers*. More and more, computers are being used in all types of crimes, to include traditional crimes of violence and theft. The investigator of the future must be aware that critical evidence, which can help him prove or disprove the crime, may be locked away in a computer or external storage media and often requires more analysis than part-time, in-house "computer experts" can provide. The successful investigator will recognize that *computer evidence is forensic evidence* that must be professionally analyzed.

BACKGROUND

Computers, especially desktop and easily portable laptop-style *personal computers,* are rapidly proliferating throughout society. In the year 2000, 80% of all Americans used personal computers at home. Virtually all businesses use computers in some way, if for nothing else than to record sales transactions or as a word processor for their correspondence. Yet many law enforcement and investigative agencies do not have dedicated computer crime units. Of those that do, few have the in-house resources either to completely understand and analyze the sometimes complex issues that arise or to fully exploit the information that the computer storage media might contain. The criminal element, on the other hand, is full of individuals who exploit the strengths and weaknesses of computers and find them to be vulnerable targets or, paradoxically, powerful tools.

Many articles have been written about computer security and computer crime involving computer security, but few address the potential for the application of computer technology in traditional crimes and the value and availability of evidence that can be obtained from a victim's or suspect's computer. For the legal professional, law enforcement investigator, or corporate security professional, a thorough knowledge of the potential for computers to be used in criminal activity of all types is critical to combat the many forms of computer crime.

POTENTIAL CRIMINAL APPLICATIONS OF A COMPUTER

Computers can be used as the *target, tool,* or *instrument* of a crime. Increasingly, valuable information is kept on a company's computers, and is often the *target* of theft, destruction, or alteration by disgruntled employees, industrial spies, or external hackers. Contrary to popular belief, the outside "hacker" who breaks into a corporation's computer system via phone lines and modem connections is rarely as successful as the "trusted insider" who already has access to the system and exploits it for his or her own purposes. Employees being hired away from one company are sometimes asked to bring copies of computer disks with them to the competing company that contain sensitive or valuable data files pertaining to clients, financial records, or research data. Corporate and industrial espionage via computer is increasing. The modern spy no longer needs to use sophisticated miniature cameras or microfilm: Hundreds of pages of computer-stored documents can be carried on a commonly available pocket size floppy disk. In February 1989, a U.S. Army soldier defected to East Germany, taking with him two floppy disks containing key portions of the U.S. General War Plans for Europe, making him the first computer spy in U.S. history.[4] Disgruntled or careless employees can bring computer viruses into the company's computer system and wreak havoc if effective safeguards are not employed. Corporations are learning that information has value, and can easily be compromised, stolen, or destroyed.

The computer can be a powerful *tool* used to commit crimes as well, as evidenced by the debit card "cloning" mentioned earlier in this article. In addition, high-resolution scanners are allowing persons to copy legitimate documents, alter the data, and thereby forge new documents with the fraudulent data. In 1994, an individual in Dallas, Texas was found to be creating authentic-looking temporary Texas driver's licenses using his scanner and a laser printer. Insurance cards, money orders, checks, and other documents can be duplicated using easily obtainable graphic editing and publishing programs. Computer-stored financial information can be manipulated to cover up embezzlement and thefts. In early 1993, officials at Reese Air Force Base in Texas discovered that a low-level computer operator had altered computerized auditing reports and account records to steal $2.1 million. He was caught only after flaunting his wealth by buying numerous high-priced sports cars.[5]

Computers are also increasingly used as the *instrument* of the crime by recording and storing information pertaining to the criminal act itself. Just as legitimate individuals and businesses use computers to handle their data, records, and correspondence, nonlegitimate businesses and individuals will also. Illegal bookmaking operations find a computer invaluable for recording bets, computing the "line" of bets, and figuring the payoffs, all while calculating the percentage kept for the "house," regardless of how the bets are paid. As early as 1984, law enforcement officials in southern Texas raided an illegal bookmaking operation, expecting to find a typical backroom operation with several operators manning the usual multiple phones, bet boards, and rice-paper betting slips. Instead, they were surprised to find just a six-button phone and a middle-aged, pot-bellied man and his wife, who were entering the bets on a small Apple computer.

Prostitution rings, boiler-room telemarketing fraud operations, and other illegal activities find computers essential for recording and tracking their data. Individuals accustomed to using a computer to type documents and enter and record data also use their computers for their illegal activity. Child molesters have been known to write up their activities in electronic journals, and suicide notes have been found on the deceased's personal computer as early as 1984. Computer-literate criminals utilize the latest technology to further their illegal enterprises just as much as the honest businessperson, and documents are no longer exclusively written on paper.

In each of the cases and examples mentioned, professional analysis of the computer system or storage media was instrumental to solving the case or prosecuting the individuals. This is because at some point in time, the *evidence* of the criminal activity ended up on something tangible somewhere. Files, programs, or documents may not be easily readable, or they may be hidden or even deleted. Often, hidden audit trails exist that can indicate what files or programs were used or accessed, and date/time stamps on files, if verified, can be valuable indicators of the usage of the computer system, which can tie suspects to the illegal activity. Special tools or techniques may be required to resurrect these files or analyze the systems. In each case, this must be done professionally, by knowledgeable analysts who have the academic and experiential credentials to be credible witnesses when the issue of data recovery comes to court.

Many commonly available utility programs can write to the hard disk or otherwise change data during the process of analysis and should not be used for extensive analysis of seized evidence. Rules of evidence, as established by the courts and legal doctrine, must be followed. Especially, defense or opposing lawyers must have the ability to have this evidence analyzed as well. This means that however analysis of computer evidence is performed by the police agency or prosecutor, the results must not alter or destroy the original evidence, and such results must be duplicable in court.

EXAMPLES OF COMPUTER-RELATED CRIME

In sex offenses, computers can be used as both a tool and an instrument. Pedophiles and child molesters utilize computer technology to record and store their collections of child pornography and child-related documents. Computer programs can be used to hide or encrypt the pictures of files so that only the pedophile can have normal, easy access to them. Sophisticated image-manipulating software programs allow for editing and enhancement of these photos. Separate pictures of children can be merged with traditional adult pornography. The combined result depicts the children interacting with the adults in the picture in a sexual fashion. In addition, new and different pictures and files can be transferred to and traded with other pedophiles using modem connections and bulletin board systems (BBSs), often with complete freedom from detection for the pornographer. Pedophiles have also been known to make contacts with potential victims through publicly accessible BBS messages, sometimes employing masquerades and phony identities to help facilitate contact with their victims. One child molester used his computer, loaded with children's games and programs, as a "bag of candy" to entice young girls to sit in his lap and play on the computer while he fondled them. Analysis of these systems can often prove or disprove such allegations and can lead the investigator to other suspects and places to search.

Criminals often find clever ways to use computers to help them in their illegal endeavors, but this does not mean they are "whiz kids" or geniuses, as some have been called. In 1987 a group of burglars used a computer, a modem, and a program called a "War Games Auto-Dialer" (named after the movie showing use of the program) to record the results of random calls to houses in a given area at several times during the day. After a while, the group had recorded blocks of time at several homes where the phone was not answered — indications that no one was home during those times. They then burglarized those homes, confident that they would be vacant. When caught by police for pawning one stolen item, professional analysis of the computer system and disks revealed the full extent of their activity, effectively linking them to every burglary.

Legal issues, long since established, require new interpretations when computers are involved. Around Christmas 1988, a woman's 13-month-old daughter was admitted to the Emergency Room at Zweibrucken Air Base, Germany, for injuries resulting in severe brain damage. Initial investigation indicated classic child abuse and that the woman's husband was a prime suspect. The next day the woman brought to investigators a computer-generated printout of a diary in which she indicated that the child's injuries were caused by hospital personnel, babysitters, and others. Diaries are admissible in court as exceptions to the hearsay rule: They can be accepted as a recording of events if the diary entry was made at the time the events occurred. Detailed forensic analysis of the computer disk containing the diary, including analysis of the date/time tagging of the files, proved she had manufactured the entire diary the night before in an attempt to divert suspicion from her husband. Hundreds of hours of investigative manpower were saved by proving her diary was an electronic forgery.[6]

WHAT CAN INVESTIGATORS DO?

How is the modern investigator then to deal with this evidence? First and foremost, investigators needs to remain investigators and recognize that they must still answer the basic questions essential to solving or proving any criminal case, such as who, what, where, when, why, and how. Regardless of how much technology changes the nature of the crime, the basic rules of investigation remain. The difference brought about by modern computer technology is that the evidence may now take new forms and may not always be instantly recognizable or readable. The modern investigator must be able to recognize that computers and their associated storage media may be integral to any category of crime, not just white-collar fraud or high-tech computer hacking.

Second, when gathering evidence in an investigation, investigators need to incorporate wording in subpoenas, search warrants, and affidavits to include computer technology. When a computer is being used as a tool to commit the crime, the search warrant should include sufficient description to enable investigators to seize the actual hardware (i.e., the physical components of the computer) and associated peripherals, such as scanners, printers, and other items, being used to perform the illegal activity. Usually, the main reason for search and seizure of a suspect's computer is for the information pertaining to the illegal activity that may be stored on the computer and associated storage media. Sometimes, non-computer-literate magistrates or judges may need to be educated as to how a computer can be used to commit traditional noncomputer crimes (e.g., cloning of credit cards) or to forge checks and other important documents. This can be done in an affidavit by adding explanatory paragraphs from a recognized computer crime expert. In all cases, the most important rule in preparing search warrants is to specify that the particular information being sought can be found in written or electronic form. This phrase enables the investigator to build a case for seizure of the suspect's entire computer system and associated peripherals and storage media, without being too general, because the specific information being sought has been identified in the warrant. This key phrase should be included in all search warrants, not just those in which computer evidence is expected. Investigators may unexpectedly encounter computer evidence in any case category.[7]

Next, computer evidence is both delicate and sturdy and is vulnerable to unseen dangers. All investigators should be aware of the many methods and ways computer evidence can be accidentally or deliberately erased or deleted. Entire systems have been booby-trapped to prevent their analysis by authorities. Before executing a search or gathering computer evidence at a crime scene, investigators should try to establish enough background intelligence on the suspect(s) to determine whether they are computer knowledgeable enough to booby-trap their systems or otherwise thwart a search of their computer. In one case, a computer hacker wrapped wire into and around the door frame and threshold of his bedroom door, then connected it to the light switch. In doing so he created a giant electromagnetic "degaussing" field that could have scrambled the contents of any computer disks or tapes brought through the door by investigators after seizure. Stray electromagnetic fields from other common sources, such as bell-ringing telephones and radio transmitters in the trunks of police vehicles, can also inadvertently destroy the information on computer disks and tapes. Even in evidence lockers, computer evidence can be damaged by high levels of humidity, excessive heat, or rough handling. Yet, as delicate as computer evidence can be, it can also be remarkably sturdy. Technicians at the Air Force Office of Special Investigations were able to piece together a floppy disk that had been cut up into a dozen pieces by a suspect using pinking shears. The end result was recovery of nearly all of the data files on the disk — enough to get the suspect convicted of the murder of his wife.

Finally, after computer evidence is seized, it must be analyzed properly to extract all possible information. Homicide detectives do not perform their own blood typing or DNA analysis on biological evidence collected at crime scenes; narcotics investigators do not run extensive analytical tests on unknown substances to determine whether or not what they seized during a raid was a controlled substance. In both cases, investigators send properly collected evidence to a reputable lab for professional analysis by trained technicians who can testify to their results as experts in the courtroom. The same should hold true for computer evidence. Many investigators today have desktop personal computers available to them, and many have become quite proficient at using them, but most do not have in-depth professional training and experience in computer science and systems analysis. Unfortunately, these same computer-literate investigators often try to perform their own analysis on the seized computer evidence. In addition, investigators may encounter networked systems of multiple desktop computers or mainframe systems with which they are completely unfamiliar. "Do-it-yourself" forensic analysis of computer evidence is full of perils and pitfalls for the investigator and can enable defense attorneys to question the results of such evidentiary analysis by the same investigator who is running the investigation, especially if he is not professionally trained in computer systems or forensic analysis.

Notes

1. Associated Press, "Va. Executes Former Naval Officer," *The Washington Post,* June 18, 1993.
2. Stephen Buckley and Graciela Sevilla, "Boy's Disappearance Remains a Puzzle," *The Washington Post,* May 30, 1993, p. 1A.
3. Sandra Sanchez, "Two Suspects Held in Fake ATM Scam," *USA Today,* July 1, 1993.
4. See *United States v. Peri,* (33 M.J. 927 (ACMR 1991).
5. Robert Green, "Ground Zero: How Much Will DoD's Security Mania Cost Us?" *Government Computer News,* June 21, 1993.
6. Air Force Office of Special Investigations file number 8970D8-1183, January 23, 1989.
7. For an excellent article on preparing warrants and affidavits, see John Gales Sauls, "Computer Searches and Seizures, Challenges for Investigators," *FBI Law Enforcement Bulletin,* June 1993, pp. 24–32.

Chapter 10

A Tale of Two Spies: The Outside Hacker and the Trusted Insider

Karl J. Flusche

From 1986 to 1988, several computer hackers located in Hannover, Germany, worked their way into more than 40 computer systems here in the United States, mostly military and federal government research-related systems. They downloaded hundreds of files consisting of thousands of pages of material, looking for military secrets pertaining to the latest weapons and other defense systems. They sold these printouts to a Soviet KGB agent in East Berlin. Although they managed to penetrate scores of computers during this two-year period, not one page of the material they stole was classified. Sensitive information, yes, but all of it publicly available. In February 1989, a young 22-year-old U.S. soldier, Michael A. Peri, abruptly left his unit in Fulda, Germany and calmly climbed the barbed-wire fence separating East and West Germany. In his black duffel bag was a laptop computer he had stolen from his unit, along with several floppy disks. Two of the disks contained hundreds of pages of classified U.S. secret documents, including the General War Plans that the United States would follow in any ground war with Soviet forces in Germany. In his 10-minute defection, Peri delivered more information to the enemy than all the efforts by the "Hannover Hackers."

HANNOVER HACKERS

The Hannover Hackers were a group of five, semi-computer-literate young men with little in common. The main hacker, Markus Hess, began hacking into the German national communications systems at first "just for fun." As he learned more and more by trial and error, he discovered "back

0-8493-1248-5/02/$0.00+$1.50
© 2002 by CRC Press LLC

doors" into many systems, ways he could enter the system using common passwords generally used for maintenance. Soon Hess found himself able to hack into the Mitre Corporation's computer in Bedford, MA. He used Mitre's computer as a jumping-off point to enter U.S. computer systems, especially military computer systems, allowing Mitre to pick up the tab for his long-distance hacking. Karl Koch, a.k.a. "Hagbard," who introduced Hess to hacking, saw there was money to be made by obtaining and selling military information, and he enlisted the aid of three other hackers — Hans Huebner, a.k.a. "Pengo," Peter Carl, and Dirk Bresinsky — to help make contacts with the Soviet KGB and make deliveries. Over the course of more than two years, Hess and Hagbard attempted to break into more than 440 U.S. computers by guessing at passwords and, once in, recreating the security password file to give themselves "master" access to the computer the next time they entered. All this activity was being observed by Dr. Clifford Stoll in Berkeley, CA, who — after accidentally discovering Hess's and his friends' efforts — tried unsuccessfully for most of the two years to get a law enforcement agency interested in investigating the activity.

Although the break-in activity of the hackers was wrong, there was no definable loss: The files being copied and examined by Hess and his friends were unclassified, publicly available files. Hess and the others were not authorized to enter the computers, but current laws did not define what they were doing as offenses. Hagbard got Pengo and Carl to travel to East Berlin and contact the Soviet Agricultural Attaché (i.e., the KGB), who paid them in money and cocaine, using a bus locker to make the transfers. Despite selling the printed files to the KGB for thousands of dollars, not one page of copied documents was classified. Hess and Hagbard effectively scammed the KGB into paying for documents they could have obtained openly. Because they were obtained by computer, the KGB apparently was more attracted to them because they pointed out systems that could be exploited.

Eventually, Hess and Hagbard were caught by the German equivalent of the FBI, the BundesKriminalAmpt (BKA), and indicted for espionage, along with the others. A search of Hess's apartment on June 29, 1987, yielded a computer, printed documents, and 100 floppy disks. Interagency squabbles between the FBI, BKA, and others resulted in the evidence never being analyzed, and Hess got off the first time around. On March 2, 1989, the Germans charged all five with espionage. Pengo and Hagbard cooperated with the BKA and escaped prosecution, but Hagbard committed suicide just a few months later. The others were tried and convicted in German courts. Dr. Stoll went on to write a book, testify before the U.S. Congress, and achieve a modicum of fame. The network system exploited by the Hannover Hackers was known then as the Arapanet. We now know it as the Internet.

Many aspects of this investigation went wrong because of unclear laws on computer crime and a lack of awareness about what crimes can be committed or aided by computer. Many of the investigators on the case were untrained in computer crime investigation and evidence handling. In this case, Hess and his friend tried to commit espionage and obtain military secrets to sell to the KGB, but they were unsuccessful. Law enforcement agencies could not or would not recognize the value of computer information or how to cooperate to solve this case. Hess and others like him are still "out there" waiting to exploit computer systems and the information they contain.

DEFECTION OF PERI

Late at night on February 21, 1989, Specialist Michael A. Peri, of the 11th Armored Cavalry Regiment, Fulda, Germany, left his unit and his country behind and quietly walked into East Germany. A few minutes earlier, he had walked into the vault room of his unit, where the most secret of documents are kept, and walked out with a laptop computer, telling the guard he was only "borrowing" it. He had also removed two floppy disks from the vault, each with a label describing it as classified. He removed the labels replacing them with game labels, checked out a jeep using a set of forged orders, and drove to the border. He climbed the barbed-wire fence and after walking up and down the line trying to find an East German patrol without success, finally gave himself up to two sentries in an East German guard tower — after he woke them up. He gave them the laptop computer, showing them first how to turn it on and calling up one of the documents from the floppy disks on the screen. The guards called over their commander, and soon Peri was in East Berlin cooperating with the East German Intelligence Service.

After 11 days, Peri was dissatisfied with how the East Germans were treating him: He expected to be greeted and treated as a hero but instead was treated rather coldly. The East Germans could have thought he was a "provocateur" of the U.S. — deliberately attempting to fake a defection for the purpose of giving them false information. At any rate, Peri asked for and was granted permission to leave, going from East Berlin to Austria. After spending the night in an expensive hotel room, Peri went back to his unit and turned himself in, taking with him the laptop and floppy disks he got back from the East Germans.

Peri refused to cooperate with investigators, who at first did not realize he had delivered any documents to the East Germans. Indeed, an inventory of the vault from which Peri had stolen the laptop showed that no documents were missing. Only after analysis of the floppy disks and laptop did the picture become clear. The disks were undocumented copies taken from a secretary's desk, and each contained hundreds of pages of secret portions of the U.S. General War Plans. The laptop contained many classified and sensitive documents as well. Most important, analysis of the laptop computer showed evidence of an audit trail of what documents were printed and when — evidence that proved that Peri and/or his East German partners printed out each document. In July 1989, Peri was tried and convicted by Courts Martial and received 30 years at the military prison at Ft. Leavenworth. To this day Peri is unrepentant: He told follow-up investigators in 1993 that if he had it to do again, he would, and this time he would make sure to take more disks.

COMPARISONS

In both cases, the stolen information originated on the computer. There the similarities end. Of the 440 systems the Hannover Hackers tried to enter, they only succeeded in about 10% of the cases (those that had left simple, common, or maintenance passwords active). Hess never successfully hacked into any system that used even the most basic of security measures. The Hannover Hackers were outsiders who did not know what information each system contained; they were literally "hunting and pecking" for whatever information they could find. Once into a system, they would search for files containing key words such as "SDI" or "Star Wars," "nuclear," and "missile." Peri, on the other hand, knew exactly which disks contained secret information and took only those two disks he thought he could get away with.

The method of transfer of the information in the two cases is interesting. Peri took the laptop and disks only. He never took any paper documents. Investigators were at first hindered because their audit of documents showed all classified documents were accounted for. The Hannover Hackers, for some reason, printed the documents out and made the transfer via a locker in a West Berlin bus terminal. Investigative methods were substantially different as well. In the Hannover Hacker case, authorities were confused and unable to apply existing laws to the hacking activity. They kept trying to place a dollar value on the information taken and did not realize the value of computer information. Even after seizure of the disks from Hess's apartment, German BKA did not have an in-house expert to analyze the disks and refused to allow the U.S. expert to conduct any such analysis. In the Peri case, investigators properly safeguarded the laptop computer and disks and allowed analysis of the evidence only by a trained expert who uncovered the necessary evidence, in a way admissible by the court.

Today's investigator cannot be the expert in every field and every method of investigation. The wise investigator will, however, be able to recognize the many methods criminals may use to commit crime by computer. Modern investigators will bring in experts as needed to help resolve the complex issues that may result from these high-tech cases. Many law enforcement agencies and prosecutors may not have the in-house expertise or experience to successfully investigate and prosecute these crimes, placing more burden on professional private investigators to fill in the gaps. The best publicly available account of the Hannover Hackers is *The Cuckoo's Egg*, by Clifford Stoll. The Peri case was analyzed by the Community Research Center under contract to the FBI/CIA. The results were published in limited distribution under the title *Project Slammer: Computer Crime and Security Incident Study, Michael A. Peri, June 3, 1993*. It is not available publicly but may be obtained under provisions of the Freedom of Information Act.

After reading this and the preceding chapter, "Computer Crime and Analysis of Computer Evidence," you now have an understanding of some of the many issues surrounding the computer and its involvement in criminal activity. Just as investigators and other professionals learn how to investigate using the computer, so will thieves learn their computer lessons. Criminals are like cockroaches — they are always there, trying new ways to take from us what we do not safeguard. The investigator must still be ready to stomp on them when the computerized light of truth shines.

Chapter 11
Federal Laws Affecting IS Auditors

Frederick Gallegos

INTRODUCTION

In recent years, advances in network environments' technologies have made security and privacy issues — once only of interest to the legal and technical expert — the concern of virtually every user of the information superhighway. Such concerns are often brought to the attention of the IS audit and control specialist. This article presents security and privacy legislation as they relate to the networked environment and the Internet. Current federal legislation, which affects the online community on these topics, is discussed, as well as the government's role in the networked society and the effect that it has had on the networked environment in recent years.

FEDERAL SECURITY LEGISLATION

Numerous pieces of legislation have been proposed or enacted regarding the security of electronic data. Among these are the Computer Fraud and Abuse Act and the Computer Security Act of 1987.

The Computer Fraud and Abuse Act

The Computer Fraud and Abuse Act was first enacted in 1984 as a response to computer crime, and later amended in 1986. The government's response to network security and network-related crimes was to revise the act in 1994 under the Computer Abuse Amendments Act to cover such crimes as trespass (i.e., unauthorized entry) onto an online system, exceeding authorized access, and exchanging information on gaining unauthorized access. Most recently, in 1996, the Computer Fraud and Abuse Act was amended by the National Information Infrastructure Protection Act. Although the act was intended to protect against attacks in a network environment, it also has its faults.

0-8493-1248-5/02/$0.00+$1.50
© 2002 by CRC Press LLC

The act requires that certain conditions be present for the crime to be a violation. Only if these conditions are present, does the crime fall under violation of the act. The three types of attack covered under the act, and the conditions that must be met, include:

1. *Fraudulent trespass.* A trespass is made with an intent to defraud that results in furthering the fraud and in the attacker obtaining something of value.
2. *Intentional destructive trespass.* A fraudulent trespass is combined with an action that intentionally causes damage to a computer, computer system, network, information, data, or program, or action that results in denial of service and causes at least $1000 total loss in the course of a year.
3. *Reckless destructive trespass.* Trespassing is combined with reckless actions (although not deliberately harmful) that cause damage to a computer, computer system, network information, data, or program, or results in denial of service and that causes at least $1000 total loss in the course of a year.

Each of these three definitions is geared toward a particular type of attack. Fraudulent trespass is a response against crimes involving telephone fraud committed through a computer system, such as using a telephone company computer to obtain free telephone service. This condition helps prosecute individuals responsible for the large financial losses suffered by companies such as AT&T. The other two usually apply to online systems and have been implemented to address problems of hackers, crackers, worms, viruses, and any other type of intruder that can damage, alter, or destroy information. The two attacks differ only in that one is a deliberate act with intent to cause damage. Penalties, under Section 1030(c) of the act, vary from a one year's imprisonment for reckless destructive trespass on a nonfederal computer to as much as 20 years' imprisonment for an intentional attack on a federal computer in which the information obtained is used to "the injury of the United States, or to the advantage of any foreign nation" (i.e., cases of espionage).

The penalties are less severe for reckless destructive trespass than for intentional destructive trespass. The reason for this situation is that the reckless attacker, who may not necessarily intend to cause damage, must still be punished for gaining access to restricted places. However, terminology creates some confusion in prosecuting the trespasser. For example, in *United States v. Morris*, it was determined that intent applied to access and not to damages. The implication is that if the intentional part of the violation is applied to access and not to the damage, the culprit can potentially be prosecuted under the lesser charge. For example, it would be difficult for prosecutors to prove that an individual intentionally released a virus over a network. The individual could claim to have been conducting a security test, during which a procedure was accidentally initiated, releasing a virus over the network. In other words, "intentional" could refer to system access, but it may not apply to damage. In this case, the lesser penalty of "reckless destructive trespass" may be applied. In some cases, however, even intentional trespass could be defended by claiming the violation was due to negligence and would therefore be subject to the less severe penalties. This loophole of intent is large enough for a serious violator to slip through. All states have closed a portion of that loophole through statutes prohibiting harassment or stalking, including by way of electronic mail.

The Computer Fraud and Abuse Act has become a general-purpose statute for prosecuting Internet crimes. It has been used in conjunction with other statutes. These statutes are in the United States Code, Title 18, and include embezzlement, malicious mischief, theft, false statements, accessory after the fact, and conspiracy. In August 2000, a false news release regarding Emulex was released on the Internet and caused a severe impact on the stock value to the extent that trading was halted on the exchange. The financial impact was considerable. This action is currently being investigated under the statute. Preliminary information is that this false information was released by a broker who profited by almost $250,000.

The Computer Security Act of 1987

The Computer Security Act of 1987 was drafted because of congressional concerns surrounding public awareness of computer security-related issues and because of disputes over the control of unclassified information. The general purpose of the act was a declaration from the government that improving the security and privacy of sensitive information in federal computer systems would be in the public interest. The act established a security program for protecting sensitive information in federal government computer systems. The program developed standards and guidelines for unclassified federal computer systems and facilitated such protection. The Computer Security Act also assigns responsibility for developing government-wide security standards, guidelines, and security training programs for the National Bureau of Standards (now the National Institute of Standards and Technology, or NIST) by amending the Act of March 3, 1901, and the Federal Property and Administrative Services Act of 1949. It further established a Computer System Security and Privacy Advisory Board within the Commerce Department. Federal agencies were required to identify those computer systems containing sensitive information and to develop security plans for those systems. Finally, the act provided for periodic training in computer security for all federal employees and contractors who managed, used, or operated federal computer systems. The Computer Security Act is particularly important because it is fundamental to the development of federal standards for safeguarding unclassified information. It is also important in addressing issues concerning government control of cryptography.

The act was also a legislative response to overlapping responsibilities for computer security among several federal agencies. Some level of responsibility for federal computers rested with the Office of Management and Budget (OMB), the General Services Administration (GSA), and the Commerce Department. The OMB maintained overall responsibility for computer security policy. The GSA issued regulations for the physical security of computer facilities and oversaw technological and fiscal specifications for security hardware and software. The National Security Administration (NSA) was responsible for the security of information that is classified for national security purposes. Such overlapping responsibilities impeded the development of one uniform federal policy covering the security of unclassified information.

The Computer Security Act gives authority for developing standards and guidelines to NIST. The intent was to refrain from giving the NSA a dominant role; however, this activity and overall implementation of the act have not been simple tasks. The Office of Technology Assessment found that the Computer Security Act has not been without problems. Although the agencies followed the rules set forth by the act regarding security plans and training, they did not necessarily follow the intent of the act. For example, although agencies developed their initial security plans, they did not regularly review them because the act does not require the periodic review or updating of these plans as technologies change. Because of this, the required security plans can become outdated and, ultimately, less effective and may be unable to properly address the new problems associated with computer security.

As stated, the Computer Security Act was intended to give NIST the lead in developing security standards and guidelines and to define the role of NSA as technical advisor to NIST. The NSA, however, has sought to undermine NIST's authority. In 1989, the two agencies developed and signed the controversial Memorandum of Understanding in an attempt to clarify the role that the two agencies play in regard to standards and guidelines for information security and to create a joint NIST and NSA technical working group to develop the Clipper Chip. This memorandum, however, has been viewed as an attempt by the NSA to undercut NIST's authority and transfer control back to itself. As a result, the Office of Technology Assessment (OTA) has viewed the NSA as the leader in the development of cryptographic standards and technical guidelines for unclassified information security, and NIST has not demonstrated enough leadership to challenge this assumption. This could have a significant effect in the area of privacy violation; if the NSA is viewed as the authority in this area, guidelines and procedures are likely to favor those that are beneficial to national security and possibly weaken the mandate of the Computer Security Act. This, in turn, could lead to the implementation of policies and procedures made in the name of national security and law enforcement but that could infringe on an individual's privacy rights.

PRIVACY ON THE INFORMATION SUPERHIGHWAY

Companies and agencies can retrieve a tremendous amount of information on any individual. People, corporations, and government are active in trading personal information for their own gain. A Virginia resident filed suit in state court against *US News & World Report*, challenging the right of the magazine to sell or rent his name to another publication without his express written consent. Criminals, competitors, and basically anyone else can buy a person's IRS form for $500. Individuals share private information on a daily basis. The following section analyzes how this has affected the network world and the Internet.

The large number of users on the Internet has resulted in the availability of an enormous amount of private information on the network. This information is available for the taking by anyone who might be interested. A person's bank balance, Social Security number, sexual orientation, political leanings, and medical record are there for anyone who might want such information. In October 1995, it was revealed that someone had developed a list of 250,000 Internet addresses showing what chat groups people were visiting, along with the Web sites they logged onto. The list was then put up for sale to any parties interested in the information. Someone has been collecting information and making it available for use, and a large number of these individuals are not following any sort of fair information practice. Are they entitled to this information? What is the government's policy regarding the privacy of an individual and keeping a strong security policy? Is the government in a position to monitor communications on the information superhighway? How will this affect its citizens' right to privacy as guaranteed by the U.S. Constitution? The following section addresses these issues and focuses on the security-based measures that have affected the ideal of individuals' right to privacy.

Privacy Legislation and the Federal Government Privacy Act

In addition to the basic right to privacy guaranteed an individual under the Constitution, safeguards against an invasion of personal privacy were enacted by the government in the Privacy Act of 1974. This act places certain requirements on federal agencies, including:

1. Permitting individuals to determine which records pertaining to themselves are collected and maintained by federal agencies
2. Permitting individuals to prevent records pertaining to themselves and obtained for a particular purpose from being used or made available for another purpose without consent
3. Permitting individuals to gain access to information pertaining to themselves in federal agency records and to correct or amend them
4. Requiring federal agencies to collect, maintain, and use any personal information in a manner that ensures that such action is for a necessary and lawful purpose, that the information is current and accurate, and that safeguards are provided to prevent the misuse of the information

In light of the provision, the Privacy Act should protect many individuals against the distribution of private information on the part of any agency. This, however, is not always the case, because the act outlines various general and specific exemptions. Because of these exemptions, law enforcement agencies, as well as other commercial agencies, may have some rights to private information.

Under Section (j), General Exemptions, of the Privacy Act, information maintained by certain agencies, such as the Central Intelligence Agency (CIA), are thus exempt from the provision for national security reasons. In addition to the CIA, any agency that performs an activity pertaining to the enforcement of criminal laws is also exempt from the provisions of the act. This appears to imply that these agencies can make inquiries for the sake of "national security" whenever they wish. Section (k), Special Exemptions, exempts protection from certain information with regard to positions, appointments, and promotions in federal service jobs or positions in the armed forces.

The point of this seems to be that even the Privacy Act is an important part of safeguarding individual privacy rights, and there are many exemptions under which it may be lawful for certain information to be disclosed. This could give various agencies, both federal and nonfederal, the means to obtain and disclose information on any individual simply because the agencies fall under one of the many exemptions that the privacy act allows.

Electronic Communication Privacy Act

In the area of computer networking, the Electronic Communications Privacy Act is one of the leading pieces of legislation against the violation of private information as applicable to online systems. Before analyzing some of the implications that this act has had on the network community, the more complicated provisions defined by the act are discussed.

For example, Section 2511 of the act prohibits the interception and disclosure of wire, oral, or electronic communications and the manufacture or possession of the intercepting devices prohibited under Section 2512. Section 2516, however, authorizes and makes exceptions for the interception of wire or electronic communications under certain circumstances. Despite the exceptions noted under Section 2516, Section 2515 prohibits the use as evidence of intercepted wire or oral communications. Even if evidence is allowed to be intercepted and collected, it seems that agencies cannot introduce that evidence in court.

Regarding government intervention in online privacy, under Section 2701, it is unlawful for anyone (including the government) to access stored communications without proper authority (i.e., a warrant). However, an exception is made in this provision. Under Section 2701(c)(a)(1), it is stated that the person or entity providing a wire or electronic communications service can intercept communications with prior user consent. Under Section 2701(b)(6)(B) on disclosure, such a person can then report the information to a law enforcement agency if such contents appear to pertain to the commission of a crime (again with the stipulation of prior consent). Upon reading this clause, many people may think that clearly anyone desiring privacy would not give prior consent, but what about cases in which consent is given when the contract is agreed on? Some services include fine print on the terminal screen at the time the user first joins the service. This fine print may contain statements regarding privacy rights as they apply to that specific service. Customers not scrutinizing the fine print closely enough may set themselves up for having their private information intercepted by and disclosed to others. For these reasons, potential customers should read the policy guidelines when signing up for an online service.

The point of seizure of private information stored on a computer without a warrant was made clear in the landmark case of Steve Jackson Games, Inc. versus U.S. Secret Service. Secret Service officials raided the office of Steve Jackson Games as part of a nationwide investigation of data piracy in 1990. Agents first violated privacy rights by searching and seizing messages without proper authority and without a warrant. It was then found, when the gaming company received a copy of the Secret Service warrant affidavit, that it was based solely on suspicion of guilt by "remote association." The author of the game GURPS Cyberpunk had corresponded with a variety of people, from computer security experts to computer hackers. That was enough to put him on a federal list of "dangerous hoodlums." More than three years later, a federal court awarded more than $50,000 in damages and $250,000 in attorney's fees after ruling that the raid had been careless, illegal, and completely unjustified. This was an important case on the topic because it was the first step toward establishing that online speech is entitled to Constitutional protection and that law enforcement agents cannot seize and hold a bulletin board service with impunity.

In summary, the Electronic Communications Privacy Act, although of fair intention (i.e., to protect privacy rights), may have too many exceptions to be fully effective for the user and law enforcement agencies alike. Ideally, any information regarding a person's private affairs should be kept from being shared by others, but this is not always easy to do. In addition, although law enforcement officials can obtain access to private information, it is difficult at times for authorities to base their prosecution solely on electronic communication.

The Communications Decency Act of 1996

The Communications Decency Act bans the making of "indecent" or "patently offensive" material available to minors by way of computer networks. The act imposes a fine of up to $250,000 and imprisonment for as many as two years. The decency act specifically exempts from liability any person who provides access or connection to or from a facility, system, or network that is not under the control of the person violating the act. The act also specifically states that an employer shall not be held liable for the actions of an employee unless the employee's conduct is within the scope of his or her employment.

Privacy

The Supreme Court uses to imply the constitutionality of privacy are in the First, Third, Fourth, Fifth, Ninth, Tenth, and Fourteenth Amendments. These amendments, when used individually or combined for certain circumstances, provide the individuals' right to privacy but, at the same time, the court may decide in some cases that the right to privacy did not exist. While the Constitution may be looked on for some privacy guidance, it should not be relied on solely to protect an individual's rights of privacy. From this determination then, federal and state laws will need to be developed to protect an individual's privacy.

Legislative Actions

Because there is no constitutional amendment that deals directly with privacy, legislation needs to be enacted to protect the individual's rights. Some of the legislative activities dealing in this area are:

- The Privacy Act of 1974 and amended Privacy Act of 1994
- Privacy Protection Act of 1980
- Freedom of Information Act and Electronic Freedom of Information Act Amendments of 1996

- The Fair Credit Reporting Act of 1970 and Amendments of 1996
- Electronic Communication Privacy Act of 1986 and Amendments of 1999
- Children's Online Privacy Protection Act of 1998
- Computer Matching and Privacy Protection Act of 1988
- The Equal Employment Opportunity Act
- The Family Education Rights Act of 1974
- 18 U.S.C. 2721-2725 for State Department of Motor Vehicles
- The Lanham Acton trademark registration
- The Computer Security Act of 1987
- Child Pornography Prevention Act of 1996
- Copyright Infringement Act of 1999
- Ecomonic Espionage Act of 1999
- Amended Electronic Funds Transfer Act of 1999
- Amended Mail and Wire Fraud Statues of 1999
- Electronic Rights for the 21st Century Act

As mentioned, the Privacy Act of 1974 uses the "fair information principles" as policy for federal agencies. For records of individuals that are maintained by federal agencies, certain rules and policies must be followed. For information to be disclosed, the individual must consent to that disclosure, with the exception of certain instances. These exceptions extend:

1. To the officers and employees of that agency who have the need for the information to perform their duties
2. To the Census Bureau to plan for its census
3. To a recipient who has provided the agency with advance adequate written assurance that the record will be used solely as statistical research or reporting record, and the record is to be transferred in a form that is not individually identifiable
4. To a person pursuant to a showing of compelling circumstances affecting the health or safety of an individual
5. To the Comptroller General, or any of his authorized representatives, in the course of the performance of the duties of the General Accounting Office
6. Pursuant to the order of a court of competent jurisdiction

Although the Privacy Act allows for some exceptions, any disclosure needs to follow certain documentation. The information to be noted includes the date, nature, and purpose of each disclosure of each record and the name and address of the person or agency to which the disclosure was made. The act also allows for individuals to have access to all their records and to be able to copy the information. The individual is also allowed to request that amendments to the records be made. Requests shall be processed within ten days and, if they are denied, the reasons must be stated to the individual to allow for a response. The exceptions for access to records are in instances where a civil action or proceeding is reasonably anticipated.

The Privacy Act states that the agencies must also follow certain requirements to ensure that their systems will adequately protect the information. The guidelines for training the agencies' personnel were developed by the NSA in NSTISSI No. 4011 National Training Standard for Information Systems Security (INFOSEC) Personnel, 4012 National Training Standard for Designated Approving Authority (DAA), 4013 National Training Standard for System Administrators in Information Systems Security (INFOSEC), and 4014 National Training Standard for Information Systems Security Officers (ISSO). These are minimum standards of training, and further training and documentation may be required by the various agencies.

The Freedom of Information Act permits individuals the right to access all federal records — with a number of exceptions. Some of these exceptions are designed to protect privacy. Exception 6 prevents access of "personnel and medical files and similar files the disclosure of which would constitute a clearly unwarranted invasion of privacy," and exception 7 prevents release of "records or information compiled for law enforcement purposes [which] ... could reasonably be expected to constitute an unwarranted invasion of privacy." The Supreme Court has ruled in favor of these exemptions in The Freedom of Information Act and has even made them more stringent in the release of certain information.

The Fair Credit Reporting Act sets requirements for consumer credit reporting agencies and the users of that information regarding the preparation and distribution of the information. As amended, the act provides that the information must be correct, and that the burden of proof to verify potentially false information falls on the credit-reporting agency. The user of the credit information must inform the consumer if an unfavorable decision was based on the credit report and provide the address of the credit agency. The consumer is then entitled to a copy of that report from the reporting agency.

As mentioned earlier, the Electronic Communication Privacy Act of 1986 broadens the federal privacy protections to electronic and computer communications. All forms of electronic communication are protected under this act. It prevents the capture and revelation of the contents of that communication. The exception is that private employers may intercept and read private e-mail that is sent over the organization's network. Many people feel this is an invasion of privacy, but the organization's contention (with the courts agreeing) is any communication sent over their network should be business related, and as such they have a right to monitor for unauthorized use of the system.

The 18 U.S.C. 2721-2725 for State Department of Motor Vehicles provides residents with a means to prohibit the disclosure of information on lists that are rented for marketing purposes or to other people. Certain provisions allow a selected list of organizations access to that information even if the individual does not want it released.

The Electronic Rights for the 21st Century Act establishes "standards and procedures regarding law enforcement access to location information, decryption assistance for encrypted communications and stored electronic information, and other private information, to affirm the rights of Americans to use and sell encrypted products as a tool for protecting their online privacy for other purposes." This act protects privacy in networked computer systems and balances the needs of law enforcement to have access to certain communication and information in particular situations. It also encourages the use of encryption to protect the communications and data of the individuals.

Current Legislative Activity

While these acts may not seem to completely protect the individuals' rights to privacy, there are significant ongoing legislative activities to meet the demand for privacy protection. They have come about as a result of concern by citizens and business. Several recent studies have identified the following as major sources of computer fraud:

- Internet services
- Work-at-home offers
- Credit card offers
- Advance fee loans
- Business opportunities
- Computer equipment and software

As a result of the above, the House of Representatives and the Senate have been very busy in developing draft legislation. The following is a list of recent legislation:

1. H.R.10. Financial Services Act of 1999. Major bank, securities, etc. merger bill. Requires FTC to issue interim reports on consumer privacy.
2. H.R.97. Personal Privacy Protection Act. Stalkerazzi bill. Prohibits physical intrusion into privacy for commercial purposes (a.k.a. press).
3. H.R.180. Integrity in Voter Registration Act of 1999. A bill to amend the National Voter Registration Act of 1993 to require each individual registering to vote in elections for federal office to provide the individual's Social Security number.

4. H.R.191. Creates tamperproof Social Security card (a.k.a. National ID Card) used for employment verification.
5. H.R.220. Freedom and Privacy Restoration Act of 1999. Limits use of SSN, prohibits creation of government IDs. Referred to the Committee on Ways and Means, and in addition to the Committee on Government Reform.
6. H.R.279. Federal Employment Applicant Drug Testing Act. Requires drug testing of all applicants for federal jobs.
7. H.R.306. Genetic Information Nondiscrimination in Health Insurance Act of 1999. A bill to prohibit discrimination against individuals and their family members on the basis of genetic information or a request for genetic services.
8. H.R.307. A bill to amend Section 552a of Title 5, United States Code, to provide for the maintenance of certain health information in cases where a health care facility has closed or a health benefit plan sponsor has ceased to do business.
9. H.R.313. Consumer Internet Privacy Protection Act of 1999. A bill to regulate the use by interactive computer services of personally identifiable information provided by subscribers to such services.
10. H.R.358. Patients' Bill of Rights Act of 1999. Requires health plans and insurers to protect confidentiality of medical records and allow patient access.
11. H.R.367. Social Security On-Line Privacy Protection Act of 1999. Limits disclosure of SSNs by interactive computer services.
12. H.R.369. Children's Privacy Protection and Parental Empowerment Act of 1999. Prohibits the sale of personal information about children without their parents' consent.
13. H.R.448. Patient Protection Act of 1999. Sets rules of confidentiality on health care information.
14. H.R.514. Wireless Privacy Enhancement Act of 1999. Prohibits interception of wireless communications, scanners.
15. H.R.516. Know Your Customer Sunset Act. Prohibits government from implementing the "Know Your Customer" rules.
16. H.R.518. Bank Secrecy Sunset Act. Prohibits government from implementing the "Know Your Customer" rules, ends provisions of the Bank Secrecy Act that requires disclosure of information to government.
17. H.R.631. SSI Fraud Prevention Act of 1999. Expands access to state, bank, and Medicare information for data matching purposes.
18. H.R.649. Real Estate Transaction Privacy Promotion Act. Prohibits a lender from requiring a borrower in a residential mortgage transaction to provide the lender with unlimited access to the borrower's tax return information.

19. H.R.850. Security and Freedom Through Encryption (SAFE) Act. Relaxes export controls on encryption, prohibits mandatory key escrow, creates criminal penalty for using crypto in a crime.
20. H.R.1057. Medical Information Privacy and Security Act. Sets general rules on the use and disclosure of medical records.
21. S. 6. Patients' Bill of Rights Act of 1999. Requires health plans and insurers to protect confidentiality of medical records and allow patient access.
22. S. 187. Financial Information Privacy Act of 1999. Requires FDIC to set privacy rules.
23. S. 240. Patients' Bill of Rights Act of 1999. Requires health plans and insurers to protect confidentiality of medical records and allow patient access.
24. S. 300. Patients' Bill of Rights Plus Act. Sets privacy protections. Prohibits genetic discrimination.
25. S. 403. Prohibits implementation of "Know Your Customer" regulations by federal banking agencies.
26. S. 466. American Financial Institutions Privacy Act of 1999. Prohibits implementation of "Know Your Customer" rules unless approved by an Act of Congress; requires study on privacy issues.
27. S. 573. Medical Information Privacy and Security Act. Comprehensive medical privacy bill.
28. S. 578. Health Care PIN Act. Weaker comprehensive medical privacy act. Provides for limited protections on medical records, easy access to records by industry (EPIC Bill Track).

Court Decisions

Court decisions that affect a person's privacy vary from court district to court district. Not all courts accept the decisions from other courts. In some cases, this may lead the plaintiff to "shop" for a court that appears to be making decisions in the direction of their favor.

In *Katz v. United States,* the use of an electronic listening device by federal authorities was found to have infringed on Katz's Fourth Amendment rights. The court defined private as what a reasonable expectation of privacy is.

In *Whalen v. Roe,* the court balanced the needs of a person's privacy with that of a genuine governmental need to prevent illegal activities. The state had taken several actions to protect the confidentiality of the information. Although the patient's information was being recorded, the processing and distribution of the information was clearly protected.

In *Rogan v. City of Los Angeles,* the purpose of the case was to show that even if the data in the FBI computer crime file is incorrect or incomplete, it can still be used to obtain warrants for arrest and to detain a person. However, processes need to be in place so that when complete or corrected information is discovered, the information is updated in a timely manner. The individual has a right that the information be corrected as soon as possible to prevent infringement of other rights.

State Laws Impacts

Various state laws also cover the issue. Alaska, California, and Indiana each have their own version of a "Fair Information Practices Act." In general, these allow citizens the right to access and correct files about themselves. It also limits the circumstances in which the information can be disclosed. Colorado's agencies must keep certain records confidential; these include personnel, medical, library material, and the address and phone number of public school children. In Florida, each state agency must have its own IT security personnel to develop policies and perform security audits. In general, each state allows its citizens to view the information collected on them and to provide a mechanism to correct any false data.

Relationship to Information Systems

The author has shown the relationship between the hierarchy of laws and who interprets and enforces them. Although more recent legislative activities may directly reveal how the protection of data privacy is related to information systems and technology, some of the older legislation needs to be determined or interpreted in the various court systems. The Freedom of Information Act was not developed for access with a personal computer, but later legislative activities provided for a large quantity of information to be made available on the Internet. The provisions to secure an individual's privacy in relation to information technology was also clarified.

Another note regarding the many legislation acts: they mainly pertain to federal and state agencies. The Fair Credit Reporting Act of 1970 amended in 1996, the Electronic Communication Privacy Act of 1986, and the Electronic Rights for the 21st Century Act are the main standouts that protect an individual's privacy without a relationship to any federal or state agencies. Some of the newer legislation being introduced provides a broader spectrum of coverage, but it appears that data collected by other organizations can be assembled and disseminated at their choosing.

Because many organizations are using "database marketing," significant amounts of information on consumers are being collected. At this point, the consumer feels like there is a loss of control of information and their personal privacy is being invaded. Business contends that consumers are getting fair value for the information through better products and services.

While much of the data is used within the organization, there is the possibility that the information can be sold or rented to other parties. It is this factor that disturbs individuals.

Consumers are also using the Internet in increasing numbers. Sites are able to store and profile information about the visitors to their sites. A former FTC Commissioner stated that self-regulation on the Internet to protect privacy is not going to work. "Privacy advocates are calling on the FTC to halt online profiling until legal protection can be established." With pressure from privacy advocates, it is a matter of time before action is taken by the regulatory bodies to prevent the random collection of data profiling. Privacy groups have also come up with the following guidelines for E-commerce and media sites:

1. Do not buy or barter profiles or identity from advertisers or other merchant sites. Wait for customers to identify themselves and say what they want.
2. Do not sell or share profiles or the identity of registered customers with other sites. Keep customers' trust and their data confidential.
3. Do not participate in plans that build "cooperative databases" that pool information on visitors using techniques such as cookie synchronization.
4. Stop ad networks and advertisers from using clickstream data on sites. Specifically, banish from sites all clear GIF "Web bugs" that report surfer movements.
5. Support the ability of consumers to visit and use sites anonymously. Sites should not require cookies or registration as a condition of use. Anonymous payment schemes are encouraged.
6. Destroy old server logs or aggregate the clickstream data so as to remove personally identifiable information.

When a customer logs into a site to visit or make a purchase, the site can collect data through the knowledge and without the knowledge of the user. One site this author visited while using a Cal Poly computer revealed system information, permanent TCP/IP numbers, network, programs installed, and other information. The purpose of the site was to show how insecure the use of the Internet can be; on the bottom of the page was a statement that said "Aren't you glad I'm not malicious?" This was disturbing because it meant that their Java applet that was contained on the Web page was allowed to run unchecked through the system. If a user has personal information about themselves, such as bank accounts, credit cards, etc., a site with similar applets can capture that information.

RealNetworks recently had a class action suit filed against them for violation of "federal and state law by misrepresenting the use and collection of personal data by users of the RealJukebox Software" (*Wired News*).

The federal law that is claimed to be violated is the Computer Fraud and Abuse Act. The software program, which is widely used, ran an undetected program to collect, store, and transmit data about the user back to Real-Networks. This is a case of an invasion of privacy that is using another law to provide protection.

Because data collection is so widespread on the Web, other companies are coming out with their own solutions to help solve the issue. Currently, there are no standards or guidelines to follow, so competing privacy systems may confuse Web users. The solutions range from providing rankings of the privacy policies that companies have to the actual blocking of information that is sent back and the creation of aliases to fill out Web forms.

CONCLUSION AND RECOMMENDATIONS

Information systems auditors and management must be aware of this area. The growth of federal laws dealing with the age of information and 21st century cyberbusinesses has exploded, as this chapter discusses. The real questions businesses must ask themselves include: Which laws directly impact us? With which of them do we have to ensure compliance?

Because of the increasingly easy and relatively inexpensive methods of data collection and usage, many organizations are gathering consumer information. It is clear to see why consumers are concerned about their privacy when cases such as the one brought against RealNetworks develop. If the coding was not discovered, the data use and collection would continue undetected by the users of that software product. While other laws may be used alone or in conjunction to protect an individual's privacy, a unified legal framework to help protect consumers' privacy should be developed. Although a framework such as the European Unions Directive for information privacy may be too stringent, it can be used as a guide to develop the United States' own standards. The need for privacy must be balanced with the need for information by organizations in order to promote the growth of E-commerce. It is in everyone's best interest to develop privacy standards for the Internet. Consumers will feel secure in providing their information to the businesses they choose to deal with, and organizations will gather the information needed to develop better products and to better compete in the marketplace. Once this balance is in place, along with the confidence of both the consumer and the E-business, the E-commerce sector will really explode.

Traditional, as well as new, security methods and techniques are not functioning as they were intended. Although many products are efficient in securing the majority of attacks on a network, no single product is able to protect a system from every possible intruder. Current security legislation, although addressing the issue of unwanted entry onto a network, may also allow for ways by which some criminals can escape the most severe penalties for violating authorized access rules. Moreover, some legislation does not require periodic review, thus allowing for various policies and procedures to become outdated. The computer networking industry is continually changing. Because of this dynamic nature, laws, policies, procedures, and guidelines must constantly change with it.

Regarding privacy in the online world, private information has begun to leak out of systems as if it were flowing from an open faucet. Some of today's legislation protects the user against invasion of privacy, but some of it contains too many exceptions and exclusions. In addition, government continues to use state-of-the-art techniques for gathering information for national security purposes. New bills and legislation continue to attempt to find a resolution to these problems, but new guidelines, policies, and procedures must be established. Further, laws must be enforced to their full extent if they are to protect a citizen's right to privacy as guaranteed under the Constitution.

Consequently, if security products are not safe from intruders and if current laws are not always efficient in correcting the problem, a user may not know how to protect his or her privacy. Although nothing completely guarantees a system's security, establishing and implementing an effective security policy provides a means to monitor unauthorized access. An effective policy would include:

1. Specifying required security features
2. Defining reasonable expectations of privacy regarding such issues as monitoring activities
3. Defining access rights and privileges and protecting assets from losses, disclosures, or damages by specifying acceptable use guidelines for users, in addition to providing guidelines for external communications (i.e., networks)
4. Defining responsibilities of all users
5. Establishing trust through an effective password policy
6. Specifying recovery procedures
7. Requiring that violations be recorded
8. Providing users with support information
9. Requiring operational and IT audits to ensure compliance

Chapter 12
Computer Forensics
Michael J. Corby

The computer forensics specialty is like the American TV show *Quincy: Medical Examiner* gone space age. Instead of putting facts together about a dead body from a few shreds of evidence, computers and their output are used to figure out the cause of a failure and possibly the perpetrator of a crime. This field has been evolving and developing since the mid-1980s. With the proliferation of computer use, the need for computer forensics has become a necessary and natural consequence of both law enforcement and operations failure prevention. It is only now that the business community is evaluating ways to incorporate this practice into an effective security policy.

The exact nature of computer forensics has been open to interpretation. The most basic definition is the collection, preservation, and analysis of computer-related evidence. Judd Robbins, a computer forensics trainer, has offered a more comprehensive definition:

> Computer forensics is simply the application of computer investigation and analysis techniques in the interests of determining potential legal evidence. Evidence might be sought in a wide range of computer crime or misuse, including but not limited to theft of trade secrets, theft of or destruction of intellectual property, and fraud. Computer specialists can draw on an array of methods for discovering data that resides in a computer system, or recovering deleted, encrypted, or damaged file information. Any or all of this information may help during discovery, depositions, or actual litigation.[1]

This definition allows for various applications that support the underlying practice that indicates there is no "right" way of conducting a computer forensic examination. In fact, much computer forensics work is part science and part art form.

The main priority and goal of this discipline is to provide solid legal evidence that can be admitted into a court of law and can be understood by laypeople. Kenneth Rosenblatt, Deputy District Attorney for Santa Clara County, California (Silicon Valley), offers the following commentary on this situation that is particularly appropriate:

0-8493-1248-5/02/$0.00+$1.50
© 2002 by CRC Press LLC

135

There are a few guidelines and standard practices which present great frustration for forensics investigators. One reason for the lack of standards stems from certain methods producing different results on different computer equipment. Furthermore, the pace that technology is being developed prohibits the standardization of little; practices are at risk of becoming outdated quickly.[2]

In addition to the delicacy of collecting, analyzing, and preserving evidence, the examiner must conduct an examination under great time constraints to recover operations and still maintain the integrity and admissibility of evidence. In other words, the chain of custody of evidence (where handling of evidence is logged and documented to prove that the evidence was not altered or compromised) is maintained throughout the entire analysis. Steps taken in a logically organized and well-documented manner diffuse a potential objection to compromised evidence and improve the potential for that evidence to withstand courtroom scrutiny. The steps used for criminal investigation are also highly valuable in investigating the root cause of "flukes" or sporadic failures in the system environment.

SCOPE OF COMPUTER FORENSICS

Like the *Quincy* TV show, the initial investigation may not even hint at a possible crime or misbehavior. If the investigation is initiated with the expectation that data collection will need to withstand the scrutiny of a court trial, the processed audit trail and conclusions drawn will be well established and can be reviewed and confirmed by experts. These experts might be court witnesses, internal auditors, regulators, operations managers, or administrators. Events that warrant forensic analysis are not based simply on crimes but can be the result of human behavior, physical events, or organizational or operational issues.

Human Behavior

The term "computer forensics" often involves investigating and prosecuting those with criminal motivations. Possible frauds, thefts, or denial-of-service attacks are types of incidents that merit forensic examination. Although the potential for criminal prosecution increases, success may not. The burden of proof is highest in criminal cases requiring that evidence collected be of the highest quality. Human behavior can be as simple as a violation of company policy. It can also deny dependable service, compromise data or process integrity, violate privacy and trade secret agreements, or break the law. An event can occur because of a variety of human behavioral actions based largely on the "seven deadly sins," notably those of greed, jealousy, or revenge. Take a look at the following underlying behaviors associated with suspect activity:

- Blackmail and extortion
- Fraud
- A disgruntled or surly employee
- "Dropping the dime"
- Sabotage or corporate espionage

Blackmail and extortion are synonymous. These actions can be targeted at an employee who holds sole responsibility for a critical function in the organization (e.g., Information Systems, Finance, or Human Resources). An individual with significant responsibility can be threatened to use his or her position to commit a crime against his or her company. Let it be said that a huge percentage of the time, this temptation is one that is never considered. However, for some, this option is considered, especially if the employee has his or her reputation on the line. The direct source of the blackmail and extortion starts with the decision by a person (the blackmailer) to use knowledge of the person with the power (the blackmailee) for his or her own personal gain. For example, one person may learn of another's skeleton in a closet and, in turn, threaten to post the information on the Internet unless there is compensation to keep the information from public attention. This malicious action is difficult to counteract and may leave few options for the victim. A corrupt person uses blackmail to force a person in power to prevent publication of a wrongdoing or an embarrassing act. It is also possible for someone to extort information, services, or financial gain out of a person in power who has done nothing wrong. In this case, the defense of allegations may be difficult to prove and may result in costly legal fees and a severe distraction from regular duties. It may actually be easier to capitulate to the extortionist's demands than to wage a viable defense. To combat this potential threat, the organization can periodically require staff to rotate responsibility among several people. The sensitive nature of the area will determine the number of people with access to its information and responsibilities. This separation of duties removes a concentration of power in the hands of one person while allowing for checks and balances within the group. If the "person with the power" changes frequently, the potential to wrongfully use that power is reduced.

Fraud can be defined by combining the definitions of *Black's Law,* *American College,* and *Random House* dictionaries, and court citations as:

> A perversion of the truth to induce a person to part with something valuable belonging to them using false or misleading representations. Elements of fraud include a false representation of a past or present fact by the defendant; a plaintiff action based upon reliance of that representation; and damages suffered by a plaintiff from the reliance of the misrepresentation.[3]

Computers and their link to the Internet can provide the fraudster with anonymity and validation in the same keystroke. Unfortunately, it can also render a very efficient mechanism for communicating with a vastly large number of possible victims, complete with an escape hatch to disappear with little or no traces. It is for these reasons that fraud runs rampant and will, in all likelihood, explode within this medium. Computer fraud has the advantage of being cloaked, thereby making it extremely difficult to detect and prove even if detected. As a result, at this stage, a proactive approach may be most successful; namely, educating the public and the workplace to the potential for fraud, coupled with firm, clear, and decisive security policies within the workplace. Guarding against fraud requires constant vigilance because of its cyclical nature. In fact, enforcing good security practices, as a whole, is a cyclical procedure. The environment must be evaluated for the risk areas, policies are then created to address them, a logging system is created to document any incidents, the policies are audited for effectiveness, and then the process repeats. Security and fraud are both dynamic disciplines and require vigor, adaptability, patience, and creativity. Prudent programs strike a balance between these demands.

The disgruntled employee presents a particularly challenging problem to overall security. In this situation, the disgruntled employee has an agenda to retaliate against a company for some perceived wrong that he or she believes has occurred. The employee's motivation is much greater, thereby making him or her far more persistent than a hacker would be in "getting the job done." Vengeance is an undaunted ally to the disgruntled employee. Furthermore, a disgruntled employee is privy to the inner workings of the company, making it much easier to exploit company weaknesses to render harm. The damage exacted by a disgruntled employee can be particularly harmful — if not lethal. Erecting defenses against this threat has proven difficult. Formal security policies that are *enforced* can prove to be the difference between the damaging consequences of a disgruntled employee and preemptively thwarting them.

A surly employee who demonstrates cynical or negative behavior can become a disgruntled employee and be a perpetrator of more serious actions, including theft, damage, sabotage, or fraud. Good employees usually do not make a complete reversal of behavior and turn bad. Most people develop an attitude of revenge, spite, or bitter retaliation as part of a progressively more emotional campaign to retaliate against what is a perceived wrongdoing. Failure to get a raise or promotion, termination or layoff of a good friend, or hiring a new employee at a rumored higher salary can trigger a campaign to "get even." The attitude can deteriorate over time until even criminal action seems reasonable. Employers must be aware of this festering bad attitude and give employees every chance to verbalize their fears, anger, and objections. This safety valve may not resolve the employee's dilemma and can result in resignation or termination, but it can also help to prevent damage or criminal action. Again, the best method for reducing the potential for a bad incident lies in proper training and providing readily available information support services. It is crucial to encourage managers and co-workers who are unsure of a particular course of action to ask first in order to act knowledgeably.

The term "dropping the dime" is a street term that refers to an observer's formally recorded information about an incident or a person committing a criminal act. He or she may become aware of the situation by chance or even by direct involvement. To address this potentially complex situation, the investigator or security officer must first ascertain the credibility of the informant. By establishing credibility, the investigator can begin to determine the extent of the situation, the players involved, and even the very existence of the situation. It is possible that an employee might fabricate a story to implicate another employee, hoping that ill consequences will befall the accused. By taking the employee's story at face value, many resources can be wasted on an investigation and can even result in liability. In some situations, the informant might feel the need to retaliate against the criminal element involved in damaging or defrauding the company; he or she might perceive some wrong has been perpetrated against him or her. Therefore, by "blowing the whistle" on the entire operation, the spoils are denied to all. In this scenario, the informant can potentially get away with the crime while his or her cohorts suffer the consequences of termination and possible criminal prosecution. To avoid this potentially embarrassing situation, company investigators must carefully (but quickly) evaluate the complaint and the overall situation.

Finally, sabotage and corporate espionage are rapidly becoming issues that security professionals must be equipped to handle. The explosion of the Internet and the subsequent restructuring of the corporate environment have made it extremely difficult to secure the corporate perimeter against those who have a hidden agenda. Sabotage is carried out by an employee or an outsider who has gained access to the company's information network with the intention of subverting a company's products, services, or overall purpose. Industrial corporate espionage agents make their presence known and often frequent places (real or virtual) where a company's trade secrets are intentionally acquired, traded, and sold. The best defense for limiting the impact and damage of such acts, once again, lies with sound security policies and practices that are regularly enforced. Audit trails and extensive logging must be implemented and regularly evaluated to determine that policies are followed and change those that have proven ineffective.

Physical Events

Computer forensics can evoke an image of people in lab coats with magnifying glasses or detectives stumbling around in a data center, poking and prodding disk drives. However, in the corporate world, computer forensics is often applied in a less clinical environment where forensic methods can diagnose the cause of incidents that stem from physical occurrences. The industry has known for years that physical events such as floods, fires, earthquakes, and other natural disasters can all wreak havoc with a system unless proper security and recovery controls and measures are in place. To respond to this, electrical or mechanical failures of computer systems (mainly hardware) have been addressed by systems managers who focus on the practice of backing up all data at regular intervals and rerouting communication activities to reduce the disruption and loss of services to end users. In some highly vulnerable applications such as banking ATM control, expensive fault-tolerant computers have been implemented. There are instances where physical access to work areas may be limited or denied because of obstructions (e.g., environmental hazards such as faulty wiring, unstable buildings, etc.). Many disaster recovery plans have been intricately written to mitigate the effects of these events and are often handled by activating satellite locations (hot and cold sites) and remote access capabilities. Often, simple events such as component theft and damage can be disruptive and cause serious service interruptions.

The financial impact of these problems can be addressed through insurance coverage, regular system backups, restricted access, and physical security (e.g., guards, video camera surveillance, etc.), but many times a physical event goes unidentified. The data center technicians walk around, talk to each other, and after a few minutes, shrug their shoulders and re-initiate the system or restart the application. This author has been told several times by a software technician to simply reboot the computer and try again. Maybe the reboot operation resolves the problem, but why did it occur in the first place? My estimate is that over 90 percent of the causes of computer glitches are never really known. Maybe they actually are flukes, unexpected data, random communication signals, or accidental keystrokes; but what if they are more malevolent? What if these glitches are failed attempts to gain access or the result of malicious code gone bad?

Forensics can be used very effectively to explain the real cause of these disruptions, especially when they affect many people. Too often, the server or shared processor is simply restarted in an effort to restore service as quickly as possible. If only some evidence were captured that could help determine the cause of the interruption, future recurrences of the same problem could be minimized. System weaknesses could be discovered and eliminated, thereby reducing the risk of future disruptive acts. Forensics is not just for the criminal, but the natural chaos surrounding physical disaster recovery as well.

Organizational Issues

All organizations have general system maintenance functions that occur periodically. These events can also cause inevitable problems. Whenever the computer hardware or operating system is upgraded, there is increased potential for disruption. Installing new hardware and application software can also bring its own set of headaches. Even a good project manager develops plans to minimize and prevent the problems that accompany compatibility problems or other unknowns. (Nevertheless, to paraphrase the popular idiom, "unpredictable occurrences happen." If I had a penny for every time a "routine" change that should pose "no problem" caused a disruption in service, I would not be a millionaire, but I bet I would have a pretty nice dinner.)

If technical changes are commonplace, organizational changes are even more so. People leave their jobs, new people are hired, and people move around within an organization. There are learning curves, procedures that slip through the cracks, and little-known facts galore. These potentially disruptive events can often be as devastating as fires, earthquakes, or white-collar crimes. Forensic evaluation cannot discount these events from causing problems as well.

Operational Issues

Last, but not least, normal operation is not 100 percent reliable. Sometimes, programs have errors in them that cause the system to stop or abruptly "hang" or "crash." Behind every interruption is a cause. Computers do not think for themselves. They do not know revenge, spite, or getting even (although one sometimes has to wonder). Murphy's law, however, has no doubt been burnt into their microchips so that they will fail when it is most critical that they run perfectly.

Although the first inclination is to call any operational malfunction a "computer error," forensic analysis should be conducted to determine if there was a preventable condition or if, as mentioned before, the failure was the result of an unsuccessful criminal attempt. If the system that is affected houses strategic, sensitive, or critical financial data, a forensic analysis and report should be completed for every operational disruption, even if the cause is obvious.

DIRECT AND INDIRECT RESULTS OF DISRUPTIVE EVENTS

The costs to an operation, either business or organizational, as a result of an incident's occurrence can range from minimal to destructive. These results can take the form of loss of service, discontinuity of reporting, or profit loss. None of these results is pleasant. One could detail an extensive cost justification for computer forensics to be employed after each event, but that kind of study is thankfully not part of the recovery process. Suffice it to say, disruptions are to be minimized. Where forensics can be of real value is when the forensic process is reviewed and procedures are put in place *before* the disruption occurs. Details of how this is done are given in the next section. For now, consider each of the results.

Loss of Service

Any disruption caused by an incident can result in a loss of service. The extent of the disruption can range from a minor inconvenience to the complete and prolonged loss of core business functions. Often, the degree of disruption depends on how dependent the business is on the computerized information network. For example, a mailing list company that relies solely on accurate and timely maintenance of its databases of addresses and client information would be brought to the brink of disaster if an event occurs that cripples the operation of those databases. This is a clear example of the heavy reliance on computerized information. Many industries — notably investment, freight movement, railroad, air traffic control, etc. — behave the same way. However critical it is to a particular industry or operation, computing has become an integral function of most businesses and organizations. The widespread use of desktop computers is a clear manifestation of this dependence within organizations — both public and private. Loss of service directly translates into a drop in personal productivity. First, there is the period of uncertainty regarding whether the system is "up" or "down." This may be 5 to 15 minutes. Next is the "water cooler" discussion that results when people who are denied computer service congregate at the coffee maker or water cooler talk to about the system or its reliability or relate stories about the last disruption. This can go on for a while. Finally, someone in the group places a phone call or gets the system functioning again. Even if nothing criminal has happened or the disruption has been minimal, a potentially large number of people may have been inconvenienced and the business has just lost tens to hundreds of hours of employee productivity, for which salary dollars have been spent. Some may call this the cost of doing business, but if the disruption was purposely caused, it could also be called theft or sabotage.

Discontinuity of Reporting

Business operation is often hampered when information does not flow freely between functions and among people. When computer services are interrupted, the organization must put aside standard practices and begin running in an alternative mode. Invariably, productivity is impacted and the bottom line is accordingly affected. If this frequently occurs in a business setting, results will be unacceptable.

In addition, over the past several years, organizations have implemented functional reporting systems that depend on computer data to provide managers and administrators with key operating data. Many times, these systems have formed a closed-loop feedback system where operational changes generate performance data, which is then analyzed by management to determine if the operational change was effective. Interruptions in the collection of the data points and fluctuations in productivity caused by computer interruptions can skew these results and lead management to incorrect or flawed conclusions.

Either by forcing alternate methods of communication or by causing "gaps" in the data collected from normal operations, interruptions can change the results from success to failure in a short period of time. Again, proper forensic analysis of the reasons for interruptions can help minimize future occurrences and can also help identify changeable factors that minimize the effect of these interruptions.

Productivity, Profit, and Loss

Almost any company can be successful if everything works as planned and there are no operating surprises. Rarely, if ever, is this the case for very long. Many daily events directly impact productivity levels, which translates into profit losses due to the slowing or obstruction of normal organizational activities. Irrespective of the organization's mission (for profit, nonprofit, or public service), computer failures can cripple or destroy mission objectives. Without dependable and reliable systems, the success of an organization hangs in the balance. It is a responsible and appropriate organization that takes interruptions seriously and employs prudent methods to determine the cause of interruptions and reduce their potential for recurrence. If, in fact, the interruption was caused on purpose, it is similarly prudent to take personnel or legal action to dissuade the perpetrator or others from completing the same or similar acts in the future.

There are no excuses for not taking precautions and employing procedures that stabilize and maximize productivity. By taking care of the workplace activity, it usually follows that profits or nonfinancial benefits (employee pride, creativity, reputation, or fulfillment) are maximized and the potential for loss — financial or otherwise — is minimized. Using computer forensics to some degree simply makes good business sense.

ELEMENTS OF FORENSIC ANALYSIS

Computer forensics is not just figuring things out, but rather a structured process of evidence preservation, damage control, and system restoration. Much of what is completed during a forensic investigation cannot be predefined because it is highly dependent on the unique events as they exist and the technical skills of the investigator. Nonetheless, some standard procedures can be followed that make good sense in completing any specific forensic analysis activities. A computer forensic analyst must be well versed in pre-event activities, recovery methods, and determining the cause of an interruption or event.

Pre-Event Preparation

Effective computer forensics does not start when the event occurs. Sure, maybe this is when most organizations think of such activity and the result may actually be useful, but the cost is usually very high and the effectiveness is often less than 100 percent. The reasons for this are threefold:

1. Data that could have been a key resource in identifying facts surrounding the event may not have been captured by the system logs and audit trails.
2. Pressure from business operations results in a quick rush to restore system operation. As part of the start-up process, the problem can be exacerbated and key signals of what happened can be destroyed.
3. The opportunity for research and investigation of several theories is limited because of the time involved in reviewing the information and the potential destruction of the logs or evidentiary data in testing the theory.

To provide the elements needed for an optimal forensic evaluation, the system must be prepared to capture, preserve, and effectively analyze the operational information immediately preceding the event. Logging and documenting everything includes inventories of hardware, files, applications, door positions, locks, and access controls. This will supply a reference that can hold up in court if necessary. Trust nothing to memory, which becomes less clear over time and may be successfully invalidated by an astute attorney.

Backups, logs, and audit trails are generally available for all systems and even for some components such as network connectors and modems. Knowing how to activate these logs and where to record the information provided by them is key to effectively capturing data. Frequently, when a system is restarted, logs are erased or overwritten, thus destroying evidence. Care must be exercised to avoid this crucial loss. The most effective way to do this is to not restart or reboot the system. The entire data structure and system boot sequence should be left unchanged while the data is copied to alternate media. Several software programs exist to do this, but there are some limitations. For example, if the system that was affected is running Windows NT and uses the NTFS file system, data is not available by booting from a regular DOS disk. For Windows NT and Novell LAN servers, the following simple and usually cost-effective methods are recommended:

- Keep the system startup data, audit logs, and other volatile information on a single disk drive. Nothing else should be kept on that drive.
- When an event occurs, the first steps would be to secure the site to determine if any physical evidence is available or if safety precautions must be taken (e.g., if the computer has been booby-trapped). If the computer is powered on prior to the incident's occurrence, any volatile data available would be copied.
- Restoration will occur on mirror-image copies; the second copy (and maybe others) can be used to evaluate evidence, list and review logs, and identify events that happened immediately before the event occurred.

Once these steps have been followed, research can be conducted, and the system should be restored to normal operation without risking the loss of key forensic data. Pre-event planning should facilitate this data recovery and restoration process.

Similar methods can be adapted to other types of systems, including minicomputer and even mainframe operating environments.

Remember that all who handle the evidence must have been documented as doing so in order to prove that if called upon in court, records will show that the evidence was not altered, damaged, or corrupted.

Post-Event Recovery

Damage control is also important to minimize the event's impact, which can (and will) translate into financial loss, productivity/service reduction, and loss of customer confidence. All can be especially damaging for the long-term success of an organization if lowered customer confidence results in loss of repeat business. Crucial to any operation is the ability to quickly restore the system to its pre-event operational status. This must occur with minimal discontinuity and disruption to activity while limiting any further loss. In business, it can be difficult to balance management's decision to absorb the cost of evidence destruction and future prosecution possibilities in the face of a short-term desire to minimize operation disruption, productivity levels, profit loss, etc. For this reason, a forensics expert must be "tough" in the face of adversity. The challenge of the hunt is many times stopped short because of a business decision to accept the risk of future events or to minimize the cost (financial and public relations) of any investigation and possible prosecution.

Nevertheless, if the pre-event plans have been put in place and are followed, the system can typically be restored to normal operation in a relatively short time period, with all evidence intact and all records preserved properly.

Many tools and methods are available to help guide the prompt recovery of an affected system while still maintaining the evidence necessary to identify the cause and potential to prosecute perpetrators. An example of what can be done on the scene of a potential crime investigation is outlined in the following summary.

Collect Evidence.

- *Conduct a "no touch" examination* of the physical site that includes observations and recordings. When entering the site, each detail of the scene must be recorded and preserved. It is a good idea to bring video or still-camera equipment to provide visual backup for written records. The placement of the computer equipment, keyboard, mouse, computer output, references, cables and wires, and switches may all be important items of evidence. Written logs must be created, initialed, witnessed, or corroborated and then filed in a secure place. Evidence bags can be useful if there are items that are removed from the scene.

- *Conduct an examination, disk "cloning," and evidence collection.* Install "Write-Block" to ensure one does not accidentally write to the hard drive. Furthermore, no programs should be executed from the hard drive of the suspect computer — a "safeboot" diskette is useful in preventing the computer from booting from the native hard drive. Install guest drivers for either Jaz or Zip drives where evidence is to be stored. Utilities that conduct a complete binary copy (e.g., Safeback, CPR Recovery Tools) are best because they preserve not only the files, but also the file slack — encrypted, hidden, and deleted files — and other subtle factors that can be important in the analysis phase (file-by-file copies are also possible). Two drives should be available for capturing evidence. Once copied, one "clone" can be replaced in the computer and one "clone" can be taken to an evidence research lab. The original should be placed in a sealed bag or envelope and, if appropriate, turned over to law enforcement or a court official for preservation as evidence. The original may be investigated further for fingerprints and even advanced magnetic remanence collection of overwritten files. If the computer is powered on, some additional evidence may be available. Remember that if the computer is suspected of being used for a crime, some common utilities and functions may be altered such that their use by an unsuspecting investigator could destroy incriminating evidence. Use utility programs that are brought to the scene to view logs, files that have been opened, and a history of what has transpired since the system was last activated. Some files may be rewritten or destroyed when the system is next powered on, so those files should be copied to the Jaz or Zip drive. Once the evidence has been collected, power-down the computer and take a physical inventory of the computer's hardware.

- *Restoring operation.* Often, the system restoration takes first priority, but in forensics, restoration should only be initiated after the evidence has been preserved. This may be a rigorous procedure if the subject is unaware of the investigation. Photos or videotape can be handy in restoring the desk to its exact former appearance. If the system was turned on, one should restore it to its condition as left by the user. The only exception to full restoration would be a case where network or online connections may further compromise the company's integrity or security. For example, if the crime was providing online availability of confidential data, that data should not be made available. Options to trap the offender can be used, including false databases or tracking methods that can identify who is involved in the crime. These trapping methods should be approached with caution. Technical, legal, and law enforcement advice should be sought before proceeding with any of these activities.

These crucial activities may be rigorous and time consuming, but they are essential for a successful analysis and potential prosecution. Only after the evidence has been preserved can an analysis begin with the objective to find the cause or trace the criminal's activities.

Finding the Cause

Discovering the real cause of an event is the long-term objective of any forensic examination. This analysis can be relatively short term or extensive, depending on the size of the system being examined; anything from a stand-alone PC to a mainframe determines the need for in-depth forensic analysis. The skills of forensic investigators, the equipment, and the time to launch a thorough and successful examination can all impact the time necessary to reach a conclusion. Often, the most surprising factor in a forensic evaluation is that computer forensics is both time and labor intensive. Determining a cause may be quick and easy, but doing so in a way that will be admissible in court can take much longer due to the need to record and validate every action. As computing capabilities increase in storage and application capacity, the amount of information that must be disseminated will also increase greatly.

Computer forensics investigation requires substantial training. Fortunately, most aspects are not "rocket science" because of its methodical nature. Also, too much technology increases the risk that a judge or jury may not understand such highly complicated methods. Still, technical tools must be used to determine what the information collected can reveal. Everything should be examined, including deleted files, encryption, hidden files, and directories. Tools can be acquired to help this examination process.

The fundamentals apply to most operating environments, but they must be adapted to the specific environment and suspected cause of each occurrence. The only constant factor in a forensic investigation is that there are no absolutes. Even the most skilled computer forensics expert experiences situations that can stop an investigation. Three common situations are:

- The loss value is small compared to the cost of investigation and prosecution.
- The legal case against the perpetrator (if identified) is too weak to prosecute.
- The system's technology being examined surpasses the capabilities of current forensic tools.

Furthermore, the tools, system conditions, and environment parameters vary with each event. No two investigations are ever exactly the same.

FINAL OBJECTIVES OF FORENSICS

Proof in Court[4]

Proving an incident's occurrence and identifying a perpetrator under a legal reading can be particularly challenging. In addition to the amount of resources expended on forensics (time, labor, money, etc.), the overall process is taxing. The United States and many other countries are founded on the presumption of innocence. Each court system is different; legislation has not advanced at the same clip as technology, and attorneys and legal counsel are not all equally well trained in computer technology and white collar crime. The U.S. legal system still demonstrates a lack of understanding on the part of the key players within the legal system — magistrates, attorneys, juries, etc. There are instances where there are knowledgeable participants, much to the delight of the techno-expert, but they are not yet the norm. Some courts are more receptive to prosecuting this type of crime, while others are still resistant to the technological advances within this society. Current legislation tends to be vague and limited. Of course, technology's rapid advancement challenges any standardization and regulation. Laws handle tangible issues, while free-flowing information is difficult to quantify and legislate. This is apparent with the issue of jurisdiction in the United States — state, federal, and international — which is complicated by data "crossing" state lines in committing a criminal act. Jurisdiction is extremely complex. Fortunately, some steps have been taken both at the federal and state levels to attempt to catch up with the wave of computer crime. International boundaries remain the most daunting aspect of prosecution, to the point where some cases may not even be viable. As a result, diplomatic channels must be employed to bolster this effort. It is a start, but there is much work to be done in this area. Until then, forensic analysts must continue to be especially careful and meticulous in gathering computer evidence.

Proof As a Business Function

Proving and determining why an event occurred as a function of computer security is smart business practice. Using computer forensics procedures as proactive tools can enhance and strengthen security policies. Furthermore, by finding the source of the incident, policies, practices, and programs can be implemented to mitigate and even prevent future occurrences. By running a tighter ship, system reliability can directly impact future success (e.g., profits, services, and general customer satisfaction and confidence). *Computer forensics can improve security but cannot, on its own, create good security.* For computer forensics to be conducted at an optimal level, standard security practices must be constructed and enforced on a regular basis. Logging and auditing are two particularly crucial security practices that greatly enrich the effectiveness of computer forensics. Computer forensics, as part of the business function, requires diligence, methodical procedures, and a bit of technological savvy.

The journey begins. As the frequency of computer events continues to increase, computer forensics will become an integral function within any well-organized organization. When computer forensics begins to emerge as a viable business function, insurers, investors, and venture capitalists will begin to include forensics capability in their evaluation of companies during due diligence. The results, as usual, will be seen in financial terms. Then we will really see computer forensics flourish as a business specialty.

CONCLUSION

Computer forensics is indeed on the cutting edge of technology — not as a high-tech advanced specialty, but as a viable and necessary business function of the twenty-first century. Computer crimes committed over the Internet, the computer knowledge gained by the general public (for good or bad), and the use of computers in traditional criminal activities such as drug trafficking, vice activities, and good old theft and murder have put the computer in the company of traditional criminal tools. Industry needs to treat computers the same way it would treat any business risk, with knowledge and measured intelligence.

What makes computer forensics especially appealing is the continued mystery surrounding the computer systems environment in general. As criminals get smarter, the business community stays the same but simply uses computers more. The next time a system "freezes," "crashes," or "bombs," think ... was it another computer glitch or did someone just try to steal money, data, or knowledge? It is like the story of the mosquito (which may or may not be true, but makes a nice story.)

> The male mosquito makes noise but does not bite, while the female mosquito needs your blood to mature newly hatched eggs, but is silent. So the next time you are laying awake on a summer night and hear a mosquito, do not worry, it is a male and will not bite you. However, if you are laying awake and hear nothing ...

Notes

1. Judd Robbins, "An Explanation of Computer Forensics by Judd Robbins" [article online]; available from http://www.knock-knock.com/forens01.htm.
2. Kenneth S. Rosenblatt, *High-Technology Crime: Investigating Cases Involving Computers,* San Jose: KSK Publications, 1995, 224.
3. "Fraud — A Criminal Offense" [definition online]; available from http://www.uslaw-books.com/books/fraud.htm.
4. David L. Carter, Computer Crime Categories, *FBI Law Enforcement Bulletin,* July 1995, 21–26; Kenneth S. Rosenblatt, *High-Technology Crime,* San Jose: KSK Publications, 1995; John G. Sauls, Computer Searches and Seizures: Challenges for Investigators, *FBI Law Enforcement Bulletin,* June 1993, 24–32.

Chapter 13

The Dangerous Precedent Set in the Use of Electronic Identifiers

John R. Vacca

The use of tracking technology (electronic identifiers to track digital evidence left behind from the attacks) to apprehend a programmer charged with authoring the Melissa virus, as well as the perpetrators of the Distributed denial of service (DDOS) attacks that Yahoo! recently suffered,[1] may have created a dangerous precedent for electronic privacy, according to legal experts.[2] In the Yahoo! case, hunting down the hackers who launched the denial of service attacks against Web sites will not be easy. The attacks paralyzed popular sites such as Yahoo!, eBay, Amazon, CNN.com, and ZDNet.com. In the Melissa case, the perpetrator, 30, of Aberdeen, New Jersey, was arrested and arraigned in April 1999, following a national manhunt. According to the New Jersey Attorney General's office, the perpetrator's arrest was made as a direct result of information provided by America Online, Inc. (AOL) through their use of electronic identifier technology. Let's look at some of this technology.

TYPES OF ELECTRONIC IDENTIFIERS

There are many types of electronic identifiers. In the AOL case, for example, the online services enterprise led investigators to a phone number and then the newsgroup where the macro virus was first posted. At this point, a controversial Microsoft document electronic identification technology (the Global Unique Identifier, or GUID) appears to have played a major role in the Melissa manhunt.

0-8493-1248-5/02/$0.00+$1.50
© 2002 by CRC Press LLC

How GUID Tracking Technology Works

The Global Unique Identifier, or GUID, is a unique serial number[3] in files created by some Microsoft (MS) applications. It eventually led to the author of Melissa.[4] How?

Office 97 and Office 2000 are chief among the MS applications containing the capability. They assign each document a different identifier. Of course, that, in itself, would not pinpoint any particular machine, or user — unless, that is, the system contains an Ethernet adapter, the device used to connect a PC to a local area network. If it does, the GUID serial number is created by adding additional digits to a single, and unchanging, address hardwired into the adapter. That means every GUID from a single Ethernet adapter also contains the same 12 digits.

This ability to link documents with a specific Ethernet adapter address was first disclosed by software tools maker Phar Lap Software, Inc. It is almost impossible to match a single Ethernet card address to a specific computer. Plus, the GUID *fingerprint* only identifies the original creator of the document, not those who may later modify it. And anyone with a special program code editor can change the GUID on any document.

Nevertheless, in the case of Melissa, luck may have overcome these obstacles. In investigating Melissa, Phar Lap posted a newsgroup inquiry. Furthermore, a Swedish computer science student who saw the posting told Phar Lap representatives that Melissa reminded him of three other viruses posted in 1997.

Together, they were able to track the virus to a specific Web site. In the end, the serial number was able to guide the FBI to Melissa's flesh-and-blood creator based on the digital evidence that was left behind after the attack.

According to the Electronic Privacy Information Center (EPIC),[5] the virtual tracking of the Melissa perpetrator gave an indication of how electronic identifiers such as Intel's ID chip could be used by law enforcement agencies. It definitely sets a potentially frightening precedent according to EPIC.

Intel's ID Chip

Intel reversed its plans to incorporate an ID number on its Pentium III chips after outcries from privacy advocates. Critics of Intel Corp.'s plan to place identification numbers on each of its Pentium III processors feel the protection scheme Intel devised for the plan would not have compensated for its technical shortcomings.

According to security experts at the consulting firm of Counterpane Internet Security, Inc.,[6] while Intel had worked to mask the ID number during legitimate queries from Web servers, the scheme would not safeguard against abuses of the ID number and would probably have been open to spoofing or hacking. There is no such thing as tamper-resistant software on a general purpose computer. If your computer can see the instructions, then you can see them too. Intel does have a technology for tamper-resistant software (they presented it at an academic workshop last year), but it is very mediocre.

The concern is not from the legitimate methods Web sites will use to query the ID, but from illegitimate methods. Intel's scheme was to rely on software code that scrambles the ID number uniquely for every Web site visited. Among other concerns is the fear that the ID number could be spoofed (software could have spit a randomized forgery instead of the real number) — and that the scheme itself is subject to hacking.

While the scheme might be very difficult to crack, the concern among security experts is that Intel's protections could be hacked, and that the hack would be distributed all around the Net. This system is only as secure as the smartest hacker. All it takes is for one person to defeat the tamper resistance. There is always someone who manages to unravel the protection. There is not a copy-protected piece of software that has not been stripped of its protections and posted to hacker bulletin boards. This will not be any different.

Masking ID Numbers

Concerns that the identification number Intel Corp. has put on Pentium III processors could have been used to track Web activity might have been overstated, as Intel's ID mechanism masks the ID number from any Web site requesting it, according to security experts who have worked with Intel.

In fact, any two Web sites verifying the number will get different results, making it almost impossible to correlate their visitor lists. The ID mechanism also would have operated outside of Windows by using a proprietary software agent that was intended to prevent spoofing of the ID number.

According to security experts at Rainbow Technologies, Inc., this approach makes the ID number far more complex than a car's license plate or vehicle ID number. The processor number says if you write down a license plate number and someone else does, they will be different numbers.

As previously stated, these factors might mitigate the concerns of privacy groups such as the Electronic Privacy Information Center, which declared a boycott of Intel products over the ID numbers in Pentium IIIs.

Intel subsequently withdrew plans to include the ID number in response to those concerns. EPIC and others feared that the ID number could have been used for surveillance of consumer Web surfing. Another common concern was that the ID number could be easily faked in software, rendering the concept useless.

Technology to keep the ID number blinded was developed by Rainbow Technologies, Inc., for its own hardware *dongles,* which for years have been sold to corporations for PC security. Intel approached Rainbow in 1998 to develop the security setup for the ID number.

According to Rainbow, very early on, when Intel described it, they were very, very careful to address certain concerns. The final scheme was defined after deep scrutiny by Intel and Rainbow, addressing problems such as traceability on the Web.

Under Intel's scheme, every Web server has a unique randomized ID number that is transmitted along with a request to verify a PC's ID number. At this point, a trusted agent intercepts the request and submits it to the microprocessor. The agent then takes the Web and Pentium numbers, runs a complex set of calculations, and returns a third number, which is uploaded to the server.

It is this third number that is used to identify a particular Pentium. The process will return the same number every time that particular machine accesses the server in question, verifying the machine's identity.

But, because every Web server has a different ID, the hashed number uploaded from the PC will differ from one site to the next. No site will know the Pentium's actual ID number, nor will any two servers use the same hashed number to represent a particular Pentium.

The setup also prevents spoofing of the serial number, another fear among privacy advocates. The agent that intercepts the ID request is an example of tamper-resistant software, which is difficult to replicate or alter and manages to tap the processor ID number without divulging the number to the outside.

Tamper-resistant software is a black art, and several enterprises in the security industry have tried their hand at it. Think of them (tamper-resistant agents) as armor around something. They can always be taken apart and defeated, but the effort becomes too much.

Microchip Electronic Identifiers

What if China used the same identifying technologies to track dissidents? Let's go one step further: What if China started implanting microchip electronic identifiers under the skin of their private citizens and all newborns? As you can see, there are lots of human rights implications, as well as violations.

Recently, I.D.ology announced that its PELIT[7] microchip (electronic animal identifier) has been approved for injection into cattle by both the FDA and USDA. This expands the utility of the PELIT (Permanent Electronic Livestock Identification Tag) which, once injected, becomes a lifetime identifier for each animal as well as humans. Each PELIT has its own unique number which it transmits to an antenna when it has been activated by a low power radio wave sent by the antenna.

The PELIT is injected beneath the skin either in the lower left rear leg or under the scutiform cartilage at the base of the left ear; both of these locations are approved by the USDA. Though either position may be used, I.D.ology has found that placement in the lower leg clearly separates the microchip from edible portions of the animal, a major criterion specified by the FDA. Another concern centers on the chemical analysis of the PELIT, which after spectrographic study was found not to be injurious to animals consuming rendered portions containing PELIT materials or to humans consuming said animals. In addition, animals bearing injected electronic identifiers that are sold or presented for slaughter must be identified as such to the establishment, and the location of the electronic identifier must be provided. If used in place of all other identifiers at slaughter, the identifying number contained on the PELIT must be made available to government officials.

I.D.ology has been developing system applications based on the PELIT where the computer automatically records data and sorts animals for task-oriented objectives. These applications reduce labor requirements and enhance management control. This is a major shift for a dairy, for example, from the historic use of the computer just to expedite recordkeeping. I.D.ology's systems utilize the PELIT coupled with the stationary *Big Matt* and portable *CompuReader* to provide real-time information to the computer, milk meters, weigh scales, or cutting gates.

Electronic Digital Signature Identifiers

Another form of electronic identifier is known as a *digital signature*. The term "digital signature" is defined as an encrypted electronic identifier, created by a computer, and intended by the party using it to have the same force and effect as the use of a manual signature.

In many states, the use of a digital signature will have the same force and effect as the use of a manual signature if and only if it embodies all of the following attributes:

- It is unique to the person using it.
- It is capable of verification.
- It is under the sole control of the person using it.
- It is linked to data in such a manner that if the data are changed, the digital signature is invalidated.
- It conforms to regulations adopted by the Secretary of State of that state.

Other Generic Electronic Identifiers

Finally, there are many generic types of electronic identifiers. These are mainly used by universities and usually consist of:

- Access control (login/logon)
- Student ID numbers
- PIN numbers

Access Control (Login/Logon)

The SUNet ID provides access control to the Stanford University Network (SUNet) and its services, and identifies authorized users of these services. Each member of the Stanford electronic community creates a unique SUNet ID and password for him or herself. SUNet IDs provide access to the following services:

- E-mail (SUNetID@leland.stanford.edu)
- Storage space within Stanford's distributed file system
- World Wide Web, including serving of personal Web pages on the Leland system and access to Stanford Web Resources
- Usenet newsgroups
- Printing
- Axess[8]

On the other hand, at the University of Texas at Austin, their access control electronic identifier consists of the following security policy steps:

1. The security administrator(s) of each computer installation will assign a unique electronic identifier (ID) to each user of the computers in the installation.
2. Each user of an electronic ID will establish a password, known only to the user. The individual user will be responsible for the confidentiality of the password and for any breaches of security committed via access gained by the electronic ID.
3. The computer installation will develop mechanisms that assures that each user of an electronic ID which provides access to confidential or sensitive information changes the password regularly. The procedure for changing passwords will be published by the computer installation.

4. The computer installation is responsible for revoking access provided to the electronic IDs of persons no longer requiring access to the information resources managed by the computer installation.

5. The computer installation will maintain a record of persons authorized to use applications that process confidential and often sensitive information stored on its computer system(s).

6. Administrative Computing Services will provide a mechanism that (a) disables (i.e., logs off) an electronic ID after a specified period of inactivity; and (b) locks an electronic ID after multiple unsuccessful attempts to logon to the administrative computer system.

Student ID Numbers

Meanwhile, at Stanford University, the student ID is a number assigned to a student's academic record and is required for any inquiries he or she make. The ID number is printed on the student's registration commitment letter, Stanford University ID card, and all enrollment/grading-related documents distributed by the Registrar's Office. The student ID number is unique and considered directory information; therefore, it is not private.

PIN Numbers

Finally, a student's personal identification number (PIN), in combination with the Stanford University Identification Number and SUNet ID, uniquely identifies the student and serves in place of his signature on electronic forms such as those within Axess. The student's initial default PIN is a five-digit number: the month and day of birth preceded by a leading zero. For instance, if the student was born on October 9, his PIN is 01009. Note the two leading zeros, as the first character of the PIN is 0 and the numeric representation for October is 10. The first time the student uses the PIN in a FOLIO system,[9] he or she will be prompted to change it. It is expected that users will change the PIN to numbers known only to them. The new number must be five or more characters. Students should protect the privacy of their records by changing their PINs when prompted.

Students may change their PINs at any time and as often as they like by leaving Axess. Then, in FOLIO, they type SET PIN on the FOLIO command line. Next, they follow the simple on-screen instructions. If they have forgotten their PINs, they must bring a photo ID to the Registrar's Office during business hours or contact the office by e-mail.

A student's ID number is not secret, but the SUNet ID password and PIN must remain confidential. It is a violation of University policy to misrepresent oneself in any way. Students may, therefore, lose student privileges or be subject to other disciplinary action if they use another student's SUNet ID/password or PIN.

BAD PRECEDENT

Cases such as Melissa and the recent hacker attacks always occur in the context where people might agree with the outcome — such as catching the person believed responsible for a damaging virus. The Melissa virus perpetrator's arrest could be a case of hard cases making bad law.

While it is very important to demonstrate to virus writers that if they write damaging code they will be caught and punished, the problem is that there is no guarantee that enterprises will not do these kind of things for less lofty reasons. There is no guarantee that privacy policies will not change based on what is in their best interests at the time.

When the process becomes legitimized, you have created a precedent. AOL, which was roundly criticized in 1999 for inadvertently releasing a user's identity to U.S. Navy investigators, had a policy to protect customers' privacy. Nevertheless, AOL made the decision that the Melissa virus perpetrator was not a person they wanted to protect.

Therefore, it is quite obvious that the Melissa virus perpetrator's case *definitely* broke new ground. However, it is not new that AOL cooperates with law enforcement in investigations, but some of the elements of the investigation are new, such as the GUID.

A case like this points out to the average consumer how the software in their lives can compromise their privacy. That is a serious area of concern.

Congress Questions Arrest

In the aftermath of the Melissa virus case, ongoing tensions between civil liberties and the interests of law enforcement again roiled Capitol Hill, leading members of Congress to question openly the FBI's pursuit of the Melissa virus perpetrator. The House Subcommittee on Technology had called the FBI Infowar Chief, a computer scientist, and three computing experts from the federal sector to talk about what Congress could do to help prevent a repeat performance of the Melissa e-mail meltdown.

As expected, the Infowar Chief, officials from the National Institute of Standards and Technology, the CERT Coordination Center at Carnegie Mellon University, and the General Accounting Office all said government and enterprises needed to work together closely in order to stop computer intrusions of all kinds. Subcommittee members agreed, but some quickly bridled at the notion that law enforcement should follow a digital trail wherever it liked.

Seeking Serial Number Source

Members of Congress grilled the Infowar Chief for details of how the FBI's National Infrastructure Protection Center had traced a string of documents used to create the virus back to the Melissa virus perpetrator. Members of Congress were especially concerned about a unique serial number within the virus itself that came from the Melissa virus perpetrator's use of Microsoft's popular Word 97 word processor.

Members of Congress asked if the Infowar Chief had a court order for all the documents the FBI had seized. Congressional members also wanted to know how America Online had helped in fingering the Melissa virus perpetrator, who had an account on the service.

Members of Congress were just a little disquieted about the way this investigation was pursued. In other words, would the FBI, in hot pursuit of this virus and the author of it, be permitted to go into congressional computers?

The Infowar Chief replied that the FBI needed either permission from a computer owner or a court warrant to get the information it wanted. Congressional members pressed the Infowar Chief for details of how he had caught Melissa's creator, but the 30-something infowarrior demurred that the information related to an ongoing investigation. To date, only New Jersey police have brought formal charges against the Melissa virus perpetrator.

Privacy Vs. Police Efforts

Other members of Congress raised questions about conflicts between complete privacy and police efforts to track wrongdoers online. Privacy concerns were among the biggest reasons people still buy things with cash. Online, people want a similar alternative. Our society is very concerned about privacy and anonymity and giving people space in which to act. But, almost every member of Congress wanted to know why computers were so insecure. The answer has many sides. In short, though, it boils down to this: because too few customers asked for secure systems, too few makers saw the need for them.

CONCLUSION AND SUMMARY

This chapter considered the problem of the legitimate use of electronic identifier technology. The use of tracking technology to apprehend a suspect is legitimate, so long as investigators have probable cause and obtain the appropriate court orders.

Of greater concern is the fact that different jurisdictions even within the United States have different standards regarding electronic privacy. The fact that they were able to and did use the identifier and Internet logs used by America Online demonstrates the extent to which peoples' movements on the Internet can be tracked — and the potential dangers.

BUSINESS ORGANIZATION ISSUES

Finally, the Melissa virus case and the upcoming hacker cases (if they ever get caught) are generally going to give us an interesting glimpse into how individuals can be tracked on the Internet. The GUID is one of those tools, but so are the recordkeeping procedures of ISPs such as AOL. These are the first case studies that we are going to have of the use of various devices to combat anonymity.

Notes

1. Yahoo! was down for nearly three hours in February 2000, the apparent victim of a distributed denial of service attack. The site was inundated with up to a gigabyte of data a second — more than most E-commerce sites face in a year. No data was lost, and no one has stepped forward to claim responsibility.
2. Some legal experts have raised a red flag about computer code that paves the way for virtual tracking.
3. A basic explanation of the Microsoft serial number that connected Melissa to its source.
4. Melissa is the name of the macro virus that has caused so much malicious mischief.
5. EPIC, ACLU, and EFF have asked a federal appeals court to block new rules that would permit the FBI to dictate the design of the nation's communication infrastructure. The challenged rules would enable the Bureau to track the physical locations of cellular phone users and potentially monitor Internet traffic. The appellate brief challenges an FCC order implementing the Communications Assistance to Law Enforcement Act (CALEA).
6. Consulting firm specializing in cryptography and computer security.
7. A low-cost, injectable microchip sealed in a protective capsule.
8. Axess is a student information system available via the Web.
9. FOLIO is a computer system at Stanford that provides access to a variety of information resources for Stanford students, faculty, and staff.

Chapter 14
Jurisdictional Issues in Global Transmissions

Ralph Spencer Poore

In the information age where teleconferences replace in-person meetings, where telecommuting replaces going to the office, and where international networks facilitate global transmissions with the apparent ease of calling one's next-door neighbor, valuable assets change ownership at the speed of light. Louis Jionet, Secretary-General of the French Commission on Data Processing and Liberties stated: "Information is power and economic information is economic power." Customs officials and border patrols cannot control the movement of these assets. But does this mean companies can transmit the data that either represents or is the valuable asset without regard to the legal jurisdictions through which they pass? To adequately address this question, both the legal issues and the practical issues involved in transnational border data flows are discussed in this article.

LEGAL ISSUES

All legally incorporated enterprises have Official Books of Record. Whether these be in manual or automated form, these are the records that governmental authorities turn to when determining the status of an enterprise. The ability to enforce a subpoena or court order for these records reflects the effective sovereignty of the nation in which the enterprise operates. Most countries require enterprises incorporated, created, or registered in their jurisdiction to physically maintain Official Books of Record within their borders. For example, a company relying on a service bureau in another country for data processing services may cause the official records to exist only in that other country. This could occur if the printouts reflected only a historic position of the company, perhaps month-end conditions, where the current position of the company — the position on which management relies — exists only through online access to the

0-8493-1248-5/02/$0.00+$1.50
© 2002 by CRC Press LLC

company's executive information system. From a nation's perspective, two issues of sovereignty arise:

- The other country might exercise its rights and take custody of the company's records — possibly forcing it out of business — for actions alleged against the company that the company's "home" nation considers legal.
- The company's "home" nation may be unable to enforce its access rights.

Another, usually overriding factor, is a nation's ability to enforce its tax laws. Many nations have value-added taxes (VATs) or taxes on publications, computer software, and services. An organization's data may qualify as a publication, as computer software, or even as services in some jurisdictions. Thus, many nations have an interest in the data that flows across their borders because it may qualify for taxation. In some cases, the tax is a tariff intended to discourage the importation of computer software or publications in order to protect the nation's own emerging businesses. More so than when the tax is solely for revenue generation, protective tariffs may carry heavy fines and be more difficult to negotiate around. With the advent of Internet businesses, determining a business' nexus for tax purposes has become even more complex. Such business may have income, franchise, and inventory or property tax issues in addition to sales tax, excise tax, and import or export duties. Business taxes, registration or license fees, and even reporting requirements depend on the applicability of a given jurisdiction.

National security interests can include controlling the import and export of information. State secrecy laws exist for almost all nations. The United States, for example, restricts government classified data (e.g., Confidential, Secret, Top Secret), but also restricts some information even if it is not classified (e.g., technical data about nuclear munitions, some biological research, some advanced computer technology, and — to varing degrees — cryptography).

Among those nations concerned with an individual's privacy rights, the laws vary greatly. Laws such as the United State's Privacy Act of 1974 (5 USC 552a) have limited applicability (generally applying only to government agencies and their contractors). The United Kingdom's Data Protection Act of 1984 (1984 c 35 [*Halsbury's Statutes,* 4th edition, Butterworths, London, 1992, Vol. 6, pp. 899–949]), however, applies to the commercial sector, as does the 1981 Council of Europe's Convention for the Protection of Individuals with Regard to Automatic Processing of Personal Data (an excellent discussion of this can be found in Anne W. Brandscomb's *Toward a Law of Global Communications Networks*, The Science and Technology section of the American Bar Association, Longman, New York, 1986). Privacy laws generally have at least the following three characteristics:

- They provide notice to the subject of the existence of a database containing the subject's personal data (usually by requiring registration of the database).
- They provide a process for the subject to inspect and to correct the personal data.
- They provide a requirement for maintaining an audit trail of accessors to the private data.

The granularity of privacy law requirements also varies greatly. Some laws (e.g., the U.S. Fair Credit Reporting Act of 1970 [see 15 USC 1681 *et seq.*]), require only the name of the company that requested the information. Other laws require accountability to a specific office or individual. Because the granularity of accountability can differ from jurisdiction to jurisdiction, organizations may need to develop their applications to meet the most stringent requirements (i.e., individual accountability). In this author's experience, few electronic data interchange (EDI) systems support this level of accountability (*UNCID Uniform Rules of Conduct for Interchange of Trade Data by Teletransmission,* ICC Publishing Corporation, New York, 1988). All protective measures and audit measures are described as options, with granularity left to the discretion of the parties.

To further complicate data transfer issues, patent, copyright, and trade secret laws are not uniform. Although international conventions exist (e.g., General Agreement on Tariffs and Trade [GATT]), not all nations subscribe to these conventions, and the conventions often allow for substantial differences among signatories. Rights one might have and can enforce in one jurisdiction might not exist (or might not be enforceable) in another. In some cases, the rights one has in one jurisdiction constitute an infringement in another jurisdiction. For example, one may hold a United States registered trademark on a product. A trademark is a design (often a stylized name or monogram) showing the origin or ownership of merchandise and is reserved to the owner's exclusive use. The Trade-Mark Act of 1946 (see 15 USC 1124) provides that no article shall be imported that copies or simulates a trademark registered under United States laws. A similar law protecting, for example, trademarks registered in India might prevent one from using the trademark in India if a similar or identical trademark is already registered there.

Disclosure of information not in accordance with the laws of the jurisdictions involved may subject the parties to criminal penalties. For example, the United Kingdom's Official Secrets Act of 1989 clearly defines areas wherein disclosure of government secrets is a criminal offense. Most nations have similar laws (of varying specificity), making the disclosure of state secrets a crime. However, technical information considered public in one jurisdiction might be considered a state secret in another. Similarly, biographical information on a national leader may be mere background information for a news story in one country but viewed as espionage by another country. These areas are particularly difficult because most governments will not advise one in advance as to what constitutes a state secret (as this might compromise the secret). Unless an organization has a presence in each jurisdiction sensitive to these political and legal issues to whom one can turn for guidance, competent legal advice should be sought before transmitting text or textual database materials containing information about individuals or organizations.

From a business perspective, civil law rather than criminal law may take center stage. Although the United States probably has the dubious distinction as the nation in which it is easiest to initiate litigation, lawsuits are possible in most jurisdictions worldwide. No company wants to become entangled in litigation, especially in foreign jurisdictions. However, when information is transmitted from one nation to another, the rules can change significantly. For example, what are the implied warranties in the receiving jurisdiction? What constitutes profanity, defamation, libel, or similar actionable content? What contract terms are unenforceable (e.g., can one enforce a nondisclosure agreement of ten years' duration)?

In some jurisdictions, ecclesiastical courts may have jurisdiction for offenses against a state-supported religion. Circumstances viewed in one jurisdiction as standard business practice (e.g., gifts) may be viewed in another jurisdiction as unethical or illegal. Even whether an organization has standing (i.e., may be represented in court) varies among nations. An organization's rights to defend itself, for example, vary from excellent to nil in jurisdictions ranging from Canada to Iran, respectively.

Fortunately, companies can generally choose the jurisdictions in which they will hold assets. Most countries enforce their laws (and the actions of their courts) against corporations by threat of asset seizure. A company with no seizable assets (and no desire to conduct future business) in a country is effectively judgment-proof. The reverse can also be true; that is, a company may be unable to enforce a contract (or legal judgment) because the other party has no assets within a jurisdiction willing to enforce the contract or judgment. When contracting with a company to develop software, for example, and that company exists solely in a foreign country, one's organization should research the enforceability of any contract and, if there is any doubt, require a bond be posted in one's jurisdiction to ensure at least bond forfeiture as recourse.

Specific and General Jurisdiction

In September 1997, in *Bensusan Restaurant Corp. v. King* (1997 U.S. App. Lexis 23742 (2d Cir. Sept. 10, 1997)), the 2d U.S. Circuit Court of Appeals held that a Missouri resident's Web site, accessed in New York, did not give rise to jurisdiction under New York's long arm statute. The court ruled there was no jurisdiction because the defendant was not physically in New York when he created the offending Web page. However, a similar case in California with a similar ruling was reversed on appeal (*Hall v. LaRonde,* 1997 Cal. App. Lexis 633 (Aug. 7, 1997)). Citing the changing "role that electronic communications plays in business transactions," the court decided that jurisdiction should not be determined by whether the defendant's communications were made physically within the state, instead concluding that "[t]here is no reason why the requisite minimum contacts cannot be electronic."

To comply with due process, the exercise of specific jurisdiction generally requires that the defendant intentionally took advantage of the benefits of the jurisdiction, and thus could have expected to be hauled into court in that jurisdiction. The nature of electronic communications and their growing role in commerce have contributed to findings that defendants' Internet communications constitute "purposeful availment" (legalese for intentionally taking advantage of the benefits) and establish jurisdiction. For example, in *California Software Inc. v. Reliability Research Inc.* (631 F. Supp. 1356 (C.D. Cal. 1986)), the court held that a nonresident's defamatory e-mail to a resident was sufficient to establish specific jurisdiction. The court noted that, as modern technology makes nationwide commercial transactions more feasible, it broadens the scope of jurisdiction.

Courts have also pointed out the distinguishing features of the Internet when holding that a Web site gives rise to specific jurisdiction for infringement claims arising out of the site's content. In *Maritz Inc. v. Cybergold Inc.* (947 F. Supp. 1328, 1332, 1334 (E.D. Mo. 1996)), the court suggested that Web site advertising more likely amounts to purposeful availment than advertising by direct mail or an "800" telephone number, noting the "different nature" of electronic communications.

Conceivably, a Web site could reflect contacts with a state's residents that were sufficiently continuous and systematic to establish general jurisdiction over the site owner. Courts have held, however, that the mere creation of a Web site does not create general jurisdiction. See, for example, *McDonough v. Fallon McElligott, Inc.* (1996 U.S. Dist. Lexis 15139 (S.D. Cal. Aug. 6, 1996)). Further, courts have held in more traditional contexts that merely placing advertisements in nationally distributed periodicals, or communicating through a national computer-based information system, does not subject a nonresident to jurisdiction. See, for example, *Federal Rural Elec. Ins. Corp. v. Kootenai Elec. Corp.* (17 F.3d 1302, 1305 (10th Cir. 1994)).

This area of law is evolving rapidly, with many jurisdictions asserting what amounts to extraterritorial jurisdiction on the basis of electronic transactions into, through, or out of their territory. The Council of Europe's Convention for the Protection of Individuals with Regard to Automatic Processing of Personal Data is but one of many examples. The entire area of cryptography, for example, is another. In January 1999, France dramatically eased its long-standing restriction on the use of cryptography within its jurisdiction. This announcement came only six weeks after France joined with 32 other countries signing an update of a document known as the Wassenaar Agreement. Signatories to this agreement promised to tighten restrictions on the import or export of cryptography. The so-called "long arm" provisions of many laws and the lack of concensus among nations on important issues — including privacy, intellectual property rights, communications security, and taxes — will challenge (or plague) us for the foreseeable future.

TECHNICAL ISSUES

Any nation wishing to enforce its laws with regard to data transmitted within or across its borders must have the ability (1) to monitor/interecept the data, and (2) to interpret/understand the data. Almost all nations can intercept wire (i.e., telephone/telegraph) communications. Most can intercept radio, microwave, and satellite transmissions. Unless an organization uses exotic technologies (e.g., point-to-point laser, extremely low frequency [ELF], super high frequency, spread spectrum), interception remains likely.

The second requirement, however, is another matter. Even simple messages encoded in accordance with international standards may have meaning only in a specific context or template not inherent in the message itself. For example, "142667456043052" could be a phone number (e.g., 1-426-674-5604 x3052), or a social security number and birthday (e.g., 142-66-7456 04/30/52), or dollar amounts ($14,266.74 $560,430.52), or inventory counts by part number (PN) (e.g., PN 142667 Quantity 45, PN 604305 Quantity 2), or zip codes (e.g., 41266, 74560, 43052). Almost limitless possibilities exist even without using codes or ciphers. And this example used human-readable digits; many transmissions may be graphic images, object code, or compressed text files completely unintelligible to a human "reading" the data on a datascope.

From the preceding, one might conclude that interception and interpretation by even a technologically advanced nation are too great a challenge. This is, however, far from true. Every "kind" of data has a signature or set of attributes that, when known, permits its detection and identification. This includes encrypted data, where the fact of encryption is determinable. Where transmitting or receiving encrypted messages is a crime, a company using encryption risks detection. Once the "kind" of data is determined, applying the correct application is often a trivial exercise. Some examples of such strong typing of data include:

- Rich-text format (RTF) documents and most word processing documents
- SQL transactions
- Spreadsheets (e.g., Lotus 1-2-3, Microsoft Excel)
- DOS, Windows, UNIX, and other operating system executables
- Standardized EDI messages
- ASCII vs. EBCDIC

If this were not the case, sending data from one computer to another would require extensive advanced planning at the receiving computer — severely impacting data portability and interoperability, two attributes widely sought in business transactions.

Countries with sufficient technology to intercept and interpret an organization's data can pose an additional problem beyond their law enforcement: that of government-sponsored industrial espionage. Many countries have engaged in espionage with the specific objective of obtaining technical or financial information of benefit to that country's businesses. A search of news accounts of industrial espionage resulted in a list that included the following countries: Argentina, Cuba, France, Germany, Greece, India, Iran, Iraq, Israel, Japan, North Korea, Peoples Republic of China, Russia, South Korea, and Turkey. Most of these countries have public policies against such espionage, and countries such as the United States find it awkward to accuse allies of such activities (both because the technical means of catching them at it may be a state secret and because what one nation views as counter-espionage, another nation might view as espionage).

Protective Technologies

For most businesses, the integrity of transmitted data is more important than its privacy. Cryptographic techniques a business might otherwise be unable to use because of import or export restrictions associated with the cryptographic process or the use of a privacy-protected message can be used in some applications for data integrity. For example, the Data Encryption Standard (DES), when used for message authentication in accordance with the American National Standard X9.9 for the protection of electronic funds transfers between financial institutions, may be approved by the U.S. Department of the Treasury without having to meet the requirements of the International Trade in Arms Regulations (ITAR). (Note that technological advances can also impact this; for example, the key space exhaustion attack in January 1999 of a DES Challenge was successful in 22.25 hours. Both the U.S. and French governments made policy changes that permit stronger cryptography for export and import that had previously been permitted.)

Integrity measures generally address one or both of the following problems:

- Unauthorized (including accidental) modification or substitution of the message
- Falsification of identity or repudiation of message

The techniques used to address the first problem are generally called message authentication techniques. Those addressing the second class of problems are generally called digital signature techniques.

Message authentication works by applying a cryptographic algorithm to a message in such a way as to produce a resulting message authentication code (MAC) that has a very high probability of being affected by a change to any bit or bits in the message. The receiving party recalculates the MAC and compares it to the transmitted MAC. If they match, the message is considered authentic (i.e., received as sent); otherwise, the message is rejected.

Because international standards include standards for message authentication (e.g., ISO 9797), an enterprise wanting to protect the integrity of its messages can find suitable algorithms that should be (and historically have been) acceptable to most jurisdictions worldwide. With some exceptions, even the Data Encryption Algorithm (DEA), also known as the Data Encryption Standard (DES), can be used in hardware implementations of message authentication. For digital signature, this may also be true, although several excellent implementations (both public key and secret key) rely on algorithms with import/export restrictions. The data protected by digital signature or message authentication, however, is not the problem, as both message authentication and digital signature leave the message in plaintext. Objections to their use center primarily on access to the cryptographic security hardware or software needed to support these services. If the cryptographic hardware or software can be obtained legally within a given jurisdiction without violating export restrictions, then using these services rarely poses any problems.

Digital signature techniques exist for both public key and secret key algorithm systems (also known respectively as asymmetric and symmetric key systems). The purpose of the digital signature is to authenticate the sender's identity and to prevent repudiation (where an alleged sender claims not to have sent the message). The digital signature implementation may or may not also authenticate the contents of the signed message.

Exhibit 1.   Sample Codebook

Code	Meaning
RED SUN	Highest authorized bid is
BLUE MOON	Stall; we aren't ready
WHITE FLOWER	Kill the deal; we aren't interested
JUNE	1
APRIL	2
JULY	3
DECEMBER	4
AUGUST	5
JANUARY	6
MARCH	7
SEPTEMBER	8
NOVEMBER	9
MAY	0

Privacy measures address the concern for unauthorized disclosure of a message in transit. Cipher systems (e.g., DEA) transform data into what appear to be random streams of bits. Some ciphers (e.g., a Vernam cipher with a key stream equal to or longer than the message stream) provide almost unbreakable privacy. As such, the better cipher systems almost always run afoul of export or import restrictions. The United States is currently working on the Advanced Encryption Standard (AES) to replace DES. One of the policy issues with the AES will be its exportability, as it will allow 128- 192- and 256-bit encryption keys. (The National Institute of Standards and Technology expects AES to be available by 2003.)

In some cases, the use of codes is practical and less likely to run into restrictions. As long as the "codebook" containing the interpretations of the codes is kept secret, an organization could send very sensitive messages without risk of disclosure if intercepted en route. For example, an oil company preparing its bid for an offshore property might arrange a set of codes as shown in Exhibit 1. The message "RED SUN NOVEMBER MAY MAY" would make little sense to an eavesdropper, but would tell the company representative that the maximum authorized bid is 900 (the units would be prearranged, so this could mean $900,000).

Other privacy techniques that do not rely on secret codes or ciphers include:

- Continuous stream messages (the good message is hidden in a continuous stream of otherwise meaningless text). For example,

THVSTOPREAXZTRECEEBNKLLWSYAINNTHELAUNCHGBMEAZY

contains the message "STOP THE LAUNCH." When short messages are sent as part of a continuous binary stream, this technique (one of a class known as steganography) can be effective. This technique is often combined with cipher techniques when very high levels of message security are needed.

- Split knowledge routing (a bit pattern is sent along a route independent of another route on which a second bit pattern is sent; the two bit streams are exclusive-OR'ed together by the receiving party to form the original message). For example, if the bit pattern of the message one wishes to send is 0011 1001 1101 0110, a random pattern of equal length would be exclusive-OR'ed with the message 1001 1110 0101 0010, to make a new message 1010 0111 1000 0100. The random pattern would be sent along one telecommunication path and the new message would be sent along another, independent telecommunication path. The recipient would exclusively OR the two messages back together, resulting in the original message. Because no cryptographic key management is required and because the exclusive-OR operation is very fast, this is an attractive technique where the requirement of independent routing can be met.

- The use of templates (which must remain secret) that permit the receiver to retrieve the important values and ignore others in the same message. For example, in the string used above,

THVSTOPREAXZTRECEEBNKLLWSYAINNTHELAUNCHGBMEAZY

used with the following template

XXXXXXXNNXXXNNXXXXXXXXXXXNXXXNXXXXXXXXXXXXXXX

where only the letters at the places marked with "N" are used, reveals a different message, RETREAT.

The first technique can also be effective against traffic analysis. The second technique requires the ability to ensure independent telecommunication routes (often infeasible). The third technique has roughly the same distribution problems that codebook systems have; that is, the templates must be delivered to the receiver in advance of the transmission and in a secure manner. These techniques do, however, avoid the import and export problems associated with cryptographic systems.

In addition to cryptographic systems, most industrialized nations restrict the export of specific technologies, including those with a direct military use (or police use) and those advanced technologies easily misused by other nations to suppress human rights, improve intelligence gathering, or counter security measures. Thus, an efficient relational database product might be restricted from export because oppressive third-world nations might use it to maintain data on their citizens (e.g., "subversive activities lists"). Restrictions on software export can sometimes be averted by finding a nation in which the desired product is sold legally without the export restriction. (Note: check with legal counsel in your enterprise's official jurisdiction as this work-around may be illegal — some countries claim extraterritorial jurisdiction or claim that their laws take precedence for legal entities residing within their borders.) For example, the Foreign Corrupt Practices Act (see 15 USC 78) of the United States prohibits giving gifts (i.e., paying graft or bribes) by U.S. corporations even if such practice is legal and traditional in a country within which that U.S. corporation is doing business. Similarly, if the People's Republic of China produces clones of hardware and software that violate intellectual property laws of other countries but that are not viewed by China as a punishable offense, using such a product to permit processing between the United States and China would doubtlessly be viewed by U.S. authorities as unacceptable.

THE LONG VIEW

New technologies (e.g., Software Defined Digital Network [SDDN] and Frame Relay) will make networks increasingly intelligent, capable of enforcing complex compliance rules and allowing each enterprise to carefully craft the jurisdictions from which, through which, and into which its data will flow. North America, the European community, Japan, and similar "information-age" countries will see these technologies before the turn of the century. But many nations will not have these capabilities for decades.

Most jurisdictions will acquire the ability to detect cryptographic messages and process cleartext messages even before they acquire the networking technologies that would honor an enterprise's routing requests. The result may be a long period of risk for those organizations determined to send and receive whatever data they deem necessary through whatever jurisdictions happen to provide the most expeditious routing.

The use of public key infrastructures (PKIs) and the reliance on certificate authorities (CAs) for electronic commerce will force many changes in international law. The jurisdictional location of a registration authority (RA), for example, may dictate whose personal data can be captured for registration. In a ruling by the EC Privacy Council early in 1999 with regard to IP addresses, it was determined that a static IP address constituted privacy-protected data, just as a name and mailing address would. The existence of a CA in a jurisdiction might constitute a nexus for an assertion of general jurisdiction or for taxation if the certificates signed by this CA are used for commercial purposes. Although this technology promises solutions to many problems — including restricting access to data on a selective basis that could bind jurisdictions — it also introduces rapid change and complexity with which societies (and legal systems) are already struggling.

SUMMARY

Data flows daily from jurisdiction to jurisdiction, with most organizations unaware of the obligations they may incur. As nations become more sophisticated in detecting data traffic transiting their borders, organizations will face more effective enforcement of laws, treaties, and regulations — ranging from privacy to state secrets, and from tax law to intellectual property rights. The risk of state-sponsored industrial espionage will also increase. Because organizations value the information transferred electronically, more and more organizations will turn to cryptography to protect their information. Cryptography, however, has import and export implications in many jurisdictions worldwide. The technology required to intelligently control the routing of communications is increasingly available, but will not solve the problems in the short term. Rather, the advancing technology will complicate matters further in two ways:

1. Where the controls become available, it will make indefensible their non-use.
2. Where the controls are used, it will make the jurisdictions intentional, thereby strengthing the state's case that it has jurisdiction.

With more legal entities asserting jurisdiction, conflict of laws cases will increase. Implicit contracts will become extremely hazardous (e.g., an e-mail message might be sufficient to constitute a contract, but what are its default terms?). Ultimately, the need for effective commerce will prevail and jurisdictional issues will be resolved. But, for the near term, jurisdictional issues in global transmissions remains a growth industry for legal professionals, politicians, lobbyists, tax accountants, and electronic commerce consultants.

Companies will need to exercise care when they place their data on open networks, the routings of which they cannot control. They will need to understand the jurisdictions in which and through which their global information infrastructure operates. The information security professional will want to have competent legal assistance on his or her team and to stay well-informed. The effectiveness of the enterprise's information security program is now irreversibly intertwined with the jurisdictional issues of global electronic commerce.

Chapter 15
Anonymity on the Internet: *ACLU of Georgia v. Miller*
Edward H. Freeman

The Internet allows anyone with a computer and a telephone line to talk to total strangers anywhere in the world. In the pure democracy of the Internet, chat sessions can become virtual masquerade parties, where users can express their own personalities or create new ones, depending on the circumstances and their individual whims. This can all take place based on the anonymity that is intrinsic to the Internet.

It is simple for the Internet user to communicate or exchange information anonymously or under a false identity. In about five minutes, anyone can create an account on www.hotmail.com, a leading source of free e-mail boxes. Hotmail asks several general questions about the mailbox owner (name, city, state, gender, birthday, occupation, but not a street address). It is easy to enter false data, and the identifying information is never verified by anyone. Unused e-mail boxes are simply abandoned by the user at will.

There are many advantages to the ability to communicate anonymously in cyberspace. Countless online support groups are readily available for victims of every human condition, illness, and situation. The freedom to discuss problems candidly and without fear of embarrassment, ridicule, or harassment has helped thousands cope with trying personal situations. Anonymity also helps users maintain their privacy and security as well as preventing the gathering of personal information about the user.

As with any new technology, it was inevitable that the anonymity of the Internet would be misused. Fraud, slander, child molestation, and other crimes have become common over the Internet. Criminals can create a virtual identity and contact thousands of potential victims at almost no cost.

0-8493-1248-5/02/$0.00+$1.50
© 2002 by CRC Press LLC

This chapter deals with anonymity on the Internet. It discusses the State of Georgia's attempt to restrict anonymity and the court challenge to that attempt brought by the ACLU. The chapter also deals with the constitutionally guaranteed right to freedom of speech, especially in cyberspace. Specific recommendations for confidential communications are included. Actual court cases are cited as examples throughout the chapter.

FACTS OF THE CASE

In 1996, the Georgia legislature passed the Georgia Computer System Protection Act (the Act) to combat computer-related crime. The Act prevented individuals from disguising their identities or even acting anonymously with respect to Internet communications. The Act made it a misdemeanor for

> Any person ... knowingly to transmit any data through a computer network ... for the purpose of setting up, maintaining, operating, or exchanging data with an electronic mailbox, home page, or any other electronic information storage bank or point of access to electronic information if such data uses any individual name ... to falsely identify the person.[1]

On September 24, 1996, a group of organizations and individuals, including the Georgia branch of the American Civil Liberties Union, challenged the constitutionality of the Act and filed suit in the federal district court in Georgia to have the Act overturned. Along with other points, the plaintiffs alleged in their brief that the Act:

- Unconstitutionally prohibited protected speech by placing restrictions on anonymous Internet use
- Violated constitutional rights to freedom of association and privacy by restricting the use of pseudonyms and pen names
- Restricted protected expression by prohibiting anonymous access to online information
- Was too vague to be applied because it did not define "names that 'falsely identify' their user"

The State of Georgia opposed the move to have the Act overturned. The state claimed that:

- The conduct prohibited by the bill did not apply to anonymous communications on the Internet but only to fraudulent computer use.
- The Act was directed only to false or misleading speech, which is not protected by the First Amendment.

Judge Marvin H. Shoob granted the ACLU's request for an injunction against the Act.[2] The court held that the statute's prohibition of anonymous Internet communications was a restriction on free speech based on the content of the speech. When the government wishes to curtail speech based on its content, it must follow a very strict and rigid analysis. The U.S. Supreme Court has consistently held that government should not suppress ideas because they are unpopular or offensive or merely to stifle dissenting viewpoints. As Justice Holmes wrote, there must be a "free trade of ideas." Truth will be accepted through the "competition of the market."[3]

In addition, the statute was too broad because "it was not drafted with the precision necessary for laws regulating speech. On its face, the act prohibits such protected speech as the use of false identification to avoid social ostracism, to prevent discrimination and harassment, and to protect privacy … a prohibition with well-recognized First Amendment problems."[4] The state decided not to appeal Judge Shoob's ruling, so the ruling became the final and definitive statement on the constitutionality of the Act.

RATIONALES FOR ANONYMITY ON THE INTERNET

ACLU of Georgia v. Miller highlighted the role and the results of anonymity on the Internet. The ability to post messages on the Internet anonymously has many possible consequences. Some people find it easier to put forward ideas in this way, particularly if they are unsure of themselves or of their ideas. Such individuals can get responses without fear of humiliation or repercussions.

On computer bulletin boards, there are advantages to being able to converse and to get to know people anonymously. Most Web sites for singles recommend anonymity as a method of self-protection until the parties involved reach a level of mutual trust. A cancer patient should not be required to identify himself to research medical data on the Internet. Whistleblowers should be protected from vindictive supervisors, government agencies, and corporations.

There is, of course, a more sinister side to anonymity. Countless individuals have been victimized by shady Internet moneymaking schemes, through which anonymous criminals can swindle the unsuspecting and simply relocate electronically to continue their activities. The nature of the Internet defies standard laws of jurisdiction, especially where such swindles are involved. It is often difficult to determine which state court should hear a case, especially when the parties to the transaction are from different states and the transaction itself occurred on the Internet.[5]

Opponents of anonymity focus their arguments on several points. Disclosure helps audiences assess the truthfulness, objectivity, and accuracy of a speaker's words. As an example, an e-mail message in defense of higher oil prices might be less credible if the author works for a major oil company. Disclosure also discourages users from publishing wild, unsubstantiated claims; writing libelous documents; or speaking in the name of a respected authority. It may also serve to limit hate speech that the speaker knows to be offensive.[6] Several online discussion groups have adopted a policy of filtering out all anonymous messages, but such a policy is often difficult to enforce without extensive reference checking.

PROTECTION OF ANONYMITY AND THE LAW

Although the Constitution does not specifically guarantee it, there is a long and respected tradition of anonymous political writings in America, going back to before the American Revolution. Thomas Paine's *Common Sense,* which is recognized as the first work to spark Americans to consider independence from Britain, was first published signed simply "An Englishman." Alexander Hamilton, John Jay, and James Madison wrote *The Federalist Papers* under the joint pseudonym "Publius."[7] Before the Civil War, many writers on both sides of the slavery issue shielded themselves anonymously or with pseudonyms.

The Supreme Court has long realized that compelled disclosure of personal information could lead to embarrassment, stigmatization, or even physical danger, although there will always be those who abuse the right. The First Amendment's guarantees of free speech and freedom of assembly have been understood for many years to provide protection for certain levels of anonymity.[8]

In 1958, the Supreme Court upheld the right of the National Association for the Advancement of Colored People (NAACP) to keep from disclosing its membership list to the Alabama state government.[9] The Court recognized "the vital relationship between freedom to associate and privacy in one's associations." The NAACP's right to pursue its lawful interests privately and to associate freely with others was considered more important than Alabama's request for the membership lists. This viewpoint was confirmed two years later when the Court invalidated a Los Angeles ordinance against the distribution of anonymous leaflets.[10]

In a 1995 ruling, *McIntyre v. Ohio Campaign Commission,*[11] the Supreme Court struck down an Ohio statute prohibiting the distribution of campaign literature that did not indicate the name and address of those responsible for its issuance. Mrs. McIntyre had been fined for handing out anonymous leaflets that urged defeat of a school tax. In its analysis, the Court ruled that anonymity "exemplifies the purpose behind the Bill of Rights, and of the First Amendment in particular: to protect unpopular individuals from retaliation — and their ideas from suppression — at the hand of an intolerant society."

There is a direct parallel between Mrs. McIntyre's pamphlets and an unsigned e-mail on a political topic. In *ACLU v. Reno,*[12] the Court emphasized that Internet speakers should have the same rights to anonymity as pamphleteers:

> Through the use of chat rooms, any person with a phone line can become a town crier with a voice that resonates farther than it could from any soapbox. Through the use of Web pages, mail exploders, and newsgroups, the same individual can become a pamphleteer .... We agree with its conclusion that our cases provide no basis for qualifying the level of First Amendment scrutiny that should be applied to this medium.

ANONYMOUS REMAILERS

An anonymous remailer is simply a computer connected to the Internet that forwards electronic mail or files to other addresses on the network. Before the message is retransmitted, it also strips off the header part of the message, which shows the origin and author of the message. The only information that the receiver can tell about a message's origin is that it passed through the remailer.[13] If the recipient wants to respond to the original e-mail, the identifying information is also stripped away before the message is sent. Without the identifying information in the header, there is no way of tracing a message back to its originator without involving the remailer.

There are many legitimate reasons why an honest person might choose to forward certain messages through a remailer. For example, an employee for a manufacturing firm might want to express an opinion about her company's dangerous products without fear of losing her job. Job hunters have found the Internet an excellent method of contacting numerous companies, but they may not want their current employers to know their intent. Government employees can use the Internet to expose corruption and bureaucratic blunders without fear of retaliation.

Dozens of remailing services are available on the Internet. Some are free to the user (supported by advertisers) and some charge a fee for the service. Most reliable remailers will refuse messages that are obscene or threatening.[14]

RECOMMENDATIONS

Most casual e-mail users do not need anonymity or encryption to protect their interests. For those users whose activities require such precautions or who are particularly zealous about protecting their privacy, the following recommendations may prevent problems:

- Create two or more separate e-mail boxes. One box should be for routine use (i.e., correspondences with trusted friends) and the other for confidential matters. The e-mail address of the confidential box should not have any reference to the name of the user.

- For a short-term project or for temporary use, it may be beneficial to create a temporary e-mail box. When the specific need no longer exists, simply discontinue use of this box.
- Be careful about revealing too much personal information over the Internet. As an example, some Web sites for prescription medications will mail a discount coupon for their product. The information about the request may eventually be sold and could cause problems if it ever becomes necessary to change health insurance providers.
- Supermarket cards allow users to save money on grocery purchases, but at a cost in terms of privacy. The market has a complete record of all purchases made, sometimes over a period of years. When you apply for such a card, use a fictitious name and address.
- Never use a credit card for any purchase that might prove embarrassing if it became public.
- If you do choose to request coupons or other information over the Internet and have them sent to you by ordinary mail, rent a mailbox at the Post Office or at a public mailbox service. Have the information sent there and use a fictitious name. If the soliciting organization insists that you give it a telephone number, use the number for your local time-of-day service or a pay phone at your local bowling alley.
- Be very discreet with personal contacts over the Internet. Assume the worst when making contacts. If you choose to meet an Internet "friend," do so in a public place.
- Never assume that any method of remailing messages is 100 percent confidential. Remember that remailers located in the United States are subject to state and federal subpoenas and other court orders. Such remailers could be forced to surrender confidential data about your correspondences. Consider the use of a foreign-based remailer that is not subject to U.S. law. The physical location of a remailer can usually be determined by the last part of the Internet address.
- Consider the use of a remailing service that features encryption technology.
- Never send or receive personal correspondences on your employer's e-mail or intranet system. The courts have consistently ruled that such correspondences are the property of the organization. Employees have been dismissed for statements made in personal e-mails sent over the corporate network (i.e., inappropriate language and vulgar jokes). There is no expectation of privacy for such transmissions.
- Legitimate remailer administrators do not tolerate and will not transmit messages containing serious harassment or criminal activity. Such communications are always inappropriate and are often illegal. Be sure that your correspondences do not violate the laws of common decency.

CONCLUSION

In a free, essentially uncontrollable environment such as the Internet, anonymity is easy to obtain and just as easy to misuse. Traditionally, anonymity is considered a basic constitutional right, especially when political free speech is involved.

Numerous court cases created the right to anonymity in print and other media. *ACLU v. Georgia* extended the right to anonymity to the Internet under the protection of the First Amendment. Problems linked to anonymity, such as difficulty in tracing hackers and perpetrators of online fraud, must find solutions that do not restrict anonymity on the Internet.

Notes

1. GA. CODE. ANN. § 16-9-93.1 (1996).
2. *ACLU of Georgia v. Miller,* 977 F. Supp. 1228 (N.D. Ga. 1997)
3. *Abrams v. United States,* 250 U.S. 616 (1919).
4. *ACLU* at 1233.
5. Edward H. Freeman, "Issues of Jurisdiction in Cyberspace," *Information Systems Security,* Winter 1999, p. 20.
6. Note, "Disclosure as a Legislative Device," *Harvard Law Review,* 76, 1273, 1963.
7. Jonathan D. Wallace, "Nameless in Cyberspace: Anonymity on the Internet," *The Laissez Faire City Times*, January 3, 2000.
8. A. Michael Froomkin, "Anonymity and Its Enmities," *J. Online L.,* Art 4. Par. 54, 1995.
9. *NAACP v. Alabama ex rel. Patterson,* 357 U.S. 449 (1958).
10. *Talley v. California,* 362 U.S. 60 (1960).
11. *McIntyre v. Ohio Elections Commissions,* 415 U.S. 334 (1995).
12. *ACLU v. Reno,* 117 S. Ct 2329 (1997).
13. Charles Arthur, "Identity Crisis on the Internet," *New Scientist,* March 11, 1995.
14. A full discussion of remailing can be found at www.andrebacard.com/remail.html.

Chapter 16
The Continuing Disintegration of Confidentiality

Belden Menkus

The concepts of confidentiality and privacy are easy to confuse. They are not identical. However, they are interrelated. The former encompasses the latter.

- Confidentiality is the ability to limit the knowledge of a particular act, condition, or segment of information to a finite number of specific entities or individuals.
- Privacy is the ability to function apart from undesired observation or oversight by others.

Neither condition is absolute, especially in an interrelated society. Neither condition is an inherent right that can be exercised freely by either an individual or an organization.

There is no unconditional privilege to refuse to disclose some types of information. In the United States, grand juries and other entities can use the courts to compel organizations and individuals to disclose information that, in an earlier era, would have been kept confidential without question. And regulatory agencies such as the U.S. Securities and Exchange Commission are continuing to require that organizations reveal more of various types of information.

Both confidentiality and privacy are conditions that must be claimed through a conscious act and can be lost through inaction or even through failure on the part of an organization's executives to exercise due diligence. The scope of an organization's involvement with both confidentiality and privacy is broader than that of an individual. The organization must protect confidentiality and privacy as they pertain to both the information that belongs to the enterprise and information that the venture may have

0-8493-1248-5/02/$0.00+$1.50
© 2002 by CRC Press LLC

access to legitimately but that belongs to others. (It may be the possession of employees, customers, or suppliers.)

IMPLICATIONS FOR IS AUDITING

The IS auditor's ability to rely on the continued confidentiality of both the organization's data and those that relate to its customers and suppliers is one of the implied assumptions behind the control structure in most organizations. (This supposition applies, as well, to data relating to students, in the case of educational institutions.) This presumption is one of the major components of the auditor's ability to conclude that an enterprise can be expected to continue to function effectively.

The problem is it appears, increasingly, that this assumption of confidentiality may not be true. Especially, this seems to be the case with such things as customer and medical patient histories, tax accountability documentation, personal bank account transaction records, data on details of the way in which lawyers deal with their clients, and student activity and course performance records.

CONFIDENTIALITY COMPROMISE INCIDENTS

Various types of confidentiality compromises have taken place already. Following are accounts of some of these incidents.

Customer Histories

The records of the involvement of some 50,000 members of Canada's Loyalty Group customer loyalty venture were displayed on a World Wide Web (Web) site, despite the claim that this data was confidential. The information included in the Web page included the names, telephone numbers, and addresses of individuals who had filled out online applications for Air Canada's Air Miles program. Also displayed were the numbers of motor vehicles that these persons owned and the types of credit cards that they held. In its apology for the confidentiality compromise which had occurred, the Loyalty Group pointed out that this display did not include the actual card numbers.

According to a computer hacker who identifies himself as Space Rogue, FAO Online, the Web site of the upscale FAO Schwarz toy retailer, has been revealing the home and electronic mail addresses and the telephone numbers of its electronic commerce customers. (Space Rogue claims to be a member of LOpht, a Boston-based computer hacker collective and the editor of the Internet's *Hacker News Network*.)

The FAO Online flaw was not revealed by some form of transaction surveillance within, or by the auditing of, the information-processing application. Rather, according to Brooke Atkins, the FAO Schwarz Public Relations vice president, the vulnerability was disclosed by one of its customers. This person unintentionally changed a particular number in the FAO Online URL. This resulted in an open display of the customer's data. The incident occurred when the customer attempted to purchase a toy from the FAO Schwarz online catalog.

FAO Online resides, according to Atkins, on a Web server that is protected with SSL (Secure Sockets Layer, a Netscape message content encryption and authentication software product) and a firewall. (This arrangement will protect an electronic commerce mechanism against a possible compromise by an intruder, but it will not compensate for an inadequate implementation of an information-processing application.) After making purchases, an FAO Schwarz customer prints a record of the transaction, adds the credit-card number and expiration date to this printout, and sends a facsimile copy of the final record to FAO Schwarz to complete the transaction.

Medical Patient Records

Thousands of patient records at Ann Arbor's University of Michigan Medical Center were accessible through the institution's Web site for at least nine weeks until a student, who was searching in the site for background on a specific doctor, was linked to a database that included patient names, residential addresses, telephone numbers, Social Security numbers, employment status, and details of treatment for specific medical conditions. The medical center had been using this information to schedule patient appointments with individual staff members.

Children who attend the Ranfurly Primary School in Victoria, Australia, have been drawing on discarded copies of the printout of pathology patient examinations at the Mildura Base Hospital. The contents of these records included patient names, residential addresses, birth dates, and the details of actual tests. A hospital executive said that the disposition of the printout copies stemmed from the 1994 privatizing of the hospital's pathology services.

Canadian Taxpayer Personal Financial Records

The Supreme Court of Canada has upheld the claimed right of Revenue Canada to investigate the personal finances of private citizens who are believed to be engaged in tax fraud. It overturned unanimously a Federal Court of Appeals decision. Revenue Canada began an investigation of a possible evasion of $1.67 million in taxes by Angelo Del Zotto of Toronto-based Tridel Enterprises, Inc. (This fraud was believed to have taken place between 1979 and 1985.)

In 1992 Revenue Canada had applied a rarely used Income Tax Act provision that permits the agency to seize all financial records of the subject of a fraud investigation, and to order possible witnesses to appear before the agency and to give it sworn testimony. Del Zotto had lost a challenge to the seizure in a Federal Court of Canada in 1997. He claimed that the action violated his constitutional right to privacy. Later that same year, the Canadian Federal Court of Appeals had ruled for Del Zotto. The Supreme Court adopted the opinion of dissenting Appeals Court Judge Barry Strayer that the investigations in question are held in private and do not amount to an unreasonable search and seizure.

U.S. Nonprofit Taxpayer Records

The U.S. Internal Revenue Service has started to require tax-exempt non-profit organizations that have annual gross receipts of more than $25,000 to provide a copy of the service's Form 990 declaration to anyone who writes or sends a facsimile or electronic mail message asking for the information. These organizations have been required by law since 1987 to make this information accessible for inspection by the public. (There was a stipulation, of course, that the request be reasonable.)

An estimated 200,000 organizations use Form 990 each year. The information contained in it includes salaries of the five highest-paid executives, the salaries of major independent contractors, and an analysis of the funds spent on programs, compared with the organization's administrative costs and fund-raising expenses. Until now, nonprofits were required only to make this material available at their headquarters site. This meant that someone requesting the material had to travel to the headquarters site of the enterprise. Such a stipulation could be inconvenient for someone in, for example, Nashville, Tennessee, who is concerned with, say, the Form 990 of Focus on the Family, operating from Colorado Springs. Under the new requirements, organizations must send copies of the documents within 30 days after receiving a request for them, or display the tax forms on the Internet for everyone to inspect. Forms for the previous three years must be made available.

The experience of Compassion International, which also operates from Colorado Springs, gives an idea of the possible greater impact of this new required availability. Compassion International says that, since it started placing its Forms 990 on the Web in October 1998 in anticipation of the change in disclosure requirements, the organization's Forms 990 have been downloaded from the site 15 to 20 times a month.

Intellectual Property Theft

Tabloid.net, an online newspaper based in San Francisco, has charged in the local U.S. District Court that the Dallas-based Richards Group advertising agency stole one of its copyrighted creations, a talking ham sandwich. The character was used, according to the Tabloid.net suit, in an advertising campaign that The Richards Group developed for the Florida Department of Citrus in September 1998.

A depiction of a talking ham sandwich, or a link to that illustration, was included, the Tabloid.net suit asserted, in four of the weekly installments of the publication's fiction series about Vodka City. The eight-part series appeared in Tabloid.net during August and September 1997. Tabloid.net sought a share of the profits that The Richards Group made from using a comparable ham sandwich in its campaign for the Florida Department of Citrus, as well as license fees stemming from that use. Also, the suit sought to have the Florida Department of Citrus, which was named as a second defendant in the Tabloid.net suit, to cease using the ham sandwich in its advertising.

Stan Richards, an executive of The Richards Group, has denied the charge. However, Tabloid.net said in its suit that the database that supports its Web site shows that employees of The Richards Group visited the site three times between May and August 1998. And the records of the Web site indicate that The Richards Group employees made at least 37 hits during these visits.

Employee Credit Card Use Records

Leesburg, Virginia, Town Manager Steven Brown's failure to arrange payment for an American Express credit card that included an overdue account balance of almost $16,000 has cost him his job. (The reason for the overdue balance was not explained by either Brown or Virginia State Police investigator Vernon Fay, who investigated Brown's personal financial dealings.) The statement had arrived while Brown was on what was described as a family vacation in Germany. The failure to provide for paying the bill has resulted in Brown being forced to resign from the $100,000-a-year position that he had held since 1991. (This figure included the value of his benefits.)

Acting under orders from Virginia Commonwealth Attorney Robert Anderson, Fay secured a search warrant to seize the town's American Express charge records, Brown's calendars dating from 1993, and related correspondence. In addition, Fay used another search warrant to gain access to personal bank records of Brown and his wife, beginning in 1993, from the F & M Bank in Winchester, Virginia, and the Loudoun County Credit Union in Leesburg. Town records indicated that Brown had charged $83,000 in personal items since 1993. These included groceries that were bought at a local supermarket, jewelry that was purchased for Brown's wife from a home shopping channel, and a microcomputer that was acquired for use in their home.

Anderson and Fay said that at issue are such things as $5200 worth of charges by Brown, consisting of plane tickets for Brown, his wife, and his two children from Dulles International Airport to Orlando and car rentals and lodgings for the family while they were there. Brown has said that more than $4000 of the Florida charges were for town business expenses. Also, town records indicate that Brown charged $600 worth of airline tickets to Munich. Apparently, these were related to the family vacation in Germany, mentioned earlier in this chapter. But the town records give no indication that the town was repaid for this expense.

Student Attendance and Grades

Ponderosa High School, located south of Parker, Colorado, is providing 300 parents who use its Internet Student Information System with a means for keeping track online such things as their children's attendance, grades, and progress toward meeting the School District's graduation require-ments.

The parents have been issued user names and passwords, permiting them to check their child's grades, which are updated four times a year. The students' attendance and discipline records are updated nightly. In addition, parents can print out transcripts at home, check on a child's course history, and interact with teachers through electronic mail. The Parker School District paid $4000 for the pilot program software. It is estimated that it will cost an additional $100,000 to purchase the software product for all of the district's schools and another $50,000 a year to maintain the product throughout the district.

Altering Evidence

David Sandy, 44, a senior partner at London's Simmons and Simmons law firm, has been accused of copying and destroying material contained on diskettes belonging to Zafar Iqbal. Iqbal was chief executive, at the time of its collapse in 1991, of the now-defunct Bank of Credit and Commerce International. Sandy is also accused of trying to conceal Iqbal's diary from a New York City Grand Jury that is investigating the operations of the bank. According to Robert Morgenthau, the Manhattan District Attorney, Sandy went in January 1992 to Iqbal's Abu Dhabi office and removed three diskettes that contained records of Iqbal's business transactions. Sandy is alleged to have asked for the diskettes to be copied and then erased. Iqbal was convicted of relatively minor offenses and jailed, eventually, in Abu Dhabi. Later, he was released from custody because of a medical condition.

THE BASIC ISSUE IS CONTROL

The concepts of confidentiality and privacy are realized through the consistent exercise of control. This activity is an indicator of due diligence on the part of an organization's executives in being responsible for the use of information. And this exercise of control runs counter to the cyberspace myths that information has to be liberated and that it must be shared in all circumstances, even if that occurs without either the knowledge or the permission of the owner or possessor of the information. Cyberspace has been described by some Internet and Web enthusiasts as the "first true communitarian society to exist in 300 years." This outlook complicates effectively all efforts to resolve the problems which are associated with realizing both IS security and control!

What to Do

The scope and complexity of these problems can be defined by an IS audit of the enterprise's confidentiality exposure, and such a review can be carried out with a very simple work program. The basic premise of such an effort should be comparable to that which is employed in a successful fraud audit. Each of the organization's information-processing applications should be examined from the perspective of determining where and how one might jeopardize the confidentiality of its content. The IS auditor must think as a possible intruder or compromiser might think.

The possibility of confidentiality compromise may be the result of malicious intent, incompetence on the part of the user of the application, or the failure of some component of the environment in which the application functions. No matter what the cause of this compromise may be, the result of a possible confidentiality exposure must be assumed to be the same in every situation.

Attempts at Problem Resolution

There are four basic ways to reduce the organization's confidentiality exposure:

1. Define the genuinely sensitive information. Every piece of information cannot be placed in this category. Every piece of information that an organization possesses is not a trade secret. Every piece that relates to an identifiable human being does not merit protection. What is called for are reasonable and prudent actions. An organization and its executives should be able to demonstrate to a judge or an investigator that they have acted prudently. The enterprise should isolate the genuinely sensitive material from the other data that it is accumulating and retaining. Just because it is relatively easy and convenient to retain particular information does not justify doing so.

2. Identify the damage to the organization that may result from the unauthorized disclosure of the genuinely sensitive material to others. The financial cost of such a revelation is the maximum possible loss of existing or future business, plus any punitive fine that may be associated with this exposure, multiplied by the number of years over which the incident may affect the generation of new or replacement business. The impact of any loss of organizational believability that may stem from such a disclosure cannot be quantified. But both the loss and its impact should not be ignored.

3. Limit the amount of data that the organization keeps about any matter and the period for which the data is retained. Include a determination in every review that these limitations are being complied with. Remember: Information that does not continue to exist beyond reasonable limitations cannot be the subject of a subpoena issued by a court, prosecutor, or regulatory agency. An executive should be advised not to give in to the temptation of trying to hide sensitive information from the issuer of a subpoena.

4. Restrict accessibility and actual access to those individuals who need to know this sensitive information as a part of their regular job. Place the responsibility for protecting this access on the individuals who are involved, not upon the technology that is being used. Encourage the liberal internal use of firewalls. Look for attempts to tunnel through them, whether it is done for claimed convenience or to demonstrate some sort of adroit use of the technology being employed.

It is always wise and cautious to demonstrate prudence and the exercise of reasonable care when one is dealing with issues of confidentiality and privacy.

Chapter 17
Selected Security and Legal Issues in E-Commerce

Frederick Gallegos
Mohammad Al-Abdullah

Encryption can be explained as the process of transforming information into an unintelligible form and thus making it extremely difficult for others to understand the meaning of the message. Encryption can be used to disguise messages so that even if a message is diverted, it will not be revealed.[6]

Some people mistakenly think that encryption and data security are new ideas, but in reality encryption has been known and used for a long time. Julius Caesar used an alphabet cipher to make sure the enemy could not read a message if it fell into enemy hands. George Washington had his military intelligence use code books containing code numbers. Each code number represents a specific word. A person who needs to encode a message has to look up the code book to assemble a message, then when the coded message is delivered, a copy of the book is used to decode the message. These coded messages assured Washington that if a message fell into enemy hands, it could not be understood. Needless to say, these code books are important; if these code books fell into enemy hands, the security system could be breached and made useless.

These coding techniques and others are the building blocks of today's encryption algorithms used on tiny SIM cards, personal computers, or a government's multimillion-dollar super computers. Encryption is also the key building block that facilitates secure Internet electronic commerce.

ENCRYPTION AND E-COMMERCE

The Internet was not built on a secure foundation. Many of the protocols running on the Internet are not secure. Consider for example, FTP, Telnet,

0-8493-1248-5/02/$0.00+$1.50
© 2002 by CRC Press LLC

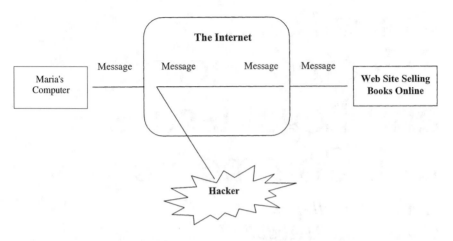

Exhibit 1.   Information Copied and Used by a Hacker

and SMTP protocols. In all of these protocols the log-ins and passwords are sent across the Internet in cleartext (unencrypted) format. Sending any message across the Internet means that at any point across the Internet, that message can be intercepted and read. Usually, hackers would use a network-monitoring tool to extract messages, such as log-ins and passwords, from a network. If the message was sent in cleartext format, then the message can be read and understood. If the message was encrypted, then it can be read but not understood. Needless to say, sometimes it is important to keep messages sent across the Internet secret.

Consider the following scenario. Maria is an avid World Wide Web surfer, and one day she reaches a Web site that advertises books for sale. Maria decides that there is a book worth buying through the Web site. So, she fills out a Web form and presses the SEND button. That Web form had fields for the name and address of the buyer in addition to the buyer's credit card number. As that information travels through cyberspace, a copy of the information is made at a workstation connected somewhere between Maria's computer and the Web site advertising the books, as illustrated in Exhibit 1. A hacker operating the workstation can then use or abuse that credit card until Maria gets her bank statement. By that time, the hacker would have charged Maria's credit card up to its maximum limit.

The financial implications of hacking are not the only reasons why messages across the Internet need to be secured. Personal information also needs to be secured via encryption. If personal information is compromised or revealed in unsecured channels, invasion of privacy might occur.

190

Skeptics of the harm that can be done by breach of privacy across the Internet should consider the "virtual murder" case. In essence, the perpetrator used the information he obtained through the Internet's chat rooms to change the Social Security Administration's records and change the status of another person to be dead on the SSA systems. The victim in this case did not know of the damage done until she tried to open a bank account.[4]

The previous scenarios are some of the main reasons why encryption is needed to protect financial information from the prying eyes of criminals and hackers. Without proper security measures, Internet E-commerce would not be accepted by the general public or corporations.

The U.S. government allows the use of encryption software and hardware within the United States. The U.S. government prohibits the export of encryption hardware and software without the prior approval of the government. Because Internet E-commerce is targeted at the global community, encryption export restriction is detrimental to everyone concerned with E-commerce. But why restrict the export of encryption products.

EXPORT RESTRICTION

Perhaps the best explanation of why the export of encryption products is prohibited is the White House statement:

> Encryption products, when used outside the United States, can jeopardize our foreign policy and national security interests. Moreover, such products, when used by international criminal organizations, can threaten the safety of U.S. citizens here and abroad, as well as the safety of the citizens of other countries. The exportation of encryption products accordingly must be controlled to further U.S. foreign policy objectives, and promote our national security, including the protection of the safety of U.S. citizen abroad.

> — The White House–Encryption Export Policy

That statement from the White House shows how seriously the U.S. government takes encryption. That is understandable considering that criminals and others use encryption to conceal their illegal communications and activities. These illegal activities include terrorist communications that relate to the safety and security of people in the United States and overseas.

Consider the following: Drug lords can coordinate with their partners on drug shipment dates and locations. Usually, law enforcement agencies can intercept these communications and catch the criminals in the act. If these criminals use encryption, then the law enforcement's ability to understand the communications is severely crippled. This leads to the criminals being able to roam free without problems.

Another more alarming scenario is the following: Usually the CIA or the NSA is able to eavesdrop on foreign communications that could be hostile to U.S. interests. That ability to eavesdrop on communications enables the U.S. government to prepare for any planned aggressions. A problem arises if foreign entities use encryption to obscure messages. That would make the job of the CIA or the NSA much more difficult. If the encryption used is of high power, then it is almost impossible to break that encryption. This would lead to possible successful attacks on U.S. government interests not only overseas but also in the country. To further clarify, consider the following statement made by RSA Laboratories:

> Cryptography is export-controlled for several reasons. Strong cryptography can be used for criminal purposes or even as a weapon of war. During wartime, the ability to intercept and decipher enemy communications is crucial. For that reason, strong cryptography is usually classified on the U.S. Munitions List as an export-controlled commodity, just like tanks and missiles.

Because the U.S. government has declared encryption products as defense articles on the U.S. Munitions List, all encryption products, hardware or software, cannot be exported without prior approval.

The Data Encryption Standard (DES) was used in the United States and overseas by financial institutions and others to encrypt data. The problem with DES is that it has become increasingly easier to break in to DES-protected messages; DES is considered weak by today's standards. Its limited key length allows hackers or criminals to compromise the DES security. Therefore, other more powerful encryption systems must be allowed to be exported for use in Internet E-commerce, as well as other financial activities.

NEW REGULATIONS

Understanding that the export restrictions are very archaic, the U.S. government decided to relax the export restrictions. This was due in part to the losses U.S. companies suffer when they are unable to sell to foreign entities. In a press release dated July 7, 1998, the commerce secretary made the following announcement:

> Commerce Secretary William Daley announced today that the Clinton Administration has finalized guidelines to allow the export of U.S.-manufactured encryption products of any bit length when used by banks, financial institutions, and their branches around the world to secure private electronic transactions. Strong encryption products — with or without recovery features — will be exportable to eligible

institutions without a license, after a one-time review, to banks and financial institutions in 45 countries. Eligible institutions include banks, security firms, brokers, and credit card companies.

These new guidelines will affect encryption exports for almost 70 percent of the world's financial institutions and the world's 100 largest banks. Today's announcement follows last year's decision to allow special treatment of encryption products used to secure financial communications and transactions.

— Bureau of Export Administration,
New Export Guidelines

Exhibit 2. List of Countries Where Encryption Products Are Not To Be Exported

Cuba	Iran	Iraq	Libya
North Korea	Syria	Sudan	

Even with the new regulations, the manufacturer of an encryption product needs to apply for a license. In addition to the license, the encryption product must not be allowed to be exported to the countries listed in Exhibit 2.

According to the Bureau of Export Administration, 45 countries are eligible to receive U.S.-produced encryption products. The Bureau of Export Administration has stated the following:

The 45 eligible countries are either members of the international anti-money laundering accord, the Financial Action Task Force, or have enacted anti-money laundering laws [see Exhibit 3]. Manufacturers and other exporters will be able to ship the products to these countries with only minimum reporting requirements. Products, which have already been reviewed, can be shipped to financial institutions of eligible countries under license exception without further review.

Exports to banks and financial institutions in countries, which are not eligible for license exception, will continue to require approval under either export licensing arrangements or individual licenses. Applications for such license arrangements will be reviewed by agencies with a presumption of approval unless agencies raise specific concerns about a country or financial end user regarding participation in money laundering, narcotics trafficking or similar concerns.

— Bureau of Export Administration,
New Export Guidelines

Exhibit 3.   List of Eligible Countries of Encryption Export

Anguilla	Antigua	Argentina	Aruba	Australia	Austria
Bahamas	Belgium	Barbados	Brazil	Canada	Croatia
Denmark	Dominica	Ecuador	Finland	France	Germany
Greece	Hong Kong	Hungary	Iceland	Ireland	Italy
Japan	Kenya	Luxembourg	Monaco	The Netherlands	New Zealand
Norway	Poland	Portugal	St. Vincent/ Grenadines	St. Kitts & Nevis	Seychelles
Singapore	Spain	Sweden	Switzerland	Trinidad & Tobago	Turkey
United Kingdom	United States	Uruguay			

GUIDELINES FOR APPLYING FOR A LICENSE

As stated earlier, manufacturers of encryption products need to apply for licenses. According to the Bureau of Export Administration (BXA), the following guidelines help in applying for a Mass Market Classification Request (license) for a particular encryption product. If these guidelines are not followed, the license will be delayed. In addition to the delay in obtaining the license, there is no guarantee that the license will be granted. The guidelines are as follows:

BXA-748P: Application Form (must be TYPED)

- Blocks 1–3: Name, telephone, and fax number of the person to whom questions should be addressed.
- Block 4: The date the application was submitted to BXA
- Block 5: Mark the classification request box
- Block 6: Mark the applicable fields
- Block 7–8: Leave blank
- Block 9: Type "Mass Market Encryption Software"
- Blocks 10–13: Leave blank
- Block 14–15: Be sure that the information is filled out correctly because this is where the official CCATS documents from BXA will sent once the classification process is completed. If both blocks are filled out, the CCATS will go the individual identified in Block 15.
- Blocks 16–21: Leave blank
- Block 22:
  - (a): Requested ECCN — typical classifications include 5D002, EAR99, 5D995 (BXA will reclassify if necessary)
  - (b): n/a
  - (c): Model name
  - (d)–(h): n/a
  - (i): Name of manufacturer

— (j): Provide a brief technical description that includes the basic purpose of the software and the type of encryption utilized in the software (e.g., 40-bit RC2/RC4 for secure e-mail, 56-bit SET for specific financial fields, SSL protocol, etc.)

Please DO NOT type "see letter of explanation" or "see brochure," because this description is entered verbatim into official documents.

- Block 23: Leave blank
- Block 24: Type any additional information

Should you want more than one item classified on this same form, please use form 748P-A and follow the same instructions for Block 22 for each of the additional items.

Submission of Supporting Documents

- The supporting documents should accompany the 748P. A copy of the supporting documents must also be express mailed to the following address (failure to comply will result in delays):
  Attn. Mass Market Encryption Request Coordinator
  P.O. Box 246
  Annapolis Junction, MD 20701-0246
- If you submit the forms electronically, please send and/or fax the supporting documents to BXA (202-482-4094) and NSA.
- Important Information to Include in the Supporting Documents

A. Technical Description that includes:

- The data encryption algorithm: name of algorithm, key length (where applicable state the number of rounds; e.g., 40-b9t RC5 algorithm with 5 round)
- Exchange technique: name of algorithm, type (e.g., public key, symmetric key password-based), key length (for symmetric key), modulus length (for public key)

B. Verify in the letter of explanation that:

- The encryption is not user modifiable.
- The software is distributed only in object code (name of the programming language and/or operating system(s) would also be useful).
- The software cannot perform multiple encryption during a single encryption session (e.g., 40-bit RC2 encryption followed by 40-bit RC4 encryption).
- The mass market software requirements are met in that:
  1. The product is generally available to the public by over-the-counter purchases, telephone orders, mail-order transactions, Internet transactions, or similar means.

2. The product is designed for installation by the end user without further substantial support by the supplier.
3. Provide a brief description of what the product does as a whole, not just how the encryption works.

By following the above guidelines and including all the necessary information, the classification process will proceed unhindered. Failure to comply generally means unwanted, unnecessary delays.

— The Bureau of Export Administration

CRITICIZING THE NEW REGULATIONS

Of course, as the case with every new policy there is criticism that helps shed some light on the new policies. According to the Center For Democracy and Technology (CDT) Executive Director Jerry Berman, the U.S. encryption policy offers the following:

- Decontrol of 56-bit (DES-level) encryption — would permit export of 56-bit products and their equivalent (including 1024-bit asymmetric systems) to most countries after a one-time governmental review.
- Export relief for specific industry segments — would permit export of stronger products to subsidiaries of U.S. companies, health and insurance industries, and unspecified "electronic-commerce" users.
- Exemptions for "recoverable" products — would permit export of encryption products of unlimited strength if those products include backdoor access to plaintext, use key recovery, or allow access to plaintext through a system administrator or other person independent of the user.

CDT welcomes these efforts to address the concerns raised about current U.S. policy. However, the new regulations leave significant privacy concerns unanswered:

- 56-bit (DES level) encryption will not adequately protect online privacy and security. Expert cryptographers have argued for years that 56-bit encryption is not sufficient to protect privacy online. Just this summer, a group of California researchers created a DES Cracker that broke a 56-bit length encrypted message in just 56 hours, using minimal resources.
- Granting export relief for industry groups leaves the little guy out. Individuals, human rights workers, or other noncommercial groups who have a compelling interest in using strong encryption without backdoor access built in will not get relief under the new proposal.
- Administration policy continues to use export controls to force the adoption of vulnerable key-recovery systems. The new regulations would continue the Administration's efforts to require key recovery

or other plaintext-access features in the encryption products that most individuals use. An expert's report on "The Risks of Key Recovery" (http://www.cdt.org/crypto/risks98) recently argued that such recovery technologies introduce new security risks.

• Standards for government access are not specified. Privacy cannot be protected under a recovery system without a clear understanding of the legal protection governing access to plaintext — a discussion that is absent from this proposal.

— The Center for Democracy and Technology

MAJOR COUNTRIES THAT HAVE IMPORT RESTRICTIONS ON CRYPTOGRAPHY

As explained earlier, the U.S. government has laws that regulate the export of encryption products. In addition to these regulations, manufacturers of encryption products need to consider the countries that the encryption product will be shipped to. Exhibits 2 and 3 list the countries that encryption products can or cannot be shipped. Furthermore, there are countries that regulate the import of encryption products to their lands. According to RSA Laboratories, France, Israel, Russia, and South Africa all have restrictions against importing encrypting products. RSA has stated the following:

> France, Israel, Russia, and South Africa all have import restrictions on cryptography. Some countries, such as France and Singapore, require vendors to obtain a license before importing cryptographic products. Many governments use such import licenses to pursue domestic policy goals. In some instances, governments require foreign vendors to provide technical information to obtain an import license. This information is then used to steer business toward local companies. Other governments have been accused of using this same information for outright industrial espionage.

This demonstrates the complications involved with encryption products to be used for E-commerce or other uses. Therefore, it is important for developer and corporations to have solid legal counsel that is not only versed in the U.S. government laws and regulations but also in international laws and regulations.

CONCLUSION

The question here would be what would happen if a developer started selling or exporting a newly developed encryption software or hardware without prior approval of the appropriate regulating government agencies? Simply put, the developer would be in court for quite some time. Consider the legal case against Zimmerman, who released his Pretty Good Privacy encryption software without prior approval from the appropriate government agencies.

Therefore, it is important to fully comply with government regulations to avoid legal problems with the federal government. Not only will a court case brought against a developer be a time drain, but it will also be a financial drain that could put the developer or his company into bankruptcy. In addition to considering U.S. government regulations, developers need to think about international laws, since other countries have strict regulations against all encryption products. That only stresses the fact that encryption is a legal challenge as well as a technical challenge.

Bibliography

1. The Bureau of Export Administration. *Helpful Hints When Applying for Mass Market TSU Exception.* [Online]. Available: http://207.96.11.93/factsheets/ammhints.html [1998, November 23].
2. The Bureau of Export Administration. *New Export Guidelines.* [Online]. Available: http://207.96.11.93/press/98/ENCDaley.htm [1998, November 23].
3. The Center for Democracy and Technology. *New Administration Encryption Controls Leave Individual Privacy Concerns Unanswered.* [Online]. Available: http://www.cdt.org/crypto/statement/CDTstatement091698.html. [1998, November 20].
4. Poulsen, Kevin (1998). *ZDTV: Cyber Crime. Death Input.* [Online]. Available: http://www.zd-net.com/zdtv/cybercrime/chaostheory/story/0,3700,2144830,00.html. [1998, October 6].
5. RSA Laboratories. *RSA Laboratories' Frequently Asked Questions About Today's Cryptography.* [Online]. Available: http://www.rsa.com/rsalabs/faq/html/questions.html. [1998, November 29].
6. Pfleeger, Charles. *Security in Computing, 2nd Ed.* Prentice Hall PTR. 1997.
7. The White House. *Encryption Export Policy.* [Online]. Available: http://www.bxa.doc.gov/Encryption/m961115.htm [1998, November 23].

Chapter 18
Security Awareness Program and Information Security Roles

Thomas R. Peltier

Development of security policies, standards, procedures, and guidelines is only the beginning of an effective information security program. A strong security architecture will be less effective if there is no process in place to make certain that the employees are aware of their rights and responsibilities. All too often, security professionals implement the "perfect" security program, and then forget to factor the customer into the formula. In order for the product to be as successful as possible, the information security professional must find a way to sell this product to the customers. An effective security awareness program could be the most cost-effective action management can take to protect its critical information assets.

Implementing an effective security awareness program will help all employees understand why they need to take information security seriously, what they will gain from its implementation, and how it will assist them in completing their assigned tasks. The process should begin at new-employee orientation and continue annually for all employees at all levels of the organization.

KEY GOALS OF AN INFORMATION SECURITY PROGRAM

For security professionals there are three key elements for any security program: *integrity, confidentiality*, and *availability*. Management wants information to reflect the real world and to have confidence in the information available to them so they can make informed business decisions. One of the goals of an effective security program is to ensure that the

0-8493-1248-5/02/$0.00+$1.50
© 2002 by CRC Press LLC

Exhibit 1. Fortune 500 Managers Rate the Importance of Information

Deloitte & Touche	Rate 1–3	Ernst & Young
1	Availability	2
3	Confidentiality	3
2	Integrity	1

1 = Most important, 2 = next, 3 = least

organization's information and its information processing resources are properly protected.

The goal of confidentiality extends beyond just keeping the bad guys out; it also ensures that those with a business need have access to the resources they need to get their jobs done. Confidentiality ensures that controls and reporting mechanisms are in place to detect problems or possible intrusions with speed and accuracy.

In a pair of recent surveys, the Big Four Accounting firms of Ernst & Young and Deloitte & Touche interviewed Fortune 500 managers and asked them to rank (in importance to them) information availability, confidentiality, and integrity. As can be seen from Exhibit 1, the managers felt that information needed to be available when they needed to have access to it. Implementing access control packages that rendered access difficult or overly restrictive is a detriment to the business process. Additionally, other managers felt that the information must reflect the real world. That is, controls should be in place to ensure that the information is correct. Preventing or controlling access to information that was incorrect was of little value to the enterprise.

An effective information security program must review the business objectives or the mission of the organization and ensure that these goals are met. Meeting the business objectives of the organization and understanding the customers' needs are what the goal of a security program is all about. An awareness program will reinforce these goals and will make the information security program more acceptable to the employee base.

KEY ELEMENTS OF A SECURITY PROGRAM

The starting point with any security program is the implementation of policies, standards, procedures, and guidelines. As important as the written word is in defining the goals and objectives of the program and the organization, the fact is that most employees will not have the time or the desire to read these important documents. An awareness program will ensure that the messages identified as important will get to all of those who need them.

Having individuals responsible for the implementation of the security program is another key element. To be most effective, the enterprise will need to have leadership at a minimum of two levels. There is a strong need to identify a senior level manager to assume the role of Corporate Information Officer (CIO). In a supporting capacity, an information security coordinator responsible for the day-to-day implementation of the information security program and reporting to the CIO is the second key player in the overall security program. Because a security program is more than just directions from the IT organization, each business unit should have its own coordinator responsible for the implementation of the program within that business unit.

The ability to classify information assets according to their relative value to the organization is the third key element in an information security program. Knowing what information an organization has that is sensitive will allow the informed implementation of controls and will allow the business units to use their limited resources where they will provide the most value. Understanding classification levels, employee responsibilities (owner, custodian, user), intellectual property requirements (copyright, trade secret, patent), and privacy rights is critical. An effective awareness program will have to take this most confusing message to all employees and provide training material for all nonemployees needing access to such resources.

The fourth key element is the implementation of the basic security concepts of separation of duties and rotation of assignments. *Separation of duties* — No single individual should have complete control of a business process or transaction from inception to completion. This control concept limits the potential error, opportunity, and temptation of personnel, and can best be defined as segregating incompatible functions (e.g., accounts payable activities with disbursement). The activities of a process are split among several people. Mistakes made by one person tend to be caught by the next person in the chain, thereby increasing information integrity. Unauthorized activities will be limited because no one person can complete a process without the knowledge and support of another. *Rotation of assignments* — Individuals should alternate various essential tasks involving business activities or transactions periodically. There are always some assignments that can cause an organization to be at risk unless proper controls are in place. To ensure that desk procedures are being followed and to provide for staff backup on essential functions, individuals should be assigned to different tasks at regular intervals.

One of the often-heard knocks against rotation of assignments is that it reduces job efficiency. However, it has been proven that an employee's interest declines over time when doing the same job for extended periods. Additionally, employees sometimes develop dangerous shortcuts when they have been in a job too long. By rotating assignments, the organization can compare the different ways of doing the task and determine where changes should be made.

The final element in an overall security program is an employee awareness program. Each of these elements will ensure that an organization meets its goals and objectives. The employee security awareness program will ensure that the program has a chance to succeed.

SECURITY AWARENESS PROGRAM GOALS

In order to be successful, a security awareness program must stress how security will support the enterprise's business objectives. Selling a security program requires the identification of business needs and how the security program supports those objectives. Employees want to know how to get things accomplished and to whom to turn for assistance. A strong awareness program will provide those important elements.

All personnel need to know and understand management's directives relating to the protection of information and information processing resources. One of the key objectives of a security awareness program is to ensure that all personnel get this message. It must be presented to new employees as well as existing employees. The program must also work with the Purchasing people to ensure that the message of security is presented to contract personnel. It is important to understand that contract personnel need to have this information, but it must be handled through their contract house. Work with Purchasing and Legal to establish the proper process.

All too often the security program fails because there is little or no follow-up. There is usually a big splash with all the fanfare that kicks off a new program. Unfortunately this is where many programs end. Employees have learned that if they wait long enough, the new programs will die from lack of interest or follow-up. It is very important to keep the message in front of the user community and to do this on a regular basis. To assist you in this process, there are a number of "Days" that can be used in conjunction with your awareness program.

- May 10 — International Emergency Response Day
- September 8 — Computer Virus Awareness Day
- November 30 — International Computer Security Day

Keeping the message in front of the user community is not enough. The message must make the issues of security alive and important to all employees. It is important to find ways to tie the message in with the goals and objectives of each department. Every department has different objectives and different security needs. The awareness message needs to reflect those concerns. We will discuss this in more detail shortly.

Find ways to make the message important to employees. When discussing controls, identify how they help protect the employee. When requiring employees to wear identification badges, many security programs tell the employees that this has been implemented to meet security objectives. What does this really mean? What the employees should be told is that the badges ensure that only authorized persons have access to the workplace. By doing this, the company is attempting to protect the employees. Finding out how controls support or protect the company's assets (including the employees) will make the security program message more acceptable.

Finally, a security program is meant to reduce losses associated with either intentional or accidental information disclosure, modification, destruction, and or denial of service. This can be accomplished by raising the consciousness of all employees regarding ways to protect information and information processing resources. By ensuring that these goals are met, the enterprise will be able to improve employee efficiency and productivity.

IDENTIFY CURRENT TRAINING NEEDS

To be successful, the awareness program should take into account the needs and current levels of training and understanding of the employees and management. There are five keys to establishing an effective awareness program. These are:

1. Assess the current level of computer usage.
2. Determine what the managers and employees want to learn.
3. Examine the level of receptiveness to the security program.
4. Map out how to gain acceptance.
5. Identify possible allies.

To assess the current level of computer usage, it will be necessary to ask questions of the audience. While sophisticated work stations may be found in employees' work areas, their understanding of what these devices can do may be very limited. Ask questions as to what the jobs are and how the tools available are used to support these tasks. It may come as a surprise to find that the most sophisticated computer is being used as a glorified 3270 terminal.

Be an effective listener. Listen to what the users are saying and scale the awareness and training sessions to meet their needs. In the awareness field, one size (or plan) does not fit everyone.

Work with the managers and supervisors to understand what their needs are and how the program can help them. It will become necessary for you to understand the language of the business units and to interpret their needs. Once you have an understanding, you will be able to modify the program to meet these special needs. No single awareness program will work for every business unit. There must be alterations and a willingness to accept suggestions from nonsecurity personnel.

Identify the level of receptiveness to the security program. Find out what is accepted and what is meeting resistance. Examine the areas of noncompliance and try to find ways to alter the program if at all possible. Do not change fundamental information security precepts just to gain unanimous acceptance; this is an unattainable goal. Make the program meet the greater good of the enterprise and then work with pockets of resistance to lessen the impact.

The best way to gain acceptance is to make your employees and managers partners in the security process. Never submit a new control or policy to management without sitting down with them individually and reviewing the objectives. This will require you to do your homework and to understand the business process in each department. It will be important to know the peak periods of activity in the department and what the manager's concerns are. When meeting with the managers, be sure to listen to their concerns and be prepared to ask for their suggestions on how to improve the program. Remember the key here is to partner with your audience.

Finally, look for possible allies. Find out what managers support the objectives of the security program and identify those who have the respect of their peers. This means that it will be necessary to expand the area of support beyond physical security and the audit staff. Seek out business managers who have a vested interest in seeing this program succeed. Use their support to springboard the program to acceptance.

A key point in this entire process is to never refer to the security program or the awareness campaign as "my program." The enterprise has identified the need for security, and you and your group are acting as the catalysts for moving the program forward. When discussing the program with employees and managers, it will be beneficial to refer to it as "their program" or "our program." Make them feel that they are key stakeholders in this process.

In a presentation used to introduce the security concept to the organization, it may be beneficial to say something like:

> Just as steps have been to taken to ensure the safety of the employees in the workplace, the organization is now asking that the employees work to protect the second most important enterprise asset — information. If the organization fails to protect its information from unauthorized access, modification, disclosure, or destruction, the organization faces the prospect of loss of customer confidence, competitive advantage, and possibly jobs. All employees must accept the need and responsibility to protect our property and assets.

Involve the user community and accept their comments whenever possible. Make information security their program. Use what they identify as important in the awareness program. By having them involved, the program truly becomes theirs and they are more willing to accept and internalize the process.

SECURITY AWARENESS PROGRAM DEVELOPMENT

Not everyone needs the same degree or type of information security awareness to do their jobs. An awareness program that distinguishes between groups of people and presents only information that is relevant to that particular audience will have the best results. Segmenting the audiences by job function, familiarity with systems, or some other category can improve the effectiveness of the security awareness and acceptance program. The purpose of segmenting audiences is to give the message the best possible chance of success. There are many ways in to segment the user community. Some of the more common methods are provided for you here.

- *Level of awareness* — Employees may be divided up based on their current level of awareness of the information security objectives. One method of determining levels of awareness is to conduct a "walkabout." A walkabout is conducted after normal working hours and looks for certain key indicators. Look for just five key indicators:
  1. Offices locked
  2. Desks and cabinets locked
  3. Work stations secured
  4. Information secured
  5. Recording media (diskettes, tapes, CDs, cassettes, etc.) secured
- *Job category* — Personnel may be grouped according to their job functions or titles:
  1. Senior managers (including officers and directors)
  2. Middle management
  3. Line supervision
  4. Employees
  5. Others
- *Specific job function* — Employees and personnel may be grouped according to:
  1. Service providers
  2. Information owners
  3. Users
- *Information processing knowledge* — As discussed above, not every employee has the same level of knowledge on how computers work. A security message for technical support personnel may be very different from that for data entry clerks. Senior management may have a very different level of computer skills than their office administrator.

- *Technology, system, or application used* — To avoid "religious wars," it may be prudent to segment the audience based on the technology used. Mac users and users of Intel-based systems often have differing views, as do MVS users and UNIX users. The message may reach the audience faster if the technology used is considered.

Once the audience has been segmented, it will be necessary to establish the roles expected of the employees. These roles may include information owners, custodians of the data and systems, and general users. For all messages it will be necessary to employ the KISS process; that is, Keep It Simple, Sweetie. Inform the audience, but try to stay away from commandments or directives. Discuss the goals and objectives using real-world scenarios. Whenever possible, avoid quoting policies, procedures, standards, or guidelines.

Policies and procedures are boring, and if employees want more information, they can access the documents on the organization intranet. If you feel that you must resort to this method, you have missed the most important tenet of awareness: to identify the business reason *why*. Never tell employees that something is being implemented to "be in compliance with audit requirements." This is, at best, a cop out and fails to explain in business terms why something is needed.

METHODS USED TO CONVEY THE AWARENESS MESSAGE

How do people learn and where do people obtain their information? These are two very important questions to understand when developing an information security awareness program. Each one is different. If we were implementing a training program, we would be able to select from three basic methods of training:

1. Buy a book and read about the subject.
2. Watch a video on the subject.
3. Ask someone to show you how.

For most employees, the third method is best for training. They like the hands-on approach and want to have someone there to answer their questions. With security awareness, the process is a little different. According to findings reported in *USA Today*, over 90 percent of Americans obtain their news from television or radio. To make an awareness program work, it will be necessary to tap into that model.

There are a number of different ways to get the message out to the user community. The key is to make the message stimulating to the senses of the audience. This can be accomplished by using posters, pictures, and videos. Because so many of our employees use television as their primary source of information, it is important to use videos to reinforce the message. The use of videos will serve several purposes.

With the advent of the news-magazine format so popular in television today, our employees are already conditioned to accept the information presented as factual. This allows us to use the media to present the messages we consider important. Because the audience accepts material presented in this format, the use of videos allows us to bring in an informed outsider to present the message. Many times our message fails because the audience knows the messenger. Being a fellow worker, our credibility may be questioned. A video provides an expert on the subject.

There are a number of organizations, such as Commonwealth Films and Mediamix Productions, that offer computer and information security videos. You might want to consider having a senior executive videotape a message that can be run at the beginning of the other video. Costs for creating a quality in-house video can be prohibitive. A 20-minute video that is more than just "talking heads" can run $90,000 to $100,000. Check out the quality and messages of the vendors discussed later in this chapter.

An effective program will also take advantage of brochures, newsletters, or booklets. In all cases, the effectiveness of the medium will depend on how well it is created and how succinct the message is. One major problem with newsletters is finding enough material to fill the pages each time you want to go to print. One way to present a quality newsletter is to look for vendors to provide such material. The Computer Security Institute offers a document titled *Frontline*. This newsletter is researched and written every quarter by CSI's own editorial staff. It provides the space for a column written by your organization to provide information pertinent for your organization. Once the materials are ready, CSI sends out either camera-ready or PDF format versions of the newsletter. The customer is then authorized to make unlimited copies.

As we discussed above, many organizations are requiring business units to name information protection coordinators. One of the tasks of these coordinators is to present awareness sessions for their organizations. An effective way to get a consistent message out is to "train the trainers." Create a security awareness presentation and then bring in the coordinators to train them in presenting the corporate message to their user community. This will ensure that the message presented meets the needs of each organization and that they view the program as theirs.

It will be necessary to identify those employees who have not attended awareness training. By having some form of sign-in or other recording mechanism, the program will be assured of reaching most of the employees. By having the coordinator submit annual reports on the number of employees trained, the enterprise will have a degree of comfort in meeting its goals and objectives.

PRESENTATION KEY ELEMENTS

While every organization has its own style and method for training, it might help to review some important issues when creating an awareness program. One very important item to keep in mind is that the topic of information security is very broad. Do not get overwhelmed with the prospect of providing information on every facet of information security in one meeting. Remember the old adage, "How do you eat an elephant? One bite at a time."

Prioritize your message for the employees. Start small and build on the program. Remember you are going to have many opportunities to present your messages. Identify where to begin, present the message, reinforce the message, and then build to the next objective. Keep the training session as brief as possible. It is normally recommended to limit these sessions to no more than 50 minutes. There are a number of reasons for this: biology (you can only hold coffee for so long), attention spans, and productive work needs. Start with an attention-grabbing piece and then follow up with additional information.

Tailor the presentations to the vocabulary and skill of the audience. Know to whom you are talking and provide them with information they can understand. This will not be a formal doctoral presentation. The awareness session must take into account the audience and the culture of the organization. Understand the needs, knowledge, and jobs of the attendees. Stress the positive and business side of security — protecting the assets of the organization. Provide the audience with a reminder (booklet, brochure, or trinket) of the objectives of the program.

TYPICAL PRESENTATION FORMAT

In a program that hopes to modify behavior, the three keys are: tell them what you are going to say; say it; and then remind them of what you said. A typical agenda appears in Exhibit 2.

Start with an introduction of what information security is about and how it will impact their business units and departments. Follow with a video that will reinforce the message and present the audience with an external expert supporting the corporate message. Discuss any methods that will be employed to monitor compliance to the program and provide the audience with the rationale for the compliance checking. Provide them with a time for questions and ensure that every question either gets an answer or is recorded and the answer provided as soon as possible. Finally, give them some item that will reinforce the message.

Information Security Awareness
Date
Time
Place

Agenda:

Introduction	**CIO**
Goals and Objectives	**ISSO**
Video	
Questions/Answer	**All**
Next Steps	**ISSO**

Exhibit 2. Typical Security Awareness Meeting Agenda

WHEN TO DO AWARENESS

Any awareness program must be scheduled around the work patterns of the audience. Take into account busy periods for the various departments and make certain that the sessions do not impact their peak periods. The best times for having these sessions is in the morning on Tuesday, Wednesday, and Thursday. A meeting first-thing Monday morning will impact those trying to get the week's work started. Having the session on Friday afternoon will not be as productive as you would like. Scheduling anything right after lunch is always a worry. The human physiological clock is at its lowest productivity level right after lunch. If you turn out the lights to show a movie, the snoring may drown out the audio. Also, schedule sessions during off-shift hours. Second- and third-shift employees should have the opportunity to view the message during their work hours just as those on the day shift do.

SENIOR MANAGEMENT PRESENTATIONS

While most other sessions will last about an hour, senior management has less time, even for issues as important as this. Prepare a special brief, concise presentation plus in-depth supporting documents. Unlike other presentations, senior management often does not want the "dog and pony show." They may not even want presentation foils to be used. They prefer that you sit with them for a few minutes and discuss the program and how it will help them meet their business objectives. Quickly explain the purpose of the program, identify any problem areas and what solutions you propose. Suggest a plan of action. Do not go to them with problems for which you do not have a solution. Do not give them a number of solutions and ask them to choose. You are their expert and they are expecting you to come to them with your informed opinion on how the organization should move forward.

Exhibit 3. Three Groups

Group	Best Techniques	Best Approach	Expected Results
Senior Management	Cost justification Industry comparison Audit report Risk analysis	Presentation Video Violation reports	Funding Support

Line Supervisors	Demonstrate job performance
	  benefits
	Perform security reviews
		Presentation
		Circulate news
		  articles
		Video
			Support
			Resource help
			Adherence

Users	Sign responsibility statements Policies and procedures	Presentation Newsletters Video	Adherence Support

THREE TYPES OF PRESENTATIONS (EXHIBIT 3)

Senior management will be expecting a sound, rational approach to information security. They will be interested in the overall cost of implementing the policies and procedures and how this program stacks up against others in the industry. A key concern will be how their policies and procedures will be viewed by the audit staff and that the security program will give them an acceptable level of risk.

Line supervisors are focused on getting their job done. They will not be interested in anything that appears to slow down their already tight schedule. To win them over, it will be necessary to demonstrate how the new controls will improve their job performance process. As we have been stressing since the beginning, the goal of security is to assist management in meeting the business objectives or mission. It will be self-defeating to tell supervisors that the new policies are being implemented to allow the company to be in compliance with audit requirements. This is not the reason to do anything, and a supervisor will find this reason useless. Stress how the new process will give the employees the tools they need (access to information and systems) in a timely and efficient manner. Show them where the problem-resolution process is and who to call if there are any problems with the new process.

Employees are going to be skeptical. They have been through so many company initiatives that they have learned to wait. If they wait long enough and do nothing new, the initiative will generally die on its own. It will be necessary to build employees' awareness of the information security policies and procedures. Identify what is expected of them and how it will assist them in gaining access to the information and systems they need to complete their tasks. Point out that by protecting access to information, they can have a reasonable level of assurance (remember, never use absolutes) that their information assets will be protected from unauthorized access, modification, disclosure, or destruction.

The type of approach chosen will be based on whether your organization has an information security program in place and how active it is. For those organizations with no information security program, it will be necessary to convince management and employees of its importance. For organizations with an existing or outdated program, the key will be convincing management and employees that there is a need for change.

THE INFORMATION SECURITY MESSAGE

The employees need to know that information is an important enterprise asset and is the property of the organization. All employees have a responsibility to ensure that this asset, like all others, must be protected and used to support management-approved business activities. To assist them in this process, employees must be made aware of the possible threats and what can be done to combat those threats. The scope of the program must be identified. Is the program dealing only with computer-held data or does it reach to all information wherever it resides? Make sure the employees know the total scope of the program. Enlist their support in protecting this asset. The mission and business of the enterprise may depend on it.

INFORMATION SECURITY SELF-ASSESSMENT

Each organization will have to develop a process by which to measure the compliance level of the information security program. As part of the awareness process, staff should be made aware of the compliance process. Included for you here is an example of how an organization might evaluate the level of information security within a department or throughout the enterprise.

INFORMATION PROTECTION PROGRAM AND ADMINISTRATION ASSESSMENT QUESTIONNAIRE

Rating scale:

1 = Completed
2 = Being implemented
3 = In development
4 = Under discussion
5 = Haven't begun

BUSINESS ORGANIZATION ISSUES

Factors	Rating/Value 1 2 3 4 5
A. ADMINISTRATION	
1. A Corporate Information Officer (CIO) or equivalent level of authority has been named and is responsible for implementing and maintaining an effective IP program.	1 2 3 4 5
2. An individual has been designated as the organization information protection coordinator (OIPC) and has been assigned overall responsibility for the IP program.	1 2 3 4 5
3. The OIPC reports directly to the CIO or equivalent.	1 2 3 4 5
4. IP is identified as a separate and distinct budget item (minimally 1 to 3 percent of the overall ISO budget).	1 2 3 4 5
5. Senior management is aware of the business need for an effective program and is committed to its success.	1 2 3 4 5
6. Each business unit, department, agency, etc., has designated an individual responsible for implementing the IP program for the organization.	1 2 3 4 5
B. PROGRAM	
1. The IP program supports the business objectives or mission statement of the enterprise.	1 2 3 4 5
2. An enterprise-wide IP policy has been implemented.	1 2 3 4 5
3. The IP program is an integral element of the enterprise's overall management practices.	1 2 3 4 5
4. A formal risk analysis process has been implemented to assist management in making informed business decisions.	1 2 3 4 5
5. Purchase and implementation of IP countermeasures are based on cost/benefit analysis utilizing risk analysis input.	1 2 3 4 5
6. The IP program is integrated into a variety of areas both inside and outside the "computer security" field.	1 2 3 4 5
7. Comprehensive information-protection policies, procedures, standards, and guidelines have been created and disseminated to all employees and appropriate third parties.	1 2 3 4 5
8. An ongoing IP awareness program has been implemented for all employees.	1 2 3 4 5
9. A positive, proactive relationship between IP and audit has been established and is actively cultivated.	1 2 3 4 5
C. COMPLIANCE	
1. Employees are made aware that their data processing activities may be monitored.	1 2 3 4 5
2. An effective program to monitor IP program-related activities has been implemented.	1 2 3 4 5
3. Employee compliance with IP-related issues is a performance appraisal element.	1 2 3 4 5
4. The ITD Project Team members have access to individuals who have leading-edge hardware/software expertise to help the Project Team, as needed.	1 2 3 4 5

5. The application development methodology addresses IP   1 2 3 4 5
requirements during all phases, including the initiation or
analysis (first) phase.
6. The IP program is reviewed annually and modified where   1 2 3 4 5
necessary.

OTHER FACTORS

1.   1 2 3 4 5

2.   1 2 3 4 5

3.   1 2 3 4 5

TOTAL SCORE

Interpreting the Total Score: Use this table of risk assessment questionnaire score ranges to assess resolution urgency and related actions.

If the Score Is...	And...	The Assessment Rate is ...	Actions Might Include...
21 to 32	• Most activities have been implemented • Most employees are aware of the program	Superior	• Annual reviews and reports to management • Annual recognition days (Computer Security Awareness Day) • Team recognition may be appropriate!
32 to 41	• Many activities have been implemented • Many employees are aware of the program and its objectives	Excellent	• Formal action plan must be implemented • Obtain appropriate sponsorship • Obtain senior management commitment
42 to 62	• Some activities are under development • An IP team has been identified	Solid	• Identify IP program goals • Identify management sponsor • Implement IP policy
63 to 83	• There is a plan to begin planning • Some benchmarking has begun	Low	• Identify roles and responsibilities • Conduct formal risk analysis
84 to 105	• Policies, standards, procedures are missing or not implemented • Management and employees are unaware of the need for a program	Poor	• Conduct risk assessment • Prioritize program elements • Obtain budget commitment • Identify OIPC

CONCLUSION

Information security is more than just policies, standards, procedures, and guidelines. It is more than audit comments and requirements. It is a cultural change for most employees. Before employees can be required to comply with a security program, they first must become aware of the program. Awareness is an ongoing program that employees must have contact with on at least an annual basis.

Information security awareness does not require huge cash outlays. It does require time and proper project management. It also requires defining information security roles and responsibilities. Keep the message in front of the employees. Use different methods and means. Bring in outside speakers whenever possible, and use videos to your best advantage.

Chapter 19
Information Security Standards: Deluge and Dearth

Ralph Spencer Poore

Avalanche! With new information doubling every five years (soon to be every two and a half years!), information security professionals may find themselves buried in an information avalanche. Where a new security standard in the financial services area could, in the past, safely take three to five years in the making, we now frown when it takes two years. Where we would, historically, rarely work on even two standards in parallel, we now must work on a dozen. Prior to 1986, the Internet Engineering Task Force (IETF) did not exist. Today, we have thousands of Requests for Comment (RFC) documents, many of which are on the IETF standards track. With the American National Standards Institute (ANSI) accredited standards bodies, with the International Standards Organization (ISO), with the International Telecommunications Union (ITU), and other national and international standards bodies, the information security professional faces hundreds of security- or privacy-related standards, guidelines, or regulatory initiatives each year.

Few of us have the luxury of attending all the meetings, reviewing all of the documents, and voting on all of these initiatives. Even with my focus narrowed to cryptographic issues, I invest more than 250 hours each year just to standards development and review. New standards include Public Key Cryptography for the Financial Services Industry: The Elliptic Curve Digital Signature Algorithm (ECDSA) (X9.62), Cryptographic Message Syntax (X9.73), Attribute Certificates (X9.45), ISO Retail Message format changes (ISO 8583), along with Banking–Certificate Management Part 1: Public Key Certificates (ISO WD 15782-1) and the Common Criteria (ISO/IEC 15408). Other initiatives include the Generally Accepted System Security Principles (GASSP), the American Institute of Certified Public Accountants'

0-8493-1248-5/02/$0.00+$1.50
© 2002 by CRC Press LLC

(AICPA) WebTrust™, the OCC's new privacy rules... well, the list is nearly endless. Our field is broad and its harvest immense.

So there would seem to be an avalanche of standards. Yet our industry has almost no professional standards (except, perhaps, a few codes of conduct associated with membership in specific organizations). We also lack a single organization that represents the standards arena for information security standards (e.g., Financial Services has X9 whose secretariat is the American Bankers Association. The accounting profession has the AICPA. Medical doctors have the American Medical Association. Lawyers have the American Bar Association).

This is not to denigrate the fine work of the International Information Systems Security Certification Consortium [(ISC)^2] whose CISSP, Common Body of Knowledge (CBK), and training efforts have made giant strides for our profession. Nor do I minimize the work of the Information Systems Security Association (ISSA) and its local chapters. Nonetheless, no group is currently recognized as the authority (i.e., standards secretariat) for our profession (at least within the United States). The absence of such coordination results in a patchwork of security, risk management, and privacy standards, generally along technology or business-application lines. Additionally, the people who work on the myriad of standards bodies attempting to produce these standards rarely have information security as their core competency. We should not be surprised (and I for one am not) that they must revisit many of these standards when they fail in practice.

Some argue that information security is application dependent, that standards must proceed from an industry point of view. Others might point to technology standards and press the case that information security is platform dependent. While both arguments have merit, the existence of both a CBK and the GASSP support my contention that universal information security standards are feasible even if exceptions are inevitable. Generalized information security standards (e.g., the United Kingdom's BS 7799) exist.

RECOGNIZED, AUTHORITATIVE STANDARDS

One of the many important uses of recognized, authoritative standards is found in the area of risk mitigation, especially with regard to litigation. Relying on expert witnesses in the absence of authoritative standards leads to confused juries, judges, and even confused litigants and may result in bad case law (which may become *de facto* standards!). Here, however, is the crux of the matter. Information security standards issue forth from a variety of sources with little to no coordination. This permits "standards shopping" where an organization seeks "standards" that support their *status quo* or their intended course of action. While this may provide an organization with some cover or risk mitigation, selecting from among potentially conflicting standards ultimately leads to second-guessing (e.g., why did you choose X and not Y?). Where an organization has documented well-considered arguments answering why it chose the standards it selected, the process may even strengthen its case. However, the process may also support the conclusion that the choices were motivated by lack of management support (e.g., apathy), insufficient research (e.g., ignorance), budgetary constraints (e.g., corporate greed), or poor planning (e.g., "quick and dirty"). The latter finding is most likely the conclusion an adversary in court would attempt to imply.

COMPUTER FORENSICS AND TESTIMONY

With a plethora of disjointed — if not directly conflicting — standards, standards compliance becomes a Picassoesque montage: chaotic caricatures vaguely representing criteria against which audits and evidential matters struggle for footing. While we may, at the least, prove the efficacy of a technical standard through formal testing — for example, demonstrating its interoperability — many information security objectives presume upon the exists of standards not in evidence. Three simple examples should suffice to illustrate this point. First, although few dispute the theory of stratification under which we specify some data for greater protection than other data, to what objective, recognized body of standards would the information security practitioner turn? Second, professionals rely on a trade vocabulary. To the extent that important terms lack a common understanding within the profession, communication among members of the profession is impeded. We do not lack glossaries posted by various organizations attempting to standardize our understanding — (see for example:

- http://csrc.nist.gov/publications/-secpubs/rainbow/tg004.txt
- http://www.setsolutions.com/-security.htm
- http://www.sans.org/newlook/-resources/glossary.htm
- the Technical Guide for ABA/ASC X9 Standards Definitions, Acronyms and Symbols (TR-1–2000) available through www.x9.org.

Important terms, however, remain poorly defined and used without specificity. "Integrity" and "privacy" are two examples.

Those in my readership who have had the privilege of hearing Donn Parker present on the subject of information integrity or who have read one or more of his articles on the subject may have first believed that they understood what an information security practitioner meant when he used the term "integrity" only to discover their naïveté. The term "privacy" may face the same fate as "virtual" and "inflammable" both of which are now commonly used as antonyms of their original meanings (i.e., "virtual" originally meant "true, real" and "inflammable" originally meant "resistant to fire, not subject to flame"). I read articles about digital certificates and how their use ensures privacy. This notwithstanding the amount of private data many certificates contain (e.g., gender, date of birth, name, company name, or affiliation) and the purpose of strong authentication (and therefore identification) provided through the proper use of digital certificates.

I also review products that allege privacy protection for data when they provide for the assured release of the data to third parties over which the product can exercise no control. If "privacy" now means giving our identity and related personal information to third parties with a high degree of assurance, then perhaps I misunderstood the entries in my Random House dictionary.

Third, we have standards for evaluating security products (although such standards often have conflicting requirements); however, we have little guidance on when to require what level of security product. The government does a somewhat better job — at least within areas that process classified data — in specifying product security levels. Nevertheless, outside of government, the information security practitioner has little guidance.

The Common Criteria (ISO/EC 15408:1999) provides for information security evaluation levels 1 through 7. A financial institution should run its applications on an operating system platform that meets what level? Your human resources application software should meet what level?

Although an oversimplification, these two rhetorical questions illustrate the dearth of practical guidance. Similarly, a vendor may have its cryptographic products evaluated under the Federal Information Processing Standards (FIPS) 140-1 (possibly 140-2 by publication date). When should a company require a level-4 device instead of a level-3 or even level-2 device?

Clearly, we have many questions that information security standards could address. When computer forensics and evidential processes can rely on these answers, we face fewer problems, especially when we must testify with regard to issues of negligence. Objective criteria created through a consensus standards process better serve forensic and evidential processes.

INFORMATION SECURITY PRACTITIONERS WITHOUT STANDARDS

Without standards that provide risk-based guidance (or other objective[1] criteria), information security practitioners make decisions based on factors that often prove opaque to their management. These factors may include ignorance, bias, perceived constraints, misplaced reliance, and personal motives.

Ignorance

The practitioner may lack a sufficient depth or breadth of experience on which to base the security judgment. While we all have limited knowledge, we are not equally adept at knowing when we do not know. We do not all have timely access to information security expertise and may feel pressured to "know" even when we do not. Standards provide a measure of protection against our ignorance — unless, of course, we are ignorant of the standards!

Bias

The practitioner may favor one vendor over another without regard to the merits of their respective products. If you know only one vendor, this probably reflects the previously discussed ignorance instead of bias. However, when we do not have objective criteria on which we may base our decisions, other factors may take precedence. The vendor that remembers your favorite sports event or takes you to lunch most often could have the appropriate product, but it does not logically follow that it does.

Perceived Constraints

The practitioner may perceive budget, time, political, or other constraints and act as if these constraints constitute criteria without confirming this with management. Standards can help the practitioner address otherwise assumed limitations by allowing the practitioner to frame the discussion in terms of standards compliance. If the limitations are real, then management — and not the information security practitioner — should make the risk-acceptance decision. In my experience, we often assume limitations that management would disavow in the event of a security failure. Best practice is to document these constraints. Your ability to test these constraints with management, however, improves as your ability to cite independent authority improves. For many organizations, the least you can do is the least you can get away with doing.

Misplaced Reliance

Without authoritative sources, the practitioner may attempt to rely on anecdotal information. The pressure to seek an independent authority may cause some to accept representations of industry behavior as *de facto* standards. This may place the reputation of the information security practitioner in jeopardy. Intentional hoax and misinformation abound. Even accurate information on industry behavior may prove to be an unworthy *de facto* standard, a standard under which your employer receives no comfort. For an historic example of this, you should review the *T. J. Hooper* case (53 F.2d 107–109). In that early 1900s case, two tugboats pulling an ore barge off the Atlantic coast were caught in a storm that came up suddenly. The tugboats sank, and the crew was lost. The shipping company attempted unsuccessfully to argue that it had met industry standards, which did not require it to have as a safeguard a weather radio. The court noted that such a safeguard would have permitted timely warning, thus giving the captain an opportunity to seek a safe harbor. The court found that not having such a safeguard could not be justified based on the *de facto* standard that such ships did not have radios.[2] To avoid misplaced reliance, whether on anecdotal or unverifiable "standards," we need authoritative standards on which we may rely.

Personal Motives

While not casting aspersions on members of my own profession, I fear we may occasionally be perceived by management as building empires or succumbing to other personal motives when we cannot provide independent justification for our security selections. Authoritative standards, especially when coordinated to avoid being a smorgasbord of conflicting standards, remove personal motives from the mix.

Professional Standards

The Association of Independent Certified Public Accountants' *Code of Professional Conduct* (http://www.aicpa.org/about/code/index.htm) and the American Bar Association's *Model Rules of Professional Conduct* (http://www.americanbar.org/cpr/pubs/561-0142.html) are much more than codes of ethics. They represent systems of professional discipline with mechanisms for ongoing guidance. Two factors generally used to define a profession are

1. A common body of knowledge (we may have this)
2. An ability to police itself

For those holding either the CISSP or the CISA, nascent sets of professional standards and associated review processes are emerging. However, we have much distance to cover between a page of code of conduct and useful professional standards with an associated body of interpretations.

CONCLUSION

Without a means for the coordination of standards, the information security practitioner may find little practical difference between a dearth of standards and a deluge of standards. In the former case, the information security practitioner must rely on his own judgment, because he is unable to reference an appropriate standard. In the latter case, he must rely on his own judgment, because he must choose among conflicting standards. In either case, he places his employer at risk.

To the extent that the information security practitioner is qualified to make expert information security judgments — and therefore the employer might rightly assert the reasonableness of its reliance thereupon — the information security professional assumes the duties and liabilities of an expert. Perhaps the CISSP designation constitutes a standard criterion for the claim of information security expert. If so, I argue that CISSP designees have a vested interest in establishing professional standards similar to the interest that CPA designees had (i.e., to provide the courts and the public with accountability criteria lest they set their own criteria to the detriment of the CISSP designees). Further, we all have a stake in consensus information security standards on which we may prudently rely. For the information security professional, we reduce our professional exposure by reducing the circumstances under which we must act as experts. For our employers, we reduce their risk by basing our judgments on applicable standards. As stakeholders, we need to encourage participation in standards development.

Notes

1. Or, if an objective criterion seems too idealistic, then at least a criterion developed through consensus that supports overt judgments (i.e., clear documentation of the basis on which risk or security judgments were made).
2. The standard of seaworthiness is not dependent on statutory enactment, but changes with advancing knowledge, experience, and changed appliances of navigation: "...that the two tugs [*T. J. Hooper* and *Montrose*] were unseaworthy in not having effective radio sets, capable of receiving the forecasts of unfavorable weather broadcast along the coast...."

Chapter 20
The Role of the Chief Medical Information Officer

Victor S. Dorodny

The chief medical information officer (CMIO) functions in a multi-dimensional, convergent environment defined by the clinical, financial, business, and information technology (IT) needs of the healthcare organization, without any particular aspect being more important than the other, and with a high degree of interdependency between them.

Because most healthcare information systems directly or indirectly affect clinical processes, some healthcare organizations are appointing physicians to oversee information technology initiatives. Increasingly, executives at these provider organizations believe that having a physician at the helm of automation plans is critical for success. In the past these physician/information technology specialists often were referred to by such titles as medical director of clinical information systems, director of medical (health) informatics, and medical director of computer services (systems). Today, physician leaders in such positions usually bear the title of chief medical information officer (CMIO). The functional description of the CMIO is that of a dedicated health "informatician," an emerging specialty in healthcare, which has not to date been definitively defined. For the purposes of this chapter, an informatician is an expert in applications of information within the integrated and secure clinical and business environments, encompassing the following responsibilities: gathering, monitoring, summarizing, merging and collating, deposition, release and exchange, transmission, storage and retrieval, analysis, and dissemination of information.[1]

These physicians usually head committees that define systems requirements and select information systems that will support outcomes research; develop, implement and monitor clinical protocols; enable clinicians to access patient information at the point of care; and many others.

0-8493-1248-5/02/$0.00+$1.50
© 2002 by CRC Press LLC

BUSINESS ORGANIZATION ISSUES

The functional goal of CMIO participation on executive and user level committees is to better integrate physicians into the delivery system to achieve lower cost and improve quality of care. The CMIO achieves this goal by helping physicians pinpoint their needs and desires and then working to educate them about information technology. The CMIO searches for, collects, processes, and understands the information needs of the enterprise so that these needs can be effectively communicated to all of the stakeholders, and acts as catalyst for the processes that need to be put in place and activated for the economic survival of the enterprise.

EXECUTIVE AND USER FUNCTIONS OF THE CMIO

On executive level information services committees, the CMIO proactively participates in the performance of multiple functions:[2]

- Spearheads development of an IS strategic plan for the organization based on business strategy and goals
- Monitors the IS strategic plan in support of the organization's strategic and business plans; prioritizes projects and leads revisions as required
- Reviews and approves IS budgets
- Oversees progress of IS strategic plan implementation and overall status of specific application and technology implementations
- Communicates the IS strategic plan and the plan's implementation status to the board
- Approves IS contingency funding and other specific projects not planned
- Communicates the IS strategic plan and directives across the organization
- Approves overall corporation-defined IS policies and procedures
- Ensures the IS plan reflects the business plan of the organization on an ongoing basis

Having CMIOs chair the user-level committees helps ensure "buy-in" from the organization's stakeholders, which is critical to the success of clinical information initiatives. Their participation also promotes coordination of the multifaceted activities of the user level committee:[2]

- Establishes user groups regarding specific IS projects based on the IS plan and scheduled implementation
- Has a working knowledge of business plan and understanding of the IS plan linkage
- Provides direction and recommendations for project implementation
- Monitors IS project implementation against established schedule
- Establishes task forces as required to support research into issues regarding project implementation

- Serves as mediation group for interdepartmental IS implementations
- Provides recommendations to the executive committee as needed for specific projects
- Reviews corporationwide IS policies/procedures and makes recommendations for approval to executive committee
- Evaluates and makes recommendations concerning IS issues and proposals that are directed by either the executive committee or recommended by the user group at large

The CMIO relies heavily on expectation and "wish" management and strives to set reasonable, achievable goals without hindering enthusiasm for information systems. For instance, the chief executive officer (CEO) wishes to be freed from problems related to the Joint Commission on Accreditation of Healthcare Organizations (JCAHO) and physicians and nurses. The chief financial officer wishes problems would go away without capital expenditure. The CIO wants his or her IS problems to evaporate and, additionally, to have an unlimited budget to make it happen quickly so the CEO will stay happy. The CIO wishes medical personnel would become computer literate and use what they have without breaking it.

Generally, physicians and nurses are not concerned with the problems of the CEO or how much it is going to cost; they just wish the CIO would come up with something that is healthcare friendly. Many physicians and CIOs prefer a part-time practicing physician for these positions because of the perception of better credibility with medical staff than an administrative physician. The rationale is that the CMIO sets an example, showing other clinicians that the person imposing the frequently unwelcome changes is being equally affected by them. Or, in the lexicon of managed care, the CMIO is "sharing risk" with providers regarding the implementation of IS.

When a healthcare organization reaches a critical mass, either through marketshare growth, mergers and acquisitions, or both, it requires a dedicated (nonpracticing) CMIO. When these physicians stop practicing, they may, arguably, lose some credibility, but the vast clinical and human interaction experience they bring to the job more than offsets the potential loss. It is this experience that enables them to understand and to communicate with all of the stakeholders in a healthcare organization. The CMIO fosters the ability of a healthcare organization to deal with the changing business environment and reconfigure itself when faced with amplifying levels of disturbance. A physician with strong interpersonal and communications skills and an inquisitive mind — one who is constantly searching for ways information systems can improve physicians' abilities to practice medicine as well as their quality of life — will do well regardless whether he or she is an administrative or a practicing physician.

A word about the relevance of technical expertise. The level of computer literacy ("geekiness") is not a crucial factor in being able to obtain a position as CMIO. However, intensive on-the-job training would have to take place to enable the CMIO to perform his or her dual (clinical and technological) functions. The technical experience is helpful, especially in the areas of evaluating vendors' products in the function of defining and selecting systems. It is less relevant in their larger, strategic role in an organization.

According to William Bria, M.D., who in 1997 co-founded the Association of Medical Directors of Information Systems (AMDIS), the CMIO is becoming a leader in defining medical information and its uses by the healthcare organization rather than defining the enabling systems.[3] The reason for this forward way of thinking is the prevalence of proven technologies available to the CMIO for implementation in the organization. Dr. Richard Kremsdorf, chief of medical informatics at Catholic Healthcare West, shares Dr. Bria's point of view and believes that the primary responsibility of the CMIO is defining the applications of IT to the care processes of an entire delivery system.[3]

CHALLENGES FOR HEALTHCARE ORGANIZATIONS — YOU CAN MANAGE THINGS YOU CANNOT MEASURE!

Recent surveys of healthcare organizations and fellows of the Healthcare Information and Management Systems Society (HIMSS) estimate that between the year 2000 and year 2005, $200 billion will be spent by healthcare organizations on health information systems. Such unprecedented expenditures are driven by the healthcare industry's shift from medical risk/benefit decision-making to cost/benefit decision-making processes. In the face of continued distress in the managed care industry, healthcare organizations' reliance on information technology (IT) to reduce redundancy and inefficiency of operations is ever increasing. The implementation of IT has become the Achilles heel of many managed care organizations. Oxford Health Plan, Pacificare, and Kaiser — in trying to explain their collective half billion dollars in losses last year — have all pointed an accusing finger at their abortive efforts to modernize their information systems infrastructure.

Healthcare organizations are considering or embarking on countless initiatives to improve business office functions (billing, collection, coding, and patient registration); to integrate financial and clinical information (both transactional and analytical) into computer-based patient records that will be available across the enterprise; and to upgrade medical documentation (and inventory control) through handheld data entry devices (bar coding) (see Exhibit 1). Many of these organizations are introducing productivity-based co-pay, monitoring and controlling utilization, facilitating physicians' vacations and continued medical education rules, etc. And

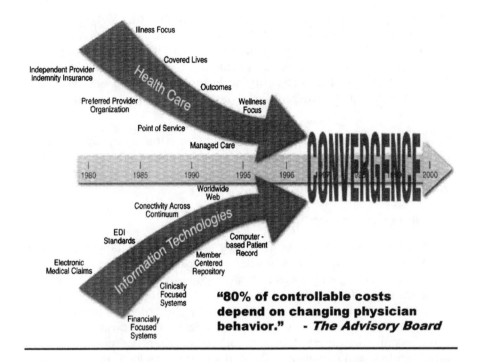

Exhibit 1.   Convergence of Healthcare and Information Technologies

they are promoting adherence to and monitoring compliance with disease management protocols, measuring outcomes (clinical and financial) against national and regional benchmarks.

Why are these healthcare organizations so involved? What are they striving for? They hope to be able to identify and analyze outliers and implement meaningful quality improvement methodologies to reduce variability. Informed decisions need to be based on real data and not on actuarial assumptions whether to accept the discounts on fee-for-service or restructure to accept capitation or global capitation (proper per-member-per-month), or to opt out of a particular contract.

By networking with hospitals, laboratories, outpatient facilities, home care providers, and skilled nursing facilities, healthcare organizations are expanding geographic access to patients or physicians with additional locations, advanced diagnostic and treatment technologies, and complementary and alternative medicine programs. In the process of developing leadership and communications skills for physicians and executives, and educating physicians to use the Internet, providers compete for quality, computer-literate support staff. The sustained growth of the health information technology sector, in part, is fueled by enormous healthcare deals that are rocking the world of enterprise integration. Mergers of mega healthcare organizations are unique in their multifaceted complexity. In order to merge two or more healthcare organizations into one cohesive enterprise, all strategic alliance partners and preferred vendors would have to afford the merging entity an optimal functional reality to avoid otherwise inevitable difficulties, complications, and related financial losses.

Seamless INFOgration, a cross-continuum, enterprisewide integration of voice, data, and imagery and secure information management, is the functional glue that would hold them together and assure their functionality and, ultimately, financial success.[4]

INFORMATION TECHNOLOGY JEOPARDY

All healthcare organizations are undergoing chaotic changes at a much faster rate than in the pre-managed care era. The growing pains experienced by these organizations are exacerbated by the ever-increasing need to provide quality care (real and perceived and, most importantly, documented, verifiable, and repeatable), and by the core functions of profitability and economic survival. Some organizations are aware of their own problems and are actively seeking solutions. Others are playing "IT Jeopardy" while getting answers (IT solutions) that are looking for questions (growing pains). Healthcare organizations desire and must have customizable, scalable proprietary solutions based on nonproprietary products, driven by healthcare communications.

The ever-growing reliance on IT to deliver these solutions is responsible for the proliferation of physicians' active participation in other-than-clinical aspects of their organizations. Furthermore, constant changes in the architecture and nature of delivery systems, contracts, reimbursement schemes, and reporting and performance requirements need to be addressed rapidly and effectively. Otherwise, the business may suffer or a new opportunity may be lost. Software designed for legacy technology, such as COBOL, Mumps, and Business Basic, all of which have been popular in healthcare applications, are not easy to modify and do not fit the changing needs of managed care. Even when a more modern language like Visual C++ is utilized, the architecture of the software may become an impediment to growth and evolution.

KNOWLEDGE-BASED HEALTH INFORMATION SYSTEMS

Knowledge-based health information systems (KBHIS©) can help fill the void in the healthcare decision-making process: the information you have is not what you need. The information you want is not what you need. The information you need is unavailable.

The concept of KBHIS was conceived and introduced to the American healthcare community to meet and specifically serve the increasingly complex requirements of healthcare information management.[5] KBHIS is based on the implementation of enterprisewide, virtual, computer-based patient record systems, providing the secure and accessible information, both analytical and transactional, that is crucial for the ability of healthcare organizations to maintain and increase their marketshare.

The complexity of knowledge-based health information systems resides in the "phase transition" — a class of behaviors in which the components of the system never quite lock in place, yet never quite dissolve into turbulence, either. These systems are both stable enough to store information, yet evanescent enough to transmit it. Even though most systems are built from "out-of-the-box" components, like children's interlocking building blocks, the end result (in shape, form, and functionality) is unique to the builder (owner) organizations but is transplantable to a large degree. They are stable from the standpoint of supporting day-to-day functioning but are probably incapable of fully addressing the current needs of the organization, and obviously would not be able to support the emerging, future needs with "major" evolution.

Knowledge-based health information systems are characterized by feedback, resiliency, self-organization, evolution, and complexity, and are subject to all applicable principles of nonlinear dynamics. This breed of systems helps define the healthcare entity because the feedback speaks to the purpose of the organization. Whatever the type of feedback, it is a form of perception that defines the system in relationship with desired outcomes. Hospitals, for example, often use feedback for control rather than to foster change. When hospitals conduct surveys, the emphasis is on gathering feedback that informs the hospital it is deviating from the path to its goal: customer satisfaction within the hospital. This is a perfect example of a regulatory, or negative, feedback loop. The patients who give the responses may not share the hospital's enthusiasm over the fact that they are sick enough to require hospitalization. In fact, it can be assumed that the patients may not want to be in the hospital at all, and yet that information is not solicited by the hospital, probably because this kind of feedback does not serve the purposes of the hospital.

The distribution and "control" of information becomes key. Information is the currency of healthcare — a dynamic element that gives order, prompts growth, and defines what is alive. Information is a unique resource because of its capacity to generate itself. For a dynamic system to remain alive, information must be continually created. Isolated health information systems wind down and decay, victims of the law of entropy. In this positive feedback loop, information increases and disturbances grow. The system, unable to deal with so much magnifying information, is being asked to change. In other words, the demand exceeds the system's capability and forces the system's managers to look for solutions to ensure optimal functionality.

For those interested in system stability, amplification (of disturbances) is threatening, and there is a need to quell the noise before eardrums burst. Yet, positive feedback and disequilibrium play a critical role in moving the healthcare system forward. True, disturbances can create disequilibrium, but disequilibrium can lead to growth. If the system has the capacity to react, change is not necessarily something to avoid.

Resiliency describes the ability of a dynamic system to reconfigure itself when faced with amplifying levels of disturbance in order to deal with new information. Neither form nor function alone dictates how the system is constructed. Instead, form and function mesh in a fluid process whereby the system may maintain itself in its present form or evolve to a new order. As the system matures, it becomes more efficient in the use of resources and better able to exist within its environment. It establishes a basic structure that supports the development of the system. Openness of information over time spawns a firmer sense of identity, one that is less permeable to externally induced change. As the system changes, it does so, in part, by referring to itself — just as centripetal force causes reversion to a center or axis. Changes do not occur randomly, but are consistent with what has gone on before — with the history and identity of the system. This consistency is so strong that in the biological system, for example, it is forced to retreat in its evolution. It does so along the same pathway, retaining a memory of its evolutionary past. This "self-reference" facilitates the inevitable "orderly" change in turbulent environments.

Self-organization describes a system's capacity for spontaneously emerging structures focusing on activities required to maintain their own integrity. Humans, for example, struggle to build layer upon layer of complex behavior, while dynamic systems unfold in a flat or horizontal fashion. In contrast to the emergence of hierarchical levels through the joining of systems from the bottom up, "unfolding" implies the interweaving of processes that lead to structure. A system manages itself as a total system through processes that maintain integrity. In health information systems, "relational holism" describes how whole systems are created among the disparate components. In this process, the parts of the information systems are forever changed, drawn together by a process of internal connectedness — hence, INFOgration (see Exhibit 2). It is no longer meaningful to talk of the individual properties of the constituent components (such as physician practice management systems or scheduling systems), as these continually change to meet the requirements of the whole system.

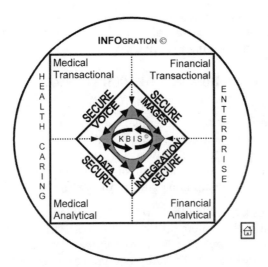

Exhibit 2. **INFOgration** (© 1997, 1998 Victor S. Dorodny, M.D., Ph.D., M.P.H. All rights reserved.)

The implications for the enterprisewide information system is similar to those of the "rubber landscape," where a change (rise, fall, reflection, or deflection) in any part of the landscape causes material changes in the entire landscape. These changes are not reversible and are not repeatable, which is good news for those healthcare organizations that might consider going back. Similarly, any changes in the IT landscape cause changes in the clinical and business landscape of the enterprise. Evolution is unending change that is inseparable from learning. Resiliency and self-organization work in tandem, fed by information to create an ordered world. The result is evolution, the organization of information into new forms. In healthcare, this is represented by standards of care and new ways to deliver that care. The same enormous energy also can be seen as a constant organization and reorganization of health information into new forms: treatment guidelines, outcomes measurement and management, cost-effectiveness studies, telemedicine, and computerized patient record systems.

Unfortunately, the concept of evolution does not provide a way to *predict* the emerging future as if we were objective observers watching from outside the system. A greater knowledge of evolution and the other systems concepts, however, offers the means to make us more aware and foster strategies for change. Complexity can be seen as the path along which evolution proceeds, or the creative border between chaos and order. This zone between two realms is created by the dynamic between building order and destroying order, moving from order to chaos. Healthcare reveals a fascinating dynamic that is ordering the system on one hand, as providers aggregate and procedures become standardized; and chaotic disordering, as a result of market forces and information technology that disrupt traditional practices.

THE CMIO AND THE BUSINESS OF HEALTHCARE

In a passage from the AMIA Proceedings 1995, the authors define the role of the information architect in medical centers. The medical informatician has a primary function "to steer the process [of clinical computing implementation] to fulfill stated objectives and build consensus where divergent forces are at work."[6] This is a challenging undertaking that can be well served by the cross-disciplinary nature of health informatics.

A 1997 survey of 140 leading provider organizations by the College of Health Information Management Executives (CHIME) revealed that 44 percent had assigned a physician to devote at least part of his or her time to information technology. It is rapidly becoming apparent that the CMIO is an important member of the executive team, and that regardless of a healthcare organization's IT strategy, closer harmony needs to be achieved among the CEO, CMIO, COO, CIO, and CFO. Each member of the executive team has his or her own "take" on the benefits of information technology. A recent study released by the Millennium Health Imperative, a think tank of executives from a variety of healthcare organizations, indicates that 71 percent of the CEOs believe there have been positive returns on their IT investment to date, but only 50 percent of the COOs and CFOs proclaim positive returns.[7] In addition, 64 percent of CEOs and 62 percent of CMOs/CMIOs say financial improvement, cost reduction, productivity, discussion support, process improvement, and integration should drive IT investment decisions. Only 27 percent of the CIOs share that perspective. CIOs who report to CFOs and COOs tend to emphasize financial and operational objectives for the next two years. Interestingly, 23 percent of respondents say the CIO reports to the CMO/CMIO.[7]

An industry survey targeted for executive level administration of complex integrated delivery networks (presented at the HIMSS 1998 Annual Conference) revealed a spate of information with regard to medical directors of information systems (see the Appendix). Again, the role of the CMIO as an educator and consensus builder among the executive team could not be overstated as the organization's willingness and capability to make IT investments are the most important factors in gaining a competitive advantage.

THE CMIO'S LIFE IN THE TRENCHES

Advocates of technology to their peers and acting facilitators between IS and clinical staffs, CMIOs may be perceived as a "magic bullet" to slay clinical computing demons. By approaching the issues from a wider band-width perspective (medical, IT, and management) as opposed to the per-spective of people with careers focused in a single domain, the CMIO is bound to run into inherent cultural and organizational conflicts. A defined position on the organizational chart and levels(s) of reporting can simplify these issues if addressed by the CMIO prior to acceptance of the job offer, but will not solve the underlying conflict of real or perceived responsibility that exceeds his or her authority. In addition, the fact that most CMIO positions have no defined budget responsibilities, exacerbates the imbal-ance. Further, such a conflict precludes the CMIO from optimally leverag-ing his or her skills for organizational success.

Some of the common pitfalls CMIOs encounter when working in the trenches is the IS department's perception of itself as the enabler that allows doctors to deliver medical care, while the CMIO is an outsider, wielding the medical sword. In turn, the CMIO, as a physician, might view the IS department as a support service to the function of the healthcare organization. These subtle psychological nuances can be very important in setting the tone and ultimately working relations between clinical and IS parts of an organization. This is actually the most difficult aspect of the job of the CMIO — a never-ending balancing act 200 feet above the ground. The good ones generate consensus from all stakeholders and become known as institutional or organizational heroes; those who are not adroit at balancing may alienate some people.

Healthcare organizations adopt one of two general approaches to healthcare informatics. The least desirable approach is to strive for phy-sicians becoming "computer proficient" and less uncooperative in the areas of database development and person–machine interaction. This approach is driven by the lack of recognition of the fact that while financial computing has not really changed much in the past few decades, clinical computing has become differentiated and highly complex. Further, many computer-proficient physicians recognize the fact that most of the "clini-cal" IT solutions on the market today are actually financial solutions mas-querading as clinical. True to the dynamic nature of these systems, neither form nor function alone dictates how the system is constructed. Instead, form and function mesh in a fluid process where the system may maintain itself in its present form or evolve to a new order.

The most desirable approach is for IS to work within the constraints of the busy clinical setting, not the other way around. The demands of staying abreast of the developments in their respective clinical fields simply pre-clude most clinicians from suddenly and dramatically changing the way they think and interact (e.g., become more IT friendly). Actually, IT is better suited to become more clinician-friendly, with user interfaces that are simple, logical, tailored to the clinical needs and accessible at the point of care.[8] These systems are self-organizing and manage themselves through processes that maintain integrity. It is here that the CMIO can impact the interaction, coexistence, and evolution of clinical computing within the constraints of a busy healthcare setting.

From a business of health standpoint, many physicians are somewhat uncomfortable with balancing practice and finance management under capitation, due to the inability to readily compare budgets to actual expenses, or to detect adverse selection or other variables resulting in abnormal expenditure patterns. Shadow capitation, or "managed care without inhaling," is the ability to convert fee-for-service data to equivalent capitation amounts. This allows physicians to compare, understand, and be able to manage changes in reimbursement and practice paradigms, and greatly eases the trauma of accepting reasonable managed care contracts. This is also useful in arriving at fair subcapitation packages.

EMERGING ISSUES

The role of the CMIO as a member of the executive team is rapidly becoming that of "data compliance manager" of a healthcare organization. The CMIO, together with the other members of the executive team, is responsible for compliance with HIPAA (Health Insurance Portability and Accountability Act) and HCFA (Health Care Financing Association) with regard to the confidentiality of health information and security of all patient-identifiable data and ORYX (the name of the JCAHO initiative to integrate performance measures into the accreditation process). "ORYX" is a term different from any other currently used in healthcare, reflecting the magnitude of the anticipated changes in the Joint Commission's accreditation process in the years ahead. The acronym itself defies interpretation, except for the fact that "oryx" is defined in the dictionary as a kind of a gazelle with sharp horns.

SUMMARY

In a practical sense, the state of the art in health information technology is best illustrated by the fact that most healthcare organizations do not know exactly what kinds of information they already have. Among those few that do know, most do not know where it is. Some of the fortunate organizations that know what they have and where it resides do not know how to get it out in useful formats. And the lucky few that do get the information they need do not know how to use it effectively to both deliver and document quality healthcare, as well as use it for competitive advantage to protect and increase their respective market share.

Today, the ideal KBHIS does not exist. The role of the CMIO is unique in its multifaceted complexity and means different things to different people in different organizations. The main functional objective of the CMIO is to foster the unending change that is inseparable from learning. As indicated earlier, the concept of evolution does not provide a way to predict the emerging future. An ongoing diligent assessment of current and emerging trends combined with out-of-the-box thinking allows for an accurate short-term forecast and projection.

In my own position as the chief medical information officer for Superior Consultant Company, Inc., a national leader in integrated healthcare and information technology management, I offer hands-on, detailed knowledge of the issues in order to assist my counterparts, as well as other members of the executive team in provider, payer, pharmaceutical, and vendor organizations.

Notes

1. Dorodny, V. S. 1999. Introducing this definition of "informatician" at the Medical Directors of Information Systems (AMDIS) Forum and Board Meeting in San Diego, CA, Feb. 16, 1999. Purpose — to define a health IT sub-specialty different from terms associated with "informatics."
2. Matthews, P. 1999. From personal communication based on unpublished work in process for the Association of Medical Directors of Information Systems (AMDIS).
3. Chin, T. L. 1998. "MCIOs, CIOs calling the doctor for clinical systems matters," *Health Data Management* 92 (Apr.).
4. Dorodny, V. S. 1998. "The piracy of privacy," *Information Security* 46 (Aug.).
5. Dorodny, V. S. 1996 (January). Sixth Annual National Managed Health Care Congress/ Information Systems and Technology Solutions Forum, Palm Springs, CA.
6. Sittig, S., and Al-Daig. 1995. "The role of the information architect in medical centers," Proceedings of AMIA.
7. Bell, C. W. 1998. "A health imperative," *Modern Healthcare* 55 (Nov. 30).
8. Silverstein, S. 1998. Director of Clinical Information, Medical Center of Delaware, personal communication.

APPENDIX: HIMSS SURVEY RETURNS

Medical Director of Information Systems

- Seventy-five percent of time dedicated to and funded by IS
- Direct report to CIO in IS role as IS medical director
- Twenty-five percent of time — practicing physician

Role.

- Clinical liaison between physicians, administration, and information systems
- Driver of new clinical ideas and clinical direction
- Provides strategic leadership in clinical systems projects

Committees.

- Chairs clinical advisory groups: groups are project specific that provide guidance and support during implementation
- Member of the technology executive committee which guides projects and funding allocation (health system executive team)

Chief Medical Information Officer position

- Thirty percent of time dedicated to and funded by IS
- Reports to CIO in IS role
- Seventy percent of time — practicing physician

Role.

- Provides direction and leadership with clinical community, systems users, and executive committees

Committees.

- Chairs clinical advisory board (multidisciplinary membership): board provides recommendations for system selections and clinical systems strategic planning efforts
- Member of the information technology governance committee: executive leadership committee responsible for approving IS projects based on the business and system strategic and budgetary plans

Physician Liaison-Health Informatics

- Volunteer support position to clinical informatics department within IS

Role.

- Provides leadership for specified clinical initiatives working with both the physician community and the other IS clinical liaisons within the clinical informatics department

Committees.

- Participates on the executive IS steering committee
- Committee responsible for maintaining and updating the IS strategic plan annually in conjunction with the corporate strategic plan. Strategic plans serve as the drivers for the annual budgetary cycle. The committee reviews and edits the IS initiatives as required to support the corporate plan. The IS strategic plan tentatively extends out four years.
- Other volunteer physician liaisons are utilized on specified project committees
- Significant trend to formalize working relations with physicians

Reporting Structure.

- Sixty-nine percent report to the CIO
- Twenty-three percent report to the medical director
- Seven percent report to other positions

Funding.

- Seventy-six percent of organizations fund physician's time
- Twenty-four percent rely on volunteers

Number.

- Fifty-six percent IS fund time for one physician
- Twenty-two percent IS fund two physicians
- Twenty-two percent IS fund more than two physicians

Health Informatician Trends

Key Success Factors Identified.

- Credible and respected by peer physicians (clout)
- Communication skills
- Leadership skills
- Understanding of corporate strategies
- Visionary
- Continue practicing medicine

Chapter 21
Information Security Management in the Healthcare Industry

Micki Krause

Proper management of the information security program addresses two very important areas: technological, because many of the controls we implement are technical security mechanisms, and people, because security is first and foremost a people issue. However, the information security manager in the healthcare industry is forced to heed another very important area: federal and state regulations.

Recently enacted government legislation, such as the Balanced Budget Act and the Health Insurance Portability and Accountability Act (HIPAA), are adding immense pressure to healthcare organizations, the majority of which have not yet adopted the generally accepted system-security principles common to other regulated industries.

This chapter will address the following issues:

- History of healthcare information systems and the inherent lack of controls
- The challenges the healthcare organization faces, *vis à vis* its information systems
- The obstacles healthcare companies must overcome in order to implement consumer-centric systems in an environment of consumer distrust of both the healthcare industry and the technology
- The multitude of privacy laws proposed
- E-commerce and the Internet
- An analysis of the proposed HIPAA security standards

0-8493-1248-5/02/$0.00+$1.50
© 2002 by CRC Press LLC

HISTORY OF HEALTHCARE INFORMATION SYSTEMS
AND THE INHERENT LACK OF CONTROLS

The goal of today's healthcare organizations' information systems is open, interoperable, standards-compliant, and secure information systems. Unfortunately, this goal does not accurately reflect the state of healthcare's information systems today. We have some very real challenges to understand and overcome.

To begin, the healthcare industry has built information systems without the sufficient granularity required to adequately protect the information for which we are custodians. Many of the existing systems require no more than a three-character log-on ID, some have passwords that are shared by all users, and most have not implemented the appropriate classification of access controls for the jobs that users perform. One healthcare organization realized that their junior claims examiners were authorizing liposuction procedures, which ordinarily are not reimbursed. However, due to a lack of granularity, the junior examiners had the same privileges as the more senior personnel and, thus, the ability to perform inappropriate actions.

Because of this lack of appropriate controls, healthcare companies have recently come to the realization that they will have to invest in retrofitting security in order to be compliant with federal regulations. Not only will they be forced to expend incremental resources in this effort, but they lose the opportunity to utilize those resources for new application development.

Unfortunately, we do not see much of an improvement in many of the commercial product offerings on the market today. Consistently, from operating systems to off-the-shelf applications, too many new products lack sufficient controls. Products from large companies, with wide deployment, such as the Windows NT operating system or the Peoplesoft application, are not built to be compliant with best practices or generally accepted system-security principles. This is poor testimony to the quality of software today. In fact, many security practitioners find it unsettling to get blank stares from their vendor representatives when they ask whether the product has the most basic of controls. Worse yet is the null response security managers receive when they ask the vendor whether or not the manufacturers have a strategy for compliance with federal regulations.

There is no doubt that along with other industries, the healthcare industry must begin to collaborate with product vendors, to ensure that new products are built and implemented by default in a secure manner.

THE CHALLENGES THE HEALTHCARE ORGANIZATION FACES, *VIS À VIS* ITS INFORMATION SYSTEMS

Another challenge facing organizations today is the pressure of keeping their networked resources open and closed at the same time, a security paradox of doing electronic commerce. Healthcare companies are forced to allow their insecure systems to be accessible to outside constituencies, trading partners, vendors, and members. In these situations, more robust authentication and access controls are mandatory, especially for those users who are not employees of the company. To exacerbate the challenge, the security manager has to reconcile decisions *vis à vis* the correct balance between access and security, especially with regard to requests for access to internal resources by external trading partners. Questions plaguing the healthcare organization include: "Should an employer have a right to see the patient-identifiable data on their employees?" For example, if a healthcare company is custodian of John Smith's medical records, and John drives a dynamite truck, should the health plan acquiesce to the employer if John's medical records indicate he has epileptic seizures? Should the employer only have this right if the safety of the public is at risk? Should the employer have access only with John's permission? The answers to these dilemmas are not clear today. Thus, health plans struggle with the overriding challenge of maintaining confidentiality of patient information, while providing reasonable access to it. Further, this balance of access and security has to be maintained across a broadly diverse infrastructure of disparate platforms and applications.

Also, there are other business partners that consistently request access to internal resources (e.g., fulfillment houses, marketing organizations, pharmacy companies). Where does it stop? How can it stop — when the competitive imperative for healthcare companies today is providing the ability to connect quickly and meaningfully with business partners and customers to improve the movement and quality of information and services?

Then, of course, there is the new frontier, the Internet, and the challenges that new technologies present. Organizations tread lightly at first, opening up their networks to the Internet by providing the ability for their employees to surf the Web. It was not long before they discovered that if an employee using a company computer on company premises downloads pornographic materials, another of their employees could sue the company for sexual harassment. Once the barn door is open, however, it is difficult to get the horses back in. Health plans faced increasing demand to accommodate electronic commerce. Surprisingly, the industry that, until very recently, considered sending files on a diskette the definition for electronic data interchange, rapidly found that they were losing membership because employers' benefits administrators were refusing to do business with plans that could not support file transfers over the Internet.

Of course, when the healthcare organization opens its kimono to the Internet, it introduces a multitude of threats to its internal network. Although most organizations implemented perimeter security with the installation of firewalls, business demands forced them to open holes in the defensive device, to allow certain types of inbound and outbound traffic. For example, one health plan encouraged its employees to enroll in courses offered on the Internet which required opening a specific port on the firewall and allowing traffic to and from the university's Internet address. In another instance, a health plan employee needed access to a nonprofit entity's Web site in order to perform Webmaster activities. In order to accomplish this, the employee utilized a service through the Internet, requiring access through the firewall. Thus, the firewall slowly becomes like Swiss cheese, full of holes. Ergo, health plans have the challenge of engaging in business with external partners while *effectively* managing the firewall.

More challenging than managing external connectivity is the security manager's task of hiring security practitioners with the necessary skills and knowledge to effectively manage the firewall. These individuals must have experience managing UNIX systems because most firewalls are built on a UNIX operating system; must know how the Internet protocols such as file transfer protocol (FTP) work through the firewall; and must have the expertise to monitor network router devices and know how to write rules for those devices, in order to accommodate business requirements while protecting the enterprise. On the other hand, as healthcare organizations seek to outsource networked resources, for example, Web sites and firewalls, the security manager must be able to provide sufficient monitoring and security oversight, to ensure that the outsourcer is meeting its contractual obligations.

It is no wonder that insurance companies are offering a myriad of secure-systems insurance programs. Cigna Insurance, for example, developed a program to offer insurance policies of up to $25 million in liability per loss, reflecting the realization that companies are not only more reliant on information systems, but with the introduction of the Internet, the risk is that much greater.

THE OBSTACLES THAT HEALTHCARE COMPANIES MUST OVERCOME IN ORDER TO IMPLEMENT CONSUMER-CENTRIC SYSTEMS IN AN ENVIRONMENT OF CONSUMER DISTRUST OF BOTH THE HEALTHCARE INDUSTRY AND THE TECHNOLOGY

In this competitive industry, the healthcare organization's mandate is to increase customer intimacy while decreasing operational costs; grant external access to internal data and applications, while most existing applications do not have the appropriate controls in place; and secure the new technologies, especially for third-party access. With all of these issues to resolve, health plans are turning toward Web-based solutions, utilizing public key encryption and digital certificate technologies. But even though health plans have the motivation to move into the Internet mainstream, there are obstacles to overcome that have, for now, slowed the adoption of Web technologies.

First, there are technological weaknesses in the Internet infrastructure. Most organizations have service-level agreements for their internal resources, which guarantee to their employees and customers a certain level of availability and response time. In the Internet space, no one entity is accountable for availability. Also, there are five major electronic junctions where the Internet is extremely vulnerable. When one junction is down, many customers feel the pain of not having reliable service. Because the Internet is not owned or operated by any one person or organization, by its very nature it cannot be expected to provide the same reliability, availability, and security as a commercial network service provider can. For example, commercial telecommunications companies provide outsourced wide area networks and deploy state of the art communications and security technologies with multiple levels of redundancy and circuitry. The Internet is like a Thomas' English muffin — a maze of nooks and crannies that no one entity controls.

Next, all of the studies show that a large majority of physicians are not comfortable with computers, let alone the Internet. The doctors are ambivalent about adopting information technology, and because there is no control over the content of the information on the net, physicians have been slow to adopt electronic mail communications with their patients on the Internet. They have legitimate concern as there is no positive assurance that we can know exactly who we are communicating with on the Internet. Thus, the healthcare providers distrust the Internet.

They are not the only persons with doubts and concerns. The perception of a lack of security and privacy by consumers is a tremendous challenge for healthcare organizations. Moreover, the media promulgates the paranoia. It is no wonder that consumers are fearful of losing their privacy when publications offer headlines such as "Naked Before the World: Will Your Medical Records Be Safe in a New National Databank?" (*Newsweek* magazine) or "The Death of Privacy: You Have No Secrets." (*Time* magazine).

Therefore, if healthcare organizations are to successfully deploy consumer-intimate Web-based applications, the biggest hurdle they have to overcome is consumer fear. This consumer fear is not a new phenomenon. For many years, public polls have shown that consumers are increasingly distrustful of organizations that collect their private information. More

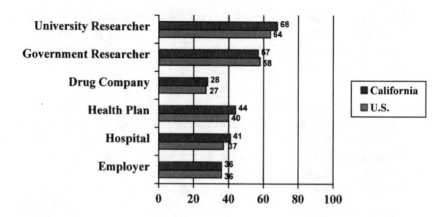

Exhibit 1.   Percent of Respondents Willing to Disclose to Following Parties

disconcerting than this, from a healthcare perspective, is that this fear is manifesting itself in negative impacts to the quality of their personal health. More and more, consumers are going out of their local areas to obtain healthcare and lying or holding back information from their health-care providers, primarily to maintain their sense of privacy and maintain some semblance of confidentiality. This reflects a real disconnect between the consumer and the custodians of the consumer data, the health plan and the doctor.

In early 1999, the Consumers' Union, the largest consumer advocacy organization in the United States, sponsored a nationwide survey. They sampled 1000 adults in the United States and a separate 1000 adults in California. The survey asked people how willing they were to disclose their personal medical information.

In Exhibit 1, we can see that the survey found that although people do concede that persons other than their immediate provider require access to their personal medical records, they display a very strong preference for restricting access. Only four of every ten asked were willing to disclose their medical information to health plans. Roughly six in ten would explicitly refuse to grant access to their information to a hospital, even if the hospital were to offer preventive care programs. Also, consumers are not happy having their employers or potential employers view their personal healthcare information. Most are not willing to offer their information to a potential employer who may be considering them for a job. Further, the drug companies are lowest on the totem pole because Americans do not want their medical data collected for the purposes of marketing new drugs.

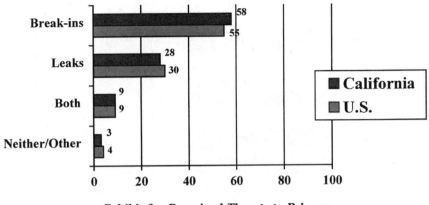

Exhibit 2. Perceived Threats to Privacy

In Exhibit 2, we see another interesting finding from the survey: most people consider electronic piracy, that is hackers, the biggest threat to their privacy. This is counter to the real threat, which is the disclosure of information by medical personnel, health plans, or other authorized users, but it is not surprising that the average consumer would be very worried about hackers, when we consider how the media exploits attempts by teenagers to hack in to the Pentagon's computers. Moreover, the vendors exacerbate these fears by playing up the evil hacker as they attempt to sell products by instilling fear, uncertainty, and doubt in our hearts and minds.

Exhibit 3 shows that most of the survey respondents perceive that if health plans and providers implement security provisions and information security management policies in order to protect medical information, it would make them more inclined to offer their personal information when it was requested. Americans believe that three specific policies should be adopted to safeguard their medical privacy:

1. Impose fines and punishments for violations
2. Require an individual's specific permission to release personal information
3. Establish security systems with security technologies, such as passwords and encryption

Further, the survey respondents were very favorable toward sending a health plan's chief executive officer to prison in the event of willful or intentional disclosure of medical information.

The Consumers' Union survey also revealed that consumers are aware — they know that their information is stored in computer databases, and they perceive computerization as the greatest threat to their privacy. In fact, more than one-half of the respondents think that the shift from paper records to electronic systems makes it *more* difficult to keep personal

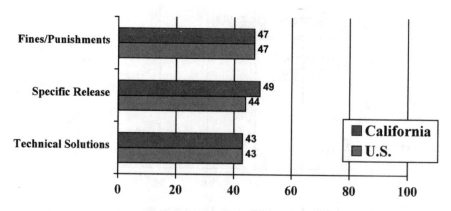

Exhibit 3. Safeguards Rated as Very Effective to Protect Privacy

medical information private and confidential. This should be of interest to any information systems manager, as computerization really provides more of an opportunity to secure data. However, perception *is* reality. Therefore, the lesson from this survey is threefold:

1. Consumers do not trust health plans or providers.
2. Consumers do not trust computers.
3. Consumers will compromise the quality of their healthcare.

All in the name of privacy.

This lesson can be an opportunistic one for the health plan security manager. Healthcare can turn those consumer fears around, and win over the public by showing them that health plans take their obligation for due diligence very seriously, and protecting consumer privacy is in perfect alignment with healthcare organizations' internal values.

Case in point: In December 1998, more people purchased goods on the Internet than ever before. The question is why? Price Coopers, the accounting firm, completed a survey early in 1999 which found that the leading factor that would persuade fearful consumers to log on to the Internet was *an assurance of improved privacy protection*. Healthcare can leverage the capabilities of security to garner that public trust. Privacy is not an arcane or a technical issue. It is, however, a major issue with consumers, and there is heightened urgency around healthcare privacy and security today, more so than ever before.

HISTORY REPEATS ITSELF

In 1972, in a similar environment of public distrust, then Department of Health and Human Services Secretary Elliot Richardson appointed an advisory board to assist the federal government in identifying approaches to protect the privacy of information in an ever-evolving computer age. The board issued a report detailing a code of fair information principles, which became the National Privacy Act of 1974.

The act outlines five separate and distinct practices:

Fair Information Privacy Principles
- "There must be a way ... to prevent information about a person that was obtained for one purpose from being used or made available for other purposes without that person's consent.
- There must be no personal data record-keeping systems whose very existence is secret.
- There must be a way for a person to correct or amend a record of identifiable information about that person.
- There must be a way for a person to find out what information about that person is in a record and how it is used.
- Any organization creating, maintaining, using, or disseminating records of identifiable personal data must ensure the reliability of the data for their intended use and must take steps to prevent misuse of the data."

Many bills and proposals concerning privacy of medical information have preceded the most prominent law, the Health Insurance Portability and Accountability Act (HIPAA), enacted in 1996. In 1995, Senator Robert Bennett (R-Utah) sponsored the Medical Records Confidentiality Act, designed to protect the privacy of medical records. Items addressed in the proposed legislation included:

1. Establishing procedures for individuals to examine their medical records and the ability to correct any errors
2. Identifying persons and entities with access to individually identifiable information as "health information trustees" and defines circumstances under which that information can be released, with or without patient authorization
3. Establishing federal certification of health information services, which must meet certain requirements to protect identifiable information
4. Providing both civil and criminal penalties, up to $500,000 and 10 years' imprisonment, for wrongful disclosure of protected information

Heightened interest in patient rights, sparked partially by tragic stories of individuals who died due to delays in medical treatment, led Senate Democratic Leader Tom Daschle to introduce the Patients' Bill of Rights in March of 1998. This law would guarantee patients greater access to information and necessary care, including access to needed specialists and emergency rooms; guarantee a fair appeals process when health plans deny care; expand choice; protect the doctor–patient relationship; and hold HMOs accountable for decisions that end up harming patients. Daschle's bill also:

- Requires plans and issuers to establish procedures to safeguard the privacy of any individually identifiable enrollee information.
- Maintains records and information in an accurate and timely manner.
- Assures the individual's timely access to such records and information.

Additionally, other organizations committed to strong privacy legislation, such as the Electronic Privacy Information Center (EPIC), have proposed multiple versions of similar bills. Most call for stringent controls over medical records. Many go beyond and call for advanced technical controls, including encryption and audit trails which record every access to every individual.

THE MULTITUDE OF PRIVACY LAWS PROPOSED IN RECENT YEARS

The federal government, very aware of its citizens' concerns, is answering their outcry with many healthcare privacy laws, proposed in recent congressional sessions. Some of the most publicized are:

- McDermott Bill, a.k.a. "Medical Privacy in the Age of New Technologies Act" — 1997
- Jeffords–Dodd Bill, a.k.a. "Health Care Personal Information Non-Disclosure Act" — 1998
- Senate Bill S.2609, a.k.a. the Bennett Bill. This proposed legislation is important to note because it addresses information in all media, whereas the other bills address the protection of information in electronic format only.
- Kennedy–Kassebaum Bill, a.k.a. the Health Insurance Portability and Accountability Act (HIPAA) — 1996

  "Electronic medical records can give us greater efficiency and lower cost. But those benefits must not come at the cost of loss of privacy. The proposals we are making today will help protect against one kind of threat — the vulnerability of information in electronic formats. Now we need to finish the bigger job and create broader legal protections for the privacy of those records."

  — The Honorable Donna E. Shalala, 1997

Kennedy–Kassebaum Bill: Background

Several iterations of congressional hearings occurred where stories were told of citizens suddenly found to be uninsurable because they had changed jobs. These instances of insurance loss led to a plethora of tragic incidents, motivating Senators Edward M. Kennedy (D-Massachusetts) and

Nancy Kassebaum (R-Kansas) to propose the legislation known as the Kennedy–Kassebaum Bill, also known as HIPAA. Because approximately two thirds of Americans are insured through their employers, the loss of a job often means the loss of health insurance — thus the justification for the term "portability," enabling individuals to port their health plan coverage to a new job. Legislators took this opportunity to incorporate privacy provisions into the bill, and thus, under HIPAA, the Health Care Financing Administration (HCFA) has issued a series of proposed rules that are designed to make healthcare plans operate securely and efficiently.

"For the Record": The Report

In 1997, the government-sponsored National Research Council report, "For the Record: Protecting Electronic Health Information," captured the essence of the status of security in the healthcare industry. The report came to several conclusions, which laid the foundation for the call from Congress and the Department of Health and Human Service, to define security standards for the healthcare industry. The report concluded:

1. Improving the quality of healthcare and lowering its cost will rely heavily on the effective and efficient use of information technology; therefore, it is incumbent on the industry to maintain the security, privacy, and confidentiality of medical information while making it available to those entities with a need.
2. Healthcare organizations, including health maintenance organizations (HMOs), insurance companies, and provider groups, must take immediate steps to establish safeguards for the protection of medical information.
3. Vendors have not offered products with inherent protective mechanisms because customers are not demanding them.
4. Individuals must take a more proactive role in demanding that their personally identifiable medical information is protected adequately.
5. Self-regulation has not proven successful; therefore, the state and federal governments must intercede and mandate legislation.
6. Medical information is subject to inadvertent or malicious abuse and disclosure, although the greatest threat to the security of patient healthcare data is the authorized insider.
7. Appropriate protection of sensitive healthcare data relies on both organizational policies and procedures as well as technological countermeasures.

Satisfying these important security and privacy considerations is the basis for the administrative simplification provisions of HIPAA. At last, the healthcare industry is being tasked to heed the cry that the citizenry has voiced for years, "Maintain my privacy and keep my personal, sensitive information private."

HIPAA ADMINISTRATIVE SIMPLIFICATION: SECURITY STANDARDS

The specific rules that apply to security standards that protect healthcare-related information (code set 6 HCPR 1317) were issued August 17, 1998, for public comment. The deadline for comment was October 13, 1998. According to HCFA, the volume of comments received was extraordinary. Plans and providers cried that implementation of the standards would be onerous and cost-prohibitive. HCFA essentially replied that "security is a cost of doing business" and the deadlines will stand. Those deadlines include adoption of security standards by 2002.

Throwing her full support behind HIPAA security standards, Shalala stated, "When Americans give out their personal health information, they should feel like they're leaving it in good, safe hands. ....Congress must pass a law that requires those who legally receive health information to take real steps to safeguard it."

Horror stories of inadvertent or malicious use or disclosure of medical information are held closely by healthcare organizations. No corporate officer wants to admit that information has "leaked" from his company. However, there are several publicized war stories in which sensitive patient healthcare information has been disclosed without proper authorization, resulting in misfortune and tragedy. For example, when former tennis star Arthur Ashe was admitted to a hospital due to chest pains, his HIV-positive status was discovered and leaked to the press, causing great embarrassment and strife not only to Ashe and his family, but to the medical institution as well.

In another instance, a claims processor brought her young teenager to work and sat her in front of a terminal to keep her occupied. The daughter accessed a database of patients who had been diagnosed with any number of maladies. The teenager concocted a game whereby she called several of the patients, pretended to be the provider, and misreported the diagnoses. One patient was told he had contracted AIDS. The man committed suicide before he could be told the report was the prank of a mischievous child.

In another instance, a healthcare maintenance employee, undergoing a nasty child custody battle with his wife's sister, gained access to his company's system, where he discovered some sensitive information about his sister-in-law, also covered by the health plan. He revealed this information in court in an attempt to discredit her. She sued the health plan for negligence and won the case.

These scenarios are not as rare as we would like to believe. The existing legal structure in healthcare does not provide for effective control of patient medical information. The federal government recognizes this and has attempted to forcefully impose stringent regulation over the protection of health information.

Under HIPAA, healthcare organizations must develop comprehensive security programs to protect patient-identifiable information or face severe penalties for noncompliance. Industry experts estimate that HIPAA will be the "next Y2K" in terms of resources and level of effort, and that annual healthcare expenditures for information security will increase from $2.2 million to $125 million over the next 3 years.

The HIPAA standards, designed to protect all electronic medical information from inadvertent or intentional improper use or disclosure, include provisions for the adoption of:

1. Organizational and administrative procedures
2. Physical security safeguards
3. Technological security measures

Health plans have until early 2002 to adopt these requirements. Although the intent of the standards should be uniform and consistent across the healthcare industry, considerable interpretation might alter the implementation of the controls from one organization to another. The HIPAA security requirements are outlined below.

1. Organizational and Administrative Procedures

1. Ensure that organizational structures exist to develop and implement an information security program. This formal, senior management-sponsored and supported organizational structure is required so that the mechanisms needed to protect information and computing resources are not overridden by a senior manager from another function, for example, Operations or Development, with their own "agendas" in mind. This requirement also includes the assignment of a Chief Security Officer responsible for establishing and maintaining the information security program. This program's charter should ensure that a standard of due care and due diligence is applied throughout the enterprise to provide an adequate level of assurance for data security (integrity/reliability, privacy/confidentiality, and availability).
2. The Chief Security Officer is responsible for the development of policies to control access to and for the release of, individually identifiable patient healthcare information. The over-arching information security policy should declare the organization's intent to comply with regulations and protect and control the security of its information assets. Additional policies, standards, and procedures should define varying levels of granularity for the control of the sensitive information. For example, some of the policies may relate

to data classification, data destruction, disaster recovery, and business continuity planning.

One of the most important organizational moves that a healthcare organization must make for HIPAA compliance is in appointing a Chief Security Officer (CSO). This person should report at a sufficiently high level in the organization so as to be able to ensure compliance with regulations. Typically, the CSO reports to the Chief Information Officer (CIO) or higher. This function is tasked with establishing the information security program, implementing best practices management techniques, and satisfying legal and regulatory requirements. Healthcare organizations seeking qualified, experienced security officers prefer or require candidates to be certified information system security professionals (CISSPs). This certification is offered solely by the nonprofit International Information Systems Security Certification Consortium (ISC²) in Massachusetts. More information about professional certification can be obtained from the organization's Web site at www.isc2.org.

3. The organization is required to establish a security certification review. This is an auditable, technical evaluation establishing the extent to which the system, application, or network meets specified security requirements. The certification should also include testing to ensure that the controls actually work as advertised. It is wise for the organization to define control requirements up front and ensure that they are integrated with the business requirements of a system, application, or network. The certification documentation should include details of those control requirements, as well as how the controls are implemented. HIPAA allows for the certification to be done internally, but, it can also be done by an external agency.

4. Establish policies and procedures for the receipt, storage, processing, and distribution of information. Realizing that information is not maintained solely within the walls of an individual organization, HIPAA calls for an assurance that the information is protected as it traverses outside. For example, an organization should develop a policy that mandates authorization by the business owner prior to sending specific data to a third-party business partner.

5. Develop a contractual agreement with all business partners, ensuring confidentiality and data integrity of exchanged information. This standard may manifest itself in the form of a confidentiality clause for all contractors and consultants, which will bind them to maintain the confidentiality of all information they encounter in the performance of their employment.

6. Ensure access controls that provide for an assurance that only those persons with a need can access specific information. A basic tenet of information security is the "need to know." This standard

requires that appropriate access is given only to that information an individual requires in order to perform his job. Organizations should establish procedures so that a business manager "owns" the responsibility for the integrity and confidentiality of the functional information (e.g., Claims) and that this manager authorizes approval for each employee to access said information.

7. Implement personnel security, including clearance policies and procedures. Several organizations have adopted human resources procedures that call for a background check of their employment candidates. This is a good practice and one that is recognized as an HIPAA standard. Employees, consultants, and contractors, who have authorized access to an organization's information assets, have an obligation to treat that information responsibly. A clearance of the employee can guarantee a higher degree of assurance that the organization can entrust that individual with sensitive information.

8. Perform security training for all personnel. Security education and awareness training is probably the most cost-effective security standard an organization can adopt. Information security analyses continually reflect that the greatest risk to the security of information is from the "insider threat."

9. Provide for disaster recovery and business resumption planning for critical systems, applications, and networks.

10. Document policies and procedures for the installation, networking, maintenance, and security testing of all hardware and software.

11. Establish system auditing policies and procedures.

12. Develop termination procedures which ensure that involuntarily terminated personnel are immediately removed from accessing systems and networks and voluntarily terminated personnel are removed from systems and networks in an expedient manner.

13. Document security violation reporting policies and procedures and sanctions for violations.

2. Physical Security Safeguards

1. Establish policies and procedures for the control of media (e.g., disks, tapes), including activity tracking and data backup, storage, and disposal.

2. Secure work stations and implement automatic logout after a specified period of nonuse.

3. Technological Security Measures

1. Assure that sensitive information is altered or destroyed only by authorized personnel.

2. Provide the ability to properly identify and authenticate users.

3. Create audit records whenever users inquire or update records.
4. Provide for access controls that are either transaction-based, role-based, or user-based.
5. Implement controls to ensure that transmitted information has not been corrupted.
6. Implement message authentication to validate that a message is received unchanged.
7. Implement encryption or access controls, including audit trails, entity authentication, and mechanisms for detecting and reporting unauthorized activity in the network.

One of the biggest challenges facing the organizations that must comply with HIPAA security standards is the proper interpretation of the regulation. Some of the standards are hazy at this time, but the fines for noncompliance are well defined. HIPAA enforcement provisions specify financial and criminal penalties for wrongful disclosure or willful misuse of individually identifiable information at $250,000 and 10 years of imprisonment per incident.

SUMMARY

The reader can see that the security manager in the healthcare industry has an ominous task, and federal regulations make that task an urgent one. However, with the adoption of generally accepted system-security principles and the implementation of best-security practices, it is possible to develop a security program that provides for a reasonable standard of due care and one compliant with regulations.

Chapter 22
Criminal Activity on the Internet

Edward H. Freeman

The development and widespread use of the Internet and e-mail have changed the methods by which organizations distribute information. The Internet has also exposed organizations to new types of criminal activity, including privacy and copyright violations, fraud, libel, and several forms of industrial espionage. This chapter discusses the legal and ethical aspects of crime on the Internet and offers specific, practical suggestions that organizations and individuals can use to reduce potential problems.

OVERVIEW

The Internet has developed into an efficient and inexpensive method to distribute and receive information. Organizations can conduct business on an instantaneous basis throughout the world. People around the world who have special interests can learn new skills, discuss common concerns, and exchange information quickly and informally.

Unfortunately, problems with criminal activity and privacy have been created with the development of the Internet. Long-time users are often disturbed by the rapid growth of the Internet. "The Internet…is becoming a tacky bazaar of junk mail, small-time scams, and now, lawyers and lawsuits."[1] The rapid development of the Internet and e-mail technology has created new legal ramifications for traditional criminal law.

This chapter discusses the development and current condition of the Internet. Criminal activity and how the courts and other government agencies have related this activity to the Internet and e-mail are addressed. The chapter defines what is necessary to prove or disprove charges of criminal activity on the Internet. Such associated issues as privacy, fraud, and copyright infringement are also discussed. Examples from court cases are offered, as well as specific, practical steps that both organizations and individuals can take to reduce or prevent potential problems.

0-8493-1248-5/02/$0.00+$1.50
© 2002 by CRC Press LLC

HISTORY AND SCOPE

The Internet was born during the mid-1970s from an attempt to connect a Department of Defense network with a series of radio and satellite networks. To transmit a message from one computer to another, the sender simply had to address the message correctly and send it over the network. The communicating computers, not the network, were responsible for ensuring that the communication was successfully completed.[2]

The development of inexpensive desktop computers and workstations has changed the scope of the computer and communications market. Organizations now expect the capability to transmit large quantities of documents and data. Certain communications (e.g., business and medical documents) must be transmitted confidentially. Other Internet items (e.g., commercial databases, bulletin boards, and advertising materials) are designed to be readily available to the public. Transmissions require a technology that screens unauthorized users and charges authorized recipients for the services that are provided. Users frequently use different brands and models of computers and operating systems, so the network must be capable of operating on numerous systems.

The Internet transmits messages between users on many networks. Communications are sent between users on the individual networks, and the Internet is used to establish the proper connection.

The Internet is not a corporation. Authority for Internet operations and policy rests with the Internet Society, a voluntary membership organization whose purpose is to promote information exchange on the Internet. The Internet Society (ISOC) has directors who work to standardize technology and allocate resources. The Internet Architecture Board and the Engineering Task Force are volunteer organizations that establish communication and network standards for the Internet. The Community Emergency Response Team serves as a central clearinghouse to which incidents can be reported. Individual networks and their management contribute their experience and ideas to develop Internet standards. If a network accepts Internet standards and considers itself so, then it will be a part of the Internet.[3]

Access to the Internet is open to anyone with a computer and a modem. The Internet itself does not collect fees from participating networks nor from individual or corporate users. Member networks establish their services and collect fees from users. Users pay the networks directly for Internet access.

The Internet is designed so that the individual user can easily get desired information although the request for information may pass through several networks. The user does not need any special computer background and is often unaware of the complexity of Internet communications.

Organizations and individuals pay for access to a regional network, which in turn pays a national provider for access. Internet service, of course, is not free, but occasionally the fees are not directly passed on to users, especially when government or advertising is involved. Fees are paid to the individual network or data provider, not to the Internet. In 2000, there were more than 20 million Internet users throughout the world, and use is growing at a phenomenal rate.

PRIVACY AND E-MAIL

E-mail allows individuals and organizations to send messages to each other. Many corporations, government agencies, and universities have introduced e-mail as an efficient alternative to the paper flow that clogs their mail rooms. Recipients of e-mail can read and delete messages without printing them. This procedure eliminates much of the clutter created by paper documents.

E-mail is frequently used for correspondence not related to business. Few employers would object if an employee occasionally sends personal messages to co-workers on the office e-mail system. A more serious question is whether an organization has the right to read an employee's e-mail and take disciplinary or legal action based on its contents. In the business environment, employees have been fired when their employers read their e-mail messages.[4] Who owns e-mail sent through an organization's network: the writer, the recipient, or the organization? Can an organization routinely monitor messages transmitted over the network?

Outside the business environment, problems related to e-mail security also exist. At the 1994 Winter Olympics in Lillehammer, Norway, three American reporters logged on to figure skater Tonya Harding's e-mail account in the Olympic Village's computer service. Although they did not read any messages, serious problems with privacy and journalistic integrity were brought into public forum.[5]

The word *privacy* does not appear anywhere in the U.S. Constitution. The Fourth Amendment states: The right of the people to be secure in their persons, houses, papers and effects, against unreasonable searches and seizures, shall not be violated, and no warrants shall issue, but upon probable cause, supported by oath or affirmation, and particularly describing the place to be searched, and the persons or things to be seized.

The restrictions in the Fourth Amendment apply only against government employees but do not restrict the activities of private employers or individuals. The Supreme Court has held that electronic listening by a government agency against its employees violated the Fourth Amendment only when the individual had a reasonable expectation of privacy.[6] In a military setting, in which security measures were extremely tight, the court held that the expectation of privacy that an engineer had in materials kept in his desk was not objectively reasonable.[7]

How does the standard of a reasonable expectation of privacy for government employees apply to computer-related material? In *Williams v. Philadelphia Housing Authority*, Williams, an attorney with the Philadelphia Housing Authority, alleged that his supervisor violated his Fourth Amendment rights by removing a computer disk from his desk while he was on leave. The disk contained Housing Authority documents written by Williams as well as personal items. Williams had been told to clear his desk before he went on leave.

The court decided that Williams did not establish a claim for unreasonable search and seizure. By retrieving the disk, the supervisor acted in her official capacity. Because the disk contained both work-related and personal documents, the court concluded it was reasonable that the supervisor reviewed the personal material in her search of official documents.

ELECTRONIC COMMUNICATIONS PRIVACY ACT OF 1986

The Electronic Communications Privacy Act of 1986[8] (ECPA) addresses unauthorized surveillance of e-mail by parties outside the government. The ECPA provides criminal sanctions for unauthorized access to electronic communications. It also restricts the actions of service providers when they handle information contained in stored messages. The ECPA makes it a federal felony to intercept, disclose, or use an electronic communication that is being transmitted. Exceptions occur when:

- One party to the message (the originator, the addressee, or the intended recipient) gives actual or implied consent for another party to read the message.
- A government agency with a warrant or administrative subpoena requests the information.[9]
- The provider of service (network operator) accesses the message in the normal course of operations, specifically for mechanical or service quality control checks.

Most observers agree that an organization that develops a network specifically for its employees can monitor its employees' communications and take specific legal action based on the contents of the message. An employee was recently dismissed for including inappropriate language and vulgar jokes in an e-mail message. Another employee was dismissed when his employer learned from e-mail messages that he had been previously employed as a stripper.

Both organizations and employees should understand their rights and responsibilities when e-mail is involved. Employees should realize that their personal and business communications can be electronically monitored in the workplace without specific notification. A potentially damaging or embarrassing message should never be sent on the e-mail network.

If an organization does choose to monitor messages, the following guidelines should be established:

- *Monitoring should be conducted only for a short period and only for a specific purpose.* Such actions should be considered only in extreme circumstances and should only be used when no other viable alternative exists.
- *Information and documents gathered should not be used for any other purpose.* Employees should not be disciplined for using e-mail for nonbusiness-related messages.
- *The procedures used should conform with legal requirements.* In addition, they should be conducted in a manner consistent with the terms of the organization's employee handbook.

The organization should realize that routine monitoring of employee messages can have a devastating effect on employee morale. If employees are concerned about the privacy of their e-mail, they will simply stop using the system. As a result, an expensive and crucial investment in the network will not fulfill its function, and the organization will not receive the many benefits of e-mail.

Both organizations and employees should be aware that e-mail messages are discoverable in legal proceedings. This means that such messages can be subpoenaed and presented as evidence in court. Employees and organizations should be aware that a backup of existing e-mail is taken on a regular basis, so that deleted messages are retained indefinitely when the computer system is backed up nightly. Individuals should not write anything on e-mail that they would not say or write publicly.

LIBEL

The Internet is a public network available to any person who has access to a computer and a modem. Anybody can log on to the Internet and send messages to other users. Control of Internet messages is more difficult because users can hide their identities by using false names.

Libel is a written, printed, or pictorial statement that damages a person by defaming his character or reputation, damaging him in his occupation, or exposing him to public ridicule. In the real world, freedom of speech is limited by the laws of libel. To date, the few libel suits involving electronic services have been settled out of court, so little legal precedent exists.

Can a network be held liable for a libelous message sent by a subscriber? In *Cubby v. CompuServe*,[10] the plaintiff sued CompuServe because a third party had allegedly posted a libelous message on the CompuServe network. The court ruled that CompuServe could not be sued for libel. Networks do not exercise editorial control over the messages that they transmit.

Although the matter has not been decided in the courts, it appears that an individual could be held liable for sending libelous e-mail messages. An article in *The Nation* states that "the Internet is not a free space when it comes to libel; it is subject to the same libel law as any publication."[11]

FRAUD

The increasing popularity of the Internet and its bulletin boards has led to new methods of conducting old fraudulent activities. A *New York Times* article announced that "the scammers, swindlers, and sharpies who hunt for unwary investors on the phone and through the mail are now prowling online computers services. But in cyberspace, where the police are few and dubious offers can be sent for under $2, such chicanery carries special twists."[12]

In one specific case, a posting on a Prodigy bulletin board claimed that E.T.C. Industries, an electric car company, was "primed for breakout." The note omitted the fact that its author was doing public relations for the company and was the son of its president. The Commissioner of Securities in Missouri issued a cease-and-desist order against E.T.C.

The Interactive Services Association and the North Securities Administrators Association are currently drafting rules that may restrict this sort of illegal activity. Investors should be especially careful about their reaction to such tips.

The Internet is especially vulnerable to credit card fraud. Kevin Mitnick, who was arrested by FBI agents in February 1995, was able to steal thousands of credit card numbers from an Internet service provider. Ivy James Lay, an MCI employee in North Carolina, programmed a microcomputer to capture more than 50,000 credit card numbers. He sold the numbers to a network of dealers, resulting in more than $50 million in fraudulent charges.[13]

Organizations must take specific steps to safeguard computers that are connected to the Internet. Firewall software screens outside requests for information so that only certain registered computers can access the internal network through the Internet. Although firewalls are not hacker-proof, they do offer substantial protection. In addition, encryption techniques can be used when sensitive information must be sent outside the internal network.

SOFTWARE PIRACY

Computer networks make it easy to copy programs and store them on computer bulletin boards. Bulletin board subscribers can then download these programs without paying for them. Many of these programs are freeware (i.e., programs donated by their creators) or shareware (i.e., programs available on a trial basis to potential users, who are expected to pay for the software if they choose to continue using it). Often, however, downloaded software is copyrighted material.

More than $1 billion worth of software is illegally downloaded every year. In one case, Windows 95 software was available for downloading nine months before it was released to the public. In another incident, David LaMacchia, a student from the Massachusetts Institute of Technology, was indicted for conspiracy to commit wire fraud after he allegedly established a bulletin board containing copyrighted versions of Excel 5.0 and Word-Perfect for Windows 6.0.[14]

On December 28, 1994, the federal court dismissed the indictment, basing its decision on two factors. LaMacchia did not make a profit from his actions, as required under the copyright act. Further, his actions did not constitute wire fraud, which would have required a fiduciary relationship between LaMacchia and the copyright owner. The court was extremely critical of his actions and called for congressional action to remedy the problem.[15]

Software developers and their trade group, the Software Publishers Association, have prosecuted several individuals, bulletin boards, and companies for illegally copying software. The federal government has indicted several bulletin board operators in the past for charging users to download pirated software. Successful prosecution is often difficult because bulletin board operators are often young students who do not charge customers and simply cannot afford to pay more than a token judgment. Most judges or juries would simply not punish operators severely. Organizations and individuals should avoid potential liability by avoiding the use of copyrighted, downloaded software.

FLAMING

Computer users express various opinions on the Internet. On occasion, the anonymity of the network encourages vulgar, verbal tirades known as *flaming*. For some users, flaming is simply a harmless method of self-expression. Most recipients ignore such messages; however, operators occasionally remove an offensive user from the bulletin board. A set of standards (known as netiquette) explains what is considered acceptable behavior for Internet users.[16]

What happens when flaming goes beyond any decent standards of proper behavior? In San Jose, California, a pedophile made contact on a bulletin board with a police detective posing as a young teenage boy. When they arranged to meet, the pedophile was arrested. More than 100 similar incidents have occurred.[17]

As one system operator said, "The Internet is expanding at logarithmatic rates. A million new users will bring a few sociopaths. Until recently, [there was] complete anarchy with self-regulation. Now some human will have to look at everything and decide what to post."[18] Unfortunately, even a single flamer can destroy the good nature and style of a bulletin board. A single individual with criminal intent can cause tremendous problems. A bulletin board operator is often forced to censor or eliminate messages from a particularly annoying or offensive user.

From a legal standpoint, a bulletin board operator has the absolute right to censor message or ban a user for any reason or even for no reason. Just as a newspaper is not required to print every opinion, a bulletin board or network operator is not required to allow all opinions.

FREE SPEECH

Individuals log on to bulletin boards to obtain information or simply to talk to others. It is often difficult to control access to the bulletin board. This has led to several cases in which the limits of free speech as they relate to cyberspace have been challenged.

Ohio police confiscated a $3000 computer belonging to Mark Lehrer, charging that children had seen pornography on his bulletin board. Lehrer did have pornographic files available, but he restricted access to users over 18 and required that users send copies of their driver's licenses. A few explicit photos were in the nonrestricted area because of a filing error. Local police recruited a 15-year-old to gain access to the files and then arrested the operator. Lehrer entered a guilty plea to a misdemeanor charge of possessing a criminal tool, specifically his computer.

In a similar matter, an uninvited Tennessee hacker broke into a California bulletin board that featured pornographic materials. The operator was charged with violation of obscenity laws, not by lenient California standards but in accordance with standards established in Tennessee. For the first time, a bulletin board operator was prosecuted where the obscene material was received instead of at its point of origin. The operator was convicted and the case is currently on appeal.[19]

The concept of free speech on the Internet, especially when users in different states are involved, will eventually be decided by the courts. At issue is a 1973 Supreme Court ruling[20] that states that obscenity must be judged by local community standards. Should alleged obscenity on a California bulletin board be judged by the standards of another state, standards that may be much stricter than in California? This is typical of the type of problem that can develop in cyberspace, in which state borders are essentially meaningless.

Internet users have all types of political beliefs; some users are libertarian in their views regarding the Internet (i.e., they believe in keeping the government out of cyberspace). This viewpoint is in opposition to the common belief that children should not be exposed to pornography. An early solution to this dilemma is not likely.[21]

HACKERS AND PASSWORD PROTECTION

E-mail can transmit hundreds of pages of text throughout the world in a few minutes. Most experts recommend, however, that particularly sensitive information (e.g., medical and financial records) be sent by alternative means. This is due in part to the lack of security on the Internet.

Although a user needs a password to send e-mail, typically no real barriers to entering another user's area and reading that person's mail exist. Hackers are expert network users who specialize in illegal access and manipulation of user areas. In 1993, there were 1334 confirmed hacking incidents on the Internet.[22]

By using privacy-enhanced mail (PEM), Internet users can use cryptography to decode and encode their messages. Under PEM, each user is given two numbers, known as keys, that lock and unlock computerized messages. One number is the public key, which is freely distributed. The other number is the private key, which is kept secret.

A user can send secure mail by typing in the recipient's public key, which is public information. The recipient then has to apply his private key to decode the message, so only that person can read the message. The system can also verify the sender's private key signature; the recipient can unlock it using the sender's public key. Messages are then secure as long as a user's private key is kept secret.[23]

To protect e-mail and other data, the following recommendations will prove useful to individuals and organizations:[24]

- *Passwords should be changed frequently.* A password should never be written down, especially next to a terminal.
- *Passwords should never be given out to anyone, especially if someone claims to be an employee of the computer network.* Such requests should be reported to the system administrator.
- *Passwords should never be included in e-mail messages.*
- *English words should not be used as passwords.* Hackers can run dictionary programs that attempt every word in the English language as a password.
- *Passwords that contain personal information* (e.g., nicknames, children's names, spouse's names, or birth dates) *should be avoided.* A hacker can determine a user's password based on personal information.
- *Immediate steps should be taken to disable an employee's password when that employee leaves the organization.*
- *Many organizations require that users change their passwords on a regular basis and not reuse them.* If a user feels that a password is no longer secure, the system administrator should be contacted for a new password. If an employee does choose to take this action, it should never be used as an indication that the employee is less than scrupulous with his or her use of the computer network.

Until a more secure method of transmitting e-mail is developed, users should remain cautious about what they send and store on the Internet. It is often a good idea to rely on alternative means of sending messages.

RECOMMENDED COURSE OF ACTION

The Internet and e-mail have drastically changed the ways in which society does business. As with any new technology, problems can develop. The following recommendations should be beneficial in reducing problems:

1. *Individuals should be extremely careful of what they send in e-mail.* If a document should not be left in clear view on a desk overnight, an alternate method to transmit the document should be used.
2. *Policies should be clearly defined.* If an organization chooses to ban personal messages from its e-mail system, this policy should be explicitly spelled out to all employees.
3. *Organizations should respect the privacy of their employees.* E-mail should not be read unless a crucial reason for doing so is evident. If such actions are necessary, they should be conducted on a short-term basis. Employee privacy and corporate personnel procedures should be honored.
4. *Organizations should be extremely careful to ensure that software is purchased from legitimate vendors.* Illegal copies of copyrighted software are frequently downloaded from bulletin boards. Use of this software could be disastrous to an organization.

Organizations and individuals must take serious steps to ensure that communications are secure and confidential. Common sense, restraint, and a high level of integrity should be exercised by all parties involved.

Notes

1. Newsletter Faces Libel Suit for "Flaming" on Internet, *Wall Street Journal,* April 22, 1994, p. B1.
2. Krol, E., *Whole Internet*, Sebastapol, CA: O'Reilly & Associates, Inc., 1994, p. 13.
3. Harowitz, S., "Building Security into Cyberspace, *Security Management*, June 1994, p. 54.
4. Nelson, C.L., Employers Have No Right to Snoop Through Mail, *Computerworld*, June 27, 1994, p. 135.
5. Hacked Off, *Sporting News*, March 7, 1994, p. 6.
6. *Katz v. U.S.,* 389 U.S. 347, 88 S.Ct. 507 (1967).
7. *Schowengerdt v. U.S.,* 944 F.2d 483, (9th Cir. 1991).
8. 18 *USC* §2510 *et seq.*
9. 18 *USC* §2703.
10. *Cubby v. CompuServe*, 776 F. Supp 135, SDNY 1991.
11. Wiener, Free Speech on the Internet, *The Nation*, June 13, 1994, p. 825.
12. Cyberspace Swindles: Old Scams, New Twists, *New York Times*, July 16, 1994, p. A35.
13. Cortese, Warding Off the Cyberspace Invaders, *Business Week*, March 13, 1995, p. 92.
14. Crimes of the Net, *Newsweek*, November 14, 1994, p. 46.
15. Gunn, Law and Disorder on the Internet, *PC Magazine*, March 14, 1995, p. 30.
16. Fisher, S., *Riding the Internet Highway*, Indianapolis, IN: New Riders Publishing, 1993, pp. 33–37.
17. "Seeking Victims in Cyberspace," *U.S. News & World Report*, September 19, 1994, p. 73.
18. Wiener, "Free Speech on the Internet," *Nation*, June 13, 1995, p. 69.
19. Ness, Big Brother @ Cyberspace, *Progressive*, December, 1994, p. 22.
20. *Miller v. California*, 413 U.S. 15 (1973).
21. Who Speaks for Cyberspace?, *The Economist*, January 14, 1995, p. 69.
22. Kierman, Internet Wide Open to Hacker Attack, *New Scientist*, April 2, 1994, p. 8.
23. Protecting E-Mail, *Technology Review*, August/September 1992, p. 11.
24. Wilson, Computing Insecurity, *Chronicle of Higher Education*, February 16, 1994, p. A25.

Chapter 23
Identity Theft: Who Are You Anyway?

Ralph Spencer Poore

When farmer Jones walked into the general store in town, the storeowner — or one of his employees — would greet him personally. The storeowner knew whether farmer Jones' credit was good, what his buying habits were, and how he would settle his account. If someone else came in pretending to be farmer Jones, he had to look and act like farmer Jones, and if he did not pull it off, he risked physical detention. Of course, there may be places today that are like the television show *Cheers* where everyone knows us. In cyberspace, however, our computer has a better chance to be known than we do.

The degree to which I must convey who I am to others directly correlates with the requirements of the transaction I attempt. Many transactions do not require me to identify myself. When I walk into a convenience store to buy a gallon of milk and I pay cash, the clerk neither requests nor needs my identification. When I attempt a transaction for which personally identifiable information is required (e.g., one requiring that I be at least 21 years of age), then either the clerk must ask for identification sufficient for the transaction or the clerk must acquire sufficient validation by personal recognizance. The latter choice (e.g., recognizing that a man with a graying beard is probably older than 21) is, at least currently, not an available choice to online merchants. In cyberspace, the apparent identity (usually obtained from the hardware or software used) becomes your identity for purposes of an online transaction.

From knowing the identity of the computer presented, you may correctly identify the person using the computer — or not. Many technologies purporting to identify and to authenticate a person ("end user") rely on the assumed relationship the user has with the computer that the user appears to be using. Cellular telephones and similar handheld computers (e.g., PDA) usually authenticate as if they were the end users. Successfully cloning such computers equates to stealing the identities of the legitimate

0-8493-1248-5/02/$0.00+$1.50
© 2002 by CRC Press LLC

owners — if only for limited purposes. Files used to authenticate a user can usually be copied to other computers. In Windows systems, for example, these include password-list files (e.g., janedoe.pwl) and certificate files (e.g., jqpublic.pfx). Hacker tools exist to crack these files. When features such as `AutoComplete` are used, a person using the computer may log in as whatever user had last logged in using `AutoComplete`. She need not know the password because the system will provide it for her. In cyberspace, gaining effective use of an identity may prove sufficient for a perpetrator to take over that identity. Authentication systems that rely on data stored on a device (e.g., the computer's hard drive) assume either or both of the following:

- Physical security controls and human procedures are sufficient to prevent unauthorized access to the device.
- The device enforces end-user authentication sufficient to ensure that only the authorized user can gain control of it.

In my experience, both of these assumptions prove to be false with an astonishing frequency.

Solving the identity theft problem requires both knowledge of how identities are authenticated and what techniques are used for identification. When weak means of authentication are used, a perpetrator has a better chance of a successful masquerade. When the technique used for identification actually identifies an entity that may not represent the person the technique alleges to identify, then an effective authentication of that entity may still prove incorrect in identifying the actual user. For example, a public key infrastructure requires both trusted roots for certificate chains and trusted means for registering users. Services such as Verisign and Entrust go to great lengths to protect the former, but may permit imposters to register. A recent and highly visible example of this was when two Verisign certificates were issued as being from Microsoft when Microsoft did not authorize Verisign to issue the certificates. The perpetrators successfully fooled Verisign into believing that they were Microsoft.

Relying on e-mail addresses, for example, as a means of identification, places the initial burden of authentication on the e-mail address issuer and a continuing burden on the system of controls that protect access to the authority to send an e-mail message using that address. Anyone can obtain an e-mail address. With some persistence, you can obtain an e-mail address that clearly represents someone else's name. Few public e-mail systems require strong authentication of your identity before they will issue you an e-mail address. In fact, free e-mail services exist for which you need not present even a means of payment (e.g., credit card number or debit card number) through which a third party (in this case a financial institution) might vouch for you.

Private e-mail systems may fair no better. In a large accounting firm with which I am familiar, one or more persons unknown succeeded in obtaining or creating e-mail user identities that they used for at least 6 months (more likely over a year) before they were detected and shutdown. Many large organizations find when they perform an operational audit of user identifiers that active identifiers remain for people who have died, retired, resigned, or been fired. User identifiers may also exist through errors in the issuance process. For example, my company may issue `rsmoore` for me by mistake, and then, when a second request is submitted for `rspoore` (because I did not get *my* identifier), it is issued. With no one to complain about `rsmoore`, it may remain active. I believe each experienced information security professional and each experienced information systems auditor will know of examples of this problem. We rely at our peril on the issuer to ensure that a valid relationship exists between the user identifier (or e-mail address) and the true identity of the person using the identifier.

When the issuer takes seriously the need to authenticate the identity of the person to whom the issuer is issuing an identifier, we begin with an excellent foundation. Regrettably, the networks on which we rely, e.g., the Internet, may build poorly on that foundation. The address resolution process permits the rerouting of an e-mail message without the knowledge or consent of the person rightfully represented by the e-mail address. By hijacking a user's messages, a perpetrator can impersonate either the originator or the recipient. Digital signatures and encrypted messages can diminish this risk but, as discussed previously, these techniques have weaknesses of their own. Although we generally rely on e-mail addresses that we recognize as if they were valid surrogates for a person we know, we should remain skeptical — especially when acting on the message would transfer assets, potentially defame, or place people or property at risk. Unfortunately, almost any level of business reliance portends harm if misplaced. The huge success of e-mail, where control failures appear low, may desensitize us to the risk and cause us to lower our guard. The hacker certainly hopes this will be the case.

I KNOW WHO I AM AND I AM NOT THAT PERSON!

Mistakes happen. An incorrect billing statement, for example, could be a simple error, or someone might have pretended to be you. Forged credit cards remain a bane to credit card issuers everywhere. Credit card issuers spend millions of dollars on holograms, card validation codes, and alert services. The integrated circuit cards (IC, the so-called "smart" cards) are the latest response in an attempt to stem the billions of dollars in fraud and abuse of credit and debit cards worldwide. With the exception of IC cards and some aspects of alert services, the attempts at preventing card forgery — and the associated identity theft — only work when the card is presented to a properly trained and vigilant human for processing.

One of the most powerful tools in preventing crime is the assurance that the perpetrator will be apprehended. Although some people are sufficiently desperate that they attempt crimes that put them on camera, in front of witnesses, or create other, clear physical evidence that will be used against them, most of us fear getting caught enough (or have sufficiently strong ethical or moral sense) that we do not commit such crimes. Cyberspace, however, tempts perpetrators by eliminating physical evidence at the scene of the crime and providing the perpetrator with a sense of anonymity. The science of computer forensics has advanced mightily as some perpetrators have discovered. Notwithstanding, the perception remains that getting caught for a cybercrime is unlikely. Weak identity controls and the perception that arrest is unlikely create a ripe environment for identity theft.

HOW DID I LOSE WHO I AM?

Identity theft can occur through the theft of card numbers, expiration dates, and your name. In most instances, this is sufficient to permit telephone, Internet, or fax-based purchases. Some merchants now require some or all of the billing address for the card as a further check of the identity. In the case of persons who communicate this information to a merchant using a means that is not secure, the customer may compromise this data. Wireless telephones and HTTP instead of HTTPS are two examples that come to mind. To the extent that the merchant provides ineffective protection for the data after receiving it, the merchant may compromise this data. The CDUniverse loss of credit card records through an exploited security weakness is but one of too many examples. In several cases, e.g., U.S. Bancorp,1 a third party may have bought your data. If the acquiring third party's controls prove ineffective, it may compromise this data. As leaky as this system is, I am astonished that identity theft remains rare — and concerned that little exists to prevent it from becoming common. Ordinary use of personally identifiable information (PII) — without extraordinary care — places it in the hands of persons unknown who remain outside of the data subject's control. With each such transaction you lose control over who you are. Generally, all that protects you is the lack of motive on behalf of those persons who gain access to your PII. In large organizations — even those with an excellent reputation for protecting customer data — there always seems to be at least one person with a motive. (For example, Bank of America's alleged problem recently with an insider at a subsidiary who may have misused access to customer data by selling it to others.)

We potentially lose control of who we are with every transaction we make that includes a transfer of PII to someone else. In the United States, privacy (i.e., control over one's own PII) is not treated as a human right; rather, it is treated as a property right. Although much is said about privacy as a Constitutional right, the Constitution (including amendments) is silent on this matter. The U.S. Supreme Court has pieced together some elements of a right to privacy largely related to search and seizure and to abortion. Notwithstanding, both the governmental sector and the commercial sector buy and sell PII — and generally do so without the consent of the data subject. New laws, e.g., the Gramm–Leach–Bliley Act (GLB) and the Health Insurance Portability and Accountability Act (HIPAA), have the potential for mandating notice (at least in some cases), but they may produce more exceptions than protections (especially the privacy rules for HIPAA, finalized April 12, 2001). You may already have received "opt out" notices under GLB from your financial institutions. However, opting out may prove of limited value in protecting your "nonpublic personal information," which is all that GLB requires a financial institution to protect. The exceptions permitted under GLB and the potential for control failures with each transfer of PII provide small comfort. In addition, an "opt out" is not retroactive. Data already sold or transferred to another organization remains gone.

WHERE DID MY IDENTITY GO?

With few exceptions, organizations are not required to keep records of their allowed transfers of PII. Even when they are required to do so, the granularity of that audit trail may prove less than useful. For example, just knowing that someone within a huge company such as GE obtained your credit history is probably insufficient for tracing where it went. Without accurate audit trails, finding and correcting errors in PII can become a nightmare. Because organizations give precedence to computer databases over the testimony of real people, an error may result in denied credit, denied employment, denied medical coverage, false arrest, improper medical treatment, defamation, unauthorized transfer of assets, and just plain bad things. Once your identifiable information leaves the firm to which you entrusted it, you have lost control. Just like closing the barn door after the horse has left, opting out proves an ineffective countermeasure once an organization has given, sold, or bartered your PII away.

WILL I RECOGNIZE MY IDENTITY IF I FIND IT?

While human error may associate errors with your identity and inadvertently cause you harm, people may exploit the poor recordkeeping and commercial market for PII to intentionally cause harm. By introducing false information into records associated with an individual, a perpetrator can create a false profile of that individual. The individual may only become aware of the false information after the information has spread to multiple databases. At that point, correcting the information may require Herculean efforts. Generally, the victim cannot recoup the costs associated with such corrective actions. The organizations duped into accepting the false information are also victims whose costs may go well beyond that of correcting the erroneous data. Any organization acting on such false information may create significant liabilities for itself, improperly allocate resources, or place assets at risk. As important as our identities are to each of us, their representations are essential to modern commerce. In fact, they have become so essential that our true identities are less important to commerce than are the representations made as our identities. If your earnings are reported under my Social Security number, then I will accrue the benefits — and probably the tax liabilities. If your name and date of birth are used to obtain credit, the fact that you knew nothing about it may not prevent an adverse credit report. And does your employer know you were arrested for prostitution and have HIV?

In cyberspace, who we are is unimportant. All that matters is who we appear to be. If the user ID and password are correct, that is who we are. If the digital signature verifies, that is who we are. If the name, account number, expiration date, and billing address we give matches what the company has on file, then we are that customer — even if we are not.

Biometrics may offer some help against identity theft. It certainly raises the stakes. How do I change my fingerprint, voiceprint, retina pattern, or even DNA if someone else gains the ability to use them? How do we protect against their misuse? All biometrics have the potential for being copied. A single cell or strand of your hair may prove sufficient to clone additional material with your DNA. The effectiveness of biometric identification depends on the effectiveness of the registration process and the security and controls over the authentication process. Associate a biometric with the wrong person and the person with that biometric becomes the person with whom its associated — at least until that person can prove through his actual biometric that he is not the person whose biometric points to him. In databases, this distinction will not exist. Computers relying on a biometric database will associate you with the entry you match. Thus, your biometric may point to an entry that is not who you claim to be or someone else's biometric may point to who you claim to be. In either case, who you are is not who you are, is it? Try explaining to the police that the near-perfect fingerprint match wrongly identifies you, especially when your fingerprints do not match what the computer says are the fingerprints for the person you claim to be. The stronger the scientific basis for authentication, the more calamitous the result when the association breaks down.

ANY IDEAS FOR PROTECTING MY PII?

Individuals can take some steps to protect their PII. They can "opt out" at each opportunity. They can write their legislators to lobby for stronger laws. They can limit what PII they release. Many organizations ask for information beyond the minimum data needed for the conduct of a given business transaction. If you decline to provide it, the transaction is not impaired. However, some employees may have trouble dealing with fields left blank. Some computerized systems have trouble with fields left blank. If patience fails, then a willingness to boycott these merchants may prevail. Surrendering to their incompetence just rewards them for insisting on PII that they do not need.

Although not releasing PII is your best protection, most of us already have PII at risk. Vigilance becomes the next best protective measure. Periodically review your credit bureau records. Carefully examine monthly billings for unauthorized or unexpected charges.

As information security professionals, we have an obligation to help our respective organizations protect PII. We need to assist our organizations' implementations of privacy policy and procedures. In many organizations, the need for proper privacy policy and procedures flows from regulations. More and more, however, organizations are realizing the potentially devastating effect that public disclosure of poor privacy practices can have. Even organizations without regulatory incentive may find merit in protecting the PII they need for their business transactions. The clear need for appropriate privacy policy only acts to remind us that security measures must enforce the policy. Empty privacy promises portend more public-relations harm than good. To protect PII requires controls in at least the domains under your control, including:

- Transmission between computers
- Storage (regardless of medium)
- Processing

Cryptographic security methods, e.g., SSL or IPSEC, may address protection while in transit, and an organization can store PII in encrypted form. A secure platform for processing usually remains problematic. However, new technologies will address this as well. As information security professionals and information system auditors, we need to invest some of our CPE requirements in keeping current on the technology and the ever-changing legal front. Protecting the privacy of PII is essential if we are to reduce the risk of identity theft. We need to design systems such that they do not rely on surrogate identities, i.e., identities of products that might be used by someone other than the expected user, because relying on such identification increases the potential for identity theft. Most of all, we need to educate our respective organizations and the public to the risks of identity theft and to the countermeasures available.

Note

1. In 1999 U.S. Bancorp was sued by a group of State Attorneys General and a separate class-action lawsuit related to alleged release of customer account information to a third-party merchant. These actions were both settled in 2000 for a total cost to U.S. Bancorp (based on U.S. Bancorp's press release) of over $7.5 million.

Chapter 24
ID Theft: When Bad Things Happen to Your Good Name

Federal Trade Commission

In the course of a busy day, you may write a check at the grocery store, charge tickets to a ball game, rent a car, mail your tax returns, call home on your cell phone, order new checks, or apply for a credit card. Chances are you do not give these everyday transactions a second thought. But someone else may.

The 1990s spawned a new variety of crooks called identity thieves. Their stock in trade is your everyday transactions. Each transaction requires you to share personal information: your bank and credit card account numbers; your income; your Social Security number (SSN); and your name, address, and phone numbers. An identity thief co-opts some piece of your personal information and appropriates it without your knowledge to commit fraud or theft. An all-too-common example is when an identity thief uses your personal information to open a credit card account in your name.

Can you completely prevent identity theft from occurring? Probably not, especially if someone is determined to commit the crime. But you can minimize your risk by managing your personal information wisely, cautiously, and with heightened sensitivity.

The Congress of the United States asked the Federal Trade Commission to provide information to consumers about identity theft and to take complaints from those whose identities have been stolen. If you have been a victim of identity theft, you can call the FTC's Identity Theft Hotline toll-free at 1-877-IDTHEFT (438-4338). The FTC puts your information into a secure consumer fraud database and may, in appropriate instances, share it with other law enforcement agencies and private entities, including any companies about which you may complain.

The FTC, working in conjunction with other government agencies, has produced this chapter to help you guard against and recover from identity theft.

HOW IDENTITY THEFT OCCURS

Despite your best efforts to manage the flow of your personal information or to keep it to yourself, skilled identity thieves may use a variety of methods — low- and hi-tech — to gain access to your data. Here are some of the ways imposters can get your personal information and take over your identity.

How identity thieves get your personal information:

- They steal wallets and purses containing your identification and credit and bank cards.
- They steal your mail, including your bank and credit card statements, pre-approved credit offers, telephone calling cards, and tax information.
- They complete a change of address form to divert your mail to another location.
- They rummage through your trash, or the trash of businesses, for personal data in a practice known as "dumpster diving."
- They fraudulently obtain your credit report by posing as a landlord, employer, or someone else who may have a legitimate need for — and a legal right to — the information.
- They get your business or personnel records at work.
- They find personal information in your home.
- They use personal information you share on the Internet.
- They buy your personal information from "inside" sources. For example, an identity thief may pay a store employee for information about you that appears on an application for goods, services, or credit.

How identity thieves use your personal information:

- They call your credit card issuer and, pretending to be you, ask to change the mailing address on your credit card account. The imposter then runs up charges on your account. Because your bills are being sent to the new address, it may take some time before you realize there is a problem.
- They open a new credit card account, using your name, date of birth, and SSN. When they use the credit card and do not pay the bills, the delinquent account is reported on your credit report.
- They establish phone or wireless service in your name.
- They open a bank account in your name and write bad checks on that account.
- They file for bankruptcy under your name to avoid paying debts they have incurred under your name or to avoid eviction.

- They counterfeit checks or debit cards and drain your bank account.
- They buy cars by taking out auto loans in your name.

MINIMIZE YOUR RISK

While you probably cannot prevent identity theft entirely, you can minimize your risk. By managing your personal information wisely, cautiously, and with an awareness of the issue, you can help guard against identity theft:

- Before you reveal any personally identifying information, find out how it will be used and whether it will be shared with others. Ask if you have a choice about the use of your information: can you choose to have it kept confidential?
- Pay attention to your billing cycles. Follow up with creditors if your bills do not arrive on time. A missing credit card bill could mean an identity thief has taken over your credit card account and changed your billing address to cover his tracks.
- Guard your mail from theft. Deposit outgoing mail in post office collection boxes or at your local post office. Promptly remove mail from your mailbox after it has been delivered. If you are planning to be away from home and cannot pick up your mail, call the U.S. Postal Service at 1-800-275-8777 to request a vacation hold. The Postal Service will hold your mail at your local post office until you can pick it up.
- Put passwords on your credit card, bank, and phone accounts. Avoid using easily available information such as your mother's maiden name, your birth date, the last four digits of your SSN or your phone number, or a series of consecutive numbers.
- Limit the identification information and the number of cards you carry to what you will actually need.
- Do not give out personal information on the phone, through the mail, or over the Internet unless you have initiated the contact or know who you are dealing with. Identity thieves may pose as representatives of banks, Internet service providers, and even government agencies to get you to reveal your SSN, mother's maiden name, financial account numbers, and other identifying information. Legitimate organizations with whom you do business have the information they need and will not ask you for it.
- Keep items with personal information in a safe place. To thwart an identity thief who may pick through your trash or recycling bins to capture your personal information, tear or shred your charge receipts, copies of credit applications, insurance forms, physician statements, bank checks, and statements that you are discarding, as well as expired charge cards and credit offers you get in the mail.

Exhibit 1. Credit Bureaus

Credit Bureau	URL	To Order Report	To Report Fraud
Equifax	http://www.equifax.com/	800-685-1111 P.O. Box 740241 Atlanta, GA 30374-0241	800-525-6285 P.O. Box 740241 Atlanta, GA 30374-0241
Experian	http://www.experian.com/	888-EXPERIAN (397-3742) P.O. Box 2104 Allen, TX 75013	888-EXPERIAN (397-3742) P.O. Box 9532 Allen, TX 75013
Trans Union	http://www.tuc.com/	800-916-8800 P.O. Box 1000 Chester, PA 19022	800-680-7289 Fraud Victim Assistance Division P.O. Box 6790 Fullerton, CA 92634

- Be cautious about where you leave personal information in your home, especially if you have roommates, employ outside help, or are having service work done in your home.
- Find out who has access to your personal information at work and verify that the records are kept in a secure location.
- Give your SSN only when absolutely necessary. Ask to use other types of identifiers when possible.
- Do not carry your SSN card; leave it in a secure place.
- Order a copy of your credit report from each of the three major credit reporting agencies every year (see Exhibit 1). Make sure it is accurate and includes only those activities you have authorized. The law allows credit bureaus to charge you up to $8.50 for a copy of your credit report.

Your credit report contains information on where you work and live, the credit accounts that have been opened in your name, how you pay your bills, and whether you have been sued, arrested, or have filed for bankruptcy. Checking your report on a regular basis can help you catch mistakes and fraud before they wreak havoc on your personal finances. See "Credit Reports" for details about removing fraudulent and inaccurate information from your credit report.

A Special Word about Social Security Numbers

Your employer and financial institution will likely need your SSN for wage and tax reporting purposes. Other private businesses may ask you for your SSN to do a credit check, such as when you apply for a car loan. Sometimes, however, they simply want your SSN for general record keeping. You do not have to give a business your SSN just because they ask for it. If someone asks for your SSN, ask the following questions:

- Why do you need my SSN?
- How will my SSN be used?
- What law requires me to give you my SSN?
- What will happen if I do not give you my SSN?

Sometimes a business may not provide you with the service or benefit you are seeking if you do not provide your SSN. Getting answers to these questions will help you decide whether you want to share your SSN with the business. Remember, though, that the decision is yours.

CHOOSING TO SHARE YOUR PERSONAL INFORMATION — OR NOT

What happens to the personal information you provide to companies, marketers, and government agencies? They may use your information just to process your order. They may use it to create a profile about you and then let you know about products, services, or promotions. Or they may share your information with others. More organizations are offering consumers choices about how their personal information is used. For example, many let you "opt out" of having your information shared with others or used for promotional purposes.

You can learn more about the choices you have to protect your personal information from credit bureaus (see Exhibit 1), state Departments of Motor Vehicles, and direct marketers.

Credit Bureaus

Pre-Screened Credit Offers. If you receive pre-screened credit card offers in the mail (namely, those based on your credit data), but do not tear them up after you decide you do not want to accept the offer, identity thieves may retrieve the offers for their own use without your knowledge.

To opt out of receiving pre-screened credit card offers, call: 1-888-5-OPTOUT (1-888-567-8688). The three major credit bureaus use the same toll-free number to let consumers choose not to receive pre-screened credit offers.

Marketing Lists. Of the three major credit bureaus, only Experian offers consumers the opportunity to have their names removed from lists that are used for marketing and promotional purposes. To have your name removed from Experian's marketing lists, call 1-800-407-1088.

Departments of Motor Vehicles

Take a look at your driver's license. All the personal information on it — and more — is on file with your state Department of Motor Vehicles (DMV). A state DMV may distribute your personal information for law enforcement, driver safety, or insurance underwriting purposes, but you may have the right to choose not to have the DMV distribute your personal information for other purposes, including for direct marketing.

Not every DMV distributes personal information for direct marketing or other purposes. You may be able to opt out if your state DMV distributes personal information for these purposes. Contact your state DMV for more information.

Direct Marketers

The Direct Marketing Association's (DMA) Mail, e-mail, and Telephone Preference Services allow consumers to opt out of direct mail marketing, e-mail marketing or telemarketing solicitations from many national companies. Because your name will not be on their lists, it also means that these companies cannot rent or sell your name to other companies.

To remove your name from many national direct mail lists, write:

Direct Marketing Association
Mail Preference Service
P.O. Box 9008
Farmingdale, NY 11735-9014

To remove your e-mail address from many national direct e-mail lists, visit http://www.e-mps.org/.

To avoid unwanted phone calls from many national marketers, send your name, address, and telephone number to:

DMA Telephone Preference Service
P.O. Box 9014
Farmingdale, NY 11735-9014

For more information, visit http://www.the-dma.org/.

IF YOU ARE A VICTIM

Sometimes an identity thief can strike even if you have been very careful about keeping your personal information to yourself. If you suspect that your personal information has been hijacked and misappropriated to commit fraud or theft, take action immediately, and keep a record of your conversations and correspondence. You may want to use the form shown in Exhibit 2. Exactly which steps you should take to protect yourself depends on your circumstances and how your identity has been misused. However, three basic actions are appropriate in almost every case.

Your First Three Steps

First, contact the fraud departments of each of the three major credit bureaus. Tell them that you are an identity theft victim. Request that a "fraud alert"

Use this form to record the steps you've taken to report the fraudulent use of your identity. Keep this list in a safe place for reference.

Credit Bureaus - Report Fraud

Bureau	Phone Number	Date Contacted	Contact Person	Comments
Equifax	1-800-525-6285			
Experian	1-888-397-3742			
Trans Union	1-800-680-7289			

Banks, Credit Card Issuers and Other Creditors (Contact each creditor promptly to protect your legal rights.)

Creditor	Address and Phone Number	Date Contacted	Contact Person	Comments

Law Enforcement Authorities - Report Identity Theft

Agency/Dept.	Phone Number	Date Contacted	Contact Person	Report Number	Comments
Federal Trade Commission	1-877-IDTHEFT				
Local Police Department					

Exhibit 2. Chart Your Course of Action

be placed in your file, as well as a victim's statement asking that creditors call you before opening any new accounts or changing your existing accounts. This can help prevent an identity thief from opening additional accounts in your name.

At the same time, order copies of your credit reports from the credit bureaus. Credit bureaus must give you a free copy of your report if your report is inaccurate because of fraud, and you request it in writing. Review your reports carefully to make sure no additional fraudulent accounts have been opened in your name or unauthorized changes made to your existing accounts. Also, check the section of your report that lists "inquiries." Where "inquiries" appear from the company(ies) that opened the fraudulent account(s), request that these "inquiries" be removed from your report. (See "Credit Reports" for more information.) In a few months, order new copies of your reports to verify your corrections and changes and to make sure no new fraudulent activity has occurred.

Second, contact the creditors for any accounts that have been tampered with or opened fraudulently. Creditors can include credit card companies, phone companies and other utilities, and banks and other lenders. Ask to speak with someone in the security or fraud department of each creditor, and follow up with a letter. It is particularly important to notify credit card companies in writing because that is the consumer protection procedure the law spells out for resolving errors on credit card billing statements. Immediately close accounts that have been tampered with and open new ones with new Personal Identification Numbers (PINs) and passwords. Here again, avoid using easily available information such as your mother's maiden name, your birth date, the last four digits of your SSN or your phone number, or a series of consecutive numbers.

Third, file a report with your local police or the police in the community where the identity theft took place. Get a copy of the police report in case the bank, credit card company or others need proof of the crime. Even if the police cannot catch the identity thief in your case, having a copy of the police report can help you when dealing with creditors.

Your Next Steps

Although there is no question that identity thieves can wreak havoc on your personal finances, there are some things you can do to take control of the situation. For example:

- **Stolen mail.** If an identity thief has stolen your mail to get new credit cards, bank and credit card statements, pre-screened credit offers, or tax information, or if an identity thief has falsified change-of-address forms, that is a crime. Report it to your local postal inspector. Contact your local post office for the phone number for the nearest postal inspection service office or check the Postal Service Web site at www.usps.gov/websites/depart/inspect.
- **Change of address on credit card accounts.** If you discover that an identity thief has changed the billing address on an existing credit card account, close the account. When you open a new account, ask that a password be used before any inquiries or changes can be made on the account. Avoid using easily available information such as your mother's maiden name, your birth date, the last four digits of your SSN or your phone number, or a series of consecutive numbers. Avoid using the same information and numbers when you create a PIN.
- **Bank accounts.** If you have reason to believe that an identity thief has tampered with your bank accounts, checks, or ATM card, close the accounts immediately. When you open new accounts, insist on password-only access to minimize the chance that an identity thief can violate the accounts. In addition, if your checks have been stolen or misused, stop payment. Also contact the major check verification companies to request that they notify retailers using their databases not to accept these checks, or ask your bank to notify the check verification service with which it does business.

National Check Fraud Service: 1-843-571-2143
SCAN: 1-800-262-7771
TeleCheck: 1-800-710-9898 or 927-0188
CrossCheck: 1-707-586-0551
Equifax Check Systems: 1-800-437-5120
International Check Services: 1-800-526-5380

- If your ATM card has been lost, stolen, or otherwise compromised, cancel the card as soon as you can and get another with a new PIN.
- **Investments.** If you believe that an identity thief has tampered with your securities investments or a brokerage account, immediately report it to your broker or account manager and to the Securities and Exchange Commission.
- **Phone service.** If an identity thief has established new phone service in your name, is making unauthorized calls that seem to come from — and are billed to — your cellular phone, or is using your calling card and PIN, contact your service provider immediately to cancel the account and/or calling card. Open new accounts and choose new PINs. If you are having trouble getting fraudulent phone charges removed from your account, contact your state Public Utility Commission for local service providers or the Federal Communications Commission for long-distance service providers and cellular providers at www.fcc.gov/ccb/enforce/complaints.html or 1-888-CALL-FCC.
- **Employment.** If you believe someone is using your SSN to apply for a job or to work, that is a crime. Report it to the SSA's Fraud Hotline at 1-800-269-0271. Also call SSA at 1-800-772-1213 to verify the accuracy of the earnings reported on your SSN, and to request a copy of your *Social Security Statement.* Follow up your calls in writing.
- **Driver's license.** If you suspect that your name or SSN is being used by an identity thief to get a driver's license or a non-driver's ID card, contact your Department of Motor Vehicles. If your state uses your SSN as your driver's license number, ask to substitute another number.
- **Bankruptcy.** If you believe someone has filed for bankruptcy using your name, write to the U.S. Trustee in the Region where the bankruptcy was filed. A listing of the U.S. Trustee Program's Regions can be found at www.usdoj.gov/ust, or look in the Blue Pages of your phone book under U.S. Government — Bankruptcy Administration. Your letter should describe the situation and provide proof of your identity. The U.S. Trustee, if appropriate, will make a referral to criminal law enforcement authorities if you provide appropriate documentation to substantiate your claim. You also may want to file a complaint with the U.S. Attorney or the FBI in the city where the bankruptcy was filed.

- **Criminal records/arrests.** In rare instances, an identity thief may create a criminal record under your name. For example, your imposter may give your name when being arrested. If this happens to you, you may need to hire an attorney to help resolve the problem. The procedures for clearing your name vary by jurisdiction.

Should I Apply for a New Social Security Number?

Under certain circumstances, SSA may issue you a new SSN — at your request — if, after trying to resolve the problems brought on by identity theft, you continue to experience problems. Consider this option carefully. A new SSN may not resolve your identity theft problems, and may actually create new problems. For example, a new SSN does not necessarily ensure a new credit record because credit bureaus may combine the credit records from your old SSN with those from your new SSN. Even when the old credit information is not associated with your new SSN, the absence of any credit history under your new SSN may make it more difficult for you to get credit. And finally, there is no guarantee that a new SSN would not also be misused by an identity thief.

WHERE THERE IS HELP...

The FTC collects complaints about identity theft from consumers who have been victimized. Although the FTC does not have the authority to bring criminal cases, the Commission can help victims of identity theft by providing information to assist them in resolving the financial and other problems that can result from this crime. The FTC also refers victim complaints to other appropriate government agencies and private organizations for further action.

If you have been a victim of identity theft, file a complaint with the FTC by contacting the FTC:

> Identity Theft Hotline: Toll-free 1-877-IDTHEFT (438-4338)
> TDD: 202-326-2502
> Mail: Identity Theft Clearinghouse
> Federal Trade Commission
> 600 Pennsylvania Avenue, NW
> Washington, D.C. 20580
> Online: www.consumer.gov/idtheft

Other agencies and organizations also are working to combat identity theft. If specific institutions and companies are not being responsive to your questions and complaints, you also may want to contact the government agencies with jurisdiction over those companies. They are listed in the Resources section of this chapter.

Federal Laws

The federal government and numerous states have passed laws that address the problem of identity theft.

The Identity Theft and Assumption Deterrence Act, enacted by Congress in October 1998 (and codified, in part, at 18 USC § 1028), is the federal law directed at identity theft.

Violations of the Act are investigated by federal law enforcement agencies, including the U.S. Secret Service, the FBI, the U.S. Postal Inspection Service, and SSA's Office of the Inspector General. Federal identity theft cases are prosecuted by the U.S. Department of Justice.

Identity Theft and Assumption Deterrence Act of 1998

The Identity Theft and Assumption Deterrence Act makes it a federal crime when someone:

> Knowingly transfers or uses, without lawful authority, a means of identification of another person with the intent to commit, or to aid or abet, any unlawful activity that constitutes a violation of federal law, or that constitutes a felony under any applicable state or local law.

Note that under the Act, a name or SSN is considered a "means of identification." So is a credit card number, cellular telephone electronic serial number or any other piece of information that may be used alone or in conjunction with other information to identify a specific individual.

In most instances, a conviction for identity theft carries a maximum penalty of 15 years imprisonment, a fine, and forfeiture of any personal property used or intended to be used to commit the crime. The Act also directs the U.S. Sentencing Commission to review and amend the federal sentencing guidelines to provide appropriate penalties for those persons convicted of identity theft.

Schemes to commit identity theft or fraud also may involve violations of other statutes, such as credit card fraud, computer fraud, mail fraud, wire fraud, financial institution fraud, or Social Security fraud. Each of these federal offenses is a felony and carries substantial penalties — in some cases, as high as 30 years in prison, fines, and criminal forfeiture.

State Laws

Many states have passed laws related to identity theft; others may be considering such legislation. Where specific identity theft laws do not exist, the practices may be prohibited under other laws. Contact your State Attorney General's office or local consumer protection agency to find out whether your state has laws related to identity theft, or visit www.consumer.gov/idtheft.

State laws that had been enacted at the time of this chapter publication are listed in Exhibit 3.

RESOLVING CREDIT PROBLEMS

Resolving credit problems resulting from identity theft can be time consuming and frustrating. The good news is that there are federal laws that establish procedures for correcting credit report errors and billing errors, and for stopping debt collectors from contacting you about debts you do not owe.

Here is a brief summary of your rights, and what to do to clear up credit problems that result from identity theft.

Credit Reports

The Fair Credit Reporting Act (FCRA) establishes procedures for correcting mistakes on your credit record and requires that your record be made available only for certain legitimate business needs.

Under the FCRA, both the credit bureau and the organization that provided the information to the credit bureau (the "information provider"), such as a bank or credit card company, are responsible for correcting inaccurate or incomplete information in your report. To protect your rights under the law, contact both the credit bureau and the information provider.

First, call the credit bureau and follow up in writing. Tell them what information you believe is inaccurate. Include copies (NOT originals) of documents that support your position. In addition to providing your complete name and address, your letter should clearly identify each item in your report that you dispute, give the facts, explain why you dispute the information, and request deletion or correction. You may want to enclose a copy of your report with circles around the items in question. Your letter may look something like the sample in Exhibit 4. Send your letter by certified mail, and request a return receipt so you can document what the credit bureau received and when. Keep copies of your dispute letter and enclosures.

Credit bureaus must investigate the items in question — usually within 30 days — unless they consider your dispute frivolous. They also must forward all relevant data you provide about the dispute to the information provider. After the information provider receives notice of a dispute from the credit bureau, it must investigate, review all relevant information provided by the credit bureau and report the results to the credit bureau. If the information provider finds the disputed information to be inaccurate, it must notify any nationwide credit bureau that it reports to so that the credit bureaus can correct this information in your file. Note that:

Exhibit 3.   State Laws Related to Identity Theft

Alaska	2000 Alaska Sess. Laws 65
Arizona	Ariz. Rev. Stat. § 13-2008
Arkansas	Ark. Code Ann. § 5-37-227
California	Cal. Penal Code § 530.5
Colorado	2000 Colo. Legis. Serv. ch. 159 (May 19, 2000)
Connecticut	1999 Conn. Acts 99
Delaware	72 Del. Laws 297 (2000)
Florida	Fla. Stat. Ann. § 817.568
Georgia	Ga. Code Ann. §§ 16-9-121
Idaho	Idaho Code § 18-3126
Illinois	720 ILCS 5/16G
Indiana	Ind. Code § 35-43-5-4 (2000)
Iowa	Iowa Code § 715A.8
Kansas	Kan. Stat. Ann. § 21-4018
Kentucky	Ky. Rev. Stat. Ann. § 160, ch. 514
Louisiana	La. Rev. Stat. Ann. § 67.16
Maine	Me. Rev. Stat. Ann. tit. 17-A, § 354-2A
Maryland	Md. Ann. Code art. 27, § 231
Massachusetts	Mass. Gen. Laws ch. 266, § 37E
Minnesota	Minn. Stat. Ann. § 609.527
Mississippi	Miss. Code Ann. § 97-19-85
Missouri	Mo. Rev. Stat. § 570.223
Nevada	Nev. Rev. State. § 205.465
New Hampshire	N.H. Rev. Stat. Ann. § 638:26
New Jersey	N.J. Stat. Ann. § 2C:21-17
North Carolina	N.C. Gen. Stat. § 14-113.20
North Dakota	N.D.C.C. § 12.1-23-11
Ohio	Ohio Rev. Code Ann. 2913.49
Oklahoma	Okla. Stat. tit. 21, § 1533.1
Oregon	Or. Rev. Stat. § 165.800
Pennsylvania	Pa. Cons. Stat. Ann. § 4120
Rhode Island	R.I. Gen. Laws § 11-49.1-1
South Carolina	S.C. Code Ann. § 16-13-500, 501
South Dakota	S.D. Codified Laws § 22-30A-3.1
Tennessee	TCA 39-14-150
Texas	Tex. Penal Code § 32.51
Utah	Utah Code Ann. § 76-6-1101-1104
Virginia	VA. Code Ann. § 18.2-186.3
Washington	Wash. Rev. Code § 9.35.020
West Virginia	W. Va. Code § 61-3-54
Wisconsin	Wis. Stat. § 943.201
Wyoming	Wyo. Stat. Ann. § 6-3-901

Exhibit 4.   Sample Dispute Letter to Credit Bureau

Dear Sir or Madam:

I am writing to dispute the following information in my file. The items I dispute also are circled on the attached copy of the report I received. (Identify item(s) disputed by name of source, such as creditors or tax court, and identify type of item, such as credit account, judgment, etc.)

This item is (inaccurate or incomplete) because (describe what is inaccurate or incomplete and why). I am requesting that the item be deleted (or request another specific change) to correct the information.

Enclosed are copies of (use this sentence if applicable and describe any enclosed documentation, such as payment records, court documents) supporting my position. Please investigate this (these) matter(s) and (delete or correct) the disputed item(s) as soon as possible.

Sincerely,

[Your name]
Enclosures: [List what you are enclosing]

- Disputed information that cannot be verified must be deleted from your file.
- If your report contains erroneous information, the credit bureau must correct it.
- If an item is incomplete, the credit bureau must complete it. For example, if your file shows that you have been late making payments, but fails to show that you are no longer delinquent, the credit bureau must show that you are current.
- If your file shows an account that belongs to someone else, the credit bureau must delete it.

When the investigation is complete, the credit bureau must give you the written results and a free copy of your report if the dispute results in a change. If an item is changed or removed, the credit bureau cannot put the disputed information back in your file unless the information provider verifies its accuracy and completeness, and the credit bureau gives you a written notice that includes the name, address and phone number of the information provider.

If you request, the credit bureau must send notices of corrections to anyone who received your report in the past six months. Job applicants can have a corrected copy of their report sent to anyone who received a copy during the past two years for employment purposes. If an investigation does not resolve your dispute, ask the credit bureau to include your statement of the dispute in your file and in future reports.

Second, in addition to writing to the credit bureau, tell the creditor or other information provider in writing that you dispute an item. Again, include copies (NOT originals) of documents that support your position. Many information providers specify an address for disputes. If the information provider then reports the item to any credit bureau, it must include a notice of your dispute. In addition, if you are correct — that is, if the disputed information is not accurate — the information provider may not use it again. For more information, consult *How to Dispute Credit Report Errors* and *Fair Credit Reporting*, two brochures available from the FTC or at www.consumer.gov/idtheft.

Credit Cards

The Truth in Lending Act limits your liability for unauthorized credit card charges in most cases to $50 per card. The Fair Credit Billing Act establishes procedures for resolving billing errors on your credit card accounts.

The Act's settlement procedures apply to disputes about "billing errors." This includes fraudulent charges on your accounts.

To take advantage of the law's consumer protections, you *must*:

- Write to the creditor at the address given for "billing inquiries," not the address for sending your payments. Include your name, address, account number, and a description of the billing error, including the amount and date of the error. Your letter may look something like the sample in Exhibit 5.
- Send your letter so that it reaches the creditor within 60 days after the first bill containing the error was mailed to you. If the address on your account was changed by an identity thief and you never received the bill, your dispute letter still must reach the creditor within 60 days of when the creditor would have mailed the bill. This is why it is so important to keep track of your billing statements and immediately follow up when your bills do not arrive on time.

Send your letter by certified mail, and request a return receipt. This will be your proof of the date the creditor received the letter. Include copies (NOT originals) of sales slips or other documents that support your position. Keep a copy of your dispute letter.

The creditor must acknowledge your complaint in writing within 30 days after receiving it, unless the problem has been resolved. The creditor must resolve the dispute within two billing cycles (but not more than 90 days) after receiving your letter.

Exhibit 5. Sample Dispute Letter to Credit Card Issuers

Dear Sir or Madam:

I am writing to dispute a billing error in the amount of $_____on my account. The amount is inaccurate because (describe the problem). I am requesting that the error be corrected, that any finance and other charges related to the disputed amount be credited as well, and that I receive an accurate statement.

Enclosed are copies of (use this sentence to describe any enclosed information, such as sales slips, payment records) supporting my position. Please investigate this matter and correct the billing error as soon as possible.

Sincerely,

[Your name]
Enclosures: [List what you are enclosing]

For more information, see *Fair Credit Billing* and *Avoiding Credit and Charge Card Fraud*, two brochures available from the FTC or at www.consumer.gov/idtheft.

Debt Collectors

The Fair Debt Collection Practices Act prohibits debt collectors from using unfair or deceptive practices to collect overdue bills that a creditor has forwarded for collection.

You can stop a debt collector from contacting you by writing a letter to the collection agency telling them to stop. Once the debt collector receives your letter, the company may not contact you again — with two exceptions: they can tell you there will be no further contact and they can tell you that the debt collector or the creditor intends to take some specific action.

A collector also may not contact you if, within 30 days after you receive the written notice, you send the collection agency a letter stating you do not owe the money. Although such a letter should stop the debt collector's calls, it will not necessarily get rid of the debt itself, which may still turn up on your credit report. In addition, a collector can renew collection activities if you are sent proof of the debt. So, along with your letter stating you do not owe the money, include copies of documents that support your position. If you are a victim of identity theft, including a copy (NOT original) of the police report you filed may be particularly useful.

For more information, consult *Fair Debt Collection*, a brochure available from the FTC or at www.consumer.gov/idtheft.

ATM Cards, Debit Cards and Electronic Fund Transfers

The Electronic Fund Transfer Act provides consumer protections for transactions involving an ATM or debit card or other electronic way to debit or credit an account. It also limits your liability for unauthorized electronic fund transfers.

It is important to report lost or stolen ATM and debit cards immediately because the amount you can be held responsible for depends on *how quickly* you report the loss.

- If you report your ATM card lost or stolen within two business days of discovering the loss or theft, your losses are limited to $50.
- If you report your ATM card lost or stolen after the two business days, but within 60 days after a statement showing an unauthorized electronic fund transfer, you can be liable for up to $500 of what a thief withdraws.
- If you wait more than 60 days, you could lose *all* the money that was taken from your account after the end of the 60 days and before you report your card missing.

The best way to protect yourself in the event of an error or fraudulent transaction is to call the financial institution and follow up in writing — by certified letter, return receipt requested — so you can prove when the institution received your letter. Keep a copy of the letter you send for your records.

After notification about an error on your statement, the institution generally has 10 business days to investigate. The financial institution must tell you the results of its investigation within three business days after completing it and must correct an error within one business day after determining that the error has occurred. If the institution needs more time, it may take up to 45 days to complete the investigation — but only if the money in dispute is returned to your account and you are notified promptly of the credit. At the end of the investigation, if no error has been found, the institution may take the money back if it sends you a written explanation.

A Special Word About Lost or Stolen Checks

While no federal law limits your losses if someone steals your checks and forges your signature, state laws protect you. Most states hold the bank responsible for losses from a forged check. At the same time, however, most states require you to take reasonable care of your account. For example, you may be held responsible for the forgery if you fail to notify the bank in a timely manner that a check was lost or stolen. Contact your state banking or consumer protection agency for more information.

Note: VISA and MasterCard voluntarily have agreed to limit consumers' liability for unauthorized use of their debit cards in most instances to $50 per card, no matter how much time has elapsed since the discovery of the loss or theft of the card.

For more information, consult *Electronic Banking* and *Credit and ATM Cards: What to Do If They Are Lost or Stolen*, two brochures available from the FTC or at www.consumer.gov/idtheft.

RESOURCES

Federal Government

Federal Trade Commission (FTC) — http://www.ftc.gov/. The FTC is the federal clearinghouse for complaints by victims of identity theft. Although the FTC does not have the authority to bring criminal cases, the Commission helps victims of identity theft by providing them with information to help resolve the financial and other problems that can result from identity theft. The FTC also may refer victim complaints to other appropriate government agencies and private organizations for action.

If you have been a victim of identity theft, file a complaint with the FTC by contacting the FTC's Identity Theft Hotline by telephone: toll-free 1-877-IDTHEFT (438-4338); TDD: 202-326-2502; by mail: Identity Theft Clearinghouse, Federal Trade Commission, 600 Pennsylvania Avenue, NW, Washington, D.C. 20580; or online: www.consumer.gov/idtheft.

FTC publications:

- *Avoiding Credit and Charge Card Fraud*
- *Credit and ATM Cards: What to Do If They Are Lost or Stolen*
- *Credit Card Loss Protection Offers: They Are The Real Steal*
- *Electronic Banking*
- *Fair Credit Billing*
- *Fair Credit Reporting*
- *Fair Debt Collection*
- *Getting Purse-onal: What To Do If Your Wallet or Purse Is Stolen*
- *How to Dispute Credit Report Errors*
- *Identity Crisis… What to Do If Your Identity Is Stolen*
- *Identity Thieves Can Ruin Your Good Name: Tips for Avoiding Identity Theft*

Banking Agencies

If you are having trouble getting your financial institution to help you resolve your banking-related identity theft problems including problems with bank-issued credit cards contact the agency with the appropriate jurisdiction. If you are not sure which agency has jurisdiction over your institution, call your bank or visit www.ffiec.gov/nic/default.htm.

Federal Deposit Insurance Corporation (FDIC) — http://www.fdic.gov/. The FDIC supervises state-chartered banks that are not members of the Federal Reserve System and insures deposits at banks and savings and loans.

Call the FDIC Consumer Call Center at 1-800-934-3342; or write: Federal Deposit Insurance Corporation, Division of Compliance and Consumer Affairs, 550 17th Street, NW, Washington, D.C. 20429.

FDIC publications:

- *Classic Cons... And How to Counter Them*
- *Pretext Calling and Identity Theft*
- *Your Wallet: A Loser's Manual*
- *A Crook Has Drained Your Account. Who Pays?*

Federal Reserve System (Fed) — http://www.federalreserve.gov/. The Fed supervises state-chartered banks that are members of the Federal Reserve System.

Call: 202-452-3693; or write: Division of Consumer and Community Affairs, Mail Stop 801, Federal Reserve Board, Washington, D.C. 20551; or contact the Federal Reserve Bank in your area. The 12 Reserve Banks are located in Boston, New York City, Philadelphia, Cleveland, Richmond, Atlanta, Chicago, St. Louis, Minneapolis, Kansas City, Dallas and San Francisco.

National Credit Union Administration (NCUA) — http://www.ncua.gov/. The NCUA charters and supervises federal credit unions and insures deposits at federal credit unions and many state credit unions.

Call: 703-518-6360; or write: Compliance Officer, National Credit Union Administration, 1775 Duke Street, Alexandria, VA 22314.

Office of the Comptroller of the Currency (OCC) — http://www.occ.treas.gov/. The OCC charters and supervises national banks. If the word "national" appears in the name of a bank, or the initials "N.A." follow its name, the OCC oversees its operations.

Call: 1-800-613-6743 (business days 9:00 a.m. to 4:00 p.m. CST); fax: 713-336-4301; or write: Customer Assistance Group, 1301 McKinney Street, Suite 3710, Houston, TX 77010.

OCC publications:

- *Check Fraud: A Guide to Avoiding Losses*

Office of Thrift Supervision (OTS) — http://www.ots.treas.gov/. The OTS is the primary regulator of all federal and many state-chartered thrift institutions, which include savings banks and savings and loan institutions.

Call: 202-906-6000; or write: Office of Thrift Supervision, 1700 G Street, NW, Washington, D.C. 20552.

Department of Justice (DOJ) — http://www.usdoj.gov/. The DOJ and its U.S. Attorneys prosecute federal identity theft cases. Information on identity theft is available at www.usdoj.gov/criminal/fraud/idtheft.html.

Federal Bureau of Investigation (FBI) — http://www.fbi.gov/. The FBI is one of the federal criminal law enforcement agencies that investigates cases of identity theft. Local field offices are listed in the Blue Pages of your telephone directory.

FBI publications:

- *Protecting Yourself Against Identity Fraud*

Federal Communications Commission (FCC) — http://www.fcc.gov/. The FCC regulates interstate and international communications by radio, television, wire, satellite, and cable. The FCC's Consumer Information Bureau is the consumer's one-stop source for information, forms, applications, and current issues before the FCC.

Call: 1-888-CALL-FCC; TTY: 1-888-TELL-FCC; or write: Federal Communications Commission, Consumer Information Bureau, 445 12th Street, SW, Room 5A863, Washington, D.C. 20554. You can file complaints via the online complaint form at www.fcc.gov, or e-mail questions to fccinfo@fcc.gov.

Internal Revenue Service (IRS) — www.treas.gov/irs/ci. The IRS is responsible for administering and enforcing the internal revenue laws. If you believe someone has assumed your identity to file federal income tax returns, or to commit other tax fraud, call toll-free: 1-800-829-0433. For assistance to victims of identity theft schemes who are having trouble filing their correct returns, call the IRS Taxpayer Advocates Office, toll-free: 1-877-777- 4778.

U.S. Secret Service (USSS) — www.treas.gov/usss. The U.S. Secret Service is one of the federal law enforcement agencies that investigates financial crimes, which may include identity theft. Although the Secret Service generally investigates cases where the dollar loss is substantial, your information may provide evidence of a larger pattern of fraud requiring their involvement. Local field offices are listed in the Blue Pages of your telephone directory.

Secret Service publications:

- *Financial Crimes Division*
- *Frequently Asked Questions: Protecting Yourself*

Social Security Administration (SSA) — http://www.ssa.gov/. SSA may assign you a new SSN — at your request — if you continue to experience problems even after trying to resolve the problems resulting from identity theft. SSA field office employees work closely with victims of identity theft and third parties to collect the evidence needed to assign a new SSN in these cases.

SSA Office of the Inspector General (SSA/OIG). The SSA/OIG is one of the federal law enforcement agencies that investigates cases of identity theft.

Direct allegations that an SSN has been stolen or misused to the SSA Fraud Hotline. Call: 1-800-269-0271; fax: 410-597-0018; write: SSA Fraud Hotline, P.O. Box 17768, Baltimore, MD 21235; or e-mail: oig.hotline@ssa.gov.

SSA publications:

- *SSA Fraud Hotline for Reporting Fraud*
- *Social Security When Someone Misuses Your Number* (SSA Pub. No. 05-10064)
- *Social Security: Your Number and Card* (SSA Pub. No. 05-10002)

U.S. Postal Inspection Service (USPIS) — www.usps.gov/websites/depart/ inspect. The USPIS is one of the federal law enforcement agencies that investigates cases of identity theft. USPIS is the law enforcement arm of the U.S. Postal Service. USPIS has primary jurisdiction in all matters infringing on the integrity of the U.S. mail. You can locate the USPIS district office nearest you by calling your local post office or checking the list at the Web site above.

U.S. Securities and Exchange Commission (SEC) — http://www.sec.gov/. The SEC's Office of Investor Education and Assistance serves investors who complain to the SEC about investment fraud or the mishandling of their investments by securities professionals. If you have experienced identity theft in connection with a securities transaction, write: SEC, 450 Fifth Street, NW, Washington, D.C., 20549-0213. You also may call 202-942-7040 or send an e-mail to help@sec.gov.

U.S. Trustee (UST) — www.usdoj.gov/ust. If you believe someone has filed for bankruptcy using your name, write to the U.S. Trustee in the region where the bankruptcy was filed. A list of the U.S. Trustee's Regional Offices is available on the UST Web site, or check the Blue Pages of your phone book under U.S. Government Bankruptcy Administration. Your letter should describe the situation and provide proof of your identity. The U.S. Trustee, if appropriate, will make a criminal referral to criminal law enforcement authorities if you provide appropriate documentation to substantiate your claim. You also may want to file a complaint with the U.S. Attorney and/or the FBI in the city where the bankruptcy was filed.

The U.S. Trustee does not provide legal representation, legal advice, or referrals to lawyers. That means you may need to hire an attorney to help convince the bankruptcy court that the filing is fraudulent. The U.S. Trustee does not provide consumers with copies of court documents. Those documents are available from the bankruptcy clerk's office for a fee.

State and Local Governments

Many states and local governments have passed laws related to identity theft; others may be considering such legislation. Where specific identity theft laws do not exist, the practices may be prohibited under other laws. Contact your State Attorney General's office (for a list of state offices, visit http://www.naag.org/) or local consumer protection agency to find out whether your state has laws related to identity theft, or visit www.consumer.gov/idtheft/.

PRIVACY POLICY

When you contact us with complaints or requests for information, you can contact us by telephone, toll-free at 1-877-ID-THEFT (438-4338); by postal mail: Federal Trade Commission, Identity Theft Clearinghouse, 600 Pennsylvania Avenue, NW, Washington, D.C. 20580; or electronically via our online complaint form, located at http://www.consumer.gov/. Before you do, there are a few things you should know.

The material you submit may be seen by various people. We enter the information you send into our electronic database. This information is shared with our attorneys and investigators. It may also be shared with employees of various other federal, state, or local authorities who may use this data for regulatory or law enforcement purposes. We may also share some information with certain private entities, such as credit bureaus and any companies you may have complained about, where we believe that doing so might assist in resolving identity theft-related problems. You may be contacted by the FTC or any of the agencies or private entities to whom your complaint has been referred. In other limited circumstances, including requests from Congress, we may be required by law to disclose information you submit.

You have the option to submit your information anonymously. However, if you do not provide your name and contact information, law enforcement and other entities will not be able to contact you to obtain additional information to assist in identity theft investigations and prosecutions.

The FTC works for the consumer to prevent fraudulent, deceptive, and unfair business practices in the marketplace and to provide information to help consumers spot, stop, and avoid them. To file a complaint, or to get free information on any of 150 consumer topics, call toll-free,

1-877-FTC-HELP (1-877-382-4357), or use the online complaint form. The FTC enters Internet, telemarketing, identity theft, and other fraud-related complaints into Consumer Sentinel, a secure, online database available to hundreds of civil and criminal law enforcement agencies in the United States and abroad.

Chapter 25

To Disclose or Not to Disclose: A Legal Primer for ISPs

Mitch Dembin
Erin Kenneally

INFORMATION PLEASE

Internet service providers (ISPs) have something that everyone wants: information. From law enforcement to marketers to criminals, information about subscribers and others who transit ISPs is valuable. Information about subscribers and others can be critical to the victims of criminal hackers trying to secure their systems and determine the identity and motives of the intruder. Yet there is a volume of misinformation about when and to whom an ISP can lawfully disclose information. All too often, the upstream ISP tells the downstream victim that information about the intruder is available but that the law requires a subpoena. This unfortunate response requires that the victim absorb the expense of retaining a lawyer and file a "John Doe" lawsuit without any assurance that the information obtained will be useful, or give up and just repair the damaged systems. Most victims choose the latter, giving the criminal hackers a tremendous boon.

In many instances, the upstream ISPs are wrong. Whether or not the law places restrictions on the voluntary disclosure of information by ISPs depends on who is asking, the category of information being requested, and whether the information relates to a system subscriber. In some circumstances, regardless of the law, user agreements will impact the decision as to whether voluntary disclosure of certain information is acceptable. The purpose of this chapter, however, is to clarify the legal restrictions and obligations of an ISP from which information is requested.

0-8493-1248-5/02/$0.00+$1.50
© 2002 by CRC Press LLC

THE TREASURE

ISPs, except as required in individual cases pursuant to court order or formal request from a qualified law enforcement agency, are under no obligation to retain information pertaining to subscribers or others who transit the ISP. ISPs cannot be required, absent a regulatory framework that does not currently exist, to create records. Nevertheless, most United States ISPs do have and retain for some period of time a treasure trove of information about subscribers and others.[1]

The federal Electronic Communications and Privacy Act (ECPA) found at Title 18, United States Code, Section 2701, *et seq.,* provides a framework to categorize information held by ISPs. The ECPA treats information possessed by ISPs as subscriber information, transactional information related to subscribers, and contents of stored electronic communications. This information is valuable to marketers, retailers, advertisers, demographers, politicians, researchers, law enforcement officers, and criminals. The ECPA, however, only applies to disclosures of such information to the government.

Subscriber information, as provided by the ECPA, consists exclusively of the name, address, local and long-distance telephone toll billing records, telephone number or other subscriber number or identity, and length of service and the types of services the subscriber or customer utilized (see 18 USC 2703(c)(1)(C)). The ECPA covers disclosure of the contents of stored electronic communications. An *electronic communication* is:

> Any transfer of signs, signals, writing, images, sounds, data, or intelligence of any nature transmitted in whole or in part by a wire, radio, electromagnetic, photoelectronic or photooptical system that affects interstate or foreign commerce.

> — 18 USC 2510(12)

Transactional information is not defined but presumably includes all other information pertaining to a subscriber, such as billing and payment information, logging and tracking information (where the subscriber traveled online and what the subscriber did while on line), and with whom the subscriber communicated with while online (excluding content).[2]

There is a class of information unaddressed by the ECPA. Criminal hackers can obtain unauthorized access to an ISP and, from there, attack other computer systems. The ISP will have log records and other evidence regarding the intruder. Because the intruder is not a subscriber, such records, other than the contents of stored communications, are not governed by the ECPA.

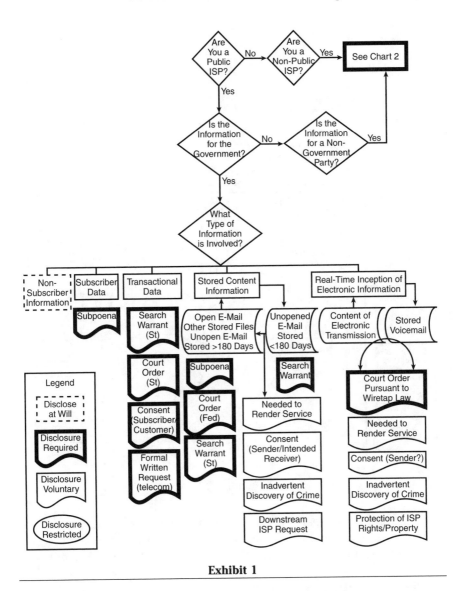

Exhibit 1

DISCLOSURE AND THE LAW

Electronic communication service providers, the legal term used by federal law for entities including ISPs, are regularly asked to disclose or sell information. Depending on who is asking and what is being asked for, and, sometimes, whether the ISP is a private or public provider, the law provides some answers regarding whether disclosure is required, forbidden, or voluntary. (See Exhibits 1 and 2.) The identity of the requestor matters most if the requestor is or represents a government entity. The law is at

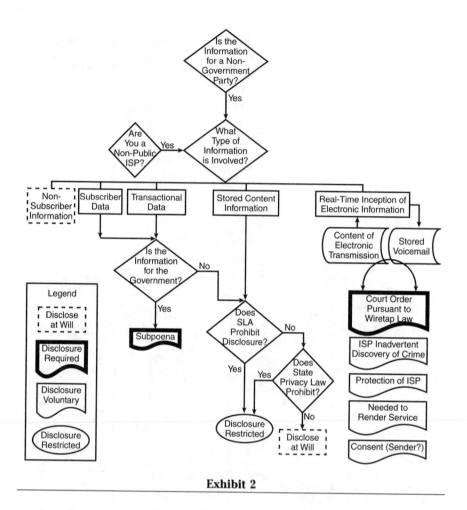

Exhibit 2

its most restrictive regarding disclosures to the government. It is an area fraught with peril for the ISP, however, because government entities routinely request broader information than allowed by the vehicle employed.

Disclosure and the Government

Subscriber Information. The federal Electronic Communications Privacy Act (ECPA) provides the exclusive means for any government authority (federal, state, or local) to obtain subscriber information, transactional information pertaining to subscribers, and stored electronic communications from electronic communication service providers. The ECPA provides the least protection for subscriber information and applies progressively greater protection for transactional information and stored contents. That protective structure is reflected by the means required of

302

the government to obtain the different levels of information and the notice requirements applicable to each level.

Recall that the definition of subscriber information in the ECPA is rather narrow. It defines subscriber information exclusively as consisting of the name, address, local and long-distance telephone toll billing records, telephone number or other subscriber number or identity, and length of service and the types of services the subscriber or customer utilized (see 18 USC 2703(c)(1)(C)). To lawfully obtain subscriber information from an ISP, the minimum requirement is that the government entity must supply a subpoena to the ISP. The subpoena can be an administrative subpoena authorized by a federal or state statute, a federal or state grand jury subpoena, or a trial subpoena. The government is not required to issue a subpoena if it chooses to use one of the major methods available under the ECPA, as discussed below. The government entity is not required to give notice to the subscriber that it is seeking or has obtained subscriber information from the ISP.[3]

Transactional Information Pertaining to a Subscriber. Recall that this class of information is everything between the rather narrow definition of subscriber information provided in the ECPA and the contents of stored communications. If an ISP extensively logs and tracks subscriber activity, that information is available to the government. If the ISP employs minimal logging and tracking, the government cannot compel the ISP to increase logging and tracking. All the government can do is compel the ISP to preserve records and other evidence in its possession for 90 days, pending the issuance of appropriate legal process to obtain the information. The 90-day period can be renewed for an additional 90 days. All that is required is a *request* from a governmental entity (see 18 USC 2703(f)). It is important to note that the request to preserve evidence only relates to information in the possession of the ISP at the time of the request. The preservation request does not and cannot require the ISP to preserve information that has not yet come into its possession (logs from the next day, for example).[4] Interestingly, there is no sanction provided in the law if the ISP discloses the existence of the preservation request (absent criminal intent).[3]

The ECPA provides four different methods for the government to obtain transactional records relating to a subscriber from an ISP (see 18 USC 2703(c)(1)(B)). The government can obtain a search warrant, a court order issued pursuant to Section 2703(d) of the ECPA, consent of the subscriber or customer, or a formal written request if the matter under investigation is a telemarketing fraud. That is, no notice to the subscriber is required of the government but, as provided above, the ISP can disclose the government's actions to anyone unless barred by court order or made with criminal intent to obstruct a lawful proceeding.

As a practical matter, most state and local government entities will obtain a search warrant for transactional information, and most federal authorities will obtain a Section 2703(d) court order for such information. Ordinarily, the court will require nondisclosure by the ISP upon application of the government in either circumstance.

Transactional Records of Nonsubscribers. Historical records relating to the activities of nonsubscribers using an ISP are not covered by the ECPA. The ISP can freely provide such information to the government, with or without a request. Moreover, as discussed below, if the ISP has been monitoring the activities of an intruder for its own protection, the records of those interceptions can also be freely provided to law enforcement authorities.

Stored Contents of Electronic Communications. The most difficult, confusing, and poorly written sections of the ECPA pertain to stored electronic communications. Real-time interceptions of electronic communications are the province of the federal wiretap law as discussed below. The ECPA applies to electronic communications in "electronic storage," and to communications maintained by a "remote computing service" only if such services are provided to the public.[5] Strangely enough, a literal reading of the statute leads one to the conclusion that private service providers, such as corporations and universities, are not constrained regarding the disclosure of stored electronic communications (see 18 USC 2702(a)). There even is case law supporting this point of view. See *Arthur Andersen LLP v. UOP*, 991 F. Supp. 1041 (N.D. Ill. 1998).

Electronic storage is defined as:

> Any temporary, intermediate storage of a wire or electronic communication incidental to the electronic transmission thereof; and any storage of such communication by an electronic communication service for purposes of backup protection of such communication.

> — 18 USC 2510(17)

Unopened electronic mail that is awaiting download by the recipient and backups of that mail are in electronic storage. Once the electronic mail is opened and remains resident on the ISP, it is considered to be held by a remote computing service. The ECPA provides that anyone who provides electronic communication services *to the public* shall not knowingly divulge to any person or entity the contents of a communication while in electronic storage by that service (see 18 USC 2702(a)(1)). Remote computing service providers, generally the same ISP holding the mail after it is opened, are also prohibited from divulging the contents of the communication if the communication is subscriber generated or subscriber received and the subscriber has not authorized the remote provider to access the contents other than as necessary to provide the storage service. Civil liability is available against the ISP and the offending government agency (see 18 USC 2707). Curiously, there is no counterpart to this provision regarding private ISPs. Consequently, an electronic communication service provider that does not provide such services to the public appears freely able to disclose the contents of stored communications to anyone other than a government entity.

The rules regarding governmental access to stored electronic communications are complicated. The rules vary if the electronic communications are opened or unopened and, if unopened, the length of time that the communication has resided on the ISP's server. Unopened electronic mail in electronic storage is provided the greatest protection under the ECPA. To obtain the contents of unopened electronic mail in electronic storage, the government entity must use a search warrant. If, however, the unopened electronic mail or communication has been in electronic storage for more than 180 days, the government can use a search warrant, a subpoena, or a Section 2703(d) court order. If the government entity uses anything other than a search warrant for contents of stored communications, it must provide notice to the subscriber or obtain a court order delaying notice (see 18 USC 2703(a), (b), and 2705).

Opened mail, regardless of vintage, if found on the ISP, is considered by the ECPA to be in the possession of a remote computing service. Opened mail is treated the same as unopened mail in electronic storage for more than 180 days. That is, the government entity can use a search warrant (no notice) or a subpoena or 2703(d) court order with notice (or delayed notice).

An important caveat relates to stored voice mail communications. Increasingly, electronic communication service providers are carrying and storing voice communications either as part of electronic mail services or through Internet telephony. Recall that an *electronic communication* is:

> Any transfer of signs, signals, writing, images, sounds, data, or intelligence of any nature transmitted in whole or in part by a wire, radio, electromagnetic, photoelectronic or photooptical system that affects interstate or foreign commerce.

> — 18 USC 2510(12)

The definition would appear to include stored voice mail even if transmitted, in whole or in part, by wire. By this reasoning, voice mail transmitted and stored by an electronic communication service provider should be available to the government on the same basis as stored electronic mail that does not contain a voice communication. And, as a practical matter, how does the ISP or the government entity seeking access to contents of stored electronic communications know, in advance, whether the contents contain voice, music, or other sound clip?

The same statute, however, also defines *wire communication*. A wire communication:

> Means any aural transfer made in whole or in part through the use of facilities for the transmission of communications by the aid of wire, cable, or other like connection between the point of origin and the point of reception (including the use of such connection in a switching station) furnished or operated by any person engaged in providing or operating such facilities for the transmission of interstate or foreign communications or communications affecting interstate or foreign commerce *and such term includes any electronic storage of such communication.*

> — 18 USC 2510(1) (emphasis added)

By this definition, stored voice mail, even if carried by an electronic communication service provider, is a wire communication and not an electronic communication. This is a difference with a distinction. Wire communications can only be obtained by the government by following the procedures of the wiretap laws — a difficult and time-consuming task. Moreover, violations of the wiretap laws carry not only civil liability but also are five-year federal felonies. Information obtained in violation of the wiretap laws, even if obtained by a private citizen, is not admissible in court. Evidence obtained in violation of the ECPA, however, is admissible in court.

At least one court has ruled that the stricter provisions of the wiretap laws apply to stored voice mail. See *United States v. Smith*, 155 F.3d 1051 (9th Cir. 1998). This can be a minefield for law enforcement officers and for ISPs.

Real-Time Interception of Electronic Communications. Absent consent of a party to the communication, there are two ways that the government can lawfully obtain the contents of intercepted communications. First, the government can obtain a court order pursuant to the applicable wiretap laws (the federal law is the minimum standard). This is no easy task. To obtain a court order authorizing the interception of electronic communications, the government agency must demonstrate, among other things, probable cause to believe that the contents of the communications relate to the commission of a federal felony offense, that traditional investigative means have been tried and have failed or that there is reason to believe that such means would fail if tried, and that the interception is designed so that only relevant communications will be intercepted. The application must be approved by a high-level official in the Department of Justice and by a United States District Judge. The interception can only continue until its object has been achieved or 30 days have passed, whichever is earlier. Extensions require the same approvals and information (see 18 USC 2510 *et seq.*).

The government can also obtain the contents of electronic communications intercepted lawfully by the electronic communication service provider. The ECPA provides that a provider of electronic communication services to the public can disclose the contents of an electronic communication in electronic storage or in remote storage to a law enforcement agency if the contents were inadvertently obtained by the service provider and appear to pertain to the commission of a crime (see 18 USC 2702(b)(6)). There is a broader exception available under the wiretap laws:

> It shall not be unlawful under this chapter for an operator of a switchboard, or on [*sic*] officer, employee, or agent of a provider of wire or electronic communication service, whose facilities are used in the transmission of a wire or electronic communication, to intercept, disclose, or use that communication in the normal course of his employment while engaged in any activity which is a necessary incident to the rendition of his service or to the protection of the rights or property of the provider of that service, ...

> — 18 USC 2511(2)(a)(i)

In essence, this means that if the ISP is monitoring the electronic communications of a subscriber (or anyone else) transiting its system in order to provide service or to protect itself, it can disclose the intercepted communications to the government. For example, an ISP learns that a hacker is transiting its system. To defend itself, the ISP institutes keystroke monitoring of the hacker. The ISP can conduct the interception and disclose the results to the government. When the business purpose for the interception ends, the government must obtain a wiretap order to continue its investigation.

Disclosure and Everyone Else under ECPA

In the preceding section, we discussed the means by which the government can obtain information from ISPs. But, as noted above, the government is not the only entity that treasures this information. What are the rules applicable to ISPs from whom information is requested when the requesting party is not the government?

Subscriber Information. The ECPA applies only when the requesting party is the government. In fact, the ECPA expressly says so:

> Except as provided in subparagraph (B), a provider of electronic communication service or remote computing service may disclose a record or other information pertaining to a subscriber to or customer of such service (not including the contents of communications covered by

> subsection (a) or (b) of this section) *to any person other than a governmental entity.*

> — 18 USC 2703(c)(1)(A)

The reference to subparagraph (B) should not provide any solace to privacy advocates; subparagraph (B) only pertains to governmental access to transactional records pertaining to a subscriber.

Under the law, therefore, an ISP can disclose subscriber information to anyone it wants other than to the government. Only their user agreements and conscience serve as bars.

Transactional Records Pertaining to Subscribers. As above, the ECPA applies only to governmental access to transactional records pertaining to subscribers. An ISP can freely disclose transactional records pertaining to subscribers to anyone it chooses, subject only to user agreements.

Transactional Records of Nonsubscribers. These records are not governed by the ECPA. The ISP can freely provide these records to anyone it chooses. And, because no subscriber agreement applies to persons who use the ISP without permission, the ISP is not constrained by whatever service agreements may exist for its subscribers.

Although seemingly obvious, ISPs are at liberty to restrict the flow of bulk, unsolicited e-mail (spam) to their subscribers. As such, curbing the flow may entail disclosing information about the offending party, whether or not that party is a subscriber. This disclosure would be supported as a protective measure under the ECPA, regardless of whether its SLA contains anti-spam provisions. Furthermore, the offending party cannot raise a constitutional claim for such disclosures because there is no First Amendment right to use private computer services to deliver unsolicited e-mail.[6]

Contents of Stored Electronic Communications. Providers of electronic communication services to the public are generally prohibited from disclosing the contents of electronic communications in electronic storage or held as a remote computing service (see 18 USC 2702(a)). Exceptions to the general prohibition are made to allow for disclosure to addressees of the communication (2702(b)(1)); pursuant to a court-ordered interception, the service provider exception or a 2703(d) court order (2702(b)(2)); consent of the originator or of an intended recipient of the communication (2702(b)(3)); downstream ISPs (2702(b)(4)); as necessary to provide service or to protect the rights or property of the service provider (2702(b)(5)); and to a law enforcement agency if the contents were inadvertently obtained and appear to pertain to the commission of a crime (2702(b)(6)).

Providers of electronic communication services that do not provide such services to the public are not constrained by the ECPA in disclosing the contents of electronic communications in electronic storage or held as a remote computing service. See *Arthur Anderson LLP v. UOP,* [cite] (N.D. Ill. 1998).

Real-Time Interception of Electronic Communications. As discussed, both the ECPA and the wiretap laws have service provider exceptions allowing for the disclosure of the contents of communications as necessary to render service or to protect the rights and property of the service provider. The ECPA provides that the provider of electronic communication services to the public can divulge the contents of electronic communications that are in electronic storage or are held by a remote computing service "as may be necessarily incident to the rendition of the service or to the protection of the rights or property of the provider of that service" (see 18 USC 2702(b)(5)). The broader provision of the wiretap laws provide that the service provider may "intercept, disclose, or use that communication in the normal course of his employment while engaged in any activity which is a necessary incident to the rendition of his service or to the protection of the rights or property of the provider of that service" (see 18 USC 2511(2)(a)(i)).

REMEDIES AND PENALTIES

Both the ECPA and the wiretap laws provide for remedies and penalties for violations. The ECPA provides only for civil remedies.[7] ISPs, subscribers, or other persons aggrieved by any knowing and intentional violation of the ECPA can recover from the person or entity that engaged in the violation equitable relief such as an injunction, damages of at least $1000 and punitive damages for willful violations, and reasonable attorney fees and litigation costs (see 18 USC 2707(a), (b), and (c)). The statute suggests that personal liability for government agents is not permitted because it provides a separate subsection requiring a government agency to initiate disciplinary proceedings against its agents that the court believes may have acted willfully (see 2707(d)). Finally, a complete defense is provided if the defendant has, in good faith, relied on a court warrant or order, grand jury subpoena, legislative or statutory authorization; an emergency request of an investigative or law enforcement officer under the wiretap laws; or a good-faith determination that the service provider exceptions provided by 18 USC 2518(3) applied.

The wiretap laws are a different matter. The intentional interception of electronic communications without legal authority, the disclosure or use of communications intercepted unlawfully and the disclosure of lawfully intercepted communications if made with intent to obstruct a criminal investigation constitute federal felonies punishable by up to five years imprisonment (see 18 USC 2511). The wiretap laws also provide for civil remedies for any person whose electronic communication is intercepted, disclosed, or used in violation of the law (see 18 USC 2520). The same good-faith defenses as apply to a civil action under the ECPA apply to civil actions brought under the wiretap laws (see 18 USC 2520).

Beyond the ECPA: Disclosure and Civil Law

The ECPA does not prohibit a public or private ISP from revealing customer information (subscriber, transactional) to nongovernmental entities. An ISP that serves the public, however, cannot voluntarily provide this customer information (subscriber, transactional, or content based) to the government without first requiring the proper legal process mandated by the ECPA. The ECPA provides for civil remedies by the aggrieved customer against their ISP and the offending government entity.

This civil remedy is a privacy protection measure to deter unfettered disclosures to government entities by public ISPs. Yet, for example, the same caution does not forestall the dissemination of data to private organizations or service providers. As mentioned, any limitations on a public or private ISP revealing this information to nongovernmental parties would reside in service level agreements (SLAs or user agreements) between the ISP and its customers. Furthermore, although courts have not yet squarely confronted the issue, state laws may further prohibit the free disclosure of customer identities. In addition, such privacy provisions might affect the compelled disclosure of users' identities attendant to the civil discovery process.

SLAs. Service level agreements (SLAs) can restrict an ISP's right to reveal customer information. These user agreements are contracts between the ISP and its customers. The terms of service and assignment of rights and responsibilities defined therein are purely within the discretion of the contracting parties.[8] Contrast this to the ECPA, whereby limits on disclosure attach automatically whenever the government obtains this information from a public provider — whether by legal process or voluntary act. That is, an ISP has no contractual liability if it discloses customer information to nongovernmental parties, unless the SLA states otherwise.[9]

Major Internet services that provide more than ports of entry to the Internet, such as message boards and chat rooms, face additional challenges to voluntary disclosure. For these types of service providers, the SLA can provide a vehicle for users to assert their right to anonymous speech and to seek protection from unwanted disclosure by ISPs.

To be sure, services providers are granted limited immunity under the Communications Decency Act (47 USC §230(c)) and Digital Millennium

Copyright Act (17 USC Section 512, 1999) for its users' defamatory content and copyright infringement, respectively. Nevertheless, regardless of whether an ISP chooses to monitor content, an ISP can thwart users' anonymity by complying with a John Doe subpoena and releasing a user's identity before that usser is notified. The issue here is not whether the ISP should comply with a valid subpoena; rather, it is unsettled whether an ISP is required to give notice to its users before disclosing their identities. As with provisions restricting disclosure at all, ISPs can be bound by notice requirements if this is addressed in the SLA. In the absence of such a provision, however, ISPs could face prohibitions under state constitutional free-speech provisions.

State Privacy Provisions. The ECPA's protection of privacy extends only to government invasions of privacy.[10] Not to belabor the point, but this is significant because it reveals that the ECPA does not create a reasonable expectation of privacy in that information. Furthermore, there is no uniform, federal requirement to notify a user if his identity is disclosed to or requested by a third party. However, this does not put ISPs beyond the reach of other sources of privacy rights that may encumber voluntary disclosure of customer data.

It is well settled that the First Amendment protects the right to anonymous speech from government interference.[11] Thus, government action is required to bring a claim under Article I of the U.S. Constitution. Likewise, the vast majority of state cases addressing this issue assume the same posture: state action is required to raise a state constitutional cause of action.[12] That is, a private party is generally not subject to constitutional requirements and thus cannot be liable to another party for infringing those rights.

There is an argument, however, that a cause of action may exist against a private-party service provider conducting itself as a public forum. Although "public forum" has not been specifically defined in the digital world, the definition would likely include service providers that directly administer Web sites, message boards, and chat areas.

This argument is derived, in part, from a California Supreme Court holding that the free speech guarantees of the California Constitution "protect speech and petitioning reasonably exercised, in shopping centers, even when the centers are privately owned."[13]

The rationale was that large shopping centers had replaced downtown business districts as community areas where large groups of people tend to congregate.

Applying this rationale to the modern Internet society, large providers such as America Online and Yahoo! have become the shopping centers of the digital realm. Their message boards and chat rooms foster community building and invite an exchange of ideas reminiscent of the open spaces, nonretail activities, and expressive uses of shopping centers. Just as malls have an incentive to attract a large number of visitors, so too do providers of these digital malls benefit from the advertising dollars that derive from a large user base.

Service providers that are within the jurisdiction of any state that adopts this legal framework may be prohibited from disclosing customer information or providing prior notice to them before complying with a subpoena.

Compelled Disclosure and John Doe Case Law. Whereas the ECPA sets forth the standards for disclosure of a person's identity to the government, there are no federal laws protecting anonymous speech online. As such, courts are struggling with standards for disclosing identities of anonymous Internet posters.

Service providers have been increasingly drawn into disputes between users who post anonymous Internet messages and the companies that are allegedly harmed by these cybersmears. Service providers are oftentimes the only harbingers of identity data, which is the centerpiece in the conflict between free speech and anonymity vs. accountability and fraud prevention. These "John Doe" lawsuits have come under fire because they are often filed solely to uncover the identity of anonymous Internet messages.[14] That is, companies are compelling the disclosure of user identities by using the civil discovery process to serve subpoenas on ISPs. To exemplify a case that arguably arose from the desire to uncover anonymous posters, Raytheon sued 21 "John Doe" defendants and subpoenaed Yahoo! for their identities. Subsequent to unmasking the defendants, it voluntarily dismissed the suit.[15]

Nevertheless, courts are split over the threshold needed to unmask an anonymous user's identity in the discovery process of a case. Recently, a federal district court started to draw lines by quashing a subpoena that would have required Web provider InfoSpace to disclose the identity of nearly two dozen anonymous message posters because they were not named in the lawsuit nor found to be central to the claim.[16] Rather, 2TheMart.com sought the identities behind the pseudonyms on one of its investment bulletin boards in attempting to defend itself in a class-action lawsuit for securities fraud. Whereas compelled disclosure to government entities carries the force of uniform, federal law (ECPA), service providers should be aware that the authority behind conformity with civil subpoenas is more tenuous.

Many providers comply with the subpoenas as a matter of course, thus affording the user no notice or opportunity to quash the subpoena.[17] In contrast, other ISPs do provide notice and time to challenge the process when served with civil subpoenas, as stated in the companies' privacy policy.[18] To be sure, ISPs are wise to comply with the civil process that mandates disclosure of users' identities; the abuse of civil discovery is an issue best left to the courts and legislatures. Nevertheless, ISPs should be aware that a subpoena is not required before disclosing user identifications to nongovernmental parties, and there is no federal requirement that notice be given to users upon receiving a civil subpoena. An ISP is only encumbered by such requirements if its SLAs or state privacy provisions speak to the issue.

CONCLUSION

Internet service providers possess information and data valuable to marketers, law enforcers, and criminals. When an ISP is asked for information, the decision whether or not to comply should be based on knowledge and reason, not myth and conjecture. The purpose of this chapter was to provide the ISP and its attorneys with an understanding of the legal framework that might affect their decision. The legal framework may change as more laws are passed regarding privacy, so it is essential that ISPs and their lawyers stay abreast of the relevant laws.

Notes

1. It is beyond the scope of this chapter to discuss the status of the laws governing retention and disclosure of information by ISPs subject to the jurisdiction of other nations. Suffice it to say that there is a raging debate in the European Union about these and related issues. See, for example, Draft Convention on Cybercrime (Draft No. 25 Rev. 5), Council of Europe, European Committee on Crime Problems, Committee of Experts on Crime in Cyber-space, December 22, 2000.
2. There is some dispute in the law enforcement community regarding the meaning of the terms applied in defining subscriber information in the ECPA. The statute exclusively defines subscriber information as provided above. Case law governing the meaning of those terms is sparse. Considering that the ECPA provides for civil penalties for unlawful disclosures, the authors advise caution and conservatism.
3. It is a popular misconception that an ISP in receipt of a subpoena is not permitted to disclose the existence or contents of the subpoena to the subscriber. Recipients of subpoenas may disclose the subpoena to anyone unless the government entity has obtained a court order prohibiting such notice (see 18 USC 2705(b)). Many law enforcement agencies request nondisclosure of the ISP, but cannot require it without a court order. Disclosure may have consequences, however, if the disclosure is made with criminal intent to corruptly obstruct the proceeding from which the subpoena issued (see 18 USC 1505).
4. Savvy government agents will determine from the ISP its normal record retention period and submit additional preservation requests before the expiration of that period to cover newly obtained information. Sometime before the expiration of the initial preservation request (plus one extension), the government entity will serve its process on the ISP for all of the information collected.
5. The ECPA does not apply to communications of any nature stored on a user's computer. A government agent with lawful access to a user's computer, by means of consent or search warrant, for example, can obtain all information maintained on that computer consistent with the terms of the consent and the warrant.
6. See, for example, *CompuServe v. Cyber Promotions,* 962 F. Supp. 1015 (S.D. Ohio 1997); *Cyber Promotions v. America Online,* 948 F. Supp. 456 (E.D. Pa. 1996).

7. The ECPA does provide a criminal penalty for intentionally accessing without authority or exceeding authorized access to a facility that provides electronic communication services and thereby obtaining, altering, or preventing authorized access to electronic communications in electronic storage (18 USC 2701(a)). Violation of this statute is a misdemeanor (18 USC 2701(b)).

8. In practice, these provisions are normally not negotiated. Rather, the user agrees to a boilerplate SLA created by the ISP in exchange for gaining an entryway to the Internet.

9. See, for example, *U.S. v. Hambrick*, 55 F. Supp. 2d 504 (1999). In reference to a state subpoena issued for the billing and user records for a user coming from a specific IP address at a specific date and time, the MindSpring ISP provided the government with the defendant's name, address, credit card number, e-mail address, home and work phone numbers, fax number, and confirmation that his account was connected at that IP address. The Court noted *in dicta* that because MindSpring had ready access to these records in the normal course of its business, nothing prevented it from revealing this information to nongovernmental actors. It added, "[t]here is nothing in the record to suggest that there was a restrictive agreement between the defendant and MindSpring that would limit the right of MindSpring to reveal the defendant's personal information to nongovernmental entities."

10. Recall (18 USC § 2703(c)(1)(A)) that ISPs are free to turn stored content and transactional data over to nongovernmental parties.

11. See *McIntyre v. Ohio Elections Comm'n*, 514 U.S. 334 (1995).

12. See *U.S. v. Cruikshank*, 92 U.S. 542 (1875).

13. *Robins v. Pruneyard Shopping Center*, 23 Cal.3d. 899 (1979), aff'd, 447 U.S. 74 (1980). Appellate courts in Colorado, Massachusetts, New Jersey, Oregon, and Pennsylvania, and a Texas trial court have interpreted their state constitutions similarly. See also *Commonwealth v. Tate*, 432 A.2d 1382 (Pa. 1981). The Pennsylvania Supreme Court held that the state constitution protects an individual's right to freedom of expression at a public forum held on the premises of a private college.

14. "[S]ince June 1988, American companies fighting ... cybersmears reportedly have been filing one or two lawsuits a week in Santa Clara County, California, the home of Yahoo! Inc." Blake Bell, Dealing with the Cybersmear, *N.Y.L.J.*, April 19, 1999, at T3.

15. See, for example, *Raytheon Co. v. John Does*, Civil Action No. 99-816 (Commonwealth of Massachusetts Superior Court, Middlesex County, filed February 1, 1999).

16. Federal District Seattle.

17. Yahoo! maintains that users have adequate notice per the company's policy statement, which reserves the right to disclose personal information. Yahoo! Privacy Policy (visited April 15, 2001) <http://docs.yahoo.com/info/privacy/>.

18. America Online, for example.

Section II
Tools and Related Technology

Chapter 26
Selecting a Cryptographic System
Marie A. Wright

Never before has there been a greater risk of unauthorized access to computer data. Corporations using computer networks face an increasing probability that their data will be compromised as the business environment expands through dial-up and internetwork connections. Sensitive data is often insecurely stored and transmitted, furthering the risk of its unauthorized disclosure or modification by employees or external intruders. These risks can be significantly reduced through the implementation of a comprehensive security plan that includes the use of cryptography.

INTRODUCTION

Cryptography is concerned with the design and use of encryption systems, and its primary objective is to ensure the privacy and authenticity of data. Encryption provides privacy by transforming data into an unintelligible form through the use of a key, which is a symbol or group of symbols that controls the encryption or decryption processes.

Some cryptographic systems allow the same key to be used for both encryption and decryption. These private key systems are so named because the disclosure of the key to anyone but the sender and the receiver will compromise the integrity of the transmitted data. Other cryptographic systems use different keys to control the encryption and decryption operations. These public key systems typically use a public encryption key and a private decryption key. Although it is easy to calculate the public key from the private key, it is computationally infeasible to calculate the private key from the public key.

Public key cryptographic systems readily provide authenticity by generating and verifying digital signatures. Of particular importance in financial

0-8493-1248-5/02/$0.00+$1.50
© 2002 by CRC Press LLC

and legal transactions, digital signatures are used to confirm the source of a message and to ensure that the message has not been inadvertently or deliberately modified.

Neither type of cryptographic system is inherently better than the other; each is used for different applications, and many practical implementations use both. Similarly, no single cryptographic system is suitable for all security needs. However, there are several key factors (e.g., the nature of the organization, the type of data maintained, the size and geographic distribution of the user population, and the system types and architectures) that render the use of some cryptographic systems more effective than others.

This chapter offers guidelines for developing a comprehensive security plan that includes cryptographic measures. It then discusses the three most widely used cryptography alternatives: the DES, the RSA algorithm, and the DSS.

SELECTING A CRYPTOGRAPHIC SYSTEM

Several steps should be followed in selecting a cryptographic system. Namely, the security manager should:

1. Identify the data to be secured, as well as the length of time security must be provided.
2. Determine the level of network security required.
3. To the extent possible, estimate the value of the data to be protected and the cost to secure it.
4. Evaluate the existing physical and logical security controls.
5. Evaluate the existing administrative security controls.
6. Determine how the cryptographic keys will be securely generated, distributed, stored, and used.

The following sections discuss these suggested guidelines in more detail.

Identifying the Data to Be Secured

Before any thought is given to implementing a cryptographic system, the quantity, type, and sensitivity of the data to be secured must be clearly identified. The volume of data that must be securely transmitted or stored and the nature of the processing involved are fundamental criteria for a cryptographic system. So, too, are the nature and operations of certain organizations (e.g., financial institutions), the types of databases maintained, and the opportunities for economic gain for potential perpetrators. Although certain data (e.g., personnel records and electronic funds transfer data) is clearly sensitive, the sensitivity of other data (e.g., inventory records) may not be as easily assessed.

Not all data requires encryption, and very little data needs to remain in encrypted form at all times. Certainly, any data that could cause competitive disadvantage, financial loss, breach of good faith, or personal injury or death if disclosed or modified in an unauthorized manner should be secured. In some cases, unencrypted sensitive data may be considered secure when stored within a large computer system with adequate access controls. However, the same data may be highly vulnerable and therefore should be encrypted when stored on a file server in a local area network or when transmitted through dial-up network connections, wide area network, satellite communications, or facsimile machines.

Determining the Level of Network Security Required

There are two ways in which encryption can be applied to networks: link encryption and end-to-end encryption. These two approaches differ in the nature of security provided.

Link encryption performs the encryption of a message immediately before its physical transmission over an individual communications link between two network nodes. A message can be transmitted over many communications links before arriving at its final destination. Within each node, the incoming message is decrypted and the routing information extracted. The message is then reencrypted using a different key and transmitted to the next node. Because the transmitted message is decrypted and encrypted at each node that it passes through, all data transmitted on the links, including the destination addresses, is encrypted. Because encryption is part of the transmission process, no special user intervention is required.

One disadvantage of link encryption is that it requires all nodes to be physically secure because the subversion of any network node will expose substantial amounts of information. In addition, key distribution and key management (discussed in a later section) are problematic in link encryption systems because each node must store the cryptographic key of every node to which it is connected.

End-to-end encryption provides a higher level of security in a network environment because the message is not decrypted until the final destination has been reached. Because the message is encrypted at the source and remains encrypted throughout its transmission, it will not be compromised if a node has been subverted. This level of encryption is more naturally suited to users' perceptions of their security requirements, because only the source and destination nodes must be secure. In addition, key management tends to be less problematic in this environment because end-to-end encryption does not require all of the network nodes to have special encryption capabilities.

However, this level of encryption does not permit destination addresses to be encrypted because each node that the message passes through must have access to the address to correctly forward the message. Therefore, end-to-end encryption is more susceptible to attacks of traffic flow analysis because the origin-destination patterns are not masked. In addition, because individual users may elect to use this method of encryption, it is not as transparent to the users as link encryption.

Furthermore, end-to-end encryption requires each system to perform compatible encryption. As a result, the use of proprietary algorithms is less feasible in this environment. The options are effectively reduced to those cryptographic systems that are compatible with existing domestic or international standards (e.g., the DES or RSA algorithms, both discussed later).

Estimating the Value of the Data to Be Protected

Because it is often difficult to assign financial values to the data to be secured, risk analysis methods typically prove to be beneficial. A risk analysis is a structured, methodical analysis of system assets and perceived threats. It realistically assesses the value of the resources to be protected, quantifies the probability of occurrence of identified system threats, calculates annual loss expectancies, and determines the cost of available security countermeasures. Undertaken by skilled professionals, a risk analysis can identify cost-effective security measures and enhance security awareness throughout the organization.

It is important to consider the impact of time on both the value of the data and the strength of the cryptographic system. Certain cryptographic algorithms are able to withstand cryptanalytic attack for longer periods of time than others. Because the value of data tends to decrease over time, variations in cryptographic strength should be carefully evaluated. A reasonable assessment of the time factors might show that a simpler and less costly cryptographic system could provide adequate security during the time that the value of the data remains at or above a critical threshold.

The use of cryptography can be an expensive means of providing data security. A realistic assessment should be made of the costs of acquiring and installing a cryptographic system, the processing costs of the encryption/decryption operations, and the costs associated with any adverse impact on data compression or data transmission rates. Cryptography should be used only when the value of the data exceeds the costs involved in securing that data.

Evaluating the Existing Physical and Logical Security Controls

Cryptography is only one component of total system security. Implemented alone, cryptography offers little protection in terms of avoiding the unauthorized disclosure of data, deterring inadvertent or deliberate modifications to data, preventing unauthorized data modifications, detecting the loss of data, or recovering after the occurrence of such events. Adequate physical and logical security controls must also be in place.

For example, access controls are of particular importance. These controls are designed to limit the number of individuals who can access the system and to constrain their activities once access is achieved. As a result, these controls should provide for the classification and isolation of data according to different levels of sensitivity, and they should allow only those individuals with authorized access rights to store, process, or retrieve data or to communicate with or make use of any system resource. Because cryptography operates as an adjunct to access controls, the security provided by a cryptographic system depends, at least in part, on the security provided by the operating system.

Evaluating the Existing Administrative Security Controls

Just as cryptography is only one facet of data security, data security is only one element of effective administrative control over system resources and operations. Safeguards — in the form of mandatory technological security mechanisms, operational and procedural controls, and accountability procedures — are required to support management control. Of particular importance to the implementation and use of cryptography are the following administrative practices:

- *Seeking expert advice before a cryptographic system is implemented.* In-house experts and knowledgeable outside consultants should be used to analyze the strengths and weaknesses of a cryptographic system in light of the organization's current and future security needs.
- *Selecting the most inexpensive cryptographic system available that meets the organization's current and projected security needs.*
- *Monitoring the technical operations of the cryptographic system after it has been implemented.* Any changes in its operations should be made with extreme caution because partial modifications often result in the degradation of cryptographic security.
- *Monitoring human interactions with the cryptographic system.* Cryptographic keys are particularly vulnerable in the hands of inexperienced or inadequately trained personnel. For this reason, the handling of cryptographic keys should be transparent to system users and operators.

Determining How the Cryptographic Keys Will Be Managed

The security provided by a cryptographic system depends on the security of the keys. In fact, the importance of the keys suggests that they be given greater protection than the data to be secured. Key management focuses on the generation, distribution, storage, and use of the cryptographic keys, and its goal is to protect the integrity of the keys.

The issue of key distribution remains the most complex problem within key management. Private key cryptographic systems require a cryptographic key to be secretly exchanged and therefore mandate rigorous key distribution procedures. When there are relatively few users, many methods could be used to distribute the limited number of keys. For example, the keys could be transported manually to the communicating sites or sent in a sealed envelope by overnight courier.

Most current systems are far more complex, however; there are a large number of users in widely dispersed communicating sites who request numerous keys and require frequent key changes. Manual key distribution is impractical for these systems. Instead, automated key distribution techniques are used.

In network environments in which terminal-host communication occurs, the host computer generates a session key for encryption purposes. The session key is generated on the request of a user at a terminal and is used only for that individual user's session at that terminal. After the session key has been generated, it is encrypted with the terminal key and transmitted from the host to the terminal. The session key is encrypted with the host's master key (or key-encrypting key) and stored at the host. Messages transmitted between the terminal and the host are encrypted and decrypted in secure modules at both sites.

In network environments with heavy data traffic and multiple communicating sites, a central key management system can be used. A standard describing this type of system has been established by the American National Standards Institute (ANSI). Published as ANSI X9.17, this key management standard is designed for use among wholesale financial institutions for electronic funds transfer systems.

The central key management system described in ANSI X9.17 calls for a key distribution architecture that uses either two or three layers of keys. In the two-layer architecture, the master key (or top-level key-encrypting key) is distributed manually, and the data keys (the cryptographic keys used to encrypt the data) are distributed automatically after they have been encrypted with the master key. The three-layer architecture also requires the master key at the top level to be distributed manually. A second layer of key-encrypting keys is then encrypted with the master key and distributed automatically. The data keys on the third layer are encrypted with the second-level key-encrypting keys and distributed automatically.

Automated key distribution may occur in point-to-point, key distribution center, or key translation center environments. In a point-to-point environment, at least one of the two communicating sites must be able to generate the top-level master key. This master key is shared by both sites so that the data keys (in the two-layer architecture) or the second-level key-encrypting keys (in the three-layer architecture) may be exchanged.

In a key distribution center environment, neither communicating site has the ability to generate the top-level master key. Instead, both communicating sites individually share a master key with the centralized key distribution facility. The site that wants to initiate communications requests the data keys from the centralized facility and provides the center with the identity of the receiving site. The center then generates two sets of data keys. The first set is encrypted with the master key shared between the center and the initiating site, and the second set is encrypted with the master key shared between the center and the receiving site. Both sets of encrypted data keys are transmitted from the center to the initiating site. This site in turn transmits the second set of keys to the receiving site.

In a key translation center environment, the initiating site has the ability to generate the data key and can encrypt it with the master key, which is shared with the centralized facility. The encrypted data key is then transmitted to the center along with the identity of the receiving site. The key translation center decrypts the encrypted data key and uses the master key shared between the center and the receiving site to reencrypt the data key. The center then transmits the reencrypted data key back to the initiating site, and from there the key is forwarded to the receiving site.

Public key cryptographic systems (e.g., the RSA algorithm, discussed later) can be used to transmit the key-encrypting keys or data keys. Because public key cryptography does not require the exchange of secret keys before the establishment of secure communications, these systems can be used to reduce the inherent complexities of key distribution.

Effective key management is one of the most crucial elements of the encryption process. Clearly, the number of individuals required to handle the keys and the manual operations involved should be kept to a minimum. Without exception, all cryptographic keys must be well protected and changed frequently to ensure the privacy and authenticity of the data.

CRYPTOGRAPHIC ALTERNATIVES

Different cryptographic systems provide varying degrees of strength. The three primary encryption algorithm currently in use are the DES, the RSA algorithm, and the Data Signature Standard (DSS), which are discussed in the following sections.

The Data Encryption Standard

One of the oldest and most widely used cryptographic systems in the United States is the Data Encryption Standard (DES). An industry staple for more than 15 years, the DES is a private key system designed to provide privacy.

The DES is used extensively by financial institutions for the encryption of financial transactions. In fact, the DES is used to encrypt most of the transaction data (valued at approximately one trillion dollars) transmitted daily over such bank networks as the FedWire and CHIPS (Clearing House Interbank Payment System).

During the late 1960s and early 1970s, there were increasing concerns within the United States that some information was being lost to foreign powers as a result of insecure communications media in the United States. In response to the perceived need for the strong method of encryption to protect computer data, IBM Corp. developed a cryptographic system known as Lucifer.

In 1973, the National Bureau of Standards (now the National Institute of Standards and Technology) made a nationwide request for submissions for an encryption algorithm that could be used to protect sensitive but unclassified data. Lucifer was submitted, and it was adopted as the national DES in 1977.

However, the DES was adopted amid controversy and bureaucratic compromise, much of which centered on the National Security Agency (NSA). As adviser on the DES project, the NSA convinced the National Bureau of Standards and IBM to weaken the key from its originally designed 128 bits to 64 bits. However, because eight of these bits are reserved for parity, the key was technically reduced to a relatively small 56 bits. In addition, the NSA advised IBM not to publish certain design criteria, leaving many to speculate that the algorithm might contain trapdoor mechanisms that could be used to circumvent or subvert its security features.

The only publicly known way to break the DES algorithm is by brute force: testing each of the cryptographic keys until the correct one is discovered. With an effective key length of 56 bits, the DES provides more than 72 quadrillion (256) unique cryptographic keys. Before computers with multiple parallel processors were introduced, testing all keys was believed to be computationally infeasible. This is no longer the case because parallel processing significantly reduces the time needed to search through all of the keys, making it possible to identify the cryptographic key currently in use. With the growth of parallel processing, DES security depends more than ever on random key selection and frequent key changes.

DES Cryptographic Process. The DES algorithm uses a 56-bit key to encipher a 64-bit block of plaintext into a 64-bit block of ciphertext. The 64 bits in the block of plaintext are initially transposed, and then divided into two equal-sized blocks. These two blocks, referred to as L32 and R32, each contain 32 bits.

The bits in blocks L32 and R32 undergo 16 iterations of an intricate cryptographic process. Each iteration begins with a transposition of the 32 bits in R32, followed by an expansion of these bits into a 48-bit block. Next, an encryption key is computed that consists of 48 of the possible 56 bits. This 48-bit key is added to the expanded 48 bits in the R32 block, and the resulting 48 bits are split into eight 6-bit blocks. The eight 6-bit blocks are then input to eight different substitution functions. Each substitution function generates one 4-bit block as output.

These eight 4-bit blocks are consolidated into a 32-bit block. The 32 bits are transposed, added to the 32 bits in L32, and stored in a temporary location in memory. The 32 bits in R32 are then transferred to L32, and the bits temporarily stored in memory are transferred to R32. This process is repeated a total of 16 times, with a different 48-bit encryption key computed for each iteration. After 16 iterations, the contents of L32 and R32 are interchanged. The bits in both blocks are transposed and then combined into a 64-bit output block of ciphertext.

The decryption process is accomplished by reversing this algorithm; the encryption process is effectively repeated with the order of the 16 keys reversed.

DES Variations. The conventional mode of the DES, previously described, is a basic block encryption method. It operates like an electronic code book (ECB) that contains 256 possible entries. The ECB form of the DES provides privacy but not authentication, because there are inherent weaknesses in its operations.

For example, the encryption process is linear in nature; given a certain key and block of plaintext, the transformation process and the resulting ciphertext output will always be the same. Because most messages have some degree of redundancy, the plaintext could be constructed by examining several output blocks. Furthermore, because each block of plaintext is encrypted as an independent entity, a block could be modified without affecting any of the other blocks.

Other modes of DES operation eliminate the repetition of ciphertext blocks and provide both privacy and authentication. The cipher block chaining mode encrypts 64-bit blocks of plaintext into 64-bit blocks of ciphertext. However, cipher block chaining overcomes the fundamental weakness of the ECB mode by using the ciphertext for each block as feedback into the next plaintext block to be encrypted. As a result, repeated output patterns are hidden through the chaining process of repetitive encryption.

An alternative to cipher block chaining is the cipher feedback mode. Cipher feedback is used to encrypt individual bits or bytes of plaintext and is typically used when the plaintext cannot be framed into 64-bit blocks. Because each DES operation encrypts a much smaller unit of plaintext, cipher feedback is considered to be a stronger, but significantly slower, method of DES encryption.

The RSA Algorithm

The RSA algorithm, named for its inventors (Rivest, Shamir, and Adleman), was developed at MIT in 1978. It has proved its reliability through years of testing and public scrutiny and is now an internationally recognized encryption standard. The RSA algorithm provides both privacy and authentication.

Currently used by more than two thirds of the U.S. computer industry, the RSA algorithm is the *de facto* public key encryption standard. The encryption key and the algorithm are made public, but the decryption key is kept private. Although the encryption and decryption keys are mathematically inverse pairs, it is computationally infeasible for an intruder to calculate the private decryption key from the known encryption key and algorithm.

RSA Cryptographic Process. The RSA algorithm is based on the fact that it is much easier to multiply two numbers than it is to factor the result. The algorithm used in the encryption process is referred to as a trapdoor one-way function. It calls for the product of two large prime numbers (integers with more than 100 decimal digits) to be computed and made public as part of the encryption key. To perform the decryption operations, however, the two prime factors must be known. Because the encryption key and algorithm are made public, the theoretical possibility exists that an intruder could determine the private decryption key through extensive mathematical analysis. In practice, however, the excessive number of calculations required to determine the decryption key renders this form of attack computationally infeasible.

The process of encryption begins with the random selection of two very large prime numbers (p and q). These numbers are multiplied, and the product (n) is made public. A calculation is then performed that computes the number of positive integers less than n that have neither p nor q as factors. The result of this calculation (x) is kept secret. Next, an enciphering integer (e) is randomly selected between the range of 2 and ($x - 1$). The resulting encryption key (e,n) is made public.

The plaintext to be encrypted is represented as a sequence of integers between 0 and ($n - 1$). The public encryption key (e,n) is used to transform each plaintext integer into a corresponding ciphertext integer. Each plaintext integer is raised to the power of e, the result is divided by n, and the ciphertext is equal to the remainder.

A private decryption key (d,n) must be used to decipher the encrypted plaintext. The deciphering integer (d) is calculated from the values of e and x, such that the product of e and d differs from 1 by a multiple of x. Decryption is accomplished by raising each ciphertext integer to the power of d. The result is divided by n, and the plaintext is equal to the remainder.

RSA Applications. Although the encryption and decryption operations in the RSA scheme are computationally slower than those of the DES, use of the RSA algorithm is preferred for such applications as key management and digital signatures. The RSA algorithm is particularly effective in the area of key management. Key distribution is a significant problem with the DES because the mechanics of the DES algorithm mandate that a secret cryptographic key be shared by both the sender and the receiver.

The RSA algorithm overcomes many of the complexities involved in distributing the private cryptographic keys. Because the RSA scheme does not require the exchange of a private key before secure communications are established, it provides an effective method of securing the DES keys.

The RSA algorithm is often used for certain financial and legal transactions because the digital signatures produced are valid for legal contracts. A digital signature provides authentication by verifying the integrity and the source of a message, as well as the identity of the sender.

The RSA algorithm provides an elegant method of producing digital signatures. The process begins with the encryption of a message with the sender's private key; this creates the digital signatures. The sender then encrypts this message with the recipient's public key for additional privacy. When the message is received, the recipient's private key is used to decrypt the message and verify its integrity. The message is then decrypted using the sender's public key; this verifies the identity of the sender and validates the digital signature. The nature of the mathematics involved in the RSA algorithm allows the encryption and decryption operations to be reversed, thus allowing plaintext that was initially encrypted using the sender's private key to be decrypted and validated with the sender's public key.

The Digital Signature Standard

The Digital Signature Standard (DSS) was introduced by the National Institute for Standards and Technology (NIST) in 1991 as the federal government's proposed standard for encrypting unclassified data. Developed by the NSA, the DSS was designed to compute and verify digital signatures, thus providing message authentication but not privacy. Despite this apparent weakness, the DSS was intended to become the nation's public key encryption standard. If it is adopted, the DSS will be used in such business practices as electronic data interchange, electronic funds transfer, electronic mail, software distribution, and software virus detection.

The need for a stronger, national cryptographic standard has been a matter of extensive debate since 1985 when the NSA announced that it would neither endorse DES-based products nor recommend recertification of the DES algorithm after 1988. The NSA justified its decision by citing potential vulnerabilities of the DES resulting from its widespread use. There was considerable reaction to the NSA's announcement from the financial community, whose concern about the security provided by the DES was overshadowed by the fact that a suitable cryptographic alternative had not been made available. The NSA rescinded its decision, and the DES was recertified through 1992.

The need to develop a stronger domestic cryptographic system has been underscored by recent technological advances, which some believe have pushed the DES close to the end of its useful life. However, introduction of the DSS was a disturbing answer to the question of how best to provide data security.

Like the DES, the DSS owes its controversial beginnings to the NSA. The DSS was unilaterally developed by the NSA, a secretive government intelligence agency responsible for monitoring foreign communications. The absence of any involvement from business or academia on the algorithm's development stands in marked contrast to the origins of the DES and RSA algorithms. Unlike these algorithms, the DSS contains no method for encrypting data and will not be subject to government-imposed export restrictions. The potential imposition of this untested security standard has caused many to conclude that the NSA is more concerned with reducing the difficulty of cryptanalyzing foreign communications than with increasing the security of corporate data communications.

NIST's role in proposing the DSS also has been the subject of intense scrutiny. The introduction of the DSS represents the government's overt rejection of the RSA algorithm. The impact of this is significant. It would be unduly expensive and complicated for businesses to use the DSS for domestic communications and the RSA scheme for international communications; yet multiple encryption technologies would have to be sustained to ensure compatible data communications. Furthermore, the DSS digital signature vertification process is slower than that of the RSA algorithm. This creates the additional problem of noticeable performance delays for those applications requiring extensive use of signature verification (e.g., credit card or banking transactions).

Signature Generation and Verification. Because it was NIST's intent to offer a public key cryptographic standard that was free of existing patents, the DSS uses a different algorithm than the RSA scheme. Although the RSA algorithm relies on the computational infeasibility of calculating the prime factors of large numbers, DSS security is based on the difficulty of calculating discrete logarithms.

The DSS uses two keys to control the digital signature generation and verification processes. The algorithm requires the sender to use a one-way hash function (i.e., a mathematical process) to generate a profile (or condensed version) of the message. The profile is encrypted with the sender's private key, creating the digital signature, which is attached to the message for transmission. When the message is received, the receiver uses the sender's public key to decrypt the profile. The receiver then uses the same hash function to create a profile of the message. If the receiver's profile matches that of the sender, the integrity of the message and the identity of the sender are authenticated.

The DSS requires all public keys to appear in a public directory, thus alowing any user to validate a sender's digital signature. To authenticate the public key registry, the DSS uses a mutually trusted arbiter (or certifying authority) to generate a certificate of credentials associating a given public key with the corresponding identity of the owner. However, details pertaining to the generation of such a certificate have not been fully specified by NIST.

CONCLUSION

Although cryptography is used as the primary means of protecting data in computer networks, it should be an integrated component of a comprehensive system security program. Selection of a cryptographic system should be undertaken after several factors have been carefully assessed, including:

- The nature and operations of the organization
- The quantity, type, sensitivity, and value of the data
- The perceived threats to the data
- The size and geographic distribution of the user population
- The level of network security required
- The effectiveness of existing physical, logical, and administrative security controls

In addition, variations in the level of security provided by different cryptographic systems should be knowledgeably evaluated. Before a cryptographic system is chosen, consideration should be given to the level of privacy and authenticity provided; the reputed strength, speed, and efficiency of the algorithm; its recognized domestic and international use; and its associated acquisition, installation, and processing costs. The optimal choice is the most inexpensive cryptographic system available that meets the organization's current and projected security needs.

Chapter 27
A New Paradigm Hidden in Steganography*

Ira S. Moskowitz
Garth E. Longdon
Li Wu Chang

Steganography, which is Greek for "covered writing," is a subset of the emerging discipline of *information hiding*.[1,5,12,13,18] It is the science of transmitting a message between two parties (Alice and Bob) in such a manner that an eavesdropper (Eve) will not be aware that the message exists. The terms "information hiding" and "steganography" are often, but incorrectly, used interchangeably. Information hiding is the broad term for the scientific discipline that studies topics such as covert and subliminal communication channels, detection of hidden information (e.g., steganography), watermarking of digital objects, and anonymity services. Unlike cryptography, which seeks to hide the *content* of the message, with steganography we seek to hide the *existence* of the message. Steganographically hidden messages are inserted into legitimate and obvious (with respect to Eve) communications between Alice and Bob. Eve's steganographic challenge, therefore, is to detect the message, not to understand it. Of course, steganography and cryptography can be used in conjunction, so that message content may be protected cryptographically, even if the steganographic "shield" fails and the existence of the message is discovered.

Paradigms Old and New

The paradigm of cryptography (the "old" paradigm) is that cryptography can be modeled, measured, and utilized by the standards of information

---

* This chapter appeared in the *Proceedings of the New Security Paradigms Workshop,* Ballycotton, County Cork, Ireland, on September 12–22, 2000, pp. 41–50, ACM Press.

theory and noise. We have Shannon[21] to thank for this. Attempts have been made to extend this paradigm to steganography.[6,16,25] We find that these extensions, although useful, do not capture all of the essence of steganography. Note that these authors never claimed that their work did. We propose a "new paradigm" for steganography, based on (1) discontinuous mathematical models, and (2) the lack of noise as a detection deterrent. This is not to say that the present steganographic models do not take, at least part of, this thinking into account. However, we feel that it is important to delineate these ideas as a new paradigm to force ourselves to think of steganography in a different light than that of cryptography. Perhaps by looking at steganography in light of our new paradigms, the present steganographic models can be "filled out" to capture more of the essence of steganography.

This chapter discusses how (part of) the old paradigm applies to covert channels, but not to the steganographic equivalent — subliminal channels. Our ideas are preliminary and works-in-progress. We invited discussion, encouragement, and criticism from the workshop participants, and received it. Because much of this community's work is based on ideas from Shannon, some may (especially the first author) find it difficult to break away from the old paradigm of continuity and noise. We are quite respectful of the existing steganographic techniques. They are a useful assortment of engineering methods that seem to work, some better than others. The few existing formal models noted above are quite new and were developed to attempt to fill a void. They are a service to the community. It is our desire to continue to study the existing models, but with our new paradigm in mind. Our ultimate goal is a mathematical model of steganography that incorporates our new paradigm.

STEGANOGRAPHY — BACKGROUND MATERIAL

This section focuses on the standard terminology for steganography and includes some simple examples.

Terminology

We will use the standard terminology for steganography as discussed at the First International Information Hiding Workshop.[19] We assume that Alice wishes to send, via steganographic transmission, a message to Bob. Alice starts with a cover message. The hidden message is called the embedded message. A steganographic algorithm combines the covermessage with the embedded message. The algorithm may or may not use a steganographic key (stegokey), which is similar to a cryptographic key in purpose and use — this is illustrated by using a dotted line in Exhibit 1. The output of the steganographic algorithm is the stegomessage. The covermessage and stegomessage must be of the same datatype, but the embedded message may be of another datatype. We sometimes make the datatype explicit in our

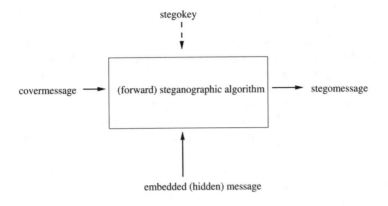

Exhibit 1. Embedding the Hidden Message

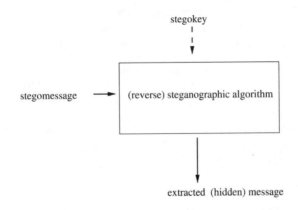

Exhibit 2. Extracting the Hidden Message

terminology; for example, "coverimage." Exhibit 1 illustrates the embedding process. In steganography, we do not make the "strong" assumption that Eve has knowledge of the steganographic algorithm. This is why there may, or may not, be a stegokey involved in the embedding and extraction of a hidden message. Eve should not be able to determine from the stegomessage that there is an embedded message in it. Of course, in steganography we often make the assumption that Eve does not have access to the covermessage. Thus, Eve should not be able to tell if she is "observing" a legitimate cover-message or a stegomessage. Both Bob and Eve receive the stegomessage. Bob reverses the embedding process to extract the embedded message. Exhibit 2 illustrates the extracting process.

We say that steganographic communication is *steganographically strong* if it is impossible for Eve to detect the steganography. It is the concept of "impossibility" that influences our new paradigm. Note that many authors refer to Eve as Wally, Wendy, Willy, etc. This is because the eavesdropper is often thought of as a warden due to the paper of Simmons.[22] We prefer to stick with eavesdropper because it is more general. Because the goal of this paper is to discuss the new paradigm associated with steganography, let us illustrate our thinking with some examples. There are certainly many more sophisticated and robust steganographic techniques than what we present here. We choose these two methods for (1) the historical significance of the first method, and (2) the simplicity and illustrative strength of both methods.

Kurak–McHugh Method

In 1992, C. Kurak and J. McHugh[14] detailed how one can hide an image inside of an image. The thrust for writing that paper was to show that one should not be too complacent about downgrading images from "private" to "public." The paper simply and graphically demonstrates that a public image that appears innocuous to a casual observer may, in fact, be hiding an embedded private image. We summarize the Kurak–McHugh method.

> Start with a bitmapped version of a greyscale image that we wish to do the hiding in (the coverimage). Next, we consider a bitmap of the image that we wish to hide. The two images are merged into a bitmap (the stegoimage). The merging is done in the following manner. The bitmaps have one byte representing each pixel. Thus there are 256 levels of grey, ranging from 0 to 255 for each pixel. Replace the n least significant bits (LSB) of each pixel in the coverimage, with the n most significant bits (MSB) from the corresponding pixel of the image to be embedded.

For simplicity's sake, we assume that the coverimage and the embedded image are of the same size so that the pixels are in bijective correspondence. In Ref. 14, the authors vary n from 1 to 4 bits. We found that $n = 1$ is insufficient for preserving the quality of the original image. (What we embed is often only an approximation of the original message that we wish to send. Questions of artistic quality and and what information we are actually trying to pass come into play here.) Values of $n > 2$ may cause Eve to notice that an image has been embedded. Therefore, we set $n = 2$ for discussion. Because the stegoimage differs from the coverimage by, at most, three grey levels (the two lowest bits affect the grey level anywhere from 0 (e.g., 2 LSB are (0,0)) to 3 (e.g., 2 LSB are (1,1)), it is visually impossible for Eve to detect the steganography. Of course, if Eve has knowledge of the algorithm, it is then trivial for Eve to detect the steganography.

Alice performs the embedding process as described above. The stegoimage can be passed to Bob in e-mail, or simply by posting the stegoimage on a Web page. Pixel byte values must be unchanged through the storage and transmission processes. Thus, with this algorithm, a lossless method such as TIFF must be used. Note that some authors have steganographic methods that apply to methods such as JPEG (see, for example, Reference 9. The Web page approach may cause Eve the least suspicion, because Eve does not know the intended recipient of any surreptitious transmission from Alice. Bob receives the image (either through e-mail or from downloading it from the Web) and then shifts every byte 6 bits to the left, thus uncovering the embedded image.

One can use the Kurak–McHugh method to deal with color images (they noted this trivial extension in their paper). Each pixel is represented by three bytes, one for each of the colors red (R), green (G), or blue (B). Every color byte is modified as for the greyscale byte. The conclusions are the same.

In terms of impact, the Kurak–McHugh paper was a huge success. If Alice is sending the stegoimage to Bob, the eavesdropper, Eve, cannot tell by looking that there is actually an embedded image hiding in the coverimage. However, is the Kurak–McHugh method steganographically strong? The answer is no.* Eve can determine and duplicate the stegoalgorithm and thus find the hidden picture. Can we modify the Kurak–McHugh method and make it steganographically strong? One would think that using the Kurak–McHugh method with cryptography would make the steganography impossible to detect. In fact, just the opposite is true, as we will discuss later. Accepting this causes us to rethink our paradigms about the use of noise — an important part of the new paradigm needed for steganography.

Our Text Hiding Method

There are many ways to hide text in an image. We present our own method which we feel is steganographically strong (but not necessarily robust). (Note that by using an image of text the Kurak–McHugh method would work.) We summarize the method in this chapter. The full details of our method and the underlying statistical analysis can be found in Reference 17.

We start with the bitmap of an image. For the sake of simplicity, we will restrict ourselves in this chapter to greyscale images with dimensions 500×500 pixels. Our text data is limited to 249 (ASCII) characters. Each character of the text is represented in binary form by a byte (eight bits) $(b_1; b_2; b_3; b_4; b_5; b_6; b_7; b_8)$. We use this representation to encode the text data. Each character is broken down into four sections of two bits each: $(b_1; b_2), (b_3; b_4), (b_5; b_6), (b_7; b_8)$. We generate a list of 1000 unique random pixel coordinates and use that list as a stegokey. Each two-bit section, from above, is then sequentially matched with a pixel from the stegokey.

---

* Note that Kurak and McHugh never made, nor implied any such claims. This was not the purpose of their paper.

Now we mimic what Kurak–McHugh, along with many others, (see, for example, Reference 13, Section 3.2.1) have done with the popular, but non-robust LSB technique.[7] We replace the two LSB of the pixel in question with the matching two-bit section. We do this for every character. We always end our text message with the null character, represented in binary as (0; 0; 0; 0; 0; 0; 0; 0). This allows us to send a message shorter than 249 characters. To extract the embedded text, the algorithm is reversed. When the reverse algorithm reads the null character, it stops the extraction process. In general, the smaller the message, the more difficult it is for Eve to detect that there is an embedded message. This is why we change no more than $1000 = (249+1) \cdot 4$ out of the available 250,000 pixels.

DETECTING STEGO: PARADIGM SHIFT 1

Now that we have some simple examples to play with, let us examine the first part of our paradigm shift. In cryptography, Eve knows that there is an encrypted message. The job for Eve is to learn as much as possible about the encrypted message. In cryptography, it is not Alice or Bob's responsibility to hide their encrypted message. Rather, it is their job to make the message unintelligible to Eve, even if Eve may be able to bring large amounts of computational resources to bear upon the problem. Shannon modeled secrecy based on probabilities and information theory. Perfect secrecy is achieved if the ciphertext and the plaintext are statistically independent. Mathematically, Shannon[21] expressed this as: Given finite messages M that are enciphered into possible cryptograms E we say that perfect secrecy is achieved iff $\forall E$, $\forall M$, $P(M|E) = P(M)$. This is a "yes or no" situation. However, in cryptography less than perfect secrecy is of great interest. This is very different than steganography (and this is the first part of our new paradigm).

The Wire-Tap Channel

Wyner[24] first described a simplified eavesdropper scenario in cryptography in terms of a wire-tapper, Eve, listening in on Alice and Bob.[8,10] Alice's transmission to Bob may be noisy, and Eve's tapping also has noise in it. Alice wishes to send k source bits S^k which are encoded into n symbols through a noisy discrete memoryless channel, channel X. Bob receives Y^n from the channel and Eve taps Z^n out of the channel. Both $X \rightarrow Y$ and $X \rightarrow Z$ have their noise characteristics modeled by the joint conditional probability $P_{Y,Z|X}$. Based on what Bob receives, he "estimates" what S^k was. Alice wishes for this estimate to differ, in probability, from S^k as little as possible. This is the probability of error. However, Eve is learning information about what Alice transmitted. This is measured as the normalized conditional entropy as $\Delta = H(S^k | Z^n)/H(S^k)$. If Eve can determine without question what Alice sent, based on what Eve received, then all probabilities are zero or one, and therefore $H(S^k \mid Z^n) = 0$, and $\Delta = 0$. This is the worst case in terms of secrecy. If Eve learns nothing about the distribution of S^k from knowing Z^n, then the two are statistically independent and Δ is maximized at the value 1. This is the best in terms of security. However, pragmatically secure communication can be done between Alice and Bob even when $\Delta = 1 - \varepsilon$, ε small. In contrast, in steganography, there is no such thing as "almost does not know there is a hidden message." Therefore, the wire-tap model differs greatly for steganography. We must call our thinking into question when it comes to things like ε-security.

Of course, Δ is very similar to *unicity distance*,[15,21] which is expressed also as a normalized entropy. This measures how much plaintext can be revealed without enabling decryption of the entire ciphertext. This is not the case in steganography. The use of a normalized entropy must be called into question when it is an either/or situation, as it is in steganography.

Existing Steganographic Models

Consider the above scenario, but substitute steganography for cryptography. Let Δ again represent the amount of "information" that Eve can learn through eavesdropping.

- Should we still use an entropy-based measure? Entropy works well for cryptography. But is it the appropriate measure for steganography?
- How should one interpret Δ? Should anything other than boundary values for Δ be useful? Non-boundary values are useful for cryptography, where we are willing to live with less than perfect secrecy, but this is not the case for steganography.

To the best of our knowledge, all existing steganographic models are based on a paradigm of entropy/information theory (which has continuous probability theory as its underlying core principle). Of course, the above wire-tapping scenario does not map exactly into a steganographic problem. Consider Exhibit 1: Let C be a random variable representing the covermessage, E a random variable representing the embedded message, and S the random variable representing the stegomessage. The idea is that, statistically, the stegomessage should appear to be similar to a covermessage. Differences in statistical profiles, or conditional entropies, would alert Eve that there is an embedded message. What concerns us is that the prevailing paradigm assumes that probability distributions can be assigned to the set of legitimate covermessages. We would like to see more published work on how these distributions are actually assigned. Also, the existing paradigm does not include the idea of "spontaneous discovery." That is, once Eve knows that there is hidden information, the game is over. Of course, we can get into a discussion (not in this chapter) of what "knows" means. Obviously, in the Kurak–McHugh method, Eve is definite in her knowledge. The process of obtaining this knowledge might very well be a continuous process (such as hypothesis testing). What is not acceptable is the idea of a "little bit discovered." This of course is different than the acceptable idea (and what the existing models use) that if one knows that all messages under consideration have a given non-zero probability of containing a hidden message that it is then appropriate to discuss subtle differences in that probability. This distinction in approach must be drawn out.

Cachin[6] uses the discrimination (relative entropy) $D(C \mid S)$ between the distributions C and S to define ε-security against a passive (just listening in) Eve; the stegosystem is ε-secure against a passive Eve iff $D(C \mid S) \leq \varepsilon$. When the discrimination is zero, then the stegosystem is perfectly secure. We take issue with the concept of ε-security *in general* (not necessarily with how it was used in Ref. 6). Is this the proper way to be thinking about steganography? Does ε-security mean that you have some knowledge that there is a hidden message, or does it mean that the odds have shifted by ε that there is a hidden message? Cachin nicely ties ε-security into hypothesis testing (detects a hidden message). However, we still feel that a continuous slide from perfection to detection is questionable. Perhaps there is a deeper concept describing this change that is not continuous. However, to defend Cachin,[6] one must keep in mind that the purpose of this paper is to define a concept of steganographic security/insecurity when one has the ability to assign probabilities to what a legitimate cover might be. The author himself expresses the need for "caution."

Ettinger[11] takes a game theoretic approach to detecting the steganography. A permitted "distortion" is allowed. This permitted distortion is allowed under the concept of "a distribution of locations." Is it possible for Eve to increase her computational efforts so that what was acceptable before is no longer acceptable? Is discovery not just a "yes/no" proposition? We must think about how and when to apply such a model. The formalism of all of the existing models seems to be correct only under the ability to assign distributions for what is a legitimate cover. (Note that the authors of those papers make no further claims.)

Zollner et al.[25] use conditional entropies to show that it is impossible to have any sort of steganographic security if Eve has knowledge of both the covermessage and the stegomessage. Without all of the fancy math, this boils down to the fact that Eve can compare covermessages and stegomessages and see that something is amiss. This is why all stegosystems are modeled with Eve only getting her hands on the stegomessage. The authors then go on to show that there must be uncertainty in the covermessage, or Eve could always tell if she had a stegomessage or a covermessage. Underlying this paper is, we feel, the *all or nothing* idea that we wish to pursue as part of our new paradigm. However, the emphasis of Ref. 25 is the need for *indeterminacy* in the set of covermessages in order to obfuscate Eve, a point that they make well!

In Refs. 2 and 3 the authors discuss the appropriateness of using an information theoretical approach for modeling steganography. They discuss how Eve's computational power could influence such a model, and also consider some upper bounds for hidden information. A parallel to a one-time pad is discussed, as it also is in Ref. 6.

Mittelholzer[16] discusses a perfect steganography scenario in light of issues of steganographic robustness — an important topic in digital watermarking. Mittelholzer also includes watermarking in his model. Although watermarking is part of the larger field of information hiding, it is not identical to steganography. For example, in watermarking, the fact that a digital watermark has been embedded in a covermessage is often a public fact. This is orthogonal to steganography. Therefore, we find it difficult to follow a model that attempts to incorporate both steganography and watermarking.

In cryptography, a small amount of discovery is allowed. In steganography, a small amount of discovery is not allowed. It is our desire to find/ design a formal model that explicitly shows that partial discovery is not allowed. Of course, uncertainty in discovery is allowed (e.g., indeterminacy). This uncertainty in discovery can be expressed probabilistically, provided that one can show that distributions can be assigned.

Covert Channels

We note that the existing paradigm for covert channels is not appropriate for steganography. Steganography can be thought of as a subliminal channel. Simmons was the first to use the term *subliminal channel* in a general sense.[22] A subliminal channel is a secondary communication between two parties, Alice and Bob, such that the primary communication is publicly known, but the secondary communication is meant to be hidden. A covert channel differs in that there is communication between Alice and Bob that exists outside of the system design. A covert channel is allowed to exist if its information theoretical capacity is below an agreed-upon upper bound. This does not, and should not, work for steganography. Once Eve knows that there is hidden communication, the subliminal channel has been discovered. There is no such thing as partially subliminal, which is similar to the concept of being a little bit pregnant. The paradigm of covert channels, the old paradigm, is similar to that of cryptography, also the old paradigm. Steganography (subliminal channels) must have a new paradigm that does not include such distinctions as a little bit discovered (non-hidden)! However, steganographic models do rely upon the fact that one can be a little bit confused — through the indeterminacy of what is a legitimate cover.

Comments

All of the above models are important and of interest. They have their various strengths and weaknesses, depending upon what aspect of steganography one is attempting to model. At present, the community has yet to agree upon one model or approach as the definitive one. We wish to discuss how a system transitions from successful steganography to unsuccessful steganography. This transition is very different from that of cryptosystems or of "safe" covert channels. This is the first part of our new paradigm (noise being the other). Our ideas are raw and in need of refinement. We enjoyed the workshop participants' feedback.

Lack of Steganography: New Paradigm Shift 1

In our view, steganographic communication exists when and only when Eve is not cognizant of the hidden message. Acceptable regions of indecision should only be allowed under the cloud of indeterminacy. The fact that one does not have the proper tools to detect the steganography should not be part of a formal model. Once Eve has any evidence that there is hidden information, the steganography has failed. This is a discontinuity. This is not to say that the underlying process may not, in fact be continuous. As in Ref. 6, it might be some sort of hypothesis that is accepted that causes Eve to detect the hidden communication. However, it is not, as in the wire-tap channel, a case where some amount of information is allowed to be leaked. This may not happen in steganography. The first part of our *new paradigm* is:

> In steganography, the discovery of hidden information is not modeled in a continuous manner. We must readdress our old paradigms for secure systems to deal with discontinuities. Standard information theoretical models do not deal with "jumps."

The idea of a discontinuity arising from a (perhaps) continuous process had disturbed us for quite a while. It was when we started investigating the much-maligned field of mathematics called "catastrophe theory"[23] that we started to get a feel for how to approach modeling our new paradigm. A successful and complete model of steganography should deal with jump discontinuities.

Consider the polynomial $y = (x - 3)^2 + \delta = x^2 - 6x + (9 + \delta)$. This is a simple quadratic whose graph is a parabola with the minimum value of δ achieved when $x = 3$. In Exhibit 3, we show the plots for three values of δ: $\delta = -1; 0; 2$. Note that the quadratic has two roots when $\delta = -1$, one root when $\delta = 0$, and no real roots when $\delta = 2$. This phenomenon is expressed

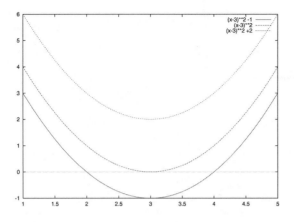

Exhibit 3. Real Roots

in general in Exhibit 4; here we plot the number of real roots against δ. Note that although δ increases in a continuous manner, the number of real roots (intersections with the x-axis) has a discontinuity at zero (non-removable singularity). This simple example shows that a continuous natural event might have some features acting in a discontinuous manner, and any attempts to model those features in a continuous manner are contrary to the will of nature — this relates quite strongly to our new paradigm. We must call the old ways of thinking into question and look for new methods with which to model steganographic systems.

Catastrophe Theory. Catastrophe theory was developed in the 1970s by the great French mathematician Rene Thom.[23] In some sense, catastrophe theory was the unsuccessful precursor to chaotic dynamical systems. As the name implies, catastrophe theory models discontinuities in a system's behavior; for example, when does a dog decide to bark, what is the difference between genius and insanity, when does the bubble burst on Internet stocks, etc.? In short, it shows how discontinuities can describe certain aspects of continuous natural systems, which is a scenario quite like what we have described with steganography. In Exhibit 5, we see the plot of the parametrized surface.

$$(r, \theta) \rightarrow \left(r\cos(\theta), r\sin(\theta), \frac{r}{2\pi}\,\theta \right), \quad r \in [0, 1], \theta \in [0, 2\pi]$$

(*Note:* This is similar to the Riemann surface of $\log(\zeta)$.) The mathematics describing Exhibit 5 are not important. Rather, the importance lies in its interpretation. Our example is motivated by Arnol'd's[4] example of the "technical proficiency-enthusiasm-achievement" scientist. Note that standard

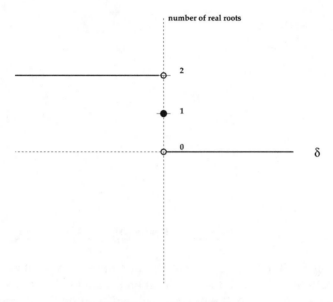

Exhibit 4.   Discontinuity

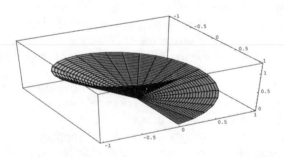

Exhibit 5.   Parametrized Surface in R^3 of Mathematician's Skill

illustrations of catastrophe theory often use "folded" surfaces — for simplicity, we just stay with "cut" surfaces. Our interpretation of Exhibit 5 is of the skill of a mathematician. The uppermost regions of the surface represent *genius,* the middle *normal,* and the bottom *prealgebraist.* Think of three-dimensional space R^3 with coordinates (r, θ, z). The coordinate r is ability, θ is effort, and z is mental state (we do not intend for this example to be exact representation of what makes up a mathematician's skill — it is for illustrative purposes only). When we project down to the polar plane, we arrive at Exhibit 6. In other words, when we only have a partial view of the mathematician's skill, it seems that there is a discontinuous

342

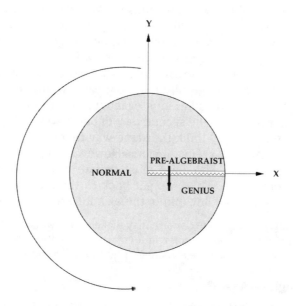

Exhibit 6. Mathematician's Skill with Hidden Variable

jump from pre-algebraist to genius, which is a view that many have of mathematicians. This is the same behavior when we looked at the roots in the previous example. It is not an exact match, but the ideas are very similar. What we see from this example is that depending upon how one views a physical system or phenomenon, it may appear discontinuous.

We are presently investigating catastrophe theory to see if it can be used as a model for steganography. One must move carefully when using catastrophe theory. Many think of it as the cold fusion of modern mathematics. However, the underlying mathematics are sound; it is the applications that must be carefully examined. It is our opinion that the new paradigm that started with catastrophe theory laid the foundations for the 1980s rage in chaos and fractals. Steganography must use a new paradigm that includes discontinuous jumps. Reliance upon the old paradigms of entropy must be examined. Now we discuss the second part of our new paradigm.

NOISE IS BAD FOR STEGANOGRAPHY: PARADIGM SHIFT 2

One can achieve perfect secrecy in cryptography using a one-time pad. If Eve intercepts the encrypted transmission, what she gets is total noise (of course, this is only true if the random number generator behaves properly). This is the best that one could hope for with respect to cryptography. This old paradigm must be examined when it comes to steganography. We thought that we could use (white) noise to assist in steganography. We found that we were wrong. This was the paradigm that we took from cryptography, and the paradigm that must be changed. In retrospect, we see that the old paradigm is obviously wrong when it comes to steganography. However, we had to learn our lesson. Note that we know of no existing models of steganography that advocate "white noise." We bring up the issue to show how different steganography is from cryptography. It is hoped that expressing the second part of our new paradigm will cause others not to erroneously think the same way that we unfortunately did (at first). In retrospect, it seems obvious. However, one can use noise, but in a controlled manner. The noise must imitate what noise a legitimate coverimage would have. Thus, we get back to the idea of some sort of indeterminacy which is a linchpin of the existing steganographic models.

> In steganography, the use of noise may make things worse, not better. One can use the inherent noise in a covermessage, but adding additional noise may cause the steganography to be discovered.

Kurak–McHugh — Again?

One can easily adjust the Kurak–McHugh method to not let Eve know what the embedded image is, even if Eve has determined that there is an embedded image. Thus, we can achieve cryptographic security when the steganography has failed. Simply encrypt the embedded bits so that the 2 LSB in the stegoimage appear as white noise. By white noise, we mean that the 2 LSB are statistically equivalent to having each pixel's 2 LSB randomly and independently generated from a uniform draw of the (decimal) values 0, 1, 2, 3. We use Blowfish[20] to do this as follows.

The 2 MSB of each pixel of the embedded image are saved into an array that is encrypted using Blowfish in cipher block chaining (CBC) mode. The encryption key is a 16-byte MD5 hash of a passphrase. The encrypted array is then stored, two bits at a time, replacing the 2 LSB of each pixel in the coverimage, thus forming the stegoimage. The embedded hidden image is recovered by a reversal of this process. The 2 LSB of each pixel are saved to an array, which is decrypted using Blowfish CBC with the decryption key being equal to the encryption key. The decrypted array is then used, two bits at a time, to form the 2 MSB of each pixel in the recovered hidden image.

Although the above approach keeps the hidden image (ignoring the 6 LSB) cryptographically secure it does not keep the hidden image steganographically secure. This is extremely important. Our experiments have shown that there are "artifacts" residing in the 2 LSB. This is independent of what image type (JPEG, TIFF, PNG, etc.) the original image was before we realized its bitmap. We discuss this below. Not all images that we used had these artifacts, but most did.

Exhibit 7.   Coverimage

Exhibit 8.   Coverimage (Shifted 6 Bits to the Left)

The effect that we demonstrate seems to hold, irrespective of the file type the image is. Exhibit 7 is the bitmapped version of a TIFF file. Exhibit 8 is the bitmap when we move every byte (R byte, G byte, B byte for each

Exhibit 9.　Image to be Embedded

pixel) from Exhibit 7, six places to the left. This forces the 2 LSB from Exhibit 7 to become the 2 MSB, and all of the other bits making up the byte to become zero. One can easily see that the bright spots from Exhibit 7 leave very visible artifacts upon the lower bit planes. Thus, to use cryptography to enforce steganographic robustness would force the encryption to mimic the artifact pattern both visually and at the more complex statistical level. However, when we attempt to embed the 2 MSB of Exhibit 9 into Exhibit 7 by encrypting as above and resulting in Exhibit 10, and then shift the bits left 6, we are left with Exhibit 11, which is white noise. Thus, it is obvious that something is "wrong" with Exhibit 10. Therefore, using cryptography without mimicking the artifact pattern of the coverimage lets Eve know that there is am embedded image in the coverimage. We do not know how to force the encryption to mimic the artifact pattern. This seems to be quite complex. Note, of course, that after decrypting the 2 MSB as given in Exhibit 10, we have the 2 MSB representation of Exhibit 9 as shown in Exhibit 12.

Discussion: New Paradigm Shift 2

From the above we note that adding totally random white noise is exactly the *wrong* thing to do with respect to steganography. In the example given above, Eve can easily, through trivial statistical tests, determine that there is something "fishy" with respect to the 2 LSB. Most legitimate images would not have the 2 LSB appear as white noise. Therefore, adding noise

Exhibit 10. Stegoimage

Exhibit 11. White Noise

to increase security — the old paradigm from cryptography — fails miserably here. The noise must be added in a manner consistent with the coverimage. This is not to say that all present models and techniques of steganography ignore this thinking. Our goal, rather, is to emphasize the

Exhibit 12.   Recovered Extracted Image

difference between the paradigms of cryptography with those of steganography. This is non-trivial and is part of our current research.

CONCLUSION

We have shown how two staples of cryptography — a continuous-information theoretic-based foundation, and the use of noise — should not be staples for steganographic modeling. Steganographic models must contain some way of dealing with (catastrophic) jumps from not knowing, to knowing, that there is hidden information. We have shown that this type behavior is possible in other continuous physical/mathematical systems. Therefore, we feel it is imperative to incorporate it into steganographic models. Adding noise during the steganographic embedding phase can cause the steganography to fail. The transition from a covermessage to a stegomessage must be carefully done so that Eve does not know that the covermessage has been tampered with. In cryptography, one need not hide the fact that a message has been encrypted. However, in steganography one must hide the fact that a message has been embedded. Because the philosophies of the two are so different, so should the guiding paradigms be different.

ACKNOWLEDGMENTS

We appreciate the helpful comments from the reviewers, R. Heilizer, A. Pfitzmann, and the workshop participants. Research supported by the Office of Naval Research, NSPW2000, Ballycotton, Co. Cork, Republic of Ireland.

References

1. R.J. Anderson, Editor: Information Hiding: First International Workshop, Vol. 1174 of *Lecture Notes in Computer Science.* Springer-Verlag, Berlin, 1996.
2. R.J. Anderson: Stretching the Limits of Steganography, In R. Anderson, editor, Information Hiding: First International Workshop, Vol. 1174 of *LNCS*, pp. 39-48. Springer-Verlag, 1996.
3. R.J. Anderson and F.A.P. Petitcolas: On the Limits of Steganography, *IEEE Journal of Selected Areas in Communications,* 16(4), 474-481, May 1998.
4. V.I. Arnol'd: *Catastrophe Theory,* Third, revised and expanded ed., Springer-Verlag, Berlin, 1992.
5. D. Aucsmith, Editor: Information Hiding: Second International Workshop, Vol. 1525 of *Lecture Notes in Computer Science.* Springer-Verlag, Berlin, 1998.
6. C. Cachin: An Information-Theoretic Model for Steganography, in D. Aucsmith, Editor, Information Hiding: Second International Workshop, Vol. 1525 of LNCS, pp. 306-318. Springer-Verlag, Berlin, 1998.
7. L. Chang and I.S. Moskowitz: Critical Analysis of Security in Voice Hiding Techniques, in Y. Han, T. Okamoto, and S. Qing, Editors, Information and Communications Security: First International Conference, Vol. 1334 of *Lecture Notes in Computer Science,* pp. 203-216, Springer-Verlag, 1997.
8. I. Csiszar: Broadcast Channels with Confidential Messages, *IEEE Transaction on Information Theory,* Vol. IT-24, No. 3, 339-349, May 1978.
9. D.L. Currie, III and C.E. Irvine: Surmounting the Effects of Lossy Compression on Steganography, in *National Information System Security Conference,* Baltimore, MD, pp. 194-201, October 1996.
10. M. van Dijk: On a Special Class of Broadcast Channels with Confidential Messages, *IEEE Transactions on Information Theory,* Vol. 43, No. 2, 712-714, March 1997.
11. J.M. Ettinger: Steganalysis and Game Equilibria, in D. Aucsmith, Editor, Information Hiding: Second International Workshop, Vol. 1525 of *LNCS,* pp. 319-328. Springer-Verlag, 1998.
12. D. Kahn: The History of Steganography, in R. Anderson, Editor, Information Hiding: First International Workshop, Vol. 1174 of *LNCS,* pp. 1-6, Springer-Verlag, Berlin, 1996.
13. S. Katzenbeisser and F. Petitcolas, Editors: Information Hiding Techniques for Steganography and Digital Watermarking. Artech House, Norwood, MA, 2000.
14. C Kurak & J. McHugh: *A Cautionary Note on Image Downgrading* in Computer Security Applications Conference, San Antonio, TX, pp. 153-159, Dec. 1992.
15. A.J. Menezes, P.C. van Oorschot, and S.A. Vanstone: *Handbook of Applied Cryptography,* CRC Press, Boca Raton, FL, 1997.
16. T. Mittelholzer: An Information-Theoretic Approach to Steganography and Watermarking, in A. Pfitzmann, Editor, Information Hiding: Third International Workshop, Vol. 1768 of *LNCS,* pp. 1-16. Springer-Verlag, Berlin, 2000.
17. I.S. Moskowitz, G.E. Longdon, and L. Chang: *A Method of Steganographic Communication,* in preparation, 2000.
18. A. Pfitzmann, editor: Information Hiding: Third International Workshop, Vol. 1768 of *Lecture Notes in Computer Science.* Springer-Verlag, Berlin, 1999.
19. B. Pfitzmann: Information Hiding Terminology, in R. Anderson, Editor, Information Hiding: First International Workshop, Vol. 1174 of *LNCS,* pp. 347-350. Springer-Verlag, Berlin, 1996.
20. B. Schneier: Description of a New Variable-Length Key, 64-Bit Block Cipher (Blowfish), in R. Anderson, Editor, Fast Software Encryption, Cambridge Security Workshop Proceedings, Vol. 809 of *LNCS,* pp. 191-204. Springer-Verlag, 1994 (Blowfish implementation written by Eric Young).
21. C.E Shannon: Communication Theory of Secrecy Systems, *Bell System Technical Journal,* 28, 656-715, 1949.
22. G. Simmons: The Prisoners' Problem and the Subliminal Channel, in D. Chaum, Editor, *Advances in Cryptology: Proceedings of Crypto 83,* pp. 51-67. Plenum Press, New York, 1984.
23. R. Thom: *Structural Stability and Morphogenesis,* W.A. Benjamin, Reading, MA, (French ed. 1972) 1975.
24. A.D. Wyner: The Wire-Tap Channel, *The Bell System Technical Journal,* 54(8), 1355-1387, October 1975.
25. J. Zollner, H. Federrath, H. Klimant, A. Pfitzmann, R. Piotraschke, A. Westfeld, G. Wicke, and G. Wolf: *Modeling the Security of Steganographic Systems,* in D. Aucsmith, Editor, Information Hiding: Second International Workshop, Vol. 1525 of *LNCS,* pp. 344-354. Springer-Verlag, Berlin, 1998.

Chapter 28

Cookies and Web Bugs: What They Are and How They Work Together

William T. Harding
Anita J. Reed
Robert L. Gray

What are cookies and what are Web bugs? Cookies are not the kind of cookies that we find in the grocery store and love to eat. Rather, cookies found on the World Wide Web are small unique text files created by a Web site and sent to your computer's hard drive. Cookie files record your mouse clicking choices each time you get on the Internet. After you type in a Uniform Resource Locator (URL), your browser contacts that server and requests the specific Web site to be displayed on your monitor. The browser searches your hard drive to see if you already have a cookie file from the site. If you have previously visited this site, the unique identifier code, previously recorded in your cookie file, is identified and your browser will transfer the cookie file contents back to that site. Now the server has a history file of actually what you selected when you previously visited that site. You can readily see this because your previous selections are highlighted on your screen. If this is the first time you have visited this particular site, then an ID is assigned to you and this initial cookie file is saved on your hard drive.

A Web bug is a graphic on a Web page or in an e-mail message that is designed to monitor who is reading the Web page or e-mail message. A Web bug can provide the Internet protocol (IP) address of the e-mail recipient, whether or not the recipient wishes that information disclosed. Web bugs can provide information relative to how often a message is being

0-8493-1248-5/02/$0.00+$1.50
© 2002 by CRC Press LLC

forwarded and read. Other uses of Web bugs are discussed in the details that follow. Additionally, Web bugs and cookies can be merged and even synchronized to a person's e-mail address. There are positive, negative, illegal, and unethical issues to explore relative to the use of Web bugs and cookies. These details also follow.

WHAT IS A COOKIE?

Only in the past few years have cookies become a controversial issue, but, as previously stated, not the kind of cookies that you find in the grocery store bearing the name "Oreos" or "Famous Amos." These cookies deal with information passed between a Web site and a computer's hard drive. Although cookies are becoming a more popular topic, there are still many users who are not aware of the cookies being stored on their hard drives. Those who are familiar with cookies are bringing up the issues of Internet privacy and ethics. Many companies such as DoubleClick, Inc. have also had lawsuits brought against them that ask the question: are Internet companies going too far?

To begin, the basics of cookies need to be explained. Lou Montulli for Netscape invented the cookie in 1994. The only reason, at the time, to invent a cookie was to enable online shopping baskets. Why the name "cookie" though? According to an article entitled "Cookies ... Good or Evil?," it is said that early hackers got their kicks from Andy Williams' TV variety show. A "cookie bear" sketch was often performed where a guy in a bear suit tried all kinds of tricks to get a cookie from Williams, and Williams would always end the sketch while screaming, "No cookies! Not now, not ever ... NEVER!" A hacker took on the name "cookie bear" and annoyed mainframe computer operators by taking over their consoles and displaying a message "WANT COOKIE." It would not go away until the operator typed the word cookie, and cookie bear would reply with a thank you. The "cookie" did nothing but damage the operator's nerves. Hence, the name "cookie" emerged.

COOKIE CONTENTS

When cookies were first being discovered, rumors went around that these cookies could scan information off your hard drive and collect details about you, such as your passwords, credit card numbers, or a list of software on your computer. These rumors were rejected when it was explained that a cookie is not an executable program and can do nothing directly to your computer. In simple terms, cookies are small, unique text files created by a Web site and sent to a computer's hard drive. They contain a name, a value, an expiration date, and the originating site. The header contains this information and is removed from the document before the browser displays it. You will never be able to see this header, even if you execute the view or document source commands in your browser. The header is part of the cookie when it is created. When it is put on your hard drive, the header is left off. The only information left of the cookie is relevant to the server and no one else.

An example of a header is as follows:

```
Set-Cookie: NAME = VALUE; expires = DATE; path = PATH;
domain = DOMAIN_NAME; secure
```

The NAME = VALUE is required. NAME is the name of the cookie. VALUE has no relevance to the user; it is anything the origin server chooses to send. DATE determines how long the cookie will be on your hard drive. No expiration date indicates that the cookie will expire when you quit the Web browser. DOMAIN_NAME contains the address of the server that sent the cookie and that will receive a copy of this cookie when the browser requests a file from that server. It specifies the domain for which the cookie is valid. PATH is an attribute that is used to further define when a cookie is sent back to a server. Secure specifies that the cookie will only be sent if a secure channel is being used.

Many different types of cookies are used. The most common type is named a visitor cookie. This keeps track of how many times you return to a site. It alerts the Webmaster of which pages are receiving multiple visits. A second type of cookie is a preference cookie that stores a user's chosen values on how to load the page. It is the basis of customized home pages and site personalization. It can remember which color schemes you prefer on the page or how many results you like from a search. The shopping basket cookie is a popular one with online ordering. It assigns an ID value to you through a cookie. As you select items, it includes that item in the ID file on the server. The most notorious and controversial is the tracking cookie. It resembles the shopping basket cookie, but instead of adding items to your ID file, it adds sites you have visited. Your buying habits are collected for targeted marketing. Potentially, companies can save e-mail addresses supplied by the user and spam you on products based on information they gathered about you.

Cookies are only used when data are moving around. After you type a URL in your browser, it contacts that server and requests that Web site. The browser looks on your machine to see if you already have a cookie file from the site. If a cookie file is found, your browser sends all the information in the cookie to that site with the URL. When the server receives the information, it can now use the cookie to discover your shopping or browsing behavior. If no cookie is received, an ID is assigned to you and sent to your machine in the form of a cookie file to be used the next time you visit.

Cookies are simply text files and can be edited or deleted from the computer system. For Netscape Navigator users, cookies can be found under (C:/Program Files/Netscape/Users/default or user name/cookie.txt) directory, while Explorer users will find cookies stored in a folder called Cookies under (C:/windows/Cookies). Users cannot harm their computer when they delete the entire cookie folder or selected files. Web browsers have options that alert users before accepting cookies. Furthermore, there is software that allows users to block cookies, such as Zero-knowledge systems, Junkguard, and others that are found at www.download.com.

For advanced users, cookies can also be manipulated to improve their Web usage. Cookies are stored as a text string, and users can edit the expiration date, domain, and path of the cookie. For instance, JavaScript makes the cookies property of the documents object available for processing. As a string, a cookie can be manipulated like any other string literal or variable using the methods and properties of the string object.

Although the cookie is primarily a simple text file, it does require some kind of scripting to set the cookie and to allow the trouble-free flow of information back and forth between the server and client. Probably the most common language that is used is Perl CGI script. However, cookies can also be created using JavaScript, Livewire, Active Server Pages, or VBScript.

Here is an example of a Javascript cookie:

```
<SCRIPT language=JavaScript>
  function setCookie (name,
   value, expires, path, domain,
   secure) {
  document.cookie = name + " =" +
   escape(value) +
  ((expires) ? "; expires =" +
   expires: "") +
  ((path) ? "; path=" + path:
   "") +
  ((domain) ? "; domain=" +
   domain: "") +
  ((secure) ? "; secure": "");
  }
</SCRIPT>.
```

Even though the design of the cookie is written in a different language than the more common Perl CGI script that we first observed, the content includes the same name-value pairs. Each one of these scripts is used to set and retrieve only their unique cookie and they are very similar in content. The choice of which one to use is up to the creators' personal preference and knowledge.

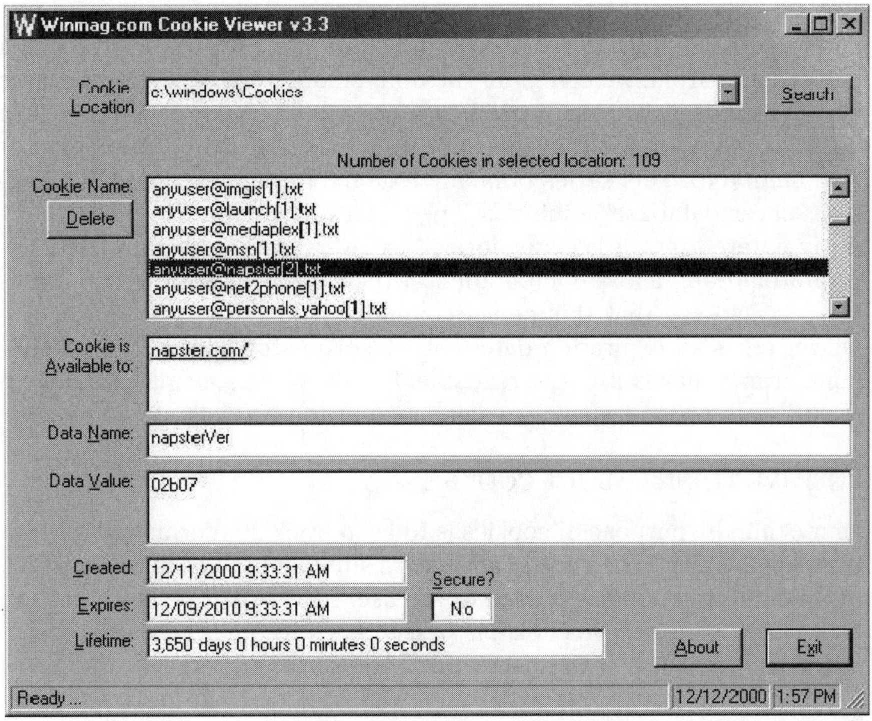

Exhibit 1. Karen's Cookie Viewer

When it comes to being able to actually view what the cookie looks like on your system, what you get to see from the file is very limited and not easily readable. The fact is that all of the information on the cookie is only readable in its entirety by the server that set the cookie. Furthermore, in most cases, when you access the files directly from your cookies.txt file or from the windows/cookies directory with a text editor, what you see looks mostly like indecipherable numbers or computer noise. However, Karen Kenworthy of Winmag.com (one super sleuth programmer) has created a free program that will locate and display all of the cookies on your Windows computer. Her cookie viewer program will display all the information within a cookie that is available except for any personal information that is generally hidden behind the encoded ID value. Exhibit 1 shows Karen's Cookie Viewer in action.

As you can see, the cookie viewer shows that we have 109 cookies currently inside our Windows/Cookie directory. Notice that she has added a Delete feature to the viewer to make it very easy for the user to get rid of all unwanted cookies. When we highlight the cookie named

355

anyuser@napster[2].txt, we can see that it indeed came from napster.com and is available only to this server. If we are not sure of the Web site a cookie came from, we can go to the domain or IP address shown in this box to decide if we really need that particular cookie. If not, we can delete it! Next we see that the Data Value is set at 02b07, which is our own unique ID. This series of numbers and letters interacts with a Napster server database holding any pertinent information we have previously entered into a Napster form. Next we see the creation date, the expiration date, and a computation of the time between the two dates. We can also see that this cookie should last for 10 years. The cookie viewer takes an expiration date that Netscape stores as a 32-bit binary number and makes it easily readable. Finally, we see a small window in regard to the security issue, which is set at the No default.

POSITIVE THINGS ABOUT COOKIES

First of all, the purpose of cookies is to keep track of information on your browsing history. When a user accesses a site that uses cookies, up to 255 bytes of information are passed to the user's browser. The next time the user visits that site, the cookie is passed back to the server. The cookie might include a list of the pages that the user has viewed or the user's viewing patterns based on prior visits. With cookies, a site can track usage patterns and customize the information displayed to individuals as they log on to the site.

Second, cookies can provide a wealth of information to marketers. By using Internet cookies, online businesses can target ads that are relevant to specific consumers' needs and interests. Both consumers and marketers can benefit from using cookies. The marketers can get a higher rate of Click-Through viewers, while customers can view only the ads that interest them. In addition, cookies can prevent repetitive ads. Internet marketing companies such as Focalink and DoubleClick implement cookies to make sure an Internet user does not have to see the same ads over and over again. Moreover, cookies provide marketers with a better understanding of consumer behavior by examining the Web surfing habits of the users on the Internet. Advanced data mining companies such as NCR, Inc. and Sift Inc. can analyze the information about customers in the cookie files and better meet the needs of all consumers.

An online ordering system can use cookies to remember what a person wants to buy. For example, if a customer spends hours of shopping looking for a book at a site, and then suddenly has to get offline, the customer can return to the site later and the item will still be in their shopping basket.

Site personalization is also another beneficial use of cookies. Let's say a person comes to the CNN.com site, but does not want to see any sports news; CNN.com allows that person to select this as an option. From then on (until the cookie expires), the person will not have to see sports news at CNN.com.

Internet users can use cookies to store their passwords and user IDs, so the next time they want to log on to the Web site, they do not have to type in the password or user ID. However, this function of cookies can be a security risk if the computer is shared among other users. Hotmail and Yahoo! are some of the common sites that use this type of cookie to provide quicker access for their e-mail users.

Cookies have their advantages, described in "Destroying E-Commerce's 'Cookie Monster' Image."[2] Cookies can target ads that are relevant to specific consumers' needs and interests. This benefits users by keeping hundreds of inconvenient and unwanted ads away. The cookies prevent repetitive banner ads. Also, through the use of cookies, companies can better understand the habits of consumer behavior. This enables marketers to meet the needs of most consumers. Cookies are stored at the user's site on that specific computer. It is easy to disable cookies. In Internet Explorer 4.0, choose the View, Internet Options command, click the Advanced tab, and click the Disable All Cookies option.

NEGATIVE ISSUES REGARDING COOKIES

The main concerns about using cookie technology are the security and privacy issues. Some believe that cookies are a security risk, an invasion of privacy, and dangerous to the Internet. Whether or not cookies are ethical is based on how the information about users is collected, what information is collected, and how this information is used. Every time a user logs on to a Web site, he or she will give away information such as service provider, operating system, browser type, monitor specifications, CPU type, IP address, and what server last logged on.

A good example of the misuse of cookies is the case when a user shares a computer with other users. For example, at an Internet café, people can snoop into the last user's cookie file stored in the computer's hard disk and potentially uncover sensitive information about the earlier user. That is one reason why it is critical that Web developers do not misuse cookies and do not store information that might be deemed sensitive in a user's cookie file. Storing information such as someone's Social Security number, mother's maiden name, or credit card information in a cookie is a threat to Internet users.

There are disadvantages and limitations to what cookies can do for online businesses and Web users. Some Internet consumers have several myths about what cookies can do, so it is crucial to point out things that cookies *cannot* do:

- Steal or damage information from a user's hard drive
- Plant viruses that would destroy the hard drive
- Track movements from one site to another site
- Take credit card numbers without permission
- Travel with the user to another computer.
- Track down names, addresses, and other information unless consumers have provided such information voluntarily

On January 27, 2000, a California woman filed suit against DoubleClick, accusing the Web advertising firm of unlawfully obtaining and selling consumers' private information. The lawsuit alleges that DoubleClick employs sophisticated computer tracking technology, known as cookies, to identify Internet users and collect personal information without their consent as they travel around the Web. In June 2000, DoubleClick purchased Abacus Direct Corporation, a direct marketing service that maintains a database of names, addresses, and the retail purchasing habits of 90 percent of American households. DoubleClick's new privacy policy states that the company plans to use the information collected by cookies to build a database profiling consumers. DoubleClick defends the practice of profiling, insisting that it allows better targeting of online ads which in turn makes the customer's online experiences more relevant and advertising more profitable. The company calls it "personalization."

According to the Electronic Privacy Information Center, "DoubleClick has compiled approximately 100 million Internet profiles to date." Consumers felt this provided DoubleClick with too much access to unsuspecting users' personal information. Consumers did not realize that most of the time they were receiving an unauthorized DoubleClick cookie. There were alleged violations of federal statutes, such as the Electronic Communication Privacy Act and the Stored Wire and Electronic Communications and Transactional Records Access Act. In March 2000, DoubleClick admitted to making a mistake in merging names with anonymous user activity.

Many people say that the best privacy policies would let consumers "opt in," having a say in whether they want to accept or reject specific information. In an article titled "Keeping Web Data Private," Electronic Data Systems (EDS) Corp. in Plano, Texas was said to have the best practices.[4] Bill Poulous, EDS's director of E-commerce policy stated, "Companies must tell consumers they are collecting personal information, let them know what will be done with it and give them an opportunity to opt out, or block collection of their data." Poulous also comments that policies should be posted where the average citizen can read and understand them and be able to follow them.

WHAT IS A WEB BUG?

A Web bug is a graphic on a Web page or in an e-mail message that is designed to monitor who is reading the Web page or an e-mail message. Like cookies, Web bugs are electronic tags that help Web sites and advertisers track visitors' whereabouts in cyberspace. However, Web bugs are essentially invisible on the page and are much smaller — about the size of the period at the end of a sentence. Known for tracking down the creator of the Melissa virus, Richard Smith, chief technology officer of www.privacyfoundation.org, is accredited with uncovering the Web bug technique. According to Smith, "Typically, set as a transparent image, and only one pixel by one pixel in size, a Web bug is a graphic on a Web page or in an e-mail message that is designed to monitor who is reading the Web page or e-mail message." According to Craig Nathan, Chief Technology Officer for Meconomy.com, the 1 ×1 pixel Web bug "is like a beacon, so that every time you hit a Web page it sends a ping or call-back to the server saying 'Hi, this is who I am and this is where I am.'"

Most computers have cookies, which are placed on a person's hard drive when a banner ad is displayed or a person signs up for an online service. Savvy Web surfers know they are being tracked when they see a banner ad. However, people cannot see Web bugs, and anti-cookie filters will not catch them. So the Web bugs can wind up tracking surfers in areas online where banner ads are not present or on sites where people may not expect to be trailed.

An example of a Web bug can be found at http://www.investorplace.com. There is a Web bug located at the top of the page. By choosing View, Source in Internet Explorer or View, Page Source in Netscape you can see the code at work. The code, as seen below, provides information about an "Investor Place" visitor to the advertising agency DoubleClick:

```
<IMG SRC="http:ad.doubleclick.net/
       activity;src=328142;
       type=mmti;
    cat=invstr;ord=<Time>
       ?"WIDTH=1
       HEIGHT=1 BORDER=0>
```

It is also possible to check for bugs on a Web page. Once the page has loaded, view the page's source code. Search the page for an IMG tag that contains the attributes WIDTH=1 HEIGHT=1 BORDER=0 (or WIDTH="1" HEIGHT="1" BORDER="0"). This indicates the presence of a small, transparent image. If the image that this tag points to is on a server other than the current server (i.e., the IMG tag contains the text SRC="http://"), it is quite likely a Web bug.

PRIVACY AND OTHER WEB BUG ISSUES

Advertising networks, such as DoubleClick or Match Point, use Web bugs (also called "Internet tags") to develop an "independent accounting" of the number of people in various regions of the world, as well as various regions of the Internet, who have accessed a particular Web site. Advertisers also account for the statistical page views within the Web sites. This is very helpful in planning and managing the effectiveness of the content, because it provides a survey of target market information (i.e., the number of visits by users to the site). In this same spirit, the ad networks can use Web bugs to build a personal profile of sites a person has visited. This information can be warehoused on a database server and mined to determine what types of ads are to be shown to that user. This is referred to as "directed advertising."

Web bugs used in e-mail messages can be even more invasive. In Web-based e-mail, Web bugs can be used to determine if and when an e-mail message has been read. A Web bug can provide the IP address of the recipient, whether or not the recipient wishes that information disclosed. Within an organization, a Web bug can give an idea of how often a message is being forwarded and read. This can prove to be helpful in direct marketing to return statistics on the effectiveness of an ad campaign. Web bugs can be used to detect if someone has viewed a junk e-mail message or not. People who do not view a message can be removed from the list for future mailings.

With the help of a cookie, the Web bug can identify a machine, the Web page it opened, the time the visit began, and other details. That information, sent to a company that provides advertising services, can then be used to determine if someone subsequently visits another company page in the same ad network to buy something or to read other material. "It is a way of collecting consumer activity at their online store," says David Rosenblatt, senior vice president for global technology at DoubleClick. However, for consumer watchdogs, Web bugs and other tracking tools represent a growing threat to the privacy and autonomy of online computer users.

It is also possible to add Web bugs to Microsoft Word documents. A Web bug could allow an author to track where a document is being read and how often. In addition, the author can watch how a "bugged" document is passed from one person to another or from one organization to another.

Some possible uses of Web bugs in Word documents include:

- Detecting and tracking leaks of confidential documents from a company
- Tracking possible copyright infringement of newsletters and reports

- Monitoring the distribution of a press release
- Tracking the quoting of text when it is copied from one Word document to a new document

Web bugs are made possible by the ability in Microsoft Word for a document to link to an image file that is located on a remote Web server. Because only the URL of the Web bug is stored in a document and not the actual image, Microsoft Word must fetch the image from a Web server each and every time the document is opened. This image-linking feature then puts a remote server in the position to monitor when and where a document file is being opened. The server knows the IP address and host name of the computer that is opening the document. A host name will typically include the company name of a business. The host name of a home computer usually has the name of a user's Internet Service Provider. Short of removing the feature that allows linking to Web images in Microsoft Word, there does not appear to be a good preventative solution. In addition to Word documents, Web bugs can also be used in Excel 2000 and PowerPoint 2000 documents.

SYNCHRONIZATION OF WEB BUGS AND COOKIES

Additionally, Web bugs and browser cookies can be synchronized to a particular e-mail address. This trick allows a Web site to know the identity of people (plus other personal information about them) who come to the site at a later date. To further explain this, when a cookie is placed on your computer, the server that originally placed the cookie is the only one that can read it. In theory, if two separate sites place a separate unique cookie on your computer, they cannot read the data stored in each other's cookies. This usually means, for example, that one site cannot tell that you have recently visited the other site. However, the situation is very different if the cookie placed on your computer contains information that is sent by that site to an advertising agency's server and that agency is used by both Web sites. If each of these sites places a Web bug on their page to report information back to the advertising agency's computer, every time you visit either site, details about you will be sent back to the advertising agency utilizing information stored on your computer relative to both sets of cookie files. This allows your computer to be identified as a computer that visited each of the sites.

An example will further explain this: When Bob, the Web surfer, loads a page or opens an e-mail that contains a Web bug, information is sent to the server housing the "transparent GIF." Common information being sent includes the IP address of Bob's computer, his type of browser, the URL of the Web page being viewed, the URL of the image, and the time the file was accessed. Also potentially being sent to the server, the thing that could be most threatening to Bob's privacy, is a previously set cookie value, found on his computer.

Depending on the nature of the preexisting cookie, it could contain a whole host of information from usernames and passwords to e-mail addresses and credit card information. To continue with our example, Bob may receive a cookie upon visiting Web Site #1 that contains a transparent GIF that is hosted on a specific advertising agency's server. Bob could also receive another cookie when he goes to Web Site #2 that contains a transparent GIF which is hosted on the same advertising agency's server. Then the two Web sites would be able to cross-reference Bob's activity through the cookies that are reporting to the advertiser. As this activity continues, the advertiser is able to stockpile what is considered to be nonpersonal information on Bob's preferences and habits, and, at the same time, there is the potential for the aggregation of Bob's personal information as well.

It is certainly technically possible, through standardized cookie codes, that different servers could synchronize their cookies and Web bugs, enabling this information to be shared across the World Wide Web. If this were to happen, just the fact that a person visited a certain Web site could be spread throughout many Internet servers, and the invasion of one's privacy could be endless.

CONCLUSION

The basics of cookies and Web bugs have been presented to include definitions, contents, usefulness, privacy concerns, and synchronization. Several examples of the actual code of cookies and Web bugs were illustrated to help the reader learn how to identify them. Many positive uses of cookies and Web bugs in business were discussed. Additionally, privacy and other issues regarding cookies and Web bugs were examined. Finally, the synchronization of Web bugs and cookies (even in Word documents) was discussed.

However, our discussions have primarily been limited to cookies and Web bugs as they are identified, stored, and used today only. Through cookie and Web bug meta data (stored data about data), a great deal of information could be tracked about individual user behavior across many platforms of computer systems. Someday we may see cookie and Web bug mining software filtering out all kinds of different anomalies and consumer trends from cookie and Web bug warehouses! What we have seen thus far may only be the tip of the iceberg.

ACKNOWLEDGMENT

Special thanks go to the following MIS students at Texas A&M University–Corpus Christi for their contributions to this research: Erik Ballenger,

Cookies and Web Bugs: What They Are and How They Work Together

Cynthia Crenshaw, Robert Gaza, Jason Janacek, Russell Laya, Brandon Manrow, Tuan Nguyen, Sergio Rios, Marco Rodriquez, Daniel Shelton, and Lynn Thornton.

Further Reading

1. Bradley, Helen. "Beware of Web Bugs & Clear GIFs: Learn How These Innocuous Tools Invade Your Privacy," *PC Privacy*, 8(4), April 2000.
2. Cattapan, Tom. "Destroying E-Commerce's 'Cookie Monster' Image," *Direct Marketing*, 62(12): 20–24+, April 2000.
3. Hancock, Bill. "Web Bugs — The New Threat!," *Computers & Security*, 18(8): 646–647, 1999.
4. Harrison, Ann. "Keeping Web Data Private," *Computerworld*, 34(19): 57, May 8, 2000.
5. Junnarkar, S. "DoubleClick Accused of Unlawful Consumer Data Use," *Cnet News*, January 28, 2000.
6. Kearns, Dave. "Explorer Patch Causes Cookie Chaos," *Network World*, 17(31): 24. July 31, 2000.
7. Kokoszka, Kevin. "Web Bugs on the Web," Available: http://writings142.tripod.com/kokoszka/paper.html.
8. Kyle, Jim. "Cookies ... Good or Evil?," *Developer News*. November 30, 1999.
9. Mayer-Schonberger, Viktor. "The Internet and Privacy Legislation: Cookies for a Treat?" Available: http://wvjolt.wvu.edu/wvjolt/current/issue1.
10. Olsen, Stefanie. "Nearly Undetectable Tracking Device Raises Concern," *CNET News.com*, July 12, 2000, 2:05 p.m. PT.
11. Rodger, W. "Activists Charge DoubleClick Double Cross," *USA Today*, July 6, 2000.
12. Samborn, Hope Viner. "Nibbling Away at Privacy," *ABA Journal, the Lawyer's Magazine*, 86:26–27, June 2000.
13. Sherman, Erik. "Don't Neglect Desktop When It Comes to Security," *Computerworld* 25: 36-37, September 2000.
14. Smith, Richard. "Microsoft Word Documents that 'Phone Home,'" Privacy Foundation. Available: http://www.privacyfoundation.org/advisories/advWordBugs.html, August 2000.
15. Turban, Efraim, Lee, Jae, King, David, and Chung H. *Electronic Commerce: A Managerial Perspective*, Prentice-Hall, Englewood Cliffs, NJ, 2000.
16. Williams, Jason. "Personalization vs. Privacy: The Great Online Cookie Debate," *Editor & Publisher*, 133(9): 26–27, February 28, 2000.
17. Wright, Matt. "HTTP Cookie Library," Available: http://www.worldwidemart.com/scripts/.

Web Site Sources

1. http://www.webparanoia.com/cookies.html
2. http://theblindalley.com/webbugsinfo.html
3. http://www.privacyfoundation.org/education/webbug.html
4. http://ciac.llnl.gov/ciac/bulletins/i-034.shtml
5. http://ecommerce.ncsu.edu/csc513/student_work/tech_cookie.html
6. http://www.rbaworld.com/security/computers/cookies/cookies.shtml
7. http://www.howstuffworks.com/cookie2.htm

Chapter 29
Online Profiling: Benefits and Concerns

Prepared Statement before the Committee on Commerce, Science, and Transportation, United States Senate

The Federal Trade Commission

Washington, D.C.

June 13, 2000

Mr. Chairman and Members of the Committee, I am Jodie Bernstein, Director of the Bureau of Consumer Protection of the Federal Trade Commission.[1] I appreciate this opportunity to discuss the Commission's report on profiling issued today.[2] The report describes the nature of online profiling, consumer privacy concerns about these practices, and the Commission's efforts to date to address these concerns. The Commission is not making any recommendations at this time.

As it has in other areas, the Commission has encouraged effective industry self-regulation, and the network advertising industry has responded with drafts of self-regulatory principles for our consideration. As discussed further in this testimony, there are real challenges to creating an effective self-regulatory regime for this complex and dynamic industry, and this process is not yet complete. The Commission will supplement this report with specific recommendations to Congress after it has an opportunity to fully consider the self-regulatory proposals and how they interrelate with the Commission's previous views and recommendations in the online privacy area.

I. INTRODUCTION AND BACKGROUND

A. FTC Law Enforcement Authority

The FTC's mission is to promote the efficient functioning of the marketplace by protecting consumers from unfair or deceptive acts or practices and to increase consumer choice by promoting vigorous competition. As you know, the Commission's responsibilities are far-reaching. The Commission's primary legislative mandate is to enforce the Federal Trade Commission Act (FTCA), which prohibits unfair methods of competition and unfair or deceptive acts or practices in or affecting commerce.[3] With the exception of certain industries and activities, the FTCA provides the Commission with broad investigative and law enforcement authority over entities engaged in or whose business affects commerce.[4] Commerce on the Internet falls within the scope of this statutory mandate.

B. Privacy Concerns in the Online Marketplace

Since its inception in the mid-1990s, the online consumer marketplace has grown at an exponential rate. Recent figures suggest that as many as 90 million Americans now use the Internet on a regular basis.[5] Of these, 69 percent, or over 60 million people, shopped online in the third quarter of 1999.[6] In addition, the Census Bureau estimates that retail e-commerce sales were $5.2 billion for the fourth quarter of 1999, and increased to $5.3 billion for the first quarter of 2000.[7]

At the same time, technology has enhanced the capacity of online companies to collect, store, transfer, and analyze vast amounts of data from and about the consumers who visit their Web sites. This increase in the collection and use of data, along with the myriad subsequent uses of this information that interactive technology makes possible, has raised public awareness and consumer concerns about online privacy.[8] Recent survey data demonstrate that 92 percent of consumers are concerned (67 percent are "very concerned") about the misuse of their personal information online.[9] The level of consumer unease is also indicated by a recent study in which 92 percent of respondents from online households stated that they do not trust online companies to keep their personal information confidential.[10] To ensure consumer confidence in this new marketplace and its continued growth, consumer concerns about privacy must be addressed.[11]

C. The Commission's Approach to Online Privacy — Initiatives Since 1995

Since 1995, the Commission has been at the forefront of the public debate concerning online privacy.[12] The Commission has held public workshops;

examined Web site information practices and disclosures regarding the collection, use, and transfer of personal information; and commented on self-regulatory efforts and technological developments intended to enhance consumer privacy. The Commission's goals have been to understand this new marketplace and its information practices, and to assess the costs and benefits to businesses and consumers.[13]

In June 1998, the Commission issued *Privacy Online: A Report to Congress* (1998 Report), an examination of the information practices of commercial sites on the World Wide Web and of industry's efforts to implement self-regulatory programs to protect consumers' online privacy.[14] The Commission described the widely accepted fair information practice principles of *Notice, Choice, Access,* and *Security.* The Commission also identified *Enforcement* — the use of a reliable mechanism to provide sanctions for noncompliance — as a critical component of any governmental or self-regulatory program to protect privacy online.[15] In addition, the 1998 Report presented the results of the Commission's first online privacy survey of commercial Web sites. While almost all Web sites (92 percent of the comprehensive random sample) were collecting great amounts of personal information from consumers, few (14 percent) disclosed anything at all about their information practices.[16]

Based on survey data showing that the vast majority of sites directed at children also collected personal information, the Commission recommended that Congress enact legislation setting forth standards for the online collection of personal information from children.[17,18] The Commission deferred its recommendations with respect to the collection of personal information from online consumers generally. In subsequent Congressional testimony, the Commission referenced promising self-regulatory efforts suggesting that industry should be given more time to address online privacy issues. The Commission urged the online industry to expand these efforts by adopting effective, widespread self-regulation based on the long-standing fair information practice principles of Notice, Choice, Access, and Security, and by putting enforcement mechanisms in place to assure adherence to these principles.[19] In a 1999 report to Congress, *Self-Regulation and Privacy Online*, a majority of the Commission again recommended that self-regulation be given more time.[20]

On May 22, 2000, the Commission issued its third report to Congress examining the state of online privacy and the efficacy of industry self-regulation. *Privacy Online: Fair Information Practices in the Electronic Marketplace* (2000 Report) presented the results of the Commission's 2000 Online Privacy Survey, which reviewed the nature and substance of U.S. commercial Web sites' privacy disclosures, and assessed the effectiveness of self-regulation. In that Report, a majority of the Commission concluded that legislation is necessary to ensure further implementation of fair information practices online and recommended a framework for such legislation.[21]

II. ONLINE PROFILING

On November 8, 1999, the Commission and the United States Department of Commerce jointly sponsored a Public Workshop on Online Profiling.[22] As a result of the Workshop and public comment, the Commission learned a great deal about what online profiling is, how it can benefit both businesses and consumers, and the privacy concerns that it raises.

A. What is Online Profiling?

More than half of all online advertising is in the form of "banner ads" displayed on Web pages — small graphic advertisements that appear in boxes above or to the side of the primary site content.[23-25] Often, these ads are not selected and delivered by the Web site visited by a consumer, but by a network advertising company that manages and provides advertising for numerous unrelated Web sites.

In general, these network advertising companies do not merely supply banner ads; they also gather data about the consumers who view their ads. This is accomplished primarily by the use of "cookies"[26] which track the individual's actions on the Web.[27] The information gathered by network advertisers is often, but not always, anonymous; that is, the profiles are frequently linked to the identification number of the advertising network's cookie on the consumer's computer rather than the name of a specific person. In some circumstances, however, the profiles derived from tracking consumers' activities on the Web are linked or merged with personally identifiable information.[28]

Once collected, consumer data is analyzed and can be combined with demographic and "psychographic"[29] data from third-party sources, data on the consumer's offline purchases, or information collected directly from consumers through surveys and registration forms. This enhanced data allows the advertising networks to make a variety of inferences about each consumer's interests and preferences. The result is a detailed profile that attempts to predict the individual consumer's tastes, needs, and purchasing habits and enables the advertising companies' computers to make split-second decisions about how to deliver ads directly targeted to the consumer's specific interests.

The profiles created by the advertising networks can be extremely detailed. A cookie placed by a network advertising company can track a consumer on any Web site served by that company, thereby allowing data collection across disparate and unrelated sites on the Web. Also, because the cookies used by ad networks are generally persistent, their tracking occurs over an extended period of time, resuming each time the individual logs on to the Internet. When this "clickstream" information is combined with third-party data, these profiles can include hundreds of distinct data fields.[30]

Although network advertisers and their profiling activities are nearly ubiquitous,[31] they are most often invisible to consumers. All that consumers see are the Web sites they visit; banner ads appear as a seamless, integral part of the Web page on which they appear and cookies are placed without any notice to consumers.[32] Unless the Web sites visited by consumers provide notice of the ad network's presence and data collection, consumers may be totally unaware that their activities online are being monitored.[33]

B. Profiling Benefits and Privacy Concerns

Network advertisers' use of cookies[34] and other technologies to create targeted marketing programs can benefit both consumers and businesses. As noted by commenters at the Public Workshop, targeted advertising allows customers to receive offers and information about goods and services in which they are actually interested.[35] Businesses clearly benefit as well from the ability to target advertising because they avoid wasting advertising dollars marketing themselves to consumers who have no interest in their products.[36] Additionally, a number of commenters stated that targeted advertising helps to subsidize free content on the Internet.[37]

Despite the benefits of targeted advertising, there is widespread concern about current profiling practices. The most consistent and significant concern expressed about profiling is that it is conducted without consumers' knowledge.[38] The presence and identity of a network advertiser on a particular site, the placement of a cookie on the consumer's computer, the tracking of the consumer's movements, and the targeting of ads are simply invisible in most cases.

The second most persistent concern expressed by commenters was the extensive and sustained scope of the monitoring that occurs. Unbeknownst to most consumers, advertising networks monitor individuals across a multitude of seemingly unrelated Web sites and over an indefinite period of time. The result is a profile far more comprehensive than any individual Web site could gather. Although much of the information that goes into a profile is fairly innocuous when viewed in isolation, the cumulation over time of vast numbers of seemingly minor details about an individual produces a portrait that is quite comprehensive and, to many, inherently intrusive.[39]

For many of those who expressed concerns about profiling, the privacy implications of profiling are not ameliorated in cases where the profile contains no personally identifiable information.[40] First, commenters feared that companies could unilaterally change their operating procedures and begin associating personally identifiable information with non-personally identifiable data previously collected.[41,42] Second, these commenters objected to the use of profiles — regardless of whether they contain personally identifiable information — to make decisions about the information individuals see and the offers they receive. Commenters expressed concern that companies could use profiles to determine the prices and terms upon which goods and services, including important services like life insurance, are offered to individuals.[43]

C. Online Profiling and Self-Regulation: The NAI Effort

The November 8th Workshop provided an opportunity for consumer advocates, government, and industry members not only to educate the public about the practice of online profiling, but to explore self-regulation as a means of addressing the privacy concerns raised by this practice. In the Spring of 1999, in anticipation of the Workshop, network advertising companies were invited to meet with FTC and Department of Commerce staff to discuss their business practices and the possibility of self-regulation. As a result, industry members announced at the Workshop the formation of the Network Advertising Initiative (NAI), an organization comprised of the leading Internet Network Advertisers — 24/7 Media, AdForce, AdKnowledge, Avenue A, Burst! Media, DoubleClick, Engage, and MatchLogic — to develop a framework for self-regulation of the online profiling industry.

In announcing their intention to implement a self-regulatory scheme, the NAI companies acknowledged that they face unique challenges as a result of their indirect and invisible relationship with consumers as they surf the Internet. The companies also discussed the fundamental question of how fair information practices, including choice, should be applied to the collection and use of data that is unique to a consumer but is not necessarily personally identifiable, such as clickstream data generated by the user's browsing activities and tied only to a cookie identification number.[44]

Following the workshop, the NAI companies submitted working drafts of self-regulatory principles for consideration by FTC and Department of Commerce staff. Although efforts have been made to reach a consensus on basic standards for applying fair information practices to the business model used by the network advertisers, this process is not yet complete. The Commission will supplement this report with specific recommendations to Congress after it has an opportunity to fully consider the self-regulatory proposals and how they interrelate with the Commission's previous views and recommendations in the online privacy area.

III. CONCLUSION

The Commission is committed to the goal of ensuring privacy online for consumers and will continue working to address the unique issues presented by online profiling. I would be pleased to answer any questions you may have.

Notes

1. The Commission vote to issue this testimony was 5–0, with Commissioner Swindle concurring in part and dissenting in part. Commissioner Swindle's separate statement is attached to the testimony.
2. My oral testimony and responses to questions you may have reflect my own views and are not necessarily the views of the Commission or any individual Commissioner.
3. 15 USC § 45(a).
4. The Commission also has responsibility under 45 additional statutes governing specific industries and practices. These include, for example, the Truth in Lending Act, 15 USC §§ 1601 *et seq.*, which mandates disclosures of credit terms, and the Fair Credit Billing Act, 15 USC §§ 1666 *et seq.*, which provides for the correction of billing errors on credit accounts. The Commission also enforces over 30 rules governing specific industries and practices, e.g., the Used Car Rule, 16 CFR Part 455, which requires used car dealers to disclose warranty terms via a window sticker; the Franchise Rule, 16 CFR Part 436, which requires the provision of information to prospective franchisees; the Telemarketing Sales Rule, 16 CFR Part 310, which defines and prohibits deceptive telemarketing practices and other abusive telemarketing practices; and the Children's Online Privacy Protection Rule, 16 CFR Part 312.

    In addition, on May 12, 2000, the Commission issued a final rule implementing the privacy provisions of the Gramm-Leach-Bliley Act, 15 USC §§ 6801 *et seq.* The rule requires a wide range of financial institutions to provide notice to their customers about their privacy policies and practices. The rule also describes the conditions under which those financial institutions may disclose personal financial information about consumers to nonaffiliated third parties, and provides a method by which consumers can prevent financial institutions from sharing their personal financial information with nonaffiliated third parties by opting out of that disclosure, subject to certain exceptions. The rule is available on the Commission's Web site at <http://www.ftc.gov/os/2000/05/index.htm#12>. *See Privacy of Consumer Financial Information*, to be codified at 16 C.F.R. pt. 313.

    The Commission does not, however, have criminal law enforcement authority. Further, under the FTCA, certain entities, such as banks, savings and loan associations, and common carriers, as well as the business of insurance, are wholly or partially exempt from Commission jurisdiction. *See* Section 5(a)(2) and (6)a of the FTC Act, 15 USC § 45(a)(2) and 46(a). *See also* The McCarran-Ferguson Act, 15 USC § 1012(b).
5. The Intelliquest Technology Panel, *Panel News*, available at <http://www.techpanel.com/news/index.asp> [hereinafter "Technology Panel"] (90 million adult online users as of third-quarter 1999). Other sources place the number in the 70–75 million user range. *See* Cyber Dialogue, *Internet Users*, available at <http://www.cyberdialogue.com/resource/data/ic/index.html> (69 million users); Cyberstats, *Internet Access and Usage, Percent of Adults 18+*, available at <http://www.mediamark.com/cfdocs/MRI/cs_f99a.cfm> (75 million users).
6. Technology Panel. This represents an increase of over 15 million online shoppers in one year. *See id.*
7. United States Department of Commerce News, *Retail E-commerce Sales Are $5.3 Billion In First Quarter 2000, Census Bureau Reports* (May 31, 2000), available at <http://www.census.gov/mrts/www/current.html>.
8. Survey data is an important component in the Commission's evaluation of consumer concerns, as is actual consumer behavior. Nonetheless, the Commission recognizes that the interpretation of survey results is complex and must be undertaken with care.

9. Alan F. Westin, *Personalized Marketing and Privacy on the Net: What Consumers Want*, Privacy and American Business at 11 (Nov. 1999) [hereinafter "Westin/PAB 1999"]. *See also IBM Multi-National Consumer Privacy Survey* at 72 (Oct. 1999), prepared by Louis Harris & Associates, Inc. [hereinafter "IBM Privacy Survey"] (72 percent of Internet users very concerned and 20 percent somewhat concerned about threats to personal privacy when using the Internet); Forrester Research, Inc., *Online Consumers Fearful of Privacy Violations* (Oct. 1999), available at <http://www.forrester.com/ER/Press/Release/0,1769,177,FF.html> (two-thirds of American and Canadian online shoppers feel insecure about exchanging personal information over the Internet).

10. *Survey Shows Few Trust Promises on Online Privacy*, Apr. 17, 2000, available at <http://www.nyt.com> (citing recent Odyssey survey).

11. The Commission, of course, recognizes that other consumer concerns also may hinder the development of E-commerce. As a result, the agency has pursued other initiatives such as combating online fraud through law enforcement efforts. *See FTC Staff Report: The FTC's First Five Years Protecting Consumers Online* (Dec. 1999). The Commission, with the Department of Commerce, recently held a public workshop and soliciting comment on the potential issues associated with the use of alternative dispute resolution for online consumer transactions. *See* Initial Notice Requesting Public Comment and Announcing Public Workshop, 65 Fed. Reg. 7,831 (Feb. 16, 2000); Notice Announcing Dates and Location of Workshop and Extending Deadline for Public Comments, 65 Fed. Reg. 18,032 (Apr. 6, 2000). The workshop was held on June 6 and 7, 2000. Information about the workshop, including the federal register notices and public comments received, is available at <http://www.ftc.gov/bcp/altdisresolution/index.htm>.

12. The Commission's review of privacy has mainly focused on online issues because the Commission believes privacy is a critical component in the development of electronic commerce. However, the FTC Act and most other statutes enforced by the Commission apply equally in the offline and online worlds. As described *infra,* n.11, the agency has examined privacy issues affecting both arenas, such as those implicated by the Individual Reference Services Group, and in the areas of financial and medical privacy. It also has pursued law enforcement, where appropriate, to address offline privacy concerns. *See FTC v. Rapp*, No. 99-WM-783 (D. Colo. filed Apr. 21, 1999); *In re Trans Union*, Docket No. 9255 (Feb. 10, 2000), *appeal docketed*, No. 00-1141 (D.C. Cir. Apr. 4, 2000). These activities — as well as recent concerns about the merging of online and offline databases, the blurring of distinctions between online and offline merchants, and the fact that a vast amount of personal identifying information is collected and used offline — make clear that significant attention to offline privacy issues is warranted.

13. The Commission held its first public workshop on privacy in April 1995. In a series of hearings held in October and November 1995, the Commission examined the implications of globalization and technological innovation for competition and consumer protection issues, including privacy concerns. At a public workshop held in June 1996, the Commission examined Web site practices regarding the collection, use, and transfer of consumers' personal information; self-regulatory efforts and technological developments to enhance consumer privacy; consumer and business education efforts; the role of government in protecting online information privacy; and special issues raised by the online collection and use of information from and about children. The Commission held a second workshop in June 1997 to explore issues raised by individual reference services, as well as issues relating to unsolicited commercial e-mail, online privacy generally, and children's online privacy.

The Commission and its staff have also issued reports describing various privacy concerns in the electronic marketplace. *See, e.g., FTC Staff Report: The FTC's First Five Years Protecting Consumers Online* (Dec. 1999); *Individual Reference Services: A Federal Trade Commission Report to Congress* (Dec. 1997); *FTC Staff Report: Public Workshop on Consumer Privacy on the Global Information Infrastructure* (Dec. 1996); *FTC Staff Report: Anticipating the 21st Century: Consumer Protection Policy in the New High-Tech, Global Marketplace* (May 1996). Recently, at the request of the Department of Health and Human Services (HHS), the Commission submitted comments on HHS' proposed Standards for Privacy of Individually Identifiable Health Information (required by the Health Insurance Portability and Accountability Act of 1996). The Commission strongly supported HHS' proposed "individual authorization" or "opt-in" approach to health providers' ancillary use of personally identifiable health information for purposes other than those for which the information was collected. The Commission also offered HHS suggestions it may wish to consider to improve disclosure requirements in two proposed forms that would be required by the regulations. The Commission's comments are available at <http://www. ftc.gov/be/v000001.htm>.

The Commission also has brought law enforcement actions to protect privacy online pursuant to its general mandate to fight unfair and deceptive practices. *See FTC v. ReverseAuction.com, Inc.,* No. 00-0032 (D.D.C. Jan. 6, 2000) (consent decree) (settling charges that an online auction site obtained consumers' personal identifying information from a competitor site and then sent deceptive, unsolicited e-mail messages to those consumers seeking their business); *Liberty Financial Companies, Inc.*, FTC Dkt. No. C-3891 (Aug. 12, 1999) (consent order) (challenging the allegedly false representations by the operator of a "Young Investors" Web site that information collected from children in an online survey would be maintained anonymously); *GeoCities,* FTC Dkt. No. C-3849 (Feb. 12, 1999) (consent order) (http://www.ftc.gov/os/1999/9902/9823015d&o.htm) (settling charges that Web site misrepresented the purposes for which it was collecting personal identifying information from children and adults).

14. The Report is available on the Commission's Web site at http://www.ftc.gov/reports/privacy3/index.htm.
15. 1998 Report at 11-14.
16. *Id.* at 23, 27.
17. *Id.* at 42-43. In October 1998, Congress enacted the Children's Online Privacy Protection Act of 1998 (COPPA), which authorized the Commission to issue regulations implementing the Act's privacy protections for children under the age of 13.
18. 15 USC § § 6501 *et seq.* §§
19. *See* Prepared Statement of the Federal Trade Commission on "Consumer Privacy on the World Wide Web" before the Subcommittee on Telecommunications, Trade and Consumer Protection of the House Committee on Commerce, U.S. House of Representatives (July 21, 1998), available at <http://www.ftc.gov/os/1998/9807/privac98.htm>.
20. *Self-Regulation and Privacy Online* (July 1999) at 12-14 (available at <http://www.ftc.gov/os/1999/9907/index.htm#13>).
21. The 2000 Report is available at <http://www.ftc.gov/os/2000/05/index.htm#22>. The Commission's vote to issue the report was 3-2, with Commissioner Swindle dissenting and Commissioner Leary concurring in part and dissenting in part.
22. A transcript of the Workshop is available at <http://www.ftc.gov/bcp/profiling/index.htm> and will be cited as "Tr. [page], [speaker]." Public comments received in connection with the Workshop can be viewed on the Federal Trade Commission's Web site at <http://www.ftc.gov/bcp/profiling/comments/index.html> and will be cited as "Comments of [organization or name] at [page]."
23. In 1999, 56 percent of all online advertising revenue was attributable to banner advertising. Online advertising has grown exponentially in tandem with the World Wide Web: online advertising revenues in the U.S. grew from \$301 million in 1996.
24. *See* Federal Trade Commission, Privacy Online: A Report to Congress (1998) at 3. The Report is available on the Commission's Web site at <http://www.ftc.gov/reports/privacy3/index.htm>.
25. *See* Jupiter Communications, Inc., Online Advertising Through 2003 (1999) (summary available at <http://www.jupitercommunications.com>).
26. A cookie is a small text file placed on a consumer's computer by a Web server that transmits information back to the server that placed it. As a rule, a cookie can be read only by the server that placed it.
27. In addition to cookies, which are largely invisible to consumers, other hidden methods of monitoring consumers' activities on the Web may also be used. One such method is through the use of "Web bugs," also known as "clear GIFs" or "1-by-1 GIFs." Web bugs are tiny graphic image files embedded in a Web page, generally the same color as the background on which they are displayed. They are one pixel in height by one pixel in length — the smallest image capable of being displayed on a monitor — and are invisible to the naked eye. The Web bug sends back to its home server (which can belong to the host site, a network advertiser or some other third party): the IP (Internet Protocol) address of the computer that downloaded the page on which the bug appears; the URL

(Uniform Resource Locator) of the page on which the Web bug appears; the URL of the Web bug image; the time the page containing the Web bug was viewed; the type of browser that fetched the Web bug; and the identification number of any cookie on the consumer's computer previously placed by that server. Web bugs can be detected only by looking at the source code of a Web page and searching in the code for 1-by-1 IMG tags that load images from a server different than the rest of the Web page. At least one expert claims that, in addition to disclosing who visits the particular Web page or reads the particular e-mail in which the bug has been placed, in some circumstances, Web bugs can also be used to place a cookie on a computer or to synchronize a particular e-mail address with a cookie identification number, making an otherwise anonymous profile personally identifiable. *See generally* Comments of Richard M. Smith; *see also Big Browser Is Watching You!*, Consumer Reports, May 2000, at 46; U.S.A. Today, *A new wrinkle in surfing the Net: Dot-coms' mighty dot-size bugs track your every move*, Mar. 21, 2000 (available at <http://www.usatoday.com/life/cyber/tech/cth582.htm>).

28. Personally identifiable data is data that can be linked to specific individuals and includes, but is not limited to such information as name, postal address, phone number, e-mail address, social security number, and driver's license number. The linkage of personally identifiable information with non-personally identifiable information generally occurs in one of two ways when consumers identify themselves to a Web site on which the network advertiser places banner ads. First, the Web site to whom personal information is provided may, in turn, provide that information to the network advertiser. Second, depending upon how the personal information is retrieved and processed by the Web site, the personally identifying information may be incorporated into a URL string that is automatically transmitted to the network advertiser through its cookie. In addition, network advertising companies can and do link personally identifiable information to non-personally identifiable information at their own Web sites by asking consumers to provide personal information (for example, to enter a sweepstakes) and then linking that information to the cookie previously placed on the consumer's computer; the linkage of personally identifying information to a cookie makes all of the data collected through that cookie personally identifiable.

29. Psychographic data links objective demographic characteristics like age and gender with more abstract characteristics related to ideas, opinions and interests. Data mining specialists analyze demographic, media, survey, purchasing and psychographic data to determine the exact groups that are most likely to buy specific products and services. *See* Comments of the Center for Democracy and Technology (CDT) at 5 n.5. Psychographic profiling is also referred to in the industry as "behavioral profiling."

30. For example, the Web site for Engage states repeatedly that its profiles contain 800 "interest categories." *See, e.g.,* <http://www.engage.com/press/releases/2qfiscal.htm>.

31. DoubleClick has approximately 100 million consumer profiles, *see* Heather Green, *Privacy: Outrage on the Web*, Business Week, Feb. 14, 2000, at 38; Engage has 52 million consumer profiles, *see* <http://www.engage.com/press/releases/2qfiscal.htm>; and 24/7 Media has 60 million profiles, *see* <http://www.247media.com/connect/adv_pub.html>.

32. Most Internet browsers can be configured to notify users that a cookie is being sent to their computer and to give users the option of rejecting the cookie. The browsers' default setting, however, is to permit placement of cookies without any notification.

33. Not all profiles are constructed by network advertising companies. Some Web sites create profiles of their own customers based on their interactions. Other companies create profiles as part of a service — for example, offering discounts on products of interest to consumers or providing references to useful Web sites on the same topic as those already visited by the consumer. *See, e.g.,* Megan Barnett, *The Profilers: Invisible Friends*, The Industry Standard, Mar. 13, 2000, at 220; Ben Hammer, *Bargain Hunting*, The Industry Standard, Mar. 13, 2000, at 232. These profiles are generally created by companies that have a known, consensual relationship with the consumer and are not addressed in this report. This report uses the term "profiling" to refer only to the activities of third-party network advertising companies.

34. Cookies are used for many purposes other than profiling by third-party advertisers, many of which significantly benefit consumers. For example, Web sites often ask for user names and passwords when purchases are made or before certain kinds of content are provided. Cookies can store these names and passwords so that consumers do not need to sign

in each time they visit the site. In addition, many sites allow consumers to set items aside in an electronic shopping cart while they decide whether or not to purchase them; cookies allow a Web site to remember what is in a consumer's shopping cart from prior visits. Cookies also can be used by Web sites to offer personalized home pages or other customized content with local news and weather, favorite stock quotes, and other material of interest to individual consumers. Individual online merchants can use cookies to track consumers' purchases in order to offer recommendations about new products or sales that may be of interest to their established customers. Finally, by enabling businesses to monitor traffic on their Web sites, cookies allow businesses to constantly revise the design and layout of their sites to make them more interesting and efficient. The privacy issues raised by these uses of cookies are beyond the scope of this report.

35. *See, e.g.,* Comments of the Magazine Publishers of America (MPA) at 1; Comments of the Direct Marketing Association (DMA) at 2; Comments of the Association of National Advertisers (ANA) at 2; Tr. 30, Smith; Tr. 120, Jaffe.

36. *See, e.g.,* Comments of the Association of National Advertisers (ANA) at 2.

37. *See, e.g.,* Comments of the Magazine Publishers of America (MPA) at 1; Comments of Solveig Singleton at 3-4; Tr. 20, Jaye; Tr. 124, Aronson.

38. *See, e.g.,* Comments of the Center for Democracy and Technology (CDT) at 2, 16; Reply Comments of the Electronic Information Privacy Center (EPIC) at 1; Comments of TRUSTe at 2; Tr. 113, Mulligan.

39. *See, e.g.,* Comments of the Center for Democracy and Technology (CDT) at 2; Reply Comments of Electronic Information Privacy Center (EPIC) at 1-2.

40. *See, e.g.,* Comments of the Center for Democracy and Technology (CDT) at 2-3; Tr. 112, Steele; Tr. 128, Smith.

41. *See* Comments of the Center for Democracy and Technology (CDT) at 2-3; Comments of Christopher K. Ridder (Nov. 30, 1999) at 6 (listing examples of sites whose privacy policies explicitly reserve the right of the site to change privacy policies without notice to the consumer); Tr. 158, Mulligan. These commenters also felt that the comprehensive nature of the profiles and the technology used to create them make it reasonably easy to associate previously anonymous profiles with particular individuals.

42. *See, e.g.,* Rebuttal Comments of the Electronic Frontier Foundation (EFF) at 2; Tr. 40-1, Catlett; Tr. 54, Smith; Tr. 62, Weitzner.

43. *See* Comments of the Center for Democracy and Technology (CDT) at 3; Comments of the Electronic Frontier Foundation (EFF) Session II at 2; Rebuttal Comments of the Electronic Frontier Foundation (EFF) at 4; Tr. 81, Feena; Tr. 114, Hill; Tr. 146-7, Steele; *see also* John Simons, *The Coming Privacy Divide*, The Standard, Feb. 21, 2000, <http://www.thestandard.com/article/display/1,1153,10880,00.html>. For example, products might be offered at higher prices to consumers whose profiles indicate that they are wealthy, or insurance might be offered at higher prices to consumers whose profiles indicate possible health risks. This practice, known as "Web-lining," raises many of the same concerns that "redlining" and "reverse redlining" do in offline financial markets. *See, e.g.,* Rebuttal Comments of the Electronic Frontier Foundation (EFF) at 4 (expressing concern about "electronic redlining"); Tr. 81, Feena (describing technology's potential use for "red-lining" [sic]); Tr. 146-7, Steele (describing risk of "electronic redlining and price discrimination").

44. Tr. 186, Jaye; Tr. 192-193, Zinman.

Chapter 30
Where Is the IDS?

Peter Stephenson

Sometimes you just get lucky. Sometimes, you are in the right place at the right time. That was the case recently when I attended the second annual workshop on Recent Advances in Intrusion Detection (RAID99). RAID99 was held at Purdue University and hosted by Gene Spafford and CERIAS (formerly COAST). Nothing can beat three days of hearing about where a technology will be in one to three years. What made this conference particularly interesting was the fact that many of the attendees were too young to rent an automobile. The intrusion detection concepts this new generation of computer scientists are working on are truly awesome. It was, however, comforting to note that there were a few participants with more gray hair than I.

Those of you who have read my material before know that I do not, generally, address serious issues in a serious or heavy-handed manner. I have always believed that a little lighthearted sarcasm is good for the soul. Certainly, I am not in the habit of reviewing conferences or workshops. I am about to do both; address a serious issue and review a workshop. I am doing this because I am convinced that one of the hottest issues for today's network managers is intrusion detection. If you consider the four-layer Intrusion Management model (Avoidance, Assurance, Detection, Investigation), you will quickly see that intrusion detection fits into the third layer (Detection).

Therefore, intrusion detection plays a cornerstone role in protecting today's networks. Understanding that role is useful in selecting appropriate intrusion-detection systems. Feedback (down the layers) and service loops (servicing a layer higher on the model) in the model connect Detection with Avoidance (feedback loop) and Detection with Investigation (service loop). This means that one task of the intrusion-detection system is Avoidance. The response taken by the intrusion-detection system avoids the consequences of the intrusion that it has detected. Additionally, the information that the intrusion-detection system is able to gather about the intrusion provides valuable input for investigation. We will examine this pair of relationships later. For now, I simply want to bring you up to

0-8493-1248-5/02/$0.00+$1.50
© 2002 by CRC Press LLC

date on some important issues in intrusion detection addressed at this interesting workshop. Consider this, if you wish, a report on the current status of intrusion detection.

The papers presented covered a broad range of topics from the practical to the arcane. In order to understand the intrusion-detection process, some fundamentals are in order. Edward Amoroso in his excellent book *Intrusion Detection* (publisher: Intrusion.net Books, http://www.intrusion. net) discusses seven fundamental issues in intrusion detection: What methods are used by intrusion-detection systems? How are intrusion-detection systems organized? What is an intrusion? How do intruders hide on the Internet (and how can their origin be traced)? How do intrusion-detection systems correlate information? How can intruders be trapped? What methods are available for incident response? Amoroso discusses each of these issues in detail in his book. An understanding of the Amoroso book is really necessary to appreciate many of the presentations at RAID99.

Basically, the presentations fell into a few distinct categories. There are several fundamental types of intrusion-detection systems. Audit trail processing is often referred to as host-based intrusion detection. On-the-fly processing, on the other hand, generally is considered network-based intrusion detection. The third basic type of intrusion detection is profiling. Variations on these three include abnormal behavior signature methods (anomaly detection) and pattern matching. It was interesting to note that most of the presentations focused on variations of network-based intrusion detection.

One significant area that did not get the coverage that I thought it should have was intrusion-detection architecture. Vendors have argued since the first intrusion-detection systems were shipped that the system should go either on the network or at the host. It depends, of course, what kind of system you sell. Coming out of this workshop, I had several distinct impressions.

First, today's commercial intrusion-detection systems (IDS) are incredibly crude. If the concepts presented at RAID99 are any indication, IDS has a long way to go. That's the bad news. The good news is that companies such as ISS are recognizing that it is important to protect both the host and the network. The latest incarnation of RealSecure is an excellent example.

Second, a lot of good work is being done on attack-resistant detection systems. There were several papers presented on attack resistance, IDS evasion, and cryptographically protected audit logs. Other good work is being done in the areas of anomaly detection, string analysis, and data mining in an intrusion-detection environment.

Third, we heard papers on IDS testing and benchmarking. Today, there are very few benchmarking suites available for testing intrusion-detection systems. Some work in that area has been done by DARPA and the Air Force.

Finally, there were discussions of privacy, intrusion-detection systems in a forensic environment, and insider misuse. These discussions, touching on "soft" IDS issues, provided the only moments of real controversy in the conference.

ARCHITECTURE

The concept of architecture embodies two specific areas of interest. First, is the topological issue. The obvious concern here is the placement of the intrusion-detection system. Should the system be host based or network based? There is a strong trend toward considering the importance of both. A leader in that approach is ISS. Personally, I think this one is a no-brainer. If for no other reason than that an intruder with physical access to the console can attack the host without accessing the network at all, there must be detection on the device. On the other hand, an attack that can be detected on the network may allow early opportunity for countermeasures. A good example of this is a denial-of-service attack. If we wait to detect the attack on the target, it may well be too late.

The second area of interest is the method of detection. Anomaly detection currently is popular in the research community. In practical application, however, it is in its infancy. Most commercial intrusion-detection systems at present deal with variations of string recognition. It is fairly clear that until there is a detailed taxonomy for intrusion detection, including a standardized vocabulary, the next efforts past string recognition will be baby steps.

There are, of course, some efforts being made to use profiling and variations on anomaly detection. Notable among these efforts is CMDS from ODS Networks. CMDS (Computer Misuse Detection System) is one of the first commercial IDS to make use of profiling. CMDS can evaluate logs for an extended period of use and determine user behavior patterns. If a particular user diverges from his or her standard behavior pattern, CMDS recognizes the changing behavior.

Because CMDS parses log entries, arguably it is simply a sophisticated string-recognition IDS. However, CMDS is able to learn and analyze changing patterns of behavior, even if it must derive its base data by parsing logs. Additionally, CMDS is able to perform intrusion detection based on policy violations. Its method of doing is fairly straightforward. It simply parses log entries and compares the results with a table of predetermined strings that indicate policy violations. The IDS then takes the appropriate predetermined action.

PRIVACY AND INTRUSION DETECTION

This was an area of particular concern, and I, for one, can certainly understand the issues. However, here is a situation, uncommon as it is, where a clear understanding of architectural issues can save the day. There was a strong contention in some quarters that the use of profiling should be avoided at all costs. The idea that monitoring users' behavior patterns is an intrusion on their privacy makes a lot of sense on the surface. One can readily imagine the potential for abuse when an organization is monitoring keystroke by keystroke the activity of its employees.

On the other hand, it certainly is arguable that the organization has a right to protect itself and its information assets from abuse by insiders. Such methods as keystroke monitoring and profiling can assist in that protection. The key, of course, is in what you monitor. If you monitor user accounts, globally, there is unquestionably the potential for abuse of individual privacy rights. If, on the other hand, you monitor the activity with an application, or on a particular platform, you are simply protecting against abuse of that resource.

Whereas profiling and monitoring of individual users imply a lack of distrust and lend themselves to error based on legitimately changing user patterns, monitoring and profiling of activity on an application relates more specifically to the way the application is used then to the activity of individual users. For example, in accessing applications on a particular platform, users may be expected to behave in manners fairly consistent with the requirements of those applications. Thus, if a particular user account on a database application begins to behave outside of that account's normal behavior patterns, we may have a reason to become suspicious. From this perspective, profiling presents enormous potential for detecting rogue employees and, perhaps more important, intruders masquerading as legitimate users (using stolen ID/password pairs).

It was somewhat disappointing that the discussion of privacy and profiling did not extend much beyond global issues. True, there was a proposal that privacy issues as regards profiling be considered at the application level. Unfortunately, there was not sufficient time to explore that approach in more detail.

BENCHMARKING

Some very promising work is being done in the dual areas of IDS taxonomy and benchmarking. Today, it is very difficult to determine exactly what a vendor's claims really mean when evaluating an intrusion-detection system. There is a real danger of heading in the direction of virus checkers (i.e., "my product catches more [viruses/attacks] then my competition's does."). In order to develop a meaningful benchmarking system, however, some consistency in such things as attack-naming conventions is necessary.

Additionally, an appropriate attack test suite is also necessary. Although there are literally thousands of attacks, as there are viruses, there are probably only a relatively small number of attacks generally seen "in the wild." While it is, of course, necessary to have the ability to test for a broad range of vulnerabilities, it is probably more important to ensure that an IDS is capable of intercepting common, frequent attack types. In this regard, Mitre Corp. is developing a common vulnerability exposure (CVE) list. The CVE is "a simplified list of vulnerabilities that aims to standardize vulnerability names in order to facilitate data sharing and comparison across vulnerability databases, such as databases from security tools and academic research" ("The Development of a Common Vulnerability Enumeration" by Stephen Christey, David Mann, and William Hill, Mitre Corp., paper delivered at RAID99).

According to those authors, a CVE is "a standardized list that:

- Enumerates and discriminates between all known vulnerabilities,
- Assigns a standard, unique name to each vulnerability,
- Exists independently of the multiple perspectives of what a vulnerability is, and
- Is publicly open and shareable, without distribution restrictions."

Mitre's draft CVE currently contains over 600 vulnerabilities. The expectation is that this common naming convention will facilitate a consistent set of tests for the efficacy of intrusion-detection systems. By discriminating between variations on attacks, such as the numerous variants in on the teardrop attack, an accurate test bench can be created. Consistency in the test suite permits consumers to compare intrusion-detection systems from different vendors consistently.

ATTACK RESISTANCE

Obviously, an intrusion-detection system is not much use if the intruder can disable or fool it. Several of the papers presented at RAID99 dealt with the issue of hardening the IDS itself to avoid compromise by an intruder. Attack resistance takes two general directions. One direction is the attack directed against the IDS. In this approach the objective is to disable the IDS completely. The second direction is evasion.

In the former, there are several possible defenses. The obvious defense is to harden the platforms and software performing intrusion detection. Research currently being conducted by the National Institute of Standards and Technology points to other approaches, most of which are extremely sophisticated. Do not expect to see the NIST research implemented in commercial intrusion-detection systems any time soon.

Likewise, work done at Lawrence Berkeley National Laboratory on IDS evasion will not likely appear in commercial IDS in the near future. That leaves us with the necessity of protecting intrusion-detection systems by protecting the platforms on which they reside and logs that they create. Such an approach takes us back to the old days of the "Orange Book" and its network companion, the "Red Book." A core principle of the C2 standard is that the security system must take measures to protect itself from compromise. Until work such as the NIST and LBNL projects find their way into commercial IDS, we will need to take traditional measures to protect the IDS from compromise.

THE IDS AS A FORENSIC TOOL

I had the opportunity to participate in a panel on intrusion detection and the law. The panel, specifically, was "Intrusion Detection Systems as Evidence." Our discussion brought up a number of important points, some of which, because of their importance, I would like to offer here. The first question we need to ask on this topic is "Why do we want an intrusion-detection system in the first place?" The traditional answer is, "To trap an intrusion attempt and take some predetermined action." A better answer, but still not the correct one in my opinion, is "To trap an intrusion attempt, take some predetermined action, and gather information for future use."

This answer gets closer to the forensic requirements of intrusion detection, but it does not address the appropriate preservation of evidence. Therefore, I would pose that the correct answer is, "To trap an intrusion attempt, take some predetermined action, gather information for future use, and treat that information as forensic evidence." Forensic evidence in the context of intrusion detection (or other computer venues for that matter) is technical data that can be used in a legal setting. That means that the data must have been properly collected and preserved. Such issues as chain of custody, appropriateness for intended use (e.g., as evidence), and completeness all play into what we mean by "properly collected and preserved."

Thus, there is an important dichotomy in how we use and construct intrusion-detection systems. The dichotomy comes from this: the IDS is probably the only thing watching at the time of an intrusion attempt. Therefore, it is probably the only thing in a position to gather all of the evidence of the intrusion attempt. However, once most intrusion-detection systems recognize the attempt as a probable attack, they take preprogrammed action and go back to waiting for the next attempt.

There are reasons for this. For one thing the logging and preserving of every step in the attack that might be construed as evidence is a resource-consuming task. The primary objective of an IDS is to protect the system. If we add the secondary objective of collecting forensically pure evidence and preserving it, we add an additional load to the intrusion-detection system that may prevent it from doing its primary job correctly. So we have an important next question to answer: assuming that the intrusion detection system has a forensic role in the first place, how do you build an IDS that performs intrusion-detection and response duties fully, while gathering and protecting evidence?

What are the appropriate intrusion-detection system responses to the challenges of collecting and managing forensic evidence? How does the intrusion-detection system deal with such issues of accuracy, purity of the collected data, chain of custody from the point of collection, and other forensic issues? Additionally, what is the point of collection? Typically, we consider the chain of custody to begin at the point where a human extracts evidence from a computer. In an intrusion-detection system, this system is extracting evidence from logs created as an attack progresses. How logs are protected is an important part of the chain of custody.

SOME AFTERTHOUGHTS AND CONCLUSIONS

Obviously, intrusion-detection systems have a long way to go. Equally obvious, there is a high degree of interest in the research community in developing sophisticated intrusion detection systems equal to the passage of protecting today's large distributed networks. Even though the IDS currently deployed in most organizations is crude by the measure of where it is going, a well-deployed, well-protected intrusion-detection system can be very effective in protecting the system. It is also clear, that the IDS belongs both on the network and on the device. In addition, there are various types of intrusion-detection systems that are appropriate for various types of intrusion-detection problems. For example, a large-scale database or ERP system with a relatively consistent user base, high sensitivity, and reasonably stable separating procedures, lends itself well to profiling solutions such as CMDS.

Host-based intrusion detection, where there are different platform types, may require host-based systems with centralized management capabilities such as Intruder Alert from Axent Technologies. Intruder Alert provides rule-based intrusion detection on the platform and, regardless of platform, may be managed from a central console.

Network-based intrusion detection is available from ISS (RealSecure) and Cisco (Net Ranger). RealSecure is both network and host based. These are all different intrusion-detection systems with different capabilities and different system requirements. They all have their strengths and weaknesses. Often, it makes sense to use these products together for the best overall protection.

Intrusion-detection systems, deployed in a large network, can be very expensive. So, an important question may be "Can we afford the investment?" Given the state of intrusions, both from inside and outside the organization, today, however, I would suggest that the more appropriate question is "Can we afford NOT to make the investment?"

Chapter 31

Internet Acceptable Use Policies: Navigating the Management, Legal, and Technical Issues

Farley Stewart

During the past few years, providing employees with access to the Internet has become a critical factor in the success of most corporations and other large organizations in the United States and around the globe. Many companies have openly embraced the widespread use of the World Wide Web, Internet e-mail, and file transfer mechanisms as highly efficient communications and research tools to boost employee productivity. In addition, a rapidly growing number of organizations are instituting private intranets and extranets to enhance their employees' internal communications and to streamline interaction with external customers and partners.

However, too many organizations have also discovered the hard way that unrestricted and unmanaged Internet access by employees can lead to dire consequences in the form of wasted time, lost productivity, misappropriation of resources, reduced morale, and the risk of diminished corporate reputation. Perhaps more important, an organization's failure to take adequate steps to define, manage, and control employees' Internet usage can also lead to severe risks in the form of potential legal and financial liabilities.

The need to protect against these risks has given rise to a new wave of significant management efforts involving corporate executives, IT managers, human resource staff, and the legal community. Although the need

0-8493-1248-5/02/$0.00+$1.50
© 2002 by CRC Press LLC

for comprehensive and enforceable Internet Acceptable Use Policies (IAUP) has now become a critical issue cutting across organizations in virtually all industry segments, all too often the IAUP policy efforts or technological implementation for policy enforcement fall short of the mark.

In some cases, the shortcoming occurs because company management fails to understand the full extent of the risk, while in other instances there is reluctance to come across like "big brother" for fear of harming the company culture. Sometimes IAUP efforts fail to adequately address the legal issues involved, and other times, the policies are simply ignored because they are too full of "legalese" to be understood by rank-and-file managers and employees. Or, even with extremely well-intentioned and well-crafted IAUPs, the failure to deploy appropriate technologies for comprehensive monitoring and management can dilute the policy's enforceability or, on the other end of the scale, can severely restrict Internet usability to the point of compromising its overall benefits.

The bottom line is that an effective IAUP must take into account the whole spectrum of these policy and technology issues, within the framework of the specific organization's unique set of goals and culture. This article takes a closer look at the benefits and risks of employee Internet usage and then explores the specific issues involved in the development and deployment of effective IAUPs and how to enforce them.

When it comes to potential employee abuse of Internet access, the most prominent concerns are loss of productivity, degradation of available computing resources, and the high risks of legal liabilities — for example, those associated with sexual or other types of harassment based upon access and display of inappropriate web content.

LOSS OF PRODUCTIVITY

The potential negative impacts from lost productivity alone represent a multibillion dollar issue for today's companies. According to estimates by research firm Computer Economics, companies lost $5.3 billion to recreational Internet surfing in 1999. As Michael Erbschloe, Computer Economics vice president of research, describes it, "Online shopping, stock trading, car buying, looking for a new house, and even visiting porn sites have become daily practices for about 25 percent of the workers in U.S. companies that have access to the Internet in their offices. The illegitimate and personal use of the Web by employees has become commonplace. And when the boss is not around, improper use of the Web is normal. The inappropriate activities even include employees starting their own e-business operations and building and promoting their own Web sites while in the office of their full-time employer."

For the most part, organizations that provide their employees with Internet access expect that there will be some small amount of personal use. In concept, this is not much different than the traditional issue of allowing some "reasonable" amount of personal calls using company telephones. In practice, however, the Internet poses a much more sweeping opportunity for abuse. For example, an employee's Web browsing for a quick ad hoc check of the stock market might seem innocuous enough on the surface, but what about when the lure of the Web draws that same employee to expand his or her activities to continual tracking of quotes, in-depth research, and online day trading?

As most of us have discovered from Web browsing, it is very easy to start off with a single objective and then, through the magic mix of hyperlinks and human curiosity, find ourselves exploring interesting new areas that we had never previously considered. To a significant extent, it is exactly that "unlimited diversity at your fingertips" phenomenon that makes the Web so compelling for millions. Unfortunately, as a growing body of research shows, the availability of compelling content can lead to compulsive behavior on the part of a significant percentage of Web users. While it is easy to understand how an otherwise valued employee might inadvertently slip into a pattern of misuse, in the long run it is incumbent upon the employer to anticipate such risks and to establish well-communicated policies and management mechanisms to help employees live up to required expectations.

If left unchecked, even a small amount of Internet abuse by only a few employees can easily turn into a widespread pattern of abuse, making it the norm. In certain situations, the misuse of Web browsing privileges can actually become a self-reinforcing social phenomenon in which even those employees who would not typically flout the rules eventually succumb to the "everybody's doing it" attitude. For example, after the peak of the Clinton–Lewinsky scandals, ZDNet reported that industry experts estimated "American companies lost $470 million in productivity to employees reading the salacious document online."

DRAIN ON COMPUTING RESOURCES AND BANDWIDTH

In addition to the loss of productivity for the employees that are directly abusing their Internet access privileges, another major concern involves the ripple effects of clogged bandwidth, degraded system performance, and overconsumption of finite computing resources that can indirectly reduce the productivity of other, non-abusing employees. In some cases, the ripple effects can be catastrophic. Consider the PointCast stir a few years back. Businesses were stunned to find that almost overnight significant percentages of their employees with access to the Internet were getting large quantities of real-time data — news stories and stock ticker data—being pushed to their desktops. They were experiencing double-digit percentage loss of bandwidth without even seeing it coming. Today, the same risk exists and is being manifested in the streaming audio, "free music over the Internet" phenomenon. Even though the music may be free to those who listen to it, it is not free to the employer who pays for the Internet connectivity. However, most of the time the performance-degrading impacts of misuse are more insidious; they slowly choke off the company's networked computing resources, while masquerading as legitimate work-related traffic.

For most organizations, the networked IT infrastructure has evolved into an indispensable part of their everyday operations, providing the underlying foundation for everything from new product development to manufacturing to finance and human resources. In addition, with the rise of E-commerce in both the business-to-consumer and business-to-business arenas, many companies now also depend vitally upon the performance of their network to support responsive communications and real-time transactions with their customers. When network performance is degraded, companies are often forced to respond with major new investments in system improvements and expanded bandwidth, even though they may be unaware that a significant part of the demand is a result of inappropriate Internet usage by employees.

LEGAL LIABILITY RISKS

Going beyond the concerns of loss of productivity and degradation of available network resources, many companies are just now coming to realize that the latent legal risks from employees' Internet abuse can potentially be astronomical. The major concern is the employer's obligation to take prudent steps to protect all employees from "hostile work environments" such as exposure to sexually oriented or hate-related information in the workplace.

As described by Frank C. Morris, Jr., director of the Employment Law Department at Epstein, Becker & Green in Washington, D.C., "Since the number of discrimination lawsuits have been on the rise, the workplace has become more politically correct. Rarely will employees engage in the same offensive conduct that was commonplace just a few years ago. As a result, potential plaintiffs have had to look elsewhere for 'smoking guns' to prove their cases, and many are now finding them with the increased presence of the Internet in the workplace."

Morris further explains, "Few employees would believe that their seemingly innocent Web-surfing could expose their employers to insurmountable liability. But it is this improper use of the Internet that is now the smoking 'e-gun' of current plaintiffs. For a plaintiff, there is nothing better than walking into court with a piece of paper illustrating a discriminatory statement, joke, or picture downloaded off the Internet and sent through e-mail."

Even though enlightened management practices have virtually eliminated yesterday's common practice of posting sexually oriented pictures on the walls of businesses, too many employees tend to think that the fleeting exposure of a similarly offensive picture on a computer screen is somehow not a problem. However, the courts have consistently held that the presence of Internet-related sexual content in the workplace does meet the definition of harassment and that the employer's failure to take appropriate preventative measures does constitute a violation of an employees' rights.

Besides hostile workplace concerns, a variety of other legal exposures can accrue to employers through their employees' misuse of the Internet. For instance, employers can potentially be held liable for employees who use company Internet connections to violate copyright laws or to post false information that libels other companies or individuals. While the case law continues to evolve in this area, there is some potential that a company could be deemed responsible for illegal activities, (e.g., fraudulent Internet scams) conducted by its employees if company equipment and Internet access were involved.

Beyond the strict legal liabilities, a company could sustain significant damage to its reputation and goodwill as a result of the negative publicity that can ensue from employee misuse of the Internet. At best, the company can simply appear to be badly managed for allowing such practices or, worse, it can actually lose business from customers worried about lack of adequate controls and security.

CRAFTING AN ORGANIZATION-SPECIFIC INTERNET ACCEPTABLE USAGE POLICY

The creation of an effective Internet Acceptable Use Policy requires a comprehensive understanding of the company's business goals, Internet usage objectives, specific risk profiles, and organizational culture. In most mid-size to large organizations, the IAUP development effort must involve a high degree of cross-departmental inputs from the executive staff, human resources, IT management, and functional departmental managers.

According to Ira G. Rosenstein, a New York-based partner in the Employment Department of Orrick, Herrington & Sutcliffe, "The Internet is a valuable tool and therefore it is very important to craft the usage policy in such a way that it reinforces productivity and employee morale, without becoming unmanageable. For example, if a policy inflexibly mandates very draconian measures for the slightest infraction, it greatly reduces management's ability to apply a measured or proportionate response to different types or levels of Internet abuses. With any policy covering areas that could be deemed the 'personal' activities of employees, it makes sense to build in some degree of discretion. However, in order to ensure that the policy is sufficiently enforceable, employers need to clearly define what does and does not constitute acceptable behaviors with regard to Internet usage."

Rosenstein adds, "In some instances, a 'zero-tolerance' stance may be necessary, such as if an employee knowingly and repeatedly accesses pornographic or hate-inciting Web sites. Obviously, these offenses are very different than going to an E-commerce site and buying the latest *New York Times* best-selling novel, especially as it relates to the liability risks of litigation from other impacted employees. The ability to distinguish between 'casual' and 'chronic' behavior is also a useful concept to build into the policy. For instance, even relatively innocuous behavior can rise to the level of a serious offense if it becomes chronic, such as the difference between an employee quickly checking out an item on eBay or spending half a day bidding and tracking various auction items."

As Frank Morris points out, "Perhaps most importantly, it is critical to remember that an Internet usage policy cannot be treated as a 'one size fits all' proposition. In order to be truly effective, the policy has to fit within the corporate culture and goals while clearly conveying its underlying rationale in a manner that makes sense to the company's employees. For example, while virtually no one would be likely to argue that any company's employees need at-work access to porn sites, the range of Internet access needed in a Web-centric E-commerce company is probably going to be wider than that required in the accounting department of a traditional manufacturing company."

NOTIFICATION, EDUCATION, AND APPLICATION

Of course, after the policy has been developed, it cannot actually become useful until it has been communicated to employees. In most companies, the initial notification takes the form of having each employee read the policy and sign an "acknowledgement of receipt" that then becomes a permanent part of that employee's personnel file. In addition to the initial notification, it may also be prudent for the companies to include short educational sessions on Internet usage policies as a formal part of new-employee orientation and training curricula.

According to Rosenstein, "Essentially the company needs to inform every employee of the policy's provisions as soon as they are given access to the Internet and then also to reinforce the employee's obligations on a regular basis. For example, some companies set up a short summary of the policy as a 'splash screen' that appears for a brief period during boot-up and whenever an employee signs on to the Internet."

Keeping in mind the overall corporate culture and ensuring that the Internet usage policy meshes smoothly within the existing management philosophies can also enhance overall understanding and compliance. The avoidance of overt legalese is important, as is the need to craft the notification methods to be consistent with other company policies. For example, while very firm and proscriptive language may be quite appropriate in some more traditional firms, it is less likely to be well received within the free-flowing environment of a Web-centric technology company. Here again, it is important to keep in mind that the ultimate objective of the IAUP effort is not so much to catch people doing something wrong as it is to proactively prevent abuse through a well-crafted and well-communicated policy.

TECHNOLOGY ISSUES IN MONITORING AND ENFORCEMENT

Often the mere existence and promulgation of a clear policy is enough to stem most forms of Internet access abuse. At the very least, it provides a firm basis for communicating with employees whenever policy violations lead to the need for corrective action. However, like any rule that is not enforced, Internet access policies that are not backed up by proactive monitoring and access control measures will quickly become hollow pronouncements — losing the ability to effectively guide users' behavior and to protect the organization from liability. Therefore, more organizations are turning to the dual strategy of publishing clear IAUPs combined with instituting comprehensive, precision Internet access control over users' Web related activities.

A May 1999 study conducted by Zona Research showed that one-third of companies use some type of screening to block employee access to sites that are not on an approved list. In its survey of more than 300 companies, Zona also found that 20 percent of the organizations use selective screening to filter sites based on the users' job categories, whereas 13 percent selectively filtered based upon the time of day.

During the past few years, the need to proactively control Web access has driven the development of a variety of Web-filtering methodologies, from plug-in software for the PC browser client to complex server software packages. However, the unrelenting growth of new Internet content combined with the need for transparent network installation and simple setup and administrative mechanisms to manage large numbers of users have often made these alternatives either too unwieldy or too ineffective for use by most businesses.

Early attempts at Internet access control focused primarily on filtering based on keywords as the means to identify objectionable or inappropriate content. This method entailed scanning text on Web pages received and matching them against lists of "bad" keywords. Given that many words can be judged only in context, these solutions had an impossible balancing act between filtering out too little or too much material. Besides the issue of inaccuracy, these keyword-based solutions failed to protect companies or users from access to other forms of inappropriate Internet content, such as pornographic images or graphics.

A major improvement came with the introduction of solutions that monitor or block access based upon the Web site being requested. When IT administrators have a chance to make the call before placing a site in a blocked category list, most of the ambiguity and inaccuracy associated with the keyword approach is eliminated. With this approach, when a user clicks on a link or enters a Web site address, it is matched against a database of inappropriate sites. If the requested site is found on the list of blocked sites, users are presented with a message stating that access to this site is contrary to company policy and specifiying who to contact if they think they have a legitimate reason for accessing that site.

Given the dynamic and explosive nature of the Internet, with thousands of new sites going online every day, this approach is viable only when coupled with a subscription service that continually provides updates for the database of inappropriate sites, preferably daily. And to ensure the updates are applied as they are delivered, the filtering tool should allow for automatic refresh of the database. Like a virus checker without the latest virus definitions applied, protection rapidly diminishes. Daily updates need to be delivered and applied over the Internet for the best protection and to save administrators a great deal of effort. Weekly or monthly CD update lists that sit on someone's desk sap a company of the protection it has paid for.

For organizations considering a database-driven solution, there are two primary types. The first blocks based upon a requested Web site's IP address (e.g., http://199.42.53.141/). The second alternative blocks based on the site's URL address (e.g., www.mycompany.com). The URL approach solves a unique problem associated with the IP address approach. When blocking by IP address, all Web sites that share an IP address, as is the case with many hosted Web sites, get blocked with the one offender. Using URLs, targeted hosted sites can not only be singled out, but specific sections of sites and even individual pages can be identified and blocked.

Regardless of the blocking approach, a filtering solution must be flexible. Not only must an IAUP adapt to a company's culture and specific needs, but so does the tool to enforce that policy. IT administrators need the ability to custom-tailor and control their filtering rules and databases. Local control of how site categories and specific sites are rated and handled is very important. The ability to tailor blocking on a group-by-group or individual user basis is needed. And being able to control access based on time of day or day of week is becoming increasingly important.

Flexibility is also needed in the range of Internet services controlled. As the variety and type of Internet content has proliferated, the issue of access control has now expanded way beyond just HTML-based Web pages. Unauthorized access to other Internet services, such as ICQ® and IRC chat, FTP downloads, RealAudio® broadcasts, and MP3 music can easily consume significant bandwidth and resources while degrading employee productivity, all without triggering any access control mechanisms in traditional Web filtering products.

Finally, to be truly effective, Internet access management technology must not only be accurate, dynamic, automatic, tailorable, and comprehensive; but it must also be affordable, transparent to the installed network hardware and software, easy to set up and maintain, not performance degrading, and scalable enough to grow with the corporate IT environment. In response to these needs, a new generation of turnkey solution is just now emerging — the Internet filtering server appliance. These are dedicated, low-cost, solid-state devices that can be dropped into virtually any network. By their nature, they can begin providing filtering protection straight from the box, yet allow for easy customization to meet just about any enterprise's needs. The best require no modification to existing desktop browsers or network servers.

By combining subscription-based filtering services with the easy installation and administration of "plug-and-protect" server appliances, these new alternatives provide highly customizable filtering mechanisms and user profiles, sophisticated monitoring and filtering of all Internet content types, plus a high degree of scalability and maintainability.

BOTTOM LINE

Given the risk of legal liability, productivity loss, and bandwidth drain, it is clear why an IAUP is needed by companies today. It is also important that the IAUP be tailored to meet the needs of each organization — one size does not fit all. If the policies are too restrictive or too lax, they run the risk of causing an employee backlash or providing inadequate corporate protection.

Once an IAUP has been established, employee communication is critical. If the employees are not clearly notified and educated as to the policy requirements, they will lack the knowledge base needed to fully comply.

Tools are then needed to help ensure compliance by all employees. Without the tools or means to monitor and enforce the policy, an IAUP will become toothless and not provide the protection desired. Like the usage policies themselves, a company's monitoring and control mechanisms must also be tailorable to meet the specific requirements of the organization and include the capability for evolving and adapting with changing requirements.

Ultimately, the organization's Internet acceptable use policies, management/supervision practices, employee training/education programs, and Internet access management technologies all have to mesh together to form a unified and proactive system for effectively managing all employees' online behavior.

Chapter 32
Ethics and the Internet
Micki Krause

The research for this chapter was done entirely on the Internet. The net is a powerful tool. This author dearly hopes that the value of its offerings is not obviated by those who would treat the medium in an inappropriate and unethical manner.

Ethics: Social values; a code of right and wrong

The ethical nature of the Internet has been likened to "a restroom in a downtown bus station," where the lowest of the low congregate and nothing good ever happens. This manifestation of antisocial behavior can be attributed to one or more of the following:

- The relative anonymity of those who use the net
- The lack of regulation in cyberspace
- The fact that one can masquerade as another on the Internet
- The fact that one can fulfill a fantasy or assume a different persona on the net, thereby eliminating the social obligation to be accountable for one's own actions

Whatever the reason, the Internet, also known as the "wild west" or the "untamed frontier," is absent of law and therefore is a natural playground for illicit, illegal, and unethical behavior.

In the ensuing pages, we will explore the types of behavior demonstrated in cyberspace, discuss how regulation is being introduced and by whom, and illustrate the practices that businesses have adopted in order to minimize their liability and encourage their employees to use the net in an appropriate manner.

THE GROWTH OF THE INTERNET

When the Internet was born approximately 30 years ago it was a medium used by the government and assorted academicians, primarily to perform

0-8493-1248-5/02/$0.00+$1.50
© 2002 by CRC Press LLC

Exhibit 1. GenX Internet Use

A Higher Percentage of Gen-Xers Use the Web...	
	Used the Web in the past 6 months
Generation X	61%
Total U.S. Adults	49%
... More Regularly...	
	Use the Web regularly
Generation X	82%
Baby Boomers	52%
... Because it is the Most Important Medium	
	Most important medium
Internet	55%
Television	39%

Source: *The Industry Standard*, M.J. Thompson, July 10, 1998.

and share research. The user community was small and mostly self-regulated. Thus, although a useful tool, the Internet was not considered "mission-critical," as it is today. Moreover, the requirements for availability and reliability were not as much a consideration then as they are now, as Internet usage has grown exponentially since the late 1980s.

The increasing opportunities for productivity, efficiency and worldwide communications brought additional users in droves. Thus, it was headline news when a computer worm, introduced into the Internet by Robert Morris, Jr., in 1988, infected thousands of net-connected computers and brought the Internet to its knees.

In the early 1990s, with the advent of commercial applications and the World Wide Web (WWW), a graphical user interface for Internet information, the number of Internet users soared. Sources such as the *Industry Standard*, "The Newsmagazine of the Internet Economy," published a Nielsen Media Research Commerce Net study in late 1998, which reported the United States Internet population at 70.5 million (out of a total population of 196.5 million).

Today, the Internet is a utility, analogous to the electric company, and "dot com" is a household expression. The spectrum of Internet users extends from the kindergarten classroom to senior citizenry, although the GenX generation, users in their 20s, are the fastest adopters of net technology (see Exhibit 1).

Because of its popularity, the reliability and availability of the Internet are critical operational considerations, and activities that threaten these attributes (e.g., spamming, spoofing, hacking and the like) have grave impacts on its user community.

UNETHICAL ACTIVITY DEFINED

Spamming, in electronic terminology, means electronic garbage. Sending unsolicited junk electronic mail, for example, such as an advertisement, to one user or many users via a distribution list, is considered spamming.

One of the most publicized spamming incidents occurred in 1994, when two attorneys (Laurence Carter and Martha Siegel) from Arizona, flooded the cyber-waves, especially the Usenet newsgroups,* with solicitations to the immigrant communities of the U.S. to assist them in the green card lottery process to gain citizenship. Carter and Siegel saw the spamming as "an ideal, low-cost and perfectly legitimate way to target people likely to be potential clients" (*Washington Post*, 1994). Many Usenet newsgroup users, however, saw things differently. The lawyers' actions resulted in quite an uproar among the Internet communities primarily because the Internet has had a long tradition of noncommercialism since its founding. The attorneys had already been ousted from the American Immigration Lawyers' Association for past sins, and eventually they lost their licenses to practice law.

There have been several other spams since the green card lottery, some claiming "MAKE MONEY FAST," others claiming "THE END OF THE WORLD IS NEAR." There have also been hundreds, if not thousands, of electronic chain letters making the Internet rounds. The power of the Internet is the ease with which users can forward data, including chain letters. More information about spamming occurrences can be found on the net in the Usenet newsgroup alt.folklore.urban.

Unsolicited Internet e-mail has become so widespread that lawmakers have begun to propose that sending it be a misdemeanor. Texas is one of 18 states considering legislation that would make spamming illegal. In February 1999, Virginia became the fourth state to pass an anti-spamming law. The Virginia law makes it a misdemeanor for a spammer to use a false online identity to send mass mailings, as many do. The maximum penalty would be a $500 fine. However, if the spam is deemed malicious and results in damages to the victim in excess of $2500 (e.g., if the spam causes unavailability of computer service), the crime would be a felony, punishable by up to 5 years in prison. As with the Virginia law, California law

---

* Usenet newsgroups are limited communities of net users who congregate online to discuss specific topics.

allows for the jailing of spammers. Laws in Washington and Nevada impose civil fines.

This legislation has not been popular with everyone, however, and has led organizations such as the American Civil Liberties Union (ACLU), to complain about its unconstitutionality and threat to free speech and the First Amendment.

Like spamming, threatening electronic mail messages have become pervasive in the Internet space. Many of these messages are not taken as seriously as the one that was sent by a high school student from New Jersey, who made a death threat against President Clinton in an electronic mail message in early 1999. Using a school computer which provided an option to communicate with a contingent of the U.S. government, the student rapidly became the subject of a Secret Service investigation.

Similarly, in late 1998, a former investment banker was convicted on eight counts of aggravated harassment when he masqueraded as another employee and sent allegedly false and misleading Internet e-mail messages to top executives of his former firm.

Increasingly, businesses are establishing policy to inhibit employees from using company resources to perform unethical behavior on the Internet. In an early 1999 case, a California firm agreed to pay a former employee over $100,000 after she received harassing messages on the firm's electronic bulletin board, even though the company reported the incident to authorities and launched an internal investigation. The case is a not so subtle reminder that businesses are accountable for the actions of their employees, even actions performed on electronic networks.

Businesses have taken a stern position on employees surfing the web, sending inappropriate messages, and downloading pornographic materials from the Internet. This is due to a negative impact on productivity, as well as the legal view that companies are liable for the actions of their employees. Many companies have established policies for appropriate use and monitoring of computers and computing resources, as well as etiquette on the Internet, or "Netiquette."

These policies are enhancements to the Internet Advisory Board's (Request for Comment) RFC 1087, "Internet Ethics," January 1989, which proposed that access to and use of the Internet is a privilege and should be treated as such by all users of the system. The IAB strongly endorsed the view of the Division Advisory Panel of the National Science Foundation Division of Network Communications Research and Infrastructure. That view is paraphrased below.

Any activity is characterized as unethical and unacceptable that purposely:

- Seeks to gain unauthorized access to the resources of the Internet
- Disrupts the intended use of the Internet
- Wastes resources (people, capacity, computers) through such actions
- Destroys the integrity of computer-based information
- Compromises the privacy of users
- Involves negligence in the conduct of Internet-wide experiments

Source: RFC 1087, "Ethics and the Internet," Internet Advisory Board, January 1989.

A sample "Appropriate Use of the Internet" policy is attached as Appendix A. Appendix B contains the partial contents of RFC 1855, "Netiquette Guidelines," a product of the Responsible Use of the Network (RUN) Working Group of the Internet Engineering Task Force (IETF).

In another twist on Internet electronic mail activity, in April 1999 Intel Corporation sued a former employee for doing a mass e-mailing to its 30,000 employees, criticizing the company over workers' compensation benefits. Intel claimed the e-mail was an assault and form of trespass, as well as an improper use of its internal computer resources. The former employee contended that his e-mail messages were protected by the First Amendment. "Neither Intel nor I can claim any part of the Internet as our own private system as long as we are hooked up to this international network of computers," said Ken Hamidi in an e-mail to *Los Angeles Times* reporters. The court found in favor of Intel, ordering Hamidi not to send unsolicited e-mail to Intel systems.

Using electronic media to stalk another person is known as "cyberstalking." This activity is becoming more prevalent, and the law has seen fit to intercede by adding computers and electronic devices to existing stalking legislation. In the first case of cyberstalking in California, a Los Angeles resident, accused of using his computer to harass a woman who rejected his romantic advances, is the first to be charged under a new cyberstalking law that went into effect in 1998. The man was accused of forging postings on the Internet, on America Online (AOL) and other Internet services, so that the messages appeared to come from the victim. The message provided the woman's address and other identifying information, which resulted in at least six men visiting her home uninvited. The man was charged with one count of stalking, three counts of solicitation to commit sexual assault, and one count of unauthorized access to computers.

In another instance where electronic activity has been added to existing law, the legislation for gambling has been updated to include Internet gambling. According to recent estimates, Internet-based gambling and gaming has grown from about a $500 million-a-year industry in the late 1990s, to what was a $6.6 billion industry in 2001, and what is expected to be a $13.6 billion industry in 2005. All 50 states regulate in-person gambling in some manner. Many conjecture that the impetus for the regulation of electronic gambling is financial, not ethical or legal.

PRIVACY ON THE INTERNET

For many years, American citizens have expressed fears of invasion of privacy, ever since they realized that their personal information is being stored on computer databases by government agencies and commercial entities. However, it is just of late that Americans are realizing that logging on to the Internet and using the World Wide Web threatens their privacy as well. Last year, the Center for Democracy and Technology (CDT), a Washington, D.C. advocacy group, reported that only one third of federal agencies tell visitors to their Web sites what information is being collected about them.

AT&T Labs conducted a study in 1999 in which they discovered that Americans are willing to surrender their e-mail addresses online, but not much more than that. The study said that users are reluctant to provide other personal information, such as a phone number or credit card number.

The utilization of technology offers the opportunity for companies to collect specific items of information. For example, Microsoft Corporation inserts tracking numbers into its Word program documents. Microsoft's Internet Explorer informs Web sites when a user bookmarks them by choosing the "Favorites" option in the browser. In 1998, the Social Security Administration came very close to putting a site online that would let anyone find out another person's earnings and other personal information. This flies in the face of the 1974 Privacy Act, which states that every agency must record "only such information about an individual as is relevant and necessary to accomplish a purpose of the agency required to be accomplished by statute or by executive order of the President."

There is a battle raging between privacy advocates and private industry aligned with the U.S. government. Privacy advocates relate the serious concern for the hands-off approach and lack of privacy legislation, claiming that citizens are being violated. Conversely, the federal government and private businesses, such as American Online, defend current attempts to rely on self-regulation and other less government-intrusive means of regulating privacy, for example, the adoption of privacy policies. These policies, which state intent for the protection of consumer privacy, are deployed to raise consumer confidence and increase digital trust. The CDT has urged the federal government to post privacy policies on each site's home page, such as is shown in Exhibit 2 from the Health and Human Services web site from the National Institute of Health (www.nih.gov).

HHS Web Privacy Notice

(as of April 13, 1999)

Thank you for visiting the Department of Health and Human Services Website and reviewing our Privacy Policy. Our Privacy Policy for visits to **www.hhs.gov** is clear:

We will collect no personal information about you when you visit our website unless you choose to provide that information to us.

Here is how we handle information about your visit to our website:

Information Collected and Stored Automatically

If you do nothing during your visit but browse through the website, read pages, or download information, we will gather and store certain information about your visit automatically. This information does not identify you personally. We automatically collect and store only the following information about your visit:

- The Internet domain (for example, "xcompany.com" if you use a private Internet access account, or "yourschool.edu" if you connect from a university's domain), and IP address (an IP address is a number that is automatically assigned to your computer whenever you are surfing the Web) from which you access our website
- The type of browser and operating system used to access our site,
- The date and time you access our site,
- The pages you visit, and
- If you linked to our website from another website, the address of that website.

We use this information to help us make our site more useful to visitors — to learn about the number of visitors to our site and the types of technology our visitors use. We do not track or record information about individuals and their visits.

Links to Other Sites

Our website has links to other federal agencies and to private organizations. Once you link to another site, it is that site's privacy policy that controls what it collects about you.

Information Collected When You Send Us an E-mail Message

When inquiries are e-mailed to us, we again store the text of your message and e-mail address information, so that we can answer the question that was sent in, and send the answer back to the e-mail address provided. If enough questions or comments come in that are the same, the question may be added to our Question and Answer section, or the suggestions are used to guide the design of our website.

We do not retain the messages with identifiable information or the e-mail addresses for more than 10 days after responding unless your communication requires further inquiry. If you send us an e-mail message in which you ask us to do something that requires further inquiry on our part, there are a few things you should know.

The material you submit may be seen by various people in our Department, who may use it to look into the matter you have inquired about. If we do retain it, it is protected by the Privacy Act of 1974, which restricts our use of it, but permits certain disclosures.

Also, e-mail is not necessarily secure against interception. If your communication is very sensitive, or includes personal information, you might want to send it by postal mail instead.

Exhibit 2.

ANONYMITY ON THE INTERNET

Besides a lack of privacy, the Internet promulgates a lack of identity. Users of the Internet are virtual, meaning that they are not speaking with, interacting with, or responding to others, at least not face to face. They sit behind their computer terminals in the comfort of their own home, office, or school. This anonymity makes it easy to masquerade as another, as there is no way of proving or disproving who you are or who you say you are.

Moreover, this anonymity lends itself to the venue of Internet chat rooms. Chat rooms are places on the net where people congregate and discuss topics common to the group, such as sports, recreation, or sexuality. Many chat rooms provide support to persons looking for answers to questions on health, bereavement, or disease and, in this manner, can be very beneficial to society.

Conversely, chat rooms can be likened to sleazy bars, where malcontents go seeking prey. There have been too many occurrences of too-good-to-be-true investments that have turned out to be fraudulent. Too many representatives of the dregs of society lurk on the net, targeting the elderly or the innocent, or those who, for some unknown reason, make easy marks.

A recent *New Yorker* magazine ran a cartoon showing a dog sitting at a computer desk, the caption reading "On the Internet, no one knows if you're a dog." Although the cartoon is humorous, the instances where child molesters have accosted their victims by way of the Internet are very serious. Too many times, miscreants have struck up electronic conversations with innocent victims, masquerading as innocents themselves, only to lead them to meet in person with dire results. Unfortunately, electronic behavior mimics conduct that has always occurred over phone lines, through the postal service, and in person. The Internet only provides an additional locale for intentionally malicious and antisocial behavior. We can only hope that advanced technology, as with telephonic caller ID, will assist law enforcement in tracking anonymous Internet "bad guys."

Attempts at self-regulation have not been as successful as advertised, and many question whether the industry can police itself. Meanwhile, there are those within the legal and judicial systems that feel more laws are the only true answer to limiting unethical and illegal activities on the Internet. How it will all play out is far from known at this point in time. The right to freedom of speech and expression has often been at odds with censorship. It is ironic, for example, that debates abound on the massive amounts of pornography available on the Internet, and yet, in early 1999, the entire transcript of the President Clinton impeachment hearings was published on the net, complete with sordid details of the Monica Lewinsky affair.

INTERNET AND THE LAW

The Communications Decency Act of 1996 was signed into law by President Clinton in early 1996 and has been challenged by civil libertarian organizations ever since. In 1997, the United States Supreme Court declared the law's ban on indecent Internet speech unconstitutional.

The Childrens' Internet Protect Act (S.97, January 1999) requires "the installation and use by schools and libraries of a technology for filtering or blocking material on the Internet on computers with Internet access to be eligible to receive or retain universal service assistance."

MONITORING THE WEB

Additionally, many commercial businesses have seen the opportunity to manufacture software products that will provide parents the ability to control their home computers. Products such as Crayon Crawler, Family-Connect, and KidsGate are available to provide parents with control over what Internet sites their children can access, while products such as WebSense, SurfControl and Webroot are being implemented by companies that choose to limit the sites their employees can access.

SUMMARY

Technology is a double-edged sword, consistently presenting us with benefits and disadvantages. The Internet is no different. The net is a powerful tool, providing the ability for global communications in a heartbeat and sharing information without boundaries, but it is also a platform for illicit and unethical shenanigans.

This chapter has explored the type of behavior demonstrated in cyberspace, antisocial behavior, which has led to many discussions about whether or not this activity can be inhibited by self-regulation or the introduction of tougher laws. Although we do not know how the controversy will end, we know it will be an interesting future in cyberspace.

APPENDIX A
APPROPRIATE USE AND MONITORING OF COMPUTING RESOURCES

Policy

The Company telecommunications systems, computer networks, and electronic mail systems are to be used only for business purposes and only by authorized personnel. All data generated with or on the Company's business resources are the property of the Company; and may be used by the Company without limitation; and may not be copyrighted, patented, leased, or sold by individuals or otherwise used for personal gain.

Electronic mail and voice mail, including pagers and cellular telephones, are not to be used to create any offensive or disruptive messages. The Company does not tolerate discrimination, harassment, or other offensive messages and images relating to, among other things, gender, race, color, religion, national origin, age, sexual orientation, or disability.

The Company reserves the right and will exercise the right to review, monitor, intercept, access, and disclose any business or personal messages sent or received on Company systems. This may happen at any time, with or without notice.

It is the Company's goal to respect individual privacy, while at the same time maintaining a safe and secure workplace. However, employees should have no expectation of privacy with respect to any Company computer or communication resources. Materials that appear on computer, electronic mail, voice mail, facsimile and the like belong to the Company. Periodically, your use of the Company's systems may be monitored.

The use of passwords is intended to safeguard Company information, and does not guarantee personal confidentiality.

Violations of company policies detected through such monitoring can lead to corrective action, up to and including discharge.

APPENDIX B
NETIQUETTE

RFC 1855
NETIQUETTE GUIDELINES

Status of This Memo

This memo provides information for the Internet community. This memo does not specify an Internet standard of any kind. Distribution of this memo is unlimited.

Abstract

This document provides a minimum set of guidelines for Network Etiquette (Netiquette) which organizations may take and adapt for their own use. As such, it is deliberately written in a bulleted format to make adaptation easier and to make any particular item easy (or easier) to find. It also functions as a minimum set of guidelines for individuals, both users and administrators. This memo is the product of the Responsible Use of the Network (RUN) Working Group of the IETF.

1.0 Introduction

In the past, the population of people using the Internet had "grown up" with the Internet, were technically minded, and understood the nature of the transport and the protocols. Today, the community of Internet users includes people who are new to the environment. These "Newbies" are unfamiliar with the culture and do not need to know about transport and protocols. In order to bring these new users into the Internet culture quickly, this Guide offers a minimum set of behaviors which organizations and individuals may take and adapt for their own use. Individuals should be aware that no matter who supplies their Internet access, be it an Internet Service Provider through a private account, or a student account at a University, or an account through a corporation, that those organizations have regulations about ownership of mail and files, about what is proper to post or send, and how to present yourself. Be sure to check with the local authority for specific guidelines.

We have organized this material into three sections: one-to-one communication, which includes mail and talk; one-to-many communications, which includes mailing lists and NetNews; and Information Services, which includes ftp, WWW, Wais, Gopher, MUDs and MOOs. Finally, we have a selected bibliography, which may be used for reference.

2.0 One-to-One Communication (Electronic Mail, Talk)

We define one-to-one communications as those in which a person is communicating with another person as if face-to-face: a dialog. In general, rules of common courtesy for interaction with people should be in force for any situation, and on the Internet it is doubly important where, for example, body language and tone of voice must be inferred. For more information on Netiquette for communicating via electronic mail and talk, check References 1, 23, 25, and 27 in the "Selected Bibliography."

2.1 User Guidelines

2.1.1 For mail:

- Unless you have your own Internet access through an Internet provider, be sure to check with your employer about ownership of electronic mail. Laws about the ownership of electronic mail vary from place to place.
- Unless you are using an encryption device (hardware or software), you should assume that mail on the Internet is not secure. Never put in a mail message anything you would not put on a postcard.
- Respect the copyright on material that you reproduce. Almost every country has copyright laws.
- If you are forwarding or re-posting a message you have received, do not change the wording. If the message was a personal message to you and you are re-posting to a group, you should ask permission first. You may shorten the message and quote only relevant parts, but be sure you give proper attribution.

405

- Never send chain letters via electronic mail. Chain letters are forbidden on the Internet. Your network privileges will be revoked. Notify your local system administrator if your ever receive one.

- A good rule of thumb: Be conservative in what you send and liberal in what you receive. You should not send heated messages (we call these "flames") even if you are provoked. On the other hand, you shouldn't be surprised if you get flamed, and it is prudent not to respond to flames.

- In general, it is a good idea to at least check all your mail subjects before responding to a message. Sometimes a person who asks you for help (or clarification) will send another message which effectively says "Never Mind". Also make sure that any message you respond to was directed to you. You might be cc:ed rather than the primary recipient.

- Make things easy for the recipient. Many mailers strip header information which includes your return address. In order to ensure that people know who you are, be sure to include a line or two at the end of your message with contact information. You can create this file ahead of time and add it to the end of your messages. (Some mailers do this automatically.) In Internet parlance, this is known as a ".sig" or "signature" file. Your .sig file takes the place of your business card. (And you can have more than one to apply in different circumstances.)

- Be careful when addressing mail. There are addresses which may go to a group but the address looks like it is just one person. Know to whom you are sending.

- Watch cc's when replying. Do not continue to include people if the messages have become a 2-way conversation.

- In general, most people who use the Internet do not have time to answer general questions about the Internet and its workings. Do not send unsolicited mail asking for information to people whose names you might have seen in RFCs or on mailing lists.

- Remember that people with whom you communicate are located across the globe. If you send a message to which you want an immediate response, the person receiving it might be at home asleep when it arrives. Give them a chance to wake up, come to work, and log in before assuming the mail did not arrive or that they do not care.

- Verify all addresses before initiating long or personal discourse. It is also a good practice to include the word "Long" in the subject header so the recipient knows the message will take time to read and respond to. Over 100 lines is considered "long".

- Know whom to contact for help. Usually you will have resources close at hand. Check locally for people who can help you with software and system problems. Also, know whom to go to if you receive anything questionable or illegal. Most sites also have "Postmaster" aliased to a knowledgeable user, so you can send mail to this address to get help with mail.

- Remember that the recipient is a human being whose culture, language, and humor have different points of reference from your own. Remember that date formats, measurements, and idioms may not travel well. Be especially careful with sarcasm.
- Use mixed case. UPPER CASE LOOKS AS IF YOU'RE SHOUTING.
- Use symbols for emphasis. That *is* what I meant. Use underscores for underlining. _War and Peace_ is my favorite book.
- Use smileys to indicate tone of voice, but use them sparingly. :-) is an example of a smiley (look sideways). Do not assume that the inclusion of a smiley will make the recipient happy with what you say or wipe out an otherwise insulting comment.
- Wait overnight to send emotional responses to messages. If you have really strong feelings about a subject, indicate it via FLAME ON/OFF enclosures. For example:
FLAME ON:
This type of argument is not worth the bandwidth it takes to send it. It's illogical and poorly reasoned. The rest of the world agrees with me.
FLAME OFF
- Do not include control characters or non-ASCII attachments in messages unless they are MIME attachments or unless your mailer encodes these. If you send encoded messages make sure the recipient can decode them.
- Be brief without being overly terse. When replying to a message, include enough original material to be understood but no more. It is extremely bad form to simply reply to a message by including all the previous message: edit out all the irrelevant material.
- Limit line length to fewer than 65 characters and end a line with a carriage return.
- Mail should have a subject heading that reflects the content of the message.
- If you include a signature keep it short. Rule of thumb is no longer than 4 lines. Remember that many people pay for connectivity by the minute, and the longer your message is, the more they pay.
- Just as mail (today) may not be private, mail (and news) are (today) subject to forgery and spoofing of various degrees of detectability. Apply common sense "reality checks" before assuming a message is valid.
- If you think the importance of a message justifies it, immediately reply briefly to an e-mail message to let the sender know you got it, even if you will send a longer reply later.
- "Reasonable" expectations for conduct via e-mail depend on your relationship to a person and the context of the communication. Norms learned in a particular e-mail environment may not apply in general

to your e-mail communication with people across the Internet. Be careful with slang or local acronyms.

- The cost of delivering an e-mail message is, on the average, paid about equally by the sender and the recipient (or their organizations). This is unlike other media such as physical mail, telephone, TV, or radio. Sending someone mail may also cost them in other specific ways like network bandwidth, disk space or CPU usage. This is a fundamental economic reason why unsolicited e-mail advertising is unwelcome (and is forbidden in many contexts).
- Know how large a message you are sending. Including large files such as Postscript files or programs may make your message so large that it cannot be delivered or at least consumes excessive resources. A good rule of thumb would be not to send a file larger than 50 Kilobytes. Consider file transfer as an alternative, or cutting the file into smaller chunks and sending each as a separate message.
- Do not send large amounts of unsolicited information to people.
- If your mail system allows you to forward mail, beware the dreaded forwarding loop. Be sure you have not set up forwarding on several hosts so that a message sent to you gets into an endless loop from one computer to the next to the next.

SELECTED BIBLIOGRAPHY

This bibliography was used to gather most of the information in the sections above as well as for general reference. Items not specifically found in these works were gathered from the IETF-RUN Working Group's experience.

1. Angell, D., and B. Heslop, *The Elements of E-mail Style,* New York: Addison-Wesley, 1994.
2. Answers to Frequently Asked Questions about Usenet" Original author: jerry@eagle.UUCP (Jerry Schwarz) Maintained by: netannounce@deshaw.com (Mark Moraes) Archive-name: usenet-faq/part1.
3. Cerf, V., "Guidelines for Conduct on and Use of Internet," at: http://www.isoc.org/policy/conduct/conduct.html
4. Dern, D., *The Internet Guide for New Users,* New York: McGraw-Hill, 1994.
5. "Emily Postnews Answers Your Questions on Netiquette" Original author: brad@looking.on.ca (Brad Templeton) Maintained by: netannounce@deshaw.com (Mark Moraes) Archive-name: emily-postnews/part1.
6. Gaffin, A., *Everybody's Guide to the Internet,* Cambridge, MA, MIT Press, 1994.
7. "Guidelines for Responsible Use of the Internet" from the U.S. House of Representatives gopher, at: gopher://gopher.house.gov:70/OF-1%3a208%3aInternet%20Etiquette.
8. How to find the right place to post (FAQ) by buglady@bronze.lcs.mit.edu (Aliza R. Panitz) Archive-name: finding-groups/general.
9. Hambridge, S., and J. Sedayao, "Horses and Barn Doors: Evolution of Corporate Guidelines for Internet Usage," LISA VII, Usenix, November 1-5, 1993, pp. 9-16. ftp://ftp.intel.com/pub/papers/horses.ps or horses.ascii>
10. Heslop, B., and D. Angell, *The Instant Internet Guide: Hands-on Global Networking,* Reading, Mass., Addison-Wesley, 1994.
11. Horwitz, S., "Internet Etiquette Tips," ftp://ftp.temple.edu/pub/info/help-net/netiquette.infohn.
12. Internet Activities Board, "Ethics and the Internet," RFC 1087, IAB, January 1989. ftp://ds.internic.net/rfc/rfc1087.txt.

13. Kehoe, B., *Zen and the Art of the Internet: A Beginner's Guide* (Netiquette information is spread through the chapters of this work) 3rd ed. Englewood Cliffs, NJ: Prentice-Hall, 1994.
14. Kochmer, J., *Internet Passport: NorthWestNet's Guide to Our World Online,* 4th ed. Bellevue, WA: NorthWestNet, Northwest Academic Computing Consortium, 1993.
15. Krol, Ed, *The Whole Internet: User's Guide and Catalog,* Sebastopol, CA: O'Reilly & Associates, 1992.
16. Lane, E. and C. Summerhill, *Internet Primer for Information Professionals: A Basic Guide to Internet Networking Technology,* Westport, CT: Meckler, 1993.
17. LaQuey, T., and J. Ryer, The Internet companion, Chapter 3 in *Communicating with People,* pp 41-74. Reading, MA: Addison-Wesley, 1993.
18. Mandel, T., "Surfing the Wild Internet," SRI International Business Intelligence Program, Scan No. 2109. March, 1993. gopher://gopher.well.sf.ca.us:70/00/Communications/surf-wild.
19. Martin, J., "There's Gold in them thar Networks! or Searching for Treasure in all the Wrong Places," FYI 10, RFC 1402, January 1993. ftp://ds.internic.net/rfc/rfc1402.txt.
20. Pioch, N., "A Short IRC Primer," Text conversion by Owe Rasmussen. Edition 1.1b, February 28, 1993. http://www.kei.com/irc/IRCprimer1.1.txt.
21. Polly, J., "Surfing the Internet: An Introduction," Version 2.0.3. Revised May 15, 1993. ftp://ftp.nysernet.org/pub/resources/guides/surfing.2.0.3.txt
22. "A Primer on How to Work With the Usenet Community" Original author: chuq@apple.com (Chuq Von Rospach) Maintained by: netannounce@deshaw.com (Mark Moraes) Archive-name: usenet-primer/part1.
23. Rinaldi, A., "The Net: User Guidelines and Netiquette," September 3, 1992. http://www.fau.edu/rinaldi/net/index.htm.
24. "Rules for posting to Usenet" Original author: spaf@cs.purdue.edu (Gene Spafford) Maintained by: netannounce@deshaw.com (Mark Moraes) Archive-name: posting-rules/part1
25. Shea, V., *Netiquette,* San Francisco: Albion Books, 1994.
26. Strangelove, M., with A. Bosley, "How to Advertise on the Internet," ISSN 1201-0758.
27. Tenant, R., "Internet Basics," ERIC Clearinghouse of Information Resources, EDO-IR-92-7. September, 1992. gopher://nic.merit.edu:7043/00/introducing.the.Internet/Internet.basics.eric-digest gopher://vega.lib.ncsu.edu:70/00/library/reference/guides/tennet.
28. Wiggins, R., *The Internet for Everyone: A Guide for Users and Providers,* New York: McGraw-Hill, 1995.

Chapter 33
Security of Wireless Local Area Networks

Amin Leiman
Martin Miller

Wireless networks have grown in popularity because they can be installed in difficult-to-wire locations and are able to support mobile workforces. However, the increased flexibility of these systems does not come without a price. Wireless LANs are exposed to an array of security threats that differ from those that confront conventional wired LANs. This chapter focuses on the critical factors that should be considered when evaluating the security of wireless LANs, including their physical configuration, type of transmission, and service availability.

INTRODUCTION

Wireless local area networks (LANs) use a network interface card with a frequency modulation transceiver to link multiple workstations. External antennae can be used to provide omnidirectional transmission between workstations. Wireless LANs are implemented using any of three types of communications technology: infrared, radio frequency, and microwave. A typical wireless LAN can be connected without any cabling; in some configurations, the wireless LAN may also be connected to a wired network.

Wireless technology allows users the freedom to move (within certain boundaries) without the restrictions imposed by trailing cables. Networks can be set up without having to lay cable, which makes it much easier to implement changes in the network configuration. Indeed, the primary reason for the growth of wireless LANs has been their configuration flexibility in difficult-to-wire locations and their ability to support mobile workforces. These benefits must be weighed against the fact that wireless systems can cost as much as two-and-a-half times the amount per workstation of conventional cabled networks.

0-8493-1248-5/02/$0.00+$1.50
© 2002 by CRC Press LLC

This chapter examines the strengths and weaknesses of various forms of wireless networking, with special emphasis given to potential security exposures. Three critical factors must be considered in evaluating the security of wireless LANs: their physical configuration, type of transmission, and service availability. The chapter discusses each of these factors and concludes by reviewing the controls best suited for securing wireless transmissions.

AN OVERVIEW OF COSTS AND BENEFITS

Infrared LANs require no Federal Communications Commission (FCC) license and are relatively secure because disruption of their required line-of-sight operation (e.g., that caused by electronic eavesdropping) will bring down the LAN. However, they use limited bandwidth, are easily disrupted (e.g., they cannot transmit through walls), and they are more expensive than conventional cabled LANs.

The radio frequency LAN does not require line-of-sight transmission, but it is easily intercepted. However, some products do provide encryption capability. Radio frequency wireless LANs require an FCC license.

The microwave transmission LAN is a technology used to bridge LANs between buildings or greater distances as an alternative to using commercial telephone lines. It is less expensive than using leased lines and is not subject to phone company rate fluctuations. However, it does require microwave and satellite dishes at both ends, both of which are subject to city zoning laws. As with radio frequency transmission, microwave transmission methods are subject to interception.

Wireless network technologies also share some general limitations as described in the following sections.

Interoperability. Interoperability is a problem with current wireless LANs. Different LANs use different technologies that are not highly compatible. For example, some vendors use the infrared part of the spectrum, while others use the radio-wave band. Those that use the radio-wave band may operate at different frequencies, which accounts for their different speeds. FCC regulations vary for different vendors' products. As a response to this situation, the Institute of Electrical and Electronics Engineers 802.11 Committee is developing a standard radio frequency protocol.

Given the diversity of interests and protocols currently being developed, it is possible that no one standard will emerge. Instead, industry-specific standards may arise, such as one for retail and another for manufacturing.

Performance. Performance of wireless LANs has generally lagged behind that of cabled LANs. Infrared LANs operate at or below 1 megabit per second (Mbps). Radio frequency LANs typically run between 2 Mbps and 3.5 Mbps, well below Ethernet's published rate of 10 Mbps. (The actual Ethernet throughput is lower than this stated rate; the variance is therefore not as great.) Despite the difference, it is expected that wireless LANs wil move to a frequency capable of boosting speeds to 16 Mbps, a pace highly comparable with the capacity of current cabled networks.

Configuration. Configuration limitations restrict the use of wireless LANs. For example, infrared LANs require line-of-sight operation. Although radio LANs can transmit through walls, to be most effective they are typically kept on the same floor within a fixed area (depending on the requirements of the specific vendor equipment used). The wireless LAN may work well in one location but may not be recognized on a network in another office. The challenge is to route a microcomputer's data to the appropriate file server when the computer is continually moving.

INDUSTRY APPLICATIONS

Wireless computing is slowly gaining broader acceptance as portables become more prominent in business settings. In addition, the development of cellular technology has led to increased interest in wireless LANs. With the growing acceptance of cellular technology, organizations have become more comfortable with the concept of processing without cables.

Often, such new technologies as wireless LANs experience dynamic growth only after a unique application is introduced that is well suited to the technology. Electronic messaging (e-mail) may be that application. Wireless messaging fits well with a growing workforce that must be able to communicate in real time. Wireless mail networks allow mobile users to communicate wherever they are without plugging into a data port. This includes participation in mail-enabled applications specifically adapted for portable computers. Electronic wireless messaging is typically accomplished by sending a message from a network through a gateway to a local switch, transmitting by satellite, from which it is downlinked to a relay station, which in turn transmits to a stationary or mobile receiver. From here, the user can download the message to microcomputers running such mail-enabled applications as dispatch and sales systems. Although wireless e-mail is a wide area network (WAN) application, it is certain to influence attitudes about the use of wireless LAN processing within the office environment.

More recent developments may help spur the growth of wireless LANs. These developments include:

- Hardware and software for notebook and laptop computers that allow access to host systems over wireless networks.
- External wireless adapters that attach to a computer's parallel port, allowing even those computers with no available slots to gain wireless access.
- Cellular technology that allows the user to carry a computer from one cell to another while the software automatically seeks and finds the next adjacent cell and makes the connection to the new server, forging a link to the first server and maintaining the logical link at all times.
- The development of a wireless LAN with transmission rates of 5.7 Mbps, which is comparable to the speeds of many wired Ethernet LANs.
- The recent plan by the Federal Communications Commission to allocate 20 MHz of radio spectrum — which would not require a license — for use in wireless networks.

Wireless technology is being applied in such diverse settings as the airline, banking, and health-care industries. For example, a major European air carrier is using a palmtop product to check passengers remotely from the curbside and parking lot at an East Coast airport, which has resulted in shorter check-in lines. A major Midwestern commercial bank transmits customer information to its branches using spread-spectrum radio frequency LANs, which has improved customer service. And a Florida hospital is considering implementing cellular technology that would allow doctors to travel throughout the hospital with palmtop computers without losing connection to the network.

SECURITY CONCERNS

Wireless LANs differ from hard-wired LANs in the physical and data link layers of the Open Systems Interconnect (OSI) reference model. In attacking hard-wired LANs, a perpetrator would need physical access to the communication medium either through the cables that connect the network or through the telephone closet. A wireless LAN communicates through the air; intercepting emanated signals in the air requires more sophisticated techniques.

The belief that airborne transmissions can be easily intercepted with readily available radio equipment is simplistic and misleading. Intercepting is one thing; understanding the intercepted data another. This is especially true if the data is sent in digital form. Many wireless LAN products have built-in security features specifically designed to prevent unauthorized access to signals in transit. Decrypting an encrypted signal requires vendor-supplied decryption devices and decryption keys as well as the technical expertise to use them effectively.

According to a U.S. Senate subcommittee report, the Electronic Communications Privacy Act of 1986 (ECPA), which prohibits the interception of electronic messages, does not cover wireless data communications. The Senate Privacy and Technology Task Force Report says that the ECPA "failed to anticipate" how the variety of private communications available to users would expand and how data would be carried by radio links. It recommends that the law be updated to protect most radio-based communications technology.[1]

The absence of laws protecting wireless communications has encouraged perpetrators to attempt unauthorized access to company data. As a consequence, businesses and other organizations have been wary of using this technology for sensitive applications. Currently, the use of wireless LANs in industry has been limited to nonsensitive applications. However, as users learn more about wireless LAN technology and methods for securing wireless communications, organizations should become more interested in using this technology for processing sensitive applications.

This chapter focuses on the three critical factors that should be considered when evaluating the security of a wireless LAN: physical configuration, type of transmission, and service availability. Each of these factors is related; therefore, the security specialist must have a clear understanding of all of them to fully appreciate the relevant security issues.

Physical Configuration

From an operational point of view, the use of wireless LANs gives the user more flexibility in changing the configuration of terminals. However, from the security perspective, this flexibility provides more avenues of potential attack. Intruders can intercept wireless transmissions without having to physically access the office in which the network is located. However, the ease of such access depends, in part, on how the wireless LAN is configured. For example, if designed correctly, an in-office wireless LAN should limit the range of access to the office area. On the other hand, a network designed to communicate between buildings is more susceptible to potential intruders because the range of possible interception is much wider.

But even then, the intruder's task is not a simple one. It requires being able to distinguish the target data from other data being transmitted at the same time. The intruder must also be able to decipher the signal. Although computers can be used to sort out the signal, this process requires significant effort and expense.

It is important to recognize that the coverage area in a wireless network is not defined by distance alone but by signal levels and co-channel interference as well. A wireless LAN may also be used to extend an existing hard-wired LAN rather than to replace it; this may add further complexity to the overall architecture.

Types of Transmission

As stated, there are three types of wireless LAN technologies: infrared (e.g., light and laser beam), radio frequency (e.g., spread spectrum), and microwave. Each of these technologies has its own security exposures. Three popular wireless LAN products on the market utilize these different technologies. The BICC Communications InfraLAN uses infrared, the NCR Corp. WaveLAN uses spread spectrum, and the Motorola Altair uses microwave technology. The following sections describe the security exposures common to each technology.

Infrared. Infrared communications require line-of-sight transmission over a limited bandwidth. For example, InfraLAN uses an optical wavelength of 870 nanometers; its range between nodes is 80 feet. Hence, a potential intruder must be in the office within the specified range and must be in a line-of-sight path, a combination of factors that can be easily achieved only by insiders.

The use of infrared technology is not licensed by the Federal Communications Commission. This increases the possibility of unauthorized use and potential interference. However, this technology is also relatively secure because disruption of its line-of-sight operation (e.g., in the event of electronic eavesdropping) will bring down the LAN. In light of the limited distance between nodes and the line-of-sight requirement, infrared-based wireless LANs are considered relatively secure.

Radio Frequency. Although radio frequency transmissions can pass through walls and partitions, radio frequency networks must usually be kept on the same floor. Because line-of-sight transmission is not required, transmitted data can be more readily intercepted. To combat this problem, some products have incorporated encryption capabilities.

By sending data over several frequencies, spread-spectrum transmission minimizes the possibility of eavesdropping. Radio frequency-based LANs currently use frequencies in the range of 902 to 928 MHz. The drawback of these frequencies is that they are also used by television, VCR extenders, and antitheft devices in stores. In the presence of such devices, the network may be disrupted. Generally, the radio signal is affected by noise and interference.

WaveLAN is one product that uses spread-spectrum technology. In an open environment, it can cover a range of 800 feet; in a semiclosed environment, it can cover a range of 250 feet. Because radio technology is well understood by many professionals, it may also be more susceptible to attempts at unauthorized access. This exposure can be mitigated by implementing such security mechanisms as encryption and access controls.

It should be noted that the Institute of Electrical and Electronics Engineers 802.11 Committee is trying to forge a standard radio frequency for use in network transmissions.

Microwave. Microwave is a communications technology used to connect LANs between buildings and over greater distances than is possible with infrared or radio frequency technologies. Altair uses microwave technology; this product is compatible with existing cable-based standards, protocols, and communication speeds, and can complement, replace, or extend such networks as Token Ring and Ethernet networks. One of Altair's strengths is its transparent operation with Ethernet architecture and such Network Operating System as Novell NetWare and Microsoft LAN Manager. Altair utilizes the FCC-licensed 18-GHz frequencies, and it can cover a range of 5000 square feet. To coordinate the use of separate frequencies, Motorola has established a centralized Altair Frequency Management Center to ensure compliance with FCC regulations.

Altair provides two built-in security features: data scrambling and restricted access. The data scrambling feature scrambles data between the control module and the user module. The restricted access feature, which is incorporated into Altair's Time-Division Multiplexing architecture, allows access only to user modules whose 12-digit IEEE 802.33 Ethernet addresses have been entered into the control module's registration table.

Because microwave use is FCC licensed and, hence, is monitored, it is considered the most secure system. As one might expect, potential intruders tend to avoid regulated environments for fear of being caught and prosecuted.

Service Availability

For a complete understanding of the security concerns affecting wireless LANs, the concept of service availability must be understood. In a simple way, service availability can be thought of in terms of the dial tone one gets when picking up a telephone — the absence of a dial tone can be the result of equipment failure, a busy circuit, or a poor signal.

Service availability can be discussed in terms of these three components: signal availability, circuit availability, and equipment availability. To tap the network using unauthorized terminal connections, the perpetrator must obtain an adequate signal, an available circuit, and the right equipment. If any of the three components of service availability is missing, access to a wireless LAN cannot be completed. However, having service availability does not automatically mean getting successful access to the network. Other factors such as network architecture and network security mechanisms affect the potential success of access attempts.

Signal Availability. In a radio frequency system, signal availability has to do with whether there is sufficient radio energy reaching the receiver to produce an acceptable bit-error rate in the demodulated signal. In an infrared system, the receiving unit must be in the line of sight of the beam. Signal availability directly relates to distance; as a node is placed beyond the effective range, the signal becomes unavailable.

Circuit Availability. Circuit availability usually depends on co-channel interference and adjacent channel interference. Co-channel interference occurs when two transmissions on the same carrier frequency reach a single receiver. (The ratio of the carrier to interference is called the carrier-to-interference ratio.) Adjacent channel interference occurs when energy from the modulated carrier spreads into the adjacent channels. The Motorola Frequency Management Center maintains a central database that tracks the location and frequency of each Altair module in the United States to lessen the possibility of interference.

One tactic of intruders is to locate the carrier frequency and purposely jam the receiver to prevent other transmissions from accessing the receiver. Wireless networks are particularly susceptible to this form of attack.

Equipment Availability. Equipment availability refers to the availability of appropriate equipment for a particular network. In the case of wireless LANs, special equipment and connectors may be required to access the network. For example, equipment proprietary to Altair is needed to access an Altair network. Therefore, an intruder cannot use a typical scanner to access and compromise the network. In addition, this equipment must be connected to the Altair LAN by means of ThinNet T connectors with terminators, which are also unique to Altair.

WIRELESS NETWORK CONTROLS

The security of a wireless LAN depends on two factors: protective security mechanisms and audit mechanisms. These controls are discussed in the following paragraphs.

Protective Security Mechanisms

As identified by the International Standards Organization in its ISO-OSI Reference Model Security Guidelines, several mechanisms can be used to provide security services in a network: encryption, cryptographic error checks, source authentication, peer-to-peer authentication, and access control. In wireless LANs, encryption and access control are the two most widely used methods of security.

Encryption. The three most common techniques of encryption are link, end-to-end, and application encryption. Link encryption encrypts and decrypts information at each physical link, whereas end-to-end encrypts the information throughout the network and decrypts it at the receiving location. Link encryption is more secure if the information is being transmitted by means of several physical links because multiple keys are required to decipher the information. Application encryption encrypts information at the application level. Among wireless LAN products that offer encryption, Altair uses end-to-end encryption to scramble data sent between the control module and the user module.

Access Controls. Access controls are used to identify network users and authorize or deny access according to prescribed guidelines. Some LAN operating systems use the workstation ID stored in network interface card, which the LAN operating system checks at log-on time. Any workstation attempting to access the network without the correct ID is disconnected from the network. Another way of providing access control is by means of a user registration table. For example, Altair requires that the 12-digit Ethernet addresses of all authorized users be entered into the control module's registration table. Any user whose code has not been so entered is denied access to the network. This feature is effective in restricting potential perpetrators from gaining network access.

Audit Mechanisms

To maintain a secure wireless LAN, a security audit should be performed in addition to ongoing monitoring activities. The security audit of a wireless LAN requires the examination of security policy, security protection mechanisms, and security administration. These areas are described in the following paragraphs.

Security Policy. Security policy governs the overall activities of the network. Without an effective policy, it is difficult to enforce protection. A security policy should specifically address the policy for accessing the wireless LAN. The policy should be as specific as possible. At a minimum, it should specify who is authorized to access the network, under what circumstances and what capacity, and when access is permitted. The policy should also establish the rules for moving workstations to ensure proper monitoring of each physical access point. The security manager should ensure that this policy is communicated to all network users and that it is adopted by them.

Security Protection. Securing a wireless LAN requires constant physical and logical protection. Physical protection involves securing the physical devices from unauthorized access. This usually requires such normal security housekeeping as providing a secure room to house the computer devices. Logical protection usually requires access controls and data encryption. It is crucial that all built-in security features be fully implemented; add-on security products (e.g., end-to-end encryption devices) should be considered as necessary.

Security Administration. Without proper enforcement, security policy and protective devices provide false assurance about the organization's level of information security. Therefore, it is important that one or more individuals be designated to act as a security administrator. The security administrator is responsible for ensuring that the organization's security policy is implemented and that all applicable security features are fully and correctly used. Strict enforcement of security policy and procedures is particularly important in a wireless LAN environment because of the relative ease with which users can change the composition of the network.

CONCLUSION

To take full advantage of the benefits of wireless networks, appropriate security measures should be instituted. With the constant development of new technologies, security exposures need to be controlled in a cost-effective manner. Although customer demands influence the development of new products, they typically do not drive the development of security features for these products. It is management's responsibility to ensure that newly acquired wireless technologies are implemented in a controlled way.

When purchasing a wireless LAN product, the quality of its security features should be carefully reviewed and tested. Because wireless LAN technology is relatively new, it is recommended that products be considered on the basis of the security mechanisms they incorporate and on the reputation of the vendor for its research and ongoing development of products. Prior to purchasing a wireless LAN product is purchased, the quality of its security features should be thoroughly evaluated and tested.

Note

1. Betts, M., Do Laws Protect Wireless Nets?, *Computerworld*, 25(24), 47, 1991.

Chapter 34
Customer Relationship Management and Data Warehousing

Duane E. Sharp

One application of technology that many organizations have adopted over the past few years to enhance customer relations is customer relationship management. This application even has its own acronym — CRM — which has taken its place in the jargon of the information technology (IT) sector.

A key objective of CRM is to establish relationships with each individual customer, rather than treating customers as a mass market based on a product-centric marketing structure. The new model, referred to as customer-centric, relates to each customer as if he or she were the *only* customer. This is a revolutionary approach for organizations that may have thousands or even millions of customers.

Today's customers are better educated, better informed, more knowledgeable about technology, and therefore more demanding when it comes to the products and services they buy. Increased competition, with little or no product/service differentiation, further adds to customer purchasing power in the new millennium.

MANAGING RELATIONSHIPS: THE CRM SOLUTION

Successfully managing customer relationships means learning about the behavior and needs of customers, anticipating future buying patterns, and finding new opportunities to add value to the relationship.

Relationship technologies are the keys to making customer transactions more personal, more individual, and more intimate. Solutions driven by data warehousing systems are designed specifically to expand and

0-8493-1248-5/02/$0.00+$1.50
© 2002 by CRC Press LLC

enhance relationships with customers — not just process their data. More than ever, relationship technologies are vital to any company wishing to deal with customers, whether through personal contact or via the Internet or other electronic media.

To be effective for both supplier and customer, the objectives of CRM should be aligned with customer needs. Why? Because customers expect a vendor relationship with value. This means looking after purchasing needs — even anticipating these needs — and responding to them.

CRM can help businesses turn detailed customer information into competitive advantage, using a data warehousing system to target and market to their customers. A well-defined CRM solution enables businesses to capture and analyze customer interactions to better understand their requirements, and to build lifetime relationships. With CRM, many organizations have been able to reduce customer "churn," understand changes in customer buying behavior or life event changes, and focus on customer value.

Organizations that achieve high ratings for customer relationships are those that make the relationship something that the customer values from one particular organization over another. To accomplish this, companies need to look at their experiences with customers — not simply the transactions and demographics, but every customer interaction. These include the phone call to a call center, the click on a World Wide Web site, and the response to a direct mail campaign.

Building data and information technology architecture around each individual customer — the customer-centric model — enables customers to enjoy a seamless and rewarding experience when doing business with a company.

CUSTOMER FEEDBACK

A recent survey by a major consulting firm examined the impact of technology on the delivery of improved customer practices and services. Predictably, the study found that technology alone does not guarantee success in enhancing customer relationships. The key is selecting the right technology to meet customer needs, and the right partner to help implement it.

More than 1300 organizations participated in this survey, which found that:

1. Organizations that improve customer satisfaction also reap a number of important side benefits.
2. Technology alone is not the key to success. Rather, organizations that focus on three areas — technology, processes, and customer needs — are the most successful.

3. Technology plays a dual role for companies, acting as both a driver and enabler of change in achieving effective CRM.
4. Companies with the greatest customer satisfaction ratings were those that integrated the best practices of the three main types of organizations: process focused, customer needs focused, and technology focused.

DEFINING THE CUSTOMER

Surveys such as this raise an important and fundamental question for organizations: Who are my customers? The answer may point an organization in several directions, because "customers" take various forms for many organizations and, in today's market, all of these customer categories enjoy a new range of purchasing power. There are four definable customer categories in most business sectors:

1. *Individual* customers who buy products directly from a company
2. *Businesses* that buy from a company
3. *Distribution channels* that buy products for resale to an end user
4. *Internal departments*

All of these customer categories have more power today than ever before, because today's market forces have made organizations more competitive. Because there is less differentiation in products and services, and more product and supplier choices, switching suppliers or products is easy. It requires little cost and often little effort. In addition, customers expect customization and they have the bargaining power to demand it.

To keep customers, "loyalty" programs and incentives that entice them to stay with a given supplier have become popular and widespread. Often, these programs become an integral part of a corporate CRM strategy.

THE PRIVACY ISSUE

The rapid growth of data warehousing as a business tool in a variety of business sectors — including financial, retailing, health care, and travel — has placed new emphasis on the issue of individual privacy, vastly increasing the opportunity and ease with which one's personal information can be compromised.

Personal privacy is becoming an increasingly important issue for consumers as they become more aware of how organizations with data warehousing systems are gathering, monitoring, and using personal data to develop customer profiles. This is an issue that must be addressed by organizations, and consumers must know that the organizations they do business with have policies and practices to protect personal information.

There are several areas of impact in a CRM system on the privacy of personal information, including:

- *Notice:* providing notice to customers of an organization's policies and practices regarding personal information
- *Collection and use limits:* how information is collected and how it is used
- *Choice/consent:* letting customers choose which personal information can be used and for what purpose(s)
- *Data quality, access, and correction:* who can access what level of personal information and who can update it
- *Data security:* what measures are taken to protect unlawful or unauthorized use of personal information
- *Accountability:* accepting responsibility for protection of personal privacy

Advances in technology have dramatically altered the global marketplace, offering significant benefits to consumers in terms of greater choice and convenience, and providing companies with availability and access to personal information on a global scale. This ready access has increased the opportunity and ease with which personal information can be obtained and compromised.

There are opportunities for enhancing customer relationships in the development of privacy policies and the implementation of privacy practices. A successful CRM system must be designed with opt-in/opt-out features on consumer data collection. Consumers must have the ability to know and understand what data is being collected. They must also be able to state how that information is being used, who has access to it, and, more generally, what an organization's privacy policies are with regard to this customer data.

Among the trade associations and industry groups that have endorsed privacy principles, the Online Privacy Alliance, located at www.privacyalliance.org on the World Wide Web, has established a set of privacy principles for online activities and electronic commerce. These privacy principles involve a combination of technology and operating procedures that address the privacy issues arising from the growth of data warehousing.

There are typically three defined layers of identification data in the logical data model used in a privacy system. These levels determine how personal data is handled in a data warehouse. Opt-out features have also been incorporated into privacy systems, enabling customers to specify which personal data can be accessed:

- *Layer 1:* The first layer in the logical data model is the individual's identity; that is, name, address, and phone number.

- *Layer 2*: The second layer is more restrictive and will contain personal information such as age, sex, and marital status.
- *Layer 3*: The third layer will contain the most sensitive data, for example, information such as race.

Control of access is the next step in the move to greater protection of personal information. This process involves the restriction of user access to private data by using database "views," with their associated security. Views are database mechanisms that restrict access to data and return appropriate subsets of data to authorized users or applications. These views protect personal data in several ways, by:

- Restricting access to personal data fields by routine users or applications
- Making personal data more anonymous for analytical applications
- Preventing access to records relating to opted-out customers to any user or application involved in direct marketing or disclosure of data to third parties

Governments have not been hesitant to regulate and legislate where citizen concerns have come to the fore. In Europe, beginning with the initial Privacy Guidelines adopted in 1980 by the Organization for Economic Cooperation and Development, there has been a steady progression from guidance for collectors of information to, more recently, national and sub-national legislation that places restrictions on the collection and use of personal data.

In 1995, the European Union (EU) adopted the European Directive on Personal Data Protection, which became effective on October 25, 1998. The directive applies restrictions to all forms of personal data processing, both electronic and non-electronic environments, and will affect all companies either operating in Europe or collecting/using European personal data. The Directive's Article 25 restricts the transfer of personal data about European citizens to third countries unless those countries have adequate personal data protection.

In the United States, privacy issues are already being legislated in several sectors, including financial, health care, and communications; and there is a threat of further legislation at the federal and state levels if companies themselves do not address the privacy/data protection concerns of the consumer. In addition, the United States has been in discussion with the EU regarding implementation of Article 25, and discussions continue regarding a proposed "safe harbor" concept for those companies that self-certify their adherence to defined personal data protection practices.

FOUR STAGES IN THE CRM PROCESS

One definition for CRM describes the process as "an enterprise approach to understanding and influencing customer behavior through continuous, relevant communication to improve customer acquisition, retention, and profitability." Based on this definition, there are four distinct stages in the development of an effective, efficient CRM process. The first stage is *interaction*, which involves a series of transactions and interactions that make up a dialog between a customer and an organization. Sales processes are examples of customer interaction.

The second stage is *relating*. This refers to the application of insightful marketing practices to create relevant interactions that build valued relationships. *Connection*, the third stage, refers to the mapping and management of interaction points between a consumer and an organization. Finally, in the *knowing* stage or *knowledge discovery*, the insight gained through capture and analysis of detailed information is used to create continuous learning.

Interacting with Customers

A series of transactions and interactions defines a dialog between a customer and an organization. This dialog may take several forms. For example, transactions could include a product order over the Web or telephone, a cash request from an ATM, a service request, or payment of a monthly bill.

An interaction could include a call for product information, placement of a product in a shopping cart without purchasing it, a complaint about the quality of a product or service, or a request for the status of a shipment. It might also involve a profile update stemming from a life-cycle event, such as a change of address, an increase in family size, or a change in marital status.

Each of these transactions and interactions represents an opportunity to build and develop a relationship with a customer. Even the shortest dialog, such as a change in telephone number or address, represents a change in a customer's lifestyle. One way of encouraging customer loyalty and retention is to use this insight to interact with a customer in a follow-up mode — with a special marketing offer, for example.

Relating to a Customer

Relating to a customer involves the application of insight to create relevant interactions that build valued relationships. This is the stage where market planning comes into play and marketing campaigns are initiated to build value for customers. This is accomplished by offering a customer something of value, to demonstrate and emphasize a desire to retain that customer.

Connecting with a Customer

Mapping and managing interaction points between a customer and an organization defines the third stage in customer relationship management. These activities involve establishing ongoing procedures for maintaining customer contact — through correspondence, phone calls, personal meetings, or any other one-on-one activity that serves to enhance customer relationships by maintaining customer contact.

Getting to Know a Customer

Learning about customers, their purchasing patterns, product preferences, and lifestyle is an important element in the CRM process and is a fundamental requirement in treating each customer as an individual. This objective can be achieved through constant analysis of each customer's transaction activity and will be built on both customer and company activity.

CRM: GLOBAL APPLICATIONS AND BENEFITS

At a number of major public and private sector organizations throughout the world, management has turned to sophisticated technologies such as data warehousing to develop and implement CRM systems. The following examples from the telecommunications, financial services, transportation, and entertainment sectors illustrate how important CRM is to these organizations.

Telecommunications

In the telecommunications field, CRM has a global reach. Pelephone of Israel, for example, has extended its traditional database management system, which was designed for transaction management for its more than 10 million customers, to a data warehouse application that has enhanced its customer relationship capabilities. Several benefits have resulted from this transformation, to include:

- All detailed customer data can be scanned.
- Multiple customer models can be developed.
- The right customers can be targeted.
- There has been a reduction in customer "churn."
- A new range of customer services is being offered.
- Customer service loyalty has been improved.
- Known and tangible paybacks have been created.

These changes in managing customer relationships enabled the company to confirm that between 50,000 and 70,000 customers remained loyal, rather than moving to the competition.

In Australia, Vodafone, the country's third largest wireless telephone company with revenues of $1 billion (AS), was faced with deregulation and strong competition. It realized that customer retention was a key requirement to its continued growth. With an effective CRM system, the company was able to retain a significant percentage of its 900,000 wireless customers, as well as reduce churn and increase marketing effectiveness, while growing its organization exponentially.

In Austria, Mobilkom, a leading analog and digital networking company, with 1.2 million users and 85 percent market share, was acquiring 30,000 new customers monthly. Nevertheless, the company faced several internal and eternal challenges as it rapidly grew. These included uncoordinated data systems for billings, long waits by customers for calls to be answered, a low level of customer satisfaction, inaccessibility of detailed data to agents who needed to answer questions, and increased competition due to deregulation.

Mobilkom met these challenges by initiating several major changes in the way in which it managed customer relationships. It implemented a data warehouse system and integrated a CTI-enabled call center with the data warehousing system. As a result of these changes, the company was able to handle four times as many calls, reduce hold time to 20 seconds, reduce call abandonment by 80 percent, empower agents, increase profits, and improve customer satisfaction ratings.

Financial Services

Typical of the large financial institutions using CRM to enhance their businesses is California-based Bank of America. This organization has continually invested in data warehousing, using its substantial storehouse of customer data to perform target marketing, resulting in significant success and increased customer retention.

By gathering data on customer habits in savings, mortgages, checking services, credit cards, loans, and time deposits, Bank of America has been able to develop effective programs for target marketing, credit risk management, portfolio analysis, and retail banking services. The ultimate benefit has been a resultant increase in new business by many millions of dollars, avoidance of risk, and increased profits.

Transportation and Travel

A number of international airlines — including American, British Airways, Quantas, US Airways, Continental, Lufthansa, and Delta — are using data warehousing in a variety of travel-oriented applications.

For example, British Airways uses a data warehousing system for complete business analysis and resource allocation. The range of information it provides includes which customers are traveling, as well as where, when, and how often; an estimate of the resources and inventory required, based on customer-centric data; and the building of a knowledge base of customer actions and transactions, which the organization can use to predict the future and manage its operation.

In addition, British Airways and the six other major international airlines use data warehousing to provide a number of business solutions beneficial to their operations, including:

- Online query of all resources and schedules
- The ability to manage planes/loads/usages
- A financial management system
- Resource planning and system scheduling
- Knowledge transfer to all levels of business users

Travel Unie is one of Europe's fastest-growing tour operators and specialized travel agencies. Use of a data warehousing system and a focus on CRM has enabled this organization to derive the following benefits:

- In-depth customer profiling, trend, and marketing analysis
- Customer service response time of less than one second
- More efficient interaction, more satisfied customers, and a higher tour-booking capability by agents (based on higher response rates from direct mail, call centers and Web sites)
- The capability to provide new products and services for elderly customers

Entertainment

Harrah's owns 18 casinos in eight U.S. states and is the most recognized and respected brand name in the casino entertainment industry. Using a sophisticated data warehousing system with an effective CRM element, Harrah's was able to:

- Understand, retain, and reward 15 million guests
- Encourage customers to remain loyal to the Harrah's brand across the country and over time
- Analyze, predict, and maximize the value of each relationship
- Compile hundreds of customer attributes to help determine customer likelihood to visit, predicted spending, opportunities for cross-selling, customer segmentation, and event data
- Analyze each customer's preference and predict which services and rewards they will respond to in the future
- Use call center access to the data warehouse to provide customers with the same service they would get on the floor of their favorite casino

CRM: A PROCESS, NOT AN EVENT

Effective and successful customer relationship management is not an event, but a process that needs to be strategically managed at all levels within an organization by everyone involved in customer relationships. Ultimately, CRM is all about increasing customer profitability by identifying detailed customer segmentation, defining marketing communication strategies, and providing the intelligent decisions to more effectively drive retention, profitability, and customer satisfaction.

Chapter 35

Anonymity, Privacy, and Trust

Ralph Spencer Poore

In the Internet realm these days, we see the terms *anonymity, privacy,* and *trust* used as if they meant the same thing. We see "trust marks" attempting to describe the privacy policy of a Web site (e.g., Truste™ and WebTrust™). And we see "privacy" described in terms of personally identifiable information (PII) leaving the control of the person whose PII it is. We have also learned that accessing a site without revealing some information useful in tracking back to us is difficult and is never the default situation.

Whether it is coded information in a Microsoft document, Pentium III serial numbers, Windows 98 identifiers, "cookies," or static IP addresses, preventing the leakage of PII when anonymity is needed or desired has become increasingly problematic. But before I delve into these issues, let's agree on some definitions.

ANONYMITY

True anonymity requires the shielding of one's identity beyond the use of pseudonyms. Whether I know you as "John" and someone else knows you as "Mr. Little" matters not if either name can be tied back to you. That includes my knowing you as "987-65-4321" or as "254.98.167.03" or as "Red Hack Trucker." A political dissident using the handle of "Free Voice" who is traced back to a specific apartment address will feel no more anonymous as a political prisoner than if the dissident had used his or her real name. Anonymity means without name, so being associated with any static appellation voids anonymity.

Anonymity in political discourse may be the most important guarantee of freedom you can have. In addition to its value in a political context, anonymity is also important in some businesses. For example, if you knew that someone had retained an expert in Pre-Columbian art to bid at an auction, you would not need to know the bidder's name to benefit from that expert whom the bidder retained. You would only need to know what bids were associated with that expert. By simply outbidding the expert

0-8493-1248-5/02/$0.00+$1.50
© 2002 by CRC Press LLC

Exhibit 1. Six Conditions Associated with Privacy

Condition	Description
1. Notice	The individual has the right to know that the collection of PII will exist
2. Choice	The individual has the right to choose not to have the data collected
3. Use	The individual has the right to know how data will be used and to restrict its use
4. Security	The individual has the right to know the extent to which the data will be protected
5. Correction	The individual has the right to challenge the accuracy of the data and to provide corrected information
6. Enforcement	The individual has the right to seek legal relief through appropriate channels to protect privacy rights

by a small margin, you would gain the benefit of the expert's expertise without paying the expert's fee. Because the expert's employer has the burden of the expert's fee, you might reason that your incremental bid over the expert's remains a bargain.

If you have children, you may wish to protect their identities. Stalking on the Internet is already reported to be a problem. Rather than allow any PII, they are best protected by anonymity. Another example where anonymity proves beneficial is in health-related reporting. To obtain accurate data for research and policy issues related to sexually transmitted diseases or illicit drug use, the respondents must believe that they will not be identified. Whether anonymity is used to protect personal liberties, to protect trade secrets, or to improve the quality of responses, we will need systems designed to ensure nonattribution.

PRIVACY

When you must have a relationship with attribution, the personally identifiable information (PII) that results is considered private only to the extent that you control to whom access is granted. A "Privacy Policy" does not establish privacy and may, in fact, specify that privacy is not provided. The European Union's Privacy Directive specifies six conditions associated with privacy. Exhibit 1 describes each briefly.

Although the U.S. Supreme Court has several rulings deriving a right to personal privacy (generally from the Fourth, Ninth [rarely], and Fourteenth Amendments) and although the United States has a law known as the *Privacy Act*, almost every so-called privacy law at the federal level is either an expansion of authority to invade privacy (e.g., wiretaps) or limited in scope and remedy. Real privacy protection — to the extent we have it in the United States at all — has been left primarily to state legislation. (On an ironic note, many states not only provide little relief, they actually sell the PII that citizens of those states are forced by law to provide to the state!) The United States follows a contract-law model that effectively grants ownership of PII to the collector of such data, not to the person whose personally identifiable information it is. The European Union model provides the individual with rights over such data that may not be abridged by contract. This has placed the EU and the United States at more than just opposite sides of the Atlantic. With Canada's adoption of the EU position on privacy, the United States is further isolated in its stance.

The approach to privacy seemingly adopted by the majority of commercial Internet sites with a U.S. nexus is to provide notice (i.e., a privacy policy statement) but not to accommodate any of the other privacy principles listed in Exhibit 1. Some sites have provided a means for opting out of data releases to other third parties and some even provide a means for opting out of receiving e-mail solicitations from the company itself. However, civil litigation appears to be the only enforcement mechanism where the cause for action is breach of contract. Although other legal theories will no doubt be tried, using litigation as the enforcement mechanism — except in egregious cases where a class action is warranted — will provide us with little comfort. The need to establish monetary damages, the voluntary nature of the release of PII with its implicit acceptance of the site's terms and conditions, and the technical barriers most plaintiffs would have to overcome to prove that a specific site released the data, make litigation less than ideal as the enforcement mechanism.

The most common approach individuals have taken to combat the loss of PII is to misrepresent PII to sites. This varies from small misrepresentations to "color" the data (so you can tell if the site provided your data to someone else) to complete fictions. This data pollution may harm companies who attempt to rely on this data and may harm the individuals who use these techniques to protect their privacy. Most commercial transactions include warranties, may include the need for recall notices or upgrades, and may involve the potential for refunds, reversals, rebates, or returns/exchanges. To facilitate these, the company needs a valid means of reaching the customer and the customer needs to be able to prove that he or she is the valid purchaser. Providing false credentials may void warranties and interfere with other recourse to which the consumer would otherwise be entitled. False demographic information may cause a company to misapply marketing dollars or to make incorrect inventory decisions. The lack of trust fostered by poor privacy practices may harm both parties.

TRUST

In the context of privacy, trust is the assurance that PII will be used only as agreed and will be protected against unauthorized access. Ideally, trust would extend to the enforcement of choice and to the provision of means for the review and correction of PII. However, most of the trust-mark processes, e.g., Truste, WebTrust, Better Business Bureau™, and the Ernst & Young Cyber Process Certification™, are not inherently assertions of privacy. Rather, they relate to assertions by management with regard to specific policies or practices among which might be privacy. The specific privacy policy or practice, if it is included in the trust-mark process, need not actually promote privacy; rather, it may confirm that PII *is* sold, leased, or given to third parties.

Critical to the success of any trust-mark is the reputation of the organization granting such a mark. If I create a site, for example, www.privacy-is-I.org, and I create my own privacy assurance trust-mark, what is its value to the general public? Unless my advertising campaign causes the public to view my trust-mark as synonymous with privacy (and unless Web site owners actually use my trust-mark), it will have no value regardless of the quality of the privacy assertion it represents. In this regard, organizations with an existing reputation for "trust" and a recognized name in the marketplace begin with an advantage. Public accounting firms, security and privacy associations, consumer advocacy or arbitration groups, and financial institutions are among the organizations prepositioned to offer trust-mark services. However, the initial recognition as a potential guarantor of trust is an ephemeral advantage. It will not last unless the quality of the privacy assertion supports the trust-mark. The "goodness" associated with a brand (or trust-mark) is an emotional binding that may change rapidly and pejoratively. Well before the twentieth century, a cross with the ends bent at right angles was a good luck symbol. The swastika took on quite a different meaning after its use by the Nazis. If a trust-mark becomes associated with practices inimical to privacy or if a trust-mark becomes associated with an infamous failure of trust, its value transforms to a liability. Rehabilitation of such marks may prove infeasible.

TECHNOLOGY ISSUES

The Internet provides an inherently hostile environment for anonymity, privacy, and trust. You may feel that your PC acts as a shield behind which you may hide. After all, you do not see, hear, smell, taste, or touch what is at the other end of your electronic connection. This apparent anonymity may give you a sense of privacy that is unwarranted. The person allegedly responsible for the Melissa virus clearly did not believe that AOL could determine who he was. Just point your browser to http://www.junkbusters.com or to http://www.anonymizer.com/snoop.cgi and test to see what information your browser volunteers to a Web site. This is without the site attempting to exploit protocol or system weaknesses associated with some releases and implementations of ActiveX, JavaScript, and other add-ons, plug-ins, or downloaded processes. Further, a combination of technologies may allow an Internet service provider (ISP) or Internet gateway to which you establish a PPP connection to gather additional information through features such as Caller ID, PIN registry (captures telephone number), reverse directories, and route traces. Where a careful hacker can make this quite a rabbit chase, the normal user will not (and may not know how).

Much is discussed about the use of cryptography, e.g., Pretty Good Privacy (PGP), to protect identity. In fact, the use of public-key cryptography provides a means for improving the certainty with which an identity is known. After all, we use digital signatures to prove identity and to support nonrepudiation. Symmetric-key cryptography is better suited to protecting anonymity where each session key is a one-time-only key.

We may enlist technology to counter technological threats to privacy. For example, we may use services that randomize IP addresses and that strip IP addresses from messages. However, the protocols used in the Internet are rich with "identifiers" and applications we commonly use may embed serial numbers, our names and organizations' names, or similar identifiers. (For examples, use a text editor and look at documents produced by Word, WordPro, WordPerfect, Excel, Lotus 1-2-3, and your mail program.) To address the *transmission* of such documents, symmetric key cryptography — e.g., SSL a.k.a. TLS or virtual private network (VPN) or other tunneling protocol — may provide adequate privacy protection. If the document recipient is not to know your identity, you must go to much greater lengths.

TRUSTED AGENTS

When you allow an organization to store PII and potentially to use that data on your behalf, you have created an "agent" or representative (somewhat like the English model of the butler). This agent need only give out its identity to others, e.g., merchants, when it completes a transaction you have requested. To be a trusted agent, it must protect your PII and it must act only in accord with your directions. One company promoting a trusted agent service is @YourCommand. This company addresses the security of PII via an IdentitySafe™. It otherwise acts as an intermediary substituting its identity for the identity of its clients. Other companies provide some elements of privacy protection through various models of agency. However, the truly difficult problems arise in commerce where a product must be selected, purchased, shipped, and received without compromising more than the least amount of PII required. Payment and receipt mechanisms pose the most challenge. Merchants desire payment and the least risk of repudiation. That generally requires a degree of identity authentication at odds with anonymity, but feasible in almost any privacy model. Product delivery could always be accomplished through the use of mail drops, i.e., service providers whose location you can use instead of your own. However, to use your actual address for deliveries without giving it to the merchant (and potentially losing control over it) requires the use of a trusted agent or freight-forwarding company.

Wherever trust is needed, a guardian of trust is also needed. In the United States, businesses and investors rely on independent auditors. The use of independent audit organizations to attest to the "trusted agent's" policy and enforcement is one important means for ensuring customers that the site or service is, in fact, worthy of trust. Government agencies could also act in this role (although the size and scope of Internet commerce do not recommend it to this solution). A new breed of "trust brokers" may also step into this arena — companies that exist solely to provide anonymity or privacy services and otherwise do not participate in the commercial transaction.

SUMMARY

Many organizations offer services under the rubric of "anonymity" or "privacy." (See, for example, http://www.privacyrights.org/links.htm.) For commercial sites to have privacy policies is in vogue. However, few privacy policies actually assert that your personally identifiable information (PII) will remain secret and under your control. Many applications automatically insert PII into the documents they create. Popular Internet protocols at almost all layers provide data potentially linking the sender's identity to the message. These protocols may, in some cases, also provide potentially identifying information on the recipient (making return messages — even automatic responses to unsolicited messages — a possible source of information leakage). Providing privacy-friendly Internet services independent of individual Web sites and in spite of user naiveté remains a worthy goal. Commercial and governmental organizations will continue to ask the information security professional to investigate alleged security violations or incidence of fraud or abuse. Strong authentication and audit trails with excellent attribution make this easier. Freedom, however, cannot exist in an Orwellian world in which privacy does not exist. I hope that we as information security professionals can assist organizations in balancing security and privacy needs. I further hope that we can invent systems that will support anonymity without endangering security. Or, if we cannot, that we accept the security risks as a prudent price for a free society. I solicit your opinions. Please feel free to send e-mail to me at rspoore@ralph-s-poore.com.

Chapter 36
Web Certification: A Benchmark for Trustworthy Commerce

Benjamin Wright

One of the great and lasting effects of the Internet revolution is the triumph of the Transmission Control Protocol/Internet Protocol (TCP/IP) and the tools that support it, such as Web browsers. Internet technologies have become the common denominator in the networking world and the platform for the leading edge of electronic commerce. Folks yearn to use the public Internet and its offspring, private intranets, to transact business.

The problem is security. Although the market is awash with security products, businesses do not know what is and is not secure, and they do not know how much security is enough. ICSA Labs has crafted a solution in the form of a program for certifying the security of Web installations. The Web certification program will give qualifying Web site owners and administrators peace of mind that they have taken reasonable steps to ward off abuse and meet the duties expected of them by law.

The ICSA Labs sets baseline requirements that a Web site must satisfy to attain and maintain certification. Requirements include organizational policies, backup facilities, proper installation of encryption, a detailed checklist of loopholes that must be closed on the site (to thwart eavesdroppers), and so on. Certification also entails opening the site to on- and off-site inspection by qualified auditors.

Certification is not, however, a one-time exercise. It is a way of life. It expects Web administrators to perform and review their security housekeeping on a regular basis.

0-8493-1248-5/02/$0.00+$1.50
© 2002 by CRC Press LLC

The process of obtaining Web certification educates Web administrators and their staff about specific, real-world threats to their Web site, tells them in a concrete way how to close off those threats, and then informs them whether they have successfully done so.

Although vendors of some devices suggest that they solve all security worries, it is not realistic. No single device addresses all or even most risks, and absolute security is unattainable. What is attainable is a comprehensive routine of vigilance over one's Web environment, with a view to foreclosing all but the most determined and unlikely threats.

PROVING RECORDS

From a legal perspective, the greatest difference between electronic commerce and paper-based commerce is the medium on which transaction records are maintained. Whereas paper records are physical and inherently difficult to change, electronic records are not. Electronic records are believable only to the extent they reside in a controlled, secure environment. When the day comes that the security professional must prove to a court or an auditor (e.g., one representing a state sales tax authority) what occurred on the organization's Web site — who agreed to buy what, when, and at what price — complete archives and evidence of the integrity of the site are critical. Certification (e.g., ICSA Labs certification or AICPA's WebTrust) can aid Web administrators in their carrying burden of proof.

A computer record is admissible as evidence in legal proceedings on the condition that the environment in which the record was created and preserved can be shown. This principle is illustrated in the Iran-Contra trial of John Poindexter, a former National Security Advisor. The prosecutor in the trial alleged that Poindexter had, at a certain time in the past, transmitted to Oliver North an electronic mail message that encouraged North to lie in testimony before Congress.

To prove the existence and content of the message, the prosecutor needed to show the judge and jury a record of the message and persuade them it was credible. The prosecutor did this by retrieving a record, stored on magnetic tape by the technician who operated the network in question. Then, to show that this record could be believed (that it was not a fabrication), the prosecutor asked the technician to describe in court the many different security features in the e-mail system that tended to make the record reliable. These features included, among other things, the use of passwords and an audit trail and the employment of a record custodian (the technician himself) who had no incentive to falsify his records. Based on this description of the secure computing environment, the judge allowed the e-mail record to be admitted into evidence, which contributed to Poindexter's eventual conviction.

It is easier to establish a secure computing environment if the Web administrator has achieved and maintained a credible certification. Although nothing can guarantee that records will be believed, a history of certification helps show the user to be reasonably diligent in protecting the environment in which the records existed.

WEB ADMINISTRATOR'S DUTY OF CARE

Suppose the security administrator maintains a Web site on behalf of someone else, such as a merchant or an association of commodity brokers. In other words, he is an "agent" for his client. Under the law of agency, he could be held responsible for security breaches if he failed to prevent them.

Given this as the law, some might advise the Web administrator simply to take all the steps he can to foil any hackers who may target his site. The logical conclusion to that advice, however, is that he should unplug his site from the Internet. But, of course, that is silly. So, for the practical-minded Web administrator, the issue is, "What are the reasonable steps to take?" That is not an easy issue to resolve — very difficult to do in a vacuum. Web certification can lend guidance, as it can impart a sense for what is realistic security and what is not.

An agent using electronic systems must implement controls to prevent asset loss and system abuse. The precautions an agent could use to make records and preserve assets are endless. How far must the agent go? Agency law generally holds agents liable for their negligence, or failure to exercise the requisite standard of care. The law defines that as the "standard of care and ... skill which is standard ... for the kind of work which [the agent] is employed to perform and, in addition, ... any special skills that he has."[1]

Although it may be early to declare a specific certification the indisputable industry standard, the ICSA Labs Web Certification Program, in the absence of a universally recognized standard, can be very helpful in court. ICSA Labs certification reflects a disciplined, carefully considered approach. A court should respect that approach as substantial evidence of what constitutes standard or due diligence on the part of a Web professional.

Clearly, a court expects more of a stockbroker's site than it does of a hot dog vendor's. Web certification should evolve to account for that difference. But, in either case, Web administrators play from a stronger hand in court if they can show they began their security work from an authoritative baseline such as ICSA Labs Web Certification.

In the United States, another law bears remembering. The Foreign Corrupt Practices Act (FCPA) places sweeping recordkeeping and control requirements on every publicly held company. Such a company must "make and keep books, records, and accounts, which, in reasonable detail, accurately and fairly reflect the transactions and dispositions of assets of the" company. In addition, the company must do the following:

> Devise and maintain a system of internal accounting controls sufficient to provide reasonable assurances that
>
> (i) transactions are executed in accordance with management's general or specific authorization;
>
> (ii) transactions are recorded as necessary (I) to permit preparation of financial statements in conformity with generally accepted accounting principles or any other criteria applicable to such statements, and (II) to maintain accountability for assets;
>
> (iii) access to assets is permitted only in accordance with management's general or specific authorization; and
>
> (iv) the recorded accountability for assets is compared with existing assets at reasonable intervals and appropriate action is taken with respect to any differences.

In other words, the system by which the company makes and memorializes its commitments must be controlled and secured. In *SEC v. World-Wide Coin Investments, Ltd.*, a case finding a violation of the FCPA's recordkeeping and control provisions, the court observed the following about a hapless company named World-Wide Coin (a memorable name for a company bearing a lesson for firms doing business on the World Wide Web):

> [T]he internal recordkeeping and accounting controls of World-Wide [have] been sheer chaos. ... For example, there has been no procedure implemented with respect to writing checks: employees have had access to presigned checks; source documents were not required to be prepared when a check was drawn; employees have not been required to obtain approval before writing a check; and, even when a check was drawn to "cash," supporting documentation was usually not prepared to explain the purpose for which the check was drawn. [T]here has been no separation of duties in the areas of purchase and sales transactions, and valuation procedures for ending inventory. [E]mployees have not been required to write source documents relating to the purchase and sale of ... inventory. Because of this total lack of an audit trail with respect to these transactions and the disposition of World-Wide's assets, it has been virtually impossible to determine if an item has been sold at a profit or a loss.

These oversights exposed the company's executives to liability for misappropriation of corporate assets. An analogous lack of control in a Web commerce environment can yield the same result.

AUTHORITATIVE GUIDANCE

The ICSA Labs Web Certification Program serves a need that did not exist before. Although electronic commerce is not entirely new, its transaction on the Web is. Traditional electronic commerce transpired within the comfortable confines of closed, intimate trading communities. Commerce on the Web, on the other hand, is open to the world at large. Any of 100 million people may come knocking on a Web door, some with less-than-honorable intentions. The need for security is heightened, and the nature of the required response is different from the past. A Web certification program will enhance the Web staff's ability to identify the likely dangers and gauge whether the dangers are adequately addressed on the site.

Note

1. Restatement (Second) of Agency § 379.

Chapter 37
Get It in Writing

Rebecca Herold

One element in safeguarding a shared network is having each person with access to the network sign a confidentiality/security agreement. Requesting all network users to sign a confidentiality agreement (see Exhibit 1) helps to ensure that each network user understands corporate information security policies and commits to following them. It also provides evidence to customers and potential corporate investors that a company is committed to protecting the information with which it is entrusted. This practice should be considered a selling point for any company. Additionally, it provides a way to show state, federal, and international regulators that the company has implemented information security policies and that the network users and staff have agreed to follow them. In addition, it is also common for vendors and other business partners who must disclose confidential information to the company to require the company to have all their employees and business associates sign confidentiality agreements.

The confidentiality agreement should include security and control directives that will help protect the company from unauthorized use of the network and inappropriate use of network resources and commit the network users to take effective custodial care to protect the information to which they have access. The following issues should be addressed within such an agreement:

- *Confidentiality.* Persons signing the agreement indicate that they will take all prudent measures to protect the confidentiality and privacy of the information for which they are entrusted to process.
- *Standards and procedures.* Persons signing the agreement should be told either what the security and privacy standards are for the company or where the standards can be found. Signing the agreement will indicate a person's knowledge and understanding of the standards and procedures.
- *Auditing.* Persons signing the agreement indicate their acceptance that their systems and information files are the property of the company and are subject to monitoring or auditing at any time.

0-8493-1248-5/02/$0.00+$1.50
© 2002 by CRC Press LLC

- *Enforceability.* Signing the agreement should be a requirement for employment of new hires. The agreement should indicate that failure to follow the agreement is subject to disciplinary action up to and possibly including immediate termination of employment. Additionally, noncompliance could result in legal actions against the network user, depending on the situation.
- *Review.* Persons signing the agreement need to read the document carefully and understand their obligations resulting from their signatures.

One should work closely with the company's legal department to develop the company's confidentiality agreement to best fit its business environment and state, federal, and international legal requirements. Exhibit 1 is an example of a confidentiality agreement one could use as a starting point for creating one's own corporate confidentiality agreement.

Exhibit 1.　Sample Confidentiality Agreement

Please print or type.

Company of employment:

Person given access to corporate information assets or network services:

Manager:

Date:

I am employed by, or perform business services for, the company listed above. To fulfill my job responsibilities, I will need access the company's information or network systems. In consideration of being granted access by the company, I personally agree to the following:

1. **Confidential Information.** The company may disclose some of its confidential, private, or proprietary information ("Confidential Information") to me ("Recipient"). I understand Confidential Information includes all data, corporate information, materials, customer information, products, technology, computer programs, specifications, manuals, business plans, software, marketing plans, business plans, financial information, and other information disclosed or submitted, orally, in writing, or by any other media, to me by the company. I will consider all information as Confidential unless specifically labeled as Public.

2. **Recipient's Obligations.**
   A. I agree to consider Confidential Information as confidential, private, and proprietary to the company. I shall hold such Confidential Information in confidence, shall not use the Confidential Information other than for the purposes of my business with the company, and shall disclose it only to its officers, directors, or employees with a specific business need to know. I will not disclose, publish, or otherwise reveal any of the Confidential Information received from the company to any other party whatsoever except with the specific prior written authorization of appropriate company representatives.
   B. I shall not duplicate any Confidential Information furnished in tangible form except for purposes of this Agreement. Upon the request of the company, I will return all Confidential Information received in written or tangible form, including copies, or reproductions, or other media containing such Confidential Information, within ten (10) days of such request. I may also choose to destroy any documents or other media I developed for the company that contains Confidential Information. I shall provide a written certificate to the company regarding destruction within ten (10) days following destruction.
   C. I shall use only the login ID assigned to me to access the company's computers systems.
   D. I shall log off the company's computer systems immediately upon completion of each session of service.
   E. I shall not intentionally access any information or data other than that for which I have been specifically authorized to access.
   F. I shall not intentionally spread viruses or other malicious computer code to the company's computer systems.
   G. I shall read and follow the company's information security policies.

Exhibit 1.   Sample Confidentiality Agreement (continued)

H. I further agree that I will regard all knowledge and information that I may acquire from the company, or from the company's employees or consultants, or from access to the company's premises or computers systems, respecting the company's plans, strategies, inventions, designs, methods, systems, improvements, trade secrets, and other confidential, secret, or proprietary matters, for all time and for all purposes as strictly confidential and held in trust and solely for the company's benefit and use. I will not directly or indirectly disclose Confidential Information to any person other than to the company without the company's written permission. I understand and accept that the company's network and information systems are subject to monitoring at any time.

I. I shall have no obligation under this Agreement with respect to Confidential Information that is or becomes publicly available without breach of this Agreement by me; is rightfully received by me without obligations of confidentiality; or is developed by me without breach of this Agreement; provided, however, such Confidential Information will not be disclosed until thirty (30) days after written notice of intent to disclose is given to the company along with the asserted grounds for disclosure.

3. **Term.** My obligations described in this legally binding contract will be effective immediately upon the date this agreement is signed. Further, the obligation not to disclose will not be affected by bankruptcy, receivership, assignment, attachment or seizure procedures, whether initiated by or against me, nor by the rejection of any agreement between the company and me, by my trustee in bankruptcy, or by me as a debtor-in-possession or the equivalent of any of the foregoing under local law. I agree not to disclose my participation in this undertaking, the existence or terms and conditions of the Agreement, or the fact that discussions are being held with the company.

4. **No License.** Nothing contained herein shall be construed as granting or conferring any rights by license or otherwise in any Confidential Information. It is understood and agreed that neither party solicits any change in the organization, business practice, service, or products of the other party, and that the disclosure of Confidential Information will not be considered as any intent by a party to purchase any products or services of the other party nor as an encouragement to expend funds in development or research efforts. Confidential Information may pertain to prospective or unannounced products. I agree not to use any Confidential Information as a basis upon which to develop or have a third party develop a competing or similar product.

5. **Notices.** Any notice required by this Agreement, or given in connection with it, shall be in writing and shall be given to the appropriate party by personal delivery or by certified mail, postage prepaid, or recognized overnight delivery services.

My signature below signifies my personal obligation to be bound by the terms of this agreement.

_____   _____

Signature   Date

Section III
United States of America Laws and Issues

Chapter 38

Standards for Privacy of Individually Identifiable Health Information

45 Code of Federal Regulations Parts 160 and 164

The following is an overview that provides answers to general questions regarding the regulation entitled, Standards for Privacy of Individually Identifiable Health Information (the Privacy Rule), promulgated by the Department of Health and Human Services (HHS), and process for modifications to that rule. Detailed guidance on specific requirements in the regulation is presented in subsequent sections, each of which addresses a different standard.

The Privacy Rule provides the first comprehensive federal protection for the privacy of health information. All segments of the health care industry have expressed their support for the objective of enhanced patient privacy in the health care system. At the same time, HHS and most parties agree that privacy protections must not interfere with a patient's access to or the quality of health care delivery.

The guidance provided in this section and those that follow is meant to communicate as clearly as possible the privacy policies contained in the rule. Each section has a short summary of a particular standard in the Privacy Rule, followed by "Frequently Asked Questions" about that provision. In some cases, the guidance identifies areas of the Privacy Rule where a modification or change to the rule is necessary. These areas are summarized below in response to the question "What changes might you make to the final rule?" and discussed in more detail in the subsequent sections of this guidance. We emphasize that this guidance document is only the first of several technical assistance materials that we will issue to provide clarification and help covered entities implement the rule. We anticipate that there will be many questions that will arise on an ongoing basis which we will need to answer in future guidance. In addition, the Department will issue proposed modifications as necessary in one or more rulemakings to ensure that patients' privacy needs are appropriately met. The Department plans to work expeditiously to address these additional questions and propose modifications as necessary.

Frequently Asked Questions

Q: What does this regulation do?

A: The Privacy Rule became effective on April 14, 2001. Most health plans and health care providers that are covered by the new rule must comply with the new requirements by April 2003.

The Privacy Rule for the first time creates national standards to protect individuals' medical records and other personal health information.

- It gives patients more control over their health information.
- It sets boundaries on the use and release of health records.
- It establishes appropriate safeguards that health care providers and others must achieve to protect the privacy of health information.
- It holds violators accountable, with civil and criminal penalties that can be imposed if they violate patients' privacy rights.
- And it strikes a balance when public responsibility requires disclosure of some forms of data — for example, to protect public health.

For patients — it means being able to make informed choices when seeking care and reimbursement for care based on how personal health information may be used.

- It enables patients to find out how their information may be used and what disclosures of their information have been made.
- It generally limits release of information to the minimum reasonably needed for the purpose of the disclosure.
- It gives patients the right to examine and obtain a copy of their own health records and request corrections.

Q: Why is this regulation needed?

A: In enacting the Health Insurance Portability and Accountability Act of 1996 (HIPAA), Congress mandated the establishment of standards for the privacy of individually identifiable health information.

When it comes to personal information that moves across hospitals, doctors' offices, insurers or third party payers, and state lines, our country has relied on a patchwork of federal and state laws. Under the current patchwork of laws, personal health information can be distributed — without either notice or consent — for reasons that have nothing to do with a patient's medical treatment or health care reimbursement. Patient information held by a health plan may be passed on to a lender who may then deny the patient's application for a home mortgage or a credit card — or to an employer who may use it in personnel decisions. The Privacy Rule establishes a federal floor of safeguards to protect the confidentiality of medical information. State laws which provide stronger privacy protections will continue to apply over and above the new federal privacy standards.

Health care providers have a strong tradition of safeguarding private health information. But in today's world, the old system of paper records in locked filing cabinets is not enough. With information broadly held and transmitted electronically, the rule provides clear standards for all parties regarding protection of personal health information.

Q: **What does this regulation require the average provider or health plan to do?**

A: For the average health care provider or health plan, the Privacy Rule requires activities, such as:

- Providing information to patients about their privacy rights and how their information can be used.
- Adopting clear privacy procedures for its practice, hospital, or plan.
- Training employees so that they understand the privacy procedures.
- Designating an individual to be responsible for seeing that the privacy procedures are adopted and followed.
- Securing patient records containing individually identifiable health information so that they are not readily available to those who do not need them.

Responsible health care providers and businesses already take many of the kinds of steps required by the rule to protect patients' privacy. Covered entities of all types and sizes are required to comply with the final Privacy Rule. To ease the burden of complying with the new requirements, the Privacy Rule gives needed flexibility for providers and plans to create their own privacy procedures, tailored to fit their size and needs. The scalability of the rules provides a more efficient and appropriate means of safeguarding protected health information than would any single standard. For example,

- The privacy official at a small physician practice may be the office manager, who will have other non-privacy-related duties; the privacy official at a large health plan may be a full-time position, and may have the regular support and advice of a privacy staff or board.

451

- The training requirement may be satisfied by a small physician practice's providing each new member of the workforce with a copy of its privacy policies and documenting that new members have reviewed the policies; whereas a large health plan may provide training through live instruction, video presentations, or interactive software programs.
- The policies and procedures of small providers may be more limited under the rule than those of a large hospital or health plan, based on the volume of health information maintained and the number of interactions with those within and outside of the health care system.

Q: Who must comply with these new privacy standards?

A: As required by Congress in HIPAA, the Privacy Rule covers health plans, health care clearinghouses, and those health care providers who conduct certain financial and administrative transactions electronically. These electronic transactions are those for which standards are required to be adopted by the Secretary under HIPAA, such as electronic billing and fund transfers. These entities (collectively called "covered entities") are bound by the new privacy standards even if they contract with others (called "business associates") to perform some of their essential functions. The law does not give HHS the authority to regulate other types of private businesses or public agencies through this regulation. For example, HHS does not have the authority to regulate employers, life insurance companies, or public agencies that deliver social security or welfare benefits. The "Business Associate" section of this guidance provides a more detailed discussion of the covered entities' responsibilities when they engage others to perform essential functions or services for them.

Q: When will covered entities have to meet these standards?

A: As Congress required in HIPAA, most covered entities have two full years from the date that the regulation took effect — or, until April 14, 2003 — to come into compliance with these standards. Under the law, small health plans will have three full years — or, until April 14, 2004 — to come into compliance.

The HHS Office for Civil Rights (OCR) will provide assistance to help covered entities prepare to comply with the rule. OCR maintains a Web site with information on the new regulation, including guidance for industry, such as these frequently asked questions, at http://www.hhs.gov/ocr/hipaa/.

Q: Do you expect to make any changes to this rule before the compliance date?

A: We can and will issue proposed modifications to correct any unintended negative effects of the Privacy Rule on health care quality or on access to such care.

In February 2001, Secretary Thompson requested public comments on the final rule to help HHS assess the rule's real-world impact in health care delivery. During the 30-day comment period, we received more than 11,000 letters or comments — including some petitions with thousands of names. These comments are helping to guide the Department's efforts to clarify areas of the rule to eliminate uncertainties and to help covered entities begin their implementation efforts.

Q: What changes might you make in the final rule?

A: We continue to review the input received during the recent public comment period to determine what changes are appropriate to ensure that the rule protects patient privacy as intended without harming consumers' access to care or the quality of that care.

Examples of standards in the Privacy Rule for which we will propose changes are:

- *Phoned-In Prescriptions* — A change will permit pharmacists to fill prescriptions phoned in by a patient's doctor before obtaining the patient's written consent (see the "Consent" section of this guidance for more discussion).
- *Referral Appointments* — A change will permit direct treatment providers receiving a first time patient referral to schedule appointments, surgery, or other procedures before obtaining the patient's signed consent (see the "Consent" section of this guidance for more discussion).
- *Allowable Communications* — A change will increase the confidence of covered entities that they are free to engage in whatever communications are required for quick, effective, high quality health care, including routine oral communications with family members, treatment discussions with staff involved in coordination of patient care, and using patient names to locate them in waiting areas (see the "Oral Communications" section of this guidance for more discussion).
- *Minimum Necessary Scope* — A change will increase covered entities' confidence that certain common practices, such as use of sign-up sheets and X-ray lightboards, and maintenance of patient medical charts at bedside, are not prohibited under the rule (see the "Minimum Necessary" section of this guidance for more discussion).

In addition, HHS may reevaluate the Privacy Rule to ensure that parents have appropriate access to information about the health and well-being of their children. This issue is discussed further in the "Parents and Minors" section of this guidance.

Other changes to the Privacy Rule also may be considered as appropriate.

Q: How will you make any changes?

A: Any changes to the final rule must be made in accordance with the Administrative Procedures Act (APA). HHS intends to comply with the APA by publishing its rule changes in the *Federal Register* through a Notice of Proposed Rulemaking and will invite comment from the public. After reviewing and addressing those comments, HHS will issue a final rule to implement appropriate modifications.

Congress specifically authorized HHS to make appropriate modifications in the first year after the final rule took effect in order to ensure the rule could be properly implemented in the real world. We are working as quickly as we can to identify where modifications are needed and what corrections need to be made so as to give covered entities as much time as possible to implement the rule. Covered entities can and should begin the process of implementing the privacy standards in order to meet their compliance dates.

CONSENT [45 CFR § 164.506]

Background

The Privacy Rule establishes a federal requirement that most doctors, hospitals, or other health care providers obtain a patient's written consent before using or disclosing the patient's personal health information to carry out treatment, payment, or health care operations (TPO). Today, many health care providers, for professional or ethical reasons, routinely obtain a patient's consent for disclosure of information to insurance companies or for other purposes. The Privacy Rule builds on these practices by establishing a uniform standard for certain health care providers to obtain their patients' consent for uses and disclosures of health information about the patient to carry out TPO.

General Provisions

- Patient consent is required before a covered health care provider that has a direct treatment relationship with the patient may use or disclose protected health information (PHI) for purposes of TPO. Exceptions to this standard are shown in the next bullet.
- Uses and disclosures for TPO may be permitted without prior consent in an emergency, when a provider is required by law to treat the individual, or when there are substantial communication barriers.

- Health care providers that have indirect treatment relationships with patients (such as laboratories that only interact with physicians and not patients), health plans, and health care clearinghouses may use and disclose PHI for purposes of TPO without obtaining a patient's consent. The rule permits such entities to obtain consent, if they choose.
- If a patient refuses to consent to the use or disclosure of their PHI to carry out TPO, the health care provider may refuse to treat the patient.
- A patient's written consent need only be obtained by a provider one time.
- The consent document may be brief and may be written in general terms. It must be written in plain language, inform the individual that information may be used and disclosed for TPO, state the patient's rights to review the provider's privacy notice, to request restrictions and to revoke consent, and be dated and signed by the individual (or his or her representative).

Individual Rights

- An individual may revoke consent in writing, except to the extent that the covered entity has taken action in reliance on the consent.
- An individual may request restrictions on uses or disclosures of health information for TPO. The covered entity need not agree to the restriction requested, but is bound by any restriction to which it agrees.
- An individual must be given a notice of the covered entity's privacy practices and may review that notice prior to signing a consent.

Administrative Issues

- A covered entity must retain the signed consent for 6 years from the date it was last in effect. The Privacy Rule does not dictate the form in which these consents are to be retained by the covered entity.
- Certain integrated covered entities may obtain one joint consent for multiple entities.
- If a covered entity obtains consent and also receives an authorization to disclose PHI for TPO, the covered entity may disclose information only in accordance with the more restrictive document, unless the covered entity resolves the conflict with the individual.
- Transition provisions allow providers to rely on consents received prior to April 14, 2003 (the compliance date of the Privacy Rule for most covered entities), for uses and disclosures of health information obtained prior to that date.

Frequently Asked Questions

Q: **Are health plans or clearinghouses required to obtain an individual's consent to use or disclose PHI to carry out TPO?**

A: No. Health plans and clearinghouses may use and disclose PHI for these purposes without obtaining consent. These entities are permitted to obtain consent. If they choose to seek individual consent for these uses and disclosures, the consent must meet the standards, requirements, and implementation specifications for consents set forth under the rule.

Q: **Can a pharmacist use PHI to fill a prescription that was telephoned in by a patient's physician if the patient is a new patient to the pharmacy and has not yet provided written consent to the pharmacy?**

A: The Privacy Rule, as written, does not permit this activity without prior patient consent. It poses a problem for first-time users of a particular pharmacy or pharmacy chain. The Department of Health and Human Services did not intend the rule to interfere with a pharmacist's normal activities in this way. The Secretary is aware of this problem, and will propose modifications to fix it to ensure ready patient access to high quality health care.

Q: **Can direct treatment providers, such as a specialist or hospital, to whom a patient is referred for the first time, use PHI to set up appointments or schedule surgery or other procedures before obtaining the patient's written consent?**

A: As in the pharmacist example above, the Privacy Rule, as written, does not permit uses of PHI prior to obtaining the patient's written consent for TPO. This unintended problem potentially exists in any circumstance when a patient's first contact with a direct treatment provider is not in person. As noted above, the Secretary is aware of this problem and will propose modifications to fix it.

Q: **Will the consent requirement restrict the ability of providers to consult with other providers about a patient's condition?**

A: No. A provider with a direct treatment relationship with a patient would have to have initially obtained consent to use that patient's health information for treatment purposes. Consulting with another health care provider about the patient's case falls within the definition of "treatment" and, therefore, is permissible. If the provider being consulted does not otherwise have a direct treatment relationship with the patient, that provider does not need to obtain the patient's consent to engage in the consultation.

Q: **Does a pharmacist have to obtain a consent under the Privacy Rule in order to provide advice about over-the-counter medicines to customers?**

A: No. A pharmacist may provide advice about over-the-counter medicines without obtaining the customers' prior consent, provided that the pharmacist does not create or keep a record of any PHI. In this case, the only interaction or disclosure of information is a conversation between the pharmacist and the customer. The pharmacist may disclose PHI about the customer to the customer without obtaining his or her consent (§ 164.502(a)(1)(i)), but may not otherwise use or disclose that information.

Q: **Can a patient have a friend or family member pick up a prescription for her?**

A: Yes. A pharmacist may use professional judgment and experience with common practice to make reasonable inferences of the patient's best interest in allowing a person, other than the patient, to pick up a prescription (see § 164.510(b)). For example, the fact that a relative or friend arrives at a pharmacy and asks to pick up a specific prescription for an individual effectively verifies that he or she is involved in the individual's care, and the rule allows the pharmacist to give the filled prescription to the relative or friend. The individual does not need to provide the pharmacist with the names of such persons in advance.

Q: **The rule provides an exception to the prior consent requirement for "emergency treatment situations." How will a provider know when the situation is an "emergency treatment situation" and, therefore, is exempt from the Privacy Rule's prior consent requirement?**

A: Health care providers must exercise their professional judgment to determine whether obtaining a consent would interfere with the timely delivery of necessary health care. If, based on professional judgment, a provider reasonably believes at the time the patient presents for treatment that a delay involved in obtaining the patient's consent to use or disclose information would compromise the patient's care, the provider may use or disclose PHI that was obtained during the emergency treatment, without prior consent, to carry out TPO. The provider must attempt to obtain consent as soon as reasonably practicable after the provision of treatment. If the provider is able to obtain the patient's consent to use or disclose information before providing care, without compromising the patient's care, we require the provider to do so.

Q: **Does the exception to the consent requirement regarding substantial barriers to communication with the individual affect**

457

requirements under Title VI of the Civil Rights Act of 1964 or the Americans with Disabilities Act?

A: No. The provision of the Privacy Rule regarding substantial barriers to communication does not affect covered entities' obligations under Title VI or the Americans with Disabilities Act. Entities that are covered by these statutes must continue to meet the requirements of the statutes. The Privacy Rule works in conjunction with these laws to remove impediments to access to necessary health care for all individuals.

Q: **What is the difference between "consent" and "authorization" under the Privacy Rule?**

A: A consent is a general document that gives health care providers, which have a direct treatment relationship with a patient, permission to use and disclose all PHI for TPO. It gives permission only to that provider, not to any other person. Health care providers may condition the provision of treatment on the individual providing this consent. One consent may cover all uses and disclosures for TPO by that provider, indefinitely. A consent need not specify the particular information to be used or disclosed, nor the recipients of disclosed information.

Only doctors or other health care providers with a direct treatment relationship with a patient are required to obtain consent. Generally, a "direct treatment provider" is one that treats a patient directly, rather than based on the orders of another provider, and/or provides health care services or test results directly to patients. Other health care providers, health plans, and health care clearinghouses may use or disclose information for TPO without consent, or may choose to obtain a consent.

An authorization is a more customized document that gives covered entities permission to use specified PHI for specified purposes, which are generally other than TPO, or to disclose PHI to a third party specified by the individual. Covered entities may not condition treatment or coverage on the individual providing an authorization. An authorization is more detailed and specific than a consent. It covers only the uses and disclosures and only the PHI stipulated in the authorization; it has an expiration date; and, in some cases, it also states the purpose for which the information may be used or disclosed.

An authorization is required for use and disclosure of PHI not otherwise allowed by the rule. In general, this means an authorization is required for purposes that are not part of TPO and not described in § 164.510 (uses and disclosures that require an opportunity for the individual to agree or to object) or § 164.512 (uses and disclosures for which consent, authorization, or an opportunity to agree or to object is not required). Situations in which an authorization is required for TPO purposes are identified and discussed in the next question.

All covered entities, not just direct treatment providers, must obtain an authorization to use or disclose PHI for these purposes. For example, a covered entity would need an authorization from individuals to sell a patient mailing list, to disclose information to an employer for employment decisions, or to disclose information for eligibility for life insurance. A covered entity will never need to obtain both an individual's consent and authorization for a single use or disclosure. However, a provider may have to obtain consent and authorization from the same patient for different uses or disclosures. For example, an obstetrician may, under the consent obtained from the patient, send an appointment reminder to the patient, but would need authorization from the patient to send her name and address to a company marketing a diaper service.

Q: **Would a covered entity ever need an authorization rather than a consent for uses or disclosures of PHI for TPO?**

A: Yes. The Privacy Rule requires providers to obtain authorization and not consent to use or disclose PHI maintained in psychotherapy notes for treatment by persons other than the originator of the notes, for payment, or for health care operations purposes, except as specified in the Privacy Rule (§ 164.508(a)(2)). In addition, because the consent is only for a use or disclosure of PHI for the TPO purposes of the covered entity obtaining the consent, an authorization is also required if the disclosure is for the TPO purposes of an entity other than the provider who obtained the consent. For example, a health plan seeking payment for a particular service from a second health plan, such as in coordination of benefits or secondary payer situations, may need PHI from a physician who rendered the health care services. In this case, the provider typically has been paid, and the transaction is between the plans. Since the provider's disclosure is for the TPO purposes of the plan, it would not be covered by the provider's consent. Rather, an authorization, and not a consent, would be the proper document for the plan to use when requesting such a disclosure.

Q: **Will health care providers be required to determine whether another covered entity has a more restrictive consent form before disclosing information to that entity for TPO purposes?**

A: No. Generally, a consent permits only the covered entity that obtains the consent to use or disclose PHI for its own TPO purposes. Under the Privacy Rule, one covered entity is not bound by a consent or any restrictions on that consent agreed to by another covered entity, with one exception. A covered entity would be bound by the consent of another covered entity if the entities use a "joint consent," as permitted by the Privacy Rule (§ 164.506(f)).

In addition, it is possible for several entities to choose to be treated as a single covered entity under the rule, as "affiliated entities." Because affiliated entities are considered to be one covered entity under the rule, there would be only one consent and each entity would be bound by that consent (§ 164.504(d)).

Q: What is the interaction between "consent" and "notice"?

A: The consent and the notice of privacy practices are two distinct documents. A consent document is brief (may be less than one page). It must refer to the notice and must inform the individual that he has the opportunity to review the notice prior to signing the consent. The Privacy Rule does not require that the individual read the notice or that the covered entity explain each item in the notice before the individual provides consent. We expect that some patients will simply sign the consent while others will read the notice carefully and discuss some of the practices with the covered entity.

Q: May consent for use or disclosure of PHI be provided electronically?

A: Yes. The covered entity may choose to obtain and store consents in paper or electronic form, provided that the consent meets all of the requirements under the Privacy Rule, including that it be signed by the individual. Paper is not required.

Q: Must a covered entity verify a signature on a consent form if the individual is not present when he signs it?

A: No.

Q: May consent be obtained by a health care provider only one time if there is a single connected course of treatment involving multiple visits?

A: Yes. A health care provider needs to obtain consent from a patient for use or disclosure of PHI only one time. This is true regardless of whether there is a connected course of treatment or treatment for unrelated conditions. A provider will need to obtain a new consent from a patient only if the patient has revoked the consent between treatments.

Q: If an individual consents to the use or disclosure of PHI for TPO purposes, obtains a health care service, and then revokes consent before the provider bills for such service, is the provider precluded from billing for such service?

A: No. A health care provider that provides a health care service to an individual after obtaining consent from the individual may bill for such service even if the individual immediately revokes consent after the service has been provided. The Privacy Rule requires that an individual be permitted to revoke consent, but provides that the revocation is not effective to the extent that the health care provider has acted in reliance on the consent. Where the provider has obtained a consent and provided a health care service pursuant to that consent with the expectation that he or she could bill for the service, the health care provider has acted in reliance on the consent. The revocation would not interfere with the billing or reimbursement for that care.

Q: **If covered providers that are affiliated or part of an organized health care arrangement are located in different states with different laws regarding uses and disclosures of health information (e.g., a chain of pharmacies), do they need to obtain a consent in each state that the patient obtains treatment?**

A: No. The consent is general and only needs to be obtained by a covered entity (or by affiliated entities or entities that are part of an organized health care arrangement) one time. The Privacy Rule does not require that the consent include any details about state law, and therefore, does not require different consent forms in each state. State law may impose additional requirements for consent forms on covered entities.

Q: **Must a revocation of a consent be in writing?**

A: Yes.

Q: **The Privacy Rule permits a covered entity to continue to use or disclose health information which it has on the compliance date pursuant to express legal permission obtained from an individual prior to the compliance date. Is a form, signed by a patient prior to the compliance date of the rule, that permits a provider to use or disclose information for the limited purpose of payment sufficient to meet these transition provision requirements?**

A: Yes. A provider that obtains permission from a patient prior to the compliance date to use or disclose information for payment purposes may use the PHI about that patient collected pursuant to that permission for purposes of TPO. Under the transition provisions, if prior to the compliance date, a provider obtained a consent for the use or disclosure of health information for any one of the TPO purposes, the provider may use the health information collected pursuant to that consent for all three purposes after the compliance date (§ 164.532(b)). Thus, a provider that obtained consent for use or disclosure for billing purposes would be able to draw on the data obtained prior to the compliance date and covered by the consent form for all TPO activities to the extent not expressly excluded by the terms of the consent.

Q: **Are health plans and health care clearinghouses required by the Privacy Rule to have some form of express legal permission to use and disclose health information obtained prior to the compliance date for TPO purposes?**

A: No. Health plans and health care clearinghouses are not required to have express legal permission from individuals to use or disclose health information obtained prior to the compliance date for their own TPO purposes.

MINIMUM NECESSARY [45 CFR §§ 164.502(B), 164.514(D)]

General Requirement

The Privacy Rule generally requires covered entities to take reasonable steps to limit the use or disclosure of, and requests for protected health information (PHI) to the minimum necessary to accomplish the intended purpose. The minimum necessary provisions do not apply to the following:

- Disclosures to or requests by a health care provider for treatment purposes.
- Disclosures to the individual who is the subject of the information.
- Uses or disclosures made pursuant to an authorization requested by the individual.
- Uses or disclosures required for compliance with the standardized Health Insurance Portability and Accountability Act (HIPAA) transactions.
- Disclosures to the Department of Health and Human Services (HHS) when disclosure of information is required under the rule for enforcement purposes.
- Uses or disclosures that are required by other law.

The implementation specifications for this provision require a covered entity to develop and implement policies and procedures appropriate for its own organization, reflecting the entity's business practices and workforce. We understand this guidance will not answer all questions pertaining to the minimum necessary standard, especially as applied to specific industry practices. As more questions arise with regard to application of the minimum necessary standard to particular circumstances, we will provide more detailed guidance and clarification on this issue.

Uses and Disclosures of, and Requests for PHI

For uses of PHI, the policies and procedures must identify the persons or classes of persons within the covered entity who need access to the information to carry out their job duties, the categories or types of PHI needed, and conditions appropriate to such access. For example, hospitals may implement policies that permit doctors, nurses, or others involved in treatment to have access to the entire medical record, as needed. Case-by-case review of each use is not required. Where the entire medical record is necessary, the covered entity's policies and procedures must state so explicitly and include a justification.

For routine or recurring requests and disclosures, the policies and procedures may be standard protocols and must limit PHI disclosed or requested to that which is the minimum necessary for that particular type of disclosure or request. Individual review of each disclosure or request is not required.

For non-routine disclosures, covered entities must develop reasonable criteria for determining, and limiting disclosure to, only the minimum amount of PHI necessary to accomplish the purpose of a non-routine disclosure. Non-routine disclosures must be reviewed on an individual basis in accordance with these criteria. When making non-routine requests for PHI, the covered entity must review each request so as to ask for only that information reasonably necessary for the purpose of the request.

Reasonable Reliance

In certain circumstances, the Privacy Rule permits a covered entity to rely on the judgment of the party requesting the disclosure as to the minimum amount of information that is needed. Such reliance must be reasonable under the particular circumstances of the request. This reliance is permitted when the request is made by:

- A public official or agency for a disclosure permitted under § 164.512 of the rule.
- Another covered entity.
- A professional who is a workforce member or business associate of the covered entity holding the information.
- A researcher with appropriate documentation from an Institutional Review Board (IRB) or Privacy Board.

The rule does not require such reliance, however, and the covered entity always retains discretion to make its own minimum necessary determination for disclosures to which the standard applies.

Treatment Settings

We understand that medical information must be conveyed freely and quickly in treatment settings, and thus understand the heightened concern that covered entities have about how the minimum necessary standard applies in such settings. Therefore, we are taking the following steps to clarify the application of the minimum necessary standard in treatment settings. First, we clarify some of the issues here, including the application of minimum necessary to specific practices, so that covered entities may begin implementation of the Privacy Rule. Second, we will propose corresponding changes to the regulation text, to increase the confidence of covered entities that they are free to engage in whatever communications are required for quick, effective, high quality health care. We understand that issues of this importance need to be addressed directly and clearly to eliminate any ambiguities.

Frequently Asked Questions

Q: **How are covered entities expected to determine what is the minimum necessary information that can be used, disclosed, or requested for a particular purpose?**

A: The Privacy Rule requires a covered entity to make reasonable efforts to limit use, disclosure of, and requests for PHI to the minimum necessary to accomplish the intended purpose. To allow covered entities the flexibility to address their unique circumstances, the rule requires covered entities to make their own assessment of what PHI is reasonably necessary for a particular purpose, given the characteristics of their business and workforce, and to implement policies and procedures accordingly. This is not a strict standard and covered entities need not limit information uses or disclosures to those that are absolutely needed to serve the purpose. Rather, this is a reasonableness standard that calls for an approach consistent with the best practices and guidelines already used by many providers today to limit the unnecessary sharing of medical information.

The minimum necessary standard is intended to make covered entities evaluate their practices and enhance protections as needed to prevent unnecessary or inappropriate access to PHI. It is intended to reflect and be consistent with, not override, professional judgment and standards. Therefore, we expect that covered entities will utilize the input of prudent professionals involved in health care activities when developing policies and procedures that appropriately will limit access to personal health information without sacrificing the quality of health care.

Q: **Won't the minimum necessary restrictions impede the delivery of quality health care by preventing or hindering necessary exchanges of patient medical information among health care providers involved in treatment?**

A: No. Disclosures for treatment purposes (including requests for disclosures) between health care providers are explicitly exempted from the minimum necessary requirements.

The Privacy Rule provides the covered entity with substantial discretion as to how to implement the minimum necessary standard, and appropriately and reasonably limit access to the use of identifiable health information within the covered entity. The rule recognizes that the covered entity is in the best position to know and determine who in its workforce needs access to personal health information to perform their jobs. Therefore, the covered entity can develop role-based access policies that allow its health care providers and other employees, as appropriate, access to patient information, including entire medical records, for treatment purposes.

Q: **Do the minimum necessary requirements prohibit medical residents, medical students, nursing students, and other medical trainees from accessing patients' medical information in the course of their training?**

A: No. The definition of "health care operations" in the rule provides for "conducting training programs in which students, trainees, or practitioners in areas of health care learn under supervision to practice or improve their skills as health care providers." Covered entities can shape their policies and procedures for minimum necessary uses and disclosures to permit medical trainees access to patients' medical information, including entire medical records.

Q: **Must minimum necessary be applied to disclosures to third parties that are authorized by an individual?**

A: No, unless the authorization was requested by a covered entity for its own purposes. The Privacy Rule exempts from the minimum necessary requirements most uses or disclosures that are authorized by an individual. This includes authorizations covered entities may receive directly from third parties, such as life, disability, or casualty insurers pursuant to the patient's application for or claim under an insurance policy. For example, if a covered health care provider receives an individual's authorization to disclose medical information to a life insurer for underwriting purposes, the provider is permitted to disclose the information requested on the authorization without making any minimum necessary determination. The authorization must meet the requirements of § 164.508.

However, minimum necessary does apply to authorizations requested by the covered entity for its own purposes (see § 164.508(d), (e), and (f)).

Q: **Are providers required to make a minimum necessary determination to disclose to federal or state agencies, such as the Social**

Security Administration (SSA) or its affiliated state agencies, for individuals' applications for federal or state benefits?

A: No. These disclosures must be authorized by an individual and, therefore, are exempt from the minimum necessary requirements. Further, use of the provider's own authorization form is not required. Providers can accept an agency's authorization form as long as it meets the requirements of § 164.508 of the rule. For example, disclosures to SSA (or its affiliated state agencies) for purposes of determining eligibility for disability benefits are currently made subject to an individual's completed SSA authorization form. After the compliance date, the current process may continue subject only to modest changes in the SSA authorization form to conform to the requirements in § 164.508.

Q: **Doesn't the minimum necessary standard conflict with the Transactions standards? Does minimum necessary apply to the standard transactions?**

A: No, because the Privacy Rule exempts from the minimum necessary standard any uses or disclosures that are required for compliance with the applicable requirements of the subchapter. This includes all data elements that are required or situationally required in the standard transactions. However, in many cases, covered entities have significant discretion as to the information included in these transactions. This standard does apply to those optional data elements.

Q: **Does the rule strictly prohibit use, disclosure, or requests of an entire medical record? Does the rule prevent use, disclosure, or requests of entire medical records without case-by-case justification?**

A: No. The Privacy Rule does not prohibit use, disclosure, or requests of an entire medical record. A covered entity may use, disclose, or request an entire medical record, without a case-by-case justification, if the covered entity has documented in its policies and procedures that the entire medical record is the amount reasonably necessary for certain identified purposes. For uses, the policies and procedures would identify those persons or classes of person in the workforce that need to see the entire medical record and the conditions, if any, that are appropriate for such access. Policies and procedures for routine disclosures and requests and the criteria used for non-routine disclosures would identify the circumstances under which disclosing or requesting the entire medical record is reasonably necessary for particular purposes. In making non-routine requests, the covered entity may also establish and utilize criteria to assist indetermining when to request the entire medical record.

The Privacy Rule does not require that a justification be provided with respect to each distinct medical record.

Finally, no justification is needed in those instances where the minimum necessary standard does not apply, such as disclosures to or requests by a health care provider for treatment or disclosures to the individual.

Q: In limiting access, are covered entities required to completely restructure existing workflow systems, including redesigns of office space and upgrades of computer systems, in order to comply with the minimum necessary requirements?

A: No. The basic standard for minimum necessary uses requires that covered entities make reasonable efforts to limit access to PHI to those in the workforce that need access based on their roles in the covered entity.

The Department generally does not consider facility redesigns as necessary to meet the reasonableness standard for minimum necessary uses. However, covered entities may need to make certain adjustments to their facilities to minimize access, such as isolating and locking file cabinets or records rooms, or providing additional security, such as passwords, on computers maintaining personal information.

Covered entities should also take into account their ability to configure their record systems to allow access to only certain fields, and the practicality of organizing systems to allow this capacity. For example, it may not be reasonable for a small, solo practitioner who has largely a paper-based records system to limit access of employees with certain functions to only limited fields in a patient record, while other employees have access to the complete record. Alternatively, a hospital with an electronic patient record system may reasonably implement such controls and, therefore, may choose to limit access in this manner to comply with the rule.

Q: Do the minimum necessary requirements prohibit covered entities from maintaining patient medical charts at bedside, require that covered entities shred empty prescription vials, or require that X-ray light boards be isolated?

A: No. The minimum necessary standards do not require that covered entities take any of these specific measures. Covered entities must, in accordance with other provisions of the Privacy Rule, take reasonable precautions to prevent inadvertent or unnecessary disclosures. For example, while the Privacy Rule does not require that X-ray boards be totally isolated from all other functions, it does require covered entities to take reasonable precautions to protect X-rays from being accessible to the public. We understand that these and similar matters are of special concern to many covered entities, and we will propose modifications to the rule to increase covered entities' confidence that these practices are not prohibited.

Q: Will doctors' and physicians' offices be allowed to continue using sign-in sheets in waiting rooms?

A: We did not intend to prohibit the use of sign-in sheets, but understand that the Privacy Rule is ambiguous about this common practice. We, therefore, intend to propose modifications to the rule to clarify that this and similar practices are permissible.

Q: What happens when a covered entity believes that a request is seeking more than the minimum necessary PHI?

A: In such a situation, the Privacy Rule requires a covered entity to limit the disclosure to the minimum necessary as determined by the disclosing entity. Where the rule permits covered entities to rely on the judgment of the person requesting the information, and if such reliance is reasonable despite the covered entity's concerns, the covered entity may make the disclosure as requested.

Nothing in the Privacy Rule prevents a covered entity from discussing its concerns with the person making the request, and negotiating an information exchange that meets the needs of both parties. Such discussions occur today and may continue after the compliance date of the Privacy Rule.

ORAL COMMUNICATIONS [45 CFR §§ 160.103, 164.501]

Background

The Privacy Rule applies to individually identifiable health information in all forms, electronic, written, oral, and any other. Coverage of oral (spoken) information ensures that information retains protections when discussed or read aloud from a computer screen or a written document. If oral communications were not covered, any health information could be disclosed to any person, so long as the disclosure was spoken.

Providers and health plans understand the sensitivity of oral information. For example, many hospitals already have confidentiality policies and concrete procedures for addressing privacy, such as posting signs in elevators that remind employees to protect patient confidentiality.

We also understand that oral communications must occur freely and quickly in treatment settings, and thus understand the heightened concern that covered entities have about how the rule applies. Therefore, we are taking a two-step approach to clarifying the regulation with respect to these communications. First, we provide some clarification of these issues here, so that covered entities may begin implementing the rule by the compliance date. Second, we will propose appropriate changes to the regulation text to clarify the regulatory basis for the policies discussed below in order to minimize confusion and to increase the confidence of covered entities that they are free to engage in communications as required for quick, effective, and high quality health care. We understand that issues of this importance need to be addressed directly and clearly in the Privacy Rule and that any ambiguities need to be eliminated.

General Requirements

Covered entities must reasonably safeguard protected health information (PHI) — including oral information — from any intentional or unintentional use or disclosure that is in violation of the rule (see § 164.530(c)(2)). They must have in place appropriate administrative, technical, and physical safeguards to protect the privacy of PHI. "Reasonably safeguard" means that covered entities must make reasonable efforts to prevent uses and disclosures not permitted by the rule. However, we do not expect reasonable safeguards to guarantee the privacy of PHI from any and all potential risks. In determining whether a covered entity has provided reasonable safeguards, the Department will take into account all the circumstances, including the potential effects on patient care and the financial and administrative burden of any safeguards.

Covered entities must have policies and procedures that reasonably limit access to and use of PHI to the minimum necessary given the job responsibilities of the workforce and the nature of their business (see §§ 164.502(b), 164.514(d)). The minimum necessary standard does not apply to disclosures, including oral disclosures, among providers for treatment purposes. For a more complete discussion of the minimum necessary requirements, see the fact sheet and frequently asked questions titled "Minimum Necessary."

Many health care providers already make it a practice to ensure reasonable safeguards for oral information — for instance, by speaking quietly when discussing a patient's condition with family members in a waiting room or other public area, and by avoiding using patients' names in public hallways and elevators. Protection of patient confidentiality is an important practice for many health care and health information management professionals; covered entities can build upon those codes of conduct to develop the reasonable safeguards required by the Privacy Rule.

Frequently Asked Questions

Q: If health care providers engage in confidential conversations with other providers or with patients, have they violated the rule if there is a possibility that they could be overheard?

A: The Privacy Rule is not intended to prohibit providers from talking to each other and to their patients. Provisions of this rule requiring covered entities to implement reasonable safeguards that reflect their particular circumstances and exempting treatment disclosures from certain requirements are intended to ensure that providers' primary consideration is the appropriate treatment of their patients. We also understand that overheard communications are unavoidable. For example, in a busy emergency room, it may be necessary for providers to speak loudly in order to ensure appropriate treatment. The Privacy Rule is not intended to prevent this appropriate behavior. We would consider the following practices to be permissible, if reasonable precautions are taken to minimize the chance of inadvertent disclosures to others who may be nearby (such as using lowered voices, talking apart):

- Health care staff may orally coordinate services at hospital nursing stations.
- Nurses or other health care professionals may discuss a patient's condition over the phone with the patient, a provider, or a family member.
- A health care professional may discuss lab test results with a patient or other provider in a joint treatment area.
- Health care professionals may discuss a patient's condition during training rounds in an academic or training institution.

  We will propose regulatory language to reinforce and clarify that these and similar oral communications (such as calling out patient names in a waiting room) are permissible.

Q: **Does the Privacy Rule require hospitals and doctors' offices to be retrofitted, to provide private rooms, and soundproof walls to avoid any possibility that a conversation is overheard?**

A: No, the Privacy Rule does not require these types of structural changes be made to facilities.

Covered entities must have in place appropriate administrative, technical, and physical safeguards to protect the privacy of PHI. "Reasonable safeguards" mean that covered entities must make reasonable efforts to prevent uses and disclosures not permitted by the rule. The Department does not consider facility restructuring to be a requirement under this standard. In determining what is reasonable, the Department will take into account the concerns of covered entities regarding potential effects on patient care and financial burden.

For example, the Privacy Rule does not require the following types of structural or systems changes:

- Private rooms.
- Soundproofing of rooms.

- Encryption of wireless or other emergency medical radio communications which can be intercepted by scanners.
- Encryption of telephone systems.

Covered entities must provide reasonable safeguards to avoid prohibited disclosures. The rule does not require that all risk be eliminated to satisfy this standard. Covered entities must review their own practices and determine what steps are reasonable to safeguard their patient information.

Examples of the types of adjustments or modifications to facilities or systems that may constitute reasonable safeguards are:

- Pharmacies could ask waiting customers to stand a few feet back from a counter used for patient counseling.
- Providers could add curtains or screens to areas where oral communications often occur between doctors and patients or among professionals treating the patient.
- In an area where multiple patient-staff communications routinely occur, use of cubicles, dividers, shields, or similar barriers may constitute a reasonable safeguard. For example, a large clinic intake area may reasonably use cubicles or shield-type dividers, rather than separate rooms.
- In assessing what is "reasonable," covered entities may consider the viewpoint of prudent professionals.

Q: Do covered entities need to provide patients access to oral information?

A: No. The Privacy Rule requires covered entities to provide individuals with access to PHI about themselves that is contained in their "designated record sets." The term "record" in the term "designated record set" does not include oral information; rather, it connotes information that has been recorded in some manner.

The rule does not require covered entities to tape or digitally record oral communications, nor retain digitally or tape recorded information after transcription. But if such records are maintained and used to make decisions about the individual, they may meet the definition of "designated record set." For example, a health plan is not required to provide a member access to tapes of a telephone "advice line" interaction if the tape is only maintained for customer service review and not to make decisions about the member.

Q: Do covered entities have to document all oral communications?

A: No. The Privacy Rule does not require covered entities to document any information, including oral information, that is used or disclosed for treatment, payment or health care operations (TPO).

The rule includes, however, documentation requirements for some information disclosures for other purposes. For example, some disclosures must be documented in order to meet the standard for providing a disclosure history to an individual upon request. Where a documentation requirement exists in the rule, it applies to all relevant communications, whether in oral or some other form. For example, if a covered physician discloses information about a case of tuberculosis to a public health authority as permitted by the rule in § 164.512, then he or she must maintain a record of that disclosure regardless of whether the disclosure was made orally by phone or in writing.

Q: Did the Department change its position from the proposed rule by covering oral communications in the final Privacy Rule?

A: No. The proposed rule would have covered information in any form or medium, as long as it had at some point been maintained or transmitted electronically. Once information had been made electronic, it would have continued to be covered as long as it was held by a covered entity, whether in electronic, written, or oral form.

The final Privacy Rule eliminates this nexus to electronic information. All individually identifiable health information of the covered entity is covered by the rule.

BUSINESS ASSOCIATES [45 CFR §§ 160.103, 164.502(E), 164.514(E)]

Background

By law, the Privacy Rule applies only to health plans, health care clearinghouses, and certain health care providers. In today's health care system, however, most health care providers and health plans do not carry out all of their health care activities and functions by themselves; they require assistance from a variety of contractors and other businesses. In allowing providers and plans to give protected health information (PHI) to these "business associates," the Privacy Rule conditions such disclosures on the provider or plan obtaining, typically by contract, satisfactory assurances that the business associate will use the information only for the purposes for which they were engaged by the covered entity, will safeguard the information from misuse, and will help the covered entity comply with the covered entity's duties to provide individuals with access to health information about them and a history of certain disclosures (e.g., if the business associate maintains the only copy of information, it must promise to cooperate with the covered entity to provide individuals access to information upon request). PHI may be disclosed to a business associate only to help the providers and plans carry out their health care functions — not for independent use by the business associate.

What Is a "Business Associate"

- A business associate is a person or entity who provides certain functions, activities, or services for or to a covered entity, involving the use and/or disclosure of PHI.
- A business associate is not a member of the health care provider, health plan, or other covered entity's workforce.
- A health care provider, health plan, or other covered entity can also be a business associate to another covered entity.

The rule includes exceptions. The business associate requirements do not apply to covered entities who disclose PHI to providers for treatment purposes — for example, information exchanges between a hospital and physicians with admitting privileges at the hospital.

Frequently Asked Questions

Q: **Has the Secretary exceeded the statutory authority by requiring "satisfactory assurances" for disclosures to business associates?**

A: No. The Health Insurance Portability and Accountability Act of 1996 (HIPAA) gives the Secretary authority to directly regulate health care providers, health plans, and health care clearinghouses. It also grants the Department explicit authority to regulate the uses and disclosures of PHI maintained and transmitted by covered entities. Therefore, we do have the authority to condition the disclosure of PHI by a covered entity to a business associate on the covered entity's having a contract with that business associate.

Q: **Has the Secretary exceeded the HIPAA statutory authority by requiring "business associates" to comply with the Privacy Rule, even if that requirement is through a contract?**

A: The Privacy Rule does not "pass through" its requirements to business associates or otherwise cause business associates to comply with the terms of the rule. The assurances that covered entities must obtain prior to disclosing PHI to business associates create a set of contractual obligations far narrower than the provisions of the rule, to protect information generally and help the covered entity comply with its obligations under the rule. For example, covered entities do not need to ask their business associates to agree to appoint a privacy officer, or develop policies and procedures for use and disclosure of PHI.

Q: **Is it reasonable for covered entities to be held liable for the privacy violations of business associates?**

A: A health care provider, health plan, or other covered entity is not liable for privacy violations of a business associate. Covered entities are not required to actively monitor or oversee the means by which

473

the business associate carries out safeguards or the extent to which the business associate abides by the requirements of the contract.

Moreover, a business associate's violation of the terms of the contract does not, in and of itself, constitute a violation of the rule by the covered entity. The contract must obligate the business associate to advise the covered entity when violations have occurred.

If the covered entity becomes aware of a pattern or practice of the business associate that constitutes a material breach or violation of the business associate's obligations under its contract, the covered entity must take "reasonable steps" to cure the breach or to end the violation. Reasonable steps will vary with the circumstances and nature of the business relationship.

If such steps are not successful, the covered entity must terminate the contract if feasible. The rule also provides for circumstances in which termination is not feasible, for example, where there are no other viable business alternatives for the covered entity. In such circumstances where termination is not feasible, the covered entity must report the problem to the Department.

Only if the covered entity fails to take the kinds of steps described above would it be considered to be out of compliance with the requirements of the rule.

PARENTS AND MINORS [45 CFR § 164.502(G)]

General Requirements

The Privacy Rule provides individuals with certain rights with respect to their personal health information, including the right to obtain access to and to request amendment of health information about themselves. These rights rest with that individual, or with the "personal representative" of that individual. In general, a person's right to control protected health information (PHI) is based on that person's right (under state or other applicable law, e.g., tribal or military law) to control the health care itself.

Because a parent usually has authority to make health care decisions about his or her minor child, a parent is generally a "personal representative" of his or her minor child under the Privacy Rule and has the right to obtain access to health information about his or her minor child. This would also be true in the case of a guardian or other person acting *in loco parentis* of a minor.

There are exceptions in which a parent might not be the "personal representative" with respect to certain health information about a minor child. In the following situations, the Privacy Rule defers to determinations under other law that the parent does not control the minor's health care decisions and, thus, does not control the PHI related to that care.

- When state or other law does not require consent of a parent or other person before a minor can obtain a particular health care service, and the minor consents to the health care service, the parent is not the minor's personal representative under the Privacy Rule. For example, when a state law provides an adolescent the right to consent to mental health treatment without the consent of his or her parent, and the adolescent obtains such treatment without the consent of the parent, the parent is not the personal representative under the Privacy Rule for that treatment. The minor may choose to involve a parent in these health care decisions without giving up his or her right to control the related health information. Of course, the minor may always have the parent continue to be his or her personal representative even in these situations.

- When a court determines or other law authorizes someone other than the parent to make treatment decisions for a minor, the parent is not the personal representative of the minor for the relevant services. For example, courts may grant authority to make health care decisions for the minor to an adult other than the parent, to the minor, or the court may make the decision(s) itself. In order to not undermine these court decisions, the parent is not the personal representative under the Privacy Rule in these circumstances.

In the following situations, the Privacy Rule reflects current professional practice in determining that the parent is not the minor's personal representative with respect to the relevant PHI:

- When a parent agrees to a confidential relationship between the minor and the physician, the parent does not have access to the health information related to that conversation or relationship. For example, if a physician asks the parent of a 16-year-old if the physician can talk with the child confidentially about a medical condition and the parent agrees, the parent would not control the PHI that was discussed during that confidential conference.

- When a physician (or other covered entity) reasonably believes in his or her professional judgment that the child has been or may be subjected to abuse or neglect, or that treating the parent as the child's personal representative could endanger the child, the physician may choose not to treat the parent as the personal representative of the child.

Relation to State Law

In addition to the provisions (described above) tying the right to control information to the right to control treatment, the Privacy Rule also states that it does not preempt state laws that specifically address disclosure of health information about a minor to a parent (§ 160.202). This is true whether the state law authorizes or prohibits such disclosure. Thus, if a physician believes that disclosure of information about a minor would endanger that minor, but a state law requires disclosure to a parent, the physician may comply with the state law without violating the Privacy Rule. Similarly, a provider may comply with a state law that requires disclosure to a parent and would not have to accommodate a request for confidential communications that would be contrary to state law.

Frequently Asked Questions

Q: **Does the Privacy Rule allow parents the right to see their children's medical records?**

A: The Privacy Rule generally allows parents, as their minor children's personal representatives, to have access to information about the health and well-being of their children when state or other underlying law allows parents to make treatment decisions for the child. There are two exceptions: (1) when the parent agrees that the minor and the health care provider may have a confidential relationship, the provider is allowed to withhold information from the parent to the extent of that agreement; and (2) when the provider reasonably believes in his or her professional judgment that the child has been or may be subjected to abuse or neglect, or that treating the parent as the child's personal representative could endanger the child, the provider is permitted not to treat the parent as the child's personal representative with respect to health information.

Secretary Thompson has stated that he is reassessing these provisions of the regulation.

Q: **Does the Privacy Rule provide rights for children to be treated without parental consent?**

A: No. The Privacy Rule does not address consent to treatment, nor does it preempt or change state or other laws that address consent to treatment. The Rule addresses access to health information, not the underlying treatment.

Q: **If a child receives emergency medical care without a parent's consent, can the parent get all information about the child's treatment and condition?**

A: Generally, yes. Even though the parent did not provide consent to the treatment in this situation, under the Privacy Rule, the parent would still be the child's personal representative. This would not be so only when the minor provided consent (and no other consent is required) or the treating physician suspects abuse or neglect or reasonably believes that releasing the information to the parent will endanger the child.

HEALTH-RELATED COMMUNICATIONS AND MARKETING
[45 CFR §§ 164.501, 164.514(E)]

General Requirements

The Privacy Rule addresses the use and disclosure of protected health information (PHI) for marketing purposes in the following ways:

- Defines what is "marketing" under the rule;
- Removes from that definition certain treatment or health care operations activities;
- Set limits on the kind of marketing that can be done as a health care operation; and
- Requires individual authorization for all other uses or disclosures of PHI for marketing purposes.

What Is Marketing

The Privacy Rule defines "marketing" as "a communication about a product or service a purpose of which is to encourage recipients of the communication to purchase or use the product or service." To make this definition easier for covered entities to understand and comply with, we specified what "marketing" is not, as well as generally defined what it is. As questions arise about what activities are "marketing" under the Privacy Rule, we will provide additional clarification regarding such activities.

Communications That Are Not Marketing

The Privacy Rule carves out activities that are not considered marketing under this definition. In recommending treatments or describing available services, health care providers and health plans are advising us to purchase goods and services. To prevent any interference with essential treatment or similar health-related communications with a patient, the rule identifies the following activities as not subject to the marketing provision, even if the activity otherwise meets the definition of marketing. (Written communications for which the covered entity is compensated by a third party are not carved out of the marketing definition.)

Thus, a covered entity is not "marketing" when it:

- Describes the participating providers or plans in a network. For example, a health plan is not marketing when it tells its enrollees about which doctors and hospitals are preferred providers, which are included in its network, or which providers offer a particular service. Similarly, a health insurer notifying enrollees of a new pharmacy that has begun to accept its drug coverage is not engaging in marketing.

- Describes the services offered by a provider or the benefits covered by a health plan. For example, informing a plan enrollee about drug formulary coverage is not marketing.

Furthermore, it is not marketing for a covered entity to use an individual's PHI to tailor a health-related communication to that individual, when the communication is:

- Part of a provider's treatment of the patient and for the purpose of furthering that treatment. For example, recommendations of specific brand-name or over-the-counter pharmaceuticals or referrals of patients to other providers are not marketing.
- Made in the course of managing the individual's treatment or recommending alternative treatment. For example, reminder notices for appointments, annual exams, or prescription refills are not marketing. Similarly, informing an individual who is a smoker about an effective smoking-cessation program is not marketing, even if that program is offered by someone other than the provider or plan making the recommendation.

Limitations on Marketing Communications

If a communication is marketing, a covered entity may use or disclose PHI to create or make the communication, pursuant to any applicable consent obtained under § 164.506, only in the following circumstances:

- It is a face-to-face communication with the individual. For example, sample products may be provided to a patient during an office visit.
- It involves products or services of nominal value. For example, a provider can distribute pens, toothbrushes, or key chains with the name of the covered entity or a health care product manufacturer on it.
- It concerns the health-related products and services of the covered entity or a third party, and only if the communication:
  — Identifies the covered entity that is making the communication. Thus, consumers will know the source of these marketing calls or materials.
  — States that the covered entity is being compensated for making the communication, when that is so.
  — Tells individuals how to opt out of further marketing communications, with some exceptions as provided in the rule. The covered entity must make reasonable efforts to honor requests to opt-out.
  — Explains why individuals with specific conditions or characteristics (e.g., diabetics, smokers) have been targeted, if that is so, and how the product or service relates to the health of the individual. The covered entity must also have made a determination that the product or service may be of benefit to individuals with that condition or characteristic.

For all other communications that are "marketing" under the Privacy Rule, the covered entity must obtain the individual's authorization to use or disclose PHI to create or make the marketing communication.

Business Associates

Disclosure of PHI for marketing purposes is limited to disclosure to business associates that undertake marketing activities on behalf of the covered entity. No other disclosure for marketing is permitted. Covered entities may not give away or sell lists of patients or enrollees without obtaining authorization from each person on the list. As with any disclosure to a business associate, the covered entity must obtain the business associate's agreement to use the PHI only for the covered entity's marketing activities. A covered entity may not give PHI to a business associate for the business associate's own purposes.

Frequently Asked Questions

Q: **Does this rule expand the ability of providers, plans, marketers and others to use my PHI to market goods and services to me? Does the Privacy Rule make it easier for health care businesses to engage in door-to-door sales and marketing efforts?**

A: No. The provisions described above impose limits on the use or disclosure of PHI for marketing that do not exist in most states today. For example, the rule requires patients' authorization for the following types of uses or disclosures of PHI for marketing:

- Selling PHI to third parties for their use and re-use. Under the rule, a hospital or other provider may not sell names of pregnant women to baby formula manufacturers or magazines.
- Disclosing PHI to outsiders for the outsiders' independent marketing use. Under the rule, doctors may not provide patient lists to pharmaceutical companies for those companies' drug promotions.

These activities can occur today with no authorization from the individual. In addition, for the marketing activities that are allowed by the rule without authorization from the individual, the Privacy Rule requires covered entities to offer individuals the ability to opt-out of further marketing communications.

Similarly, under the business associate provisions of the rule, a covered entity may not give PHI to a telemarketer, door-to-door salesperson, or other marketer it has hired unless that marketer has agreed by contract to use the information only for marketing on behalf of the covered entity. Today, there may be no restrictions on how marketers re-use information they obtain from health plans and providers.

Q: Can telemarketers gain access to PHI and call individuals to sell goods and services?

A: Under the rule, unless the covered entity obtains the individual's authorization, it may only give health information to a telemarketer that it has hired to undertake marketing on its behalf. The telemarketer must be a business associate under the rule, which means that it must agree by contract to use the information only for marketing on behalf of the covered entity, and not to market its own goods or services (or those of another third party). The caller must identify the covered entity that is sponsoring the marketing call. The caller must provide individuals the opportunity to opt out of further marketing.

Q: When is an authorization required from the patient before a provider or health plan engages in marketing to that individual?

A: An authorization for use or disclosure of PHI for marketing is always required, unless one of the following three exceptions apply:
- The marketing occurs during an in-person meeting with the patient (e.g., during a medical appointment).
- The marketing concerns products or services of nominal value.
- The covered entity is marketing health-related products and services (of either the covered entity or a third party), the marketing identifies the covered entity that is responsible for the marketing, and the individual is offered an opportunity to opt out of further marketing. In addition, the marketing must tell people if they have been targeted based on their health status, and must also tell people when the covered entity is compensated (directly or indirectly) for making the communication.

Q: How can I distinguish between activities for treatment, payment or health care operations (TPO) vs. marketing activities?

A: There is no need for covered entities to make this distinction. In recommending treatments, providers and health plans advise us to purchase good and services. The overlap between "treatment," "health care operations," and "marketing" is unavoidable. Instead of creating artificial distinctions, the rule imposes requirements that do not require such distinctions. Specifically:
- If the activity is included in the rule's definition of "marketing," the rule's provisions restricting the use or disclosure of PHI for marketing purposes will apply, whether or not that communication also meets the rule's definition of "treatment," "payment," or "health care operations." For these communications, the individual's authorization is required before a covered entity may use or disclose PHI for marketing unless one of the exceptions to the authorization requirement (described above) applies.

- The rule exempts certain activities from the definition of "marketing." If an activity falls into one of the definition's exemptions, the marketing rules do not apply. In these cases, covered entities may engage in the activity without first obtaining an authorization if the activity meets the definition of "treatment," "payment," or "health care operations." These exemptions are described above, in the section titled "Communications That Are Not Marketing," and are designed to ensure that nothing in this rule interferes with treatment activities.

Q: Do disease management, health promotion, preventive care, and wellness programs fall under the definition of "marketing"?

A: Whether these kinds of activities fall under the rule's definition of "marketing" depends on the specifics of how the activity is conducted. The activities currently undertaken under these rubrics are diverse. Covered entities must examine the particular activities they undertake, and compare these to the activities that are exempt from the definition of "marketing."

Q: Can contractors (business associates) use PHI to market to individuals for their own business purposes?

A: The Privacy Rule prohibits health plans and covered health care providers from giving PHI to third parties for the third party's own business purposes, absent authorization from the individuals. Under the statute, this regulation cannot govern contractors directly.

RESEARCH [45 CFR §§ 164.501, 164.508(F), 164.512(I)]

Background

The Privacy Rule establishes the conditions under which protected health information (PHI) may be used or disclosed by covered entities for research purposes. A covered entity may always use or disclose for research purposes health information which has been de-identified (in accordance with §§ 164.502(d), 164.514(a)–(c) of the rule) without regard to the provisions below.

The Privacy Rule also defines the means by which individuals/human research subjects are informed of how medical information about themselves will be used or disclosed and their rights with regard to gaining access to information about themselves, when such information is held by covered entities. Where research is concerned, the Privacy Rule protects the privacy of individually identifiable health information, while at the same time, ensuring that researchers continue to have access to medical information necessary to conduct vital research. Currently, most research involving human subjects operates under the Common Rule (codified for the Department of Health and Human Services (HHS) at Title 45

Code of Federal Regulations Part 46) and/or the Food and Drug Administration's (FDA) human subjects protection regulations, which have some provisions that are similar to, but more stringent than and separate from, the Privacy Rule's provisions for research.

Using and Disclosing PHI for Research

In the course of conducting research, researchers may create, use, and/or disclose individually identifiable health information. Under the Privacy Rule, covered entities are permitted to use and disclose PHI for research with individual authorization, or without individual authorization under limited circumstances set forth in the Privacy Rule.

Research Use/Disclosure Without Authorization: To use or disclose PHI without authorization by the research participant, a covered entity must obtain one of the following:

- Documentation that an alteration or waiver of research participants' authorization for use/disclosure of information about them for research purposes has been approved by an Institutional Review Board (IRB) or a Privacy Board. This provision of the Privacy Rule might be used, for example, to conduct records research, when researchers are unable to use de-identified information and it is not practicable to obtain research participants' authorization; or
- Representations from the researcher, either in writing or orally, that the use or disclosure of the PHI is solely to prepare a research protocol or for similar purposes preparatory to research, that the researcher will not remove any PHI from the covered entity, and representation that PHI for which access is sought is necessary for the research purpose. This provision might be used, for example, to design a research study or to assess the feasibility of conducting a study; or
- Representations from the researcher, either in writing or orally, that the use or disclosure being sought is solely for research on the PHI of decedents, that the PHI being sought is necessary for the research, and, at the request of the covered entity, documentation of the death of the individuals about whom information is being sought.

A covered entity may use or disclose PHI for research purposes pursuant to a waiver of authorization by an IRB or Privacy Board provided it has obtained documentation of all of the following:

- A statement that the alteration or waiver of authorization was approved by an IRB or Privacy Board that was composed as stipulated by the Privacy Rule;
- A statement identifying the IRB or Privacy Board and the date on which the alteration or waiver of authorization was approved;

- A statement that the IRB or Privacy Board has determined that the alteration or waiver of authorization, in whole or in part, satisfies the following eight criteria:
  - The use or disclosure of PHI involves no more than minimal risk to the individuals;
  - The alteration or waiver will not adversely affect the privacy rights and the welfare of the individuals;
  - The research could not practicably be conducted without the alteration or waiver;
  - The research could not practicably be conducted without access to and use of the PHI;
  - The privacy risks to individuals whose PHI is to be used or disclosed are reasonable in relation to the anticipated benefits, if any, to the individuals, and the importance of the knowledge that may reasonably be expected to result from the research;
  - There is an adequate plan to protect the identifiers from improper use and disclosure;
  - There is an adequate plan to destroy the identifiers at the earliest opportunity consistent with conduct of the research, unless there is a health or research justification for retaining the identifiers or such retention is otherwise required by law; and
  - There are adequate written assurances that the PHI will not be reused or disclosed to any other person or entity, except as required by law, for authorized oversight of the research project, or for other research for which the use or disclosure of PHI would be permitted by this subpart.
- A brief description of the PHI for which use or access has been determined to be necessary by the IRB or Privacy Board;
- A statement that the alteration or waiver of authorization has been reviewed and approved under either normal or expedited review procedures as stipulated by the Privacy Rule; and
- The signature of the chair or other member, as designated by the chair, of the IRB or the Privacy Board, as applicable.

Research Use/Disclosure With Individual Authorization. The Privacy Rule also permits covered entities to use and disclose PHI for research purposes when a research participant authorizes the use or disclosure of information about him or herself. Today, for example, a research participant's authorization will typically be sought for most clinical trials and some records research. In this case, documentation of IRB or Privacy Board approval of a waiver of authorization is not required for the use or disclosure of PHI.

To use or disclose PHI created from a research study that includes treatment (e.g., a clinical trial), additional research-specific elements must be included in the authorization form required under § 164.508, which describe how PHI created for the research study will be used or disclosed. For example, if the covered entity/researcher intends to seek reimbursement from the research subject's health plan for the routine costs of care associated with the protocol, the authorization must describe types of information that will be provided to the health plan. This authorization may be combined with the traditional informed consent document used in research.

The Privacy Rule permits, but does not require, the disclosure of PHI for specified public policy purposes in § 164.512. With few exceptions, the covered entity/researcher may choose to limit its right to disclose information created for a research study that includes treatment to purposes narrower than those permitted by the rule, in accordance with his or her own professional standards.

Frequently Asked Questions

Q: Will the rule hinder medical research by making doctors and others less willing and/or able to share information about individual patients?

A: We do not believe that the Privacy Rule will hinder medical research. Indeed, patients and health plan members should be more willing to participate in research when they know their information is protected. For example, in genetic studies at the National Institutes of Health (NIH), nearly 32 percent of eligible people offered a test for breast cancer risk decline to take it. The overwhelming majority of those who refuse cite concerns about health insurance discrimination and loss of privacy as the reason. The Privacy Rule both permits important research and, at the same time, encourages patients to participate in research by providing much needed assurances about the privacy of their health information.

The Privacy Rule will require some covered health care providers and health plans to change their current practices related to documenting research uses and disclosures. It is possible that some covered health care providers and health plans may conclude that the rule's requirements for research uses and disclosures are too burdensome and will choose to limit researchers' access to PHI. We believe few providers will take this route, however, because the Common Rule includes similar, and more stringent requirements, that have not impaired the willingness of researchers to undertake federally-funded research. For example, unlike the Privacy Rule, the Common Rule requires IRB review for all research proposals under its purview, even if informed consent is to be sought. The Privacy Rule requires documentation of IRB or Privacy Board approval only if patient authorization for the use or disclosure of PHI for research purposes is to be altered or waived.

Q: **Are some of the criteria so subjective that inconsistent determinations may be made by IRBs and Privacy Boards reviewing similar or identical research projects?**

A: Under the Privacy Rule, IRBs and Privacy Boards need to use their judgment as to whether the waiver criteria have been satisfied. Several of the waiver criteria are closely modeled on the Common Rule's criteria for the waiver of informed consent and for the approval of a research study. Thus, it is anticipated that IRBs already have experience in making the necessarily subjective assessments of risks and benefits. While IRBs or Privacy Boards may reach different determinations, the assessment of the waiver criteria through this deliberative process is a crucial element in the current system of safeguarding research participants' privacy. The entire system of local IRBs is, in fact, predicated on a deliberative process that permits local IRB autonomy. The Privacy Rule builds upon this principle; it does not change it.

In addition, for multi-site research that requires PHI from two or more covered entities, the Privacy Rule permits covered entities to accept documentation of IRB or Privacy Board approval from a single IRB or Privacy Board.

Q: **Does the Privacy Rule prohibit researchers from conditioning participation in a clinical trial on an authorization to use/disclose existing PHI?**

A: No. The Privacy Rule does not address conditions for enrollment in a research study. Therefore, the Privacy Rule in no way prohibits researchers from conditioning enrollment in a research study on the execution of an authorization for the use of pre-existing health information.

Q: **Does the Privacy Rule permit the creation of a database for research purposes through an IRB or Privacy Board waiver of individual authorization?**

A: Yes. A covered entity may use or disclose PHI without individuals' authorizations for the creation of a research database, provided the covered entity obtains documentation that an IRB or Privacy Board has determined that the specified waiver criteria were satisfied. PHI maintained in such a research database could be used or disclosed for future research studies as permitted by the Privacy Rule — that is, for future studies in which individual authorization has been obtained or where the rule would permit research without an authorization, such as pursuant to an IRB or Privacy Board waiver.

Q: **Will IRBs be able to handle the additional responsibilities imposed by the Privacy Rule?**

A: Recognizing that some institutions may not have IRBs, or that some IRBs may not have the expertise needed to review research that requires consideration of risks to privacy, the Privacy Rule permits the covered entity to accept documentation of waiver of authorization from an alternative body called a Privacy Board — which could have fewer members, and members with different expertise than IRBs.

In addition, for research that is determined to be of no more than minimal risk, IRBs and Privacy Boards could use an expedited review process, which permits covered entities to accept documentation when only one or more members of the IRB or Privacy Board have conducted the review.

Q: **By establishing new waiver criteria and authorization requirements, hasn't the Privacy Rule, in effect, modified the Common Rule?**

A: No. Where both the Privacy Rule and the Common Rule apply, both regulations must be followed. The Privacy Rule regulates only the content and conditions of the documentation that covered entities must obtain before using or disclosing PHI for research purposes.

Q: **Is documentation of IRB and Privacy Board approval required before a covered entity would be permitted to disclose PHI for research purposes without an individual's authorization?**

A: No. The Privacy Rule requires documentation of waiver approval by either an IRB or a Privacy Board, not both.

Q: **Does a covered entity need to create an IRB or Privacy Board before using or disclosing PHI for research?**

A: No. The IRB or Privacy Board could be created by the covered entity or the recipient researcher, or it could be an independent board.

Q: **What does the Privacy Rule say about a research participant's right of access to research records or results?**

A: With few exceptions, the Privacy Rule gives patients the right to inspect and obtain a copy of health information about themselves that is maintained in a "designated record set." A designated record set is basically a group of records which a covered entity uses to make decisions about individuals, and includes a health care provider's medical records and billing records, and a health plan's enrollment, payment, claims adjudication, and case or medical management record systems. Research records or results maintained in a designated record set are accessible to research participants unless one of the Privacy Rule's permitted exceptions applies.

One of the permitted exceptions applies to PHI created or obtained by a covered health care provider/researcher for a clinical trial. The Privacy Rule permits the individual's access rights in these cases to be suspended while the clinical trial is in progress, provided the research participant agreed to this denial of access when consenting to participate in the clinical trial. In addition, the health care provider/ researcher must inform the research participant that the right to access PHI will be reinstated at the conclusion of the clinical trial.

Q: **Are the Privacy Rule's requirements regarding patient access in harmony with the Clinical Laboratory Improvements Amendments of 1988 (CLIA)?**

A: Yes. The Privacy Rule does not require clinical laboratories that are also covered health care providers to provide an individual access to information if CLIA prohibits them from doing so. CLIA permits clinical laboratories to provide clinical laboratory test records and reports only to "authorized persons," as defined primarily by state law. The individual who is the subject of the information is not always included as an authorized person. Therefore, the Privacy Rule includes an exception to individuals' general right to access PHI about themselves if providing an individual such access would be in conflict with CLIA.

In addition, for certain research laboratories that are exempt from the CLIA regulations, the Privacy Rule does not require such research laboratories if they are also a covered health care provider to provide individuals with access to PHI because doing so may result in the research laboratory losing its CLIA exemption.

Q: **Do the Privacy Rule's requirements for authorization and the Common Rule's requirements for informed consent differ?**

A: Yes. Under the Privacy Rule, a patient's authorization will be used for the use and disclosure of PHI for research purposes. In contrast, an individual's informed consent as required by the Common Rule and FDA's human subjects regulations is a consent to participate in the research study as a whole, not simply a consent for the research use or disclosure of PHI. For this reason, there are important differences between the Privacy Rule's requirements for individual authorization, and the Common Rule's and FDA's requirements for informed consent. Where the Privacy Rule, the Common Rule, and/ or FDA's human subjects regulations are applicable, each of the applicable regulations will need to be followed.

RESTRICTIONS ON GOVERNMENT ACCESS TO HEALTH INFORMATION [45 CFR §§ 160.300; 164.512(B); 164.512(F)]

Background

Under the Privacy Rule, government-operated health plans and health care providers must meet substantially the same requirements as private ones for protecting the privacy of individual identifiable health information. For instance, government-run health plans, such as Medicare and Medicaid, must take virtually the same steps to protect the claims and health information that they receive from beneficiaries as private insurance plans or health maintenance organizations (HMO). In addition, all federal agencies must also meet the requirements of the Privacy Act of 1974, which restricts what information about individual citizens — including any personal health information — can be shared with other agencies and with the public.

The only new authority for government involves enforcement of the Privacy Rule itself. In order to ensure covered entities protect patients' privacy as required, the rule provides that health plans, hospitals, and other covered entities cooperate with the Department's efforts to investigate complaints or otherwise ensure compliance. The Department of Health and Human Services (HHS) Office for Civil Rights (OCR) is responsible for enforcing the privacy protections and access rights for consumers under this rule.

Frequently Asked Questions

Q: **Does the rule require my doctor to send my medical records to the government?**

A: No. The rule does not require a physician or any other covered entity to send medical information to the government for a government database or similar operation. This rule does not require or allow any new government access to medical information, with one exception: the rule does give OCR the authority to investigate complaints and to otherwise ensure that covered entities comply with the rule.

OCR has been assigned the responsibility of enforcing the Privacy Rule. As is typical in many enforcement settings, OCR may need to look at how a covered entity handled medical records and other personal health information. The Privacy Rule limits disclosure to OCR to information that is "pertinent to ascertaining compliance." OCR will maintain stringent controls to safeguard any individually identifiable health information that it receives. If covered entities could avoid or ignore enforcement requests, consumers would not have a way to ensure an independent review of their concerns about privacy violations under the rule.

Q: **Why would a Privacy Rule require covered entities to turn over anybody's personal health information as part of a government enforcement process?**

A: An important ingredient in ensuring compliance with the Privacy Rule is the Department's responsibility to investigate complaints that the rule has been violated and to follow up on other information regarding noncompliance. At times, this responsibility entails seeing personal health information, such as when an individual indicates to the Department that they believe a covered entity has not properly handled their medical records.

What information would be needed depends on the circumstances and the alleged violations. The Privacy Rule limits OCR's access to information that is "pertinent to ascertaining compliance." In some cases, no personal health information would be needed. For instance, OCR may need to review only a business contract to determine whether a health plan included appropriate language to protect privacy when it hired an outside company to help process claims.

Examples of investigations that may require OCR to have access to protected health information (PHI) include:

- Allegations that a covered entity refused to note a request for correction in a patient's medical record, or did not provide complete access to a patient's medical records to that patient.
- Allegations that a covered entity used health information for marketing purposes without first obtaining the individuals' authorization when required by the rule. OCR may need to review information in the marketing department that contains personal health information, to determine whether a violation has occurred.

Q: **Will this rule make it easier for police and law enforcement agencies to get my medical information?**

A: No. The rule does not expand current law enforcement access to individually identifiable health information. In fact, it limits access to a greater degree than currently exists. Today, law enforcement officers obtain health information for many purposes, sometimes without a warrant or other prior process. The rule establishes new procedures and safeguards to restrict the circumstances under which a covered entity may give such information to law enforcement officers.

For example, the rule limits the type of information that covered entities may disclose to law enforcement, absent a warrant or other prior process, when law enforcement is seeking to identify or locate a suspect. It specifically prohibits disclosure of DNA information for this purpose, absent some other legal requirements such as a warrant. Similarly, under most circumstances, the Privacy Rule requires covered entities to obtain permission from persons who have been the victim of domestic violence or abuse before disclosing information about them to law enforcement. In most states, such permission is not required today.

Where state law imposes additional restrictions on disclosure of health information to law enforcement, those state laws continue to apply. This rule sets a national floor of legal protections; it is not a set of "best practices."

Even in those circumstances when disclosure to law enforcement is permitted by the rule, the Privacy Rule does not require covered entities to disclose any information. Some other federal or state law may require a disclosure, and the Privacy Rule does not interfere with the operation of these other laws. However, unless the disclosure is required by some other law, covered entities should use their professional judgment to decide whether to disclose information, reflecting their own policies and ethical principles. In other words, doctors, hospitals, and health plans could continue to follow their own policies to protect privacy in such instances.

Q: Must a health care provider or other covered entity obtain permission from a patient prior to notifying public health authorities of the occurrence of a reportable disease?

A: No. All states have laws that require providers to report cases of specific diseases to public health officials. The Privacy Rule allows disclosures that are required by law. Furthermore, disclosures to public health authorities that are authorized by law to collect or receive information for public health purposes are also permissible under the Privacy Rule. In order to do their job of protecting the health of the public, it is frequently necessary for public health officials to obtain information about the persons affected by a disease. In some cases they may need to contact those affected in order to determine the cause of the disease to allow for actions to prevent further illness.

The Privacy Rule continues to allow for the existing practice of sharing PHI with public health authorities that are authorized by law to collect or receive such information to aid them in their mission of protecting the health of the public. Examples of such activities include those directed at the reporting of disease or injury, reporting deaths and births, investigating the occurrence and cause of injury and disease, and monitoring adverse outcomes related to food, drugs, biological products, and dietary supplements.

Q: How does the rule affect my rights under the federal Privacy Act?

A: The Privacy Act of 1974 protects personal information about individuals held by the federal government. Covered entities that are federal agencies or federal contractors that maintain records that are covered by the Privacy Act not only must obey the Privacy Rule's requirements but also must comply with the Privacy Act.

PAYMENT [45 CFR 164.501]

General Requirements

As provided for by the Privacy Rule, a covered entity may use and disclose protected health information (PHI) for payment purposes. "Payment" is a defined term that encompasses the various activities of health care providers to obtain payment or be reimbursed for their services and for a health plan to obtain premiums, to fulfill their coverage responsibilities and provide benefits under the plan, and to obtain or provide reimbursement for the provision of health care.

In addition to the general definition, the Privacy Rule provides examples of common payment activities which include, but are not limited to:

- Determining eligibility or coverage under a plan and adjudicating claims;
- Risk adjustments;
- Billing and collection activities;
- Reviewing health care services for medical necessity, coverage, justification of charges, and the like;
- Utilization review activities; and
- Disclosures to consumer reporting agencies (limited to specified identifying information about the individual, his or her payment history, and identifying information about the covered entity).

Frequently Asked Questions

Q: **Does the rule prevent reporting to consumer credit reporting agencies or otherwise create any conflict with the Fair Credit Reporting Act (FCRA)?**

A: No. The Privacy Rule's definition of "payment" includes disclosures to consumer reporting agencies. These disclosures, however, are limited to the following PHI about the individual: name and address; date of birth; social security number; payment history; account number. In addition, disclosure of the name and address of the health care provider or health plan making the report is allowed. The covered entity may perform this payment activity directly or may carry out this function through a third party, such as a collection agency, under a business associate arrangement.

We are not aware of any conflict in the consumer credit reporting disclosures permitted by the Privacy Rule and FCRA. The Privacy Rule permits uses and disclosures by the covered entity or its business associate as may be required by FCRA or other law. Therefore, we do not believe there would be a conflict between the Privacy Rule and legal duties imposed on data furnishers by FCRA.

Q: Does the Privacy Rule prevent health plans and providers from using debt collection agencies? Does the rule conflict with the Fair Debt Collection Practices Act?

A: The Privacy Rule permits covered entities to continue to use the services of debt collection agencies. Debt collection is recognized as a payment activity within the "payment" definition. Through a business associate arrangement, the covered entity may engage a debt collection agency to perform this function on its behalf. Disclosures to collection agencies under a business associate agreement are governed by other provisions of the rule, including consent (where consent is required) and the minimum necessary requirements.

We are not aware of any conflict between the Privacy Rule and the Fair Debt Collection Practices Act. Where a use or disclosure of PHI is necessary for the covered entity to fulfill a legal duty, the Privacy Rule would permit such use or disclosure as required by law.

Q: Are location information services of collection agencies, which are required under the Fair Debt Collection Practices Act, permitted under the Privacy Rule?

A: "Payment" is broadly defined as activities by health plans or health care providers to obtain premiums or obtain or provide reimbursements for the provision of health care. The activities specified are by way of example and are not intended to be an exclusive listing. Billing, claims management, collection activities and related data processing are expressly included in the definition of "payment." Obtaining information about the location of the individual is a routine activity to facilitate the collection of amounts owed and the management of accounts receivable, and, therefore, would constitute a payment activity. The covered entity and its business associate would also have to comply with any limitations placed on location information services by the Fair Debt Collection Practices Act.

Last revised: July 6, 2001

Chapter 39

Health Privacy Regulation Enhances Protection of Patient Records but Raises Practical Concerns

Testimony before the Committee on Health, Education, Labor, and Pensions, U.S. Senate

Statement of Leslie G. Aronovitz, Director, Health Care — Program Administration and Integrity Issues, February 8, 2001

Mr. Chairman and Members of the Committee:

We are pleased to be here today as you discuss the new federal regulation covering the privacy of personal health information. Advances in information technology, along with an increasing number of parties with access to identifiable health information, have created new challenges to maintaining the privacy of an individual's medical records. Patients and providers alike have expressed concern that broad access to medical records by insurers, employers, and others may result in inappropriate use of the information. Congress sought to protect the privacy of individuals' medical information as part of the Health Insurance Portability and Accountability Act of 1996 (HIPAA).[1] HIPAA included a timetable for developing comprehensive privacy standards that would establish rights for patients with respect to their medical records and define the conditions for using and disclosing identifiable health information. In December 2000, the Department of Health and Human Services (HHS) released the final regulation on privacy standards.[2] The regulation requires that most affected entities comply by February 26, 2003.[3]

In April 2000, we testified on HHS' proposed privacy regulation.[4] At that time, we noted that the comments made by the affected parties reflected two overriding themes. The first was a widespread acknowledgment of the importance of protecting the privacy of medical records. The second reflected the conflicts that arise in attempts to balance protecting patients' privacy and permitting the flow of health information for necessary uses. Last month, the Committee requested that we obtain the perspectives of affected parties regarding the regulation. My remarks today will focus on (1) the rights of patients and the responsibilities of the entities that use personal health information, as set forth in the federal privacy regulation, and (2) the concerns of key stakeholders regarding the regulation's major provisions. In gathering this information, we contacted 17 national organizations representing patients, health care providers, accrediting bodies, state officials, employers, insurance companies, and research and pharmaceutical groups.[5] (A list of these organizations is in Exhibit 1.) We also reviewed the regulation and spoke with HHS officials responsible for implementing it. We performed our work in January 2001 in accordance with generally accepted government auditing standards.

In brief, the regulation acts as a federal floor (to be superseded by state privacy regulations that are more stringent) in establishing standards affecting the use and disclosure of personal health information by providers, health plans, employers, researchers, and government agencies. Patients will have increased knowledge about, and potential control over, what information is shared, with whom, and for what purposes. At the same time, entities that receive personal health information will be responsible for ensuring that the information is effectively protected.

Most groups we interviewed acknowledged that HHS was responsive in addressing many of their comments on the draft regulation. However, given the newness, breadth, and complexity of the regulation, they also expressed uncertainty about all that organizations may need to do to comply. Many raised questions about the requirements for entities to obtain patient consent or authorization prior to disclosing or using personal health information. Other concerns focused on how regulated entities will apply the privacy provisions to their business associates. Most groups focused on the HIPAA provision that more stringent state privacy

Exhibit 1.   Organizations Interviewed

We included the following organizations in our review:

American Association of Health Plans
American Benefits Council
Academy for Health Services Research and Health Policy
American Civil Liberties Union
American Health Information Management Association
American Hospital Association
American Medical Association
American Pharmaceutical Association
Association of American Medical Colleges
Blue Cross and Blue Shield Association
Health Insurance Association of America
Health Privacy Project
Joint Commission on Accreditation of Healthcare Organizations
Merck-Medco Managed Care, L.L.C.
National Association of Insurance Commissioners
National Partnership for Women and Families
Pharmaceutical Research and Manufacturers of America

requirements preempt the federal regulation. Some groups favored this flexibility, whereas others asserted that the lack of a single set of privacy standards will add regulatory burden. Finally, many organizations raised questions about the feasibility and cost of implementing the regulation in the time allotted.

BACKGROUND

The federal privacy regulation is the second of nine administrative simplification standards to be issued under HIPAA that HHS has released in final form.[6] In addition to information privacy, the standards are to address transaction codes and medical data code sets; consistent identifiers for patients, providers, health plans, and employers; claims attachments that support a request for payment; data security; and enforcement. Taken together, the nine standards are intended to streamline the flow of information integral to the operation of the health care system while protecting confidential health information from inappropriate access, disclosure, and use.

HIPAA required the Secretary of HHS to submit recommendations to the Congress on privacy standards, addressing (1) the rights of the individual who is the subject of the information; (2) procedures for exercising such rights; and (3) authorized and required uses and disclosures of such information. HIPAA further directed that if legislation governing these privacy standards was not enacted within three (3) years of the enactment of HIPAA — by August 21, 1999 — the Secretary should issue regulations on the matter. HHS submitted recommendations to Congress on September 11, 1997, and when legislation was not enacted by the deadline, issued a draft regulation on November 3, 1999. After receiving over 52,000 comments on the proposed regulation, HHS issued a final regulation on December 28, 2000.

Two key provisions in HIPAA defined the framework within which HHS developed the privacy regulation.

- HIPAA specifically applies the administrative simplification standards to health plans, health care clearinghouses (entities that facilitate the flow of information between providers and payers), and health care providers that maintain and transmit health information electronically. HHS lacks the authority under HIPAA to directly regulate the actions of other entities that have access to personal health information, such as pharmacy benefit management companies acting on behalf of managed care networks.[7]
- HIPAA does not allow HHS to preempt state privacy laws that are more protective of health information privacy. Also, state laws concerning public health surveillance (such as monitoring the spread of infectious diseases) may not be preempted.

HIPAA does not impose limits on the type of health care information to which federal privacy protection would apply. At the time the proposed regulation was issued, HHS sought to protect only health data that had been stored or transmitted electronically, but it asserted its legal authority to cover all personal health care data if it chose to do so.[8] HHS adopted this position in the final regulation and extended privacy protection to personal health information in whatever forms it is stored or exchanged — electronic, written, or oral.

PRIVACY REGULATION ESTABLISHES NEW RIGHTS AND RESPONSIBILITIES

The new regulation establishes a minimum level of privacy protection for individually identifiable health information that is applicable nationwide. When it takes full effect, patients will enjoy new privacy rights, and providers, plans, researchers, and others will have new responsibilities.[9] Most groups have until February 26, 2003, to come into compliance with the new regulation, while small health plans[10] were given an additional year.

Patients' Rights

The regulation protecting personal health information provides patients with a common set of rights regarding access to and use of their medical records. For the first time, these rights will apply to all Americans, regardless of the state in which they live or work. Specifically, the regulation provides patients the following:

- *Access to their medical records.* Patients will be able to view and copy their information, request that their records be amended, and obtain a history of authorized disclosures.
- *Restrictions on disclosure.* Patients may request that restrictions be placed on the disclosure of their health information. (Providers may choose not to accept such requests.) Psychotherapy notes may not be used by, or disclosed to, others without explicit authorization.
- *Education.* Patients will receive a written notice of their providers' and payers' privacy procedures, including an explanation of patients' rights and anticipated uses and disclosures of their health information.
- *Remedies.* Patients will be able to file a complaint with the HHS Office for Civil Rights (OCR) that a user of their personal health information has not complied with the privacy requirements.[11] Violators will be subject to civil and criminal penalties established under HIPAA.

Responsibilities of Providers, Health Plans, and Clearinghouses

Providers, health plans, and clearinghouses — referred to as covered entities — must meet new requirements and follow various procedures, as follows:

- *Develop policies and procedures for protecting patient privacy.* Among other requirements, a covered entity must designate a privacy official, train its employees on the entity's privacy policies, and develop procedures to receive and address complaints.
- *Obtain patients' written consent or authorization.* Providers directly treating patients must obtain written consent to use or disclose protected health information to carry out routine health care functions.[12] Routine uses include nonemergency treatment, payment, and an entity's own health care operations.[13] In addition, providers, health plans, and clearinghouses must obtain separate written authorization from the patient to use or disclose information for nonroutine purposes, such as releasing information to lending institutions or life insurers.[14]
- *Limit disclosed information to the minimum necessary.* Covered entities must limit their employees' access to identifiable health information to the minimum needed to do their jobs. When sharing personal health information with other entities, they must make reasonable efforts to limit the information disclosed to the minimum necessary to accomplish the purpose of the data request (such as claims payment). However, they may share the full medical record when the disclosure is for treatment purposes.

- *Ensure that "downstream users" protect the privacy of health information.* Covered entities must enter into a contract with any business associates with which they share personal health information for purposes other than consultation, referral, or treatment.[15] Contracts between covered entities and their business associates must establish conditions and safeguards for uses and disclosures of identifiable health information. Covered entities must take action if they know of practices by their business associates that violate the agreement.
- *Adhere to specific procedures in using information for fundraising or marketing.* Covered entities may use protected patient information to develop mailing lists for fundraising appeals, but they must allow patients to choose not to receive future appeals. Similarly, while patient authorization is required to transmit personal health information to a third party for marketing purposes, a covered entity (or its business associate) can itself use such data for marketing on behalf of a third party without authorization. In such cases, the entity must identify itself as the source of the marketing appeal, state whether it is being paid to do so, and give recipients the opportunity to opt out of receiving additional marketing communications.
- *Protect unauthorized release of medical records to employers.* Group health plans must make arrangements to ensure that personal health information disclosed to the sponsors, including employers, will not be used for employment-related purposes, such as personnel decisions, without explicit authorization from the individual.[16] Furthermore, where staff administering the group health plan work in the same office as staff making hiring and promotion decisions, access to personal health information must be limited to those employees who perform health plan administrative functions.

Responsibilities of Researchers

The regulation sets out special requirements for use of personal health information that apply to both federal and privately funded research:

- Researchers may use and disclose health information without authorization if it does not identify an individual. Information is presumed to be de-identified by removing or concealing all individually identifiable data, including name, addresses, phone numbers, Social Security numbers, health plan beneficiary numbers, dates indicative of age, and other unique identifiers specified in the regulation.
- Researchers who seek personal health information from covered entities will have two options. They can either obtain patient authorization or obtain a waiver from such authorization by having their research protocol reviewed and approved by an independent body — an institutional review board (IRB) or privacy board. In its review, the

independent body must determine that the use of personal health information will not adversely affect the rights or welfare of the individuals involved, and that the benefit of the research is expected to outweigh the risks to the individuals' privacy.

Responsibilities and Rights of Federal Agencies and State Governments

HHS and others within the federal government will have a number of specific responsibilities to perform under the regulations. Although it no longer falls to the states to regulate the privacy of health information, states will still be able to enact more stringent laws.

- Federal and state public officials may obtain, without patient authorization, personal health information for public health surveillance; abuse, neglect, or domestic violence investigations; health care fraud investigations; and other oversight and law enforcement activities.
- HHS' OCR has broad authority to administer the regulation and provide guidance on its implementation. It will decide when to investigate complaints that a covered entity is not complying and perform other enforcement functions directly related to the regulations. HIPAA gives HHS authority to impose civil monetary penalties ($100 per violation up to $25,000 per year) against covered entities for disclosures made in error. It may also make referrals for criminal penalties (for amounts of up to $250,000 and imprisonment for up to 10 years) against covered entities that knowingly and improperly disclose identifiable health information.

CONCERNS BY STAKEHOLDERS REFLECT COMPLEXITY OF THE REGULATION

Among the stakeholder groups we interviewed, there was consensus that HHS had effectively taken into account many of the views expressed during the comment period. Most organizations also agreed that the final regulation improved many provisions published in the proposed regulation. At the same time, many groups voiced concerns about the merit, clarity, and practicality of certain requirements.

Overall, considerable uncertainty remains regarding the actions needed to comply with the new privacy requirements. Although the regulation, by definition, is prescriptive, it includes substantial flexibility. For example, in announcing the release of the regulation, HHS noted that "the regulation establishes the privacy safeguard standards that covered entities must meet, but it leaves detailed policies and procedures for meeting these standards to the discretion of each covered entity." Among the stakeholder groups we interviewed, the topics of concern centered on conditions for consent, authorization, and disclosures; rules pertaining to the business associates of covered entities; limited preemption of state laws; the costs of implementation; and HHS' capacity to provide technical assistance.

Consent and Disclosure Provisions Attracted a Range of Concerns

Several of the organizations we contacted considered the regulation's consent, authorization, or disclosure provisions a step forward in the protection of personal health information. However, several groups questioned the merits of some of the provisions. For example, representatives of patient advocacy groups — the National Partnership for Women and Families, the Health Privacy Project, and the American Civil Liberties Union — were concerned that the regulation permits physicians, hospitals, and other covered entities to market commercial products and services to patients without their authorization. One representative noted that commercial uses of patient information without authorization was an issue that provided the impetus for federal action to protect health privacy in the first place. Another representative commented that public confidence in the protection of their medical information could be eroded as a result of the marketing provisions. One representative also concluded that allowing patients the opportunity to opt out in advance of all marketing contacts would better reflect the public's chief concern in this area. HHS officials told us that this option exists under the provision granting patients the right to request restrictions on certain disclosures but that providers are not required to accept such patient requests.

Several organizations questioned whether the scope of the consent provision was sufficient. For example, American Medical Association (AMA) representatives supported the requirement that providers obtain patient consent to disclose personal health information for all routine uses, but questioned why the requirement did not apply to health plans. Plans use identifiable patient information for quality assurance, quality improvement projects, utilization management, and a variety of other purposes. The association underscored its position that consent should be obtained before personal health information is used for any purpose and that the exclusion of health plans was a significant gap in the protection of this information. [The] AMA suggested that health plans could obtain consent as part of their enrollment processes.

The American Association of Health Plans (AAHP) also expressed concerns about the scope of consent, but from a different perspective. AAHP officials believe that the regulation may limit the ability of the plans to obtain the patient data necessary to conduct health care operations if providers' patient consent agreements are drawn too narrowly to allow such data sharing. They suggested two ways to address this potential problem. First, if the health plans and network providers considered themselves an "organized health care arrangement,"[17] access to the information plans needed could be covered in the consent providers obtained from their patients. Second, plans could include language in their contracts with physicians that would ensure access to patients' medical record information.

Several organizations also had questions about how the consent requirement might be applied. For example, the American Pharmaceutical Association (APhA) raised concerns about how pharmacies could obtain written consent prior to treatment — that is, filling a prescription for the first time. The American Health Information Management Association (AHIMA) similarly noted the timing issue for hospitals with respect to getting background medical information from a patient prior to admission. HHS officials told us that they believe the regulation contains sufficient flexibility for providers to develop procedures necessary to address these and similar situations.

Research organizations focused on the feasibility of requirements for researchers to obtain identifiable health information. The regulation requires them to obtain patient authorization unless an independent panel reviewing the research waives the authorization requirement.[18] Although this approach is modeled after long-standing procedures that have applied to federally funded or regulated research,[19] the regulation adds several privacy-specific criteria that an institutional review board or privacy board must consider. The Association of American Medical Colleges and the Academy for Health Services Research and Health Policy expressed specific concerns over the subjectivity involved in applying some of the additional criteria. As an example, they highlighted the requirement that an independent panel determine whether the privacy risks to individuals whose protected health information is to be used or disclosed are reasonable in relation to the value of the research involved.

Relationships Uncertain Regarding Covered Entities and Their Business Associates

Several groups were concerned about the requirement for covered entities to establish a contractual arrangement with their business associates — accountants, attorneys, auditors, data processing firms, among others — that includes assurances for safeguarding the confidentiality of protected information. This arrangement was HHS' approach to ensure that the regulation's protections would be extended to information shared with others in the health care system. Some provider groups we spoke with were confused about the circumstances under which their member organizations would be considered covered entities or business associates.

Some groups, including the Health Insurance Association of America (HIAA) and the Blue Cross and Blue Shield Association (BCBSA), questioned the need for two covered entities sharing information to enter into a business associate contract. The regulation addresses one aspect of this concern. It exempts a provider from having to enter into a business associate contract when the only patient information to be shared is for treatment purposes. This exemption reflects the reasoning that neither entity fits the definition of business associate when they are performing services on behalf of the patient and not for one another. An example of such an exemption might include physicians writing prescriptions to be filled by pharmacists.

Some groups also commented on the compliance challenges related to the business associate arrangement. For example, the representatives of the Joint Commission on Accreditation of Healthcare Organizations (JCAHO) noted that it would need to enter into contracts for each of the 18,000 facilities (including hospitals, nursing homes, home health agencies, and behavioral health providers) that it surveys for accreditation. However, JCAHO officials hope to standardize agreements to some extent and are working on model language for several different provider types. They explained that, because assessing quality of care varies by setting, JCAHO would need more than one model contract.

Views Divided on Partial Preemption of State Laws

Most of the groups we interviewed cited as a key issue the HIPAA requirement that the privacy standards preempt some but not all state laws. Although every state has passed legislation to protect medical privacy, most of these laws regulate particular entities on specific medical conditions, such as prohibiting the disclosure of AIDS test results. However, a few states require more comprehensive protection of patient records. The patient advocacy groups we spoke with believe that partial preemption is critically important to prevent the federal rule from weakening existing privacy protections. According to the Health Privacy Project, the federal regulation will substantially enhance the confidentiality of personal health information in most states, while enabling states to enact more far-reaching privacy protection in the future.

Despite the limited scope of most state legislation at present, other groups representing insurers and employers consider partial preemption to be operationally cumbersome and argue that the federal government should set a single, uniform standard. Organizations that operate in more than one state, such as large employers and health plans, contend that determining what mix of federal and state requirements applies to their operations in different geographic locations will be costly and complex.

Although they currently have to comply with the existing mix of state medical privacy laws, they view the new federal provisions as an additional layer of regulation.[20] A representative of AHIMA remarked that, in addition to state laws, organizations will have to continue to take account of related confidentiality provisions in other federal laws (for example, those pertaining to substance abuse programs) as they develop policies and procedures for notices and other administrative requirements.

The final regulation withdrew a provision in the proposed regulation that would have required HHS to respond to requests for advisory opinions regarding state preemption issues. HHS officials concluded that the volume of requests for such opinions was likely to be so great as to overwhelm the Department's capacity to provide technical assistance in other areas. However, they did not consider it unduly burdensome or unreasonable for entities covered by the regulation to perform this analysis regarding their particular situation, reasoning that any new federal regulation requires those affected by it to examine the interaction of the new regulation with existing state laws and federal requirements.

Stakeholders Believe Compliance Challenges May Be Costly

Several groups in our review expressed concern about the potential costs of compliance with the regulation and took issue with HHS' impact analysis. In that analysis, the Department estimated the covered entities' cost to comply with the regulation to be $17.6 billion over the first 10 years of implementation. Previously, HHS estimated that implementation of the other administrative simplification standards would save $29.9 billion over 10 years, more than offsetting the expenditures associated with the privacy regulation. HHS therefore contends that the regulation complies with the HIPAA requirement that the administrative simplification standards reduce health care system costs.

HHS expects compliance with two provisions — restricting disclosures to the minimum information necessary and establishing a privacy official — to be the most expensive components of the privacy regulation, in both the short and the long term. Exhibit 2 shows HHS' estimates of the costs to covered entities of complying with the privacy regulation.

We did not independently assess the potential cost of implementing the privacy regulation, nor had the groups we interviewed. However, on the basis of issues raised about the regulation, several groups anticipate that the costs associated with compliance will exceed HHS' estimates. For example, BCBSA representatives contended that its training costs are likely to be substantial, noting that its member plans encompass employees in a wide range of positions who will require specialized training courses. [The] AHA cited concerns about potentially significant new costs associated with developing new contracts under the business associate provision. Other provider groups anticipated spending additional time with patients to explain the new requirements and obtain consent, noting

Exhibit 2. HHS' Cost Estimates for Implementing the Privacy Regulation (Millions of Dollars)

Requirements	First-Year Costs (2003)	10-Year Costs (2003–2012)
Disclose only minimum necessary information	$926.2	$5,756.7
Designate a privacy official	723.2	5,905.8
Develop policies and procedures	597.7	597.7
Establish business associate contracts	299.7	800.3
Train employees in privacy policies	287.1	737.2
Track authorized disclosures	261.5	1,125.1
Obtain consent to use patient information	166.1	227.5
De-identify protected health information	124.2	1,177.4
Modify health information for employer use (applies to group health plans)	52.4	52.4
Prepare and distribute notice of privacy practices	50.8	391.0
Obtain IRB or privacy board approval for research	40.2	584.8
Implement a process for individuals to file complaints	6.6	103.2
Amend patient medical records on request	5.0	78.8
Process patient requests to inspect and copy their medical records	1.3	16.8
Total	**3,542.0**	**17,554.7**

Source: Federal Register, Dec. 28, 2000, page 82761.

that these activities will compete with time for direct patient care. Several groups, including AHA, AAMC, and AHIMA, expressed concerns about being able to implement the regulation within the two-year time frame.

Despite their concerns, several groups discussed possible actions that could help mitigate the anticipated administrative burden. For example, [the] AHA plans to develop model forms for patient consent forms, notices explaining privacy practices, business associate contracts, and compliance plans. Representatives of [the] APhA similarly intend to give their members model forms, policies, and procedures for implementing the regulation. [The] AMA expects to provide guidance to physicians and help with forms and notices on a national level, and noted that the state medical associations are likely to be involved in the ongoing analysis of each state's laws that will be required.

HHS' Capacity to Assist with Implementation Questioned

Representatives of some organizations we contacted commented that they were unsure how the Department's OCR will assist entities with the regulation's implementation. They anticipate that the office, with its relatively small staff, will experience difficulty handling the large volume of questions related to such a complex regulation. OCR officials informed us that the office will require additional resources to carry out its responsibilities and that it is developing a strategic plan that will specify both its short- and its long-term efforts related to the regulation.

To carry out its implementation responsibilities, HHS requested and received an additional $3.3 million in supplemental funding above its fiscal year 2001 budget of approximately $25 million. According to OCR, this amount is being used to increase its staff of 237 to support two key functions: educating the public and those entities covered by the rule about the requirements and responding to related questions. OCR officials told us that its efforts to date include presentations to about 20 organizations whose members are affected by the regulation, a hotline for questions, and plans for public forums.

OCR officials said the office had received about 400 questions since the regulation was issued. Most of these inquiries were general questions relating to how copies of the regulation can be obtained, when it goes into effect, and whether it covers a particular entity. Other questions addressed topics such as the language and format to use for consent forms, how to identify organized health care arrangements, whether the regulation applies to deceased patients, and how a patient's identity should be protected in a physician's waiting room. According to OCR officials, technical questions that cannot be answered by OCR staff are referred to appropriate experts within HHS.

CONCLUSION

The final privacy regulation represents an important advancement in the protection of individuals' health information. It offers all Americans the opportunity to know and, to some extent, control how physicians, hospitals, and health plans use their personal information. At the same time, these entities will face a complex set of privacy requirements that are not well understood at this time. Some of the uncertainty expressed by stakeholder groups reflects the recent issuance of the regulation. With time, everyone will have greater opportunity to examine its provisions in detail and assess their implications for the ongoing operations of all those affected. In addition, on a more fundamental level, the uncertainty stems from HHS' approach of allowing entities flexibility in complying with its requirements. Although organizations generally applaud this approach, they acknowledge that greater specificity would likely allay some of their compliance concerns.

Mr. Chairman and Members of the Committee, this concludes my prepared statement. I will be happy to answer any questions you may have.

UNITED STATES OF AMERICA LAWS AND ISSUES

GAO Contact and Acknowledgments

For future contacts regarding this testimony, please call Leslie G. Arono-vitz, Director, Health Care — Program Administration and Integrity Issues, at (312) 220-7600. Other individuals who made contributions to this statement include Hannah Fein, Jennifer Grover, Joel Hamilton, Rosamond Katz, Eric Peterson, Daniel Schwimer, and Craig Winslow.

Notes

1. P.L. 104-191, 264, 110 Stat. 1936, 2033.
2. 65 *Fed. Reg.* 82,462 (2000). The regulation can also be accessed at http://aspe.hhs.gov/admnsimp/.
3. The regulation was to become effective on February 26, 2001. However, it is unclear whether the Administration's moratorium delaying the effective dates of regulations that have been published in the *Federal Register* will apply to the HHS privacy regulation.
4. Privacy Standards: Issues in HHS' Proposed Rule on Confidentiality of Personal Health Information (GAO/T-HEHS-00-106, Apr. 26, 2000).
5. In addition to interviewing selected groups, we also received information volunteered from other organizations.
6. A regulation governing electronic transactions was issued on August 17, 2000.
7. The regulation does not govern workers compensation carriers, life insurers, Web sites that do not provide health treatment or insurance services, and other entities that collect and maintain health information. An unknown number of providers are not covered entities because they do not electronically transmit any of the standard financial or administrative transactions specified in HIPAA. Although likely to be few overall, members of this group, including some physicians providing occupational health care for employers, could have control over sensitive patient information.
8. In our previous testimony we specifically examined HHS' legal authority to include personal health information that had never been stored or transmitted electronically. We determined that the Department was correct in its conclusion that HIPAA did not restrict the potential scope of the regulation on this basis.
9. The Privacy Act of 1974 (5 USC 552a) established privacy protections for the use of personal health information by federal agencies.
10. Small health plans are defined in the regulation as those with annual receipts of $5 million or less.
11. The regulation does not authorize patients to sue to enforce privacy standards. However, a patient may bring a claim in a state where such actions are permitted under statute or common law.
12. A consent is written in general terms and references the notice that patients receive regarding the use of protected health information. Providers may make patient consent a condition of receiving treatment.
13. Health care operations are a provider's or health plan's management and other activities necessary for support of treatment or payment. For example, a hospital may use personal health information to teach or train staff, conduct research on treatments, or assure quality.
14. The regulation specifies certain situations in which providers and plans require neither a written consent nor authorization before health information is used or disclosed. Examples include health system oversight, public health activities, certain research studies, law enforcement, and facilities' patient directories (patient must be given opportunity to opt out).
15. A business associate is any person or organization that performs a function involving the use or disclosure of identifiable health information on behalf of a covered entity or provides legal, actuarial, accounting, or other services. Physicians on hospital medical staffs are not considered business associates of the hospital.

16. Group health plans include employee welfare benefit plans (both insured and self-insured) subject to the Employee Retirement Income Security Act (ERISA). Employee health benefit plans are excluded if they have fewer than 50 participants.
17. An organized health care arrangement involves clinical or operational integration among legally separate covered entities, which often need to share protected health information for the joint management and operations of the arrangement.
18. Authorization is not required for "de-identified" information. However, several organizations were concerned that the regulation's provisions for de-identification specify the removal of information that could be important for research purposes, such as a patient's county, city, or zip code.
19. The Federal Policy for the Protection of Human Subjects, referred to as the Common Rule, describes conditions under which research may be conducted without obtaining an individual's authorization to use identifiable health information.
20. In the case of employee health plans, which are covered by ERISA, the federal preemption of state laws that "relate to" those plans will continue to apply. Therefore, a state law that established more stringent privacy protections than the federal privacy regulation may or may not supplant the regulation for ERISA plans in the state, depending on the facts and circumstances involved.

Chapter 40

Financial Services Modernization Act
Summary of Provisions
Gramm–Leach–Bliley

TITLE I: FACILITATING AFFILIATION AMONG BANKS, SECURITIES FIRMS, AND INSURANCE COMPANIES

- Repeals the restrictions on banks affiliating with securities firms contained in sections 20 and 32 of the Glass–Steagall Act.
- Creates a new "financial holding company" under Section 4 of the Bank Holding Company Act. Such holding company can engage in a statutorily provided list of financial activities, including insurance and securities underwriting and agency activities, merchant banking and insurance company portfolio investment activities. Activities that are "complementary" to financial activities also are authorized. The non-financial activities of firms predominantly engaged in financial activities (at least 85 percent financial) are grandfathered for at least 10 years, with a possibility for a five year extension.
- The Federal Reserve may not permit a company to form a financial holding company if any of its insured depository institution subsidiaries are not well capitalized and well managed, or did not receive at least a satisfactory rating in their most recent CRA exam.
- If any insured depository institution or insured depository institution affiliate of a financial holding company received less than a satisfactory rating in its most recent CRA exam, the appropriate Federal banking agency may not approve any additional new activities or acquisitions under the authorities granted under the Act.
- Provides for State regulation of insurance, subject to a standard that no State may discriminate against persons affiliated with a bank.
- Provides that bank holding companies organized as a mutual holding companies will be regulated on terms comparable to other bank holding companies.

- Lifts some restrictions governing nonbank banks.
- Provides for a study of the use of subordinated debt to protect the financial system and deposit funds from "too big to fail" institutions and a study on the effect of financial modernization on the accessibility of small business and farm loans.
- Streamlines bank holding company supervision by clarifying the regulatory roles of the Federal Reserve as the umbrella holding company supervisor, and the State and other Federal financial regulators which "functionally" regulate various affiliates.
- Provides for Federal bank regulators to prescribe prudential safeguards for bank organizations engaging in new financial activities.
- Prohibits FDIC assistance to affiliates and subsidiaries of banks and thrifts.
- Allows a national bank to engage in new financial activities in a financial subsidiary, except for insurance underwriting, merchant banking, insurance company portfolio investments, real estate development and real estate investment, so long as the aggregate assets of all financial subsidiaries do not exceed 45 percent of the parent bank's assets or $50 billion, whichever is less. To take advantage of the new activities through a financial subsidiary, the national bank must be well capitalized and well managed. In addition, the top 100 banks are required to have an issue of outstanding subordinated debt. Merchant banking activities may be approved as a permissible activity beginning 5 years after the date of enactment of the Act.
- Ensures that appropriate anti-trust review is conducted for new financial combinations allowed under the Act.
- Provides for national treatment for foreign banks wanting to engage in the new financial activities authorized under the Act.
- Allows national banks to underwrite municipal revenue bonds

TITLE II: FUNCTIONAL REGULATION

- Amends the Federal securities laws to incorporate functional regulation of bank securities activities.
- The broad exemptions banks have from broker-dealer regulation would be replaced by more limited exemptions designed to permit banks to continue their current activities and to develop new products.
- Provides for limited exemptions from broker-dealer registration for transactions in the following areas: trust, safekeeping, custodian, shareholder and employee benefit plans, sweep accounts, private placements (under certain conditions), and third party networking arrangements to offer brokerage services to bank customers, among others.

- Allows banks to continue to be active participants in the derivatives business for all credit and equity swaps (other than equity swaps to retail customers).
- Provides for a "jump ball" rulemaking and resolution process between the SEC and the Federal Reserve regarding new hybrid products.
- Amends the Investment Company Act to address potential conflicts of interest in the mutual fund business and amendments to the Investment Advisers Act to require banks that advise mutual funds to register as investment advisers.

TITLE III: INSURANCE

- Provides for the functional regulation of insurance activities.
- Establishes which insurance products banks and bank subsidiaries may provide as principal.
- Prohibits national banks not currently engaged in underwriting or sale of title insurance from commencing that activity. However, sales activities by banks are permitted in States that specifically authorize such sales for State banks, but only on the same conditions. National bank subsidiaries are permitted to sell all types of insurance including title insurance. Affiliates may underwrite or sell all types of insurance including title insurance.
- State insurance and Federal regulators may seek an expedited judicial review of disputes with equalized deference.
- The Federal banking agencies are directed to establish consumer protections governing bank insurance sales.
- Preempts state laws interfering with affiliations.
- Provides for interagency consultation and confidential sharing of information between the Federal Reserve Board and State insurance regulators.
- Allows mutual insurance companies to re-domesticate.
- Allows multi-state insurance agency licensing.

TITLE IV: UNITARY SAVINGS AND LOAN HOLDING COMPANIES

- *De novo* unitary thrift holding company applications received by the Office of Thrift Supervision after May 4, 1999, shall not be approved.
- Existing unitary thrift holding companies may only be sold to financial companies.

TITLE V: PRIVACY

- Requires clear disclosure by all financial institutions of their privacy policy regarding the sharing of non-public personal information with both affiliates and third parties.

- Requires a notice to consumers and an opportunity to "opt-out" of sharing of non-public personal information with nonaffiliated third parties subject to certain limited exceptions.
- Addresses a potential imbalance between the treatment of large financial services conglomerates and small banks by including an exception, subject to strict controls, for joint marketing arrangements between financial institutions.
- Clarifies that the disclosure of a financial institution's privacy policy is required to take place at the time of establishing a customer relationship with a consumer and not less than annually during the continuation of such relationship.
- Provides for a separate rather than joint rulemaking to carry out the purposes of the subtitle; the relevant agencies are directed, however, to consult and coordinate with one another for purposes of assuring to the maximum extent possible that the regulations that each prescribes are consistent and comparable with those prescribed by the other agencies.
- Allows the functional regulators sufficient flexibility to prescribe necessary exceptions and clarifications to the prohibitions and requirements of Section 502.
- Clarifies that the remedies described in Section 505 are the exclusive remedies for violations of the subtitle.
- Clarifies that nothing in this title is intended to modify, limit, or supersede the operation of the Fair Credit Reporting Act.
- Extends the time period for completion of a study on financial institutions' information-sharing practices from 6 to 18 months from date of enactment.
- Requires that rules for the disclosure of institutions' privacy policies must be issued by regulators within 6 months of the date of enactment. The rules will become effective 6 months after they are required to be prescribed unless the regulators specify a later date.
- Assigns authority for enforcing the subtitle's provisions to the Federal Trade Commission and the Federal banking agencies, the National Credit Union Administration, the Securities and Exchange Commission, according to their respective jurisdictions, and provides for enforcement of the subtitle by the States.

TITLE VI: FEDERAL HOME LOAN BANK SYSTEM MODERNIZATION

- Banks with less than $500 million in assets may use long-term advances for loans to small businesses, small farms and small agribusinesses.
- A new, permanent capital structure for the Federal Home Loan Banks is established. Two classes of stock are authorized, redeemable on 6-months and 5-years notice. Federal Home Loan Banks must meet a

5 percent leverage minimum tied to total capital and a risk-based requirement tied to permanent capital.

- Equalizes the stock purchase requirements for banks and thrifts.
- Voluntary membership for Federal savings associations takes effect 6 months after enactment.
- The current annual $300 million funding formula for the REFCORP obligations of the Federal Home Loan Banks is changed to 20 percent of annual net earnings.
- Governance of the Federal Home Loan Banks is decentralized from the Federal Housing Finance Board to the individual Federal Home Loan Banks. Changes include the election of chairperson and vice chairperson of each Federal Home Loan Bank by its directors rather than the Finance Board, and a statutory limit on Federal Home Loan Bank directors' compensation.

TITLE VII: OTHER PROVISIONS

- Requires ATM operators who impose a fee for use of an ATM by a non-customer to post a notice on the machine that a fee will be charged and on the screen that a fee will be charged and the amount of the fee. This notice must be posted before the consumer is irrevocably committed to completing the transaction. A paper notice issued from the machine may be used in lieu of a posting on the screen. No surcharge may be imposed unless the notices are made and the consumer elects to proceed with the transaction. Provision is made for those older machines that are unable to provide the notices required. Requires a notice when ATM cards are issued that surcharges may be imposed by other parties when transactions are initiated from ATMs not operated by the card issuer. Exempts ATM operators from liability if properly placed notices on the machines are subsequently removed, damaged, or altered by anyone other than the ATM operator.
- Clarifies that nothing in the Act repeals any provision of the CRA.
- Requires full public disclosure of all CRA agreements.
- Requires each bank and each non-bank party to a CRA agreement to make a public report each year on how the money and other resources involved in the agreement were used.
- Grants regulatory relief regarding the frequency of CRA exams to small banks and savings and loans (those with no more than $250 million in assets). Small institutions having received an outstanding rating at their most recent CRA exam shall not receive a routine CRA exam more often than once each 5 years. Small institutions having received a satisfactory rating at their most recent CRA exam shall not receive a routine CRA exam more often than once each 4 years.

- Directs the Federal Reserve Board to conduct a study of the default rates, delinquency rates, and profitability of CRA loans.
- Directs the Treasury, in consultation with the bank regulators, to study the extent to which adequate services are being provided as intended by the CRA.
- Requires a GAO study of possible revisions to S Corporation rules that may be helpful to small banks.
- Requires Federal banking regulators to use plain language in their rules published after January 1, 2000.
- Allows Federal savings associations converting to national or State bank charters to retain the term "Federal" in their names.
- Allows one or more thrifts to own a banker's bank.
- Provides for technical assistance to microenterprises (meaning businesses with fewer than 5 employees that lack access to conventional loans, equity, or other banking services). This program will be administered by the Small Business Administration.
- Requires annual independent audits of the financial statements of each Federal Reserve bank and the Board of Governors of the Federal Reserve System.
- Authorizes information sharing among the Federal Reserve Board and Federal or State authorities.
- Requires a GAO study analyzing the conflict of interest faced by the Board of Governors of the Federal Reserve System between its role as a primary regulator of the banking industry and its role as a vendor of services to the banking and financial services industry.
- Requires the Federal banking agencies to conduct a study of banking regulations regarding the delivery of financial services, and recommendations on adapting those rules to online banking and lending activities.
- Protects FDIC resources by restricting claims for the return of assets transferred from a holding company to an insolvent subsidiary bank.
- Provides relief to out-of-State banks generally by allowing them to charge interest rates in certain host states that are no higher than rates in their home states.
- Allows foreign banks generally to establish and operate Federal branches or agencies with the approval of the Federal Reserve Board and the appropriate banking regulator if the branch has been in operation since September 29, 1994, or the applicable period under appropriate State law.
- Expresses the sense of the Congress that individuals offering financial advice and products should offer such services and products in a nondiscriminatory, nongender-specific manner.
- Permits the Chairman of the Federal Reserve Board and the Chairman of the Securities and Exchange Commission to substitute designees

to serve on the Emergency Oil and Gas Guarantee Loan Guarantee Board and the Emergency Steel Loan Guarantee Board.

- Repeals Section 11(m) of the Federal Reserve Act, removing the stock collateral restriction on the amount of a loan made by a State bank member of the Federal Reserve System.
- Allows the FDIC to reverse an accounting entry designating about $1 billion of SAIF dollars to a SAIF special reserve, which would not otherwise be available to the FDIC unless the SAIF designated reserve ratio declines by about 50 percent and would be expected to remain at that level for more than one year.
- Allow directors serving on the boards of public utility companies to also serve on the boards of banks.

Chapter 41

Gramm–Leach–Bliley (GLB) Financial Services Modernization Act

Miguel O. Villegas
John B. Van Borssum

"Indeed, the most effective means to counter technology's erosion of privacy is technology itself. … We may even see the deployment of technologies that permit individuals to make choices calibrating their degree of privacy in conducting individual transactions. … Given choices in the marketplace that include price, quality and differing degrees of privacy, I have little doubt that privacy would be valued and sought after."

— Remarks by Alan Greenspan, Chairman of the Federal Reserve
at the Conference on Privacy in the Information Age,
Salt Lake City, Utah, March 7, 1997

No one needs to be reminded that the right to privacy is a much-cherished possession. As this century dawns, advances in technology have introduced threats to personal privacy in ways that no one ever imagined. What many of us are not aware of is just how available information is about our private lives. Organizations have always been concerned about security of critical information. Companies often discipline employees who gain access to data and information not within the scope of their job function. However, we need to ask whether those that do have access privileges are using this information correctly and ethically.

The Fourth Amendment to the U.S. Constitution says that "The right of the people to be secure in their persons, houses, papers, and effects, against unreasonable searches and seizures, shall not be violated, and no

0-8493-1248-5/02/$0.00+$1.50
© 2002 by CRC Press LLC

warrants shall issue, but upon probable cause, supported by oath or affirmation, and particularly describing the place to be searched, and the persons or things to be seized."

Basically, the Fourth Amendment prohibits law enforcement and other government officials from searching people's homes and offices or seizing their property without reasonable grounds to believe that a crime has been committed. In most cases, police can conduct a search of a person's home or office only after they have obtained a written search warrant from a judge, detailing where they will search and what they expect to find. We believe in this right. However, when it comes to businesses or institutions who do not necessarily search peoples homes, we need to realize that they have access to information that threatens security of our "persons, houses, papers, and effects." Or does it?

Amitai Etzioni in his book *Limits of Privacy* writes that the "threat to privacy arises not from the state, the villain that champions of privacy traditionally fear most, but rather from the quest for profit by some private companies, privacy merchants."

With the advent of the Gramm–Leach–Bliley Financial Services Modernization Act (the GLB Act) and the Health Insurance Portability and Accountability Act (HIPAA), the focus on privacy, nonpublic personal information (NPPI) has become a growing concern in the information security, audit, and management communities.

One can have security without privacy; an organization can attempt to protect everything in its custody. However, privacy cannot exist without security because, once the permission to use information is obtained, there must be measures in place to ensure that privacy. The authors believe that security without privacy is inefficient and privacy without security is ineffective.

WHAT IS NPPI?

Basically, nonpublic personal information is data about individuals (customers, employees, or the general public) not otherwise available via public sources. For example, NPPI might include a person's name, age, place of birth, citizenship, gender, address/ZIP code, income, credit card number, marital status, or children.

There is other NPPI that, if not controlled, leads to a breach of a person's confidentiality. This includes, but is not limited to, information such as sexual preference, union membership, purchase history, credit history, medical records, marital records, income history, employment history/status, and family historical records.

Consumer concerns about loss of privacy have led to regulatory investigations of numerous companies regarding their data collection and sharing practices. These concerns have led to the passage of laws in many countries protecting personal privacy. In the United States, Congress and many state legislatures, having already passed privacy laws, are currently considering stronger legislation that will change the way business is conducted. In 2001, an organization engaged in online activities — especially those in which customer information is heavily utilized for personalization and marketing efforts — risks violating new legal requirements, enraging consumer advocacy groups, and losing the trust and confidence of consumers.

Actually, many organizations today underestimate consumer concern, while relying heavily on consumer personal information. Examples of business NPPI abuse include:

- Stock in the online banner ad placer, DoubleClick, was negatively impacted after reports of invasive information practices. The practice known as profiling gives marketers the ability to know the household, and in many cases the precise identity, of the person visiting any one of the 11,500 sites that use DoubleClick's ad-tracking "cookies."
- Amazon.com tracked buying habits of corporate employees and was subjected to much criticism, with some companies threatening to stop buying if Amazon did not revise its practices.
- The bankrupt Web site Toysmart.com settled the FTC's charge of alleged privacy policy violations — selling client lists.[9]

Historically, the legal requirements of privacy legislation have been slow in coming. However, they are now being passed with amazing frequency. The following laws were enacted that provide key aspects to security and privacy.

- Fair Credit Reporting Act (1970)
- Privacy Act (1974)
- Family Educational Rights and Privacy Act (1974)
- Right to Financial Privacy Act (1978)
- Cable Communications Privacy Act (1986)
- Electronic Communications Privacy Act (1986)
- Video Privacy Protection Act (1988)
- Telephone Consumer Fraud Protection Act (1991)
- Driver's Privacy Protection Act (1994)
- Telecommunications Act (1996)
- Children's Online Privacy Protection Act (1999)
- Health Insurance Portability and Accountability Act (1996)
- Gramm–Leach–Bliley Financial Services Modernization Act (1999)
- Wireless Communications and Public Safety Act (1999)

GRAMM–LEACH–BLILEY (GLB) FINANCIAL SERVICES MODERNIZATION ACT

Banks and financial services companies have a "call to action" with the Financial Services Modernization Act of 1999 (GLB). The regulations were published in 2000 and early 2001 and mandated that all financial institutions comply with the Act by July 1, 2001.

Requirements for providing "notice," "choice," and a board-approved information security program to support the Act are challenging tasks. Ensuring enterprisewide compliance with the Act is mandatory.

When enacting the privacy and security components of the GLB, Congress intended to create a uniform standard of notification to consumers as to their rights in controlling the use of NPPI obtained by financial institutions and other organizations that perform financial transactions as a substantial part of their business operations. The GLB Act is primarily aimed at the newly consolidated financial services companies, banking institutions, securities firms, and insurance companies. The GLB Act also applies to title companies, retailers who maintain their own credit operations, and third-party intermediaries who become custodians of other companies' records as part of an outsourced service.

GLB Act Title V relies on enforcement by the "Federal functional regulators" (collectively the Securities and Exchange Commission, Federal Reserve Board, Federal Deposit Insurance Corporation, Office of the Comptroller of the Currency, Office of Thrift Supervision, and National Credit Union Association), the Federal Trade Commission, and state insurance commissioners to regulate the financial privacy practices of companies within their respective functional jurisdictions (GLB Act § 505). The consequences of violations could therefore include administrative orders, fines, compensation, and the revocation or denial of licenses to offer regulated financial services. There even could be criminal penalties for knowingly and intentionally violating the statute.

GLB REQUIREMENTS SUMMARY

1. Provide customers with annual notice and choice about the use of their nonpublic personal information.
2. Allow customers to view the financial institution's privacy policies and practices on the Web, in writing and at other critical touch-points throughout the organization. There is no requirement to post on a Web site unless cookies are collected. However, an organization can make its privacy notice available on the site (even exclusively if the customer agrees to receive it in that manner).
3. If applicable, provide customers reasonable opportunity and procedures for "opting out" of the financial institution's sharing of their

personal information with non-affiliated third parties throughout the organization.

4. Banks and similar financial institutions must develop a board-approved information security program that supports the institution's privacy program.

Organizations that qualify as "financial institutions" under the broadest possible interpretation were on notice that they also must have provided their customers with the details of their privacy policy and any required opt-out procedures by the July 2001 deadline. Concurrent with this process, companies must have also begun assessing their internal practices and procedures on how customer information is handled between affiliated companies and unrelated third parties.

While Title V of the GLB Act primarily deals with privacy-related issues surrounding financial institutions' use of nonpublic personal information, the Act emphasizes that sound information security principles are a critical prerequisite to a thorough data privacy program. The provisions of GLB Title V declare that applying appropriate administrative, technical, and physical safeguards must protect nonpublic personal information. Specifically, Section 501(b) of the GLB states that each governing agency must establish appropriate standards for financial institutions to:

1. Ensure the security and confidentiality of customer records and information
2. Protect against any anticipated threats or hazards to the security or integrity of such records
3. Protect against unauthorized access to or use of such records or information that could result in substantial harm or inconvenience to any customer

In compliance with these requirements, the banking regulators published security guidelines in February 2001. The document is entitled, "Interagency Guidelines Establishing Standards for Safeguarding Customer Information and Rescission of Year 2000 Standards for Safety and Soundness." A soft copy of this document in Adobe format is available on the World Wide Web at the following URL address:

http://www.federalreserve.gov/boarddocs/press/boardacts/2001/20010117/

FINANCIAL PRIVACY

The GLB sets specific requirements for financial institutions. They must provide consumers with information about the kinds of nonpublic personal information they collect and whether they disseminate NPPI to third parties. The regulatory guidance proscribes specific wording that institutions must use in providing this information to consumers. Many privacy experts have decried this wording as being too generic to give consumers real information about the type and use of their personal information. They further have pointed out that the permitted exception for sharing information with third-party financial institutions with which they have a joint marketing agreement permits "business as usual."

NPPI in Financial Services

The fact of the matter is that there is little information housed on a financial institution's databases that is not nonpublic information as defined in the regulation. The very existence of an account relationship is NPPI. Social security numbers, reports from consumer reporting agencies, account numbers, and account balances would definitely be classified as NPPI.

Name and address are typically considered NPPI because an institution would need to verify whether the data is generally available to the public. This could require searching through telephone directories to determine if a name is listed as John Doe vs. J Doe; J Doe might be Jane Doe. Many telephone directories list only the city and not the street address — typically requested by the individual. Telephone numbers often are not published at all, usually because the consumer does not want to share this information.

Of course, in addition to researching whether the information is available, the institution would then be required to code individual fields as public or private. Clearly, this would be an onerous task. Rather than conduct the research necessary to determine what is publicly available or code individual data fields, the vast majority of institutions treat all information as NPPI.

Opt-Out Notices

Included with the disclosure that institutions provide to consumers, they must also offer an "opt-out" capability if they plan to share NPPI with third parties in ways that are not permitted exceptions. The opt-out gives a consumer the right to limit the use of NPPI. This creates significant record-keeping requirements for the institutions. Individual account or customer records must be coded with the opt-out preference.

That opt-out preference must then act as a filter when preparing a list of customers to be shared with third parties. Institutions must record the opt-out preference in a timely manner and maintain sufficient records to demonstrate to regulators that the institution does not share NPPI inappropriately. These examinations are only beginning in the second half of 2001 so no one really knows how much detail the regulators will require to prove this negative. The examination checklist indicates that the institution will need to provide its opt-out list and sample data files to the examiner. This would indicate that regulators would test the integrity of the list and its efficacy in limiting the disclosure of NPPI.

Annual Notices

A financial institution is further required to provide an annual notice of its privacy statement to its customers and update its privacy statement when it changes significantly. Regulators have perceived these requirements as having various economic impacts on institutions, depending on size and whether or not the institution shares NPPI. In most cases, institution costs have exceeded $100,000 to develop the policies, print and mail disclosures, make system changes, and create procedures to manage opt-out directives.

Privacy and Information Security

Every financial institution must develop and maintain an information security program with appropriate administrative, technical, and physical safeguards to protect the security, integrity, and confidentiality of customer information.

For banking institutions (including commercial banks, Internet banks, thrifts, and credit unions), GLB regulatory requirements were actually published in two documents: one dealing with financial privacy and the second with maintaining sufficient information safeguards to ensure effective protection of NPPI. The second document, published in February 2001, provides the requirements for an information security program. The banking regulators offered detailed guidance to develop the information security program. The SEC did not publish similar guidance and the following sections pertain primarily to banking institutions.

Board Ratification of the Information Security Program

The board of directors must formally ratify the program, and there must be at least an annual report to the board on the status of the program. This clearly gives the board responsibility for ensuring that the company's policies regarding NPPI are enforced. If there was any doubt of the importance attached with GLB compliance, the fact there are criminal penalties for willful and intentional violations of the Act this should remove that doubt.

The information security program must be designed to:

- Ensure that the security and confidentiality of customer information is maintained
- Protect against any anticipated threats or hazards to the security and integrity of such information
- Protect against unauthorized access to or use of NPPI that could cause substantial harm or inconvenience to any customer

These are demanding objectives that encompass information protection and application integrity. The key concept of information privacy is that the use of NPPI must be authorized; that is, permission to use information must be granted. The information security provisions of the regulation mandate that adequate protection must also be afforded. In other words, an institution can face regulatory sanction even if it has a comprehensive privacy program but fails to secure the information from unauthorized change or disclosure.

While the information security program must target customer information, we recommend that our clients' programs also address their company-private information, such as business plans, employment records, etc.

Risk Assessment

Like other recent bank regulatory guidance, the information security program must be risk based. It begins with a comprehensive assessment of threats to customer information. In this assessment, the institution must identify what could happen to customer information, and then assess the likelihood and impact of the threat. The next logical step in the risk assessment is to inventory any preemptive measures the institution has taken to reduce the resultant risk. We have suggested to clients that certain definitions systematize this assessment.

- *Likelihood*: the frequency of this threat causing a privacy lapse in typical financial institutions
- *Impact*: the magnitude of that lapse (e.g., service disruption, embarrassment, legal action, or fraud) if the information is disclosed inappropriately
- *Control*: a mechanism that reduces the likelihood or impact of a privacy lapse
- *Resultant risk*: a mathematical formula similar to Likelihood + Impact − Control

Most of our clients apply this discipline throughout their information security risk assessment because any compromise of an institution's data is likely to involve customer information. The information security program must be designed to safeguard against both internal and external access to customer information as the next section of the regulation details.

Evaluate the Program

The regulation requires that the information security program be adjusted as appropriate. This means that new products and services must be evaluated with customer privacy in mind. As new business risks are identified, there needs to be an evaluation of the institution's response to that threat. If new controls are warranted, there should be a plan to put them in place.

The institution also needs to consider the impact of mergers and establishing new relationships with service providers and joint marketers.

If a new control would be more reliable in reducing risk, it needs to be evaluated from a cost-benefit perspective. The benefits will now include regulatory compliance and protection from criminal liability if customer information is involved.

Manage and Control Risk

The information security program must include an analysis of the following eight key areas:

1. Access controls present in customer information systems must be sufficient to prevent the disclosure of NPPI. The regulation specifically directs this toward employee access. Are system security parameters stringent? Do application security mechanisms effectively limit employee access to customer information needed to perform authorized job duties?
2. Physical restrictions must be in place to allow access only to authorized individuals. Do you need to adopt clean desk procedures or implement new barriers into customer service areas that have hard-copy of customer information?
3. Encryption of customer information while in transit or in storage must be considered if there is a likelihood that unauthorized individuals can obtain the information. This can be a significant issue for many institutions. Historically, encryption has been implemented to protect the institution's assets (ATM and funds transfer traffic), but now it must be expanded to include the explicit obligation to protect customer information routinely exchanged between business units. Do you transmit account information using electronic mail systems through the Internet? If you fail to maintain adequate operating system security, must you then encrypt all databases that house customer information?
4. There must be change control procedures to maintain the integrity of systems housing customer information. How does your programming staff get its test data? Because they probably cannot demonstrate a business need to have actual customer information, is it anonymized before being provided to applications development staff? Are algorithms and edits tested to ensure that the integrity of customer information is maintained?

5. Segregation of duties must be maintained to protect customer information so that employees only have access to information that is needed to perform authorized job duties. You must also have a reasonable program in place to ensure that those being hired have the integrity and scruples to handle customer information appropriately. How stringent are your background investigations? Does your plan of organization not only limit the possibility of fraud, but also access to customer information?

6. Monitoring for unauthorized attempts to obtain customer information is a critical part of the information security program. Many institutions receive volumes of data every day about security violations — some external, but most internal. How effective is the institution at identifying trends and sifting through intentional and inadvertent security breaches?

7. If you detect a security breach, you must have a program in place to respond to the incident. This normally involves a high-level assessment of the severity followed by counseling an employee or blocking a security lapse. We further suggest to clients that they create a formal program to escalate security events, including dealing with the media should there be a public intrusion into the institution's systems. Do you routinely report attempted intrusions into your information systems on a Suspicious Activity Report?

8. There must be measures in place to protect against the destruction, damage, or loss of customer information as a result of an environmental hazard or technology failure. How current is your business resumption plan? Do you have adequate backups of data files that house customer information?

While these eight key areas are easy to understand, they have significant implications when being deployed in an organization.

Employee Awareness and Training

Once the information security program is developed, the institution's employees must be trained to comply with it. For most institutions, this is relatively straightforward. Financial institutions pride themselves on the trust relationships they have nurtured. The fiduciary relationship that exists is typically engrained into the culture through employee handbooks, codes of conduct, and general policy and procedure. There is a benefit to an institution to ensure that its employees know that information security is important, and that they have a responsibility to not share passwords, and to report unusual requests or suspected security breaches.

Periodic Testing

The information security program must include provisions for periodic testing of its effectiveness. This means audits and management certification that the information security program is being followed. When a significant lapse is detected, prompt action needs to be taken to rectify the situation. The reviews should be risk based.

Oversee Service Providers

Third-party relationships need to be managed. Often there is a shared responsibility within an organization when it comes to sharing customer information. Marketing, technology, business management, and legal all have a role to play. A relationship must be governed by a contract that creates an obligation on the third party to protect customer NPPI. For banking institutions, any contract signed after March 5, 2001, must have confidentiality clauses present. Contracts that were signed on or before March 5 that do not address confidentiality must be renegotiated with confidentiality clauses by July 1, 2003. Institutions regulated by the Securities and Exchange Commission have until July 1, 2002, to bring contracts signed prior to July 1, 2000, into compliance with confidentiality terms.

An institution must use appropriate due diligence when selecting a service provider. If it is a managed service, does it provide an SAS-70 report that addresses its information security program? If not, does the institution have the contractual right to conduct its own audit for information security? Many of the marketing uses of customer information are contracted with smaller print and mailing houses. The institution needs to satisfy itself that its customer information will not be divulged. This might require an onsite visit before providing customer NPPI to the vendor.

The institution needs to have a monitoring capability to ensure that its customer data is not being reused despite the contractual limitations. Institutions have historically "salted" data given to third parties to detect unauthorized usage. This practice now has renewed emphasis given the need to manage these third parties' use of customer information.

The information security program envisioned by banking regulators is comprehensive and creates a significant documentation burden. While the Securities and Exchange Commission does not set out a similarly detailed program, its objectives are the same. In both cases, financial institutions have a clear mandate to protect customer information from unauthorized disclosure.

SUMMARY

At first glance, it appears that the GLB Act has imposed another set of regulations for security and confidentiality of information that ultimately translates to more infrastructure expenditures and administrative costs for compliance. Although this may be true, there is a return on investment to the financial institution, not the least of which includes customer satisfaction and trust. Privacy and security have in recent customer surveys ranked in the top three concerns.

As technology changes and as we become even more dependent on technology for our daily lives, new laws and new controls will evolve. There still remains more to be accomplished in the privacy arena; however, we believe that the GLB has taken efficacious steps to the desired end.

The GLB compliance and reporting requirements have created additional costs for institutions. These costs include:

- Annual notices and opt-out procedures, when required
- Maintaining a formal information security program
- Training staff
- Monitoring third parties
- Performing due diligence before contracting with a service provider
- Testing security systems
- Adjusting security programs due to technology changes

In April 2001, the federal banking regulators released their examination checklist for examining compliance with the GLB. It largely details the examination steps for the privacy aspects of the GLB that were published in June 2000. The actual examination will be part of the safety and soundness reviews as they are scheduled into financial institutions. The information security program will be examined as part of the IT examination. It seems reasonable to anticipate that the risk assessment will be a critical part of the examination for protecting customer information. Institutions will need to ensure that they have addressed the eight key areas, along with training and third-party provider oversight.

Chapter 42
Overviews of Privacy-Related U.S. Laws and Regulations

Rebecca Herold

Are you aware of the multitude of privacy-related laws and regulations that exist in the United States? You need to have a working knowledge of at least the existence of such laws if you are:

- Updating or creating security or privacy policies or procedures for your organization
- A multinational company
- Planning a divestiture
- Planning an acquisition or merger
- Preparing for a major system or application change or upgrade
- Considering major changes to your Human Resources policies or procedures
- Considering the installation of a new communications system
- Planning a new marketing strategy
- Preparing to gather customer/client information
- Preparing to use existing customer/client information in ways other than was intended at the time of collection

The following is a listing of current privacy-related federal laws in addition to those described in previous chapters in this book. Keep in mind when scanning this list that each state also has its own privacy-related laws and regulations for which you need to be aware when doing business there. A nice listing of some of the state laws is found in this book in Chapter 24, entitled "ID Theft: When Bad Things Happen to Your Good Name."

0-8493-1248-5/02/$0.00+$1.50
© 2002 by CRC Press LLC

1. Title VII, Civil Rights Act (1964)

This defines discrimination, and protects constitutional rights in public facilities and public education, in addition to prohibiting discrimination in federally assisted programs. The Equal Employment Opportunity Commission (EEOC) was created as the agency to administer this directive. For more information, see:

- http://www.usbr.gov/laws/civil.html

2. Age Discrimination in Employment Act (ADEA) of 1967

This law restricts employers from asking the age of potential employees. The following site contains the full details:

- http://www.eeoc.gov/laws/adea.html

3. Federal Contract Compliance Regulations (1968)

This executive order applies to companies with federal contracts or subcontracts of certain specified sizes. Such companies must not discriminate based on sex, religion, race, color, or national origin. More details can be found at the following site:

- http://www.dol.gov/dol/esa/public/regs/unifiedagenda/ofccp/ofcpua.htm

4. Fair Credit Reporting Act (1970)

This law regulates the methods used to obtain credit information about job applicants or employees. Some good sites for full information include:

- http://www.ftc.gov/bcp/conline/pubs/credit/fcra.htm
- http://www.ftc.gov/os/statutes/fcrajump.htm

5. Equal Employment Opportunity Act (1972)

These guidelines address employment selection techniques that may be used to discriminate based on race, ethnicity, religion, age, or sex. Full details can be found at:

- http://www4.law.cornell.edu/uscode/42/2000e.html

6. Employee Retirement Income Security Act of 1974 (ERISA)

This law contains directives regarding the protection of personal security and privacy over employee records. A good site for additional information is:

- http://www.dol.gov/dol/pwba/public/regs/fedreg/final/2000029766.htm

7. Privacy Act (1974)

This legislation provides requirements for federal agencies specifying safeguards to protect individuals against invasion of personal privacy. Some good sites for full information on this act include:

- http://www.usdoj.gov/foia/privstat.htm
- http://www.doeal.gov/opa/pa/pahomepg.htm

8. Freedom of Information Act (1974); amended in 1996

This is a federal statute that provides any person with the right to request access to *federal* agency records that apply to that person, with nine exemptions contained in the law and three law enforcement exclusions. It is important to note this does not apply to the executive branch or judicial branch records. Some good sites that contain full information about this statute include:

- http://www.usdoj.gov/oip/foia_updates/Vol_XVII_4/page2.htm
- http://www.foia.state.gov/about.asp

9. Family Educational Rights and Privacy Act of 1974 (FERPA)

This is also known as the "Protection of the Rights and Privacy of Parents and Students" code, as well as the "Buckley Amendment." This is a spending clause statute that provides parents with the right to access "any and all official records, files, and data directly related to their children, including all material that is incorporated into each student's cumulative record folder, and intended for school use or to be available to parties outside the school or school system, and specifically including, but not necessarily limited to, identifying data, academic work completed, level of achievement (grades, standardized achievement test scores), attendance data, scores on standardized intelligence, aptitude, and psychological tests, interest inventory results, health data, family background information, teacher or counselor ratings and observations, and verified reports of serious or recurrent behavior patters." A couple of good sites with further information about this statute include:

- http://www.ed.gov/offices/OESE/SDFS/actguid/infshare.html
- http://www.ed.gov/offices/OM/fpco/Legislativehistory.html

10. Right to Financial Privacy Act (1978)

These regulations require law enforcement to use written request procedures to request financial records from a financial institution, and details the conditions under which the requests can be made. Two good sites for this act are:

- http://www.fdic.gov/regulations/laws/rules/6500-2550.html#7091

- http://www.dol.gov/dol/allcfr/Title_29/Part_19/toc.htm

11. Privacy Protection Act (1980)

This law governs searches and seizures conducted by government officers and employees while performing investigations or prosecuting criminal offenses. Information about this law can be found at:

- http://www4.law.cornell.edu/uscode/42/2000aa.html

12. Paperwork Reduction Act (1980)

One of the purposes of this law is to ensure that the federal government's creation, collection, maintenance, use, dissemination, and disposition of information follows applicable laws such as those addressing privacy and confidentiality, and security of information. The full text of this act is located at:

- http://www.rdc.noaa.gov/~pra/pralaw.htm

13. Cable Communications Policy Act (1984)

This requires the privacy of cable television subscriber records. A Web site with further information is:

- http://www.fcc.gov/Bureaus/Cable/Informal/cablinfo.txt

14. Omnibus Crime Control Act (1984)

This law created the Office of Justice Programs (OJP), some of which address matters such as data privacy, confidentiality, security, and the interstate exchange of criminal records. Part of this law requires telephone companies to cooperate with law enforcement agencies for their wiretapping needs. Discussion of this act can be found in the description of the OJP at:

- http://www.usdoj.gov/jmd/osdbu/doing.htm

15. Electronic Communications Privacy Act (1986)

This law basically extends the protections provided by the Wiretap Act of 1968 to cover electronic communications and communications systems. These include satellite, radio, and data communications. A Web site with further information is:

- http://www4.law.cornell.edu/uscode/18/1367.html

16. Computer Security Act (1987)

This law requires federal agencies to ensure the privacy and security of information stored and processed on their computer and network systems. As part of this, federal agencies must have security standards, conduct security research and training, and develop formal security plans. An additional component of the law is the requirement of a federal Privacy Advisory Board. The text of this law is located at:

- http://csrc.nist.gov/secplcy/csa_87.txt

17. Computer Matching and Privacy Protection Act (1988)

This law requires federal agencies to establish methods to detect discrepancies in individual's records that are stored in multiple databases. It amends the Privacy Act by detailing requirements for federal agency use and exchange of information contained in existing agency databases. Further details can be found at:

- http://www.irs.gov/plain/bus_info/tax_pro/irm-part/part01/ 30463.html
- http://www.iitf.nist.gov/ipc/privacy.htm

18. Video Privacy Protection Act (1988)

This law protects the privacy of video rental transactions and records. Full information can be found at:

- http://www.accessreports.com/statutes/VIDEO1.htm

19. Employee Polygraph Protection Act (1988)

This law makes it illegal for employers to require employees or job applicants to take a lie detector test, or take disciplinary actions based on an employee refusing to take a lie detector test. Full details are found at:

- http://www.dol.gov/dol/esa/public/regs/compliance/whd/ whfs36.html

20. Telephone Consumer Protection Act (1991)

This law places restrictions on the activities of telemarketers, including the time they may make calls, the disclosure of the marketer's identity, and the descriptions and costs of the telemarketer's products or services. For further information, see:

- http://www.fcc.gov/ccb/consumer_news/pl102243.html

21. Civil Rights Act (1991)

One purpose of this law is to to provide appropriate remedies for intentional discrimination and unlawful harassment in the workplace. Full details are found at:

- http://www.eeoc.gov/laws/cra91.html

22. Cable Act (1992)

The privacy protections from the Cable Communications Policy Act of 1984 were expanded to include cable companies that provide cellular and wireless services. Information about this act is located at:

* http://netec.mcc.ac.uk/BibEc/data/Papers/dukdukeec97-32.html

23. Americans with Disabilities Act of 1992 (ADA)

This law requires employers to store health information about employees in a secure and segregated personnel file. Such information is to be classified or treated as confidential. A good overview of this law can be found at the following site:

* http://www.eeoc.gov/facts/fs-ada.html

24. Driver's Privacy Protection Act (1994)

This law places restrictions on how state motor vehicle lists and data can be used. The judicial system, government agencies, and law enforcement may have access. However, the public and public organizations (e.g., marketing researchers) are restricted on how they can use the motor vehicle lists. Additional information can be found at the following site:

* http://www.nydmv.state.ny.us/dppact.htm

25. Communications Assistance for Law Enforcement Act (CALEA) of 1994

This law requires telecommunications carriers to help law enforcement agencies when they need lawful interception of transmissions. This law is found at:

* http://www.fcc.gov/wtb/csinfo/calea.html

26. NII Privacy Principles (1995)

The National Information Infrastructure's principles for protecting and using personal information. These are meant to provide guidance to NII participants who draft laws, create industry code addressing information practices, and design programs that use personal information. Further information is located at:

* http://www.iitf.nist.gov/ipc/ipc/ipc-pubs/niiprivprin_final.html

27. Communications Decency Act (1996)

This law makes it a federal crime to use any telecommunications equipment, including faxes, e-mail, and all equipment covered in the Communications Act of 1934, to annoy, threaten, or harass the people contacted using these technologies. A controversial law, it has been challenged as being unconstitutional. More information about this law can be found at:

- http://www.senate.gov/~leahy/press/199606/960612b.html
- http://www.ntia.doc.gov/opadhome/overview.htm

28. Consumer Credit Reporting Reform Act (1996)

A component of this law requires consumer reporting agencies to perform their business ensuring fairness, impartiality, and respect for consumer privacy. Additional information can be found at:

- http://www.ftc.gov/os/statutes/fcra.htm

29. Fair Debt Collection Practices Act (1996)

This law places restrictions on the release of federal debt information to credit bureaus. More information can be found at:

- http://www.ftc.gov/os/statutes/fdcpa/fdcpact.htm

30. Telecommunications Act (1996)

The purpose of this law is to promote competition and reduce regulation to lower prices and obtain higher quality services for American telecommunications consumers, in addition to encouraging the rapid deployment of new telecommunications technologies. A component of this law prohibits discrimination in actions performed to undertake this law. Further information can be found at:

- http://thomas.loc.gov/cgi-bin/query/z?c104:S.652.ENR
- http://www.ed.gov/Technology/fcc.html

31. Title 21 Code of Federal Regulations (21 CFR Part 11) Electronic Records; Electronic Signatures (1997)

This is a Compliance Policy Guide (CPG) from the Food and Drug Administration (FDA) describing how to comply with the regulations for electronic records and electronic signatures. This guide can be found at the following Web sites:

- http://www.fda.gov/ora/compliance_ref/part11/frs/background/11cfr-fr.htm
- http://www.fda.gov/ohrms/dockets/dockets/00d1539/rpt0002.pdf

32. Identity Theft and Assumption Deterrence Act (1998)

This law prohibits individuals from knowingly transferring or using another person's means of identification (such as name, driver's license, social security number, date of birth, passport, biometric data, etc.) for the purpose of committing or intent to commit illegal activities. Further information can be found at:

- http://www.ftc.gov/os/2000/09/idthefttest.htm

33. Children's On-Line Privacy Protection Act (COPPA) (1998)

This law makes it illegal for online service or Web site operators to purposefully collect personal information about children under several specified circumstances. Full details of the act can be found at the following Web sites:

- http://www.ftc.gov/bcp/conline/pubs/buspubs/coppa.htm
- http://www.itpolicy.gsa.gov/itpolicy/1.pdf

34. Financial Modernization Services Act (1999)

This is the House of Representatives' version of the bill that has become better known by the Senate's Gramm–Leach–Bliley (GLB) version of the bill. The text for this act is located at:

- http://banking.senate.gov/docs/reports/s900es.htm

35. Comparison of Financial Modernization Services Act and Gramm–Leach–Bliley Act

This document provides an interesting comparison between these two separate, but closely related, bills. The comparison is located at:

- http://banking.senate.gov/conf/compare.pdf

36. Federal Trade Commission Act of 1914 (updated in 1999)

This act created the Federal Trade Commission, defined its powers and duties, and included directives governing confidentiality. Information about this act can be found at:

- http://www.fda.gov/opacom/laws/ftca.htm

37. Patients' Bill of Rights (introduced in 1999)

This is a hotly debated bill that had not been passed as of August 2001. It is included it in this chapter because of its close ties to the active HIPAA regulations. An interesting site with further information about this bill is:

- http://www.senate.gov/~dpc/patients_rights/

38. Electronic Communications Privacy Act (2000)

This proposed law (an amendment to the Electronic Communications Privacy Act of 1986) requires judicial oversight when law enforcement officials monitor the electronic communications (such as e-mail) of suspected criminals. The law also prohibits illegally obtained electronic communications from being used as evidence in trials. A Web site that discusses this bill is:

- http://www.cbo.gov/showdoc.cfm?index = 2539&from = 2&sequence = 0

39. Children's Internet Protection Act (CIPA) (S.97) (2000)

This act allows no federal funds to be given to any local educational agency (e.g., schools, libraries, etc.) to pay for costs associated with accessing the Internet unless policies and procedures are in place to prevent children ("minors") from accessing any obscenity, pornography, or other information via the Internet connection that may be considered harmful to children. The text of this law is found at:

- http://www.fcc.gov/ccb/universal_service/chipact.doc

40. Government Information Security Reform Act (2000)

The goal of this act is to ensure adequate security and management for federal operations and assets resources. A good description of the act is located at:

- http://www.fedcirc.gov/docs/Securit.PDF

41. Electronic Signatures in Global and National Commerce Act (2000)

This act governs the use of electronic records and signatures used in interstate and foreign commerce. The details are found at:

- http://www.itpolicy.gsa.gov/itpolicy/7.pdf

Chapter 43
U.S. Bills Under Consideration

Rebecca Herold

Many of the chapters in this book reference a variety of active U.S. bills that address specific information privacy issues. This is a very hot topic. To determine the importance of privacy to the public, one can jsut look at the number of active bills that members of Congress have introduced at the urging of their constituencies.

At the time this book was compiled (late July 2001), there were 50 active bills in the 107th U.S. Congress that concerned privacy issues, were related to privacy, or had privacy requirements as a portion of the bill. Companies need to act proactively and review this list, determine the bills that would impact their organizations, determine the extent of impact to their organization, and either prepare to comply with them or lobby their legislative representatives to vote against the bill.

The list, ranked in comparative relevance to the topic of privacy, follows.

1. Expressing the sense of the House of Representatives that machine-readable privacy policies and the Platform for Privacy Preferences Project specification, commonly known as the P3P... (Introduced in the House) [H.RES.159.IH]
2. Privacy Commission Act (Introduced in the House) [H.R.583.IH]
3. Citizens' Privacy Commission Act of 2001 (Introduced in the Senate) [S.851.IS]
4. Student Privacy Protection Act (Introduced in the Senate) [S.290.IS]
5. Instant Check Gun Tax Repeal and Gun Owner Privacy Act of 2001 (Introduced in the Senate) [S.906.IS]
6. Consumer Privacy Protection Act (Introduced in the House) [H.R.2135.IH]
7. Resolved by the Senate and House of Representatives of the United States of America in Congress assembled, That Congress disapproves the rule submitted by the Department of Health... (Introduced in the House) [H.J.RES.38.IH]

0-8493-1248-5/02/$0.00+$1.50
© 2002 by CRC Press LLC

8. Personal Information Privacy Act of 2001 (Introduced in the House) [H.R.1478.IH]
9. Financial Institution Privacy Protection Act of 2001 (Introduced in the Senate) [S.450.IS]
10. Computer Security Enhancement Act of 2001 (Introduced in the House) [H.R.1259.IH]
11. Social Security Number Privacy Act of 2001 (Introduced in the Senate) [S.324.IS]
12. Consumer Internet Privacy Enhancement Act (Introduced in the House) [H.R.237.IH]
13. Wireless Telephone Spam Protection Act (Introduced in the House) [H.R.113.IH]
14. E-Government Act of 2001 (Introduced in the Senate) [S.803.IS]
15. Personal Pictures Protection Act of 2001 (Introduced in the House) [H.R.1655.IH]
16. Consumer Credit Report Accuracy and Privacy Act of 2001 (Introduced in the House) [H.R.2031.IH]
17. Online Privacy Protection Act of 2001 (Introduced in the House) [H.R.89.IH]
18. Financial Information Privacy Protection Act of 2001 (Introduced in the Senate) [S.30.IS]
19. Who Is E-Mailing Our Kids Act (Introduced in the House) [H.R.1846.IH]
20. Wireless Privacy Protection Act of 2001 (Introduced in the House) [H.R.260.IH]
21. Law Enforcement Officers Privacy Protection Act (Introduced in the House) [H.R.199.IH]
22. Social Security On-Line Privacy Protection Act (Introduced in the House) [H.R.91.IH]
23. Upper Mississippi River Basin Conservation Act of 2001 (Introduced in the House) [H.R.1800.IH]
24. Identity Theft Protection Act of 2001 (Introduced in the House) [H.R.220.IH]
25. Privacy Act of 2001 (Introduced in the Senate) [S.1055.IS]
26. Health Information Technology and Quality Improvement Act of 2001 (Introduced in the Senate) [S.705.IS]
27. Electronic Privacy Protection Act (Introduced in the House) [H.R.112.IH]
28. To modify the deadline for initial compliance with the standards and implementation specifications promulgated under Section 1173 of the Social Security Act, and for other purposes (Introduced in the House) [H.R.1975.IH]
29. Social Security Number Privacy and Identity Theft Prevention Act of 2001 (Introduced in the Senate) [S.1014.IS]

30. Social Security Number Privacy and Identity Theft Prevention Act of 2001 (Introduced in the House) [H.R.2036.IH]
31. Consumer Online Privacy and Disclosure Act (Introduced in the House) [H.R.347.IH]
32. Social Security Number Misuse Prevention Act of 2001 (Introduced in the Senate) [S.848.IS]
33. Internet Toy Safety Awareness Act (Introduced in the House) [H.R.604.IH]
34. Internet Tax Nondiscrimination Act (Introduced in the Senate) [S.288.IS]
35. Spyware Control and Privacy Protection Act of 2001 (Introduced in the Senate) [S.197.IS]
36. National Homeland Security Agency Act (Introduced in the House) [H.R.1158.IH]
37. Internet Tax Moratorium and Equity Act (Introduced in the Senate) [S.512.IS]
38. Internet Tax Moratorium and Equity Act (Introduced in the House) [H.R.1410.IH]
39. Expressing the sense of the House of Representatives on the importance of promoting fair, efficient, and simple cross-border tax collection regimes that maintain market neutrality and... (Introduced in the House) [H.RES.151.IH]
40. Child Support Distribution Act of 2001 (Introduced in the Senate) [S.918.IS]
41. To amend part C of title XI of the Social Security Act to provide for coordination of implementation of administrative simplification standards for health care information (Introduced in the Senate) [S.836.IS]
42. To authorize assistance for mother-to-child HIV/AIDS transmission prevention efforts (Introduced in the House) [H.R.684.IH]
43. Federal Communications Commission Reform Act (Introduced in the House) [H.R.646.IH]
44. Gun Show Background Check Act of 2001 (Introduced in the Senate) [S.767.IS]
45. Human Rights Information Act (Introduced in the House) [H.R.1152.IH]
46. Expressing the sense of Congress that the 2008 Olympic Games should not be held in Beijing unless the government of the People's Republic of China releases all political prisoners, ... (Reported in the House) [H.CON.RES.73.RH]
47. Child Support Distribution Act of 2001 (Introduced in the House) [H.R.1471.IH]
48. Civil Rights Amendments Act of 2001 (Introduced in the House) [H.R.217.IH]

49. Veterans' Hospital Emergency Repair Act (Introduced in the House)
    [H.R.811.IH]
50. Human Cloning Prohibition Act of 2001 (Introduced in the Senate)
    [S.790.IS]

One can find the details of these bills by visiting http://thomas.loc.gov.

Chapter 44

Internet Security and Privacy

Testimony before the Senate Judiciary Committee

James X. Dempsey, Senior Staff Counsel, Center for Democracy and Technology

May 25, 2000

Chairman Hatch, we thank you and Senator Leahy for the opportunity to testify today on the important issue of Internet security and privacy. We congratulate both of you, and Senator Schumer, for your leadership and foresight in beginning to grapple with these difficult issues, both from the law enforcement perspective and from the consumer privacy perspective. S.2448 and the other introduced bills have served to launch an important dialogue. Consensus has not been achieved yet, and we share with you today some of our concerns about various proposals that are being put forth, but CDT is committed to working with you, Mr. Chairman, and other members of this Committee, to develop narrowly focused and properly balanced legislation.

The Center for Democracy and Technology is a non-profit, public interest organization dedicated to promoting civil liberties and democratic values on the Internet. Our core goals include ensuring that the Constitution's protections extend to the Internet and other digital information technologies, and that public policies and technical solutions provide individuals with control over their personal information online. CDT also coordinates the Digital Privacy and Security Working Group (DPSWG), a forum for more than 50 computer, communications, and public interest organizations, companies and associations working on information privacy and security issues.

Our main points today are three-fold:

- While law enforcement must have sufficient authority to fight crime in cyberspace, we must recognize that the Internet industry is in the best position to prevent hacking crimes and protect critical infrastructures by building more secure products and networks.
- Given the tremendous increase in surveillance power brought about by the new technology, we must avoid expansions of government surveillance authority and instead must strengthen the weak and outdated privacy standards controlling government monitoring of communications and access to stored records.
- For consumer privacy, we must seek a solution suited to the rapidly changing Internet, combining the privacy-enhancing potential of the technology itself, self-regulation driven by consumer demands for privacy, and federal legislation that sets baseline standards and provides remedies against the bad actors and outliers.

We focus in this testimony primarily on the Fourth Amendment issues, where this Committee, along with the rest of society, is confronted with what might seem to be a dilemma: how to fight crime on the Internet without intruding on privacy.

A starting point in resolving this apparent dilemma is to recognize that the Internet is a uniquely decentralized, user-controlled medium. Hacking, unauthorized access to computers, denial of service attacks, and the theft, alteration or destruction of data are all already federal crimes, and appropriately so. But Internet security is not a problem primarily within the control of the federal government. Particularly, it is not a problem to be solved through the criminal justice system. Internet security is primarily a matter most effectively addressed by the private sector, which has built this amazing medium in such a short time without government interference. It is clear that the private sector is stepping up its security efforts, with an effectiveness that the government could never match, given the rapid pace of technology change and the decentralized nature of the medium. The tools for warning, diagnosing, preventing and even investigating infrastructure attacks through computer networks are uniquely in the hands of the private sector. In these ways, Internet crime is quite different from other forms of crime. While the potential for the government to help is limited, the risk of government doing harm through design mandates or further intrusions on privacy is very high.

Second, while the Justice Department frequently complains that digital technologies pose new challenges to law enforcement, it is clear, if you look at the Justice Department's record, that the digital revolution has been a boon to government surveillance and collection of information. In testimony on February 16, 2000, before the Senate appropriations subcommittee, FBI

Director Freeh outlined the Bureau's success in many computer crime cases. Online surveillance and tracking led to the arrest of the Phonemasters who stole calling card numbers; the Solar Sunrise culprits, several of whom were located in Israel; an intruder on NASA computers, who was arrested and convicted in Canada; the thieves who manipulated Citibank's computers and who were arrested with cooperation of Russian authorities; Julio Cesar Ardita, who was tracked electronically to Argentina; and the creator of the Melissa virus, among others. Computer files are a rich source of stored evidence: in a single investigation last year, the FBI seized enough computer data to nearly fill the Library of Congress twice. Electronic surveillance is going up, not down, in the face of new technologies. The FBI estimates that over the next decade, given planned improvements in the digital collection and analysis of communications, the number of wiretaps will increase 300 percent. Last year, the largest rate of increase in government intercepts under Title III involved newer electronic technologies, such as e-mail, fax and wireless devices. Online service providers, Internet portals and Web sites are facing a deluge of government subpoenas for records about online activities of their customers. Everywhere we go on the Internet we leave digital fingerprints, which can be tracked by marketers and government agencies alike. The FBI in its budget request for FY 2001 seeks additional funds to "data mine" these public and private sources of digital information for their intelligence value.

Considering the broad sweep of the digital revolution, it is apparent that the major problem now is not that technology is outpacing government's ability to investigate crime, but, to the contrary, that changes in communications and computer technology have outpaced the privacy protections in our laws. Technology is making ever-increasing amounts of information available to government under minimal standards falling far short of Fourth Amendment protections.

Nonetheless, the Justice Department is seeking further expansions in its surveillance authorities. But surely, before enacting any enhancements to government power, we should ensure that current laws adequately protect privacy. For example, the government wants to extend the pen register statute to the Internet and create a "roving" pen register authority. Yet, the current standard for pen registers imposes no effective control on the government, reducing judges to mere rubber-stamps. And pen registers as applied to Internet communications are even more revealing. In this and other cases, we must tighten the standards for government surveillance and access to information, thus restoring a balance between government surveillance and personal privacy and building user trust and confidence in these economically vital new media. CDT is prepared to work with the Committee and the Justice Department to flesh out the needed privacy enhancements and to convene our DPSWG working group as a forum for building consensus.

BACKGROUND: FOURTH AMENDMENT PRIVACY PRINCIPLES

To understand how far current privacy protections diverge from the principles of the Constitution, we should start with the protections accorded by the Fourth Amendment. If the government wants access to your papers or effects in your home or office, it has to meet a high standard:

- The government must obtain a warrant from a judge based on a showing of probable cause to believe that a crime has been, is being or is about to be committed and that the search will uncover evidence of the crime. The warrant must "particularly" describe the place to be searched and the things to be seized.
- The government must provide you with contemporaneous notice of the search and an inventory of items taken. See *Richards v. Wisconsin,* 520 U.S. 385 (1997); *Wilson v. Arkansas,* 514 U.S. 927 (1995).

These rules apply in the computer age, so long as you keep information stored on your hard drive or disks in your home or office.

The Supreme Court held in 1967 that wiretapping is a search and seizure and that telephone conversations are entitled to protection under the Fourth Amendment. *Katz v. United States,* 389 U.S. 347 (1967), *Berger v. New York,* 388 U.S. 41 (1967). Congress responded by adopting Title III of the Omnibus Crime Control and Safe Streets Act of 1968, requiring a court order based on a finding of probable cause to intercept wire or oral (i.e., face-to-face) communications. 18 USC §2510 *et seq.* However, Congress did not require the contemporaneous notice normally accorded at the time of a search and seizure. This was a fateful decision, but, the government argued, to give contemporaneous notice would defeat the effectiveness of the surveillance technique. In part to make up for the absence of notice, and recognizing the other uniquely intrusive aspects of wiretapping, Congress added to Title III requirements that go beyond the protections of the Fourth Amendment. These additional protections included: permitting the use of wiretaps only for investigations of a short list of very serious crimes; requiring high-level Justice Department approval before court authorization can be sought; requiring law enforcement agencies to exhaust other, less intrusive techniques before turning to eavesdropping; directing them to minimize the interception of innocent conversations; providing for periodic judicial oversight of the progress of a wiretap; establishing a statutory suppression rule; and requiring detailed annual reports to be published on the number and nature of wiretaps.[1]

After it ruled that there was an expectation of privacy in communications, the Supreme Court took a step that had serious adverse consequences for privacy: It held that personal information given to a third party loses its Fourth Amendment protection. This rule was stated first in a case involving bank records, *United States v. Miller,* 425 U.S. 435 (1976), but it is wide-ranging and now serves as the basis for government access to all of the records that together constitute a profile of our lives, both online and offline: credit, medical, purchasing, travel, car rental, etc. In the absence of a specific statute, these records are available to law enforcement for the asking and can be compelled with a mere subpoena issued without meaningful judicial control.

In 1979, a third piece of the privacy scheme was put in place when the Supreme Court held that there is no constitutionally protected privacy interest in the numbers one dials to initiate a telephone call — data collected under a device known as a "pen register." *Smith v. Maryland,* 442 U.S. 735, 742 (1979). While the Court was careful to limit the scope of its decision, and emphasized subsequently that pen registers collect only a very narrow range of information, the view has grown up that transactional data concerning communications is not constitutionally protected. Yet, in an increasingly connected world, a recording of every telephone number dialed and the source of every call received can provide a very complete picture "a profile" of a person's associations, habits, contacts, interests and activities. (Extending this to e-mail and other electronic communications can, as we explain below, be even more revealing.)

In 1986, as cellular telephones service became available and e-mail and other computer-to-computer communications were developing, this Committee recognized that the privacy law was woefully out of date. Title III anachronistically protected only wire and voice communications: it did not clearly cover wireless phone conversations or e-mail. In response, under the leadership of Senator Leahy, Congress adopted the Electronic Communications Privacy Act of 1986 (ECPA). ECPA did several things: it made it clear that wireless voice communications were covered to the same degree as wireline voice communications. It extended some, but not all, of Title III's privacy protections to electronic communications intercepted in real-time.

ECPA also set standards for access to stored e-mail and other electronic communications and transactional records (subscriber identifying information, logs, toll records). 18 USC § 2701 *et seq.* And it adopted the pen register and trap and trace statute, 18 USC § 3121 *et seq.,* governing real-time interception of "the numbers dialed or otherwise transmitted on a telephone line." (A pen register collects the "electronic or other impulses" that identify "the numbers dialed" for outgoing calls and a trap and trace device collects "the originating number" for incoming calls.) To obtain such an order, the government need merely certify that "the information likely to be obtained is relevant to an ongoing criminal investigation." 18 USC §§ 3122-23. (There is no constitutional or statutory threshold for opening a criminal investigation.) The law states that the judge "shall" approve any request signed by a prosecutor.

ECPA did not, however, extend full Title III protections to e-mail sitting on the server of an ISP. Instead, it set up a two-tiered rule: e-mail in "electronic storage" with a service provider for 180 days or less may be obtained only pursuant to a search warrant, which requires a finding of probable cause, but the additional protections of Title III — limited number of crimes, high level approval, judicial supervision — do not apply. E-mail in storage for more than 180 days and data stored on a "remote computing service" may be obtained with a warrant or a mere subpoena. In no case is the user entitled to contemporaneous notice. The e-mail portions of ECPA also do not include a statutory suppression rule for government violations and do not require annual reports of how often and under what government access, which are critical for public or congressional over-sight.

MAPPING THE FOURTH AMENDMENT ONTO CYBERSPACE

Remarkably, ECPA was the last significant update to the privacy standards of the electronic surveillance laws. Astonishing and unanticipated changes have occurred since 1986:

- The development of the Internet and the World Wide Web as mass media
- The convergence of voice, data, video, and fax over wire, cable and wireless systems
- The proliferation of service providers in a decentralized, competitive communications market
- The movement of information out of people's homes or offices and onto networks controlled by third parties
- The increasing power of hand-held computers and other mobile devices that access the Internet and data stored on networks

As a result of these changes, personal data is moving out of the desk drawer and off of the desktop computer and out onto the Internet. Unless Congress responds, the Fourth Amendment protections would remain available only in the home when increasingly information is not stored there anymore. It is time to adopt legislative protections that map Fourth Amendment principles onto the new technology.

It is clear that the surveillance laws' privacy protections are too weak:

- Data stored on networks is not afforded full privacy protection. Once something is stored on a server, it can be accessed by the government without notice to the user, and without probable cause.
- The standard for pen registers is minimal — judges must rubber stamp any application presented to them.
- Many of the protections in the wiretap law, including the special approval requirements and the statutory rule against use of illegally obtained evidence, do not apply to e-mail and other Internet communications.
- ISP customers are not entitled to notice when personal information is subpoenaed in civil lawsuits; notice of government requests can be delayed until it is too late to object.
- Inconsistent standards apply to government access to information about one's activities depending on the type of technology used. For example, watching the same movie via satellite, cable TV, Internet cable modem, and video rental is subject to four different privacy standards.

In addition, there are many ambiguities, some of which have existed since ECPA was enacted, others caused by technology's continuing evolution since 1986. For example, does the pen register statute apply to e-mail or Web communications? If so, what are "the numbers dialed or otherwise transmitted?" To get e-mail addresses and Web addresses (URLs), can the government serve a pen register order on the ISP or must it use an order under ECPA? What information is collected under a pen register order and from whom in the case of a person who is using the Internet for voice communications? What standard applies if the person has a cable modem? Is an Internet portal an electronic communications service under ECPA? Are search terms covered by ECPA? Does ECPA cover government access to information about one's activity at an e-commerce site? Do people have a constitutionally protected privacy interest in their calendars stored on Internet Web sites? At best, the answers are unclear.

The importance of these questions is heightened by the fact that transactional or addressing data for electronic communications like e-mail and Web browsing can be much more revealing than telephone numbers dialed. First, e-mail addresses are more personally revealing than phone numbers because e-mail addresses are unique to individual users. Furthermore, if the pen register authority applies to URLs or the names of files transmitted under a file transfer protocol, then the addressing information can actually convey the substance or purport of a communication. For example, a search for "heart disease" information through a search engine creates a URL that indicates exactly what content a Web surfer is exploring.

OUTLINING THE NECESSARY PRIVACY ENHANCEMENTS

To update the privacy laws, Congress should start with the following issues:

- Increase the standard for pen registers. Under current law, a court order is required but the judge is a mere rubber stamp — the statute presently says that the judge "shall" approve any application signed by a prosecutor saying that the information sought is relevant to an investigation. Instead, the government should be required to justify its request and the order should issue only if the judge affirmatively finds that the government has shown that the information sought is relevant and material.
- Assuming that the pen register authority applies to Internet service providers, define and limit what personal information is disclosed to the government under a pen register or trap and trace order.
- Add electronic communications to the Title III exclusionary rule in 18 USC §2515 and add a similar rule to the Section 2703 authority. This would prohibit the government from using improperly obtained information about electronic communications.
- Require notice and an opportunity to object when civil subpoenas seek personal information about Internet usage.
- Improve the notice requirement under ECPA to ensure that consumers receive notice whenever the government obtains information about their Internet transactions.
- Require statistical reports for §2703 disclosures, similar to the reports required under Title III.
- Make it clear that Internet queries are content, which cannot be disclosed without consent or a probable cause order.
- Provide enhanced protection for information on networks: probable cause for seizure without prior notice, opportunity to object for subpoena access.

COMMENTS ON S.2448

S.2448 represents an effort to address a range of Internet privacy and security concerns without creating an unwieldy bill. We appreciate the Chairman's decision to stay away from some contentious issues, particularly the Justice Department's request for "roving" pen registers for the Internet, and we hope you will work to keep the bill from being weighted down with other proposals that would expand government surveillance power without adequate privacy standards.

In many ways, we have a robust computer crime law. The Computer Fraud and Abuse Act was originally passed in 1984 and was amended in 1986, 1994 and 1996. It protects a broad range of computers and is quite comprehensive. By its terms, it clearly covers the recent "love bug" virus, the Melissa virus and the denial of service attacks in February, even those that were created and launched from overseas.

The main effect of S.2448's criminal provisions would be to extend federal jurisdiction over minor computer abuses not previously thought serious enough to merit federal resources. Currently, federal jurisdiction exists for some computer crimes only if they result in at least $5,000 of aggregate damage or cause especially significant damage, such as any impairment of medical records, or pose a threat to public safety. Any virus affecting more than a few computers easily meets the $5,000 threshold. S.2448 would eliminate even this low threshold.

Specifically, the bill would make it a felony to send any transmission intending to cause damage or to intentionally access a computer and recklessly cause damage, punishable for up to 3 years in prison, even if the damage caused is negligible. In addition, the bill would make it a misdemeanor to intentionally access any computer and cause damage, even unintentional damage, again regardless of the extent of such damage.

Perhaps unintentionally, these changes would federalize a range of *de minimis* intrusions on another's computer:

- Somebody borrows a friend's computer without permission and changes some files as a joke.
- A student, noticing that someone at the school library's public terminal failed to completely log out of their account, gains access to that student's account and accidentally erases some files.
- A computer science graduate student, in the process of testing a new computer security tool, gains access to another computer on campus without permission and then changes some files to show they were there.

It is highly unlikely that the FBI and the Justice Department could ever have the resources to prosecute such minor computer offenses. The provisions will have to be applied selectively, and the risk becomes high, therefore, that the provisions will be applied in unfair ways.

The elimination of any thresholds is particularly questionable in light of sections of S.2448 that would amend the forfeiture law in ways that could result in seizure by the government of the house in which sat a computer used in hacking and expand wiretap authority by making all computer crimes a predicate for wiretaps.

Another part of S.2448 permits the U.S. Attorney General to provide computer crime evidence to foreign law enforcement authorities "without regard to whether the conduct investigated violates any Federal computer crime law." It is unclear whether this expands the Justice Department's investigative authority to investigate lawful conduct in the U.S. at the request of foreign governments.

On the consumer privacy side, S.2448 has other provisions that would bring about some improvements in privacy, although there are some problems with the bill.

Sec. 302 would prohibit satellite TV service providers from disclosing information about their customers and their viewing habits unless the customers have affirmatively agreed ("opted-in") to such sharing. This is a step towards addressing one of the many areas of inconsistency in our privacy laws. Currently, federal law protects the subscriber information and viewing habits of a cable TV subscriber but not a satellite TV viewer. Sec. 302 would create privacy protections for viewers of satellite TV. However, we are distressed to see that an exception in Sec. 203 allows disclosure to the government without notice and an opportunity to object, thereby giving satellite TV viewers less protection than existing law affords to cable TV subscribers.

Sec. 304 would require commercial Web sites to give visitors notice of data collection and sharing practices and "the opportunity, before the time that such information is initially disclosed, to direct that such information not be disclosed to such person." Again, enforceable requirements of notice and opt-out would be a step forward over current law. However, the bill does not address two other key elements of online privacy — access and security.

Further, we believe that it is possible to avoid the current dichotomy between opt-out and opt-in. On the Internet, a better way to think of privacy is in terms of meaningful choice, since the technology can eliminate the transaction costs and other burdens on industry associated with opt-in rules in the offline world. Indeed, some online service providers have adopted an opt-in policy as part of their business model. Given the rapid change that is occurring as businesses respond to persistent high levels of consumer concern about privacy, we would not want federal legislation to freeze opt-out into place.

Sec. 306 would make fraudulent access to personally identifiable information a crime The provision covers anyone who "knowingly and with an intent to defraud ... causes to be disclosed to any person, personally identifiable information ... by making a false ... statement ... to a customer of an interactive computer service." The Committee should make it clear whether the "with intent to defraud" language is enough to exclude from the crime a Web site's collection of information under a privacy statement that is no longer being adhered to.

JUSTICE DEPARTMENT PROPOSALS

Our greatest concern, however, is with Justice Department and other proposals for expansions in government surveillance or data access authority. One area of serious concern is Sen. Schumer's bill S.2092, which, in its current form, extends pen register authority over the Internet in broad and ill-defined ways. S.2092 also would give every federal pen register and trap and trace order nationwide effect, without limit and without requiring the government to make a showing of need, creating a sort of "roving pen register." We have shared our privacy concerns with Sen. Schumer, along with our specific recommendations for improvements, and we hope that a more balanced bill could be agreed upon. We have prepared for Sen. Schumer and interested parties a detailed memo, which I would request be made a part of the record of this hearing.

S.2092 focuses on pen registers, which collect the numbers dialed on outgoing calls, and trap and trace devices, which collect the phone numbers identifying incoming calls. These surveillance devices have long been used by law enforcement in the plain old telephone world. Because they are not supposed to identify the parties to a communication nor whether the communication was even completed, the standard for approval of a pen register is very low: the law provides that a judge "shall" approve any request by the government that claims the information sought is "relevant" to an investigation. This really says that the court must rubber stamp any government request.

The pen register and trap and trace statute only applies to the numbers dialed or otherwise transmitted on the telephone line to which the device is attached. S.2092 would extend the pen register and trap and trace authority to all Internet traffic. It does so with very broad terminology, stating that the pen register can collect "dialing, routing, addressing or signaling information," without further definition. It needs to be made clear that pen registers do not sweep in search queries or URLs that identify specific documents viewed online or include personal information.

It is time to give the pen register statute real privacy teeth, requiring the government to actually justify its requests to a judge's satisfaction. Also, if nationwide service is to be available, it should be on the basis of a specific showing of need, and should be limited both by time and other parameters.

CONCLUSION

We do not need a new Fourth Amendment for cyberspace. The one we have is good enough. But we need to recognize that people are conducting more and more of their lives online. They are storing increasing amounts of sensitive data on networks. They are using technology that can paint a full profile of their personal lives. The pricetag for this technology should not include a loss of privacy. It should not be the end of the privacy debate to say that technological change takes information outside the protection of the Fourth Amendment as interpreted by the courts 25 years ago. Nor is it adequate to say that individuals are voluntarily surrendering their privacy by using new computer and communications technologies. What we need is to translate the Fourth Amendment's vision of limited government power and strong protections for personal privacy to the global, decentralized, networked environment of the Internet. This should be the Committee's first task.

Endnotes

1. Over time, though, many of these additional protections have been substantially watered down. The list of crimes has been expanded, from the initial 26 to nearly 100 today and more are added every Congress. Minimization is rarely enforced by the courts. The exhaustion requirement has been weakened. Evidence is rarely excluded for violations of the statute. Almost every year, the number of wiretaps goes up — 12 percent in 1998 alone. Judicial denials are rare — only 3 in the last 10 years. The average duration of wiretaps has doubled since 1988. So even in the world of plain old telephone service we have seen an erosion of privacy protections. The fragility of these standards is even more disconcerting when paired with the FBI's "Digital Storm" plans for digital collection, voice recognition and key word searching, which will reduce if not eliminate the practical constraints that have up to now limited the volume of information that the government can intercept.

Chapter 45

Independent Review of the Carnivore System for the Department of Justice

IIT Research Institute

IIT Research Institute and the Illinois Institute of Technology Chicago–Kent College of Law (herein abbreviated as IITRI), under contract to the Department of Justice (DoJ), evaluated a Federal Bureau of Investigation (FBI) system known as Carnivore. Carnivore is a software-based tool used to examine all Internet Protocol (IP) packets on an Ethernet and record only those packets or packet segments that meet very specific parameters. IITRI was asked to report on whether Carnivore:

- Provides investigators with all, but only, the information it is designed and set to provide in accordance with a given court order
- Introduces any new, material risks of operational or security impairment of an Internet Service Provider's (ISP's) network
- Risks unauthorized acquisition, whether intentional or unintentional, of electronic communication information by: (1) FBI personnel or (2) persons other than FBI personnel
- Provides protections, including audit functions and operational procedures or practices, commensurate with the level of the risks.

In addition, IITRI considered the concerns of interested organizations and citizens. IITRI studied recent testimony; examined material on Internet sites; and met with representatives of the American Civil Liberties Union,

Electronic Privacy Information Center, and the Center for Democracy and Technology. IITRI determined that this report must also address:

- All potential capabilities of the system, independent of intended use
- Controls on, and auditability of, the entire process by the FBI, the DoJ, and the courts
- Fault tolerance and integrity of the data
- Roles, actual and potential, of other parties and systems; e.g., the ISP or alternative implementations
- Functions of Carnivore within a suite of similar products

SCOPE

IITRI determined that the scope of the evaluation had to include how Carnivore is applied as well as its technical capabilities. IITRI evaluated the understanding of court orders by the field investigator, the implementation of the court order as commands to the acquisition software, the acquisition minimization performed by the software, and the handling and post-processing of acquired data. Questions of constitutionality of Carnivore-type intercepts and trustworthiness of law enforcement agents were outside the scope of this evaluation.

The Carnivore IITRI evaluated is a snapshot of an on-going development. Carnivore is evolving to improve its performance, enhance its capabilities, and keep pace with Internet development and court rulings. The current version (Carnivore 1.3.4 SP3) was deployed to meet an immediate requirement that commercial products could not satisfy while development continued. The next version, Carnivore 2.0, is in alpha test. Source code for v2.0 was provided to IITRI. This report covers an evaluation only of version 1.3.4.

APPROACH

IITRI approached the evaluation in four coordinated, but largely independent, aspects.

1. IITRI evaluated the process used to translate court orders into commands for Carnivore, implement the collection, and verify that only permitted information was gathered. This aspect considered various use scenarios including full content and pen register intercepts. It included interviews with FBI developers, the deployment team, field agents who have used Carnivore, and ISPs who have hosted it.
2. IITRI evaluated the system architecture especially with respect to security. This aspect considered alternative implementations and the capabilities of commercial products.
3. IITRI examined the Carnivore source code to determine what functions have been implemented and what limitations have been built in.

4. IITRI installed the system in its Information Technology Laboratory (IT Lab) and experimentally determined system capabilities. Tests focused on capabilities of Carnivore, but included using two post-processing programs — Packeteer and CoolMiner — that, with Carnivore, are collectively known as the DragonWare suite.

OBSERVATIONS

Carnivore is a system used to implement court-ordered surveillance of electronic communication. It is used when other implementations (e.g., having an ISP provide the requested data) do not meet the needs of the investigators or the restrictions placed by the court. Carnivore can be used to collect full content of communications under 18 USC §§ 2510-2522 and 50 U.S.C §§ 1801-1829 or only address information (i.e., pen register) under 18 USC §§ 3121-3127 and 50 U.S.C §§ 1841-1846. Law enforcement agents follow a rigorous, detailed procedure to obtain court orders and surveillance is performed under the supervision of the court issuing the order.

As in all technical surveillance, the FBI applies a strict separation of responsibility when using Carnivore. Case agents establish the need and justification for the surveillance. A separate team of technically trained agents installs the equipment and configures it to restrict collection to that allowed by the court order. In the case of Carnivore, all installations have been performed by the same small team. Case agents are motivated to solve or prevent crimes, but technically trained agents are motivated by FBI policy and procedures to ensure that collection adheres strictly to court orders and will be admissible in court as evidence.

The Carnivore architecture (Exhibit 1) comprises: (1) a one-way tap into an Ethernet data stream; (2) a general purpose computer to filter and collect data; (3) additional general purpose computers to control the collection and examine the data; and (4) a telephone link to the collection computer. The collection computer is typically installed without a keyboard or monitor. pcAnywhere, a standard commercial product from Symantec Inc., allows the additional computers to control the collection computer via the telephone link. The link is protected by an electronic key such that only a computer with a matching key can connect. Carnivore software is typically loaded on the collection computer while Packeteer and CoolMiner are installed on the control computers. All computers are equipped with Jaz drives for removable data storage.

When placed at an ISP, the collection computer receives all packets on the Ethernet segment to which it is connected and records packets or packet segments that match Carnivore filter settings.

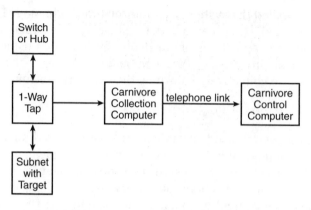

Exhibit 1.   Carnivore Architecture

The one-way tap ensures that Carnivore cannot transmit data on the network, and the absence of an installed Internet Protocol (IP) stack ensures that Carnivore cannot process any packets other than to filter and optionally record them. Carnivore can neither alter packets destined for other systems on the network nor initiate any packets.

Control computers are located at law enforcement sites. When connected by modem to the collection computer, a control computer operator can set and change filter settings, start and stop collection, and retrieve collected information. Using Packeteer and CoolMiner, the operator can reconstruct target activity from the collected IP packets. In pen mode, the operator can see the TO and FROM e-mail addresses and the IP addresses of computers involved in File Transfer Protocol (FTP) and Hypertext Transfer Protocol (HTTP) sessions. In full-collection mode, the operator can view the content of e-mail messages, HTTP pages, FTP sessions, etc. Carnivore operators are anonymous to the system. All users are logged in as "administrator" and no audit trail of actions is maintained.

Carnivore software has four components: (1) a driver derived from sample C source code provided with WinDis 32, a product of Printing Communications Associates, implements preliminary filtering of IP packets; (2) an application program interface (API); (3) a dynamic link library (DLL) written in C++ provides additional filtering and data management; and (4) an executable program written in Visual Basic provides a graphical user interface. Functionality is placed in the driver whenever possible to enhance performance. Evolution of the source code between v1.3.4 and v2.0 clearly indicates that all processing will eventually take place in the driver. The DLL provides entry points for functions such as INITIALIZE, START, STOP, and SHUTDOWN. The user interface is divided into basic (Exhibit 2) and advanced (Exhibit 3) screens. The basic screen allows an

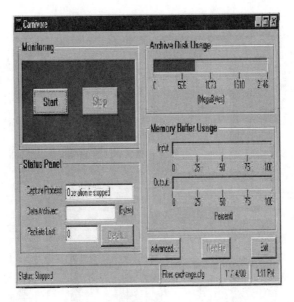

Exhibit 2.   Basic Carnivore Screen

operator to start and stop collection, view collection statistics, and segment the output file. The advanced screen allows the operator to define and redefine the filter parameters that control what Carnivore collects.

IITRI verified by code walkthrough, and later by experiment, that Carnivore works as described by the DoJ. Parameters set in the user interface were reflected in the configuration file. Data passed by the filter and DLL reflect the configuration file. While IITRI did not perform an automated analysis to verify that all code segments are executed and that no hidden code exists, IITRI did verify manually that the driver API and DLL entry points provide only the functionality required to implement the features we observed. Given that the advertised functionality provides ample capability to perform unauthorized surveillance, IITRI concluded there was little incentive to hide capabilities in the code.

IITRI installed Carnivore version 1.3.4 in its IT Lab. The test configuration, shown in Exhibit 4, mimics the typical installation at an ISP. The Carnivore tap was placed in a subnetwork containing traffic from the target, but as little other traffic as possible. The subnetwork provided both static and dynamic IP addressing of target and non-target users. IITRI ran a series of tests covering both pen register and full collection scenarios envisioned by the FBI developers. IITRI also ran a series of tests for scenarios not envisioned by the FBI to determine the full capabilities of the device.

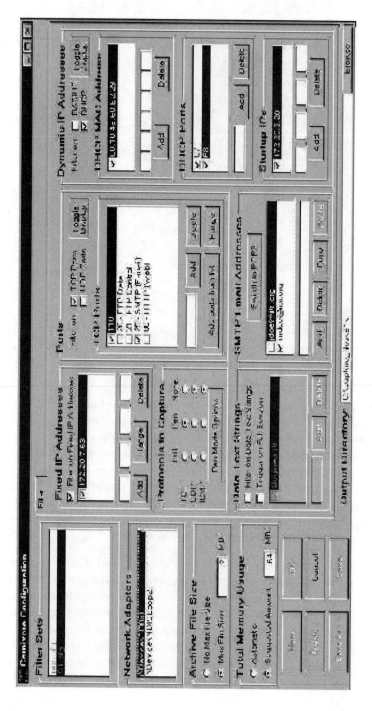

Exhibit 3. Advanced Carnivore Screen

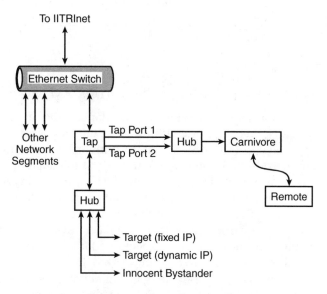

Exhibit 4. Carnivore Test Configuration

Carnivore accepts packets unless they are rejected by the filter. Proper operation relies on the ability of the operator to configure the filter correctly and fully. With the default settings, no packets are accepted. However, if a single radio button is selected to place the software in full mode collection for transmission control protocol (TCP) traffic, then all TCP traffic is collected.

As more filters are selected and configured, the volume of collection is reduced. For example, only selected ports might be collected and Simple Mail Transfer Protocol and Post Office Protocol 3 might be limited to certain user names. In normal operation, filters are also used to limit collection to specific IP addresses, but selecting the filters is established by FBI procedures, not by the software.

The other DragonWare components, Packeteer and CoolMiner, work together to display the output of Carnivore in a meaningful manner. Packeteer processes the raw output of Carnivore to reconstruct higher-level protocols from IP packets. CoolMiner develops statistical summaries and displays either pen register or full content information via an Internet browser. After initially verifying via hex-dumps that these programs were reporting the test output correctly, IITRI used them to evaluate the majority of the test scenarios. In cases where the CoolMiner output was not as expected, the raw data from Carnivore was inspected. A few software bugs were found in the Packeteer and CoolMiner programs. These bugs actually cause the collected data to be underreported. An examination of the raw Carnivore output revealed that the correct data were collected. These bugs have been reported to the FBI.

CONCLUSIONS

In response to the DoJ's four questions, IITRI concludes:

1. When Carnivore is used in accordance with a Title III order, it provides investigators with no more information than is permitted by a given court order. When Carnivore is used under pen trap authorization, it collects TO and FROM information, and also indicates the length of messages and the length of individual field within those messages possibly exceeding court-permitted collection.
2. Operating Carnivore introduces no operational or security risks to the ISP network where it is installed unless the ISP must make changes to its network to accommodate Carnivore. Such changes may introduce unexpected network behavior.
3. Carnivore reduces, but does not eliminate, the risk of both intentional and unintentional unauthorized acquisition of electronic communication information by FBI personnel, but introduces little additional risk of acquisition by persons other than FBI personnel.
4. While operational procedures or practices appear sound, Carnivore does not provide protections, especially audit functions, commensurate with the level of the risks.

In response to broader concerns, IITRI concludes:

- Carnivore represents technology that can be more effective in protecting privacy and enabling lawful surveillance than can alternatives such as commercial packet sniffers.
- Multiple approvals are currently required by FBI and DoJ policy (but not currently by statute) before a court order that might involve a Carnivore deployment is requested; significant post-collection organizational and judicial controls exist as well.
  - The supervising judge can, and regularly does, independently verify that traffic collected is only what was legally authorized.
  - Civil litigation, and potential criminal prosecution of agents involved in over-collection, provide further post-collection external controls protecting against misusing Carnivore. However, the statutory suppression remedy available for illegal interception of other communications in Title III is not expended to electronic communications.
- While the system was designed to, and can, perform fine-tuned searches, it is also capable of broad sweeps. Incorrectly configured, Carnivore can record any traffic it monitors.

- Carnivore examines IP traffic and determines which packets are allowed by its filter settings.
  - It accumulates no data other than that which passes its filters.
  - It restricts packets to specific types from or to specific users.
  - It incorporates features to detect dropped packets and guards against inadvertently potentially missing the sign-off of a dynamically assigned IP address.
- Carnivore does not have nearly enough power "to spy on almost everyone with an e-mail account." In order to work effectively, it must reject the majority of packets it monitors. It also monitors only the packets traversing the wire to which it is connected. Typically, this wire is a network segment handling only a subset of a particular ISP's traffic.
- IITRI did not find adequate provisions (e.g., audit trails) for establishing individual accountability for actions taken during use of Carnivore.
- The current implementation of Carnivore has significant deficiencies in protection for the integrity of the information it collects.
  - The relationship among Carnivore filter settings, collected data, and other investigative activities may be difficult to establish.
  - Lack of physical control of the Carnivore collection computer engenders some risk of compromise.
  - FBI tools to view, analyze, and minimize raw Carnivore output contain several material weaknesses. During testing, IITRI found several bugs.
  - Carnivore does not consistently recover from power failures.
  - There is no time synchronization within Carnivore.
- No formal development process was used for Carnivore through version 1.3.4. Consequently, technical issues such as software correctness, system robustness, user interfaces, audit, and accountability and security were not well addressed.
- Carnivore does not:
  - Read and record all incoming and outgoing e-mail messages, including sender, recipients, message subject, and body. It stores packets for later analysis only after they are positively linked by the filter settings to a target.
  - Monitor the Web-surfing and downloading habits of all the ISP's customers, including Web searches for information or people. It can only record for later evaluation some HTTP files retrieved by a target.
  - Monitor or read all other electronic activity for that ISP, including instant messages, person-to-person file transfers, Web publishing, FTP, Telnet, newsgroups, online purchases, and anything else that is routed through that ISP. It can only record a subset of such files for a specific user.

- Carnivore cannot:
  - Alter or remove packets from the network or introduce new packets
  - Block any traffic on the network
  - Remove images, terms, etc. from communications
  - Seize control of any portion of Internet traffic
  - Shut down or shut off the communications of any person, Web site, company, or ISP
  - Shut off accounts, ISPs, etc. to "contain" an investigation
- Carnivore has significant performance limitations, most of which result from design decisions to enable precise collection.
- The FBI may have legitimate reasons to oppose public release of Carnivore. The current version has technical limitations that could be exploited to defeat surveillance if they were revealed.

RECOMMENDATIONS

Although IITRI specifically excluded questions of constitutionality and of illegal activity by the FBI from this evaluation, IITRI is concerned that the presence of Carnivore and its successors without safeguards as recommended below: (1) fuels the concerns of responsible privacy advocates and reduces the expectations of privacy by citizens at large; and (2) increases public concern about the potential unauthorized activity of law enforcement agents. To reduce these concerns, IITRI makes the following recommendations to add protections that are commensurate with the level of risks inherent in deploying a system such as Carnivore:

- Continue to use Carnivore versus other techniques when precise collection is required because Carnivore can be configured to reflect the limitations of a court order.
- Retain centralized control of Carnivore at the federal level and require DoJ approval of all applications that involve Carnivore systems capable of full content collection.
- Provide separate versions of Carnivore for pen register and full content collection.
- Provide individual accountability and audit trail for all Carnivore actions.
- Enhance physical control of Carnivore when it is deployed.
- Explicitly bind collected data to the collection configuration by recording the filter settings with each collected file and add a cyclic redundancy check or, preferably, a cryptographic checksum to the recorded file.
- Employ formal development processes to improve traceability of requirements, improve configuration management, and reduce potential errors in future versions of Carnivore.

- Provide checks in the user interface software to ensure that settings are reasonable and consistent.
- Work toward public release of Carnivore source code by eliminating exploitable weaknesses. Until public release, continue independent evaluation to assess effectiveness and risks of over- and under-collection. Fix known software bugs in Packeteer and CoolMiner, and make those programs available to other parties, e.g., defense attorneys, with a need to examine Carnivore data.

Notes

See http://www.usdoj.gov/jmd/publications/carniv_final.pdf for the full text of the report. Contract No. 00-C-0328 for the Department of Justice.

Section IV
International Laws and Issues

Chapter 46
The European Data Protection Directive: A Roadblock to International Trade?

John R. Vacca

Since the summer of 1998, U.S.-based multinationals have separately geared up for an unprecedented legal wrangle with Europe over the issue of personal data privacy. In some industry sectors, the problem may escalate into a complex trade war that could ultimately paralyze the transfer and handling of sensitive personal data between the United States and all European countries.

The impending battleground comes in the wake of a new Europe-wide privacy regime that went into effect in the fall of 1998. The new rules (collectively known as the European Data Protection Directive[1]) will oblige every country in Europe to conform to a common set of standards binding all governments and corporations to a rigorous observance of privacy. Internationally, the Directive has vast ramifications for enterprises such as banks, travel and leisure enterprises, outsourcing enterprises, credit card enterprises, Internet commerce enterprises, and multinationals, all of whom move vast amounts of personal data around the globe. Add to this list Internet sites, telephone systems, and laptop computers containing personal data, and a major challenge to the global economy is apparent.

0-8493-1248-5/02/$0.00+$1.50
© 2002 by CRC Press LLC

E-PRIVACY STANDARD

The intent of the regime is to create a harmonized set of national privacy standards that will ensure the free flow of personal data across Europe's internal borders. In addition, the Directive establishes strict guidelines for the international export of data from Europe. In most cases, European citizens must give their *unambiguous* consent before an enterprise or agency can process their personal data. Further, the processing of sensitive personal information (e.g., religion, sexual preference, trade union membership, health data) will be prohibited outright unless the person in question gives *explicit* consent.

Article 25 of the Directive stipulates that transfers of data may occur only to countries with an *adequate* (that is, equivalent) level of protection. If data is transferred to insecure environments, its flow may be paralyzed by a national data protection commissioner. Many European countries have already engaged these requirements. For example, Berlin's commissioner has already delayed a credit card cobranding deal between Citibank and German National Railways.

Even though the Directive is a protection mechanism in its own right, European countries are moving to enshrine the instrument into national law. Some countries, such as Italy and Greece, have already passed compatible national laws. The U.K. government passed a bill that amends the 1984 Data Protection law in accordance with the Directive. And most northern European countries already have strong privacy laws in force, with plans to strengthen them further in the near future.

An important *finality* principle in European law means that a data processor cannot use data for any purpose other than that for which it was originally intended. For example, if a European gives personal details to a supermarket for the purpose of obtaining a reward card, the enterprise cannot use that data to check financial status. Or if a European registers to enter a Web site, the enterprise hosting the site cannot sell that information to a direct marketing enterprise.

Such practices are commonplace in the United States, and the privacy commissioners of European countries do not like it. Brussels has gone so far as to give an ultimatum to Washington: adopt strong privacy laws, or stand the risk of losing countless trillions of dollars of business with Europe.

RESPONSE OF THE UNITED STATES

The Directive has caused a number of concerns in the United States, which has no general private-sector privacy regulations and instead relies on models of industry self-regulation. Europe has stated unequivocally that it will demand a much stronger level of privacy protection in the United

States before it allows its data to be transferred to U.S.-based enterprises that trade in sensitive personal information. Many U.S. enterprises have already experienced difficulties complying with these rules.

The most straightforward means of achieving this stronger level of protection would be to establish a national privacy law covering both the government and the private sector. Although Article 26 of the Directive permits limited nonlegislative methods of protection (specifically, using contract solutions or gaining prior consent from individuals for the transfer of personal data), Europe is generally looking to the U.S. government to forge a transatlantic harmony by establishing a national privacy regulator — something the Clinton Administration did not do.

Larger U.S. enterprises, particularly banks, are already making a substantial investment in the development of legal approaches to the problem, including model contracts for different industry sectors. However, these are unlikely to satisfy the most rigorous of the European data protection authorities. Consequently, there is a growing sense that the position of U.S. government authorities and industry representatives is fundamentally at odds with the European privacy standard. This situation is already disrupting certain dataflows between Europe and the United States, and may well destabilize ongoing contract arrangements and investment.

Nevertheless, the Clinton Administration maintained a steadfast opposition to the Directive. Clinton's former adviser on electronic commerce, Ira Magaziner, routinely threatened to take Europe to the World Trade Organization for setting up what he called a trade barrier. Meanwhile, a small army of industry consultants have lined up to tell Washington that effective self-regulation is the only acceptable formula. According to lobbyists for the direct marketing and banking industries, the measures Europe is demanding are cumbersome, expensive, and un-American.

The new battleground soon became a game of brinkmanship, with Administration authorities claiming they could either out-bluff the Europeans or, at worst, cut a deal in the interests of U.S. enterprises. What they misunderstood was that the deals had already been done. European nations had firmly embedded these new privacy rights in law. Washington can no more make a deal to dilute European law than Brussels can cut a deal with Washington to dilute the First Amendment.

Ultimately, any of Europe's 491 million citizens can make a claim of abuse of personal data and pursue the claim right through to the European Court of Justice. At any point in this long process, enterprise contracts can be suspended, injunctions against dataflows can be made, and compensation can be claimed. Each privacy watchdog is required by law to act on behalf of citizens whose rights have been violated. If the national watchdog (or, indeed, Brussels itself) fails in this duty, the Court of Justice can be invoked.

This prospect has sounded a warning to everyone doing business with Europe. The right of personal privacy entitles any European citizen to throw a wrench in the works of enterprise dealings between Europe and the rest of the world. The idea of millions of such rogue elements may destabilize some commercial negotiations.

THE HEATING UP OF THE E-PRIVACY BATTLE

In 1998, in what could well be a sign of things to come, Sweden's privacy watchdog, Anitha Bondestam, instructed American Airlines (AA) to delete all health and medical details on Swedish citizens after each flight unless *explicit consent* from them could be obtained. These details (allergies, asthma notification, dietary needs, disabled access, and so on) are routinely collected at the point of booking. Bondestam's order meant that AA would be unable to transmit this information to the SABRE central reservation system in the United States.

AA appealed to the County Administrative Court (in Sweden), arguing that it was impractical to obtain consent. In any event, the airline argued, people would be inconvenienced if they had to repeat the information each time they flew.

The court was unconvinced by the argument. Inconvenience, it concluded, does not constitute an exemption from the long-held legal rules for the protection of data. AA lost the case, and launched a second appeal to Sweden's Administrative Court of Appeal. This case also was lost, and the matter is now before the Sweden's national Supreme Court. In the meantime, all export and processing of medical data to the reservation system is now banned.

In a last-ditch effort to placate the Europeans, the U.S. Department of Commerce announced its own privacy scheme: a *safe harbor* strategy that would encourage enterprises to adopt a privacy code in return for guarantees of immunity from Europe. It came as no surprise to Brussels-watchers that every privacy commissioner in Europe condemned the plan. Some (particularly those in Germany) even called for stronger European privacy protections. However, the U.S. Department of Congress persisted in discussions with the European Commission. During the first half of 2001, the European Commission approved of the Safe Harbor certification program.

The response from U.S. enterprises has ranged from ambivalence to hostility. Most enterprises have refused to heed the European position, choosing instead to hire more lobbyists and more lawyers. As the contest moved toward stalemate, the London-based watchdog group Privacy International (PI)[2] waded into the melee with a threat to take legal action in Europe to paralyze data flows relating to 36 of the world's biggest multinationals.

PI's list of target enterprises includes such U.S. industry giants as Electronic Data Systems, Ford, Hilton International, Microsoft, and United Airlines, many of which subsequently complained to the U.S. enterprise press that the threat was causing concern and uncertainty.

PI commenced its action in late November 1998 by assembling a team of experts to analyze the data processing activities of these enterprises to identify breaches of European privacy law. Once that analysis was complete, the enterprise lodged specific complaints with the relevant privacy commissioners, demanding that the dataflows (banking, Internet-based or telecommunications) be immediately prohibited.

The message to U.S. enterprises and the federal government is clear: privacy is now a core legal right in Europe. For the United States, which has pioneered the idea of a global economy, there is a clear choice between isolation and a forward-looking reform that will create a new global privacy standard in everyone's interest.

OBSERVATIONS AND RECOMMENDATIONS

An important goal of this article has been to give an accurate account of the effects of the European Data Protection Directive on the United States and on third-world countries. The hope is that the analysis and description contained here have provided a wide range of interested parties with a better basis for deciding what steps to take in the new millennium.

In this portion of the article, the following preliminary observations and recommendations are made. First, the discussion focuses on the differing information cultures in Europe and the United States and explains the dilemmas concerning enforcement that face both data protection officials and the regulated community. Finally, a number of specific policy recommendations are made.

The Dilemmas of Enforcement and Differing Information Cultures

To simplify somewhat, much of the debate about the Directive comes down to a choice between overly broad laws (the European tendency) and insufficiently broad laws (the American tendency). Under the European approach, there are many routine and desirable transfers of information that would apparently be prohibited under the Directive. For example, the Directive, as written, would appear to prohibit carrying many laptop computers out of Europe, would pose a major obstacle to the collection by investment banks of important information about enterprises, and would call into doubt many mainframe and intranet applications that involve processing in the United States or in third-world countries. On the other

573

hand, the U.S. privacy laws can be described, with some merit, as haphazard, incomplete, and lax. It strikes many people as odd, for example, that video rental records are often regulated more strictly than sensitive medical data.

The differences in laws are, to a significant extent, a reflection of different information cultures. Americans historically have had a strong suspicion of government and a relatively strong esteem for markets and technology. The United States has an almost religious attitude toward free-speech rights under the First Amendment along with a strong tradition of keeping government records and proceedings open to the public. Europeans, by contrast, have given government a more prominent role in fostering social welfare but have placed more limits on the unfettered development of markets and technology. Many European governments regulate themselves less strictly than the United States in matters such as open-meeting and freedom-of-information laws. European governments are often more strict, however, in regulating the press and other private-sector uses of information.

The implementation of the Directive has precipitated a clash between the differing information cultures. In the European view, the United States has disappointingly weak protection of individual rights to privacy. In order to protect these fundamental rights, it is better to err on the side of protective regulation. In the U.S. view, the Directive contemplates that many enterprises will have to engage in costly compliance where there is little or no social harm from the regulated practices. It would be better, on this view, to seek other ways to protect against important privacy problems without subjecting so many enterprises to strict legal mandates.

Beyond this clash of information cultures, there is now tremendous uncertainty as to how strictly the Directive will be enforced. When the Directive was promulgated, there was a hope among at least some Europeans that the United States and third-world countries would promulgate new privacy laws that would meet the adequacy test. It is now clear that comprehensive privacy laws, although perhaps desirable, are unlikely to be passed in the immediate future in the United States.

This lack of new legislation has left the European Union (EU) in a dilemma. On the one hand, the EU with its Directive has taken a unified stand that privacy is a fundamental human right, requiring careful legal protection. Under the Directive, to protect these important rights, it is required that transfers to third-world countries be allowed only where there is adequate protection. The logical consequence of this position is that violations of adequate protection are to be taken seriously. Enterprises and other organizations must carefully comply with the Directive and national laws as written. As expressed in numerous speeches by senior

EU officials, the political will of Europe should not be doubted in this area. Access to the enormous EU market will be conditioned on compliance with data protection laws. A tough stance on privacy is needed to push European and other enterprises to live up to their obligations.

The dilemma facing the European data protection regime is starting to become clear. On the one hand, the regime is designed to protect important human rights. On the other hand, no European official wishes to create a major trade war or prohibit practices that are desirable or vital to both European and other economies.

The desire to avoid confrontation and economic harm results in a quite different set of statements from those supporting the European data protection regime. The United States should not be alarmist about the Directive. Data protection laws have existed in Europe for many years, without major problems. The history of data protection enforcement is one of sensible and incremental implementation, characterized by encouragement for good privacy practices but few penalties on individual enterprises. Enterprises that are conscientious about privacy should not worry about technical violations of the language of the Directive. The mildest form of this view is that the Directive is simply one more effort to encourage European and other enterprises to seek to make progress in protecting privacy.

The problem of course is that Europe cannot, at the same time, strictly enforce the letter of the Directive and announce that enterprises can routinely violate it. It violates the rule of law and fundamental fairness to enforce strictly against some while allowing others to violate the same law in the same way. This sort of enforcement is the opposite of transparent — reading the rules gives people no opportunity to know what is permitted or forbidden. A particular worry is that enforcement of an overly broad law will be done selectively in an unfair way. An often-expressed concern of U.S.-based enterprises is that they might be targeted for enforcement under the Directive, even when they follow the same privacy practices as their Europe-based competitors. This targeting of U.S.-based enterprises may fit the perception that U.S. enterprises are less careful about privacy issues, and it may be politically popular in Europe.

The dilemma of the European Union is mirrored in the dilemma facing the huge array of enterprises that are expected to comply with the Directive. On the one hand, if the Directive is actually going to be enforced as written, these enterprises must take immediate and substantial measures to comply. New consent forms must be drafted, operations of mainframes and other information processing might be shifted to Europe, and many internal procedures must be amended. Policies for use of enterprise laptops must be adopted. A comprehensive internal audit must be done of flows of personal information from the EU to the United States, the third world, and all other countries that arguably lack adequate protection. Some product lines that require intensive use of personal information in order to be profitable, might have to be dropped. National laws within the EU must be carefully examined (even though some have not yet been adopted), so that there is compliance with each country's requirements.

On the other hand, if the Directive is primarily hortatory (advising), these crash efforts to comply will seem expensive and unnecessary to many enterprises. Many enterprise persons have expressed the view that "they just can't do that" — the EU will simply not be willing or able to enforce the Directive as written. Because so many categories of data are affected by the Directive, for so many enterprises, some enterprises might make the practical decision not to comply. These enterprises might correctly judge that the risks of expensive enforcement actions are low. Privacy practices might be adopted where they help the bottom line, but not otherwise. Of course, in this scenario, enterprises will knowingly engage in routine violations of a law. But some enterprises might rather do that than undergo the expense and disruption of complying.

RESOLVING THE POLICY DILEMMAS

The challenge for policymakers and the regulated community is how to resolve these dilemmas, how to steer a sensible course between the unattractive options of harsh enforcement and public flouting of the law. At this point, some preliminary ideas about the type of policies to follow should be considered.

Sectors with Significant Privacy Legislation

A number of sectors have significant privacy legislation in the United States. Notable examples include individual credit histories, video rentals, cable television records, telephone records, and student records. Enforcement provisions are included in many of these laws. For these sectors, there is an especially strong argument that the United States has adequate protection as a matter of law and practice. It may be reasonable to ask the Working Party or the Commission to give some sort of guidance to this effect.

Sectors with Functional Similarity

There are some sectors in which realistic assessment of actual practices suggests a functional similarity between privacy practices in Europe and the United States. For example, there is a strong expectation of confidentiality when auditors have access to an enterprise's records. However, no one expects the auditors to take the files and use them for direct marketing or other enterprise purposes. This expectation of confidentiality is backed up by well-established self-regulatory bodies and also likely by legal action in the event of misuse of the data. In this and other sectors, it would be extremely helpful to get guidance from the Working Party, the Commission, or national supervisory authorities stating that there is adequate protection.

Codes of conduct may be a useful supplement to data protection laws for sectors in which there is functional similarity. The International Standards Organization (ISO) is now beginning the process of drafting one such code of conduct. Current discussion versions of the ISO code would include a significant role for outside auditing of an enterprise's privacy practices. The audits might disclose publicly any material breach of an enterprise's promise to abide by the code. Other codes might also be developed outside of the ISO process, perhaps on a sector-by-sector basis. Where the codes have adequate protection of privacy and reasonable terms for enforcement, the EU would seem to have achieved its primary goal — having controllers of information abide by transparent and enforceable privacy rules.

One objection made by some European officials has been to express doubt about how enforceable such codes would be. In the view of some persons, there may be difficulties under current European law in empowering the data subject to bring suit for violations of these codes. This is clearly a European problem however, that falls squarely within European law. Many or most of the enterprises that would adopt the codes will have enough enterprise contacts in Europe to satisfy jurisdictional requirements. It would thus seem entirely within the power of European legislatures to eliminate current barriers to enforcement actions. On this issue, the Europeans do not need to wait for the United States and third-world countries to pass new privacy laws. If the EU considers the problem serious enough, it can fix the problem itself.

One decisive advantage of the codes of conduct is that it enables enterprises that wish to comply with the Directive to do so. There is no need to wait for the U.S. Congress to pass a comprehensive privacy law. There is no need to wait for data protection agencies, which may be heavily burdened in implementing the Directive, to give prior consent to each transfer or category of transfer. Enterprises that wish to be good citizens in regard to data protection can take responsibility for adopting fair information practices. By contrast, if compliance with codes of conduct is not considered enough to comply with the Directive, there will be far weaker incentives for enterprises to seek to comply. If even substantial and good-faith efforts by controllers still leave the enterprise in violation, practical managers may decide that the effort to comply is not worthwhile.

Sectors Where Transfers Can and Should Be Approved by Data Protection Authorities

There are major and vital transfers of personal information to the main-frame processing centers. However, none of the exceptions in Article 26(1) is very effective at allowing desirable categories of transfers. Examples include credit cards, telephone calling records, Internet service providers, and airline reservation systems. For this rather limited set of industries, it is recommended that data protection authorities approve categories of transfers pursuant to contracts, as provided by Article 26(2).

Routine Transfers Where the Benefits Outweigh the Likely Privacy Harms

The scope of the Directive is so broad that it includes many transfers of information in which one would ordinarily expect the benefits of the transfer to outweigh the cost in privacy terms. The Directive as written often does not suggest any way to permit these beneficial transfers. One clear example of this phenomenon is the use of laptop computers. It might be possible to give guidance authorizing the routine carrying of laptops and personal organizers out of Europe, while crafting some language to address the occasional worrisome cases. Indeed, as suggested by one European official, it is possible for a modern laptop to transport a sensitive medical database out of Europe. Despite this exceptional case, most enterprise uses of laptops are desirable and pose minimal risks to privacy interests. Routine users of these laptops should be notified that they are not violating European law. Failure to give such notice would make millions of persons into lawbreakers, undermining respect for the data protection regime.

An analogous situation may exist for the gathering of enterprise information about individuals. Investment bankers and other analysts in financial markets, for example, consider it a core part of their function to analyze enterprises and their key personnel. Research to date has uncovered little basis for thinking that this market analysis is legal under the Directive. Use of information for hostile takeovers is even more difficult to fit within the Directive. Although the transparency of financial markets is generally thought to depend on an effective flow of material of enterprise information, the data protection rules pose an ill-defined and potentially significant hurdle to this flow. Clarification is badly needed, and much of the enterprise information should likely be considered lawful for transfer.

A more difficult issue for data protection may be the rise of client/server architecture, intranets, and extranets. On the one hand, these technologies are spreading rapidly and seem likely to be an integral feature of the information society. These technologies are likely to be vital to development of new service industries, and failure to use them would disadvantage enterprises in countries where they are not considered fully legal. On the other hand, these technologies diffuse power away from controllers and place the ability to transfer personal information into the hands of a growing number of persons, many of whom have little data protection expertise. In contrast to mainframe computing centers, the number and variety of enterprises using the newer technology makes it more difficult for data protection authorities to authorize each transfer or category of transfer under Article 26(2). Once again, clarification from data protection officials is important to receive in advance, so enterprises can decide whether and in what way to invest in these important technologies consistent with the data protection regime.

CLARIFICATION OF THE ARTICLE 26 EXCEPTIONS AND OTHER PROVISIONS

In some areas, Article 26(1) language does not provide clear guidance. In part, this lack of guidance is the inevitable result of a new legislative framework. Some of the uncertainties, moreover, will be resolved by the national laws implementing the Directive. There are many places, however, where people in good faith might differ about what is required under the Directive. A few examples include:

- The definition of each of the exceptions in Article 26(1), perhaps especially for *unambiguous consent*
- The definition of for the purposes of direct marketing under Article 14
- The decision about what a transfer is to a third party for purposes of Articles 11 and 14
- The legality of secondary use in a third country of data that is transferred pursuant to Article 26
- The meaning of the journalistic exception in Article 9
- The application of the medical and research exceptions to pharmaceutical enterprises

As the Directive begins to be implemented, data protection authorities can play an enormously helpful role in educating the regulated community about its interpretations of these provisions. For instance, with respect to consent by data subjects, the Commission or national authorities might create a best practices area on a Web site and in print. This best practices material can include sample language that clearly passes muster under the consent requirements. It can present a convenient place for reporting of any actions by national authorities either approving or disapproving of specific approaches to securing data subject consent. Through this and related approaches, the data protection community can perform an educational mission, helping those enterprises that wish in good faith to comply with applicable law.

A variety of other measures might simultaneously be taken to help clarify the data protection rules. The Working Party will continue to offer expert reports on its views about implementation of the Directive. To the extent these reports give clear guidance about what is both permitted and forbidden under the Directive, controllers will be in a better position to comply with the law while continuing sensible practices that pose low risks to privacy interests. National legislation might address some of the legitimate concerns raised in this chapter and elsewhere. Eventually, as contemplated in the Directive itself, revisions of the Directive might be appropriate to handle problems that arise in practice.

THE INTERNET

There is reason for officials to be cautious about early enforcement of the Directive against Internet applications. Jurisdictional issues are in the early stages of being resolved. For operations in third-world countries, there will often be substantial doubt about whether the controller is on notice of the asserted applicability of EU law.

THE POLITICAL AND LEGAL PROCESS FOR RESOLVING DISPUTES

Finally, it is not clear what to recommend about the process for resolving data protection issues between Europe and third-world countries. It is a challenge to determine how best to conduct diplomatic efforts to avoid a trade war and come to a sensible resolution of the issues.

It is hoped that government officials will be able to regulate community and other interested parties to come to a better resolution of outstanding differences about the Directive. Interested persons on both sides of the Atlantic should wish to find better-tuned ways to protect legitimate privacy interests, while also allowing the vital flows of information that are essential to the Information Age.

Notes

1. The new European Data Protection Directive places strict controls on the dissemination of personal data. It also puts Europe at odds with the United States, with billions of dollars in trade capital hanging in the balance.
2. Privacy International is a human rights group formed in 1990 as a watchdog on surveillance by governments and enterprises. PI is based in London and has an office in Washington, D.C. PI has conducted campaigns in Europe, Asia, and North America to counter abuses of privacy by way of information technology (e.g., telephone tapping, ID card systems, video surveillance, data matching, police information systems, and medical records).

Organizations

1. Citigroup, Inc., 153 E. 53rd St., New York, NY 10043.
2. World Trade Organization, 154 rue de Lausanne, 1211 Geneva 21, Switzerland.
3. Court of Justice of the European Communities, Palais de la Cour de Justice, Boulevard Konrad Adenauer, Kirchberg, L-2925 Luxembourg.

4. Sabre Holdings, Inc., 4255 Amon Carter Boulevard, Fort Worth, Texas 76155.
5. Privacy International Washington Office, 666 Pennsylvania Ave, SE, Suite 301, Washington, D.C. 20003.
6. European Union, Delegation of the European Commission to the United States, 2300 M Street NW, Washington, D.C. 20037.
7. International Organization for Standardization (ISO), 1, rue de Varembé, Case postale 56, CH-1211 Genève 20, Switzerland.

Chapter 47

Data Privacy Directive 95/46 EC: Protecting Personal Data and Ensuring Free Movement of Data

Lawrence D. Dietz *

To what extent have Member States of the European Union (EU) implemented legislation to comply with the Data Privacy Directive issued by the EU in 1995? How does the legislation of the United Kingdom, Germany, and Italy compare individually and collectively? And has the European Union succeeded thus far in achieving its goal of protecting individual data privacy and acting as a legal catalyst to ensure freedom of movement of this data throughout the European Union and its position as an institution and global commercial player?

INTRODUCTION AND METHODOLOGY

Directive 95/46 EC (herein after "the Directive") is generally credited with two firsts: the first piece of European Union (EU) legislation to directly address human rights and the first legislation to address the issue of protecting personal data. The General Directive was formulated for the dual purposes of providing protection of personal data and ensuring the free movement of this data throughout the European Community (EC).

---

* © 2002 by Lawrence D. Dietz. Used by permission.

To a great extent, the passage of the Directive was driven by the recognition by the Member States (MS), and subsequently the European Union, that trans-border data flow would be an important foundation of electronic commerce within the European Union. Further, the MS, Council, and Parliament, as well as the Commission realized that a pan-European approach to data protection was needed to foster trade within the European Community by simplifying the legal requirements associated with that protection. It was further reasoned that a General Directive such as 95/46 EC would provide sufficient guidance for the Member States to draft their own harmonizing data protection legislation.

Notwithstanding the significance of electronic commerce, it also appears that these political actors were motivated by the concerns of citizens who needed to be assured of the sanctity of their personal information (data) collected, stored, and processed in multiple locations by a myriad of organizations. Through compliance with harmonized legislation, individuals could be assured of their protection. Also, businesses and government organizations would be fully aware of their responsibilities and duties in connection with the collection, storage, processing, and distribution of personal data.

This chapter explores the motivating factors behind the drafting and passage of the Directive. It will then compare the legislation passed by several key MS to determine if indeed the legislation is harmonized and carries out the letter and spirit of the Directive.

Analysis begins with an explanation of the Directive and its key constituent parts. Then the laws of the United Kingdom, Germany, and Italy are analyzed, compared, and contrasted. The United Kingdom was selected because it was an early proponent of data protection legislation and because of the historically close relationship between U.K. legislation and U.S. common law and legislation. The volume of trade generated by and between these two nations is a significant portion of world trade. The United Kingdom was also selected because it is the home of the University of Leicester, the host institution for this research work.

Germany was selected because it represents a significant trade volume and because it often finds itself on opposite sides of legal arguments. Italy was selected to represent MS whose economies are less robust and more typical of southern European countries.

In performing initial research for this chapter, it became clear that there were a number of sources for legislation of the MS. Most were in the native language of the nation. However, there were a few sources with English translation. Several sources were employed, including both the Internet and a single text that contained English translations of legislation from several nations.[1]

Subsequent to the analysis of the directives, this chapter offers commentary on a scholarly work and a few selected cases. The chapter continues with an overall assessment as to how well the European Union has succeeded thus far in achieving its goal of protecting individual data privacy and acting as a legal catalyst to ensure freedom of movement of this data throughout the European Union. Finally, the conclusion assesses how effective this body will be in positioning the European Union as an institution and as a global commercial player.

DATA PROTECTION AND SOCIETY

In May 1999, *The Economist* proclaimed, "But exercising control over who knows what about you has also come to be seen as an essential feature of a civilised society."[2] The quote comes from an article entitled "The End of Privacy." The article promulgated a thesis that, although there will be a significant range of benefits to be garnered from harnessing information technology, benefits that include improved productivity, reduced crime, better health care, and an incredible array of entertainment, these benefits would come at a price. That price would be "less and less privacy." The article describes how privacy has been eroded for some time and predicts that the trend will accelerate sharply.

The accelerating pace of technology, in particular the Internet, is bringing about a number of fundamental changes in the way citizens live, work, and play. In addition, allied technologies in related fields such as video, entertainment, digital rights protection, electronic commerce, and others are putting pressure on new models of society and the legal system that is supposed to support them.

The inviting nature and ease of use of today's Internet technology is in marked contrast to the locked and foreboding computer rooms of years past. Information is being collected today that was largely left unrecorded in the past. Much of this information is being supplied by individuals without regard for the information's subsequent use or for the length of time the information is retained by the collector. This last point becomes especially significant in light of new technologies that extend the retention period for electronic information to an almost limitless time frame. New storage technologies such as storage area networks (SANs) enable large organizations with wide-ranging information technology (IT) infrastructures to harness the power of mainframes and their supporting storage devices as well as servers and other systems to store the increasing mountains of data collected and processed by the organizations.

Routine collection of information is going almost unnoticed in today's society. Electronic transactions such as telephone calls, faxes, electronic funds transfers (EFTs), and others are relentless tracked by IT systems.

Citizens using these media are offered no choice but to leave an electronic trail.

Governments are also involved in routine electronic surveillance. The governments of Australia, Canada, Great Britain, New Zealand, and the United States reportedly have a system dubbed "Echelon" that is able to monitor satellite telecommunications traffic for specific words and phrases. Domestic law enforcement agencies of various countries are also reportedly involved in passive interception. As recently as November 2000, a special panel investigated the U.S. Federal Bureau of Investigation's (FBI) Carnivore system because of allegations that it was overly broad in its intercept capabilities.

Consumers, in particular, have been subject to a widening array of technology-based privacy invasions. As noted above, collecting information over the Internet via the World Wide Web has become a daily occurrence. The Web has also reduced the barriers to entry for many online businesses. This has also reduced profit margins and forced online businesses to become more competitive. One way to become more competitive is to be more efficient in terms of targeting messages and potential buyers.

It is possible to compare the clickstream (moves through Web sites made by a mouse) and online transaction data with profiles of the Web site. This data comparison allows sellers to determine what products are most likely to be purchased by which consumers. A major market research firm, Zona Research (Redwood City, California), claimed that returns from targeted promotions such as these will be as high as 35 percent, while returns from traditional direct mail programs will be only 5 percent.[3] However, there is no data available to validate whether or not the consumers in question actually consented to this profiling or if the sellers or analysis product providers violated any privacy promises made to their customers or Web site visitors.

Data privacy is a major concern of online shoppers. Forrester Research (Cambridge, Massachusetts) surveyed a large contingent of online purchasers and prospective online purchasers. They found that 67 percent of the people surveyed were concerned about data privacy and because of that issue, they spent $US2.8 billion less in 1999 than they would have if they were not so concerned.

In addition to the interests of buyers and sellers, law enforcement plays a role in privacy erosion. Law enforcement wants to be able to lawfully and effectively acquire evidence of crimes. As legitimate and illegitimate activities migrate onto the information highway, those charged with enforcing the law and apprehending criminals are finding it difficult to collect, analyze, and present electronic evidence. While some issues here relate to admissibility, such as exceptions to the hearsay rules, others relate to the privacy of individuals and legal persons.

Some governments such as the United States have already started down the road of giving law enforcement "special rights." Title III of the U.S. Omnibus Crime Control and Safe Streets Act (1968) gives law enforcement the ability to circumvent individual rights under certain circumstances if a court order is in effect at the time with only "sound reason" as the justification. From an electronic perspective, the Electronic Communications Privacy Act (ECPA) of 1986 gives law enforcement the right to collect originating telephone numbers and information about the messages, but not the content of them.

The issue of legislating privacy norms has been a nettlesome one. The EU Directive has been a landmark piece of legislation, but not one that has been universally accepted. Part of the dilemma comes from the fact that the Internet has grown so fast, complex, and pervasive that global and national legal systems have been unable to keep up with it. Most judges and lawmakers are unfamiliar with technology and reluctant to tread new ground, especially when they fear their decisions will be ultimately overturned on appeal. It is also difficult to determine what are the expectations of privacy held by consumers and businesses and how or if those expectations should be reduced to law. Even in the United States where a market-driven or self-regulation approach is favored, there were a reported 300 or so Internet privacy bills being circulated in the U.S. Congress during July 2000.[4]

The legislation issue is complicated by individual promises made by Internet businesses to their Web site visitors and customers. These promises are in the form of policies that the businesses post on their Web sites. While voluntary in nature, they are often considered a part of the terms and conditions governing online transactions. Significant confusion has arisen concerning enforcement of these privacy policies. New variations of privacy problems seem to arise daily, with the latest being a rash of sales of the databases of failing (or failed) dot.com companies. These databases often contained information that was subject to the privacy policy the company had posted on its Web site. Consumers find that promises are not being honored. Sometimes, defendants are difficult to find and even more difficult to prosecute.

EU citizens are turning to national legislation (as will be discussed later) while American citizens are turning to the U.S. Federal Trade Commission and consumer suits to enforce their rights and pursue grievances. A key challenge to these legal actions is the difficulty of determining a legal definition of privacy.

DATA PROTECTION AND THE EUROPEAN UNION

The European Union was addressing the importance of data protection even prior to the issuance of the Directive in 1995. Data protection was deemed to be a part of general human rights law and there was a clear relationship between data protection and specific rights and interests granted by the European Convention on Human Rights (ECHR). This is particularly important in the context of EU law because these requirements as embodied in the substantive law are a part of the "general principles of Community law," meaning that they take on overriding constitutional importance within the legal order of the European Community.[5]

Article 6(2) of the Treaty of the European Union states that "The Union shall respect fundamental rights, as guaranteed by the European Convention for the Protection of Human Rights and Fundamental Freedoms signed in Rome on 4 November 1950 and, as they result from the constitutional traditions common to the Member States, as general principles of Community law."[6] This gave the Convention a strong foundation within EU law.

By way of background, the Convention for the Protection of Human Rights and Fundamental Freedoms entered into force in September 1953. It formalized a legal process for the collective enforcement of civil and political rights and freedoms stated in the United Nations Universal Declaration of Human Rights of 1948. Contracting States at the Convention agreed to a system of enforcement administered by the European Commission of Human Rights (set up in 1954), the European Court of Human Rights (set up in 1959), and the Committee of Ministers of the Council of Europe. Under the 1950 Convention Contracting States and, where the Contracting States had accepted the right of individual petition, individual applicants (individuals, groups of individuals, or nongovernmental organizations) could lodge complaints against the Contracting States for alleged violations of their Convention rights.

The complaints were first examined by the Commission to determine admissibility. Where admissible and there had been no prior friendly settlement, the Commission drew up a report establishing the facts and expressing an opinion on the merits of the case. The report was transmitted to the Committee of Ministers. Where the Respondent State had accepted the compulsory jurisdiction of the Court, the Commission and any Contracting State concerned had a period of three months following the transmission of the report to the Committee of Ministers within which to bring the case before the Court for a final, binding adjudication. Individuals were not entitled to bring their cases before the Court. If a case was not referred to the Court, the Committee of Ministers decided whether there had been a violation of the Convention and, if appropriate, awarded just satisfaction to the victim. The Committee of Ministers also had responsibility for supervising the execution of the Court's judgments.[7]

A number of other key international documents have addressed and stressed the link between data protection and human rights. They included the UN Guidelines for the regulation of computerized personal data files (E.CN.4/1190/72) adopted by the General Assembly on November 20, 1990, and by the Organization for Economic Cooperation and Development (OECD) Guidelines for the Protection of Privacy and Transborder Flows of Personal Data contained in a Recommendation of the Council of Europe Convention for the Protection of Individuals with regard to Automatic Processing of Personal Data (Strasbourg, January 28, 1981, ETS No. 108).

While these documents bring to the fore the notion of the human rights concept of respect for private life and freedom of expression, they do not provide clear definitions and allude to other rights that are allied to data protection.

For example, the aim of the OECD Guidelines is to reconcile the tension between privacy and the free flow of information. This is elaborated in the Explanatory Memorandum to the Guidelines which states in paragraph 25:

> As stated in the Preamble, two essential basic values are involved: the protection of privacy and individual liberties and the advancement of free flows of personal data. The Guidelines attempt to balance the two values against one another; while accepting certain restrictions to free transborder flows of personal data, they seek to reduce the need for such restrictions and thereby strengthen the notion of free information flows between countries.

The Explanatory Memorandum also detailed a number of other critical points. New needs for protection have emerged in addition to the classic abuse or disclosure of intimate personal data. They noted that record keepers had the obligation of informing the general public about activities and rights concerning data collection and processing and that these organizations ought to inform consumers of their rights with respect to accuracy of the data. The intent of the Guidelines could best be summed up by an extract from paragraph 2:

> Generally speaking, there has been a tendency to broaden the traditional concept of privacy ('the right to be left alone') and to identify a more complex synthesis of interests which can perhaps more correctly be termed privacy and individual liberties.

The Preamble to the Council of Europe Convention makes clear that the convention was convened "to reconcile the fundamental values of the respect for privacy and the free flow of information between peoples." The Convention issued an explanatory report that stated that the Convention imposed restrictions on freedom of information as a way to protect "other individual rights and freedoms," especially the right for individual privacy. Articles 8 and 10 of the EHCR were cited, as well as Article 19 of the International Covenant on Civil and Political Rights.

Article 8 delineates that "Everyone has the right to respect for his private and family life, his home and his correspondence." It would be a rather easy jump to see how this might affect e-mail and how data protection would be as fundamental a right with regard to e-mail as it is to snail mail. However, nothing is without exception, and individual rights and freedoms may succumb to the greater needs of society such as national security, public safety, prevention of crime or disorder, the protection of health or morals, or protection of the rights of others. These societal needs would auger as exceptions to individual freedom and would allow the government to intervene by violating individual rights where it felt that the societal needs were greater.

Overall, however, legislation and case law prior to the issuance of the Directive was inconclusive and vague. An exact definition of what exactly was meant by private life was not in the offing. However, there have been a few cases which addressed the issue.

In the case of *X v. Federal Republic of Germany* (1973), the Commission held that mere collecting of information and holding it by the police was not in conflict with Article 8, even if the subject had no criminal record. The main issue in this case was the lack of disclosure of the information. The court apparently felt that as long as the information was not disclosed to the detriment of the subject, there was no harm done.[8] Six years later, the court was to justify disclosure of information collected by the police to a court as a legitimate exercise of government activity.

Two cases followed. In *Leander v. Sweden,* the police maintained information in a secret register about an applicant for a job in a museum on a Swedish naval base. This information was used as the basis for denying the applicant the job. Leander had asked for access to the file with the intent to correct any false information and refute allegations, but was denied access. While the court noted that the refusal to allow Leander access to the information was an interference with his personal life, the court held that the national security implications of the case were special circumstances meriting this action. The court noted that it must be assured that there are adequate and effective guarantees against abuse to condone the use of a secret surveillance system. Under the circumstances, the court ruled that Leander's rights under Article 8 were not denied.[9]

Notwithstanding the court's ruling and reasoning, there was no attempt by the holding agency (the police) to actually validate the information. In 1997, the Swedish admitted in an article published by *The Guardian* that the file against Leander "turned out to be a gossipy and mistake-filled assemblage of harmless information."[10]

It is particularly interesting to note that the court supported the position of the record holder to collect, hold, and report such information, yet never did anyone actually question the validity of the information being held. This brings to the fore the issue of recovery by an aggrieved party. Leander was denied a job based on false information to which he did not have access. Given this scenario he could claim an injury; but where could he seek redress? As will be seen later, the claim of injury would be made in the country where it occurred. However, because there was no data protection law in place at the time, the best Leander can hope for now would be to file a negligence suit against the police that may or may not be dismissed due to sovereign immunity to tort prosecution.

Another case in the area concerns a Mr. Gaskin, who, as a child, was reared by government authorities. Gaskin claimed that he was ill-treated by these authorities and sought the records necessary to provide him with information about his childhood. The British system required consent of the contributor — in this case the very people that Gaskin would be accusing of mistreatment and perhaps child abuse. The court went on to discuss the principle of proportionality and its application where the contributor does not answer the complaint or withholds consent. Under these circumstances, the respect for the private and family life of the plaintiff (Gaskin) was not honored and was therefore a breach of paragraph 8 of the Convention.[11]

An allied area where there has been limited case activity is in the processing of information on groups where there is an impact on the right to freedom of thought, conscience, and religion (Article 9); the right to freedom of expression (Article 10); and the right to freedom of association (Article 11). The nub is whether the activity related to information collection and processing interferes with the group's ability to exercise its rights. The types of organizations that are most likely to be affected are political, trade union, and religious groups.

In *Church of Scientology v. France,* the Commission decided that there was "no appearance of a violation of Articles 9, 10, and 11 of the Convention."[12] The court seemed to be confirming the earlier stance that only where the information-related activities harm the plaintiff is there an action. This may be a difficult and perhaps unjust conclusion because it becomes increasingly more difficult to determine if there actually has been an interference with freedom of association as an example. There is no way of telling if an organization would be stronger but for the information activity. As the Internet grows in importance as a communications medium, especially among "unpopular" organizations, the interests of the state in discovering and preventing illegal acts will come into direct conflict with a group's ability to exercise its freedom of thought, conscience, and religion (Article 9); freedom of expression (Article 10); and freedom of association (Article 11).

Overall, it would seem that data protection rights and general principles of law should protect private life. People should be able to find out who has information about them, the accuracy of this information, and its use, especially concerning decisions that affect their well-being. Decisions of this type include job applications, loan and credit applications, etc. Citizens should have the ability to challenge these decisions based on ensuring that the information is timely, relevant, and accurate. Information concerning religious, political, or other potentially controversial positions or opinions held by citizens should be similarly protected, especially where the rights to freedom of thought, conscience, religion, expression, and association are concerned. In addition, discrimination on any of these grounds must be guarded against and prevented to ensure that citizens are not harmed.

The European Commission was being pushed to establish its own Directive as far back as mid-1970s. However, the European Community (now Union) was not authorized to address criminal law or involve provisions for "national security" because these were viewed as the exclusive provinces of the Member States. In 1982, the European Community passed a watered-down Recommendation (OJ 1981 L246/31) that simply asked individual Member States to follow the Council of Europe Convention. In 1990, it was feared that the lack of data protection would mean that Europe would degenerate into feudal states where personal data could be collected, processed, and disseminated unfettered. This they felt would be a death knell to the single market concept. The EEC Commission issued a package of proposals in 1990 in furtherance of their goal to orchestrate common data protection guidelines within the European Community.

The essence of the package was that a directive with resultant harmonized legislation would be the most effective means to achieving the goal of consistency. The draft was labeled "over-ambitious" because it required Member States to implement significant changes in their national legislation, and Parliament subsequently voted a number of changes to the draft.

With all of this as a backdrop, one can now turn to analyzing the Directive.

AN EXPLANATION OF DIRECTIVE 95/46/EC

Introduction and Overview

The full title of the Directive is: *Directive 95/46 of the European Parliament and the Council of 24 October 1995 on the Protection of Individuals with*

Regard to the Processing of Personal Data and on the Free Movement of Such Data. The Directive contains 33 articles in eight chapters. It was drafted to provide guidance to the MS (Member States) on minimum acceptable standards within the European Community for balancing the "fundamental rights and freedoms of natural persons" against a desire to "neither restrict nor prohibit the free flow of personal data between MS."

As with any other piece of EU legislation, the Directive was a compromise and, as such, contained less than complete answers and guidance in many areas, yet is the basis for national legislation and an increasingly important bulwark in natural trade.

To be regarded as successful in its efforts to provide clear guidance to the MS, the Directive should adequately address the following key issues:

- It should be clear and complete to ensure that individuals and organizations will be able to understand their rights and responsibilities.
- It should clearly indicate the extent of liability that can be imposed for failure to adhere and should offer concise advice on liability minimization and avoidance.
- While maintaining a technology neutral perspective, it should apply guidance to help organizations determine what procedural and technology measures are appropriate.
- It should provide adequate protection to EC citizens, yet should also be adaptive to global markets without imposing undue hardship on potential trading partners.
- It should offer guidance and baselines for national legislation. Furthermore, knowledgeable EU personnel should be available as a resource to provide continuing guidance to EU-based organizations and give appropriate attention to potential non-EU trading partners.

The next section examines the Directive and comments on aspects of how its provisions meet or fail to meet the criteria noted above. In subsequent sections, national legislation is examined to assess its compliance with the Directive, its harmonizing effect, and the likely effect that national legislation will have on information processing and trading.

Chapter I: General Provisions

Chapter I outlines the objectives and scope of the Directive, discusses the applicability of national law, and sets down key definitions. The objectives were discussed previously. The key point is that the Directive is designed to protect rights of "natural persons." By extension, this implies that "legal persons" or organizations would have to seek protection under natural law. It could also be argued that once a person is deceased, the Directive and perhaps national laws no longer cover him or her.

Prior to exploring definitions, it is important to point out that the Directive does not just extend to information processed by IT, but also applies to manual systems. The use of a generic term such as "filing system" expands the scope of the Directive significantly. Furthermore, the use of comprehensive descriptions, such as "shall apply to the processing of personnel data wholly or partly by automatic means, and to the processing otherwise than by automatic means of personal data which form part of a filing system or are intended to form a filing system,"[13] also has the effect of broadening the scope.

Extension to manual systems is important because organizations will now have to retroactively ensure that their records-handling processes and procedures are in compliance (assuming that the national legislation has the same scope). For many organizations, this will be a time-consuming, expensive, and even onerous process. However, if the information is to be protected, then it must be protected based on its sensitivity and importance, and not on where it is located. This retroactive application to manual systems is likely to have the secondary effect of causing organizations to examine their records-generating and -keeping procedures.

Another aspect of this wide net is the potential to include personal data collected from new and as yet unaccepted technology. Video surveillance, television Internet appliances, personal digital assistants (PDAs), and cell phones are all products of technology that may generate personal information which might come subject to national legislation passed to comply with the Directive.

One of the greatest services performed by the Directive is laying out definitions. Article 2 contains definitions that run to the heart of the Directive by describing the *dramatis personae* that play a part in the information processing cycle.

The Directive describes what information (data) must be protected. In Article 2(a), the notion of information relating to "an identifiable person" is described. This is taken to mean a natural person directly identified by an identification number, or indirectly by one or more facts that relate to that person's "physical, physiological, mental, economic, cultural, or social identity."[14]

Be advised that the identification does not extend to all circumstances, but only to the use of "reasonable efforts" by the controller. The controller is defined in Article 2(d) as the natural or legal person, public authority, agency, or other body that, alone or jointly with others, determines the purposes and means of processing the personal data. A controller is a senior individual within organizations, most likely a director or senior manager. He or she supervises organizations as well as individuals. Consequently, in a dispute, the trier of fact will look to the capabilities of the controller and similarly situated controllers to determine what constitutes "reasonable efforts." While this may seem awkward, in practice it is likely to stimulate industry norms to the benefit of all involved.

Another key definition is processing of data, which means "any operation or set of operations" performed on the personal data by any means.[15] While Articles 5 and 6 address the issues of Fair and Lawful Processing and Purpose of the Processing and Compliance, the broad definition of Article 2(b) would appear to extend protection to a wide range of applications. The key is that the data controller has determined a purpose for the processing.

The "processor" as defined by Article 2(e) is the person who or organization that processes personal data on behalf of the controller. As such, the processor can be another department in the controller's organization, a separate company that is retained to process information on behalf of the controller, or a public authority or agency that performs operations on behalf of the data controller. Processors are required to provide guarantees to the controller concerning confidentiality and security. This will be addressed later in the discussion covering Articles 16 and 17.

A "third party" under Article 2(f) refers to parties that are under the direct authority of the controller or processor and are authorized to process the data. Third parties here merely receive the data for a specific purpose but do not perform any other processing. Examples might include an Internet service provider (ISP) or a managed services provider (MSP) that provides firewall and other security-type services for the controller or processor. Information is disclosed to recipients who are further defined under Article 2(g). The major aspect of identifying the recipient is to inform the data subject (the individual whose data the information is) as to whom the information will be disclosed and for the notification of the official supervising authority pursuant to Chapter 10, Article 18.

The Data subject's consent in accordance with Article 2(h) is critical. This must be a fully informed and free process. Full and fair notice is a mandatory prerequisite to consent. In addition, the consent requires an affirmative action by the data subject. This model is often described as an "opt-in" model, wherein the data subject must specifically do something to signify assent. The opposite is the more "American" model, known as an "opt-out" model, in which an individual must specifically decide not to consent. Typically, this may involve a process on the Internet in which a U.S. citizen would have to specifically indicate he or she does not want to receive direct mail materials; whereas, an EU citizen would have to indicate that they wanted to receive the materials. Consent according to the Directive must be specific for a specific purpose. Implied is that the specific consent for the specific purpose constitutes permission only for those operations in support of the specific purpose. Any other use of the information would be considered outside the scope of consent granted by the data subject and therefore a potential cause of action under appropriate national law.

Article 4 is the jurisdictional predicate within the Directive. It explains which national law must be applied in the described situations. Its goal is to simplify the choice of law for citizens and data controllers alike. The location of a data controller within the territory of a MS subjects the controller in that case to the national law of the MS in which he or she is located. Controllers in multiple MS must ensure that they conform to the respective laws of each. A spirit of cooperation between data protection authorities was established in Article 28(6). It states, "The supervisory authorities shall cooperate with one another to the extent necessary for the performance of their duties, in particular by exchanging all useful information."[16]

By way of example, a controller established in Italy who processes data in France must respect Italian law; however, that will fall under the jurisdiction of French authorities for any and all operations carried out within the Republic of France. A special variation within the Directive advises that data processed within an embassy (due to international public law) must be processed according to the nation it represents rather than the host nation where it resides.

Affected processing requires some type of operation, storage, or copy. Mere transit of data through a country or across its borders does not trigger national legislation.

Chapter II, Section I: General Rules on Lawfulness of the Processing of Personal Data

In Article 6(1)(b), MS are admonished that personal data must be "collected for specified, explicit and legitimate purposes and not further processed in a way incompatible with those purposes."[17] The article goes on to say that processing for historical, statistical, or scientific purposes will not be considered as incompatible as long as MS provide "appropriate safeguards." Commentators often site the principle of subsidiarity as the guiding principle behind the fact that MS must determine what lawful and fair processing means in their particular jurisdictions.[18] *Fair* in this case means that all reasons for the collection, processing, and disclosure of the data must be fully disclosed.

The purpose specification aspect of Article 6 means that controllers must fully inform data subjects concerning the purpose of collection. The controller must also inform the supervisory authorities. Once the controller has notified the supervisory authorities, those authorities now have the tools and gauges to determine if the processing is legitimate and the data quality meets acceptable standards. This formal process also gives the data subject a clear idea of what is happening to the data and can serve to set the stage for legal redress should the collecting, processing, or disclosure stray from the reported descriptions.

The use limitation principle ensures that the data is employed for only the stated purposes. The data compliance principle states that "MS shall provide that personal data must be: (c) adequate, relevant and not excessive in relation to the purposes for which they are collected and/or further processed."[19] This provision requires the establishment of the logical nexus between the data collected, processed, or disclosed and the stated purpose therefore.

The data quality principle addresses the accuracy and completeness of the data, while the conservation principle provides retention guidance. Data quality guidelines require that the controller (or his delegatee) ensures that the data collected actually relates to the purpose, that the data is up-to-date, and that reasonable steps are taken to ensure that inaccurate or incomplete data is dealt with.

When the data is kept for a period longer than required for the purpose given consent, the data must be rendered anonymous, meaning that it can no longer be associated with an identifiable person.

The controller is the individual responsible for compliance. This responsibility can be delegated to the processor, but it is likely that the controller will not be able to avoid liability merely by delegating. The controller will have to perform reasonable audits, checks, etc. to ensure that compliance is being maintained.

Chapter II, Section II: Criteria for Making Data Processing Legitimate

Chapter II, Articles 7(a) through 7(f) describe a prerequisite prior of legal processing and multiple variations of legal processing. These articles set down criteria for legitimate processing, which is of course the only type of processing permitted. Under Article 7(a), a data subject's specific and unambiguous consent constitutes grounds for legal processing. There are a number of alternative grounds, as detailed in Articles 7(b) through and including 7(f).

If a data subject is a party to a contract or has taken steps prior to entering into a contract, then the collection, processing, and disclosure considered necessary for the performance of the contract are considered legitimate. Article 7(c) provides that processing of personal data is legal when it is necessary for compliance with a legal obligation. The notion of a data subject's vital interests — meaning those interests that are "essential for the data subject's life" — is the province of Article 7(d). Article 7(e) indicates that processing of personal information in the public interest, or in the exercise of an official authority (vested in the controller or in a third party) as defined by national law, is also considered legal processing.

Article 7(f) is a catchall. It allows MS to determine when personal data can be processed or disclosed in the context of normal business activities without regard to whether the activities are of a commercial or nonprofit nature. The key requirement imposed by the article is to balance the fundamental rights and freedoms of the data subject against the interests at hand. An important aspect is that a data subject can object to the processing of data about him and may have a means to "opt out."

Chapter II, Section III: Special Categories of Processing

Sensitive data is an important subset of personal data. As described in Article 8(1), this is data that reveals racial or ethnic origin, political opinions, religious beliefs, trade union membership, health, or sex life details.[20] This information is regarded as sensitive because it could expose the data subject to discrimination as well as infringe on the very fundamentals of privacy. Health information, as defined by this article, would include past or present information on physical or mental state as well as any abuse of drugs or alcohol. However, the Directive recognizes that even this information may have to be processed under certain conditions and sets down exceptions or derogations that provide for the processing of this sensitive data under specific conditions.

Aspects of the derogations include situations in which the data subject has given his or her explicit consent and this consent is not prohibited by law (Article 8(2)(a)). The processing is necessary to allow the controller to fulfill obligations under employment law and according to national law and its safeguards (Article 8(2)(b)).

Other exceptions include times when the data subject is unable to give consent and when processing is necessary to protect the vital (life-threatening) interests of the data subject. An interesting exception is posed by Article 8(2)(d).[21] Under this exemption, nonprofit organizations organized for political, philosophical, religious, or trade union purposes and that provide guarantees may process information relating "solely to the members of the body or to persons who have regular contact with it in connection with its purposes and that the data are not disclosed to a third party without the consent of data subjects."

This section is significant because it seems to stand for the propositions that nonprofit organizations associated with generating sensitive data or that could identify data subjects' sensitive data or protected information have the need to process information for their own benefit. Implied is that these organizations have obtained appropriate consent from the data subject and that there is no commercialization of the data. Often the

Directive takes positions that discriminate among commercial, nonprofit, and government entities as to their rights and responsibilities with respect to the data and the data subject.

Other derogations include data made public or employed in legal claims, medical utilization of the data, and additional exemptions "for reasons of substantial public interest." This might be a broad category that extends from health and social protection to matters of national security.

With regard to criminal records and data "relating to offences, criminal convictions or security measures," the Directive notes that only an official national authority can maintain a complete register of criminal convictions. As a further safeguard, the Directive requires controllers employing derogations from Articles 8(1) and 8(5) to notify the data commissioner. This requirement is made to ensure that this sensitive information is properly safeguarded and processed.

Article 9 codifies protection of freedom of expression in journalistic, artistic, or literary endeavors by admonishing MS to provide exemptions for these purposes under Chapters II, IV, and VI. The general rule is that the freedom of expression must be balanced against the right to privacy; however, specific guidance is not provided. This is especially troublesome if data collected under the journalistic exemption is then employed for commercial means. While journalistic efforts can be balanced toward disclosure, commercial efforts would not be protected to that extent and the rights of the data subject would be more pronounced.

Chapter II, Section IV: Information to Be Given to the Data Subjects

Articles 10 and 11 offer guidance to the MS as to the minimum information that must be provided by the data controller (or designated representative) to the data subject. MS can, of course, require that additional information be supplied to the data subject. The Directive does not provide guidance as to "how" the data subject must be informed. This lack of guidance may give rise to variations in national laws, such as whether or not a mere mouse-click constitutes an acknowledgment by data subjects that they have been informed. Minimum information that must be provided according to Article 10 includes the identity of the controller (or designiated representative), purpose of the processing, potential recipients of the data, and the existence of right of access and right to rectify data. Other points include whether providing the information is obligatory or voluntary and the potential consequences of failing to provide the information.[22]

Chapter II, Section V: The Data Subject's Right of Access to Data

Member States must provide data subjects with access to information and must guarantee that data subjects will have the ability for "rectification, erasure or blocking of the data" because the data is inaccurate or incomplete. In addition to these rights, third parties must be notified of any rectification, erasure, or blocking "unless this proves impossible or involves a disproportionate effort."[23]

Article 12 pays attention to balancing the right of the subject against cost to the data controller in its guidance. However, as national laws are enforced and "aggrieved plaintiffs" turn to the courts, it is likely the disproportionate effort will be defined in several gradations. Balancing the subject's need for privacy and accurate data against profits may prove to be an interesting dilemma. This is likely to become even more interesting when the defendant is unpopular or not a national of the country in which the litigation is being pursued.

Chapter II, Section VI: Exemptions and Restrictions

Member States are authorized to adopt legislation limiting rights and obligations. The caveat to these restrictions is that more powerful individual or public interests must justify them. Article 13(1) lists the following interests: (a) national security, (b) defense, and (c) public security. These are self-explanatory and will not be discussed further.

Regulated professions and the need to prevent, investigate, detect, and prosecute criminal offenses and ethical breaches are noted as another important exemption in Article 13(1)(d). Other exemptions under Article 13(1) include important economic or financial interests of a MS or the EU (13(1)(e)) and exercise of official authority (13(1)(f)). The protection of the rights and freedoms of data subjects is addressed by Article 13(1)(g). Family law matters may emerge as a key area for paragraph (g) given the fluid nature of immigration. Medical data and health professional access may also be important areas. The United States has singled out health care information as one of the few instances requiring legislation and has implemented the Health Information Portability and Accountability Act (HIPAA) to that end. Finally, the article defines the use of data for developing statistics as long as there is no risk of data subject privacy breach and that the data is only retained for the period necessary to create the statistics.[24]

Chapter II, Section VII: The Data Subject's Right to Object

Article 14 authorizes MS (Member States) to grant data subjects with the right to object to processing if they can show compelling and legitimate grounds to do so. "Compelling" is taken to mean a detrimental effect on the data subject and "legitimate" to mean that the processing is not legal according to national law.

Member States are also supposed to provide data subjects with the right to object to any processing relating to direct marketing. The potential impact on electronic commerce of Article 14(b) is significant. Its immediate effect has been the European opt-in model of consent, as previously explained. The EU was particularly keen on these provisions, as shown by the fact that controllers are required to inform the data subject concerning the purposes of direct marketing, thereby giving them the opportunity to object at that time. The controller is also obligated to notify the data subject if the data will be disclosed to a third party to allow that party to pursue direct marketing. In these situations, the data subject can object to the disclosure.

Decisions made by automated processes are addressed in Article 15. Paragraph (1) gives data subjects the ability to employ non-automated factors to respond to automated individual decisions that have a negative impact on the data subject. For this provision to be invoked, the automated processes must be used to evaluate personal aspects of the data subject such as credit worthiness, work performance, etc. It must be solely the result of automated processing and must have been taken against the data subject with a resulting significant negative effect on the data subject. Typical situations include mortgage approvals, loan granting, and insurance policy approval. As more and more transactions take place on the Internet, it is reasonable to expect more, totally automated processes in our daily lives. This is likely to give this rather short section a disproportionate share of attention.

Chapter II, Section VIII: Confidentiality and Security of Processing

Article 16 specifies that processing can only take place under the specific instructions of the data controller. Other processing is considered unlawful. Article 17 is a technology-neutral provision authorizing MS to "implement appropriate technical and organizational measures to protect personal data."[25] These measures must be "appropriate to the risks represented by the processing and the nature of the data to be protected." This guidance is broad to say the least. It is implied that the data controller performs a risk assessment appropriate to the situation. Assessments here need to take into account the normal principles of negligence: gravity of the harm, likelihood to occur, cost of prevention, duty of care, and reasonable care.

There are no generally accepted standards of risk assessment and an analysis of risk assessment is beyond the scope of this chapter. Suffice to say that accidental or unlawful destruction or accidental loss, alteration, unauthorized disclosure, or unlawful processing are likely to trigger litigation.

With respect to the choice of processor, Article 17 specifies that the controller must choose a processor that will provide sufficient guarantees in terms of technical and organizational security. Furthermore, the relationship between controller and processor must be a legal one with specific stipulations concerning processors actions and obligations. This legal relationship must be established "in writing or in another equivalent form."[26]

Chapter II, Section IX: Notification

Article 18(1) authorizes MS (Member States) to establish a national supervisory authority. Controllers or their representatives must describe the nature of the processing to be performed to enable the supervisory authorities (commonly called commissioners) to monitor and enforce compliance with appropriate national law.

Member States are authorized to simplify notification, decide when notification is optional, and determine when to exempt controllers from notification under certain circumstances. Minimum contents of the notification are stated in the Directive. MS may add to these requirements as well. Key elements are the identity and location of the controller as is presumably the designation of the controller, as an authorized recipient for legal documents and notices. The purpose of the processing as well as a description of the category or categories of data subject and of the data relating to them, are other key elements. Recipients of the data, proposed third-country destinations of the data, and a general description of the security measures comprise a third element.[27]

Article 19 also states that MS are to specify the notification procedures, but does not provide guidance as to what these procedures should to be. However, "MS are to determine which processing operations are to present specific risks to the rights and freedoms of data subjects and shall check that these processing operations are examined prior to the start thereof."[28] These checks should be carried out prior to the processing and after notification by the data controller. In addition to Directive provisions, MS are authorized to pass legislation wherein they define what they deem to be appropriate safeguards.[29]

Under the general principle that processing operations are to be publicized, Article 21 addresses the records and record-keeping requirements of the supervisory authority. A register is to be maintained that at a minimum, lists the information required by Article 19(1)(a) to (e).

Chapter III: Judicial Remedies, Liability and Sanctions

Remedy guidance to the MS is flexible. Article 22 merely states that MS will provide a judicial remedy for breaches of the rights guaranteed by national law. Under Article 23(1), data subjects can seek damages from the data controller for unlawful processing operations or for acts "incompatible with the national provisions adopted pursuant to this Directive."[30]

Controllers may claim lack of responsibility as a defense to the damage claim and be exempted from liability if this is proven in accordance with Article 23(2). Article 24 authorizes a penalty in the form of sanctions that can be imposed against a data controller who has been found to cause damage to the data subject.

Chapter IV: Transfer of Personal Data to Third Countries

The fundamental principle of transfer of data for subsequent processing in a third-party country is that the country in question must provide at least as much data protection to the data subject and his or her data as the data subject would receive in the European Union. MS can vary the requirements and restrictions on data transfer through national legislation. They may require stricter provisions and specify the terms and conditions precedent for a lawful data transfer. Limits on restrictions to third-party countries cannot be more stringent than found in the MS itself.

Article 25(2)[31] describes what is meant by *adequacy of protection*. The guidance suggests a case-by-case approach to decide what is "adequate" in each circumstance. Article 25 suggests that "particular consideration shall be given to the nature of the data, the purpose and duration of the proposed processing operation or operations, the country of origin and country of final destination, the rules of law, both general and sectoral in force in the third country in question, and the professional rules and security measures which are compiled with in that country."

In practical terms, this puts a burden on both the national supervisory authority and the national legislation because determination of "professional rules and security measures" may be difficult to determine in each case. Technical assessments are often beyond the competency of jurists; thus they must depend on national legislation to provide the rule of law against which compliance can be measured. Overall, the destination country is the focus of attention. That third-party country's environment is the one to be tested. Transit points are not considered at all unless the data would be exposed due to security vulnerabilities. The country of origin is not as important, although if the data originates outside countries providing data protection levels commensurate with the European Union, there might be some consideration of this fact in the overall assessment.

Security precautions considered might encompass encryption, including any use of the public key infrastructure (PKI), personal identification numbers (PIN), etc. MS have the responsibility of determining adequacy. The MS and the Commission must notify each other of third-party countries if it is determined that they are not providing adequate protection.

MS must take measures to prevent transfer of data to such a country. The Commission is empowered to negotiate with the third-party country to remedy the situation.[32]

However, as with other provisions, the transfer prohibition is not absolute and Article 26 sets forth a number of derogations. Key among these exemptions are where the data subject has given unambiguous consent to the transfer,[33] where the processing is necessitated to implement pre-contractual measures requested by the data subject,[34] or when the transfer is necessary for the performance of an already-concluded contract in the interests of the data subject and the data controller or a third party.[35] These exemptions are complemented by the public interest/legal claim exemption, the vital interest exemption, and data from public registers.[36]

Codes of Conduct

The essence of Article 27 is that the MS (Member States) are encouraged to facilitate the organization of groups of controllers with affinities (e.g., trade associations) to submit drafts of their codes of conduct to the national authority. The national authority would respond by providing opinions on the codes and their compliance with the national legislation. It was reasoned that sectoral codes would be more responsive to sector-specific issues and thereby provide the practical touch needed to make the national law workable.

The notion is laudable, but it must be pointed out that these codes would be voluntary. Failure by a member to comply with a sectoral code of conduct would only be relevant to legal action if the noncompliance violated the national law as well.

Chapter VI: Supervisory Authority and Working Party

Previously addressed was the establishment of the supervisory authority. Article 28(2) provides that these authorities must be consulted when administrative measures and regulations for data protection are being developed. Article 28(3) states that the investigative power, effective powers of intervention, and the power to engage in legal proceedings are the minimum set of powers that must be conferred on these authorities by the MS.[37]

The authority is vested with the power to hear claims and must report its activities to the public at regular intervals. The competency of the authority in data protection matters is confirmed, as is the need for MS to impose a duty of "professional secrecy" on the members and staff of the supervisory authority.[38]

An advisory body to the Commission, called the Working Party, was established in Articles 29 and 30. It is composed of representatives from the supervisory authorities of the MS. The practical effect of such a body appears to be informative in nature rather than influential.

Chapter VII: Community Implementing Measures

A committee composed of representatives of the MS and a representative of the Commission is vested with decision-making ability concerning the Directive. While this Committee receives advice from the Working Party, it is not compelled to heed or act on it. The Commission representative brings matters to the Committee, and the Committee then follows Commission rules in acting on them.

Chapter VIII: Final Provisions

Articles 32 and 33 address implementing and monitoring the implementation of the Directive. They explain the interrelationship between the national laws of the MS and their implementation. In addition, these article detail the need for cooperating and information flow between the MS and the Commission.

THE UNITED KINGDOM DATA PROTECTION ACT OF 1998

Overview

The United Kingdom Data Protection Act (UKDPA) is a faithful implementation of the EU Directive and supersedes the Data Protection Act of 1984. The 1998 Act follows the directive in extending protection of data in manual systems as well as automated ones. The Act received Royal Assent on July 24, 1998, but did not come into effect until March 1, 2000, due to the significant amount of secondary legislation (technically called Statutory Instruments, or SI) required for its implementation. The Act takes into account the need for transition and offers relief for automated processing that began prior to October 24, 1998. In that case certain provisions of the Act will not apply until October 24, 2001, for manual records and October 24, 2007, in the case of selected automated records.

The UKDPA is simple in concept. Data controllers must respect the rights of data subjects by following the provisions of the Act and adhering to the eight fundamental "Data Protection Principles." The Act is enforced through an impartial government entity, the Data Protection Commissioner, who reports directly to Parliament. The Commissioner has the authority to interpret provisions of the Act. However, this power is not absolute, as the Act is also subject to interpretation by the Data Protection Tribunal and the Courts.

The essence of the Act is embodied in the eight fundamental Data Protection Principles:

1. Personal data shall be processed fairly and lawfully and, in particular, shall not be processed unless:

   a. At least one of the conditions in Schedule 2 is met, *and*

   b. In the case of sensitive personal data, at least one of the conditions in Schedule 3 is also met.

2. Personal data shall be obtained only for one or more specified and lawful purposes, and shall not be further processed in any manner incompatible with that purpose or those purposes.

3. Personal data shall be adequate, relevant, and not excessive in relation to the purpose or purposes for which they are processed.

4. Personal data shall be accurate and, where necessary, kept up to date.

5. Personal data processed for any purpose or purposes shall not be kept for longer than is necessary for that purpose or those purposes.

6. Personal data shall be processed in accordance with the rights of data subjects under this Act.

7. Appropriate technical and organizational measures shall be taken against unauthorized or unlawful processing of personal data and against accidental loss or destruction of, or damage to, personal data.

8. Personal data shall not be transferred to a country or territory outside the European Economic Area unless that country or territory ensures an adequate level of protection for the rights and freedoms of data subjects in relation to the processing of personal data.[39]

Key Differences Between the 1994 and 1998 Acts

The Registrar is given an expanded role and renamed the Commission. Enforcement is extended to all data controllers whether or not they are registered. Conditions precedent for processing now vary, depending on whether the data is personal or sensitive. Sensitive data is employed to describe components of personal data that are considered worthy of special protection. Data subjects are given additional rights, such as the right to prevent processing of data for direct marketing, the right to compensation for damage and distress and in some cases compensation for destruction of the data.

Data controllers are given more responsibility while mere data processors have less. The term "processing" has been significantly expanded to include organizing, adapting, and altering data; and the retrieval, combining, blocking, or erasing of the data. Even a mere glance at a video display unit (VDU) is considered processing.

As with these differences, others are introduced to comply with the EU Directive. A good example is the special treatment for use of the data in journalism, literature, and art and the restriction on transferring the personal data outside the European Union.

GERMANY

No Legislation Passed to Implement the EU Directive

According to the Der Bundesbeauftragte für den Datenschutz, the Federal Ministry of the Interior is in charge of the implementation of the European Data Protection Directive 95/46/EC. The German government has so far missed the implementation deadline of October 24, 1998. It is now following a two-phase approach:

1. A first step toward implementing the directive and addressing in a couple of progressive data protection issues such as regulations on video surveillance, chip cards, anonymization, pseudonymization, and data protection audit to be completed by approximately mid-year 2001
2. A general revision of German data protection law; at a minimum, a master plan is expected before the end of 2002.[40]

However, the Federal Data Protection Act of December 20, 1990 (BGBl.I 1990 S.2954), amended by law of September 14, 1994 (BGBl. I S. 2325), is in force and it is instructive to review key portions of the act as a prelude to the implementation of the two-phase plan noted above.

Comments on the German Federal Data Protection Act (As Amended)

The Act applies to public and private bodies. The provisions concerning consent of the data subject are noteworthy because of the need for written consent (absent special circumstances such as interfering with a scientific study) and the fact that the consequences of withholding consent must be provided to the data subject.[41]

Section 7 of the Act limits compensation by public bodies to DM 250,000 (£79,926 or U.S.$118,188 as of December 23, 2000). Given the nature of awards in today's litigious society, this seems like a pittance. No such limit is placed on private bodies; however, the burden of proof is on the "controller of the data file," the likely defendant. This juxtaposition of burden of proof may be sufficient to stimulate settlement rather than proceed with litigation.[42]

Section 11 (Commissioned Processing or Use of Personal Data) states that when a data processor is employed by the data controller, the act imposes responsibility for compliance on the principal. This is in tune with the EU Directive and follows the same logic as the United Kingdom's 1998 Act.

Section 19, Provision of Information to the Data Subject, is interesting for its exemptions as stated under (4) and bears a striking similarity to exemptions noted in the EU Directive.

- This would be prejudicial to the proper performance of the duties of the controller of the data file.
- This would impair public safety or order, or otherwise be detrimental to the Federation or a Land.
- The data or the fact that it is being stored must be kept secret in accordance with a legal provision or by virtue of their nature, in particular on account of an overriding justified interest of a third party, and for this reason the interest of the data subject in the provision of information must be subordinated.[43]

Paragraph (5) goes on to state that reasons need not be given for the refusal to provide information if the statement of the actual and legal reasons on which the decision is based would jeopardize the purpose pursued by refusing to provide information. In such case, it shall be pointed out to the data subject that he or she can appeal to the Federal Commissioner for Data Protection. Finally, paragraph (7) states that the information shall be provided free of charge.

The German Act provides some very detailed technical guidance in the annex to the first sentence of Section 9 of the act. While not detailing particular technology requirements, it does provide ten control points for data controllers to employ.

ITALY

The initial foray into data protection legislation in Italy began in 1993 when a bill on the subject passed almost unanimously in the House of Deputies, but was halted in the Senate due to strong opposition by private-sector organizations opposed to protection of data relating to legal persons. The bill was subsequently modified in line with the EU Directive and, after some minor changes, was adopted as Data Protection Act No. 674 of 31.12.1996.

Passage of the Italian Data Protection Act was no doubt stimulated by the fact that Italy was temporarily excluded from the benefits conferred by the Schengen Agreement because Italy did not have appropriate data protection legislation.

The introduction to the act contains a particularly forward-looking statement: "Privacy becomes a fundamental component of the electronic citizenship which will be a basic feature of the next millennium."[44]

The Italian Data Protection (DP) authority is called *Il Garante*. Article 30 prescribes that the Chamber of Deputies elects two of the four members and the Senate elects the other two. The *Garante* then elects its chairman. It is felt that this type of mechanism, whereby the legislature is responsible for electing the DP authority, provides a highly neutral venue for the election and helps ensure the independence of the organization.

From a definitional point of view, Article 1 adds a few new definitions to EU jargon: communication, dissemination, anonymous data, and blocking. The essential difference between communication and dissemination is that communication refers to disclosing to known individuals, and dissemination refers to disclosure of personal information to "unidentified subjects." Anonymous data refers to data that can no longer be associated with a particular data subject, and blocking means keeping personal data with temporary suspension of any other processing.

The Act applies to legal bodies and associations. Part of the enforcement schema is apparent from Article 9 (Modalities for the Collection and Quality of Personal Data), paragraph (e), which details alternative methodologies under which data subjects could be identified by others. This attention to individual identity is part of the spirit of EU data protection — that is, insulating individuals from potential harm due to exposure of their beliefs, attitudes, religion, or other personal data characteristics that can associate an individual with a group or belief that might subject them to discrimination.

Article 3 addresses the issue of personal processing. Under this article, data processed by individuals for personal reasons is excluded from the act, provided that the data is not intended for systematic communication or dissemination. Ultimately, the results of actions brought under this article may come down to the question of fact as to what constitutes "systematic communication or dissemination." Extending the argument a bit, it is possible that the individual processor might claim that his freedom of expression would be hampered if he were required to report even systematic dissemination.

Article 5 of the Act covers processing of data without electronic means. The effect of this provision is to broaden coverage to manual (including verbal) means of processing. It would be interesting to see how this provision might apply to the manual processing of punched cards in situations where the voter can be identified from the card itself. Notwithstanding the recent U.S. election, a more practical example might be the election of officers of a trade association or religious organization where the identity of the voter is on the manual ballots that are to be tabulated. It would appear that this is one of the situations in which this provision would apply.

Article 26 advises data controllers that they are not required to notify the *Garante* concerning the processing and discontinuation of processing of data relating to legal persons, bodies, or associations. This provision was no doubt inserted to mollify data controllers of these organizations and to address the concerns of the Senate prior to the passage of the current Act.

The notification burden has been reduced or eliminated in other situations as well. Nonprofit public bodies, journalists, and those performing temporary processing benefit from a legislative decree authorizing simplified notification for them. There are also 16 other situations for which no notification whatsoever is necessary. These include when the processing is necessary to comply with obligations laid down by laws, data included in or retrieved from public registers, and an order to comply with specific obligations concerning accounting, salaries, social security, and fiscal issues to those necessary for canvassing support for bills proposed or advocated by legal persons, associations, etc. who might have a political, philosophical, religious or trade association character.[45]

Article 31, Data Subject's Rights, paragraph (3), notes that "anyone who is interested in" the rights of a deceased person can exercise their rights. The notion of "interested" may turn out to be too broad, although this may be left to the test of time.

The *Garante* has the ability to rule against the data subject and in favor of a data controller where it finds that a data subject's rights are manifestly disproportionate to the effort that the data controller would have to exert to honor them.[46]

Overall, the Italian Data Protection Act is in line with the EU Directive. However, there are instances in which the act favors the rights of legal persons over data subjects. This may be a reflection of the Italian legal culture, or it may reflect the influence that private organizations wield in Italian politics. In either event, data controllers subject to the Italian Act as well as others would be well advised to adhere to the requirements of the most stringent act to reduce the risk of violating one or more laws.

SCHOLARLY WORKS

Unfortunately, this author was not able to discover many significant scholarly legal works on the subject of European Union data protection. The only major paper found was entitled "Reconsidering the Premises of Labour Law: Prolegomena to an EU Regulation on the Protection of Employee's Personal Data," by Spiros Simitis and published in the *European Law Journal*.[47]

Simitis takes a critical look at the conflicts between employers and employees that might arise concerning the needs, collection, processing, and use of employee data by employers. He feels that labor law is an area where there must be constant vigilance on behalf of employees due, in part, to the inherently unequal bargaining position of employer and employee. Simitis argues that the goals of collective agreements and mandatory legislation should be to improve the knowledge base and competence of employees with respect to their data protection rights.

The following quote forms much of the basis for Simitis' argument: "Experience, moreover, shows that data-bases, once established, generate uses that had never originally been contemplated."[48] The author goes on to indicate that the collection and processing of data in the name of production optimization and administrative efficiency have combined with technological advances in employee monitoring to pose real hazards to employees, chiefly because this collected data might be used for pursuing personnel policy purposes. Simitis concludes that national laws at best provide partial answers and are often contradictory. While he commends the Council of Europe for its recommendations and the International Labour Office for its Code of Practice, he notes that they are a "best possible solution for the shortest period of time."[49]

The European Union position was praised as the European Union reconfirmed the need for regulation expressed in earlier declarations (Recommendation No. R (89)2 adopted by the Committee of Ministers of the Council of Europe on January 18, 1989) and the repeated intention to present proposals for regulations. There are several principles to be stressed by these regulations. Key among them is the processing of data only for explicit purposes that would be stated in advance of such processing, the duty to provide data subjects with sufficient information to allow them to assess the scope and implications of the processing, and the right of access to learn the context of the processing.

According to Simitis, vagueness has been the hallmark of much of the European Union's efforts. However, the Directive concerning processing of personal data and the protection of privacy in the telecom sector[50] is a clear step toward eliminating vagueness.

The major contribution of Simitis' article is the proposal of a set of criteria to be included in subsequent regulations. The author felt that by delineating the eight major issues and key criteria within them, he would shed an objective light on the employer/employee conflict and offer guidance to legal scholars and educators. The following sections highlight Simitis' recommendations.

Scope. The mode of collection or processing, whether automated or manual, does not matter in terms of regulations. Employee rights are not contingent on the employee's role within the organization or workplace. Regulations should cover not only the term of employment, but the recruitment process and post-employment time as well. Data should be kept for only as long as needed or mandated by law. Data concerning candidates who are not hired should be erased as soon as practical and post-termination data retention should be minimal.

Addressees. It must be noted that employers are not the only potential addressees, and that contractors, agencies, and other third parties are likely recipients of collected or processed data as well. Consequently, employers must ensure that the nature of potential third parties be disclosed to employees and that these third parties are complying with the Council of Europe recommendations and the International Labour Office Code of Practice.

Finality. Processing must be strictly confined to the data necessary in connection with the particular employment relationship. The amount and type of required data will vary in accordance with the employee tasks to be performed or the context of the employer's need for the data. Vagueness must be avoided and employees must understand the intended uses of their data. It is the duty of the employer to restrict the collection and retrieval of employee data to only those purposes stated in advance. It is emphasized that the particular purpose for the data collection and processing is the nexus between the first access and subsequent use. Secondary uses such as the sale of data for marketing purposes must be explicitly prohibited.

The incorporation of this finality principle offers the advantages of allowing employees to determine the effect of processing and counteracts efforts by the employer to profit from the potential multifunctional use of the stored data.

Simitis notes that exceptions are unavoidable because employees tend to remain with employers for long periods of time, and that data collected for one reason may be useful for other reasons. I cannot concur with the notion of long-term employment. The Internet economy and immigration among EU Member States and immigration flow into the European Union attest to mobility. With respect to exceptions, alternative uses of data must be compatible with their original purpose and consideration must be given to the possibility of misinterpreting the data and potential consequences for individual employees. Simitis also notes that there are possible problems with personnel decisions made solely on the basis of automated data so that employees must have specific rights in these instances (see Rights below).

Accuracy. Employers should regularly revise the data stored and ensure its correctness. They must also periodically confirm that the information is still needed and determine if the purposes of the processing could be achieved with the help of depersonalized rather than personal data.

Collection. Employees must be the primary source of information concerning them, and they need to be aware of an employer's intention of using data from third parties. Employers should name the third parties, detail the information they expect to be provided, and get explicit consent from the employee. Special rules are needed for sensitive data. For example, information on the employees' sex lives might only be relevant if they are being charged with sexual harassment. Data concerning criminal convictions should be confined to data that is relevant for the occupation at hand. Simitis contends that the employee should be the sole source of criminal conviction information so as to restrict the data provided to relevant data only. It is likely, however, that employers would not "trust" such information from an employee and would look to a "trusted third party" to provide it. Of course, there is nothing to prevent an employer or prospective employer from searching public records for such information. Simitis also notes that aptitude tests would require informed consent as well.

Surveillance. There can be no doubt that the progress of technology has opened the door to new types of surveillance and monitoring. E-mail and voice mail are two easy examples. In addition, information developed for one purpose (telephone accounting) can also be used for monitoring. Simitis offers a few suggestions:

1. Continuous monitoring must be excluded.
2. Secret surveillance should be countenanced only if there is credible evidence of criminal offenses or serious wrongdoings.
3. Data collected via electronic monitoring, ostensibly used for the observance or retracing of the work process, should not be used to sanction individual employees or particular groups.

Transmissions. Rules need to be applied covering internal and external transmissions. Transmissions should be limited to the data required for particular functions assumed by the transmitter or addressee. As noted (see Collection), special rules should be applied to sensitive data. Employees should have a clear picture of the internal data flow. External transmissions should be limited to the minimum data required, and other communications should be limited by the terms of the employee's informed consent. Enterprises or agencies other than the one the employee is employed by must be considered external addressees for data protection purposes.

Rights. Employees must know the actual state of processing of their data, especially the purpose, addressees, and data concerned. They should have the right of access extending to all data related to the particular usage. Employers should not hamper employee access by imposing fees, unfair restrictions as to time of access, or asking employees to explain why they want to be informed or to indicate the use of the data in which they are interested. Employees should have the right to demand erasure or rectification, as well as be given the ability to comment on subjective data such as evaluation reports. Ongoing security investigations would be exempt from employee disclosure, but data from completed investigations would not.

Collective Rights. The myriad of national regulations do not offer a set of common rules on the form and content of employee participation in the decision-making process of the employer. Regulations must include informing/consulting employees prior to introducing or modifying an automated system designed to process employee data before it is put into practice. The purpose, content, and prospective uses of data from questionnaires and tests should be stated ahead of time.

Overall, Simitis does a solid job of highlighting the dilemmas and conflicts between employers and employees in the area of employment data. Most of his suggestions appear to make sense and many have been incorporated into various pieces of data protection legislation.

CASE COMMENTARY

There are relatively few case precedents in the world of data protection. Research did not find any cases related to the EU Directive or national data protection legislation per se. However, there were a few cases that might offer a glimpse of future rulings. The cases are discussed in reverse chronological order with the newest case first.

British Gas Trading Ltd. v. Data Protection Registrar, Judgment Date: March 24, 1998

This case is interesting because of the combination of jurisdictional predicates: consumer protection, data protection, and the fact that British Gas (BG) was also regulated by utilities legislation. The essence of the case centered on BG's ability to use customer data (personal data such as name, address, etc.) for marketing purposes. The Data Protection Registrar (DPR) issued an enforcement notice against BG for breach of the Data Protection Act 1984 Sch. 1, Part I, Principles 1, 2, and 3.

The nub of the case was that BG collected personal data from its customers in order to supply them with gas. The DPR argued that there was an implied term in the BG contract with its individual customers that it would not disclose any customer information without the express consent of the customers for any purpose beyond the supplying of gas or gas-related products and services.

The Data Protection tribunal held that the processing was lawful, but unfair. The court ruled that the use of personal data by BG for the purpose of giving customers the ability to opt out of future marketing programs was appropriate. Further, they stated that the fact that an individual had a supply of piped gas to his or her home did not fall into the category of information that gave rise to a duty of confidence. It was also decided that the terms of the Gas Act of 1972 gave BG's parent the power to use the information for direct mail promotions of unrelated goods and services, provided that BG genuinely thought that such use was incidental to statutory functions. Perhaps the most interesting ruling was that it would have been a paradox if the processing of personal data in order to send the opt-out leaflet to all its customers had itself amounted to unfair processing. Going forward, new customers should be informed of the type of marketing intended to be carried out and asked if they object. If no objection is made, which includes returning an opt-out box ticked or alternatively being left blank, then processing for those purposes would not be unfair. For existing customers, in view of the special position of domestic utilities, it was insufficient to send a leaflet providing them with the opportunity to object to the use of their personal data for non-gas-related purposes. It would be sufficient for customers to be informed of the type of marketing proposed, and for the customer to be given the opportunity to consent or object.[51]

Thorel (Alain), Re, Judgment date: December 29, 1997

This was a French case brought in connection with respect to files being held by police and involving special circumstances of public safety. Thorel claimed that information about him was disseminated from files held by the French authorities. The authorities responded by indicating that they did not have information about him in their general files or those of the Gendarmerie Nationale. The authorities sought to examine files specified by the plaintiff and to verify whether or not any information about him was being held therein. The plaintiff sought the disclosure of any and all information in the files as a matter of law.

The Conseil d'Etat dismissed the application for disclosure and held that the Electronic Files and Liberties Act 1978 s.39 permitted the retention of information on the grounds of state security, defense, and public safety. The Act also enabled a member of the National Commission for Information Technology and Liberties to conduct appropriate inquiries. The files in question were therefore only subject to indirect rights of access. Further, those provisions were in accordance with the Convention on the Protection of Individuals with regard to Automatic Processing of Personal Data 1981

Article 8. This permitted derogation on grounds of national security or public safety.[52]

MS v. Sweden, Judgment date: August 27, 1997

This case was brought in the European Court of Human Rights (ECHR). MS was a Swedish citizen who sustained a back injury because of an accident at work in 1981. She was pregnant at the time and consulted a doctor at the women's clinic about her injury. She was unable to work for any sustained period of time and was granted a temporary disability pension, and in 1994, a disability pension was awarded. In March 1991, the plaintiff claimed compensation from the Social Insurance Office (SIO). During the course of those proceedings, she learned that the SIO had obtained medical records from the women's clinic concerning treatment from 1981 to 1986. Her claim was rejected by the SIO in 1992 on the grounds that her sick leave had been caused by an abortion and not an industrial injury. MS' domestic appeals were rejected and she subsequently presented a complaint to the Data Protection Commission alleging that submission of her medical records to the SIO constituted an unjustified interference with her right to a private life, contrary to the European Convention on Human Rights 1950 Article 8.

The court held that MS waived the confidentiality of her medical records by asking for compensation. The asking for compensation had the effect of putting her medical condition at issue. The clinic's disclosure was bound by law and the disclosure of medical records was "necessary in a democratic society."[53]

Friedl v. Austria (A/305-B), Judgment date: January 31, 1995

This is another case from the European Court of Human Rights that balances individual right to privacy against the more compelling need for public safety. The plaintiff was involved in a demonstration wherein he was photographed and identified by the police. No charges were filed against him. He complained that Article 8 had been violated and that because there had been no effective remedy in the Austrian courts, there had also been a violation of the European Convention on Human Rights Article 13.

The court ruled that there was no violation of Article 8. While Friedl's private affairs may have been subject to scrutiny, there was a more pressing and legitimate aim at stake, namely, prevention of disorder and crime. Society has the right to maintain records relating to criminal cases whether or not there is subsequent prosecution. The courts also noted that the information in question was kept in a general administrative file, which they believed had restricted access, and not in a data processing system with presumably more open access.[54]

CONCLUSION

Overall, the European Union has done well in establishing itself as a thought leader in the area of data protection and privacy. The notion of individual rights is balanced against societal concerns, and exemptions to general rules are clearly spelled out. While some Member States have opted for a strategy of vagueness or one favoring data controllers over data subjects, others have been faithful to the Directive in letter and spirit. The U.K. Data Protection Act of 1998, in particular, seems to be complete, yet workable. Documentation offered by the British Standards Institution is also helpful in providing guidance to data controllers, data processors and data subjects alike.

Consistency of legislation by the Member States has helped in positioning the European Union as an institution and as a global commercial player. Notwithstanding the economic clout of the United States, the European Union has established itself as the leader in the legislative arena. The jockeying accompanying the Safe Harbor agreements, wherein the United States seeks to be considered eligible to receive data from the European Union although its data protection standards are not in line with those of the European Union, is a testing ground for both trading partners.

Neither the European Union nor the United States wants to stop trading with each other, although it is fair to say that each would like to be the dominant trade player. It will be interesting to see if the national interests of the Member States and their national pride in enforcing their own data protection laws will come into play as the data wars continue.

It is the author's assessment that, while not all the Member States have passed complying laws, in general it appears that the European Union has succeeded in marching toward its goal of protecting individual data privacy and acting as a legal catalyst to ensure freedom of movement of this data throughout the European Union. As the battle of E-commerce supremacy heats up, only time will tell whether the European Union will be able to stand on its principles or be forced to accept concessions in the name of economics.

Notes

1. Jan Holvast, Wayne Madsen, and Paul Roth, *The Global Encyclopaedia of Data Protection Regulation,* Kluwer Law International, London, 1999.
2. *The Economist,* May 1, 1999, p. 21.
3. *Information Week.com,* March 6, 2000, p. 23.
4. *Informationweek.com,* July 17, 2000, p. 112.
5. Rome, 4 November 1950, European Treaty Series (ETS) No. 5.
6. TEU, Article 6 (ex Article F) (2).
7. http://www.echr.coe.int/Eng/edocs/infodocrevised2.html.

8. Douwe Korff, Study on the protection of the rights and interests of legal persons with regard to the processing of personal data relating to such persons, Commission of the European Communities (Study Contract ETD/97/B5-9500/78), p. 9 (Korff).
9. Ibid.
10. *The Guardian,* December 30, 1997, EU rights law [*sic*] rests on Swedish lies.
11. Korff, p 10.
12. Korff, p 14.
13. Directive 95/46 EC, Article 3.
14. Directive 95/46 EC, Article 2(a).
15. Directive 95/46 EC, Article 2(b).
16. Directive 95/46 EC, Article 28(6).
17. Directive 95/46 EC, Article 6(1)(b).
18. *A Business Guide to Changes in European Data Protection Legislation,* Cullen International, 1998, p. 40.
19. Directive 95/46 EC, Article 6(1)(c).
20. Directive 95/46 EU, Article 8(1).
21. Directive 95/46 EU, Article 8(2) (d).
22. Directive 95/46 EU, Article 10.
23. Directive 95/46 EU, Article 12.
24. Directive 95/46 EU, Article 13.
25. Directive 95/46 EU, Article 17(1).
26. Directive 95/46 EU, Article 17(2), (3), and (4).
27. Directive 95/46 EU, Articles 18 and 19.
28. Directive 95/46 EU, Article 20(1).
29. Directive 95/46 EU, Article 20(2) and (3).
30. Directive 95/46 EU, Article 23(1).
31. Directive 95/46 EU, Article 25(2).
32. Directive 95/46 EU, Article 25(3) to (6).
33. Directive 95/46 EU, Article 26(1)(a).
34. Directive 95/46 EU, Article 26(1)(b).
35. Directive 95/46 EU, Article 26(1)(c).
36. Directive 95/46 EU, Article 26(1)(d), (e), (f).
37. Directive 95/46 EU, Article 28(3).
38. Directive 95/46 EU, Article 28(4), (5), (6), and (7).
39. Data Protection Act of 1998, Schedule 1, Part 1.
40. http://www.bfd.bund.de/information/engltext1.html.
41. German Federal Data Protection Act, Section 4: Admissibility of data processing and use.
42. Federal Data Protection Act, Section 8, Compensation by Private Parties.
43. Federal Data Protection Act, Section 19, Provision of Information to the Data Subject.
44. Protection of Individuals and other subjects with regard to the Processing of Personal Data. Law No. 675 of 31.12.96 as amended by Legislative Decree no. 123 of 09.05.97 and no. 255 of 28.07.97. Published by Garante per la profezione di dati personali, 1997.
45. *The Global Encyclopaedia of Data Protection Regulation,* Jan Holvast, Wayne Masden, and Paul Roth, Kluwer Law International, London, 1999, p. 2-Italy.
46. Ibid., p 3- Italy.
47. Spiro Simitis, Reconsidering the Premises of Labour Law: Prolegomena to an EU Regulation on the Protection of Employee's Personal Data, *European Law Journal,* 5(1), 45–62, March 1999.
48. Ibid., p. 48.
49. Ibid., p. 50.
50. Directive 97/66/EC of the European Parliament and of the Council 15 Dec. 1997, OJL 24/1.
51. [1997-98] Info T.L.R. 393.
52. [1999] E.C.C. 396.
53. (1999) 28 E.H.R.R. 313; 3 B.H.R.C. 248; (1999) 45 B.M.L.R. 133.
54. (1996) 21 E.H.R.R. 83.

Chapter 48
Safe Harbor Overview

International Trade Administration,
Department of Commerce

The European Commission's Directive on Data Protection went into effect in October, 1998, and would prohibit the transfer of personal data to non-European Union nations that do not meet the European "adequacy" standard for privacy protection. While the United States and the European Union share the goal of enhancing privacy protection for their citizens, the United States takes a different approach to privacy from that taken by the European Union. The United States uses a sectoral approach that relies on a mix of legislation, regulation, and self-regulation. The European Union, however, relies on comprehensive legislation that, for example, requires creation of government data protection agencies, registration of databases with those agencies, and in some instances prior approval before personal data processing may begin. As a result of these different privacy approaches, the Directive could have significantly hampered the ability of U.S. companies to engage in many trans-Atlantic transactions.

In order to bridge these different privacy approaches and provide a streamlined means for U.S. organizations to comply with the Directive, the U.S. Department of Commerce in consultation with the European Commission developed a "safe harbor" framework. The safe harbor — approved by the EU this year — is an important way for U.S. companies to avoid experiencing interruptions in their business dealings with the EU or facing prosecution by European authorities under European privacy laws. Certifying to the safe harbor will assure that EU organizations know that your company provides "adequate" privacy protection, as defined by the Directive.

SAFE HARBOR BENEFITS

The safe harbor provides a number of important benefits to U.S. and EU firms. Benefits for U.S. organizations participating in the safe harbor will include:

- All 15 Member States of the European Union will be bound by the European Commission's finding of adequacy.
- Companies participating in the safe harbor will be deemed adequate and data flows to those companies will continue.
- Member State requirements for prior approval of data transfers either will be waived or approval will be automatically granted.
- Claims brought by European citizens against U.S. companies will be heard in the U.S. subject to limited exceptions.

The safe harbor framework offers a simpler and cheaper means of complying with the adequacy requirements of the Directive, which should particularly benefit small and medium enterprises.

An EU organization can ensure that it is sending information to a U.S. organization participating in the safe harbor by viewing the public list of safe harbor organizations posted on the Department of Commerce's Web site (www.export.gov/safeharbor). This list became operational at the beginning of November 2000. It contains the names of all U.S. companies that have self-certified to the safe harbor framework. This list will be regularly updated, so that it is clear who is assured of safe harbor benefits.

HOW DOES AN ORGANIZATION JOIN?

The decision by U.S. organizations to enter the safe harbor is entirely voluntary. Organizations that decide to participate in the safe harbor must comply with the safe harbor's requirements and publicly declare that they do so. To be assured of safe harbor benefits, an organization needs to self-certify annually to the Department of Commerce in writing that it agrees to adhere to the safe harbor's requirements, which includes elements such as notice, choice, access, and enforcement. It must also state in its published privacy policy statement that it adheres to the safe harbor. The Department of Commerce will maintain a list of all organizations that file self-certification letters and make both the list and the self-certification letters publicly available.

To qualify for the safe harbor, an organization can (1) join a self-regulatory privacy program that adheres to the safe harbor's requirements; or (2) develop its own self-regulatory privacy policy that conforms to the safe harbor.

WHAT DO THE SAFE HARBOR PRINCIPLES REQUIRE?

Organizations must comply with the seven safe harbor principles. The principles require the following:

- *Notice:* Organizations must notify individuals about the purposes for which they collect and use information about them. They must provide information about how individuals can contact the organization with any inquiries or complaints, the types of third parties to which it discloses the information, and the choices and means the organization offers for limiting its use and disclosure.

- *Choice:* Organizations must give individuals the opportunity to choose (opt out) whether their personal information will be disclosed to a third party or used for a purpose incompatible with the purpose for which it was originally collected or subsequently authorized by the individual. For sensitive information, affirmative or explicit (opt in) choice must be given if the information is to be disclosed to a third party or used for a purpose other than its original purpose or the purpose authorized subsequently by the individual.
- *Onward Transfer* (Transfers to Third Parties): To disclose information to a third party, organizations must apply the Notice and Choice principles. Where an organization wishes to transfer information to a third party that is acting as an agent, it may do so if it makes sure that the third party subscribes to the safe harbor principles or is subject to the Directive or another adequacy finding. As an alternative, the organization can enter into a written agreement with such third party requiring that the third party provide at least the same level of privacy protection as is required by the relevant principles.
- *Access:* Individuals must have access to personal information about them that an organization holds and be able to correct, amend, or delete that information where it is inaccurate, except where the burden or expense of providing access would be disproportionate to the risks to the individual's privacy in the case in question, or where the rights of persons other than the individual would be violated.
- *Security:* Organizations must take reasonable precautions to protect personal information from loss, misuse and unauthorized access, disclosure, alteration, and destruction.
- *Data Integrity:* Personal information must be relevant for the purposes for which it is to be used. An organization should take reasonable steps to ensure that data is reliable for its intended use, accurate, complete, and current.
- *Enforcement:* To ensure compliance with the safe harbor principles, there must be (a) readily available and affordable independent recourse mechanisms so that each individual's complaints and disputes can be investigated and resolved and damages awarded where the applicable law or private sector initiatives so provide; (b) procedures for verifying that the commitments companies make to adhere to the safe harbor principles have been implemented; and (c) obligations to remedy problems arising out of a failure to comply with the principles. Sanctions must be sufficiently rigorous to ensure compliance by the organization. Organizations that fail to provide annual

self-certification letters will no longer appear in the list of participants and safe harbor benefits will no longer be assured.

To provide further guidance, the Department of Commerce has issued a set of frequently asked questions and answers (FAQs) that clarify and supplement the safe harbor principles.

HOW AND WHERE WILL THE SAFE HARBOR BE ENFORCED?

In general, enforcement of the safe harbor will take place in the United States in accordance with U.S. law and will be carried out primarily by the private sector. Private sector self-regulation and enforcement will be backed up as needed by government enforcement of the federal and state unfair and deceptive statutes. The effect of these statutes is to give an organization's safe harbor commitments the force of law *vis á vis* that organization.

Private Sector Enforcement

As part of their safe harbor obligations, organizations are required to have in place a dispute resolution system that will investigate and resolve individual complaints and disputes and procedures for verifying compliance. They are also required to remedy problems arising out of a failure to comply with the principles. Sanctions that dispute resolution bodies can apply must be severe enough to ensure compliance by the organization; they must include publicity for findings of noncompliance and deletion of data in certain circumstances. They may also include suspension from membership in a privacy program (and thus effectively suspension from the safe harbor) and injunctive orders.

The dispute resolution, verification, and remedy requirements can be satisfied in different ways. For example, an organization could comply with a private sector developed privacy seal program that incorporates and satisfies the safe harbor principles. If the seal program, however, only provides for dispute resolution and remedies but not verification, then the organization would have to satisfy the verification requirement in an alternative way.

Organizations can also satisfy the dispute resolution and remedy requirements through compliance with government supervisory authorities or by committing to cooperate with data protection authorities located in Europe.

Government Enforcement

Depending on the industry sector, the Federal Trade Commission, comparable U.S. government agencies, and/or the states may provide overarching government enforcement of the safe harbor principles. Where a company relies in whole or in part on self-regulation in complying with the safe harbor principles, its failure to comply with such self-regulation must be actionable under federal or state law prohibiting unfair and deceptive acts or it is not eligible to join the safe harbor. At present, U.S. organizations that are subject to the jurisdiction of the Federal Trade Commission or the Department of Transportation with respect to air carriers and ticket agents may participate in the safe harbor. The Federal Trade Commission and the Department of Transportation with respect to air carriers and ticket agents have both stated in letters to the European Commission that they will take enforcement action against organizations that state that they are in compliance with the safe harbor framework but then fail to live up to their statements.

Under the Federal Trade Commission Act, for example, a company's failure to abide by commitments to implement the safe harbor principles might be considered deceptive and actionable by the Federal Trade Commission. This is the case even where an organization adhering to the safe harbor principles relies entirely on self-regulation to provide the enforcement required by the safe harbor enforcement principle. The FTC has the power to rectify such misrepresentations by seeking administrative orders and civil penalties of up to $12,000 per day for violations.

Failure to Comply with the Safe Harbor Requirements. If an organization persistently fails to comply with the safe harbor requirements, it is no longer entitled to benefit from the safe harbor. Persistent failure to comply arises where an organization refuses to comply with a final determination by any self-regulatory or government body or where such a body determines that an organization frequently fails to comply with the requirements to the point where its claim to comply is no longer credible. In these cases, the organization must promptly notify the Department of Commerce of such facts. Failure to do so may be actionable under the False Statements Act (18 USC § 1001).

The Department of Commerce will indicate on the public list it maintains of organizations self-certifying adherence to the safe harbor requirements any notification it receives of persistent failure to comply and will make clear which organizations are assured and which organizations are no longer assured of safe harbor benefits.

An organization applying to participate in a self-regulatory body for the purposes of requalifying for the safe harbor must provide that body with full information about its prior participation in the safe harbor.

Chapter 49
International Privacy Laws

Rebecca Herold

There are literally thousands (perhaps tens of thousands) of laws related to privacy throughout the world. Trying to write even a brief description of each would take hundreds of pages. The best service this author can provide with regard to international privacy-related laws is to provide a listing of several of these laws and regulations and, where possible, provide a link where the reader can find more information. This is just the tip of the iceberg, and not all the laws and issues for each country are included here. However, it is hoped that this list will lead the reader to needed information via other links to sites not explicitly noted.

All the listed URLs were active as of August 2001. However, the nature of the Internet does lead to changes (sometimes often) in URLs, so it is possible that the URL listed may no longer be valid. Let the author know, via e-mail address, if there are more sites or if one of these sites is now invalid.

The following sites include not only privacy-related laws, regulations, and information for specific countries, but also regulations that govern multinational organizations. The constitutions of many countries have privacy-related directives, if not laws specific to the topic of privacy. If unable to find a particular country, check a great Web site on international constitutional law: http://www.uni-wuerzburg.de/law/.

1. **United Nations**
   a. The International Covenant on Civil and Political Rights (United Nations 1966): http://home.planet.nl/~privacy1/
   b. UN Guidelines for the Regulation of Computerized Personal Files (1990):
      http://www.datenschutz-berlin.de/gesetze/internat/aen.htm
2. **Europe**
   a. Universal Declaration of Human Rights (1948):
      http://www.udhr.org/UDHR/default.htm

0-8493-1248-5/02/$0.00+$1.50
© 2002 by CRC Press LLC

b. Council of Europe Convention for the Protection of Human Rights and Fundamental Freedoms (1950) (also known as the European Convention on Human Rights, or ECHR): http://conventions.coe.int/treaty/EN/Treaties/html/005.htm or http://home.planet.nl/~privacy1/

c. OECD Privacy Guidelines (1980): http://www.oecd.fr/dsti/sti/it/consumer/prod/CPGuidelines_final.pdf

d. Council of Europe Convention on Privacy (1981): http://home.planet.nl/~privacy1/

e. Council of Europe Committee of Ministers Recommendation No. R (89) 2 of the Committee of Ministers to Member States on the Protection of Personal Data Used for Employment Purposes (1989): http://home.planet.nl/~privacy1/

f. OECD Cryptography Guidelines (1997): http://home.planet.nl/~privacy1/

g. OECD Guidelines for Consumer Protection in the Context of Electronic Commerce (1998): http://home.planet.nl/~privacy1/

h. OECD Protection of Privacy on Global Networks (1998): http://home.planet.nl/~privacy1/

i. Council of Europe Committee of Ministers Recommendation No. R (99) 5 of the Committee of Ministers to Member States for the Protection of Privacy on the Internet (1999): http://home.planet.nl/~privacy1/

j. Recommendation 3/99 on the Preservation of Traffic Data by Internet Service Providers for Law Enforcement Purposes (EC 1999)

k. Recommendation 4/99 on the Inclusion of the Fundamental Right to Data Protection in the European Catalogue of Fundamental Rights (1999)

l. European Data Protection Authorities Panel Safe Harbor Decision (July 2000): http://forum.europa.eu.int/irc/DownLoad/kjexA9JHmvGCb4Ne1oPvK-p5jlmF3GiA/yxKyGqGa64mUcBouJ_ZJtj4ySf-VPNZ1/jH4pYxtvF37cEhDZP4cG50Yv/SHdecisionEN.pdf

m. Listing of all All CoE Recommendations, Resolutions, and documents on data protection: http://home.planet.nl/~privacy1/

n. Directive of the European Parliament and of the Council concerning the processing of personal data and the protection of privacy in the electronic communications sector (2000 draft) — (this Directive will replace 97/66/EC; European Union Directive for the Protection of Privacy in the Telecommunications Sector 97/66/EC; (1997): http://home.planet.nl/~privacy1/

o. European Union Directive 2000/31/EC on Certain Data Protection Aspects of Electronic Commerce: http://home.planet.nl/~privacy1/

p. Regulation of Investigatory Powers Act 2000: http://www.hmso.gov.uk/acts/acts2000/20000023.htm

q. **Austria**

   i. Austrian Constitution: http://www.uni-wuerzburg.de/law/au00t___.html

   ii. Dutch Privacy-Related Laws: http://home.planet.nl/~privacy1/

r. **Belgium**

   i. Homepage of the Belgian Commission for the Protection of Privacy (Privacy Data Protection Commission): http://www.privacy.fgov.be/

   ii. Belgium Article 22 of the constitution: http://www.fed-parl.be/constitution_uk.html

s. **Bulgaria:** Bulgarian Constitution: http://www.uni-wuerzburg.de/law/bu00t___.html

t. **Czech Republic:** Charter of Fundamental Rights and Freedoms: http://www.psp.cz/cgi-bin/eng/docs/laws/charter.html

u. **Denmark:** Danish Data Protection Agency: http://www.privacylaws.co.uk/linksframe.htm

v. **Estonia:** Data Protection Authority: http://www.privacylaws.co.uk/linksframe.htm

w. **Finland:** Data Protection Ombudsman: http://www.privacylaws.co.uk/linksframe.htm

x. **France:** French privacy-related laws: http://www.cnil.fr/textes/text02.htm
   (*Note*: this is written in French)

y. **Germany** (*Note*: All these sites are in German)

   i. Baden-Württemberg: Landesdatenschutzgesetz: http://www.uni-konstanz.de/misc/Gesetze/LDSG.htm

   ii. Bayern: Bayerisches Datenschutzgesetz: http://www.rewi.hu-berlin.de/Datenschutz/Gesetze/BayDSG.html

   iii. Berlin: Berliner Datenschutzgesetz: http://www.datenschutz-berlin.de/infomat/blndsg/inhbln.htm

   iv. Brandenburg: Brandenburgisches Datenschutzgesetz: http://www.brandenburg.de/land/lfdbbg/gesetze/bbgdsg.htm

   v. Hamburg: Hamburgisches Datenschutzgesetz: http://www.hamburg.de/Behoerden/HmbDSB/Recht/hmbdsg.htm

   vi. Hessen: Hessisches Datenschutzgesetz: http://www.hessen.de/hdsb/hdsg86/inhalt.htm

    vii. Niedersachsen: Niedersächsisches Datenschutzgesetz:
http://www.niedersachsen.de/MI80.htm

   viii. Rheinland-Pfalz: Landesdatenschutzgesetz:
http://www.rewi.hu-berlin.de/Datenschutz/Gesetze/rp-ldsg.html

    ix. Schleswig-Holstein: Landesdatenschutzgesetz:
http://www.rewi.hu-berlin.de/

    x. Thüringen: Landesdatenschutzgesetz als Ascii-Datei:
http://www.rewi.hu-berlin.de/Datenschutz/Gesetze/thuerdsg.txt

z. **Greece:** The Greek Data Protection Authority:
http://www.privacylaws.co.uk/linksframe.htm

aa. **Hungary:** Opinion 6/99 Concerning the Level of Personal Data Protection in Hungary Act LXIII of 1992 on the Protection of Personal Data and the Publicity of Data of Public Interest:
http://www.privacy.org/pi/countries/hungary/
hungary_privacy_law_1992.html

bb. **Iceland:** Icelandic Data Protection Commission:
http://www.gilc.org/privacy/survey/surveyak.html#Iceland

cc. **Ireland:** Data Protection Act (1988):
http://www.privacylaws.co.uk/linksframe.htm

dd. **Isle of Man:** Isle of Man Data Protection Act Isle of Man Subsidiary Legislation passed under the Data Protection Act 1986

ee. **Italy:** Italian Data Protection Act (1996):
http://www.privacy.it/ (*Note*: This is in Italian)

ff. **Lithuania:** Data Protection Inspectorate:
http://www.privacylaws.co.uk/linksframe.htm

gg. **Netherlands:**
http://www.unimaas.nl/media/um-layout/opmaak_uk.htm?
http://www.unimaas.nl/~privacy/wpr.htm

hh. **Norway:** The Data Register Act:
http://www.datatilsynet.no/ (*Note*: This is in Norwegian)

ii. **Portugal:** Data Protection Commission for Portugal:
http://www.privacylaws.co.uk/linksframe.htm
(*Note*: This is in Portuguese)

jj. **Romania:** Article 26 of Constitution:
http://www.senat.ro/ENGLEZA/constitution.html

kk. **Russia:** Russian Federation Law of the Russian Federation on Information, Informatisation and Information Protection (1995):
http://www.datenschutz-berlin.de/gesetze/internat/fen.htm

ll. **Slovakia:** Right to Privacy (Article 19 of Constitution):
http://www.uni-wuerzburg.de/law/lo00000_.html

mm. **Spain**

    i. ProHuman Rights Association of Spain (1997):
http://www.ati.es/gt/CLI/doc/CLI_ENG.html

ii. Personal Data Law User's Manual:
http://www2.rediris.es/apd/lortad.html (*Note*: This is in Spanish)
nn. **Sweden:** Data Protection Act (1973):
http://www.skolverket.se/skolnet/dalk/englag.html
(*Note*: This is in Swedish)
oo. **Switzerland**
i. Swiss Federal Constitution Art. 13 Right to Privacy:
http://194.6.168.108/framese.html
ii. Swiss Federal Law on Data Protection (1992):
http://194.6.168.108/framese.html
pp. **United Kingdom:** Data Protection Act (1998):
http://www.legislation.hmso.gov.uk/acts/acts1998/19980029.htm

3. **Canada**
   a. Privacy Legislation in Canada:
   http://www.privcom.gc.ca/fs-fi/fs2001-02_e.asp
   b. Canadian Provincial/Territorial Privacy Laws, Oversight Offices and Government Organizations:
   http://www.privcom.gc.ca/information/comms_e.asp
   c. Freedom of Information and Protection of Privacy Act:
   http://www.ipc.on.ca/francais/orders/orders-p/p-692.htm
   d. A Privacy Act for New Brunswick:
   http://www.gnb.ca/legis/busi/priv/privev.htm

4. **Africa**
   a. **Democratic Republic of the Congo:** Country Reports on Human Rights Practices –2000: http://www.state.gov/g/drl/rls/hrrpt/2000/af/index.cfm?docid = 753
   b. **Egypt:** 1999 Country Reports on Human Rights Practices:
   http://www.state.gov/www/global/human_rights/1999_hrp_report/egypt.html
   c. **Israel:** The Basic Law: Human Dignity and Freedom (1992):
   http://www.uni-wuerzburg.de/law/is12000_.html
   d. **Malawi:** Country Reports on Human Rights Practices–2000:
   http://www.state.gov/g/drl/rls/hrrpt/2000/af/index.cfm?docid = 851
   e. **Mozambique:** Country Reports on Human Rights Practices–2000:
   http://www.state.gov/g/drl/rls/hrrpt/2000/af/index.cfm?docid = 859
   f. **South Africa:** South African Constitution of 1996:
   http://www.uni-wuerzburg.de/law/sf__indx.html
   g. **Zimbabwe:** Draft Constitution of the Republic of Zimbabwe (1999):
   http://www.gta.gov.zw/Constitutional/Draft.Constitution.htm

5. **Central America and South America**
   a. **Argentina:** Articles 18, 19, and 43 of the constitution:
   http://www.constitution.org/cons/argentin.htm

    b. **Brazil:** Article 5 of the 1988 Constitution, 1990 Code of Consumer Protection and Defense: http://www.uni-wuerzburg.de/law/br00t___.html

    c. **Chile:** Law for the Protection of Private Life (CHILE 1999): http://www.urich.edu/~jpjones/confinder/Chile.htm

    d. **Colombia:** Constitutional background: http://www.uni-wuerzburg.de/law/co__indx.html

    e. **Paraguay:** Paraguay Constitution: http://www.uni-wuerzburg.de/law/pa00000_.html#I000_

    f. **Peru:** Peruvian Constitution: http://www.georgetown.edu/LatAmerPolitical/Constitutions/Peru/peru.html

    g. **Uruguay:** Constitution of Uruguay: http://www.juridicas.unam.mx/

6. **Asia**

    a. **China:** Constitution: http://www.europeaninternet.com/china/constit/chconst.php3

    b. **Hong Kong**

       i. Hong Kong's Code on Access to Information: http://www.info.gov.hk/access/code.htm#introduction

       ii. Hong Kong Personal Data (Privacy) Ordinance: http://www.privacy.com.hk/contents.html

    c. **India:** Constitution: http://www.commercenetindia.com/constitution/

    d. **Indonesia:** The Constitution of the Republic of Indonesia: http://asnic.utexas.edu/asnic/countries/indonesia/ConstIndonesia.html

    e. **Japan:** 1988 Act for the Protection of Computer Processed Personal Data Held by Administrative Organs: Japanese Constitution: http://www.uni-wuerzburg.de/law/ja__indx.html

    f. **Malaysia:** Malaysian Constitution: http://www.uni-wuerzburg.de/law/my__indx.html

    g. **Philippines:** Philippine Constitutions: http://www.chanrobles.com/philsupremelaw.htm

    h. **Russia:** Section One, Chapter 2, Article 23 of the Russian Constitution; Rights and Liberties of Man and Citizen: http://www.friends-partners.org/oldfriends/constitution/russian-const-ch2.html

    i. **Singapore:** Singapore Constitution: http://www.uni-wuerzburg.de/law/sn00000_.html

    j. **Taiwan:** Taiwan Constitution: http://www.uni-wuerzburg.de/law/tw00000_.html

7. **Australia and New Zealand**
   a. New South Wales Privacy Committee Act (1975):
      http://austlii.law.uts.edu.au/au/legis/nsw/consol_act/pca1975202/
   b. Australia Freedom of Information Act (1982):
      http://austlii.law.uts.edu.au/au/legis/cth/consol_act/
      foia1982222/index.html
   c. Australia Privacy Act (1988): http://www.austlii.edu.au/au/legis/
      cth/consol_act/pa1988108/
   d. Australia Data-matching Program (Assistance and Tax) Act
      (1990): http://www.austlii.edu.au/au/legis/cth/consol_act/
      dpata1990349/
   e. New Zealand Privacy Legislation:
      http://www.privacy.org.nz/slegisf.html
   f. Australia's Commonwealth Privacy Act (1988):
      http://www.privacy.gov.au/act/index.html
   g. Australia's Data-matching Program (Assistance and Tax) Act
      (1990): http://www.privacy.gov.au/act/index.html
   h. Australia's Medicare and Pharmaceutical Benefits Program priva-
      cy guidelines (1993): http://www.privacy.gov.au/act/index.html
   i. Australia's Telecommunications Act (1997):
      http://www.privacy.gov.au/act/index.html

Section V
Appendix

Chapter 50
Privacy Resources

Rebecca Herold

There are so many great resources available for getting further information about privacy issues that it would be impossible to provide them all here. However, I always appreciate receiving information from others about such resources and am happy to pass them on to others. This is not an exhaustive list, but I believe it is a good start, in addition to the other links in this book, in assisting your efforts to address privacy issues within your organization.

WEB SITES

- Copyright laws: http://www4.law.cornell.edu/uscode/17/
- Downloadable BXA-748P Form: http://www.bxa.doc.gov/factsheets/facts4.htm
- Encryption risks: http://www.cdt.org/crypto/risks98/
- EPIC and Privacy International Privacy Survey: http://www.privacyinternational.org/survey/index.html
- Generally Accepted System Security Principles: http://web.mit.edu/security/www/gassp1.html
- Interhack Organization: http://www.interhack.net/
- Internet Advertising Bureau: http://www.iab.net/privacy/
- ISO standards (including information about ISO 17799): http://www.iso.ch/iso/en/ISOOnline.openerpage
- List of organizations with Safe Harbor certification: http://web.ita.doc.gov/safeharbor/shlist.nsf/webPages/safe+harbor+list
- OECD Guidelines for Cryptography Policy: http://cybercrime.gov/oeguide.htm
- Official HIPAA Web Site: http://www.hcfa.gov/hipaa/hipaahm.htm
- Privacilla: http://www.privacilla.org/default.htm
- Privacy and Biometrics: http://www.ipc.on.ca/english/pubpres/speeches/cfp98.htm
- Privacy Exchange: http://www.privacyexchange.org/
- Privacy Rights Clearinghouse: http://www.privacyrights.org/
- Privacy Times: http://www.privacytimes.com/
- Privacy.Org: http://www.privacy.org/

0-8493-1248-5/02/$0.00+$1.50
© 2002 by CRC Press LLC

APPENDIX

- RFC 2079 (message header standards):
  http://www.faqs.org/rfcs/rfc2076.html
- Workplace Privacy: http://www.privacyrights.org/fs/fs7-work.htm

GOVERNMENT

- Department of Commerce:
  http://www.ntia.doc.gov/ntiahome/privacy/
- Department of Education: Parents Guide to the Internet:
  http://www.ed.gov/pubs/parents/internet/
- Federal Trade Commission: http://www.ftc.gov/privacy/index.html
- National Information Infrastructure: http://iitf.doc.gov/
- National Institute of Standards: http://csrc.nist.gov/
- National Telecommunications and Information Administration:
  http://www.ntia.doc.gov/
- Privacy Discussion Paper #2:
  http://www.gnb.ca/legis/comite/priv-ii/P2e2.htm
- Privacy Online: a report to congress:
  http://www.ftc.gov/reports/privacy3/toc.htm
- U.S. Consumer Gateway: http://www.consumer.gov/

MAIL LISTS

- EPIC-DIGEST, a weekly update of news, information, and action items
  posted on privacy.org. Subscribe at
  http://www.privacy.org/digest.php
- E-Privacy, for issues pertaining to electronic and online privacy. To
  subscribe, send e-mail to: e-privacy-subscribe@egroups.com
- ISOC-NL-PRIVACY: ISOC-NL-PRIVACY@NIC.SURFNET.NL
- Verzendlijst voor leden van ISOC over privacy: to subscribe, send mail
  to LISTSERV@NIC.SURFNET.NL with the command:

  SUBSCRIBE ISOC-NL-PRIVACY

- ISOC-PRIVACY: ISOC-PRIVACY@NIC.SURFNET.NL
- Discussielijst voor de werkgroep Privacy van de Internet Society: to
  subscribe, send mail to LISTSERV@NIC.SURFNET.NL with the command:

  SUBSCRIBE ISOC-PRIVACY

- Privacy-Forum: discussion and analysis of issues relating to privacy
  in the 21st Century. Subscribe: privacy-forum-subscribe@yahoo-
  groups.com
- Privacy newsletter: subscribe at
  http://www.securemaildrop.com/freenewsletter.html

- Privacy-Protections: discussion to guard the privacy of personal information. Subscribe at:
  http://www.newhawaii.org/10kjoinproject.htm.
- Public-Privacy: subscribe at:
  http://www.scripps.ohiou.edu/PublicPrivacy/
- SPGP Mailing List: purpose is to support SPGP for software developers.
  — List Archive: http://www.freelists.org/archives/spgp/
  — Subscribe link: spgp-request@freelists.org

ORGANIZATIONS

- Association for Interactive Media (AIM):
  http://www.interactivehq.org
- Better Business Bureau (BBB): http://www.bbbonline.com
- California Privacy: http://www.privacyrights.org/
- Center for Democracy and Technology:
  — Data Privacy: http://www.cdt.org/privacy/
  — Guide to Online Privacy: http://www.cdt.org/privacy/guide/
- CERT: http://www.cert.org/
- Consumer.net: http://consumer.net/index.asp
- Council for Internet Commerce: http://www.commercestandard.com
- CPA WebTrust: http://www.cpawebtrust.org/
- CPA WebTrust Program: http://www.cpawebtrust.org/
- Direct Marketing Association (DMA): http://www.the-dma.org/
- DMA Privacy Promise: http://www.the-dma.org/library/privacy/
- Electronic Frontier Foundation: nonprofit dedicated to protecting public interest in online privacy: http://www.eff.org
- Electronic Frontier Foundation: http://www.eff.org/
- Electronic Privacy Information Center: http://www.epic.org/
- Entertainment Software Rating Board:
  http://www.esrb.org/privacy.asp
- EPIC.org (Electronic Privacy Information Center): http://www.epic.org
- EuroISPA (European Internet Service Providers):
  http://www.euroispa.org/
- Georgetown Internet Privacy Study:
  http://www.msb.edu/faculty/culnanm/gippshome.html
- Internet PRIVACY Coalition: http://www.crypto.org/
- Italian privacy site: http://www.privacy.it/
- Network Advertising Initiative: http://www.networkadvertising.org/
- Online Privacy Alliance: http://www.privacyalliance.org/
- Organization for Economic Cooperation and Development:
  http://www.oecd.org/dsti/sti/it/secur/index.htm
- Privacy and American Business: http://www.pandab.org/
- Privacy International: http://www.privacyinternational.org/
- Privacy Laws and Business: http://www.privacylaws.co.uk/

APPENDIX

- Privacy Rights Clearinghouse: http://www.privacyrights.org/
- Privacy, INC.: software that rates a site's privacy standards based on a 1–4 star system: http://www.privacyinc.com
- Privacy.org: organization that informs consumers about privacy issues: http://www.privacy.org
- StopCarnivore.Org: http://stopcarnivore.org/
- Tech Law Journal: http://www.techlawjournal.com/
- The Center for Democracy and Technology: http://www.cdt.org/
- The Privacy Place: http://www.privacy.org/
- TRUSTe: http://www.truste.org/

About the Editor

Rebecca Herold, CISSP, CISA, FLMI, is an information security consultant. Recently, she was subject matter expert for the Central Region of Netigy Corporation. Prior to joining Netigy, she was senior systems security consultant at Principal Financial Group (PFG). She has over 12 years of information security experience. Rebecca was instrumental in developing the corporate information protection department at PFG; her accomplishments include creating and implementing the company's privacy policies and privacy awareness program; creating the company's information protection awareness program; creating the corporate anti-virus strategy and heading the first virus swat team; creating and maintaining information protection policies; creating the corporate strategy to identify and control the use of modems; creating an Internet access strategy; creating and implementing a computer incident response team (CIRT) strategy and leading the CIRT; creating the strategy for protecting customer information; creating a non-employee access strategy and policies; and establishing E-commerce security requirements for Web applications. Rebecca has written numerous magazine and newsletter articles on information security topics and has given many presentations at conferences and seminars. A few of the articles published include:

> How to Secure Remote Control Access, *Computer Security Alert,* Computer Security Institute, February 2001.
> Modem Management and Security, *Data Security Management,* Auerbach Publications, August 2000.
> How to Develop and Communicate Company Privacy Policies, *Computer Security Journal,* Computer Security Institute, Spring 2000.
> Extranet Audit and Security, *Computer Security Journal,* Computer Security Institute, Winter 1998.

Who's on the Company Network?, *Security Management,* American Society for Industrial Security, June 1998.

Rebecca has a B.S. in Math and Computer Science and an M.A. in Computer Science and Education. She is a Certified Information Systems Security Professional (CISSP), a Certified Information Systems Auditor (CISA), and a Fellow of the Life Management Institute (FLMI). She has been a member of the Information Systems Audit and Control Association (ISACA) since 1990 and has held all board positions throughout her membership in the Iowa chapter. She is also a charter member of the Iowa Infragard chapter.

Index

A

AA, see American Airlines
AAHP, see American Association of Health Plans
AAMC, 504
Academy for Health Services Research and Health Policy, 495, 501
Access control(s), 80, 144, 156
  implementing, 254
  Internet, 391
Access permissions, configuring of system for, 77
Accountant–client privilege, 95
Account numbers, 86
ACLU, see American Civil Liberties Union
ACLU of Georgia v. Miller, 173–179
  anonymous remailers, 177
  facts of case, 174–175
  protection of anonymity and law, 176–177
  rationales for anonymity on Internet, 175–176
  recommendations, 177–178
ACLU v. Reno, 176
Acquisition software, 556
Active Server Pages, 354
ActiveX, 434
ADA, see Americans with Disabilities Act of 1992
Address resolution process, 269
Adequacy of protection, 603
AdForce, 370
AdKnowledge, 370
Administrative Procedures Act (APA), 454
Administrative security controls, 321
Advanced Encryption Standard (AES), 169
Advance fee loans, 127
Advertising, benefits of targeted, 369
AES, see Advanced Encryption Standard
Africa, URL of privacy-related laws for, 629

Age Discrimination in Employment Act of 1967, 530
Agency-specific policies, 78
AHIMA, see American Health Information Management Association
AICPA Web Trust, 438
AIDS, 250, 502
Air traffic control industry, 142
Allowable communications, 453
Altair
  end-to-end encryption used by, 419
  Frequency Management Center, 417
  Time-Division Multiplexing architecture, 417
AMA, see American Medical Association
Amazon, 151
AMDIS, see Association of Medical Directors of Information Systems
Amended Electronic Funds Transfer Act of 1999, 125
Amended Mail and Wire Fraud Statues of 1999, 125
American Airlines (AA), 428, 572
American Association of Health Plans (AAHP), 495, 500
American Benefits Council, 495
American Civil Liberties Union (ACLU), 174, 398, 495
American Health Information Management Association (AHIMA), 495, 501, 504
American Hospital Association, 495
American Medical Association (AMA), 495, 500, 504
American National Standards Institute (ANSI), 322
American Pharmaceutical Association (APhA), 495, 501
Americans with Disabilities Act of 1992 (ADA), 458, 534
America Online (AOL), 151, 158, 311, 399
Anarchists, goal of, 39

O

S